Money as God?

The nature of money and its impact on society has long interested scholars of economics, history, philosophy, law, and theology alike, and the recent financial crisis has moved these issues to the forefront of current public debate. In this study, authors from a range of backgrounds provide a unified examination of the nature and the purpose of money. Chapters cover the economic and social foundations of money; the historical origins of money in ancient Greece, China, the ancient Middle East, and medieval Europe; problems of justice connected to the use of money in legal systems and legal settlements, with examples both from ancient history and today; and theological aspects of monetary and market exchange. This stimulating inter-disciplinary book, with its non-technical and lively discussion, will appeal to a global readership working in the interfaces of economics, law, and religion.

JÜRGEN VON HAGEN is Professor of Economics and Director of the Institute for International Economic Policy at the University of Bonn, Germany. His research focuses on monetary and macro-economics. As a Protestant preacher, he also has a keen interest in theology and its inter-section with economics.

MICHAEL WELKER is Senior Professor of Systematic Theology at the University of Heidelberg. He is a member of the Heidelberg Academy of Science and Humanities and a corresponding member of the Finnish Academy of Arts and Sciences. He has held guest professorships at numer-ous universities, including Princeton Theological Seminary, Harvard Divinity School, and Cambridge Divinity School. He is the author or editor of around 50 books.

Money as God?

The Monetization of the Market and its
Impact on Religion, Politics, Law, and Ethics

Edited by
JÜRGEN VON HAGEN
and
MICHAEL WELKER

CAMBRIDGE
UNIVERSITY PRESS

CAMBRIDGE
UNIVERSITY PRESS

University Printing House, Cambridge CB2 8BS, United Kingdom

Cambridge University Press is part of the University of Cambridge.

It furthers the University's mission by disseminating knowledge in the pursuit of education, learning and research at the highest international levels of excellence.

www.cambridge.org
Information on this title: www.cambridge.org/9781107617650

© Cambridge University Press 2014

First published 2014
First paperback edition 2016

A catalogue record for this publication is available from the British Library

Library of Congress Cataloguing in Publication data
Money as God? : the monetization of the market and the impact on religion, politics, law, and ethics / edited by Jürgen von Hagen and Michael Welker.
    pages   cm
Includes index.
ISBN 978-1-107-04300-8
1. Money – Philosophy.   2. Money – Social aspects.   3. Money – Moral and ethical aspects.   4. Money – Religious aspects.   I. Hagen, Jürgen von, editor of compilation.
HG220.3.M65   2014
332.401–dc23
                                                                            2013036997

ISBN 978-1-107-04300-8 Hardback
ISBN 978-1-107-61765-0 Paperback

Contents

Figures   *page* viii

Tables   ix

Contributors   x

Acknowledgments   xii

Introduction   1
JÜRGEN VON HAGEN AND MICHAEL WELKER

I.   Money and markets: economic, legal, and theological
     foundations   17

1.   Microfoundations of the uses of money   19
     JÜRGEN VON HAGEN

2.   Money and its role in a decentralized market economy   42
     PETER BERNHOLZ

3.   *Mensura et mensuratum*: money as measure and measure
     for money   60
     WOLFGANG ERNST

4.   Standardization and monetization: legal perspectives   80
     BURKHARD HESS

5.   Kohelet and the co-evolution of a monetary economy
     and religion   96
     MICHAEL WELKER

II.   Monetary exchange: historical and social roots   109

6. Money and image: the presence of the state on the routes
   of economy   111
   TONIO HÖLSCHER

7. The social world of Ecclesiastes   137
   CHOON-LEONG SEOW

8. The development of monetary systems in Palestine during
   the Achaemenid and Hellenistic Eras   159
   ULRICH HÜBNER

9. Fate's gift economy: the Chinese case of coping with the
   asymmetry between man and fate   184
   RUDOLF G. WAGNER

10. "Mothers and children": discourses on paper money
    during the Song period   219
    HANS-ULRICH VOGEL

11. "Buying Heaven": the prospects of commercialized
    salvation in the fourteenth to sixteenth centuries   233
    BERNDT HAMM

III.   Monetary exchange: ethical limits and challenges   257

12. The monetization and demonetization of the human body:
    the case of compensatory payments for bodily injuries and
    homicide in ancient Near Eastern and ancient Israelite
    law books   259
    KONRAD SCHMID

13. What price do we place on life? Ethical observations on the
    limits of law and money in a case of transitional justice   282
    GÜNTER THOMAS

14. Standardized monetization of the market and the argument
    for preferential justice   309
    PIET NAUDÉ

15. Religious faith and the market economy: a survey on faith
and trust of Catholic entrepreneurs in China 339
GAO SHINING AND YANG FENGGANG

IV.   Money, wealth, and desire 363

16. "Do not sell your soul for money": economy and eschatology
in biblical and intertestamental traditions 365
ANDREAS SCHÜLE

17. "Businessmen and merchants will not enter the places of
my Father": early Christianity and market mentality 379
EDMONDO F. LUPIERI

18. Desire in consumer culture: theological perspectives from
Gregory of Nyssa and Augustine of Hippo 414
JOHN F. HOFFMEYER

Money as God?: conclusions 440
MICHAEL WELKER AND JÜRGEN VON HAGEN

Index 442

Figures

2.1 Trilateral barter   *page* 43
2.2 Development of prices in four countries, 1790–1990   47
2.3 Development of the cost of living, 1950–1995   48

Tables

2.1 Historical examples of large under- (< 100) and
overvaluations (> 100) of currencies *page* 50
2.2 Historical episodes of hyperinflation 51
12.1 Exchange rates between 1 shekel of silver and
corresponding quantities of bronze, copper, tin, and gold
(in shekels) 264
12.2 Fines and punishments for injuries and homicide in
the CH 266
12.3 Fines and punishments for injuries and homicide in
the CU 267
12.4 Fines for injuries and unintentional homicide in the CE 268
12.5 Comparative Listing of fines and punishments for injuries
and unintentional homicide in the CU, in the CE, and in
the CH 269
15.1 Business structure of enterprises 343
15.2 Relations with administrative organs 343
15.3 Participation in religious activities 348

Contributors

Name	Affiliation
PETER BERNHOLZ	Professor Emeritus of Economics, University of Basel
WOLFGANG ERNST	Professor of Law, University of Zurich
YANG FENGGANG	Professor of Sociology and Director of the Center on Religion and Chinese Society, Purdue University, West Lafayette
BERNDT HAMM	Professor Emeritus of Theology, University of Erlangen
BURKHARD HESS	Professor of Law, University of Heidelberg
JOHN F. HOFFMEYER	Professor of Theology, Lutheran Theological Seminary, Philadelphia
TONIO HÖLSCHER	Professor of Ancient History, University of Heidelberg
ULRICH HÜBNER	Professor of Theology, University of Kiel
EDMONDO F. LUPIERI	Professor of Theology, Loyola University Chicago
PIET NAUDÉ	Professor of Religion, Port Elizabeth, South Africa
KONRAD SCHMID	Professor of Old Testament, University of Zurich
ANDREAS SCHÜLE	Professor of Old Testament, University of Leipzig
CHOON-LEONG SEOW	Professor of Old Testament, Princeton Theological Seminary

GAO SHINING   Professor of Religion, Beijing
                         Chinese Academy of Social Sciences
GÜNTER THOMAS   Professor of Theology and Ethics,
                         University of Bochum
HANS-ULRICH VOGEL   Professor of Chinese Studies, University of
                         Tübingen
JÜRGEN VON HAGEN   Professor of Economics,
                         University of Bonn
RUDOLF G. WAGNER   Professor of Chinese Studies, University of
                         Heidelberg
MICHAEL WELKER   Professor of Theology,
                         University of Heidelberg

Acknowledgments

This book documents the results of a multi-year international and interdisciplinary dialogue. The project was made possible by the Evangelische Kirche im Rheinland, Düsseldorf, Germany. We are most grateful to Präses Dr. Nikolaus Schneider, Vizepräses Petra Bosse-Huber, Vizepräses Christian Drägert, Professor Dr. Bernd Wander, and the staff of the Film Funk Fernseh Zentrum (FFFZ) for their kind support. We are also indebted to Dr. Ellen Peerenboom, Gudrun Strehlow, and the team of the Internationales Wissenschaftsforum (IWH), University of Heidelberg. We acknowledge our gratitude to Dr. Heike Springhart, who was a perfect organizer of the project over many years. Special thanks go to Henning Mützlitz, Heidelberg, who created a print-ready copy, and to Cambridge University Press for their cooperation.

Introduction

JÜRGEN VON HAGEN AND MICHAEL WELKER

Over the centuries, time and again, theologians, philosophers, poets and even sociologists have proposed that money should be regarded as a "god-term" (Kenneth Burke). They have spoken of the omnipotence of money (Georg Simmel) and pondered whether we should not organize religious faith like money (Niklas Luhmann). They propagated a "pantheism of money" (Falk Wagner) and called it the "all-determining reality."[1]

This treatment of money as a god-like phenomenon stands in sharp contrast to another tradition which, in the European context, goes back at least to Luther's polemical use of the phrase, "You cannot serve God and mammon" (Matt. 6:20, Luke 16:13) and his explanation of the first article in his Great Catechism which puts God and Mammon in strong opposition to each other: "Many a one thinks that he has God and everything in abundance when he has money and possessions; he trusts in them and boasts of them with such firmness and assurance as to care for no one. Lo, such a man also has a God, Mammon by name. It is money and possessions on which he sets all his heart and which are also the most common idols on earth. He who has money and possessions feels secure, and is joyful and undismayed as though he were sitting in the midst of paradise. On the other hand, he who has none doubts and is despondent, as though he knew of no God. For very few are to be found who are of good cheer, and who neither mourn nor complain if they have not Mammon. This care and desire for money sticks and clings to our nature, even to the grave." Luther thus demonizes money as an idol trapping humans by promising them a false security and luring them into putting their trust in material goods rather than the living God.

This tension between a tradition of deification and a tradition of demonization of money is the starting point of the research project on which this book is a report. The chief goal of this project was to bring

---

[1] See Tonio Hölschers' contribution in this book, Chapter 6 below.

1

together scholars from different academic disciplines to compare and discuss the views on money their respective disciplines offer. The project did not aim at developing a unified perspective on money shared by all disciplines. Instead, it took a multidisciplinary approach, one that accepts the differences between different disciplines and traditions, and uses these differences to promote a discourse that can affect the research and thinking in each one of them. For this end, the project involved economists, historians, lawyers, sinologists, and theologians, who met several times over a period of three years to develop and discuss their contributions.

I. Money and markets: economic, legal, and ethical foundations

In "Microfoundations of the uses of money," Jürgen von Hagen provides a thorough introduction to the economic fundamentals of monetary economies. The fundamental function of money is to be a general medium of exchange. Money is characterized by three properties: it is storable, it is accepted in exchange for goods which are desirable for consumption without being the object of consumption itself, and it is nameless. Since the use of money is costly in terms of real resources, it emerges as a social institution only if it is supported by two key characteristics of a society's trading system. The first is decentralization, implying that trade takes time. The second is a lack of trust among those trading with each other which destroys the possibility of trading on the basis of credit. Where these conditions do not hold, money will not emerge.

Von Hagen then goes on to draw out the implications of these microfoundations for the current research project. One argument concerns the ambivalent role of government in monetary economies: government can supply the trust individuals must have in an anonymous medium of exchange, but government can also abuse this trust to reap the gains from money creation. Another argument concerns the social and economic developments required for money to emerge and be sustained as a social institution. Here, von Hagen formulates a set of questions to the other researchers involved in the project.

In "Money and its role in a decentralized market economy," Peter Bernholz delves more deeply into some of the aspects developed in the previous chapter. He explains the idea of monetary trade in more detail and focuses in particular on the role of government in monetary affairs. Bernholz reviews the history of hyperinflations in the past few centuries and argues that these hyperinflations were due to attempts by the governments to over-exploit money creation as a source of revenue. This was facilitated by the move from metal-based to credit money and, later, pure fiat, or paper money. In the last part of his chapter, Bernholz discusses the perceptions of the social role of money as reflected in literature and philosophical writings. These perceptions often ascribe to money a power of changing social relations and values. This links up with the discussion in von Hagen's chapter, i.e. that this may be a misperception: changes in social relations and values due to changes in economic and trading structures are ascribed to money, because the use of money emerges as a result of these structural changes.

Wolfgang Ernst, in *"Mensura et mensuratum*: money as measure and measure for money," discusses the use of money as a unit of account, or measure of value. He begins with a review of the use of money as a unit of account in the Middle Ages, a particularly interesting period during which the "money" serving as a unit of account did not coincide with the money used as a medium of exchange, a possibility discussed earlier by von Hagen. As Ernst points out, this is a period when thinking about the value of a good was dominated by religious and ethical concepts such as the "true" or "fair" price. Money was regarded as a measure of this objective value of things, a notion that led to the postulate of monetary stability. For example, Ernst reports that Thomas Aquinas argued that, since all measures must be stable, so must money as a measure of value.

Ernst then goes on to discuss the special problems of bimetallism, where the value of different coins is tied to different precious metals rather than one (usually gold and silver), and imaginary money, where the unit of account does not correspond to the actual coins circulating. In bimetallic systems, swings in the market price of one metal against the other can cause deviations of the exchange rate between different coins from their relative face values. If these swings were persistent, the face values of the coins were adjusted or official, regulated exchange rates were applied. With imaginary money, the unit of account becomes completely abstract, while the value of the coins used as a medium of exchange itself becomes variable against the unit of account. Finally, Ernst discusses modern fiat money, where the medium of exchange is no longer tied to any commodity. He argues that fiat money can no longer be regarded as a measure value of all other things; instead, the price of all other things becomes the measure of the value of money. This contradicts the medieval notion of an objective value inherent in all things, but it is fully consistent with modern economic thinking which holds that relative prices are the result of the interplay of consumer preferences and scarcities of supply.

In "Standardization and monetization: legal perspectives," Burkhard Hess addresses the issues of standardization and the use of money from a legal perspective. Hess points out that all contractual relations which can be enforced by courts require some standardization – a definition of what is equal and common in repetitive human actions and relations is necessary for a judge to rule what is right or wrong and to award compensation for damages where necessary. Standardization is not limited to economic relations; it is found also in other parts of civil law. Standardization facilitates the settlement of conflicts, but it also comes at a price, as the standards set may be perceived as unfair by the weaker parties in a conflict. In modern legal systems, judges are empowered to intervene in such cases and impose what is perceived in society as fair conditions of exchange.

In the legal context, monetization refers to the use of money to make payments and settle accounts in commercial relationships. Beyond that, it also refers to the use of monetary payments to compensate for injustice, tort, and losses of non-tangibles. Modern legal systems use this instrument pervasively, to settle conflicts. Thus, as pointed out by Bernholz, the complaints of writers and philosophers that things that were once highly valued have lost general esteem in society and have been degraded by the fact that they can be purchased for money, may actually reflect development of standardization in legal systems more than a supposedly evil property of money. Hess uses two specific examples – monetary compensation of the loss of intangibles and monetary transfers paid to the victims of mass tort – to illustrate the conflict between justice and standardization. The second example is discussed in more detail in Günter Thomas's chapter.

Michael Welker's "Kohelet and the co-evolution of a monetary economy and religion" begins with the observations that money has been ascribed god-like features by theologians, philosophers, poets, and social scientists. A well-known example is Martin Luther, who confronts us with the imperative to choose between "God and Mammon."

Welker finds that this is a distorted view not only of money and markets, but also of God. He focuses on the biblical book of Kohelet to correct these distortions. At a first glance, Kohelet's teaching seems to be characterized by the contradiction between his emphasis on the futility of all material things on the one hand and his repeated admonition that man should enjoy the things he possesses. On the one hand, wealth and money provide neither security nor the fulfillment of human desires; on the other hand, Kohelet advises his reader to sow and reap and enjoy the fruits of his labor.

This apparent contradiction, Welker argues, is resolved by the distinction between property as wealth and property as God's gift. As a gift of God, wealth should be enjoyed. It should not, however, be brought into the sphere of the market and the monetary system, because doing so involves the risk of losing it. Property as a gift can mean much more than just material possessions; it can include non-tangibles such as talents, and cultural and social institutions. Wisdom is the art of distinguishing between properties as non-marketable gifts and properties as marketable assets which can be purchased and sold in the market.

Welker argues that Kohelet is also characterized by viewing a person's relationship with God from a perspective of profit, which is anticipated, but by no means sure. God relates to individual human beings only indirectly, by granting them, or depriving them of, possessions as gifts, and the opportunity to enjoy them. The human's role in this relationship is to actively enjoy what God has given him. Yet, from the human perspective, this relationship with God is highly unpredictable; therefore, his life is marked by a large degree of uncertainty and instability. As Welker points out, referring to Seow's commentary on the book, this view of life may be a reflection of the increased degree of social and economic mobility in the Palestinian society under the Persian empire.

II. Monetary exchange: historical and social roots

Tonio Hölscher, in "Money and image: the presence of the state on the routes of economy," investigates the historical social environments in which coined money was first invented. The first known coins were introduced in the Greek state of Lydia in the seventh century BC. Hölscher argues that their introduction fell into a period in which the Greek economy underwent a deep transformation. In the pre-monetary economy, economic transactions were based mainly on barter trade and gifts exchanged between leaders, which symbolized long-term relationships based on mutual trust. In the decades around 600 BC, a prosperous middle class emerged in the cities, whose economies were characterized by a much larger degree of the division of productive tasks among individuals and families, and where the city-states began to assume greater roles than before in public life. Public building projects – both for civic and religious purposes – were at the center of the states' activities. Hölscher argues that these state-sponsored public works promoted the development of monetary economies, as money made it possible to store large amounts of wealth and to pay large public workforces on a continuous and regular basis. Hölscher explains that in the strongly decentralized political system of Greece, the value of money was certified and assured by the same communities of citizens that acknowledged this value in everyday trade. The spreading of monetary exchange implied that exchange relations lost their personal character of gift-giving and instead became impersonal market transactions, leading to a deep transformation of Greek economic life.

Hölscher also discusses the function of coins as images circulating within and outside the territorial realm of the political authority issuing them. Throughout the centuries, Greek and, later, Roman authorities used coins to present themselves and to send messages to their citizens and beyond.

Leong Seow notes in "The social world of Ecclesiastes" how much the language of Kohelet presupposes a readership that is familiar with a society embedded in an economy characterized by a high degree of commercialization and monetary exchange. Seow places the book in the era of Persian rule over Palestine and argues that archeological evidence is (partly, at least) consistent with such an economic basis. The economy in Yehud was still largely agrarian, but it was private and profit-oriented agriculture. Seow's argument is based on his observation of Kohelet's frequent use of terms which are also found in Persian legal and economic documents, and of strong parallels between the theological concepts put forward by Kohelet and legal and political concepts prevailing under the Persian rule. In particular, Seow points out, Kohelet's view of God who is completely sovereign (and perhaps somewhat arbitrary) in what he chooses to give to or withhold from individual persons resembles the Persian kings' custom of giving and withdrawing grants to and from individual citizens.

The social world of Ecclesiastes was characterized by a large degree of social mobility and uncertainty about social positions which can also be found in the book of Kohelet. Individuals of low social rank could find and grasp opportunities to climb the social ladder and gain substantial wealth and influence, but they could also lose both quickly. Facing such opportunities, some individuals devoted their lives entirely to the accumulation of wealth, sometimes only to end up in poverty. With a larger set of economic opportunities, economic inequality increased and so did the perception of economic injustice. Both are well reflected in the writing of Kohelet. While some people were able to benefit massively from the opportunities to become rich, the average person in society felt helpless and oppressed by a powerful and arbitrary king and a rich elite.

In "The development of monetary systems in Palestine during the Achaemenid and Hellenistic Eras," Ulrich Hübner describes the history of money in Palestine, which evolves in parallel and reflects the political history of the region and the influence of external forces. Hübner argues that the introduction of coins must be interpreted as a gradual improvement of pre-monetary exchange rather than a major cultural innovation. For a long time, coins that were used in long-distance trade circulated alongside coins of local and regional origin that were used in local and regional trade only. At the same time, trade based on the exchange of metal bars that needed to be weighed continued to exist for long periods of time.

While the first coins used in Palestine were of Greek origin and date from the sixth and fifth centuries BC, Sidonian and Tyrrian coins became the leading currencies in the region during the middle of the fifth century BC and into the Roman era. In the middle of the fourth century BC, coins were minted in the province of Yehud (Judah), most likely in its capital, Jerusalem. These coins bore images that contributed to the shaping of a Yehud identity separate from the neighboring regions. They were produced until the early Ptolemaic period; local minting only started again at the end of the Seleucid Empire and the beginning of the Hasmonean rule.

"Fate's gift economy: the Chinese case of coping with the asymmetry between man and fate" by Rudolf Wagner, discusses the role of *spiritual money* offered in religious rituals in China and its interpretation. Wagner develops a view of the gift economy that relates the world of the living with the supernatural world in Chinese spiritual traditions.

In this economy, human life is regarded as an initial credit given to a human being with the expectation of man paying back in the form of morally acceptable deeds. It is based on the fundamental tenet that supernatural powers do not act randomly and that man can exchange good actions for good fate, although the specific terms and ways of this exchange are not known to human beings. The relationship between human beings and the supernatural powers involves a large degree of standardization, which is embodied in a system of *karma points* that can be earned by good and squandered by bad deeds. This standardization lends itself to the use of *spiritual money* as a currency representing the value of good deeds. Wagner emphasizes that the valuation of this currency is not tied to the value of money used in ordinary human business transactions. On the contrary, paper money is postulated to have higher value in the spiritual realm than metal coins. As in ordinary credit relations, the Chinese tradition holds that the good deeds of one person may be accredited to another and contribute to the efforts of the latter to manage and pay back his life credit.

As Wagner points out, the traditional scholarly view of this relationship between the world of the living and the supernatural world interprets it as a translation of ordinary, real-life institutions and relationships to the spiritual realm. The main point of this chapter is that the inverse can also be true and serve as a fruitful hypothesis: what is assumed to be true about the supernatural world and its relationship with human beings serves as a model for ordinary economic transactions among humans. Wagner notes that, in Chinese tradition, the enforcement of business contracts explicitly relies on the punishment of devious behavior by spiritual powers. Furthermore, the development of Chinese banking is intimately linked to the Buddhist monastic tradition and its thinking about money and interest. Finally, the use of paper money, which was first invented in China, in ordinary economic transactions, may derive from the use of spiritual paper money in religious rituals. This would involve a translation of the emphasis on truth and good moral behavior in the spiritual realm to the credibility of the promise of a stable value of a currency with no backing other than paper.

In "'Mothers and children': discourses on paper money during the Song period," Hans-Ulrich Vogel continues on the theme of paper money raised in Wagner's contribution. He reviews the debate among Chinese scholars and officials surrounding the introduction and the use of paper money in the late tenth century and from the twelfth to the seventeenth century in some Chinese provinces. Paper money was introduced as an alternative to iron and copper coins, which were inconvenient in trade due to their heavy weights. Its issuance was soon taken over by the state. Paper money regimes were plagued by the tension between the need to limit the amount of money circulating in order to preserve a stable value of money and the fiscal demands of the state. Vogel cites from a record of a discussion between a Shenzong emperor and his officials which brings out this tension very explicitly and shows that the fiscal demands of the state typically prevailed.

The review of the debates shows that paper money regimes were also plagued with counterfeiting. Excessive issuance and counterfeiting of paper money caused wealthier merchants to hoard coins, which made trading more difficult for ordinary people, as paper notes were not available in small denominations, and thus resulted in economic downturns and hardship. As a result, paper money was met with criticism and suspicion by many Chinese scholars and officials of that period.

Berndt Hamm's chapter, "'Buying Heaven': the prospects of commercialized salvation in the fourteenth to sixteenth centuries," describes the theological response to the commercial revolution and the emergence of a monetary and capitalistic economy in Europe during the eleventh to the thirteenth century and until the Reformation. On the one hand, the Church adopted concepts from commercial life in its theology, teaching that God offered man a contract by which man could buy heavenly treasures for good deeds and donations of money (rather than land, as during the times of the feudal economy), thus providing the new class of rich merchants, bankers, and tradesmen with an assurance of salvation. In contrast to the Chinese gift economy described by Wagner, this contractual relationship is characterized by a very calculable principle of *do ut des*, which is perfected in the sale of indulgences. On the other hand, the Church gave legitimacy to the new economic system and itself became heavily involved in it as a financial actor. Thus, Hamm argues, the relationship between the Church and the commercial world is a dialectic one. The Church shapes it and is shaped by it.

The commercial logic of buying salvation became the main point of attack by the Reformation, which held the principle of God's free and unmerited grace against it. Hamm argues that the Reformers' critical attitude against money must be seen against the background of common teaching that money could be used to buy salvation. Moreover, the

Reformers had a tendency to demonize money and monetary exchange precisely because the Catholic Church was so deeply involved in monetary dealings. Nevertheless, Hamm shows, Lutheran and Calvinist theology found ways to adjust to the developing capitalist economic system.

Hamm concludes that Christian religion was never a driving force behind the development of the capitalist economy in Europe, but it became an important ally in many ways, providing the economic system with legitimacy, credibility, and, thus, stability. As the capitalist economy increasingly detaches itself from this ally, Hamm suggests, it may end up losing an important pillar of stability.

III. Monetary exchange: ethical limits and challenges

In "The monetization and demonetization of the human body: the case of compensatory payments for bodily injuries and homicide in ancient Near Eastern and ancient Israelite law books," Konrad Schmid picks up an argument introduced by Burkhard Hess, i.e. the use of standardization in legal contexts, and describes how this was already practiced in Near Eastern legal codes of the eighteenth and twenty-second centuries BC. These codes spelled out compensatory payments for bodily injuries that were graded by the severity of the injury, the function of the body part injured and the social status of the person injured. The values implied by these payments varied over time. Apart from the compensatory function, the payments also seem to have served a role of deterrence and punishment.

In comparison to these ancient law codes, Schmid argues that the Israelite covenant code makes less use of compensatory payments. In particular, it does not allow for payment compensating for the taking of a human life, and it does not specify set values of payments for any bodily injury. Schmid attributes this to the fact that the Palestinian economy became monetized much later than the more developed economies in the region.

Günter Thomas continues this theme in "What price do we place on life? Ethical observations on the limits of law and money in a case of transitional justice," but he looks at it from a different angle, namely, the use of monetary payments by the state to make good injustices suffered by its citizens. The case he considers is the payment of reparations to citizens of the former German Democratic Republic who suffered from political persecution. Is such a monetary compensation possible at all?

The difficulty in this case and similar ones comes from the fact that the injustices were committed by a political regime different from the state paying reparations, and that the compensation is made by an institution rather than an individual as a moral agent. Justice is sought to be done for the victims, but not for the perpetrators. Thomas provides a detailed discussion of the complex ethical issues involved in the setting of compensatory payments for large numbers of victims. It forces the state to establish a monetary price for an imaginary unit of injustice such as a month in forced-labor camps, and thus enforces a standard of comparison on individual suffering which by definition is incomparable to any other suffering.

As Thomas points out, public art, public narrative and religion offer alternatives to monetary compensation in dealing with injustices suffered by large numbers of people. In the German case, these alternatives were neglected, and deplorably the churches did not play an active role reminding the German people of these alternatives.

Piet Naudé's "Standardized monetization of the market and the argument for preferential justice" begins with a brief review of the history of the global economic system from the mid-nineteenth century to date. Naudé argues that, despite the differences in the global trading and financial regimes over time, this history is characterized by the ever-larger differences between the center and the periphery of the global economy. While the standardized market system is based on voluntary exchange and reciprocity among equals as a conception of justice, these growing differences call for a new concept of justice, one that gives unambiguous preference to the poor. This call has been voiced by theologians in the form of liberation theology, by philosophers, most prominently by John Rawls, and recently by the economist and Nobel Laureate Joseph Stiglitz.

Naudé reviews all three strands of thinking and shows how they converge on the principle of preferential justice for the poor, despite their very different starting points and methodological approaches. Preferential justice for the poor is served when those who are better off contribute to the economic well-being of the poorest.

Naudé proposes that this principle should also be applied at the local as well as the global scale of human society and politics. The fact that this has been argued from three very different bases gives it the credibility and the specificity necessary for practical implementation. Furthermore, it is an inclusive concept of justice that makes it possible to let the poor and the rich live together in a stable society. Finally, it can be usefully applied as a benchmark against which concrete political actions and their outcomes can be measured and from which they can be defended or dismissed.

How does a Christian believer cope with an economic environment characterized by dishonesty and cheating? Gao Shining and Yang Fenggang address this question in their empirical study, "Religious faith and the market economy: a survey on faith and trust of Catholic entrepreneurs in China." They start from the observation that the spreading of the market system in a weak legal and regulatory framework in China during the past 30 years has caused a widespread moral decline in the Chinese economy. Noticing that economists have long pointed to the importance of trust for the functioning of a market economy, they ask whether and to what extent personal faith influences the behavior of Catholic entrepreneurs in situations demanding trust. To answer the question, Shining and Fenggang conducted a series of interviews with such entrepreneurs in 2006.

According to their results, personal faith is, indeed, an important factor in economic situations that involve trust, such as customer–supplier or employer–employee relations. While family ties are a prime determinant for whether or not trust is granted, faith relations seem to be of significant importance, too. They help entrepreneurs build and maintain business relations which would otherwise not be possible. In a sense, Shining and Fenggang provide empirical support for the argument with which Berndt Hamm closes his chapter, namely, that religious faith provides a source of stability for the capitalist market system.

IV. Money, wealth, and desire

In "'Do not sell your soul for money': economy and eschatology in biblical and intertestamental traditions," Andreas Schüle takes the reader back to the world of Kohelet and, subsequently, that of the apocryphal *Sapientia Salomonis* (*Wisdom of Solomon*) that comes from the intertestamental period, and finally, to that of the *4QInstructions* which belong to the Qumran texts. The thread linking these three texts is the emerging concept of an immortal human soul and an afterlife the expectation of which serves as a guide for what is valuable in this life and what is not. While these concepts are only vaguely hinted at in Kohelet, they are fully developed in *Sapientia Salomonis* and receive an eschatological dimension in the Qumran text.

Schüle demonstrates that the views of money these texts hold develop in line with the development of their concepts of the immortality of the human soul and the afterlife. While Kohelet's view of money is quite ambiguous, as Michael Welker and Leon Seoq also argue in more detail in their contributions to this book, *Sapientia Salomonis* and 4QInstructions both take a more definitely negative position in this regard. They see money and the desire for monetary wealth primarily as a dangerous force threatening to destroy the relationship between human beings and God and, therefore, human chances to enjoy a glorious afterlife.

Schüle ends by noting that the development of the concepts of immortality and afterlife marks a very dynamic change in early Judaism and that the time when this occurs coincides with a period marked by very dynamic economic development, i.e. the monetization of the Palestinian economy discussed by Welker and Seow. Without claiming causality in either direction, it is interesting to see that the development of a monetary economy was a key characteristic of the period and society which developed the idea of a precious, immortal soul.

In "'Businessmen and merchants will not enter the places of my Father': early Christianity and market mentality," Edmondo Lupieri takes this discussion one step further by considering the views of money, markets, and wealth present in the early texts of the New Testament. Terms and metaphors relating to the world of business, markets, and money abound in these texts, reflecting the fact that trade, monetization, and market activities had reached a hitherto unknown degree of development in the Palestine economy of the Roman Empire during the first century AD. But the use of these terms is rather ambiguous. Buying and selling, the basic market activities, can be spoken of both with a negative meaning of an excessive focus on material things, and with a positive meaning describing fundamental theological concepts such as the purchase of the lives of believers by the blood of Jesus Christ. Similarly, New Testament writers warn of wealth as distracting human beings from relying on God, and yet describe the Lord himself as a wealthy businessman. Similar to what we have seen in the discussions of money in Kohelet, it seems that these writers do not criticize money, markets, and even wealth themselves, but rather, the wrong uses one can make of them. Matthew seems to have the most critical view of the use of money, linking it directly to the betrayal of Jesus Christ and the hypocrisy and unfaithfulness of the Jewish religious authorities. Some textual passages hint at an economy of exchanging gifts and donations based on the fundamental fact that everything owned by human beings is a gift from God as an alternative to the prevailing market economy, but this thinking remains far less explicit and developed than the gift economy Wagner describes for the Chinese religious tradition.

Lupieri provides a detailed discussion of the New Testament episode of the cleansing of the temple by Jesus, a story that stands out if only by the fact that all four evangelists mention it. This episode has often been used to justify the claim that Jesus was opposed to trading and markets. Yet, as Lupieri explains, such a simplistic interpretation is unwarranted. The focus of the New Testament texts is much less on the trading activities themselves than on the purity and holiness of the temple, the place of God's presence.

John F. Hoffmeyer, in "Desire in consumer culture: theological perspectives from Gregory of Nyssa and Augustine of Hippo," presents a theological reflection on the main dynamic force driving today's monetary market economy: consumer desire. Through the art of advertisement, Hoffmeyer argues, businesses have managed to keep consumers in a constant state of desire, never satisfied with what they have already acquired, always discontented with what is before them, ever ready to buy new things. In the modern consumer culture, the feeling of desire itself becomes desirable, and the act of shopping provides more satisfaction than the act of consuming the object purchased on the shopping trip.

Hoffmeyer refers back to Augustine and Gregory to identify the anthropological problem underlying this culture of desiring desire. Augustine holds that, because human beings are created by God and because of the way God created them, they cannot find satisfaction unless they find rest in God. Augustine describes his own experiences before becoming a Christian in terms that resemble the unquenchable desire of the consumer in a consumer culture. Faith, for Augustine, is an insatiable desire for God, much like the consumer's desire for desire. Even more forcefully, Gregory sees the process of searching for God as the believer's true enjoyment.

There is thus an interesting parallel between the desire for desire for God and the desire for desire for consumer goods. This parallel, Hoffmeyer argues, is rooted in human nature, which does not allow human beings to find satisfaction in themselves. The problem of consumer culture, then, is not that human desires are unquenchable; the problem is that they are misdirected towards things created instead of being directed towards God, the creator. This is useful, because it can teach people to focus on the real, spiritual problems to which advertisements promise a solution without offering one. While consumer culture is characterized by a restless search for the newest object of consumption, the theological perspective teaches acceptance of the insatiability of the human desire, but rejection of the claim that (even merely temporary) satisfaction requires novelty and replaces it by the claim that (everlasting) satisfaction comes only from rest in the everlasting God. Instead of constantly chasing after the latest fad, such a perspective invites us to engage in relationships of faithfulness and commitment.

Money and markets: economic, legal, and theological foundations

1 | Microfoundations of the uses of money

JÜRGEN VON HAGEN

I Introduction

Money has long fascinated economists and non-economists alike. Non-economists are fascinated by the role of money in everyday life and the pervasiveness of words and concepts related to money in our thinking. Economists are fascinated by monetary economics as the intersection of microeconomics (the analysis of the economic behavior of individual households and firms) and macroeconomics (the analysis of the economic behavior of aggregate systems). The fundamental question of monetary economics is this: why do rational agents who are otherwise interested in consumption accept goods which are not consumable like coins, or even paper money, in exchange for consumable goods? Menger poses the problem well: "that every economic unit in a nation should be ready to exchange his goods for little metal disks apparently useless as such, or for documents representing the latter, is a process so opposed to the ordinary course of things. . . . The problem which science has here to solve consists in giving an explanation of a general, homogeneous course of action pursued by human beings when engaged in traffic, which, taken concretely, makes unquestionably for the common interest, and yet which seems to conflict with the nearest and immediate interests of contracting individuals."[1]

Answers to this problem are plentiful, and hardly any other topic in economics has generated more literature. This chapter reviews the principles of monetary economics in order to clarify the nature of money and to identify the conditions for monetary economies to emerge. Section II addresses a number of confusions related to improper definitions of money and interpretations of them. Sections III and IV review the main arguments from monetary theory concerning the social

---

[1] C. Menger, "On the Origin of Money." *The Economic Journal* 2(6) (1892): 239–40.

origins of money. Section V applies those ideas to the study of monetization in Palestine and the origins of the book of Kohelet, which forms
one of the focal points of the research program on which this book is a
report. Section VI concludes.

Within the context of this book, the purpose of the chapter is to raise
a number of research questions all aiming in the same direction: if we
can take the "standardized monetization of the market" as a given,
what are the conditions in the societies under consideration that must
have emerged historically in order to make monetization possible and
desirable? Once this question has been properly answered, it will be
possible to identify which and how many of the observed changes in
politics, religion, law, and ethics are the *effects* of monetization and
which and how many of them are consequences of the same forces that
led to monetization.

II Monetary confusions

Alison Hingston Quiggin begins her *Survey of Primitive Money* with the
dictum that "Everyone, except an economist, knows what 'money'
means, and even an economist can describe it in the course of a chapter
or so."[2] Unfortunately, things are worse than that. A cursory glance at
the large literature on money reveals that even today there is considerable and widespread confusion about the principles of money. Much
of this confusion results from the fact that discussions of money often
start from an inadequate definition of it, focusing on three functions
money supposedly fulfills in an economy. In this tradition, to which
even renowned economists adhere, money is defined as anything that
simultaneously serves as: (1) a means of payment, (2) a store of value,
and (3) a unit of account. That is, "money *is* what money *does.*"[3]

Defining money in terms of these three functions is awkward, because
it contradicts the experience that not everything that assumes these roles
in an economy is deemed *money* in practice. For example, interest-
bearing assets serve both as stores of value and mediums of exchange
in modern economies where banks offer checkable asset accounts.

---

[2] A. Hingston Quiggin, *A Survey of Primitive Money*. London: Methuen and
Company 1970, 1.
[3] O. Issing, *Einführung in die Geldtheorie*. Munich: Verlag Vahlen, 13th edn. 2003,
3. Hingston Quiggin, *A Survey of Primitive Money*, replaces the second function
as being a symbol of wealth.

Under such circumstances, "dollars" or "euros" are still the unit of account, but no longer the medium of exchange. More generally, Fama argues that there is nothing that requires an economy's medium of exchange to be its unit of account.[4] In fact, any commodity could serve as a unit of account.[5] While competition and market forces can make an economy switch from one medium of exchange to another, the choice of a unit of account is a problem markets cannot solve easily. A unit of account is an important element of communication among market participants, and its attractiveness depends on how many agents in the economy use it. Therefore, its choice involves economies of scale and network externalities different from those involved in the choice of medium of exchange. Grierson points to historical examples of divergences between a society's unit of account and its medium of exchange, e.g. Homeric Greece, where the unit of account was the ox, but where payments were made in gold. In Pharaonic Egypt, the unit of account was based on copper, but payments were executed in various commodities.[6] In parts of Germany up to the tenth century and of northwestern Europe even later, cows were the unit of account, but payments were made in metal or other goods.[7] For centuries during the Middle Ages, the Carolingian *libra* served as the unit of account, although it did not circulate physically, while the currencies that did circulate did not serve as units of account.[8] Even in modern times, such examples can be found, as in the use of "*ancien francs*" as the unit of account in France long after the introduction of new francs.

Furthermore, what is deemed *money* in practice is particularly badly suited for serving some of the functions mentioned above, an observation that can be found even in the Bible.[9] For example, with positive

---

[4] E. Fama, "Banking in the Theory of Finance." *Journal of Monetary Economics* 6 (1980): 39–58.

[5] See R. Clower, "A Reconsideration of the Microfoundations of Monetary Theory." *Western Economic Journal* 6 (1968): 1–9.

[6] P. Grierson, *The Origins of Money*. Creighton Lecture in History 1970. London: The Athlone Press 1977, 16.

[7] A. Luschin von Ebengreuth, *Allgemeine Münzkunde und Münzgeschichte des Mittelalters und der Neueren Zeit*. Munich, Berlin: R. Oldenbourg 1926, §23.

[8] See B. Sprenger, *Das Geld der Deutschen: Geldgeschichte Deutschlands von den Anfängen bis zur Gegenwart*, 3rd edn., Paderborn: Schöningh 2002; W. Ernst, "*Mensura et mensuratum*: money as measure and measure for money," Chapter 3 below.

[9] See also Grierson, *The Origins of Money*, 15.

(real) interest rates, (real) interest-bearing assets dominate money as a store of value, as noted in Luke 19:23. Furthermore, storing wealth in physical money is costly, a point noted in Matthew 6:19 and James 5:3, which is easily extended to the disadvantages of using money as a store of value in times of inflation. The risk of theft makes money a worse store of value than land or other physical assets which are more difficult to steal (see Matthew 6:19). Using money as a unit of account in the presence of (uncertain) inflation is like using measuring rods that change size constantly, the danger of which was already alluded to in the pre-monetary times of Leviticus 19:35.

Another source of confusion in the discussion about money is the tendency to think about it uni-directionally, a point noted by David Hume.[10] An example is to focus on the fact that "money is exchanged against goods," leaving out the fact that "goods are exchanged against money," which raises the true puzzle of monetary economics, namely, why "goods are not exchanged against goods."[11] For example, Wolfgang Ernst argues that the beginning of a true monetary system is the moment when monetary units are standardized and the focus is on *counting*.[12] Taking this incident as given, it neglects the fact that a monetary transaction in this case involves the exchange of a certain number of standardized pieces of *money* against a certain number of standardized units of the good under consideration. The concept that the value of *a cow* is 10 standardized pieces of *money* also requires standardization and countability of cows: a cow must be a cow. A transaction of that kind is possible only if both partners of the exchange mutually agree on the standardization.[13]

Ancient law texts provide interesting evidence for this bi-directionality. Konrad Schmid, in Chapter 12 of this volume, reports that the Sumerian Codes of Ur-Nammu (*c.*2100 BC) and Eshnunna (*c.*1800 BC) contain lists of compensation payments for bodily injuries.

[10] D. Hume, "Vom Gelde," in: K. Diehl and P. Mombert (eds.), *Vom Geld I: Ausgewählte Lesestücke zur Politischen Ökonomie*, 4th edn., Karlsruhe: Braunsche Hofdruckerei und Verlag 1923, 47–62, at 61.

[11] Clower, "A Reconsideration of the Microfoundations of Monetary Theory"; and D. Gale, *Money: In Equilibrium*. Cambridge University Press 1982.

[12] W. Ernst, "Geld: Ein Überblick aus historischer Sicht," in: *Gott und Geld: Jahrbuch für Biblische Theologie 21*, Neukirchen: Neukirchener Verlag 2006, 3–21.

[13] For the importance of standardization for the use of money, see B. Hess, "Standardization and monetization: legal perspectives," Chapter 4 below.

Payment was made in hack-silver, metal rings, disks, and other premonetary mediums of exchange. These codes obviously involve a standardization of body parts – a "hand" is a "hand" etc., and a concept of the economic loss involved in the injury. No distinctions were made in the compensation rules according to the social status of the injured person and regarding the intentionality of the act, nor according to the properties of the injured body part before the injury occurred.[14]

The later Babylonian Code of Hammurabi (*c.*1750 BC) treats bodily injuries in a strikingly different way. It distinguishes according to the social status of the injured person and the offender and reserves standardized compensation payments to cases where the offender is of higher social class than the person offended. There is still standardization of the offense in cases where the offender is of lower social status than the person offended, but in these cases (standardized) rules of *lex talionis* apply. Thus, a reduction in the degree of standardization of the offense goes along with demonetization of the penalty. The even later Covenant Code of the Second Book of Moses recognizes even less standardization of the offenses, rarely uses fixed compensatory payments, and often has fines being determined by a judge. Thus, the tendency of demonetization, together with less standardization of the offense, is carried further.[15]

A further example of the same point is the popular idea that money makes all goods comparable in the fact that they have monetary prices. The idea behind this is that two objects which are not comparable in their intrinsic values become comparable by virtue of the fact that they have monetary prices. This is obviously a fallacy. Suppose that I am unable to express the price of some object X in terms of another object Y directly, that is, I cannot state an amount of X I am willing to give up in exchange for a given quantity of Y, although I find both objects desirable. Assume, for simplicity, that "money" is the only other object apart from X and Y that exists in the world. X has a price in terms of money only if I am willing to exchange a certain quantity of money against a certain quantity of X. But this will only be true if either money itself is a

---

[14] Hingston Quiggin, *A Survey of Primitive Money*, gives numerous examples of standardized valuations of human life and bodily injuries in primitive, but also more recent, societies. She also uses bride prices as an example of standardization.

[15] K. Schmid, "The monetization and demonetization of the human body: the case of compensatory payments for bodily injuries and homicide in ancient Near Eastern and ancient Israelite law books," Chapter 12 below.

desirable object, which may be true for pieces of gold but not for paper money, or if the value of money derives from the fact that instead of spending it on X, I could spend it on Y, i.e. Y, too, has a price in terms of money. If money itself is not a desirable object, the fact that X and Y have prices in terms of money implies that X has a price in terms of Y, namely, the ratio of the two money prices. If money itself has no intrinsic value, the fact that money prices of X and Y exist implies that I have an idea of how much a given quantity of Y is worth in terms of X. Either way, the comparability of X and Y is a logical precondition for both to have well-defined prices in terms of money.

Thus, money does not make things comparable. Monetary prices require that the participants in the exchange know the value of the goods exchanged in terms of each other. In fact, money, which has no consumption value itself can only exist itself if things are comparable. More technically, money has value in the situation described above, because, in Clower's terminology, exchange relations are transitive, i.e. the fact that X can be exchanged against money, and money against Y, implies that X can be exchanged against Y. This, however, is not a special property of monetary economies. Barter economies have the same characteristic.[16]

One may, however, argue that in some instances money suggests a comparability of truly incomparable things. In their contributions to this volume, Günter Thomas and Piet Naudé discuss the use of monetary payments to make compensation for injustice and suffering inflicted by the state or a brutal political regime.[17] True respect for the victims would require that their afflictions be regarded as unique, incomparable to the afflictions suffered by others. Examples of this deep-rooted demand for true respect are seen clearly in the Book of Lamentations ("Is there any sorrow like my sorrow?" 1:12) and the anger with which Jewish organizations regularly respond to any comparison of the Holocaust with other sufferings. Yet, monetary compensation for such sufferings creates a dimension in which they can be compared, even if such comparison is not intended, namely, the

---

[16] Clower, "A Reconsideration of the Microfoundations of Monetary Theory," 84.

[17] P. Naudé, "Standardized monetization of the market and the argument for preferential justice," Chapter 14 below, and G. Thomas, "What price do we place on life? Ethical observations on the limits of law and money in a case of transitional justice," Chapter 13 below.

consumption of material things that can be afforded with the compensation payment. Thus, the real issue is the – more or less conscious – denial of those who pay compensation to truly respect the victims: by reducing their suffering to a loss of consumption which can be made good by paying money, those who pay can create for themselves the illusion that justice has been properly restored. This is a problem of social justice and consciousness thereof which the use of money makes visible, but money itself is not the cause of the problem.

Immanuel Kant argued that having a price is incompatible for anything having "dignity," because prices establish comparability whereas dignity requires incomparability.[18] In the same vein, though without proper acknowledgment to Kant, Michael J. Sandel warns that by attaching monetary prices to things, society reduces them to commodities, and that this may deny them their proper valuation with dignity and respect.[19] As Sandel puts it: "Sometimes, market values [i.e. prices] crowd out nonmarket values worth caring about."[20] For both, then, the issue is the assignment of prices to what should have dignity, which, as I have argued above, is unrelated to the use of money as a medium of exchange. The true question, Sandel notes, then, is what is the proper reach of markets? Herbert Schlossberg points to the need for a Christian ethic to answer this question: "They [Christians] should be wary of the temptation to have ever more of the world's goods for that desire is what takes away personal freedom, delivering people into the clutches of those who want power. Covetousness is the weakness that induces them to give up what should not be for sale."[21]

III The nature and origin of money

Money as a social institution

The core of the economic theory of money focuses on the question of under what circumstances "money" will have a positive value in terms

[18] I. Kant, *Grundlegung zur Metaphysik der Sitten.* Stuttgart: Reclam 1961/2008, 72–3.

[19] M. J. Sandel, *What Money Can't Buy: The Moral Limits of Markets.* London: Allen Lane 2012.

[20] Ibid., 9.

[21] H. Schlossberg, *Idols for Destruction: The Conflict of Christian Faith and American Culture.* Wheaton: Crossway Books 1993.

of consumable goods in an economy. It defines money as a good with three essential properties – not functions – one of which is physical, the others social in nature: (1) money is storable, i.e. it can be kept from one period to another without losing its value completely; (2) it is accepted and offered in exchange for many or most other goods, but the purpose of acquiring it is not (solely) to consume; and (3) it is anonymous or nameless,[22] i.e. it is not a claim on an individual person or institution. We distinguish between two kinds of money: commodity money, if the good being used as money is itself a good which could be used for consumption, such as gold coins, and fiat money, if the good being used as money has no intrinsic value, such as paper money.

As we shall see below, the first property is related to the fact that money is valued only if trading other goods involves time and time is valuable. Being storable, money can serve as a store of value, but other goods or claims on goods can do that as well without being "money." If trade indeed involves time, the features of money as being a store of value and a medium of exchange are essentially the same.[23]

Hume emphasizes the second characteristic: "Money is not a true object of trade; rather, it is a means which, by convention of human beings, serves to make the exchange of one commodity against another more easy."[24] Roscher defines money as the most marketable good in an economy.[25] Clower goes one step further,[26] and defines money as a commodity which can be traded against all other commodities, which is not generally true for other goods. This is summarized in the dictum that "money buys goods and goods buy money, but goods do not buy goods." Similarly, Jones defines monetary exchange by two characteristics: "There is one good which enters into every exchange. Any other good entering an exchange, if purchased is not resold, and if sold is not repurchased. The one exceptional good is termed the 'medium of exchange.'"[27] Yet, the requirement that "money" be accepted and offered for *all* other goods seems too strong. Kiyotaki and Wright, the founders of the modern theory of money, offer the following definition: "When a commodity is accepted in trade not to be consumed or used in

[22] Gale, *Money.*   [23] Ibid.   [24] Hume, "Vom Gelde," 48.

[25] W. Roscher, *Grundlagen der Nationalökonomie: System der Volkswirtschaft I.* Stuttgart, 15th edn., 1880, in *Economic Inquiry* 6(1) (1967): 1–8.

[26] Clower, "A Reconsideration of the Microfoundations of Monetary Theory."

[27] R. A. Jones, "The Origin and Development of Media of Exchange." *Journal of Political Economy* 84(4) (1976): 758.

production but to be used to facilitate further trade, it becomes a medium of exchange and is called commodity money. If an object with no intrinsic value becomes a medium of exchange, it is called fiat money."[28]

We may then think about the use of commodity money such as gold coins as involving two aspects: first, the exchange of other goods against gold for the simple purpose of being able to consume gold, i.e. to turn it into pieces of jewelry or to use it to embellish a building. Under this aspect, the exchange of gold against other commodities is simply an example of barter, not of a monetary economy. Second, the exchange of other goods against gold for the sole purpose of being able to exchange these coins against other goods at a later point in time, and without desiring to consume the gold. This is what makes gold coins "money."

If, in a given economy, individuals demand gold coins only to exchange them against other goods at later points in time, and gold is a scarce commodity, then the value of gold, i.e. the ratio at which individuals are willing to exchange it against other goods, must be larger than if gold were only used for consumption. Thus, for an economy to be a monetary economy rather than a pure barter economy, it must be true that some people are willing to exchange other goods for gold at a higher price than if they had to consume the gold themselves. We can then think of monetary theory as explaining this extra value. Obviously, fiat money is a special case.

To claim that gold coins have a higher value if they are money rather than durable consumption goods may seem an empirically empty statement, but it is not. It implies that those who produce money can appropriate the extra value for themselves. From this perspective, it is no surprise that governments have always tried to acquire the monopoly of money production within their sphere of power: the fact that governments are willing to spend real resources on enforcing this monopoly suggests that it has real value. Economists have often explained the fact that, from earliest history, governments have held the monopoly of producing money, by the argument that the use of money requires that its value – in terms of metallic content – is credible and that only governments had the necessary credibility. This, of course, is in stark contrast to the historical experience that governments have

---

[28] N. Kiyotaki and R. Wright, "On Money as a Medium of Exchange." *Journal of Political Economy* 974 (1989): 927–54.

often abused their monopoly of money production by debasing the currency. The argument outlined above suggests, instead, that governments hold the monopoly of money production because they are the only institution in society with the power to usurp and defend that monopoly. Furthermore, there are many empirical examples of societies in which money emerged spontaneously without government involvement, such as cigarettes in POW camps, sea shells, or cattle.[29]

Gale emphasizes the third property of money, namelessness.[30] It differentiates money from other assets which may be used in exchange for goods, e.g. IOUs or other forms of trade credit. With IOUs or trade credit, consumable goods are exchanged against the promise repayment, possibly in different goods, at a later point in time. Since IOUs and other forms of trade credit pay interest, the lender is compensated for the fact that he has to postpone consumption of the goods he will eventually receive. This makes IOUs and trade credit more attractive as mediums of exchange than non-interest-bearing coins or paper money. However, the use of IOUs and trade credit as mediums of exchange requires that the promise to pay back be credible. The borrower must have a sufficiently strong incentive to keep his commitment to paying back. Where this is not the case, IOUs and other forms of trade credit will not be used. In such situations, however, money can still be used as a medium of exchange. Accepting money in exchange for consumable goods requires the expectation that some agent in the future will do the same, but this need not be the same agent with whom the first transaction was concluded. In Gale's words, "money replaces trust" in individuals by trust in social institutions.[31]

IV The benchmark: a pure exchange economy

In this section, we review what modern monetary theory tells us about the origin of money. Gale sets the agenda by stating that "money buys goods and goods buy money, but goods do not buy goods" should be properly understood as a statement about the markets, or trading opportunities available in an economy rather than a statement about the functions of money.[32] We start from a fictitious economy that has

---

[29] K. Burdett, A. Trejos, and R. Wright, "Cigarette Money." *Journal of Economic Theory* 99 (2001): 117–42.
[30] Gale, *Money.*   [31] Ibid., 242.   [32] Ibid., 231.

no use for money and then introduce restrictions that make money valuable.

The benchmark of monetary theory is the "Arrow-Debreu" economy.[33] This is an economy populated by a finite number of consumers with preferences over a finite number of goods and initial endowments of these goods. Preferences are described by binary orderings of bundles of goods which are complete, transitive, reflexive, and convex. Each ordering is of the form "the bundle of goods x is preferred to the bundle of goods x_j." Goods are defined by their physical characteristics, including the place and time of their availability for consumption. A price system of this economy is a vector of relative prices between all goods existing in the economy. The *numéraire*, or unit of account, for calculating these relative prices is completely arbitrary, as long as it is one of the goods in the economy. The economy is competitive in the sense that all consumers take the price vector as given when they decide which goods they wish to exchange against which other goods. An individual consumer's budget constraint is the sum of all the goods in his initial endowment multiplied by their respective relative prices. It defines the set of bundles of goods which the consumer can afford given his initial endowment. All individuals are free to enter into or refrain from exchanging goods with other individuals. Consumers choose the bundle of goods they prefer most within their budget constraint by selling goods from their initial endowment and buying additional goods in exchange. Market prices are flexible and adjust, such that all markets clear, i.e. the total quantity of a good demanded is equal to the total quantity offered in all markets.

In the Arrow-Debreu economy, the system of markets is complete in the sense that all goods can be bought and sold against all other goods. Note that since goods are defined by the point in time when they are available, which need not be the point in time when they are traded, we should interpret the exchange of goods as the conclusion of contracts to deliver and accept certain goods at certain points in time, at certain locations, and under certain circumstances. That is, an individual consumer can make a contract with other consumers specifying the exchange of any two goods. An allocation of goods is a distribution of the goods existing in the economy over all consumers. Since goods are

---

[33] G. Debreu, *The Theory of Value: An Axiomatic Analysis of Economic Equilibrium.* New Haven, CT: Yale University Press 1959.

defined by the time of their availability, complete markets means that all trading takes place simultaneously in the initial period of existence of the economy. This implies that contracts can specify the exchange of goods available at different points in time. Consumers, therefore, face a lifetime budget constraint, i.e. the total value of the goods they buy must be equal to the total value they sell over their entire lifetime.

A competitive equilibrium of this economy is a price system such that all consumers choose the most preferred bundle of goods in their budget constraints and all markets clear in the sense that, for each good existing in the economy, the total quantity offered by all consumers for sale is equal to the total quantity demanded by all consumers to buy. Arrow-Debreu economies have three properties which make them easy to understand and, hence, a good benchmark for value theory: first, every competitive equilibrium is Pareto efficient. This means that no goods are wasted and no individual consumer can be made better off without making another consumer worse off. Second, every Pareto-efficient allocation can be attained as a competitive equilibrium, provided that the initial endowments are distributed among the consumers appropriately. Third, the value of each good in this economy can be expressed in terms of any other good and is given by the rate at which it can be exchanged against it. In the competitive equilibrium, it reflects the change in any consumer's well-being which would result from exchanging a small quantity of this good against the other. Thus, everything is comparable to everything else. This is a consequence of the completeness of preferences and the completeness of markets.

It is easy to see that such an economy does not have any use for money. Since all contracts are concluded simultaneously at the beginning of the economy, there is no need for money as an asset transporting value from one period to another. Hence, commodity money cannot have any value above its intrinsic value, and fiat money cannot have positive value at all, i.e. no consumer will exchange other goods for fiat money. One may be tempted to argue that fiat money could be valuable as a *numéraire*, as pricing all goods in terms of money reduces the complexity of the price system from $n(n-1)$ relative prices to n. But this is impossible, since the relative price of fiat money in terms of any other good is zero and, hence, fiat money prices are undefined.

The simplest Arrow-Debreu economies are characterized by perfect foresight, i.e. consumers know perfectly well what state they will be in, in every future period and how they can exchange goods in that state.

They can be extended to allow for an uncertain future by defining possible states of nature in each future period and probability distributions assigning each possible state a probability of its realization. This requires a modification of the notion of complete markets. The existence of complete markets now means that it is possible to conclude contracts specifying which goods a consumer exchanges for which other goods in every future period given the state he finds himself in and given a price vector. A price system is now a vector of relative prices contingent on the state of nature prevailing in each period. Again, it is possible to construct a competitive equilibrium with the same, desirable properties as before. That is, uncertainty does not give money value.

It is tempting to argue that, although the economy has no need for money, it could use fiat money if all consumers agree to assign a positive value to it, the approach taken by Woodford.[34] This is possible, but results in a very fragile outcome. Every individual accepting fiat money against other goods would have to be aware of the risk that the attitudes of other individuals might change accidentally such that they no longer accept money. If so, the individual is stuck with something for which he has no use. Given this risk, it is always safer not to accept money in the first place.

Arrow-Debreu economies embed the notions of specialization in consumption and production, i.e. the fact that individuals produce and offer things different from the things they wish to consume. This, of course, is a necessary condition for any trade to occur in a society. As Adam Smith emphasized, specialization is the key to improve productivity and, hence, economic wealth. Specialization can make trade complicated because it may require a "double co-incidence of wants":[35] an individual can trade directly with another individual if, and only if, one wants the good the other offers and vice versa. But the Arrow-Debreu economy shows that this is not a sufficient condition for the use of money. Since all trades take place simultaneously at the same place, chains of trade involving many individuals at the same time and giving each individual exactly his most desired bundle of goods within his budget constraint can easily be constructed without introducing a medium of exchange.

---

[34] M. Woodford, *Interest and Prices*. Boston, MA: MIT Press 2002.
[35] W. S. Jevons, *Money and the Mechanism of Exchange*. London: King 1875.

Trading frictions

Modern monetary theory recognizes that money can emerge only in economies characterized by trading frictions, i.e. limits on the range of trades feasible in an economy. The challenge is to spell out exactly what the economic nature of these frictions is, rather than referring to some unspecified cost of transaction or exogenous trading technology.[36]

A first friction is that trade is locally decentralized, trading takes time, and time is valuable:[37] individuals can only conclude one transaction at a time, and each transaction takes an interval of time of strictly positive length. This would be true if trading involves communication and negotiation between potential buyers and sellers and each individual has a limited capacity for communication and negotiation in each period. This is when the "double coincidence of wants," the condition that one partner of the exchange wishes to sell the good that the other wishes to buy, becomes a real restriction on trade. If individuals are strongly specialized in their endowments and their desires for consumption, they will often find themselves in situations where one wants the good another offers, but the latter does not want the good the first offers to him. Whenever this happens, the two must part without trading unless one finds a way of offering the other an acceptable compensation.

The obvious way to do this is for the first individual to promise the second to deliver the good he wants at a later point in time, i.e. to use trade credit or issue an IOU. The first individual can then consume the good he wants and continue to look for other individuals who wish to exchange his good for the good the second individual desires. The interest rate demanded on the trade credit would be the compensation demanded by the latter for the fact that he has to postpone consumption. Thus, the fact that trade is decentralized and takes time alone does not support the use of money.

The additional friction required is what Gale calls lack of trust.[38] Trade credit and IOUs will only be accepted in exchange for consumable goods if the seller can be reasonably sure that he will eventually receive what he desires. Trust can be supported in two ways: by close

---

[36] For transactions costs see J. Niehans, *The Theory of Money*. Baltimore, OH, London: Johns Hopkins University Press, 1978; for trading technologies see Clower, "A Reconsideration of the Microfoundations of Monetary Theory."

[37] Jones, "The Origin and Development of Media of Exchange."

[38] Gale, *Money*.

social ties among the trading partners, or by the strong enforcement of credit contracts by the government. Close communities, in which each individual knows the economic circumstances of the others and compliance with promises is enforced by social norms and the threat of being expelled from the community, can support trade over time based on trade credit.[39] This is well known from the fact that most exchanges among families or closed villages in developing countries are non-monetary, even if they involve credit over considerable periods of time.

At the other end of the spectrum is a trading system based on IOUs, credit cards, checkable asset accounts, and other financial assets than money. By definition, such assets are named. Trade based on named assets then requires comprehensive bookkeeping services keeping track of all credit relations an individual has entered into and a powerful institution enforcing credit contracts. Modern financial and legal systems facilitate just that.[40]

Where neither social norms nor bookkeeping services and contract enforcement exist, indirect trade can be based on a medium of exchange in situations where the double coincidence of wants does not hold.[41] Suppose two individuals meet, one of whom carries a good the other wants, while the other does not have the good the first wants for consumption. To facilitate trade, it is sufficient that the first accepts the good which the second has with the intention of exchanging it for the good he wants for consumption at a later point in time, when he meets an individual carrying that good. In this case, the good carried by the second individual becomes the medium of exchange. Obviously, the

---

[39] R. E. Kranton, "Reciprocal Exchange: A Self-Sustaining System." *American Economic Review* 86(4) (1996): 830–51, describes the trading system of the !Kung tribe in the Kalahari Desert which was based entirely on reciprocity. The huts of a !Kung village were arranged in such a way that their entrances all faced the village center, so that family life in the hut could easily be observed. When reciprocal trade vanished and was replaced by monetary exchange, villagers preferred to relocate the entrances of their huts to gain privacy.

[40] J. von Hagen and Ingo Fender, "Monetary Policy in a More Perfect Financial System." *Open Economies Review* 9 (1998): 493–531.

[41] This gives rise to the modern "search theory of money," see Miquel Faig, "Divisible Money in an Economy with Villages." Mimeo, University of Toronto, 2004; Kiyotaki and Wright, "On Money as a Medium of Exchange," 927–54; N. Kocherlakota and R. Narayana, "Money is Memory." *Journal of Economic Theory* 81 (1998): 232–51; N. Kiyotaki and R. Wright, "The Search Theoretic Approach in Monetary Economics." *American Economic Review* 83(1) (1993): 63–77.

attractiveness of the good as a medium of exchange depends crucially on the first individual's expectation that he will meet another person willing to accept that good with a sufficiently high probability. This creates a tendency for societies to settle on one or a small number of mediums of exchange. Commodities which are demanded by almost everyone in society and limited in supply are good candidates.[42] A good becomes money if it is generally accepted as a medium of exchange.

Money does not require trust in an individual's ability to deliver consumable goods in the future, as it is not a claim on an individual. Its acceptance as means of payment stems solely from the expectation that other individuals will also accept it as means of payment in the future. Monetary exchange, therefore, facilitates trade among individuals who do not expect to see each other again and do not fulfill the double coincidence of wishes. However, it does so only if individuals exchanging consumable goods for money at a given point in time are reasonably sure that there will be markets in which money can be exchanged for consumable goods at a later point in time. Monetary exchange, therefore, requires trust in the continuation of the market system and the use of the particular asset used as money. Thus, it is necessarily backed by trust in social institutions rather than trust in individuals.[43]

To conclude, monetary economies are characterized by decentralized trade involving time and lack of trust allowing trade credit. Modern monetary theory shows that monetary exchange takes place if individuals are sufficiently specialized in consumption and production in the sense that they frequently end up in situations where the double coincidence of wants does not hold, and the good serving as money does not lose its value too quickly over time.[44] The theory does not explain how monetary exchange comes into existence, i.e. what it takes for an economy to move from pure barter to monetary exchange, but it identifies the conditions under which money can be supported.

Once these conditions are met, the question arises which commodity will serve as "money." The main factor here is that the quality of a commodity should be relatively easy to identify for it to serve as a means

---

[42] See Jones, "The Origin and Development of Media of Exchange," and Menger, "On the Origin of Money."
[43] Gale, *Money.*   [44] Burdett et al., "Cigarette Money."

of payment.[45] Societies will tend to settle on the use of commodities with relatively low information costs as mediums of exchange. Standardization of the units of money such as coins lowers the cost of information and makes such coins better candidates to be chosen as money. Changes in the relationship between the quality of a commodity and the cost to acquire the information necessary to judge that quality can cause a commodity used as a means of payment in an economy to be driven out by other means of payment.

The role of government

Hume points to a twofold, special role of government in explaining monetary exchange.[46] On the one hand, governments with sufficiently large geographical domains of power have an interest in promoting monetary exchange so that they can collect taxes in money. For governments that maintain large armies or administrations, collecting taxes in kind is awkward, because it requires to transport the goods collected as taxes to the place where the army or the public servants are located. Furthermore, it restricts the set of goods the army or the public servants can be offered in compensation for their services. Thus, the development of empires of significant size raises the attractiveness of demanding tax payment in money from the citizens. As a result, citizens will trade goods for money at least partially to be able to pay their taxes, while trading on a credit basis among their closely knit local communities, a phenomenon that can still be observed today in village communities in developing countries. Furthermore, Hume argues that monetary exchange promotes specialization which, in turn, increases productivity and, hence, the tax base of an economy. Hume, therefore, urges governments to promote the use of money.

Grierson argues that, from the earliest beginnings, coined money was stamped by governments (including religious authorities) and the coins bore the symbols of government (including temples) as well as the names of governors.[47] The reason is presumably that the government was known to the potential users of the money and its reputation as a

---

[45] Ibid.; see also A. Alchian, "Why Money?" *Journal of Money, Credit and Banking* 1 (1973): 133–40, and K. Brunner and A. H. Meltzer, "The Uses of Money: Money in the Theory of an Exchange Economy." *American Economic Review* 61 (5) (1971): 784–805.

[46] Hume, "Vom Gelde."   [47] Grierson, *The Origins of Money*.

power to be reckoned with could serve as a backup for the credibility of the value of the coins in terms of their metal content. Grierson adds that the use of coins facilitated the payment of large mercenary armies as well as the execution of large-scale public works in ancient states. But the argument is less compelling than it seems. First, as Hölscher, in Chapter 6 of this volume, points out, a powerful state did not exist in the Greek cities of the seventh and sixth centuries BC, where coinage was first invented.[48] On the contrary, the large empires of Ancient Egypt and Mesopotamia did not use coined money, yet they had executed very large-scale public building projects and maintained large armies based on a well-developed, hierarchical administration. Second, the army and public-works argument risks being a circular one: mercenaries and workers on large building sites would accept coins only if they were already in use as a general means of payment. Nevertheless, Hölscher shows that, in the Greek cities, the emergence of rich temples and the emergence of coined money evolved in parallel. Thus, it is relatively small governments lacking a powerful administration that find the use of coined money convenient for paying workers engaged in public projects.

Finally, the argument is ambivalent, since the historical evidence also shows that coins had a tendency to lose metal content over time, i.e. governments stamped more coins out of a given quantity of precious metal in order to gain seignorage. It is interesting to observe that, as Hölscher points out, the Greek cities were not ruled by a strong, independent authority but by the "*polis*," the community of the citizens, and thus the users of the coins themselves. Here, the link between the community issuing coins and that using them may have been strong enough to contain the incentive for inflating the currency to gain seignorage. Modern history has shown in many examples that this is not a general characteristic of democracies, however – see Chapter 2 by Peter Bernholz in this volume.[49] After all, the inflationary bias of monetary policy in modern democracies is the main justification for "independent" central banks.[50]

---

[48] T. Hölscher, "Money and image: the presence of the state on the routes of economy," Chapter 6 below.

[49] P. Bernholz, "Money and its role in a decentralized market economy," Chapter 2 below.

[50] M. Fratianni, J. von Hagen, and C. J. Waller, "Central Banking as a Political Principal Agent Problem." *Economic Inquiry* 35 (1997): 378–94.

V Implications for "the standardized monetization of markets"

The discussion in the previous sections of this chapter raises a number of interesting points for the research agenda covered by this volume. The first is that the use of money arises from a set of characteristics of a society and its economic system such as decentralized trade, specialization in production and consumption, and the absence of institutions supporting trade credit. The use of money does not of itself create these characteristics. Therefore, money should not be mistaken as the cause of the social processes and phenomena that result in its use. An attempt to circulate money would be futile in an economy which does not support the use of money, as the conditions for monetary exchange are not fulfilled. Even for tax purposes, money would be used at the margin of such a society at best. In this regard, Seow seems to get it right when he suggests that a "democratization of commerce" would be closely tied to the emergence of a monetary economy,[51] but he is wrong in suggesting that the socio-economic changes of the time were a result of the democratization of the "use of money."[52]

Second, an important topic in several contributions to this volume concerns the setting of Kohelet in a historical period in which the use of money became a fact of everyday life, as Seow argues[53] and Spieckermann and Welker emphasize.[54] Monetary theory can help us identify the circumstances under which this would be the case. If it could be shown that, during the time of the writing of Kohelet, social and political forces created the right conditions, we could perhaps explain both the mood of futility encountered in the book and the monetization of the economy as simultaneous consequences of these forces.

What would we have to look for? The first force is the breaking up of traditional, closely knit social relations among the participants in economic exchanges, resulting in a dissolution of trust and the disappearance of trade credit. This could be due to a number of developments: greater local (and social) mobility of people, more intense trading relations with more distant and less-known partners, the decline of social values that previously provided the glue for exchanges based on

---

[51] C.-L. Seow, *Ecclesiastes*, Anchor Bible 18C, New York, 1997, 23.
[52] Ibid., 21.   [53] Ibid.
[54] H. Spieckermann and M. Welker, "Der Wort Gottes und der Wert des Besitzes für den Menschen nach Qohelet," in: *Gott und Geld*, 103.

trade credit, or the decline of traditional powers enforcing trade con-tracts among local traders. Such a process would most likely be accom-panied by a general feeling of insecurity as traditional relations and values deteriorate. In this regard, there does not seem to be agreement among historians. McNutt refers to a process of reurbanization and the emergence of a class of urban elites in Judah under Persian rule: "The introduction of this urban population, which had different ethnic con-nection, regional experiences, political affiliations, occupations and financial bases resulted eventually in a significant shift in Judah's social character."[55] Seow indicates that Persian rule radically changed the allocation of property rights, especially over land, and that the Persian king's policy of granting rights was largely discretionary.[56] Furthermore, economic and social mobility were greatly increased under Persian rule.[57] All this is consistent with a process of dissolving traditional social relations, destroying trust and favoring the introduc-tion of a monetary exchange system.

In contrast, Berquist argues that the economy of Yehud during the exilic period remained much the same as before the destruction of Jerusalem.[58] Only later, under the Persian king, Xerxes, did a more pluralistic society emerge in Yehud, as the political influence of Persia declined and the elites that had founded their social positions on their ties with the colonial power lost their ability to maintain them and to enforce social norms. Yet, Berquist describes this and the subsequent period under Artaxerxes as one of economic decline in Yehud. This decline resulted in the poor getting poorer and the social conflicts described in Nehemiah 3. At the same time, Berquist sees Yehud becom-ing increasingly isolated from other parts of the Persian empire, includ-ing the surrounding provinces. Such developments would hardly provide the basis for an emerging monetary economy.

The second force is the emergence of a greater degree of specialization in production and consumption among individuals. Acquiring a more sophisticated lifestyle, consuming a wider range of differentiated con-sumer goods, e.g. by becoming more open to foreign cultures, would be a process leading to more specialization in consumption. Adopting

---

[55] P. McNutt, *Reconstructing the Society of Ancient Israel*. London: Westminster John Knox Press 1999, 192.
[56] Seow, *Ecclesiastes*, 23.   [57] Ibid., 29.
[58] J. L. Berquist, *Judaism in Persia's Shadow*. Minneapolis: Fortress Press 1995.

technologies allowing a greater specialization according to comparative advantage would be a process leading to more specialization in production. A process of urbanization as alluded to by McNutt is consistent with that.[59] Note that the latter typically results in winners and losers and, therefore, changes in relative wealth and income positions among individuals in society. This is in stark contrast, however, with authors like Berquist, Snell, and Grabbe, who describe the economy of Yehud in the Persian period as predominantly agrarian with little social mobility.[60]

The third force is the emergence of political powers extending over greater territories than before. This would make the introduction of money coined and issued by greater powers more likely than the introduction of money coined and issued by local powers. If Seow's dating of Kohelet in the Persian period is correct (second half of the fifth and first half of the fourth century),[61] the introduction of the Persian taxation of Yehud could explain the politics behind monetization.[62] McNutt points to evidence of increased taxation under the Persian reign, leading to frequent bankruptcies and loss of land among the local populations, reinforcing the role of economic uncertainty mentioned above.[63] Yet, it is not the introduction of money which is the driving force, but the need of a rising territorial power for tax revenues.

Berquist[64] and Grabbe,[65] in contrast, suggest that Yehud was taxed heavily to supply the Persian troops engaged in Egypt with food, but such taxes would have been payable in kind and not involve the use of money. To the extent that the Persian treasury reimbursed the province for its food supplies and these reimbursements were paid in coins, payment would have been to the temple rather than to the ordinary people. Grabbe argues that the Persian kings after Darius never engaged

---

[59] McNutt, *Reconstructing the Society of Ancient Israel.*

[60] Berquist, *Judaism in Persia's Shadow*; D. C. Snell, *Life in the Ancient Near East.* New Haven, London: Yale University Press 1997; L. I. Grabbe, *A History of the Jews and Judaism in the Second Temple Period, Vol. 1: Yehud: A History of the Persian Province of Judah.* London, New York: T&T Clark International 2004.

[61] Seow, *Ecclesiastes.*

[62] See Spieckermann and Welker, "Der Wert Gottes und der Wert des Besitzes für den Menschen nach Qohelet," in: *Gott und Geld*, 103.

[63] McNutt, *Reconstructing the Society of Ancient Israel*, 190.

[64] Berquist, *Judaism in Persia's Shadow.*

[65] Grabbe, *A History of the Jews and Judaism in the Second Temple Period, Vol. 1.*

in any policies aimed at developing the economies of their colonial provinces including Yehud. Thus, it seems unlikely that they would have promoted the use of money in Yehud to encourage economic specialization and increase productivity as suggested by David Hume.

VI Conclusions

Monetary economics continues to fascinate economists and non-economists alike. In this chapter, I have reviewed the foundations of monetary theory in order to identify the social conditions under which monetary exchange will arise. These include lack of trust in individual contractual commitments due to social mobility and frequent economic interactions with strangers, economic specialization, and decentralization of economic activities. Clearly, moving from a static society with stable economic relationships and little interaction with strangers to a society in which monetary exchange emerges, can be a frightening and devastating experience, especially if it happens quickly.

Another line of thought within the research agenda covered by this volume is that money makes all things comparable and thus subjects all things to the law of market exchange. As I have pointed out in this chapter, this, again, is a fallacy. Comparability of different objects, i.e. the ability to name a price for exchange, is a precondition for the use of fiat money, not a consequence. It presupposes the willingness of the potential trading partners to negotiate the terms of trade, and which objects are negotiable and which are not is an issue of social and private values and conventions, not a characteristic of money. The existence of – possibly several – "limited purpose" moneys in many societies (Grierson)[66] is a case in point. The spreading of market exchanges into ever-more spheres of social life is a process which is separate from the use of money – a complete market system does not need money to exist. Of course, in a monetary economy, the spreading of markets implies that more and more things can be bought with money, and the existence of money in a society may facilitate the spreading of markets, but this is a secondary phenomenon.

In sum, the contribution of this chapter to the volume is a methodological one. I argue that money and the spreading of its use are consequences, not causes, of changes in social structures. Of course, this

---

[66] Grierson, *The Origins of Money*.

does not force us to negate that, once monetary exchange has emerged in a society, it will have effects on human thinking and behavior. Yet, researchers coming from other social sciences should not confuse the emergence of monetary exchange with the underlying changes in society that cause it. Monetary economics can help identify what the true causes are.

2 | Money and its role in a decentralized market economy

PETER BERNHOLZ

Introduction

Money fulfills key functions of coordinating the decisions of economic actors in decentralized market economies as a medium of exchange, a store of value, and a unit of account. Without money, the division of labor and the complicated economic texture of highly developed and, thus, wealthy countries could never have arisen. It is not my intention to repeat the analysis in Jürgen von Hagen's chapter. Instead, I will concentrate on some additional aspects.

During the process of economic development, the nature of money has changed dramatically, especially in its functions as a store of value and a means of payment. As a store of value, it is today important only in underdeveloped countries, where trustworthy, interest-bearing financial instruments are absent or rare. And as a means of payment, it has changed its nature from commodity money with an intrinsic value corresponding to its nominal value to paper money with scarcely any intrinsic value at all, to checking accounts, which, until recently, were just figures on paper and are nowadays only electronic signals, and, finally, to debit cards. This development towards more and more abstract forms of money has been the source of many benefits and problems, which will be illustrated in this chapter. Finally, some other problems of money for society will be discussed.

Solving the problem of coordination in a decentralized economy

I illustrate the possibility of a pure decentralized credit economy with the simplest example of multilateral exchange, namely, trilateral exchange among three partners. It can easily be extended to situations implying multilateral exchange with more than three participants. In Figure 2.1, we assume that the people involved in the trilateral barter have already agreed on the exchange relations of the three goods to be

O: Two pairs of shoes; D: 3kg wheat

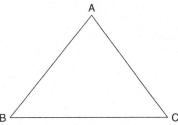

O: 3kg wheat; D: One suit   O: One suit; D: Two pairs of shoes

O: Commodities offered; D: Commodities demanded

Figure 2.1 Trilateral barter

exchanged. We further assume that the amounts offered correspond to the wishes of the respective persons. The three potential participants A, B, and C, are all offering goods which are demanded by one of the others, but, unfortunately, not by the person offering the goods wanted in exchange. In this situation the use of commodity money with full intrinsic value is a means to solve these problems. For instance, A is prepared to sell shoes to C for money, since he knows that B is ready to accept it for the 3kg of wheat he wants. And, similarly, B takes the money to buy the suit he desires from C. Obviously, this chain of transactions could also be started by B or C. Note that the existence of money allows division of a trilateral barter exchange, where all participants would have to know their offers and wishes and to meet in one place, into three bilateral transactions. In these transactions, there is no need to know about the wishes of others and to meet in one place for all transactions. But there is one condition: the person executing the first payment must have a sufficient amount of commodity money. It must be available somewhere in society. Now, as Adam Smith already observed, this is a waste of resources, since, for example, the silver for the coins has to be mined, refined, and minted. Thus, is there not a cheaper way to reach the same result?

And there is no doubt that such a solution exists. B could give the 3kg of wheat to A on credit, while B would get the suit from C on credit. Finally, A would grant credit to C for delivering the two pairs of shoes. The debts arising from these transactions could be settled at the end of the three bilateral transactions, which would lead to zero balances for all three participants. With this approach, the search and information costs connected to trilateral barter could be saved as if commodity money were used, and this without the need to spend resources for the production of silver coins.

However, this solution depends on a crucial condition: all debtors must be absolutely trustworthy to the creditors. It is obvious that this strong condition can be relaxed if paper money is used instead. The reason is that, in this case, only the issuer need be trustworthy, in the sense that he will always be able and willing to exchange the paper money into commodity money or coins at its nominal value. Note that the use of paper money implies a credit of its holder to the issuing agency. The same would be true for checking accounts which could always be exchanged into commodity money or coins.

What happens if the convertibility of the paper money into commodity money with full intrinsic value is suspended or abolished? In this case, we may refer to the paper money as a non-interest-bearing claim with infinite maturity against the issuer. But why should such a claim have any value and thus be able to function as money? Only because people are accustomed to the experience that everybody else is prepared to accept the paper money in exchange for goods and services and therefore expects that the same will be true in the future. But for this confidence to be maintained, it is necessary that the amount of paper money issued is strictly limited and that the public expects this to be the case. This means that two quite different kinds of trust have to be present.

The history of money can be described as a process leading from commodity money with full intrinsic value to more and more abstract kinds of money with less and less commodity value or chances of convertibility into such money. With every step, the need for trustworthiness of the institution issuing the money became more and more important. It is important to stress that this has been and will be a historical process. The Sumerians already used standardized silver bars as money. Later, the Lydians and the Ionian Greeks invented electron, silver, and gold coins, and spread them to ever-wider regions. The late Middle Ages saw the development of commercial bills of exchange. In China, a similar development took place. The Chinese were even the first to invent paper money and to make it inconvertible. In Europe, banknotes were first created by a private banker in Sweden, and deposits similar to checking accounts developed in late Renaissance Italy and, from the beginning of the seventeenth century, by the Bank of

Amsterdam and the Bank of Hamburg. It is also obvious that the less developed a country, the less far this process has advanced, even today. And there is always a chance that a system of exchange may revert to earlier, more primitive forms, if a sufficiently trustworthy institution issuing money does not exist, or other conditions for a functioning monetary economy are violated. Thus, the European economy returned to barter in the late Roman Empire and the early Middle Ages, and the convertibility of government notes and banknotes into gold or silver currency, which had been given up during the Napoleonic Wars, was restored by most leading countries after the end of these conflicts.

Consequences and dangers of the development of paper money and a pure credit economy

The development from money, with full intrinsic value, to paper money, has obvious advantages. Not only can the resources required to mine the copper, silver or gold needed for minting coins be used for other purposes, paper money can also be transported more easily. These costs are further reduced by paying with checks or by transfers from checking accounts, or by using credit cards. The danger of theft is absent, though criminal manipulations are now possible. Also, paper money can be falsified more easily than coins with full intrinsic value.

But these are not the main dangers. Historical evidence is abounding with examples that rulers and governments very quickly took over the monopoly to mint coins to benefit from seignorage earned in producing them. Not satisfied with this gain, they often debased the money either by reducing the weight of coins, reducing the content of the precious metal, or by increasing the nominal value of coins. As the Belgian historian Henri Pirenne[1] described it for the monetary disorders of the Middle Ages:

The progress of monetary circulation provided princes with the possibility to use it to their own advantage. Possessing the right to mint coins, they believed themselves to be authorized to use this in the interest of their treasury to the detriment of the public. The more money became indispensable for economic life, the more it was altered by those who had the right to strike it ... At the

---

[1] H. Pirenne, *Histoire economique de l'occident medievale*. Bruges: Desclées de Brouwer, 1951, 258 and 266.

end of the 12th century, the monetary disorder had reached a point that a reform imposed itself.

Clearly, the introduction of paper money would multiply these opportunities. Governments soon began to issue paper money besides the banknotes issued by private banks. And in the course of time they introduced state monopolies to issue paper money, mostly by creating central banks. A further step was the abolition of the convertibility of these notes into gold or silver at a fixed price – the gold or silver parity – which occurred mainly at the beginning of World War I and during the Great Depression.

The dangers implied in these developments were already clearly seen by leading economists during the heyday of the gold standard during the nineteenth century. The German economist, Adolph Wagner, wrote in 1868:[2]

The obstacle for an equal value, i.e., for maintaining an equal general purchasing power . . . is the impossibility to fulfill the requirements necessary for the strength of this belief. One would have to institute the most reliable guarantees to prevent that paper money would ever be used for financial purposes to create artificial purchasing power for the issuing agency without labor out of nothing; and to secure that it would be increased only according to the true necessities of the economy . . . Men would have first to be capable of unlimited self-discipline to resist any temptation to increase money arbitrarily, even if their very existence, or that of the state, were at stake.

The English economist, William St. Jevons,[3] expressed himself similarly, though he, like other economists, was concerned whether the supply of gold would always be sufficient to cover the monetary needs of a growing economy. Wagner also mentioned that inconvertible paper money would mean that many national currencies existed, whose value would fluctuate against each other; this in contrast to a general gold standard in which exchange rates can only move within narrow bands determined by the transportation and insurance costs of gold.

Historical experience has fully confirmed that these concerns were more than warranted (see Figure 2.2, and for a more detailed treatment,

---

[2] A. Wagner, *Die russische Papierwährung.* Riga: Kymmel, 1868, 43–8.
[3] W. St. Jevons, *Money and the Mechanism of Exchange.* New York: D. Appleton & Co, 1900, 229–32.

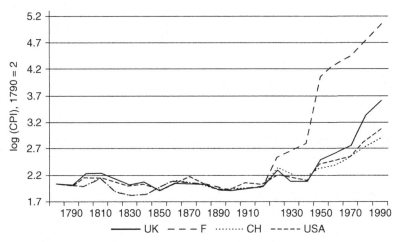

Figure 2.2 Development of prices in four countries, 1790–1990
Sources: B. Mitchell, *European Historical Statistics, 1950–1970*, 1976, 735–47;
Statistisches Bundesamt 1981 and 2000, *Statistisches Jahrbuch der Bundesrepublik Deutschland*, 704–6 ans 230 ff., respectively; US Bureau of the Census, *Historical Statistics of the United States: Colonial Times to 1970*, Bicentennial edn., 1976.

see Bernholz[4]). We turn first to the long-term development of inflation since about 1800 in several countries, which for many decades have belonged to the most highly developed economies of the world (Figure 2.2). On the vertical axis, the logarithm of the consumer price index (CPI) is depicted, whereas time is denoted on the horizontal axis. As we can see from the figure, the price levels of the United States, Great Britain, France, and Switzerland did not show an upward or downward trend before 1914, but only long-term swings. The situation changed, however, both after 1914 and after 1930. Since that time, pronounced upward trends – that is, long-term inflation – can be observed for all countries considered.

The explanation for this difference can be easily understood. Metallic standards bind the hands of rulers, governments, and politicians, since they are not able to increase the supply of silver or gold at their

---

[4] P. Bernholz, *Monetary Regimes and Inflation: History, Economic and Political Relationships*. Cheltenham, UK, and Northampton, MA: Edward Elgar, 2003, paperback edn. 2006.

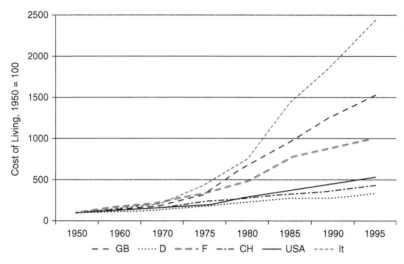

Figure 2.3 Development of the cost of living, 1950–1995

discretion. As a consequence, a monetary regime with convertibility at a fixed parity into a precious metal cannot be misused for financial purposes. This is quite different from a monetary regime based on inconvertible paper money issued by the state or its agencies.

This point is confirmed when we take a closer look at the development of inflation in some developed countries from 1950 to 1998 in terms of the CPI (Figure 2.3). The figure draws our attention to two facts: an inflationary development can be observed for the whole period, and inflation has accelerated since about 1970. After 1970, two groups of countries show different inflationary developments. The first group, consisting of Italy, France, and Great Britain, shows a higher rate of inflation than the second, consisting of Switzerland, (West) Germany, and the United States. How can these differences be explained? This is easy enough. The more stable countries were those with independent central banks,[5] whereas the central banks of the other

---

[5] For an analysis of the role of the independence of central banks, compare A. Alesina and L. H. Summers, "Central Bank Independence and Macroeconomic Performance: Some Comparative Evidence." *Journal of Money, Credit and Banking* 25(2), May 1993, 151–62. See also Michael Parkin and Robin Bade, *Central Bank Laws and Monetary Policy*. Dept. of Economics, University of Western Ontario, October 1988.

countries were dependent on the ministries of finance. They were much more dependent on political decisions.

But how can we explain the much more similar performance until 1970? We recall that the Bretton Woods agreement had established a weakened gold standard, in which only central banks had the right to change dollars into gold at a fixed parity, and vice versa, at the US Treasury. Though the United States did not follow the rules of the gold standard during this period, the Federal Reserve System was an independent central bank following a somewhat, but not very pronounced, expansionary policy. And since under the rules of the Bretton Woods monetary regime, all other central banks were required to maintain the parity of their currencies with the dollar within narrow bands, apart from occasional de- or revaluations, the development of their price levels depended mainly on the policies of the Federal Reserve System. As a consequence, inflationary developments were more similar and less pronounced than after the breakdown of the Bretton Woods system between 1971 and 1973.[6]

Again, these results show that only monetary regimes binding the hands of politicians and governments promise price stability. It is interesting to note that Adolph Wagner already had an inkling of this when he followed up the last sentence quoted above with the remark:

A somewhat greater security against the abuse of the right to issue money might perhaps be provided by one or the other constitutional form. But this certainly does not amount to a big difference.[7]

This statement may sound too pessimistic, but we see from Figure 2.2 that even relatively stable developed countries suffered from more inflation with a discretionary paper money regime and independent central banks than under the gold standard. Moreover, as the recent financial crisis since 2007 seems to prove again, the independence of central banks may be eroded or abolished during times of emergency. This is especially the case if the government becomes over-indebted in its

---

[6] For a recent discussion, see N. Kocherlakota, "Public Debt, Monetary Policy and Financial Stability. Banque de France." *Financial Stability Review*, April 16, 2012, 151–4. The dangers inherent in the development to a more and more extended credit money together with rising government debts have been vividly described by Niall Ferguson, *The Rise of Money*. London: Allen Lane, 2008, an imprint of Penguin Books.

[7] Wagner, *Die russische Papierwährung*.

Table 2.1 *Historical examples of large under- (< 100) and overvaluations (> 100) of currencies*

Periods of moderate or limited inflation differences

Country (against currency)	Spain (silver coins)	Sweden (Hamburg Mark Banco)	France (US$)	Germany (US$)	Germany (US$)	Germany (US$)	Euro area (US$)
Period	1675	1762	1925	IV, 1979	IV, 1984	I, 1995	IV, 2000
Percentage	72.27	73.31	48.73	145.89	70.68	130.6	79.43

Periods of hyperinflation

Country (against currency)	France (Basel silver coins)	Germany (US$)	Hungary 2 (US$)		Serbia (DM)
Period	9, 1795	2, 1920	30.9.1945	4, 1992	7, 1993
Percentage	30.85	30.78	27.72	21.87	15.72

own currency and is threatened by bankruptcy. Then the central bank is scarcely able to withstand the political and psychological pressures to support the government by credits and thus to give up its independence.[8]

While the gold standard provided a truly international currency, inconvertible paper monies often led to a kind of monetary nationalism. This is usually characterized by flexible exchange rates, which are subject to strong and lasting deviations from purchasing power parities (Table 2.1). When monetary nationalism leads to high inflation, however, even extreme fines and penalties cannot prevent the private sector from substituting the unstable national currency for more stable foreign ones (for a more detailed treatment, compare Bernholz[9]). This process has been called dollarization, since, in recent history, national currencies have often been substituted by the US dollar. Another

---

[8] P. Bernholz, "Die Bedeutung der Geschichte für die Wirtschaftswissenschaften und der ökonomischen Theorie für die Geschichtsforschung." *Perspektiven der Wirtschaftspolitik* 6(2) 2005, 131–50.

[9] Bernholz, *Monetary Regimes and Inflation*.

Table 2.2 *Historical episodes of hyperinflation*

Country	Year(s)	Highest monthly inflation	Country	Year(s)	Highest monthly inflation
Argentina	1989/90	196.6	Hungary	1945/46	1.295*
Armenia	1993/94	438.04	Kazakhstan	1994	57
Austria	1921/22	124.27	Kyrgyzstan	1992	57
Azerbaijan	1991/94	118.09	Nicaragua	1986/89	126.62
Belarus	1994	53.4	Peru	1988/90	114.12
Bolivia	1984/86	120.39	Poland	1921/24	187.54
Brazil	1989/93	84.32	Russia	1989/90	77.33
Bulgaria	1997	242.7	Serbia	1992/94	309000000
China	1947/49	4208.73	Soviet Union	1922/24	278.72
Congo (Zaire)	1991/94	225	Taiwan	1945/49	398.73
France	1789/96	143.26	Tajikistan	1995	78.1
Germany	1920/23	29525.71	Turkmenistan	1993/96	62.5
Georgia	1993/94	196.72	Ukraine	1992/94	249
Greece	1942/45	11288	Yugoslavia	1990	58.82
Hungary	1923/24	82.18	Zimbabwe	2008	231150889

Note: *Moldova may also be a candidate for inclusion. Producer prices rose by 64.5% in April 1994, but the data are insufficient to verify this for consumer prices.
Sources: P. Bernholz, "Die Bedeutung der Geschichte für die Wirtschaftswissenschaften und der ökonomischen Theorie für die Geschichtsforschung." *Perspektiven der Wirtschaftspolitik* 6(2) 2005, 131–50. For Zimbabwe, S. H. Hanke and A. F. Kwok, "On the Measurement of Zimbabwe's Hyperinflation." *Cato Journal* 29(2) Spring/Summer 2009.

example of this phenomenon is the replacement of the Yugoslavian dinar by the Deutschmark (DM) in the late 1980s and in the 1990s.

The dangers of paper money are understandably much more pronounced for less developed and unstable countries. Of the 30 cases of hyperinflation in history,[10] only one occurred before 1914, all others after the worldwide gold standard had been abolished (Table 2.2). By

---

[10] Hanke and Krus, using somewhat different definitions, have constructed a table containing more than 50 hyperinflations: S. H. Hanke and N. Krus, *World Hyperinflations*, Cato Working Paper no. 8, August 15, 2012.

definition, a hyperinflation is one in which the monthly rate of inflation reaches at least 50 percent in at least one month.

We conclude that the more monetary stability has been threatened, the more monetary policy was influenced by political decisions of governments, and that this damaging influence has also been greater the more the monetary system approached a pure credit system. Money with full intrinsic value enabled the decentralization of economic activity, division of labor, and the development of a market economy, since it allowed transactions to take place without trust in the debtors' future ability and willingness to pay.

But the granting of credit proved necessary to allow more extensive inter-temporal trade and to save transaction costs. With money of full intrinsic value, the damage wrought by rulers and governments was limited to debasement of coins or bullion. The historical evidence shows that the highest inflation resulting has never exceeded 8 percent per annum, reached in the late Roman Empire of the fourth century. The reason is obvious: even base metals like bronze or lead enjoy a higher value than paper.

When banknotes and checking accounts convertible into coins or bullion of full intrinsic value were introduced, another danger arose: the risk that the issuers could not meet their convertibility obligations and went into bankruptcy. This could occur since their reserves amounted to only a fraction of their debts stemming from the issue of banknotes and deposits in checking accounts. Moreover, the illiquidity of one bank could easily spread to other banks if it tried to withdraw credits of which they were debtors to meet its obligations. With the monopolization of the issue of convertible paper money by the government, this danger was diminished. In fact, central banks were often created with the aim of acting as lenders of last resort in such liquidity crises. But the government now had the right to suspend and finally abolish convertibility and to base money purely on credit granted to the state. The consequences have been sketched above. A relatively stable monetary system under these conditions could only be secured by institutionally binding the hands of politicians and government, for instance by establishing an independent central bank. But this proved to be a difficult task and presupposes a separation of powers.

We have to ask a final question. What consequences would follow if a pure credit economy without any money circulating as a means of payment were to be established? That is, if neither paper money nor coins circulate and all transactions are paid by crediting or debiting the accounts of the parties involved? An answer to this question has already been suggested more than one hundred years ago by Knut Wicksell,[11] who states that:

If the average rate of monetary interest has been fixed, even by a very small amount below that normal level [of the natural interest rate of real capital] and is maintained there, then prices will rise and rise again ... (my translation from the German).

It would be too complicated even to sketch Wicksell's proof for his assertion, but it is possible to advance some plausible arguments for his position. Assume that all persons and all organizations directly or indirectly through banks hold accounts with a Central Clearing Agency, and that all acts of buying or selling goods and services are debited or credited to these accounts. Assume, also, that everybody has a credit line, the amount of which is determined by the value of his income and his wealth. Now assume that some people, firms, and other organizations use their credit lines because of the too-low interest rate, set according to Wicksell's assumption by banks, to buy additional goods. Then, provided that markets had been in equilibrium before, prices will begin to rise because of the additional demand. As a consequence, the incomes and the wealth of some people and (or) organizations will increase. As a result, their credit lines will extend and they will be able to increase their demand again. Thus, prices will rise further, and so on. The process will accelerate as soon as people become more and more aware of rising prices and change their expectations. Thus higher and higher inflation, and finally hyperinflation, will result.[12]

It should at least provide food for thought that all hyperinflations (Table 2.2) have occurred since the abolition of the gold standard after 1914, with the exception of the French hyperinflation, which, however, also took place under a pure paper money regime. Moreover, the increasing incidence of financial crises during recent decades, noted by

[11] K. Wicksell, *Geldzins und Güterpreise*. Aalen: Scientia Verlag, 1968/1889, 61–9, 101–6, and 111–12.
[12] S. H. Hanke and A. F. Kwok, "On the Measurement of Zimbabwe's Hyperinflation." *Cato Journal* 29(2), Spring/Summer 2009.

Kindleberger and Aliber,[13] is probably also related to the emergence of money being ever-more based on credit relationships.

Note that in such an extreme system the ability of central banks to conduct monetary policy would be totally absent, since neither bank-notes nor deposits of financial institutions with them would exist any longer. But then, central banks could also no longer guarantee a relatively stable price level. It seems that some central bankers are already seeing this possible future danger, for, in a personal communication, Hans Tietmeyer, former president of the Deutsche Bundesbank, told me that because of this he insisted that the European Central Bank should be granted the right to demand the holding of minimum reserves by financial institutions with it.

A development similar to that just sketched is the development of electronic money. Though this is still limited to a small market, it seems to be growing rapidly. This can either be card-based money, or money stored on an account in the internet.[14] Since 2009, the European Union has even thought it necessary to regulate e-money services by a directive.[15]

Still, the pure credit economy sketched above seems to be slow in coming. On the one hand, it is exactly the behavior of governments which throws more and more obstacles into the path of development. Ever-higher taxes (including social security taxes) and growing regulations favor an increasing development of the shadow economy which has to rely on cash, that is, nowadays, on paper money. On the other hand, governments try to hinder this without much success by ever-tougher fines and penalties, and have also introduced strict regulations against the use of cash to prevent "money laundering" for income acquired by drug dealers and terrorist organizations. Paradoxically, if they were successful with the latter efforts, they would at the same time erode the influence of their own central banks to determine the price level.

---

[13] C. P. Kindleberger and R. Z. Aliber, *Manias, Panics, and Crashes: A History of Financial Crises*, 6th edn. Houndsmills, Basingstoke: Palgrave Macmillan, 2011.

[14] M. Zaehres, E-money. Niche market that might be expanding. Deutsche Bank, Banking & Technology Snapshot. Digital economy and structural change. www. Dbresearch.com, May 11, 2012.

[15] E-Money Directive 2009/110/EC *op. cit.*, 318.

Social consequences of the characteristics and perceptions of money

Nec quicquam insipiente fortunato intolerabilius fieri potest. (Cicero, *Lael.* 15, 54)

Utinamque posset e vita in totum abdicari, sacrum fame ... et ad repertum perniciniem vitae. (Plinius, *Historia Naturalis* 33, 6)

Auri sacra fames. (Vergil, *Aeneas* III 57)

Dummodo sit dives, barbarus ipse placet. (Ovid, *Ars armatoria* 2, 276)

Ploratur lacrimis amissa pecunia veris. (Juvenal, *Sat.* 13, 134)

Non olet. (Emperor Vespasian to his son Titus, Vespasian 13)

Neminem pecunia divitem fecit. (Seneca, *Epist.* 119, 9)

These quotations from Roman antiquity show that the often negative, or at least ambiguous, attitude towards money is not a modern development. "Money does not stink", "the most sincere tears are shed for lost money", and "even a barbarian is liked if he is rich" are the most positive statements. On the other hand, there are the complaints concerning the "cursed hunger for gold" and therefore the wish to completely ban it from human life. And of course, nobody is more contemptible than an uneducated rich person. We will discuss subsequently some of the characteristics of money which may encourage such views.

It seems fairly certain that, even in a pure credit economy, people would continue to speak of "money", though money is no longer used as a means of payment. For a unit of account would still be needed, and I am sure that this unit would be called "money", as would the accounts used for transfers to enact payments. It follows that all the characteristics rightly or wrongly assigned to money would still be dominating general thinking and perceptions.

The use of money as a general medium of exchange has important social consequences. Since money is perceived as determining the value of all goods and services, and since one can buy nearly everything with it, it is considered not only to dominate every aspect of life, but also to be of an almost metaphysical nature. Scarcely more than two hundred years after the invention of coins, the great Athenian comedian Aristophanes fully expressed this view in his *Plutus*. Plutus, the God of riches and money, is called the mightiest of all gods, who has even to be served finally by Hermes and Zeus.[16] And whereas of all things else a man may have too much – of love, of loaves of bread, art, honour, cheesecakes, dried figs, ambition, and command – this is not true of money Plutus can provide. The same idea is formulated by a well-known German sociologist about 2,400 years later:

If money would be nothing else in reality than the expression of the value of all other things, it would relate to them like an idea, which Plato imagined in fact even as a substantial metaphysical being, to empirical reality. (Simmel)[17]

As a consequence of the fact that money can buy almost everything, rich people are considered to be very powerful. "They have much money," because their wealth is calculated in terms of money. However, as soon as their money or wealth is spent on consumption, their power vanishes.

Simmel[18] explains that money conveys freedom to people. If freedom means independence from the will of others, it can be secured in a decentralized market economy with sufficient competition. Money, in contrast to barter, allows people to sell their products and services to anybody and to spend the receipts on buying goods and services from completely different persons. This fact favors impersonal relationships. The more competitors are present, the more independent individuals are from their suppliers, customers, employers, and employees. This independence also protects their dignity, since both buyer and seller enter into voluntary contracts and since both get what they desire without owing anything to the other afterwards. Moreover, such independence may be a precondition for a working democracy in complex societies. A modern liberal constitution with independent voters would hardly be possible in alternative economic regimes like a planned economy. For in such a regime citizens are necessarily dependent on some state agency, a fact which cannot but affect their behavior as voters and politicians.

The prevalence of monetary exchange has important consequences for human relations. On the one hand, money facilitates frequent economic exchanges with people we do not know and whose trustworthiness we cannot judge. On the other hand, the possibility of monetary

---

[16] Aristophanes, *Plutus*, 3 vols., English trans. B. B. Rogers. Cambridge, MA: Harvard University Press, 1977, vol. III, esp. 185–90.

[17] G. Simmel, *Philosophie des Geldes*, eds. D. P. Frisby and K. Christian Koehnke. Frankfurt: Suhrkamp, 1989, 181.

[18] Ibid., 400.

exchange can make existing relationships with other people less personal.[19] Consider marriage as an example. It can be understood as a long-term exchange of goods and services, in which the partners expect some rough balance between the goods and services received and granted by each of them over time. One would think of this intertemporal exchange as cold and horrible, if everything were calculated in monetary units. Instead, each partner is grateful for what the other person gives and responds accordingly. This traditional notion of marriage, however, is increasingly threatened in modern economies, where most other exchanges take place in the marketplace using money, and personal relationships are pushed into the background. Since both partners today have the opportunity to sell their services to outsiders, they depend less on each other for their economic well-being. Thus, for the first time in history, ordinary women today can earn enough money to support themselves even with a child. Thus, the prevalence of monetary exchange in modern society threatens the stability of traditional family structures. The relationship among friends is of a similar character. However, the use of money can also drive out negative personal feelings like hatred, for instance, in an embittered marriage. In such cases, bitter personal relationships characterizing non-monetary intertemporal exchanges may be substituted by monetary transactions, as, for instance, after a divorce.

The use of money as a unit of account also has important social consequences. It makes all goods and services comparable in value terms, even if they are of a completely different nature. An outside measure is conferred on them, which is only determined by their scarcity and the intensity of human wishes to obtain them. This fact can greatly influence our perception of things. In extreme cases, some goods may just be wanted by some people because they have a high monetary value which promises to rise even further. Stamps, old coins, paintings, and even matchboxes may simply be acquired because they can be used as a store of value, or because they increase personal prestige. And as far as they have liquid markets, they can be sold any time and the proceeds used to buy other objects or services offered. This leads to the impression that the value of one's fortune really corresponds to the value calculated in monetary units.

---

[19] For a deeper discussion of the following relationships, see C. C. von Weizsäcker, *Zeit und Geld*. Bern: Unpublished manuscript, 1995.

Simmel, as many others at the end of the nineteenth century, already described this development. He called money the most general, but also the most abstract of all instruments, since all other instruments valued in the market can be acquired with its help. And it is the most abstract instrument, since, in contrast to other instruments, it has no characteristics except its quantity.[20]

In former times, the expression "money" referred only to coins, mostly of full intrinsic value. Nowadays, when we speak of a rich person, we often say that he has "much money", though he scarcely holds any money as a means of payment, for by far most of his wealth is invested in shares, bonds, houses, landed property or production plants. But his wealth is calculated in terms of monetary units. Each year a list of the 400 richest people is published by *Fortune* Magazine, and the measuring rod of their wealth is monetary units. It is thus not surprising that most of the problematic and often strongly criticized aspects of the use of money refer to its function as a unit of account.

As a consequence of the calculation of most things in terms of money, rich people are considered as possessing great power. But this power is only a potentiality, since, if it is spent, it may rapidly vanish. Therefore, misers probably love this power so much that they don't want to spend it.[21] The problematic nature of such calculations hiding reality, as it were, behind a veil of money, can easily be seen when a crash hits the stock or the housing market. For if many people want to sell their shares or houses at the same time, prices may tumble and the former wealth calculated in monetary units reveals itself as fictitious. The big depression in Japan during the nineties of the last century, which began with a collapse of stock prices and lasted for years, is still vividly remembered, as is the worldwide tumbling of prices in the stock market beginning in 2000 and again in 2008.

The absence of any specific characteristics in money, its indifference concerning its manifold uses, the fact that it intervenes between us and the objects of our desires, its anonymity, and its use as a unit of account have certainly contributed to the measuring, weighing and calculating nature of the modern age, its more and more intellectual leaning. The abstract nature of double-entry bookkeeping is not conducive to deep feelings. And the selling of our labor services for money may also mean that we feel that our own personal traits are not adequately appreciated.

---

[20] Simmel, *Philosophie des Geldes*, 340.   [21] Ibid., 318.

On the other hand, it is only the existence of money which has allowed many cultural and institutional developments. Even the modern state would not be possible without its revenue reckoned and imposed in monetary units. Without bookkeeping depending on the calculation in monetary units, modern income and wealth taxes could not have been introduced.

The existence of money as a unit of account has also greatly contributed to the fact that the total of economic relationships could be analyzed by economics, and more and more law-like relationships be established. As Simmel expressed it in his masterly way:

For since money measures all things with merciless objectivity . . . there results a texture of factual and personal contents of life, which approaches the cosmos governed by laws of nature with its uninterrupted interrelatedness and strong causality and since it is bound together by the all-penetrating value of money . . .[22]

---

[22] Ibid., 503.

3 | Mensura et mensuratum: *money as measure and measure for money*

WOLFGANG ERNST

Introduction

One of the functions traditionally attributed to money is the measurement of the value of commodities.[1] Money is taken as a standard, a benchmark or a yardstick. The slightly naive idea is that just as a yardstick is used to measure the length of items, money can be used to "measure" their value. On closer inspection, the idea loses much of its appeal: what exactly is the quality which is "measured" by money, and does money have the necessary requirement to serve as an instrument of measurement? It is the purpose of this chapter to show that the idea of what is now called the "measurement-function" of money has a history of its own, and that – depending on the changing features of money – varying problems have hampered the use of money as a "yardstick".

Perhaps the most striking development in the field of money was the change from commodity money to fiat money (or "token money"), commodity money here taken as coins made from precious metal. Typically this would be silver, or sometimes gold, copper or some alloy of these.[2] Until well into the twentieth century money – in different ways – was related to bullion, i.e. uncoined metal of the sort used for coins, usually silver or gold. The idea of money as a yardstick originated when money was identified with coins made from bullion. Aristotle is

---

[1] See G. Ingham, *The Nature of Money*. Cambridge: Polity Press, 2004, 3; J. Tobin, "money", *The New Palgrave Dictionary of Economics*, 2nd edn., eds. S. N. Durlauf and L. E. Blume, London: Palgrave Macmillan, 2008; *The New Palgrave Dictionary of Economics Online*, Palgrave Macmillan, 16 February 2010, <http://www.dictionaryofeconomics.com/article?id=pde2008_M000217> doi: 10.1057/9780230226203.1126.

[2] On commodity money, see François R. Velde and W. E. Weber, "commodity money", *The New Palgrave Dictionary of Economics Online*, 16 February 2010, <http://www.dictionaryofeconomics.com/article?id=pde2008_C000235> doi: 10.1057/9780230226203.0268.

considered to be the first philosopher who compared money with other standards of measurement. This is the paragraph from *Ethics*:[3]

In all friendships between dissimilars it is, as we have said, proportion that equalizes the parties and preserves the friendship; e.g. in the political form of friendship the shoemaker gets a return for his shoes in proportion to his worth, and the weaver and all other craftsmen do the same. Now here a common measure has been provided in the form of money, and therefore everything is referred to this and measured by this. ...

As long as currencies consisted of metal-based coins, it would have been possible, perhaps even sensible, to see the coin itself as *mensuratum* as well as *mensura*. Each coin in turn could easily have been priced according to its metal content.[4] However, this was not the view taken in antiquity. The standard itself was not seen as subject to a reverse measurement. The monetary units were taken to be fixed or static. A second-century Roman lawyer, Javolen, stated: "Money cannot be quantified in terms of commodities in the way that a commodity, measured by quantity or number, may be assessed in money."[5]

Mensura and *mensuratum* in the Middle Ages

The idea that money is a sort of yardstick had its heyday during the Middle Ages. Money then was crucially defined by its supposed measurement-function.[6] It is easy to see why other functions of money – as a medium of exchange and as storage of wealth – did not feature as prominently in medieval monetary thought as the idea that money is a measure. Medieval coins – starting with the *denarius* standardized by Charlemagne – did not really circulate by *tale*. Due mainly to the crudeness of minting, the weight of coins was habitually checked. The use of coins was little different from the use of other commodities. Moreover, the *denarius* was a relatively small coin, a "penny". As a medium of exchange it was not ideal for

---

[3] *Nicomachean Ethics* IX, 1. The more detailed treatment of money is to be found in his *Politics* I, 8–10; cf. Scott Meikle, "Aristotle on Money," in: *What is Money?*, ed. J. Smithin, London/New York: Routledge, 2000, 156–73.

[4] In fact, the coinage standard was often stated in the number of coins made from a standard weight of silver, the so-called mint-equivalent.

[5] *Digest* 46.1.42 (my translation).

[6] J. Kaye, *Economy and Nature in the Fourteenth Century: Money, Market Exchange, and the Emergence of Scientific Thought*. Cambridge University Press, 1998, 186.

large-scale transactions. Therefore, high-value obligations were often
expressed in terms of certain weights of silver or gold, and discharged
by the delivery of *bullion*.[7] Scales and standard weights were everyday
features of medieval commerce. It is appropriate, therefore, to speak of a
"bullion-currency" which consisted of typified weights of unminted gold
and silver cast as standard bars. For storage purposes, coins and precious
metal were used more or less indiscriminately. They were often kept not in
the form of standard bars, but as *objets d'art* for church and other use
(chalices, goblets and the like). Since the work of silversmiths was cheap,
only the silver content counted. Until the late thirteenth century, when
larger coins began to be minted (these were generally made of gold, such as
the Venetian ducat), two rather different means of exchange were used
side by side. These were bullion and *pecunia numerata*, the latter consisting of small silver coins of a single denomination. Although these were all
issued as *denarii*, they were, in fact, coined by a multitude of regionally
controlled mints. Each mint's products varied greatly in style, face, and
fineness. Given the economic and monetary realities, the concurrent use
of money on the one hand and commodities on the other was not as
self-evident as in a fully monetized environment. As media of exchange
and as means to store wealth (by so-called "hoarding"), other objects,
especially bullion and silverware, could be employed as well. The main
distinguishing quality of money was that coins came as standardized units.
The association of money with other categories of measure provided a
strong   argument   against   tampering   with   monetary   standards.
Debasement, the reduction of the fineness of coins, was then a common
practice and an important source of public revenue for the ruler who
issued coins. The argument was that just as the ruler should not arbitrarily
change the measures on which the public relied, he should also refrain
from changing the "measure" money.[8]

---

[7] Looking into medieval collections of continental deed-formulas for contracts of
sale, Harald Siems encountered a characteristic difficulty in determining whether
prices fixed referred to coins or to bullion: H. Siems, *Handel und Wucher im
Spiegel frühmittelalterlicher Rechtsquellen*. Hanover: Hahn, 1992, 386.

[8] For details see W. Taeuber, *Geld und Kredit im Mittelalter*. Berlin: Heymann,
1933; repr. Frankfurt a. M.: Sauer & Auvermann, 1968, 334; on the canon law's
view, see F. Wittreck, "Conservare monetam: Geldwertstabilität im
hochmittelalterlichen Aragon im Lichte der Dekretale 'Quanto personam tuam'
(1199)," in *Währung und Wirtschaft: Das Geld im Recht. Festschrift für Hugo
J. Hahn*, ed. A. Weber, Baden-Baden: Nomos, 1997, 103 ff.

There was another precondition which greatly favored the idea that money was a kind of yardstick. Prices were perceived as being inherent qualities of commodities. Just as other qualities could be attributed to a specific commodity, so every commodity carried with it its "true" price, and this was the quality which was "measured" in terms of monetary units. Economic thought, still entangled with theological doctrine, was preoccupied with the idea of the "just" price (*justum pretium*).[9] Missing the just price entailed the risk of committing usury.[10] An enormous amount of scholarly energy was devoted to the casuistic delineation between just price transactions and usury. The linkage of commodities and services to their inherent price was not just an element of doctrinal deliberations, it was an everyday fact. For centuries it was standard practice of local, regional or national authorities to regulate prices ("tariffs") for all sorts of goods and services. For many, if not most, items, prices were not the result of a market mechanism. In this respect, scholastic theories aiming at the establishment of objectively given, pre-existing prices largely matched (and reinforced) the actual socio-political and economic realities of their time. Modern economic doctrines finally overcame the notion that prices could or should somehow be objectively attributed to goods by relying on some of their inherent qualities (e.g. production costs). This development also reflected a considerable withdrawal of public price-setting, which had been a widespread practice over many centuries. In earlier times, the modern concept that prices could – and ideally should – result from the market mechanism of supply and demand would not have been helpful for the vast commercial areas controlled by statutory tariffs, or the general notion of usury. Given the notion that objects carried with them their unique price, it is understandable that medieval scholars regarded the establishment of this price as a real process of measurement, and that money was the yardstick used to effect it.

The prevalence of the measurement idea can be found in Albertus Magnus's reasoning about monetary matters, which has the Aristotelian

[9] On the doctrine of *iustum pretium*, see Odd Inge Langholm, *Economics in the Medieval Schools*. Leiden: Brill Academic Publishers, 1993, 223 ff.; A. Lapidus, "Norm, virtue and information: individual behaviour and the just price in Thomas Aquinas' Summa theological," *The European Journal of the History of Economic Thought* 1 (1994): 435–73.

[10] J. T. Noonan, *The Scholastic Analysis of Usury*. Cambridge, MA: Harvard University Press, 1957.

writings as its starting point. As Bridrey observed with regard to Albertus Magnus, "[l]a fonction de mesure, affirmet-il, est la fonction essentielle du numéraire, qui doit exclure toute autre fonction".[11] For Albertus Magnus, the measurement function leads directly to the postulate of monetary stability:[12] "A measure must always be certain".[13] The same ideas recur in the writings of Thomas Aquinas.[14] Reciting Aristotle, he stated: "Hence money was invented for that reason, so that there is ... a measure in exchanges".[15] Thomas Aquinas also insisted on monetary stability, using the argument that "a measure in the first place needs to be permanent".[16] So the idea that money was a kind of yardstick was part and parcel of the scholastic monetary doctrine.

Learned lawyers of the high Middle Ages taught that "coins are as such certain, they are the evaluation of things".[17] Coins therefore were used only for "active appreciation" (*"appreciatio activa"*), they were not seen as being passively subjected to measurement themselves.

Problems of bimetallism: which measures which?

The term "bimetallism" is the name given to a currency system which uses two different bullions, typically gold and silver, for different coins.[18] There were many varieties of bimetallism, mostly depending on whether the relation between the two kinds of coins was officially decreed or not. Bimetallism brought new and very serious difficulties for the measurement function of money. With bimetallism, two different

---

[11] E. Bridrey, *La théorie de la monnaie au XIVe siècle*. Paris: V. Giard & E. Brière, 1906, 378.

[12] See L. Baeck, *The Mediterranean Tradition in Economic Thought*. London: Routledge, 1994, 158.

[13] *Super Ethica* V 7.

[14] F. Wittreck, *Geld als Instrument der Gerechtigkeit: Die Geldrechtslehre des Hl. Thomas von Aquin in ihrem kulturellen Kontext*. Paderborn: Ferdinand Schoeningh, 2002, 370 ff.

[15] *De regimine principum ad regem cipri* II, 13.   [16] Ibid., 429 ff.

[17] Gl. *aestimatio*, ad D. 12.3.3, *Magna Glossa*, around 1250; likewise, Baldus de Ubaldis, *Lectura super secunda parte Digesti veteris*, ad D. 12,3,3.

[18] On bimetallism, see Ingham, *The Nature of Money*; Lawrence H. Officer, "bimetallism", *The New Palgrave Dictionary of Economics, Online edn.*, 16 February 2010, <http://www.dictionaryofeconomics.com/article?id=pde2008_B000137> doi: 10.1057/9780230226203.0136.

kinds of fluctuations – influenced by different factors and hence not in tune – hampered the fitness of the money for measurement. Again and again the question was asked whether silver was the *mensura* for gold or gold the *mensura* for silver. Xenophon proposed expansion of silver mining to increase revenues for the City of Athens. He argued that the increase in supply of silver would not have the usual impact that he had observed to follow from the increased supply of other kinds of commodities (and he regarded gold as a commodity for this purpose). He argued that the demand for silver was unlimited. Hence the value of silver could not be reduced owing to an increase in the level of its supply.

Or again, in a plethoric condition of the corn and wine market these fruits of the soil will be so depreciated in value that the particular husbandries cease to be remunerative, and many a farmer will give up his tillage of the soil and betake himself to the business of a merchant, or of a shopkeeper, to banking or money-lending. But the converse is the case in the working of silver; there the larger the quantity of ore discovered and the greater the amount of silver extracted, the greater the number of persons ready to engage in the operation. ... And if it be asserted that gold is after all just as useful as silver, without gainsaying the proposition I may note this fact about gold, that, with a sudden influx of this metal, it is the gold itself which is depreciated whilst causing at the same time a rise in the value of silver.[19]

To Xenophon, silver was the inflexible standard. Gold, even in coined form, was a commodity.

In bimetallic systems, general business usage tended to single out the lead bullion which was taken as standard against which all commodities, including the other bullion, were measured. However, the relationship between one coin – the money – and the other coin – the commodity – could change over time. The older Talmudic writers held that: "The silver buys the gold". However, when the Roman silver coinage drastically deteriorated in the third century, they switched to: "The gold buys the silver".[20] Insofar as gold and silver coins could switch their roles as *mensura* and *mensuratum*, one speaks of "alternating currencies".

---

[19] Xenophon, *On revenues*, Ch. IV (trans. H. G. Dakyns, *The Works of Xenophon*. London: Macmillan, 1892).

[20] See F. M. Heichelheim, *Wirtschaftsgeschichte des Altertums*, vol. III. Leiden: Sijthoff, 1969, 1129.

Since in bimetallic systems rigid relations were decreed between gold and silver coins, a change of bullion prices could lead over time to a ratio between gold and silver that differed from the initial official exchange rate between the two types of coin. The coinage authorities could – and indeed, did – realign the exchange rate. In the medieval environment, given that there were tariffs for all sorts of goods and services, regulated "exchange rates" for different coins were just another case of statutorily fixed prices. The "price" thus fixed was called the "*valor impositus*", the "*valor extrinsecus*" or the "*bonitas extrinseca*". (None of these terms referred to the nominal value which might have been ascribed to the face of the coin.[21]) Only the small coin, typically the denarius (the *picciolo*), was not subject to a tariff. For the denarius one could still say that it was *mensura rerum venalium*, whereas the larger coins were not *mensura*, but *mensuratum*. However, realigning the gold and silver coins (and coins from different mints) by means of tariffs usually meant losing the systematic coherence between the various nominal values. These were initially set up as handy multiples (or fractions) of one another. Unless the tariff was made compulsory, business could establish its own rates of exchange, in line with the market rate for the two metals. The official rate and the business rate would then vary from each other.

Imaginary money

The *moneta imaginaria* was a system of monetary units for which no actual corresponding coinage existed. Imaginary money could be found throughout the Middle Ages and early modern times in many countries.[22] The concept of imaginary money is still entertained in modern monetary environments.[23] One example is the Carolingian libra system, which happens to match the old English system. It was a mixed decimal/duodecimal system:

1 libra = 20 solidi = 240 denarii
1 solidus = 12 denarii

[21] Taeuber, *Geld und Kredit im Mittelalter*, 253.
[22] L. Einaudi, "Teoria della moneta immaginaria nel tempo da Carlomagno alla rivoluzione francese," *Rivista di Storia Economica* 1 (1936): 1–35.
[23] The "Special Drawing Rights" (SDR) of the International Monetary Fund are imaginary money, and so was the ECU before euro coins and notes were issued.

1 pound = 20 shilling (s) = 240 pence (d)
1 shilling = 12 pence.

In the Middle Ages, coins were minted and put into circulation which, owing to their actual weight, did not fit into the system of libra, solidus, and denarius. Coins which did not conform to the standard set by the system were then handled as so-called *pagamentum*, or *moneta usualis*: everyday money, as opposed to the *moneta dativa*. The degree to which the coins were deficient in silver was then allowed for by fixing an exchange rate (by means of *adisagio*) between the actual coins and the value officially attributed to them by the system. On the one hand, there was a system of units of account, and, on the other, a multitude of coins circulating alongside one another (this phenonenom is called "variety money"). The units of account and the adding-value of actual coins were not identical. The libra served as a counting unit, a numeric shorthand for 240 denarii, but it was not at the same time a coin with exactly 240 times the silver content of one actual denarius.

Moreover, some units of account did not even exist as actual coins. For a long time, for example, there was no coin corresponding to the counting unit of the libra. The libra was *moneta imaginaria*. The system of imaginary money was used to define a monetary obligation. It was a pure "money of account". Since actual payment could only be made using existing coins, again there were "exchange rates" for the conversions of amounts of the imaginary money into various actual coins.

In this state of affairs, different monetary concepts were used to fulfill the different functions of money. For actual payments and for the purpose of storage, actual coins were used; for the measurement function, the imaginary money was relied upon. In a way, imaginary money was more advanced, at least in the isolated respect of the measurement function of money, since it was free from the technological and economic shortcomings of the coinage actually in circulation.

It is interesting to note that one could easily rely on imaginary money for the main use of money as a standard of measurement. For the purpose of an accounting exercise, all relevant items under consideration need to have values assigned to them which are in amounts of a specific currency. For this, one specific currency – one monetary system – must be chosen as a standard. A certain amount of the money of this currency is then attributed to each item. This is called the "reporting currency" (*monnaie de compte*, *money of account*, *numéraire*). The reporting currency may well be imaginary.[24] Indeed, many theorists have advanced the idea that money has a dual nature, being on one hand a medium of exchange ("concrete money" or money proper) and on the other hand the abstract monetary unit, used for computational purposes. On this view, abstract and concrete money need to be considered separately.[25]

If one sees money as a "standard", the field of accounting shows that the coherent application of this standard to all things needing to be accounted for is no mean feat. Accounting standards are intricate and often far from self-evident. Were it not for uniform accounting standards which are agreed upon and internationally implemented (e.g. the International Financial Reporting Standards, or "IFRS"), accounting would entail many arbitrary and doubtful decisions. The need to overcome these arbitrary elements, and the never-ending struggle for "true and fair" accounting standards, show that there is no such thing as an easy "measurement" of commodities. It is simplistic to believe that commodities would readily betray their values in terms of a certain number of units of account just by being held up against the yardstick of money. Money is not itself the standard which expresses the economic value of commodities; rather, it is the unit one uses when standards, such as those provided, for example, by accounting rules, are applied to commodities. If the monetary unit is comparable to a unit of measurement, like a yard, what, then, is the yardstick? It has long been taken for granted that the pricing process effortlessly attaches the "correct" monetary values to commodities. This belief has been shattered, as will be set out in the section below on fiat money.

It is easy and, indeed, commonplace today to analytically separate the abstract monetary unit of account from the use of "concrete" money as a means of exchange. As to the early history of money, there is a controversy as to which function can be seen as the driving force igniting the idea of money: was money "invented" in order to facilitate contractual transactions by providing a standardized means

---

[24] The money of account featured prominently in J. M. Keynes, *A Treatise on Money*, vol. I: *The Pure Theory of Money*. New York: Harcourt, Brace, 1930; see also Ingham, *The Nature of Money*, 24 ff.

[25] J. Schumpeter, *Das Wesen und der Hauptinhalt der theoretischen Nationalökonomie*. Leipzig: Duncker & Humblot, 1908, 342 ff.

of exchange,[26] or did communities need a common standard to express taxes, price lists, and credits in standardized units?[27] Unquestionably, money first emerged as minted coins, which at the same time served as "units of account" and means of exchange. Given that coins, once available, could equally be used on the spot for market exchanges as well as a unit defining deferred payments (and taxes), it is probably futile trying to single out one of these functions as historically anterior to the other. As to the future, theorists have already envisaged market economies relying solely on clearing systems, using the "unit of account" without tangible money circulating as a means of exchange ("pure credit economy"[28]). While we may perhaps be unable to decide which came first, we may perhaps see which lasts longer – the abstract monetary unit of account or the concrete units circulating, transaction-wise – as intermediate means of exchange.

The changing yardstick: the varying value of coins

Seen in retrospect, the fact that money consisted of coins made from precious metal was not conducive to the notion that money could be used as a yardstick. The reason for this is that the bullion coexisted in two forms: one coined and the other uncoined. There was a potential flux from one form to the other: everybody could melt coins to obtain bulk metal. The reverse process of minting, which turned bulk metal into coins, was generally a prerogative of rulers; occasionally citizens were free to have their silver turned into official coins. However, money coined from precious metal knew no territorial borders and circulated easily beyond the realm of the issuing ruler. Since the overall proportion of coined bullion could be increased by foreign minting activities, no one really controlled (or even knew) the "worldwide" ratio of coined to uncoined bullion. Hence, there was no separate supply and demand for

---

[26] This is the conventional view, going back to Aristotle (*Nicomachean Ethics* I), supported in Roman antiquity by the lawyer Julius Paulus around the turn of the second to the third century CE (*Dig.* 18,1,1). It seems not quite right to label this idea as neoclassical economics.

[27] Among modern authors, this view is supported by Ingham, *The Nature of Money*, 24 et seq.; Ingham, "'Babylonian madness': on the historical and sociological origins of money," in *What is Money?*, 16–41.

[28] K. Wicksell, *Geldzins und Gueterpreise*. Aalen: Scientia, 1968 (repr. of 1898 edn.), 61 et seq.

bulk bullion alone, excluding coins. Coins and bulk bullion were almost *one* commodity. This connection could easily override the slightly higher price which coins tended to have owing to the need to take costs of minting into account. An overall increase of the bullion – due to intensified mining activities or the discovery of new Eldorados – not only tended to bring down the price of bullion, but sometimes led to a reduction in the relative purchasing power of money. The reverse held true when metal was taken out of circulation. This happened, for example, when it was hoarded.

Surprising as it may be, the fact that supply and demand of the bullion made the coin an unreliable standard of measurement over time seems to have escaped the attention of monetary theorists for a long time. While the flux of prices was obvious, the impact of changes in the supply and demand for bullion supply on the price for bullion (and hence on the material value of coins) was by and large ignored, or outright negated. The person credited with the discovery that the extent of the bullion supply affected the value of money is Jean Bodin. What brought this to his attention was the influx of gold into Europe after the discovery of the Americas. The effects were especially felt in France with a currency of minted gold coins.[29]

Old habits die hard. People stuck to the idea that money could be used as a yardstick, even when its shortcomings had become obvious. One must not forget, however, that for a long time other standards of measurement were also far from perfect. Standards of weights, lengths and volume were at first only regulated on a local level and were extremely heterogeneous in consequence. In continental Europe it took a long time for the emerging national states to unify their standards of measurement. It was probably the combined effect of the Enlightenment (with its treatment of historical traditions as essentially arbitrary in the way they worked), modern statehood and the Industrial Revolution that led to unified standards of measurement. Increasingly, these were agreed upon at an international level and conformed to ever-higher requirements of exactness. The French standard meter of 1791 comes to mind.

---

[29] On Bodin's contribution to monetary theory, see Jérôme Blanc, "Beyond the quantity theory: A reappraisal of Jean Bodin's monetary ideas," in: A. Giacomin and M. C. Marcuzzo, eds., *Money and Markets: A Doctrinal Approach*. Routledge Studies in the History of Economics. London: Routledge, 2007, 135 et seq.

It was probably in the light of these advances that nineteenth-century authors began to question the idea that coins (and paper notes) could serve as effective standards of measurement.[30] Theodor Mommsen, in his magisterial study of the Roman currency, saw that traditional coinage allowed the values of commodities to be expressed in terms of another commodity, which in this case was silver. Hereby:

the key effect is brought about that all commodities can be related to each other in fixed, quantitative terms, in so far as they are traded at the same time and at the same place. Seen for what it really is, this is the position as regards a unified system of evaluation. It is a kind of conventional self-delusion that, in using this unified evaluation, the requirement "same time, same location" is neglected to a certain degree. For a commodity which, owing to its status as a commodity "is subject to decrease or increase [in price] is taken to be an ever valid measure of value …. One measures, indeed, with a standard which in itself expands or contracts and, at the same place, is today greater or smaller than yesterday, and which can, at the same time, be larger at this place, smaller at that.[31]

Mommsen looked forward to what we now call fiat money. He hoped for the far-off day when fiat money, stripped of all inherent value, would "measure the value of other goods nearly as perfectly as the watch measures time and the carpenter's rule space".[32] Mommsen clear-sightedly recognized that even fiat money would not be an absolute standard. Fluctuations in the demand for money owing to business cycles and the supply of fiat money in actual circulation would not necessarily keep in step with each other: "There cannot be an absolute standard of value." As he saw it, the nature of things only made it possible to approach a constant value, albeit ever-more closely. A practical approximation to that constant value was the best one could hope for.

Despite these reservations of a theoretical nature, the notion of money as a yardstick still held good in the public arena. The introduction of bank notes and their gradual acceptance as "money", which continued throughout the nineteenth century and beyond, was accompanied by

---

[30] Of course, technical progress had greatly increased the exactness of minting, as well; on the impact of technological problems, see T. J. Sargent and F. R. Velde, *The Big Problem of Small Change*. Princeton University Press, 2002, 45 et seq.

[31] T. Mommsen, *Römisches Münzwesen*. Leipzig: Weidmann, 1850, v et seq. (my translation from the German).

[32] Ibid.

heated debates about the pros and cons of the process. One argument brought forward in order to fend off the idea of paper money was the idea of a yardstick: "[T]he yardstick becomes the measure of length by having length within itself . . . So metallic money having intrinsic value is made a measure of value by its coinage based on its metallic value".[33] The argument echoes David Ricardo's statement, that "[t]here can be no unerring measure of either length, of weight, of time or of value unless there be some object in nature to which the standard itself can be referred".[34]

Fiat money and its value

In the twentieth century, coins and notes underwent a remarkable change. They ceased to have an inherent material value based on the metal or, in the case of notes, the holder's entitlement to exchange the paper note for a metal equivalent, consisting of gold. Today's money is fiat money[35] (sometimes also called "token money"). Coins and notes, as corporeal entities, no longer have any substantial value conferred on them by virtue of their silver or gold content (or by virtue of their convertibility into gold, guaranteed as long as the gold standard was upheld). Henceforth, for money as a *mensuratum*, one can no longer rely on the value of the gold or silver amount involved (which in itself had been far from perfect as a benchmark).

The value of a specific coin or note of fiat money is based on the possibility of exchanging it for another item: "[A] condition for fiat money to be held and valued today is that it will be acceptable in exchange for intrinsically useful commodities tomorrow" (James Tobin).[36] So it is essentially the purchasing power of token money which gives it its "value". This may be referred to as its "value of

---

[33] B. G. Carruthers and S. Babb, "The Color of Money and the Nature of Value: Greenbacks and Gold in Postbellum America," *American Journal of Sociology* 101 (1996): 1567, quoting an American politician named Bartley.

[34] *The Works and Correspondence of David Ricardo*, ed. P. Stufford. Cambridge University Press, 1988, 401.

[35] See N. Wallace, "fiat money", *The New Palgrave Dictionary of Economics, Online edn.* 16 February 2010, <http://www.dictionaryofeconomics.com/article?id=pde2008_F000059> doi: 10.1057/9780230226203.0563.

[36] Fn. 1, also drawing attention to the limits of this concept.

exchange".[37] Of course, money has always had this value of exchange. The only difference with commodity money is that it also had a material value, since it was made of silver or some other precious metal. The metal value having gone, the purchasing power of money is all that is left to determine its value today.

In order to look for the "value" of money, one now has no option but to look into *prices*. The theoretical concept of "prices" itself has considerably changed.[38] Prices are no longer seen as a yardstick for a "value" of a specific commodity, which one could objectively establish prior to and in the absence of any specific exchange. For the changing view of prices one may look, for example, to von Mises' contribution.[39] Von Mises objected to the notion that a barter implied the notion of equality in the value of the objects bartered, and likewise of the notion that a price, fixed in money, attributes a specific "value" to the object bought. Rather, von Mises maintained, each party signals not a *value* judgment, but a *preference*. He wants to have the object received rather than the object given. Thus buyer and seller do not *jointly* attribute the price as the monetary value to the object, they do not jointly "measure" the value of the object sold in terms of money. The buyer acts on the preference that he would rather have the object than the money paid as a price, whereas the seller signals his preference of the sum of money fixed as the price over his object. With respect to the "value" of the object, they are not in accord. "The exchange ratio, the price, is not the product of an equality of valuation, but, on the contrary, the product of a discrepancy in valuation".[40] Each of the parties to a transaction ranks the objects of the exchange according to his or her own very personal

---

[37] Some writers (e.g. J. Schumpeter, "Das Sozialprodukt und die Rechenpfennige," *Archiv für Sozialwissenschaften* 44 (1917/18): 636) have rephrased this view by stating that "[m]oney is an individual's entitlement to a share of the national product" (*"Anweisung auf das Sozialprodukt,"* Gustav Schmoelders). This is a manner of speaking only, because this "entitlement" is not legally enforceable. The notion of "money as entitlement", however, is apt to highlight that money has its value only by virtue of its convertibility into "real" commodities.

[38] The history of the doctrinal approaches to the problem of how prices are arrived at cannot be addressed here.

[39] L. von Mises, *Theorie des Geldes und der Umlaufmittel.* Berlin: Duncker & Humblot, 1911, 10 et seq. The English-speaking reader is referred to von Mises' own restatement of his views in: L. von Mises, *Human Action: A Treatise on Economics*, ed. B. Bien Greaves, vol. II. Auburn: Liberty Fund Inc., 2007, first pub. 1949, 331 et seq.

[40] Ibid., n. 39, 331.

preferences. These relative, preferential value judgments are, in von Mises' view, incompatible with the notion of a (joint) measurement. Transactions, in von Mises' view, are about ranking or scaling of preferences, and not about measurement. Therefore, he concluded, it was unscientific to speak about the value measurement as a function of money.[41] Commodities do not carry, as one quality among others, a specific quantum of value, stemming, for example, from their production cost, the labor cost involved in their production, or some level of interest rates. In other words, the quality which money was long said to measure did not even exist.

The distinction between *mensura* and *mensuratum* is thus fading. To express the value of money, at a given time, one needs to look into the prices of commodities, which in turn are given in units of money. At this state of affairs, there exists a network of exchange relations between all merchantable commodities: at a given time and in a given place, we can establish all sorts of exchange rates between different commodities, including the "exchange rates" between the monetary unit and commodities. What distinguishes money in this network of exchange rates is that all commodities have other uses which confer some kind of "value" on them, whereas money can *only* be used by exchanging it for commodities. No real needs can be satisfied using fiat money; money can only be used for the purpose of circulation.

Ascertaining money's purchasing power

How does one establish money's purchasing power, its "objective value of exchange"? The actual idea of what money is "worth" can only stem from an *expectation* of what a specific amount of money can buy.[42] This expectation must be based on observations of how much money could buy in the recent past. In establishing the up-to-date "value of exchange", or purchasing power of money, a memory element creeps in, since one needs a number of past transactions to realize the quantity of goods bought with a particular amount. Past prices have a considerable impact on today's reckoning of the purchasing power of money.

---

[41] von Mises, *Theorie des Geldes*, n. 39, 20.

[42] It has also been held that money is our means to gain an idea of the different values of commodities, a "means for the conception of value" ("*Wertvorstellungsmittel*") or for the "expression of value" ("*Wertausdrucksmittel*").

The purchasing power of money may fluctuate considerably. But these fluctuations, instead of being totally random, will tend to depart from the exchange rates established on the basis of the last observed exchanges. To quote von Mises: "The individual, in order to develop an idea of the amount of money he or she needs today, needs to know the money's objective value of exchange, as it has been established on yesterday's market".[43]

The purchasing power of money can be stated, for a given moment in time, in units of each and every commodity. One can thus single out a specific commodity which is taken as a *mensura* to state the purchasing power of money in units of this commodity. All problems start when one wants to measure the money's "objective value of exchange" (purchasing power) *as it develops over time*. Since supply and demand of the commodity which one has singled out vary over time, the standard of measurement is not at all stable. Observing the development of prices for this commodity does not allow the observation of a possible change of money's purchasing power. The solution was seen in the definition of baskets of goods: how many of the same monetary units does one need, at two different times, to purchase the same basket of goods (this is a so-called "multiple standard")? From the start of the twentieth century onwards, the question has been addressed how best to define such "baskets of commodities", in order to produce so-called general index numbers, which reflect the general change of money's purchasing power over time (as opposed to the change of prices for a specific commodity).[44] Despite the elaborate methods which have been suggested, difficulties remain. Owing to social and economic changes, the relative importance of various goods also changes over time. In order to reflect these changes, the basket of commodities needs to be redefined from time to time. This in turn compromises the long-term stability of this "standard of measurement".[45] Defining and readjusting the "basket of commodities" in order to produce general index numbers which reliably reflect the change in the general purchasing power of

---

[43] von Mises, *Theorie des Geldes*, n. 39, 93 (my translation).

[44] I. Fisher, *The Making of Index Numbers*. New York: Houghton Mifflin, 1922; for an early criticism, see G. Haberler, *Der Sinn der Indexzahlen*. Tübingen: J. C. B. Mohr, 1927.

[45] For a more recent overview, see C. L. Schultze, "The Consumer Price Index: Conceptual Issues and Practical Suggestions," *Journal of Economic Perspectives* 17 (2003): 3–22.

money has proved so difficult that it is probably reasonable to conclude that at best no more than approximations can be achieved. The idea of index numbers cannot be realized with exactness. The general index numbers, however refined, hardly provide a constant standard to measure the value of money.

As an illustration of these difficulties, an example from the politico-legal field may be in order. When compensation was sought for money kept in accounts in Switzerland which had lain dormant for half a century because the account holders had perished in the Holocaust, the current value for former accounts needed to be established. During the negotiations, all sorts of methods were proposed, none of which could really be seen as rationally persuasive.[46] (In the end, the negotiators settled for compensation set at ten times the nominal value of the accounts.)

Could one eliminate the shortcomings as to the changing exchange-value of modern money, which limits its value as a yardstick? One of the suggestions made was the so-called Index money. Index money would be a modern form of *moneta imaginaria*. The Index currency was proposed as a means to come to terms with a currency system troubled by inflation. One such proposal was made by Irving Fisher.[47] Fisher suggested adjusting the monetary unit of account, by means of indices, to its fluctuating purchasing power (this he called a "Tabular Standard"). This proposal has not found general support.

If money is not to be spent right away, but sometime in the future, one must ask oneself what this money will buy at the time it actually comes to be spent. In this respect, the value attributed to money depends on a prediction about its future purchasing power. This entails a prognosis into which all sorts of expectations (specific and general) are factored. Projections about the rates of inflation (or deflation, for that matter) are essential ingredients of today's wage negotiations between unions and employers.

Regarding the stability of the purchasing power of money, today one goes beyond detached attempts at passive monitoring. Rather, societies actively try to manage currencies so that the "objective value of exchange" changes at a specific target rate or, more realistically, at a

---

[46] See S. E. Eizenstat, *Imperfect Justice: Looted Assets, Slave Labor, and the Unfinished Business of World War II*. New York: PublicAffairs, 2003, 73–4.

[47] I. Fisher, *Stable Money: A History of the Movement*. Adelphi, NY: Octavo, 1934.

rate within a desirable target range. In a historical perspective, money today is probably much more systematically managed than ever before. The instruments and effectiveness of this management need not concern us here. If we look at the present state of affairs from the viewpoint of money as "measure", it is interesting to note, however, that the "stability" of money, rather than being taken for granted, has been recognized as an objective which needs to be actively pursued.

Enter psychology

The twentieth century has revealed yet another aspect of the problem of the "value" of money. If the "value" of modern (fiat) money derives from its purchasing power, then to get an idea of the "value" of money, everybody somehow needs to link a specific monetary unit to a set of objects which he thinks this amount of money can buy. Since the early decades of the twentieth century, there has been a growth of interest in the psychological processes which lead to the formation of ideas about the purchasing power[48] of money. The term "consciousness of the value of money" was coined.[49] It refers to the *felt* (or apparent) value of money: a monetary unit, such as a coin or a banknote, is mentally associated with commodities which one piece of this unit could buy. This association depends on very personal and selective observations. This formation of one's "consciousness of the value of money" is not a scientific process. Citizens do not rely on or conduct econometric studies. Rather, all sorts of observations, ideas and musings – rational and irrational alike – can contribute to the ad hoc "felt value of money".

Since the purchasing power of money fluctuates, the "felt value of money" would need to follow suit in order adequately to reflect such fluctuations. In fact, the "felt value of money" does not correspond to the actual development of the purchasing power of money. There is, at

---

[48] A. Wagner, *Sozialökonomische Theorie des Geldes*. Leipzig: C. F. Winter, 1909, 116. In 1900, Georg Simmel had already pointed out that the use of money ultimately depends on "states of mind", i.e. facts of a psychological nature: G. Simmel, *Die Philosophie des Geldes*, 2nd edn., Leipzig: Duncker & Humblot Verlag, 1907, 165.

[49] Pioneer works are F. Wilken, "Die Phänomenologie des Geldwertbewusstseins," *Archiv für die Sozialwissenschaft und Sozialpolitik* 56 (1926): 420 et seq.; and W. Taeuber, "Psychologie des Geldes," *Jahrbuch für Psychologie und Psychotherapie* 1 (1952): 14–36.

best, a recognition lag. In view of this discrepancy, the term "money illusion" was introduced.[50] Relying on an idea first sketched by Keynes,[51] in 1928 Irving Fisher defined monetary illusion as "... the failure to perceive that the dollar, or any other unit of money, expands or shrinks in value".[52] The money illusion has now also been looked into (and has been empirically confirmed) from a behavioral economics perspective.[53]

The disregard of inflation due to a one-sided leaning towards the nominal value of money, instead of its purchasing power, is but one type of money illusion. The reverse illusion, namely, disregarding deflation, can also occur. Monetary illusions are not without real-life economic effects. Fear of inflation has, in itself, an inflationary impact, because sellers beset by inflation fear tend to demand higher prices, reckoning that they will need "more" money once the time comes that they are going to spend it. Therefore, in managing currencies, not only inflation must be staved off, inflation expectation needs to be kept at bay as well. Realizing how important the psychological element is for a functioning currency, today one very much tries to build up and maintain the trust-worthiness of the institutions which manage the currency. Their inde-pendence and neutrality is recognized not only as a key factor for the maintenance of a sound and stable monetary environment, but also as a precondition for the public's indispensable trust in the stability of its money.

Concluding remarks

The notion of money as a yardstick, rather than being a constant of western monetary thought, has undergone quite dramatic changes. In view of the difficulties which have accompanied the evolution of this concept, it seems rather improbable that the so-called measurement

---

[50] See, for example, I. Meyer and G. Schmoelders, *Geldwertbewusstsein und Münzpolitik*. Cologne: Westdeutscher Verlag, 1957; for a more recent overview, see P. Howitt, *"money illusion"*, *The New Palgrave Dictionary of Economics*, Online edn., 16 February 2010, <http://www.dictionaryofeconomics.com/article?id=pde2008_M000225>, doi: 10.1057/9780230226203.1129.

[51] J. M. Keynes, *A Tract on Monetary Reform*. London: Macmillan, 1923.

[52] I. Fisher, *The Money Illusion*. New York: Adelphi, 1928, 4.

[53] E. Fehr and J.-R. Tyran, "Does Money Illusion Matter?" *American Economic Review* 91 (2001): 1239–62.

function of money should have been, genetically, one of the main driving forces in the origins of currencies. For a lawyer, these difficulties are even more startling, since in the legal field one tends to support the idea of nominalism, i.e. the concept that monetary obligations are unalterably defined by a number of monetary units, disregarding all intervening changes of purchase power.[54]

---

[54] See C. Proctor, *Mann on the Legal Aspect of Money*, 6th edn. Oxford University Press, 2005, 9.05–9.51.

4 | *Standardization and monetization: legal perspectives*

BURKHARD HESS

The position of the chapter

How does legal science address standardization and monetization? The following chapter tries to explore the subject from a "positivistic perspective" – this means not from the perspective of legal history or legal philosophy, but rather, from a norm-oriented point of view. By adopting this approach, the chapter must face the challenge that standardization and monetization are not judicial concepts in the traditional sense. Accordingly, a clear definition of these concepts does not exist in legal doctrine. However, the chapter adopts a traditional methodological approach of a German law professor who firstly tries to set a definition of the concepts and, secondly, transposes them in some specific areas of life from a comparative and global perspective and, finally, addresses fairness and justice in order to explore their relationship to standardization and monetization.

Let me start by setting some definitions: the common use of the word "standard" implies that it is a generally accepted set of guidelines for interoperability or communication. In the context of social sciences, standardization often describes the process of establishing standards of various kinds, or the process of improving an efficient handling of interactions between men within a society. Seen from the legal perspective, standardization can firstly be defined as a legislative technique which underlies any legal system. Legal systems are aimed at standardizing human and social relations as well as economic exchange. Legal provisions describe and regulate typical transactions within social communities and among economic entities. Typical transactions relate to economic exchange on a contractual basis: the exchange of goods and services, the lending of money, the transfer of property. In this respect, legal provisions define typical exchange situations in economic life, including pathological situations. Standardization is also found in legal proceedings where the unfolding of the process is defined by legal provisions and claim forms which must be used by the court and the parties. Therefore, standardization is the underlying legal technique of any set of legal rules (or codification). In addition, it is often used in modern contracts.[1] Standardization in legal relationships refers to binding norms which are derived from legal provisions or contractual relations.[2]

In this chapter, monetization is firstly conceived as a (sophisticated) form of standardization, which refers to the use of money instead of a barter exchange. Accordingly, monetization makes economic transactions easier.[3] In this respect, monetization directly refers to one of the basic functions of money as a media of exchange.[4] In addition to this, monetization also reflects the general attitude of modern societies of evaluating most of the individual rights against their monetary value. This corresponds to the function of money as "storage of value".[5] Yet, this function is sometimes used for the valuation of non-tangible goods (life, health, freedom) which are not freely available in a liquid market.[6] Legal literature criticizes this trend as a "commercialization" of personality and other (non-tangible) rights.[7] In this context, monetization is mainly found in the law of compensation. This specific problem will be explained in more detail by Günter Thomas (Chapter 13 below).[8]

---

[1] Claim forms and standard contracts will be explained below as typical tools of modern, sophisticated legal systems.

[2] The binding force of legal standards/norms seems to be the difference between other situations where standardization is also found.

[3] At least within a defined economic community (such as the State). International financial transactions cannot easily rely on common standards (one currency or balanced currencies). Accordingly, economic exchanges become more difficult because of the lack of standardization respective to monetization.

[4] These functions are to serve as a media of exchange, as a store of value, and as a unit of account. See Peter Bernholz, "Money and its role in a decentralized market economy", Chapter 2 above.

[5] Ibid.

[6] In modern societies, these values are more and more affected by general economization; critical of these developments is M. Sandel, *What Money Can't Buy: The Moral Limits of Markets*, London: Allen Lane (an imprint of Penguin), 2012, 163ff.

[7] See *Münchener Kommentar zum BGB*/Oetker, §249 BGB (6th edn., Nünchen, C.H. Beck 2012), nos. 40–5, with further references.

[8] G. Thomas, "What price do we place on life? Ethical observations on the limits of law and money in a case of transitional justice," Chapter 13 below.

Standardization as a legal technique

Every legal system is based on the standardization of human relations.
In this context, standardization simply means the description of repetitive human behavior.[9] Let's start with the conclusion of a contract as a
striking example. Any contract is concluded by the offer of one party
and by the acceptance of the other. This mechanism is found in all legal
systems which implement the right of the parties to conclude contracts
freely.[10] Legal systems which are based on codifications[11] provide for
explicit provisions defining the persons able to act within the system
as well as the method of how transactions within the system are performed. Accordingly, civil codes define who can conclude a contract,[12]
as well as the conditions for its conclusion.[13] Codifications regularly use
standardization for setting different types of contracts (sale, gift, lease,
loan, contract of service, contract for work and labor, progress contract, mandate, franchise, commission etc.). This example demonstrates
that standardization is the typical legal technique of these codifications.
However, the standards contained in civil codes are not binding (with
rare exceptions).[14] These standards are used as a kind of "fall-back
position". This means that parties are free to refer to the legal provisions
or to deviate from them, their contractual obligations prevail over the
corresponding legal norms, but their contract is also complemented by
the legal provisions.[15]

---

[9] According to Luhmann, standardization does not refer to human relations, but to
communication with a definite system.
[10] In the world of today, all countries, with the exception of North Korea and Cuba,
have adopted (more or less) the principle of a decentralized market economy.
[11] The idea of a codification is to provide for a comprehensive set of rules which
regulates all major aspects of a distinct judicial field – accordingly, the Civil Code
is aimed at addressing all legal relationships between private persons
(transactions, family relations, successions, etc.), see J. P. Schmidt,
"Kodifikation," in: J. Basedow, K. J. Hopt, and R. Zimmermann,
Handwörterbuch des Europäischen Zivilrechts, Tübingen: Mohr Siebeck, 2009,
986–90.
[12] Natural and legal persons; minors and adults and their capacity to enter into
contractual relationships, etc.
[13] Examples are offer, acceptance, the binding force of an offer, statutory
prohibition, public policy, and nullity of a contract.
[14] Especially by mandatory norms in the context of consumer protection.
[15] Nevertheless, the legal provisions of the codification function as default rules
which can be modified by the parties.

This technique is demonstrated by the example of Section 434 of the German Civil Code which deals with the contract for purchase. The provision reads as follows:

The good is free from defects of quality, if it corresponds at the moment of the delivery, to the agreed quality. To the extent that the quality has not been agreed the good is free of defects of quality,

if it is suitable for the use specified in the contract;

if it is suitable for the normal use and has a quality customary with goods of the same kind and which the buyer may expect in the nature of the good.

According to this provision, the question of whether the delivered good is defective is determined firstly by the agreement of the parties, secondly by the use specified in the contract (implied agreement) and, finally, by normal standards of comparable goods and by the expectation of the buyer. Thus, if the parties do not agree on the quality of the good, the Civil Code opens up a way to determine the defects of the good. Accordingly, Section 434 functionally corresponds to a fall-back provision which complements the contract of the parties.

Standardization as a basic legal technique is not limited to economic relations. It also applies to other fields which are not dominated by economic exchange, such as family law, the law of succession, or the protection of privacy. One striking example is the following rule in German family law. The German Civil Code provides for three different regimes of matrimonial relations: the so-called legal regime (which applies when the spouses do not agree otherwise) is called the "statutory property regime of the community of surplus". This means that the properties of the spouses remain separate (SS.1363, 1364 German Civil Code). However, when the matrimonial state is terminated (by the death of one spouse or by divorce) the gains obtained are equalized. The spouse who made a higher gain than the other is obliged to pay half of the amount to the other spouse, or his or her heirs. Yet, the spouses may conclude a contract governing their matrimonial relationship. In order to protect the weaker spouse and third parties, the Civil Code strictly limits the freedom of the spouses to agree on individual regimes. The Civil Code provides for only two additional regimes (complete separation of property or the complete community of property). Any additional deviation is strictly prohibited. Accordingly, the matrimonial regimes provided for by the German Civil Code are strictly standardized and limited by mandatory legal provisions.[16]

The standardization of legal relations also takes place in the common law world, i.e. in legal systems without a codified legal framework (especially England, the United States, Australia etc.).[17] In these jurisdictions, standardization is mainly achieved by claim forms and standard contracts elaborated by private parties.[18] Accordingly, an American-style contract is much more comprehensive than its continental counterpart, as it must contain all the fall-back provisions of the civil code (which – principally – does not exist in the United States). Yet, private standardization also takes place in the civil law world, as the civil codes are not comprehensive enough to address all legal questions of economic and social exchange. Accordingly, businesses (i.e. banks and insurance), but also notaries and other stakeholders, normally use standardized contracts for their legal relationships.

Private standardization is very efficient, but has its price: as the more powerful party often imposes his or her standard forms on the weaker, standard forms are not usually "fair", but often biased. Normally, parties do not negotiate on standard terms, and the terms are often agreed to without any precise knowledge of their content by the (weaker) party.[19] In the second half of the twentieth century, national and European legislations realized the dangers of "contractual standardization" and addressed this problem in different ways. In modern legal systems, standard contracts are subject to judicial review and/or administrative control; in some legal fields, especially in the laws for the protection of consumers, they are forbidden by mandatory laws.[20] The criteria for judicial review are found in explicit legal provisions

---

[16] The legal framework and its underlying principles were explained by Zöllner, *Familienrechtszeitschrift*, 1965, 113ff.

[17] Comparative law clearly distinguishes continental (civil) law and common law as so-called legal families. The main feature of the civil law's legal tradition is the reliance on written legal texts (especially codifications of private law and of civil procedure), while the common law is based on the case law of the judiciary which is evolved on a case-by-case basis, see Zweigert and Kötz, *Einführung in die Rechtsvergleichung*,Tübingen, Mohr, 1996, § 5 III, 69.

[18] An additional example is letters for credit which have evolved by the practice of international commerce and banks (without any intervention of states).

[19] Standard contracts and forms are also largely used in continental systems, because powerful parties often try to impose their claim standard forms in business relations, especially in business relationships with consumers.

[20] See sections 474–7 of the German Civil Code (2002).

(e.g. German law largely refers to the legal provisions of the Civil Code which are considered fair for both parties) and in the case law of the courts. In addition to this, European law provides for a specific directive which empowers consumer associations to seek injunctions against businessmen who use unfair standard contracts.[21] These examples show that the standardization of legal relations, especially of contracts, has become the usual situation in modern legal systems.[22]

A short remark must be added in relation to the advantages of using standard forms in the cross-border context. Let's take as an example a French merchant of wine who is suing a German client for the non-payment of a delivery. This businessman is facing enormous barriers: his lawsuit must overcome different legal systems and different languages: creditors seeking to enforce judgments in other European Member States must resort to different national procedures, use different languages, and seek translations. The outcome of these expensive and time-consuming proceedings is often unpredictable – many businessmen do not enforce their claims, but simply write them off. Standardization may overcome these obstacles: one striking example is the EC Regulation Creating a European Order for Payment,[23] which facilitates the cross-border recovery of monetary claims. It provides for a simplified procedure based on standard forms. The standard forms are available in all languages of the Community at the website of the European Commission.[24] A creditor who applies for a European Payment Order must simply fill out the standard form by inserting the names and addresses of the parties, the competent court and by specifying the respective claim (sale, rent, lease etc.).[25] The application is filed

---

[21] Directive 1998/27/EC on injunctions for the protection of consumers' interests, Burkhard Hess, *Europäisches Zivilprozessrecht*, 2010, § 10 IV, nos. 118–135.

[22] The conclusion of individual contracts only occurs in specific situations. One example of an individually negotiated contract may be found in the agreement between the German Federal Government and a private consortium on the construction of the Toll-Collect System (for the German autobahn). As the consortium did not set up the system in time, the German Government claimed damages (several billion Euros) and initiated arbitration proceedings: R. Stürner, *Juristenzeitung* 2006, 80, 82.

[23] Regulation EC 1896/2006, OJ 2006 L 399/1 et seq., Hess, *Europäisches Zivilprozessrecht*, § 10 II, nos. 39–79.

[24] This website, called the European Judicial Atlas, is accessible at: http://ec.europa.eu/justice_home/judicialatlascivil/html/epo_filling_en.htm.

[25] Only in exceptional circumstances need the applicant describe the legal nature of the claim.

directly with the competent court. For instance, a Finnish judge who receives a German creditor's application based on the German claim form may simply take the identical Finnish claim form in order to understand the meaning of the "German application". The same technique applies to the cross-border enforcement of the European Payment Order. A Payment Order of a Finnish court in its own language can be enforced directly (without any prior translation) by a German bailiff on the basis of standard forms explaining its content. This example shows that sophisticated standardization may also overcome linguistic and legal obstacles in a single market with different national cultures and languages.[26]

Monetization within legal systems: compensation and rehabilitation

In the legal context, monetization has a twofold meaning. Firstly, it refers to the legal regime of claims for payment. In legal history, the replacement of bartering by a monetary economy was often the first step towards the implementation of a legal system.[27] Several centuries later, the elaboration of the Bill of Exchange in the late twelfth century (in northern Italy) enabled merchants to engage in transactions without coins and to minimize the risk of transporting and losing large sums of money when traveling between different marketplaces.[28] The standardization of commercial contracts, especially the standardization of payments since the Middle Ages, was the main incentive for the elaboration of transnational uniform legal instruments in the nineteenth and twentieth centuries.[29] The introduction of a single currency has similar effects: it facilitates not only economic, but also legal, exchange.

---

[26] It is interesting to note that in this context, claim forms are more important than the underlying legal provisions.

[27] H. Hattenhauer, *Europäische Rechtsgeschichte*, Karlsruhe: C. F. Müller 2004, 12ff.

[28] A. Hueck and W. Canaris, *Recht der Wertpapiere*, Munich: Franz Vahlen 1986, 50ff.

[29] Modern payments are regulated by uniform standard rules (for letters of credit, independent guarantees, electronic presentations, etc.) which have been elaborated by international organizations (UNIDROIT, UNCITRAL, International Chamber of Commerce), see R. Goode, H. Kronke, E. McKendrick, and J. Wood (eds.), *Transnational Commercial Law: Text, Cases and Materials*, Oxford University Press, 2004, 331ff.

Nevertheless, it should be noted that most of the legal systems do not provide for a comprehensive definition of money; jurists prefer to describe money by its different functions.[30] The famous German law professor, Friedrich Carl von Savigny (1779–1861), described money as "a mere instrument for measuring the value of individual parts of wealth".[31] In addition, von Savigny stressed a second function of money serving as an abstract purchasing power.[32] This conception is approved by the law – all modern legal systems define money as a legal tender,[33] by setting denominations and technical specifications of coins and bills intended for circulation.[34] By virtue of the law, parties are obliged to use the legal tender as the medium of exchange. In the European Currency Union, the pertinent provision is found in Article 128 of the Treaty on the Functioning of the European Union.[35] Private law largely refers to these provisions. According to section 244 of the German Civil Code, all payments effected in Germany may be made in euros unless payment in the other currency has been expressly agreed. In order to guarantee the stability of the currency, parties are not free to agree a different tender or to stipulate that the payment shall be measured by the price of a certain commodity (depreciation or index clause).

---

[30] See *Münchener Kommentar*/Grundmann, §§ 244 and 245 BGB, paras. 1–4; F. A. Mann, *Legal Aspects of Money*, New York: Oxford University Press, 4th edn. 1982, 4–79. In this respect, jurists largely refer to the (different) conceptions of economists.

[31] Savigny, *Obligationenrecht*.

[32] See Mann, *The Legal Aspects of Money*; W. Ernst, "*Mensura et mensuratum*", Chapter 3 above.

[33] Council Regulation (EC) No. 974/98 of 3 May 1998 on the introduction of the euro, OJ 1998 L 139/1, esp. Article 10: "As from 1 January 2002, the ECB and the central banks of the participating Member States shall put into circulation banknotes denominated in euro. Without prejudice to Article 15, these banknotes denominated in euro shall be the only banknotes which have the status of legal tender in all these Member States."

[34] Council Regulation (EC) No. 975/98 of 3 May 1998 on denominations and technical specifications of euro coins intended for circulation, OJ 1998 L 139/6.

[35] Article 128(1) of the Treaty on the Functioning of the European Union reads as follows: "The ECB shall have the exclusive right to authorize the issue of banknotes within the Community. The ECB and the national central banks may issue such notes. *The banknotes issued by the ECB and the national central banks shall be the only such notes to have the status of legal tender within the Community* [emphasis added]."

However, in cross-border transactions and with regard to long-term agreements, the parties are free to stipulate index clauses.[36]

Secondly, monetization refers to the commercialization of legal entitlements and of non-tangible goods.[37] Especially in the context of the law of compensation, jurists distinguish two kinds of damages: pecuniary damages, which can be calculated in a precise sum of money, and non-monetary damages, which cannot be determined in a precise sum of money. Examples of non-monetary damages are pain and suffering, the loss of relatives, infringements of privacy etc. In practice, it is extremely difficult to evaluate non-pecuniary damages, and the legal solutions vary significantly among the legal systems.[38] The pertinent legal provisions of the German Civil Code on the compensation of damages read as follows:

Section 249 § 1
A person who is obliged to make compensation shall restore the situation which would have existed if the circumstance rendering him or her liable to compensation had not occurred.

Section 253
(1) For an injury which is not an injury to property, compensation in money may be demanded only as provided by law.
(2) In the case of injury to the body or health or in the case of deprivation of liberty or of sexual assault the injured party may also demand fair compensation in money for non-pecuniary damages.

These provisions clearly demonstrate the basic features of the German law of compensation which, as a matter of principle, provides for full compensation of the damage which is normally implemented by payment for the loss suffered. However, if the damages consist of a non-pecuniary loss, the situation is more complicated. In this constellation, the payment of money has mainly a symbolic function: it is to

---

[36] *Münchener Kommentar*/Grundmann, §§ 244 and 245 BGB, paras. 68–71 (commenting on s. 2 of the German law on prices (Preisangaben und Preisklauselgesetz)).

[37] This development is correctly criticized by Sandel, *What Money Can't Buy*, 93ff.

[38] The main differences relate to the availability of punitive and treble damages in the United States. These damages are not awarded in most of the European jurisdictions. For a recent comparison between the American and the German approach to punitive damages (and the underlying legal concepts), see V. Behr, "Myth and Reality of Punitive Damages in Germany," *Journal of Law and Commerce* 24 (2005), 197.

compensate the loss of quality of life (especially in the case of severe violations of body or health) and demonstrate a kind of "recognition" of the injury incurred. Some legal systems (especially the United States) also provide for punitive damages: they not only compensate the loss incurred, but punish the tortfeasor and deter them from committing similar torts. The main disadvantage of this kind of damages lies in the fact that the victim will get much more compensation than the loss incurred. In Germany, there is a clear trend of standardizing the compensation for non-pecuniary losses. In legal practice, monetization is implemented by so-called schedules of money for pain and suffering. These schedules are compilations of the case law on compensation awarded for pain and suffering. These compilations do not have any binding legal effect. However, lawyers, courts, and (especially) assurances are well aware of the "typical awards" and do not deviate considerably from these figures. However, judgments regularly do not refer to these compilations – the compensation of non-pecuniary damages is regularly awarded according to the circumstances of the individual case.[39] Nevertheless, the guiding value of these compilations for practice cannot be disregarded – monetization allows for a comparison of the injuries incurred.[40]

In 2007, I addressed this issue of non-pecuniary damages by referring to the example of infringement of privacy and the case law of the European Court of Human Rights on Caroline of Hanover. The European Court of Human Rights in Strasbourg held that Princess Caroline of Hanover's privacy had been severely infringed by photographers who secretly took photos of her and her children in a golf club.[41] These photos had been published by different newspapers throughout Europe without the princess's consent.[42] However, it was impossible to give a precise calculation of the damage sustained by the princess. The European Court of Human Rights held that in order to

---

[39] *Münchener Kommentar*/Oetker, § 253 BGB, para. 37.

[40] Thomas, Chapter 13 above.

[41] European Court of Human Rights, 6/24/2004, Case no. 59320/00, [2004] ECHR 294. Generally on the protection of personality rights in private international and procedural law, Hess, "Der Schutz der Privatsphäre im Europäischen Zivilverfahrensrecht," *Juristenzeitung* (2012), 189ff.

[42] While the German civil courts held that the taking of photos outside her home did not infringe her right of privacy, the European Court dissented and held that Art. 8 of the European Convention on Human Rights (which protects the privacy of a person) had been violated.

deter the photographers ("paparazzi") from infringing the privacy of victims, the national systems must grant a considerable sum of money to the victims. As a result, the princess settled the case for about €115,000.[43] However, the compensation in this case (and in comparable lawsuits) was much higher than that normally awarded to persons who had been severely injured. In Germany, bodily injured victims may recover damages for medical expenses, future medical expenses, and rather a small sum of damages for pain, suffering, and similar non-pecuniary losses. Damage awards should position the plaintiff where he would be had the damage not occurred. Damages should not enrich the plaintiff or aim to punish and deter the tortfeasor beyond the general effect that is inherent in all compensatory damages obligations.[44]

The current legal situation is not undisputed. Some years ago, the German Constitutional Court was seized by two plaintiffs whose four children had been killed by a drunk driver in a road accident.[45] The civil court had awarded the parents compensation of about €30,000 for pain and suffering.[46] The parents filed a constitutional complaint in the Constitutional Court. They argued that the Princess of Monaco had received four times more for the violation of her privacy than they had been awarded by the German civil courts, and asserted a violation of the fundamental guarantee of equal treatment (Art. 3(1) German Constitution).[47] The Constitutional Court held, however, that the case law which awarded higher compensations for infringements of the right of privacy did not impair the constitutional right. The Court

---

[43] According to the settlement, €15,000 was awarded as compensation for non-pecuniary damages, €100,000 for attorneys' fees, costs, and taxes.

[44] Behr, "Myth and Reality of Punitive Damages in Germany," 197, 199.

[45] German Constitutional Court, 1 BvR 1127/96, judgment of 3/8/2000, available at http://www.bverfg.de/.

[46] According to German civil law, this judgment was rather generous, as German law, as a rule, does not provide for any compensation for the loss (death) of close relatives.

[47] In the 1990s, Caroline of Monaco (now of Hanover) sued several European publishers for infringements of her personality rights and the rights of her children. In Germany, the civil courts changed their case law to some extent and awarded the plaintiff considerable compensation: see especially Federal Supreme Civil Court (Bundesgerichtshof), 11/15/1994, BGHZ 128, 1 (€15,000 non-pecuniary compensation for the publication of an interview which had never taken place); 12/5/1995, *Neue Juristische Wochenschrift* 1996, 984 (DM 180,000 = €90,000 for the publication of the headline: "Caroline, fighting fearlessly breast cancer": in the newspaper an article explained that Caroline was supporting a public campaign against breast cancer).

distinguished the damages for the infringement of privacy from the damage sustained by the applicants. It held that in the case of infringement of privacy, the idea of deterring future perpetrators justified the different amount of compensation.

It goes without saying that this result remains unsatisfactory. But it demonstrates the practical difficulties in evaluating non-pecuniary damages and awarding a "just compensation". During the last decade, civil courts throughout Europe have improved their case law on the compensation of non-pecuniary damages.[48] At present, there is a clear trend to increase the sums of money awarded to victims in these kinds of cases.[49] This development is sometimes described as "economization" or as "monetization" of tort law.[50]

Günter Thomas's chapter below describes the differing compensation paid to victims persecuted during the Holocaust and to persons who were persecuted by the former communist regime of the GDR.[51] He correctly stresses inconsistencies between the compensation paid to different groups of victims. Yet, from a legal perspective, the application of specific regimes may be justified by the following considerations.

First, these losses relate to the category of mass torts. Modern legal theory describes mass torts as a distinct category of the law of torts, due to the amount of the damages incurred and the number of victims. Individual handling of thousands of individual cases is not possible. Accordingly, mass claims processing on the basis of standardized criteria takes place – individual compensation is awarded on the basis of "rough justice" on the basis of an administrative procedure.

Second, the compensation is not paid by the individual perpetrator to the victim, but by public authorities. Accordingly, not private law, but

---

[48] A comprehensive critique of the current case law was given by the former presiding judge of the 6th Senate of the Federal Supreme Civil Court, Erich Steffen, who argued that the constitutional protection of personality rights implies an effective protection of these rights by the civil law. Accordingly, Steffen favors extending the amount of compensation for non-pecuniary damages: E. Steffen, "Die Aushilfeaufgaben des Schmerzensgeldes," in: R. Boettcher, W. Odersky, G. Hueck, and B. Jähnke (eds.), *Festschrift für Walter Odersky zum 65. Geburtstag*, Berlin: Walter de Gruyter, 1996, 723ff.

[49] Gottfried Schiemann, "Entwicklungen des Schadensrechts," in: Burkhard Hess (ed.), *Wandel der Rechtsordnung*, Tübingen: Mohr Siebeck, 2003, 130 et seq.

[50] Hein Kötz and Gerhard Wagner, *Deliktsrecht*, Munich: Franz Vahlen, 11th edn. 2010.

[51] See generally Burkhard Hess, *Intertemporales Privatrecht*, Tübingen: Mohr Siebeck, 1998, § 6, 250–90.

social law applies – compensation is paid mainly in order to prevent social injustice and individual plight. The payments are aimed at enabling the victims to build up a new future and to overcome physical and mental losses. A comprehensive establishment of the wrongs committed and the reparation of damages sustained are not of paramount importance in this context. Therefore, rehabilitation is of paramount importance and only an *appropriate* compensation is granted.[52]

Nevertheless, from the perspective of the individual victim, his or her individual fate and the individual losses remain of paramount importance. Sometimes the processing of mass claims in this context is felt to be "disregarding the individual case".[53] In the context of historical wrongs, the reparation of injuries by providing for financial compensation should not constitute the only redress available. In the context of rehabilitation, additional avenues for dealing with the past seem to be important, such as the recognition that injustice has been committed. The sincere excuse for unlawful conduct and for its continuing consequences may also entail acknowledgment and forgiveness. In this respect, experience shows that the coming to terms with injustices of the past cannot be done by courts alone. A broader process of remembrance in society as a whole is needed. In addition, the monetization or commercialization of historical wrongs may entail strong resistance from the victim's side. When American lawyers in the late 1990s initiated large human rights class actions against all companies which had undertaken investments in South Africa during the time of apartheid, the government of South Africa intervened in the pending proceedings in New York and contested the legitimacy of these lawsuits. The government referred to the Truth Commissions which were trying to overcome the crimes of apartheid and held that the parallel institution of judicial proceedings in other states amounted to an unwelcome interference in the internal affairs of a sovereign state.[54] Finally, the US Supreme Court

---

[52] See Article 17 of the German Unification Treaty of 1990: "The parties of this agreement affirm their intention, that a legal foundation shall be created immediately so that all persons who became the victims of politically motivated persecution or any other legal decision contrary to the rule of law shall be rehabilitated. The rehabilitation of these victims of the SED regime of injustice shall be connected to an appropriate compensatory regulation."

[53] Thomas, Chapter 13 above.

[54] See B. Hess, "Kriegsentschädigungen aus kollisionsrechtlicher und rechtsvergleichender Sicht," *Berichte der Deutschen Gesellschaft für Völkerrecht* 40 (2003), 107, 180 et seq.

held (in a footnote) that American courts should respect this statement and dismiss the lawsuits.[55] This example demonstrates that the judicial handling of historical wrongs is only one possible way of dealing with these sensitive issues.

Standardization, monetization, and the quest for justice

As explained above, the standardization of legal relations may lead to unjust results, especially when the (legal) standards do not meet the specific circumstances of the individual case and lead to unfairness and injustice. In such constellations, parties should be free to deviate from the standardization. In this respect, two different situations must be distinguished: standardization by legal provisions and standard terms. Standardization by legal provisions, as a matter of principle, is acceptable and leads to satisfactory results. As legal provisions are elaborated by legislation, the (democratically legitimated) legislator is obliged (by constitutional law) to balance the different interests and to elaborate a neutral provision which normally does not put one party at a disadvantage. Accordingly, standardization of legal relationships by legal provisions is an adequate tool for rationalizing legal transactions. In addition to this, the general principle of good faith enables the courts to deviate from the standards of the Civil Code in order to adopt the legal regime to the specific circumstances of the individual case.[56] Finally, under constitutional law, each party may have recourse to the Constitutional Court (or to similar bodies) if legislation does not sufficiently protect individual rights. The Constitutional Court may balance the conflicting rights and interests and correct imbalanced standardization of a legal system in specific circumstances.

Still, the situation of private standardization is different. In this context, the judicial (or administrative) control of standard terms is absolutely necessary for the protection of legal rights and the interests of the weaker party. As the parties normally do not negotiate all terms and

[55] US Supreme Court: *Sosa* v. *Alvarez-Machain*, 542 U.S. 692 (2004). Litigation in the Court of Appeal for the 2nd Cir. is still pending – a newly elected government of South Africa openly supported the lawsuit in New York.

[56] It must be noted, however, that the courts are not free to derogate from mandatory legal provisions by referring to the principle of good faith. However, the courts must interpret the transaction of the parties in good faith and respect their contractual arrangement.

conditions of a contract, the standard terms are not the result of a freely agreed transaction, but imposed by the stronger party on the weaker counterpart. In order to restore the balance of the contractual relations, modern legal systems empower judges to control the standard terms and to declare unfair terms void. By imposing these safeguards, modern legal systems implement the freedom of contract in private law which remains the main guarantee (and valid basis) for a fair and just legal regime between the parties.

The quest for justice is also a challenge in the context of monetization. This has been demonstrated in relation to the compensation of damages. The guiding principle of compensating all damage incurred completely does not apply in two constellations: on the one hand, the monetary compensation of non-pecuniary damages seems to be impossible, as an evaluation of this kind of damages in money is excluded. Nevertheless, all legal systems provide for monetary compensation for pain and suffering. In practice, the calculation of the compensation often remains unsatisfactory, and the sums paid are considered either as being too high (and, consequently, as an enrichment of the injured party) or as being too low (providing only for a symbolic compensation). Yet, modern law is clearly oriented towards an increasing economization or monetization of non-pecuniary damages. In legal practice, so-called schedules of compensation for pain and suffering provide for guidance and transparency. Finally, the fundamental question remains whether any infringement of non-pecuniary rights must give rise to an action for the payment of money.

The second situation refers to so-called mass torts (especially the compensation of war damages or damage incurred by dictatorial regimes). In this constellation, the number of victims and the total amount of all (individual) damages are too high and prevent full compensation of the losses incurred. Accordingly, only partial compensation is organized by providing for mass claim processing on a standardized basis which – at least partially – disregards the individual cases. Compensation paid to the victims of such "historical wrongs" often amounts to a partial, or even mere symbolic, compensation.[57] Victims often consider such "rough justice" as unsatisfactory or even as "unjust" (especially compared with the "full reparation" for victims

---

[57] In the legal literature, this situation has been described as a kind of bankruptcy of a failing state.

under the civil code).[58] Still, it should not be forgotten that these injuries are not only a matter for compensation, but should be addressed by a broader concept of reconciliation and of rebuilding a society as a whole. In this context, the quest for possible alternatives to administrative and judicial proceedings is needed.[59] On the other hand, injuries individually incurred should also be considered as part of the individual's fate. In this context, justice can also be done by non-economic redress such as rehabilitation and acknowledgment. This does not exclude, however, providing for compensation and rehabilitation (especially by social law) in order to prevent social injustice and individual plight.

---

[58] It should be noted that also in the case of an individual tort, the injured party remains uncompensated should the tortfeasor be bankrupt. This constellation also occurs in the context of mass torts, i.e. product liability cases (asbestos, cigarettes).

[59] Thomas, Chapter 13 above.

5 | Kohelet and the co-evolution of a monetary economy and religion

MICHAEL WELKER

Over the centuries, time and again, philosophers, poets, and even sociologists have proposed that money should be regarded as a "god-term".[1] They have spoken of "money as the God of our Time",[2] about the replacement of "the omnipotence of God by the omnipotence of money".[3] They have pondered whether we should not organize religious faith like money.[4] Even theologians propagated a "pantheism of money" and called it the "all-determining reality".[5]

This development was greatly influenced by Luther's polemical use of the phrase, "You cannot serve God and mammon" (Matt. 6:20, Luke 16:13)[6] and his explanation of the first article in his Great Catechism which strongly opposes God and mammon: "Many a one thinks that he has God and everything in abundance when he has money and possessions; he trusts in them and boasts of them with such firmness and assurance as to care for no one. Lo, such a man also has a God, Mammon by name. It is money and possessions on which he sets all his heart and which is also the most common idol on earth. He who has money and possessions feels secure, and is joyful and undismayed as though he were sitting in the midst of paradise. On the other hand, he who has none doubts and is despondent, as though he knew of no God.

---

[1] K. Burke, *A Grammar of Motives*, 2nd edn., New York, 1962, 355.

[2] G. Simmel, "Das Geld in der modernen Kultur," in: *Schriften zur Soziologie*, Frankfurt a. M., 1983, 78–94, at 90; cf. Simmel, *Philosophie des Geldes*, Berlin: 1900, repr. as *The Philosophy of Money*, New York and London, 2011.

[3] N. Luhmann, "Knappheit, Geld und bürgerliche Gesellschaft," *Jahrbuch für Sozialwissenschaft* 23 (1972): 186–210, 191.

[4] N. Luhmann, *Funktion der Religion*, Frankfurt a. M., 1977, 141 and 315.

[5] F. Wagner, *Geld oder Gott: Zur Geldbestimmtheit der kulturellen und religiösen Lebenswelt*, Stuttgart, 1984, esp. 144. The phrase follows R. Bultmann, "Welchen Sinn hat es, von Gott zu reden?" in: Bultmann, *Glauben und Verstehen II*, Tübingen, 1933, 26–37, at 26.

[6] See F. Bovon, *Das Evangelium nach Lukas*, EKK III/3, 70, 75ff. and 93f.; P. W. van der Horst, "Mammon," *RGG*, 4th edn., Vol. V, 720f.

For very few are to be found who are of good cheer, and who neither mourn nor complain if they have not Mammon. This care and desire for money sticks and clings to our nature, even to the grave."[7]

The fact that the deification and the plain demonization of money might be a distortion can be seen with reference to the broad spectrum of the biblical witnesses. Only twice do we find this strong opposition of God and mammon. Luke 16:11 qualifies: "If therefore you have not been faithful in the unrighteous mammon, who will commit to your trust the true riches?" At least 300 references in the biblical traditions offer a more subtle criticism than the mere demonization of the function and the potentials of money and monetary communication, or they use the symbolism of money in order to express complex spiritual processes and practices.[8] The project of this book contributes in various ways to the demythologizing of the religious talk about money and it serves the reconstruction of its functions and powers in very different contexts and traditions.

The following contribution focuses on Kohelet (Ecclesiastes) and recent interpretations of its help to understand early processes of the monetization of the market. It does not do so for exegetical and historical interests only. One of the tasks of systematic theology is to provide a critique of distorted or ideologized forms of religion. The plain demonization of the market, also in its monetized forms, is very short-sighted, if not stupid. It can also go hand in hand with a distorted form of religious thoughts and ideas, which generates a love–hate relationship with the numinous powers of the market. The equation of God and mammon (as a cipher for the monetized market) not only mirrors an economic analphabetism; it also distorts sound theological perspectives on God. The interdisciplinary exploration in some phases of the emergence of a monetized economy might offer potentials for a critique of such confusions, but also win some insights in the co-evolution of economics and religion. At the same time, this contribution bridges

---

[7] BSLK, 561. Cf. F. W. Marquardt, "Gott oder Mammon: Theologie und Ökonomie bei Martin Luther," in: Marquardt, *Einwürfe 1*, Munich, 1983, 176–216, with the problematic assertion that Luther had turned economy into a "Mammon-question" and tried to think God with reference to God's battle against Mammon.

[8] See M. Welker and M. Wolter, *Jahrbuch für Biblische Theologie*, vol. XXI (2006): *Gott und Geld*, Neukirchen-Vluyn, 2007.

the introductory contributions and the historical investigations we offer in this book.

I

While Kohelet is not the only voice in the biblical canon to speak on the topic of God and money, he is certainly an important one. A cursory examination of the text reveals the following statements:

5:9, "the lover of money will not be satisfied with money";
7:12, the idea that money (like wisdom) can provide shelter, but that wisdom (unlike money) can preserve the life of its owner;
finally, in 10:19, the statement "that money meets every need", it must be the answer for everything.

In addition to these direct reflections on money, we find a range of observations about the want of moderation of human beings, whose eyes and ears are never satisfied (1:8), about the wealthy and kings who collect treasure (2:4, etc.), and many other general statements about the unending search for profit (4:8, etc.). But above all, we find a constant lament about the futility of efforts to pile up riches only to have them consumed and enjoyed by others.

This constantly repeated observation on the final futility in the acquisition of money and riches helps us to understand Kohelet's *cantus firmus*, which opens with the verse of the framework (1:2): "'Meaningless! Meaningless!' says Kohelet, 'Utterly meaningless! Everything is meaningless'" (or: "'Vapors, vapors', says Kohelet, 'Vapors, vapors. Everything is a vapor of air'"), continues with (1:3): "What does man gain from all the fruits of his labor at which he toils under the sun?", and ends (before the two postscripts) with the closing verse of the framework (12:8): "'Vapors, vapors', says Kohelet, 'everything is a vapor of air.'"

The term "futility", "vapor", *hæbæl*, is often interpreted as dust or transience. Luther translates the passage as: "it is all utterly vain [*es ist alles ganz eitel!*]". "Vanity of vanities" is the formulation chosen by the Finnish Old Testament scholar, Aarre Lauha, in his commentary on Kohelet.[9] Diethelm Michel uses the translation: "it is all absurd!" Seven times Kohelet presents the refrain: "See, all is vanity and a

---

[9] A. Lauha, *Kohelet BKAT XIX*, Neukirchen-Vluyn, 1978, 38.

chasing after wind!" (1:14; 2:11, 17, 26; 4:4, 16; 6:9; see also 1:17 and 4:6). Sixteen times we hear the express assurance that everything is vanity. The term *hæbæl* is used thirty-eight times – perhaps even with an intended order.[10] In addition, countless further statements express the conviction (described as an "insight" or "knowledge") that to the greatest degree, everything is futile.[11] This overpowering and relativistic-sounding tone (which is peculiar within the biblical canon) not only stands in close connection with the relation to God and the "value" of God for humanity, but also to fine-tuned reflections on engaging the money economy and its underlying principles.

In his commentary on Kohelet,[12] the Princeton Old Testament scholar, Leong Seow, provides an in-depth investigation of this view of the economic world and of monetary processes. He argues that Kohelet is writing during the Persian era, during the second half of the fifth and first half of the fourth centuries. We have an impressively clear image of this period due to an astonishing wealth of epigraphic sources and archeological excavations, to which Seow refers in an illuminating way. He sees his theory confirmed not least by Kohelet's use of Persian loan-words ("*pardēs*, park or grove" in 2:5, and "*pitgām*, decree" in 8:11). According to Seow, the Persians introduced the democratization of money:

It is not that "money" was unknown in earlier periods, for silver pieces in various forms and sizes already were used as a medium of exchange in earlier times. Yet the introduction of coinage by the Persians democratized the usage of money and radically transformed the economy of the Levant. Not surprisingly, therefore, the epigraphic materials from this era show a great deal of concern with money. Contemporaneous inscriptions are replete with reference to money, most frequently mentioned in connection with taxes, wages, rent, loans, fines, inheritance, and the prices of goods and services. Money was used in everyday business transactions both large and small, given as gifts and bribes, and hoarded. Money had become not just a convenient medium of exchange; it had become a commodity.[13]

---

[10] D. Michel, *Qohelet*, Darmstadt, 1988, 127.

[11] Cf. 1:2; 2:1, 15, 19, 21, 23; 3:19; 4:8; 5:9; 6:2; 7:6; 8:1, 14; 11:8, 10; 12:8.

[12] C.-L. Seow, *Ecclesiastes*, New York and London, 1997, esp. 21ff.; see also his contribution to this volume, Chapter 7 below.

[13] Ibid., 21.

Seow gives an impressive description of the leasehold system introduced by the Persians: namely, making land and property available, and then charging duties and taxes on it. This led to the development of a hierarchy of landlords and leaseholders. Since the conditions of a lease were not automatically subject to inheritance, but needed constantly to be renewed, a connection arose between the personal, political exercise of power and monetary transactions. The largely unpredictable individual exercise of power by landowners and rent-collectors and the reliable predictability of leaseholders and income come into view simultaneously. One no longer needs the identification and accumulation of storable goods for the purpose of satisfying the needs of the powerful or for the general purpose of securing and extending power. Concerns about the weather and the success of the harvest become less important. The possibilities for using leased land to make a profit which far exceeds the rental fee – yet also a loss of crops and the rise of economic difficulties – become an everyday experience. Since leaseholders also divided up parcels of land to be sublet, a further difficulty arose: namely, being forced to live on property hardly large enough to provide a subsistence living for one's own family, let alone pay the expected fees.

The *legal system* had to be extended and reinforced, but the threat and exercise of violence were introduced on a new level and routinized to secure claims to rent and interest, even leading to the establishment of private prisons. The corruptibility of judges became as much of a problem as the arbitrariness of landowners. And since *military service* could also be enforced in lieu of payment, endangerment of (and even the risk of losing) one's own life became an embedded aspect in the financial system. Considerable risks were connected with previously non-existent chances. In some cases, even *slaves could become wealthy and exercise financial and political power*. As Kohelet observes: "I have seen slaves on horseback, while princes go on foot like slaves" (10:7).

It is uncertain whether Seow is correct in his dating of Kohelet during the period of Persian rule. The majority of scholars argue for a date during the Hellenistic period, approximately 200 years later.[14] Yet independent of these issues regarding historical dating, Seow is certainly correct that even if the dominance of the monetary economy is not *the background* here, it still represents *a thoroughly crucial context* for the

---

[14] L. Schwienhorst-Schönberger, *Das Buch Kohelet*, Berlin and New York, 1997, 24f.; T. Krüger, *Kohelet*, Neukirchen-Vluyn, 2000, 39ff.

formulation of Kohelet's message. While German-language exegesis (driven by its typically stronger focus on the history of ideas) seeks to understand Kohelet from the perspective of the dialogue with Hellenistic philosophy,[15] Seow takes a path decidedly focused on the social and cultural sciences. This path cannot be ignored, even in the event of a later dating.

With a sensitivity of observation, Kohelet sees that the unending effort to make money and hoard wealth is generally *aimed at the safeguarding of one's life, particularly for the future.* Yet this attempt to secure security is accompanied by high risks, since these increased and supposedly secured possibilities for moneymaking are often paid for with heavy, and sometimes oppressive, rent and vassalage. Furthermore, Kohelet repeatedly thematizes the dangers of dependence upon the arbitrariness of the powerful, which increases in a standardized, monetized system. Paradoxically, the chances for profit, but also for loss, increase simultaneously – so, too, with the security and insecurity of expectations, as well as independence from and dependence upon the arbitrariness of the powerful and propertied classes. The experience of life connected with an insight into the fabric of this structure is what Kohelet articulates.

Kohelet also sees that the mechanisms involved in the acquisition of money and property take on an independent nature and may also lead to an *addictive pursuit of accumulation.* With fine subtlety he argues that money is a shadow (7:12), which can certainly provide cover and cooling. But this protection is also just as uncontrollable and incalculable as the coming of the wind, or of the shade, which paradoxically is dependent upon the sun, that is, on that from which the shade is supposed to protect. Over against unending moneymaking, over against the risks connected with the increased accumulation of money, and over against the final futility of these efforts, Kohelet concludes (5:17f.): "This is what I have seen to be good: it is fitting to eat and drink and find enjoyment in all the toil with which one toils under the sun the few days of the life God gives us; for this is our lot. Likewise all to whom God gives wealth and possessions and whom he enables to enjoy them,

[15] See N. Lohfink, *Das Koheletbuch*, Würzburg, 1980; L. Schwienhorst-Schönberger, "Nicht im Menschen gründet das Glück" (Koh. 2,24), Freiburg, 1994, esp. 233ff.

and to accept their lot and find enjoyment in their toil – this is the gift of God." Kohelet repeats these statements throughout.[16]

Repeatedly, we hear his message: that a person should eat and drink and the soul should be happy in all its toils – but that this comes from God's hand. Without God's goodness no one can eat happily, drink and enjoy themselves. God gives to one the strength to enjoy life, but to the sinner he gives toil, and despite all his or her gathering and hoarding, in the end everything will be given to the one who pleases God (2:26).

Kohelet connects this ability (through God's goodness) to eat, drink and be merry – yet also the attempts to attain supposed security for the future through the unceasing accumulation of money and power – with God's eternal plan. In chapter 9:7, we find it stated expressly: "Go, eat your bread with enjoyment, and drink your wine with a merry heart; for God has long ago approved what you do." Thus the search for an orientation on God's intentions with one's own life and the whole creation (which becomes possible with wisdom and the fear of God) is to be found on a completely different level than that of the endless acquisition of money and power, than that of the pursuit of existential security through material goods.

It can be disturbing that, on the one hand, Kohelet repeatedly stresses the reliability of divine direction, the eternal perspective as well as the life-creating force of wisdom and of the fear of God. Yet on the other hand, we see a repeated stress on the inability of human beings to know the work of God, the maker of all things (11:5): "Just as you do not know the path of the wind, or how the body is formed in a mother's womb, so you cannot understand the work of God, the maker of all things." For this reason, Hartmut Gese noted a "crisis of wisdom in Kohelet" and assumed a break with the world-view of the older wisdom tradition.[17] The individual can only receive a successful life "from the hand of God" (2:24), it is "God's gift" (3:13; 5:19), it "is our lot" (3:22; 5:18; 9:9). "'God is pleased' by the acceptance of this gift."[18]

This does not mean that Kohelet preaches nothing but human passivity. He does not say, like Matthew (6:25f.): "Do not be anxious about your life, what you will eat ... Look at the birds of the air; they neither

---

[16] Cf. 2:24f.; 3:13f.; 3:22; 5:17f.; 8:15; 9:7; 11:8.
[17] H. Gese, "Die Krisis der Weisheit bei Kohelet," in Gese, *Vom Sinai zum Zion: Alttestamentliche Beiträge zur biblischen Theologie*, Munich, 1974, 168–79.
[18] Ibid., 179.

sow nor reap . . . yet your heavenly Father feeds them." Amid all the many warnings against the frailty and futility of human efforts and aspirations, of the accumulation of money and goods, of the safeguarding of future existence, we still hear Kohelet's repeated exhortations: "In the morning sow your seed, and in the evening do not let your hands be idle" (11:6). We hear his warnings: "Whoever observes the wind will not sow; and whoever regards the clouds will not reap" (11:4).

The supposed contradiction between warnings about human restlessness (directed toward comprehensive existential security) and the encouragement energetically to sow and reap and to enjoy life if this is what God has granted, can be resolved if we learn to distinguish between property as wealth (upon which one can capitalize) and property as (a non-marketable) gift.

Against this background, Kohelet's wisdom does not mean simply hold on to your property as a gift and avoid the embarrassment of converting it into wealth and thus submitting it to the monetary system! Despite the degree to which a conservative, small-farmer mentality may have flowed into Kohelet's wisdom, his message is much more subtle. On the one hand, we have the imperative: be aware of the high risks involved with the transformation of property as gift into property as wealth! On the other hand, it also encourages us to see property as God's good gift and not to admire those who are carried away by the chances and risks of wealth and the monetary system, and allow themselves to be blinded by them. They, too, stand under God's rule, but they have surrendered to the futility of human effort: everything is a vapor of air, it is all meaningless.

Does Kohelet's position allow us to derive an opposition to monetization and the market along the lines of the statement "God or Mammon"? And is this opposition bound with the living conditions of small farmers, who seek to persevere in their furrows and with their archaic barter systems? If we follow it through consistently, then Kohelet's message is significantly more innovative. It demands that human property be distinguished in accordance with that which can be converted into wealth and subjected to the channels of trade and that which (as a non-marketable gift) must be kept separate from the market. Thus, under "property as gift" we should not only think of "fields, cattle, and all I own".

From good physical health and beauty to cultivated knowledge and talents; good relations within the immediate and extended family as well as in the local political context; beneficial cultural and trustworthy social institutions; the intellectual climate; and even beautiful country-side and largely unspoiled nature – there are many conceivable "pos-sessions" which can be received partly as a gift, or which can in part be cultivated, built up, reclaimed and enjoyed through one's own efforts. Most of these possessions can (at least in part) be transformed into wealth. Often, one can do business just as well with a beautiful body and a good education as with the beautiful countryside and the resil-ience of nature.

Every total refusal of the transformation of property into wealth is as implausible as it is unrealistic. Yet the wise decision to care for and increase such possessions while at the same time perceiving them as precious, non-marketable gifts, is anything but out of touch with reality or yokelish. Instead of simply staring at the duality of "God or Mammon", we must practice differentiating property into non-marketable gifts, or assets which can be monetized. Additional orient-ing markers are required here to unpack not only the rationalities of the market, but also the insights of the theological doctrine of creation, anthropology, pneumatology, and eschatology.

II

The Judeo-Christian traditions connect the divinity of God with (sov-ereign) power, justice, wisdom, and love. These associations have become established in the theological doctrine of the "attributes of God", and have been extended by speculation regarding the universal presence of God in space and time. The Reformers, and especially Luther, warned against indulging in such speculation. Luther called such attempts to achieve insights into God *theologia gloriae* – a theol-ogy of glory – and he accused them of principle falsehood, of being a misorientation. A theology interested in truth must hold to God's revelation in Jesus Christ, and thus attempt to find God in "the cross and suffering". *Theologia crucis*, a theology of the cross, rather than a *theologia gloriae*: here we have a striking description of one of the central programs of the Reformation. In his famous 1518 Heidelberg Disputation, Luther formulated this position, arguing that it must go hand-in-hand with a comprehensive reorientation of theological and spiritual education. The universities and high schools should promote historical and philological education, and there should be restrictions on philosophical and metaphysical speculation. Bible study programs and education in the catechism should introduce even the less-educated classes of society to their own study of God's revelation in Jesus Christ. A general elementary school education, efforts at religious education in the home, and historically and philologically informed church preaching and teaching were to provide the groundwork.

In many regions of the world, it was this important anti-metaphysical fervor which ushered in extremely beneficial revolutions in education, as well as emancipation from patronizing, oligarchic religious and political systems. Yet at the same time, important sources of knowledge, both for religion and for its critical observation, have been ignored – sources which may be newly revealed by interdisciplinary work on religion and religion's potential for informing culture and society.

The biblical associations of God with (sovereign) power, justice, truth, wisdom, and love point to inherent connections between religion and politics, law, science, education, and the family – connections which go hand-in-hand not only with claims to an orienting character, but also with a need to distance religion from these organizational forms of social life. Polycontextual and multisystemic investigations into differing historical periods would be required if we wish to gain sturdy insights into this web of interdependencies and its evolution. That step (which was so important for economic processes of communication) marked by the introduction and widespread use of coinage, seems to be a helpful starting point not only for understanding some of the central dynamics of this web of interdependencies, but also for achieving fruitful insights into the co-evolution of religion, economy, and other social subsystems.[19]

In which way, and with which concepts, is God related to this emerging form of economy? Since even before this historical step of introducing a general circulation of coins was taken, there must have been some form of economical administering. What, then, were the corresponding symbolic forms upon which it was anchored? Should we search for them, and expect to find them, in the "economy" of the extended

---

[19] For some preliminary thoughts, see M. Welker, "Richten und Retten: Systematische Überlegungen zu einer unverzichtbaren Funktion der Religion," in: J. Assmann, B. Janowski, and M. Welker (eds.), *Gerechtigkeit: Richten und Retten in der abendländischen Tradition und ihren altorientalischen Ursprüngen,* Munich, 1998, 28–35.

family? Can we observe corresponding transformations in the family ethos, and have they had a subsequent effect on religion?

Against the background of such an approach, it becomes painfully clear that we have experienced a loss in our depth of field. This loss goes hand-in-hand with a general translation of the biblical semantics of love into personalist "I – Thou" conceptions, and with a reduction of love to "eros and agape", an egoistic or altruistic alter-ego relation.[20] Countless theological classics of the modern age (especially the nineteenth and twentieth centuries) use this conception in their attempts to grasp the essential aspects of inner-trinitarian relationships, "the relations between God and man", as well as "interpersonal relations". Yet this is accompanied by massive processes of the self-secularization and self-banalization of religion. Nor can one say that the widespread religious fixation in the Christian-influenced West on a semantics of love, based on partnership and the ethics of intersubjectivity (*Nahbereichsethos*), has been able to provide long-term religious stability for the nuclear family. Can we discover plausible connections between a deepened understanding of love (in the sense of a mutual honoring which opens up the relationship of love) and the "economy" of the ancient extended family – connections which may have been influenced by the change of the economy due to the general circulation of currency?

The reflections on Kohelet, with his strong interest in "profit" (in both the economic and religious sense) and his strangely distant relationship with God, aim to explore a few first steps on the way to clarifying the interdependencies between a religious and friendly/familial line of thought and that which has been influenced by the potentials of a management of affairs generally based on the use of money. In this way, they aim at helping us envisage alternatives to today's morally and politically helpless Manichaeism, which uses the rhetorical formulation: "God or Mammon!"

"No other book of the Bible views a person's relationship to God so strongly from the perspective of anticipated profit as the Book of Ecclesiastes. Yet this profit is by no means certain. To seek it involves risk, and it is perhaps even hopeless. Nonetheless, an almost unsettling

---

[20] See M. Welker, "Romantic Love, Covenantal Love, Kenotic Love," in: J. Polkinghorne (ed.), *The Work of Love: Creation as Kenosis*, Grand Rapids, London, 2001, 127–36; Welker, "Liebe," in: *Evangelisches Soziallexikon*, M. Honecker et al. (eds.), Stuttgart, Berlin, Cologne, 2001, 959–63.

calmness prevails in this book. Kohelet abandons the idea of direct contact between God and the human being. It is not that God does not exist, but rather that this contact is dangerously unpredictable." Kohelet "asks about the profit [*yitrôn*] which human beings gain from all their efforts [see 1:3]. One cannot overlook the affinity to economic language."[21]

The answer comes in a plea to take pleasure in the humble experiences of success and the enjoyment of life, and to do away with those efforts aimed at opening up comprehensive future horizons. Kohelet's recommendation is to accept with thanks "the good works [of God] as an experience of the good, and the bad works as a manifestation of God's determination to keep people ignorant their entire lives long. The attainment of insight which is possible for wisdom is limited to the partial experience of the good and to the divinely desired withholding of insight in view of the whole creation."[22]

How can one explain this individual perspective of a deeply skeptical religiosity? Is this an expression of the experience of powerlessness when confronted with the destabilization of familiar horizons of expectation? Tonio Hölscher has provided an impressive presentation of the co-evolution of the routinized use of coinage in economic systems, the development of egalitarian city-state structures, and a narrowed horizon of expectation in religious and moral orientations. The creative power and endurance of broad-reaching bonds of trust is replaced by a mesh of clearly measurable barter operations.[23] By resignation in his great religious expectations of God and modestly meting out small portions of the joys of life, does Kohelet reflect this experience?

The depotentialization of the symbiosis of religion and the extended family must be compensated for by politico-legal systems of guarantee. Should the construction of the temple, which accompanied this development, also be understood as such a compensation? The creation within a natural space of an imposing presence of possible and actual religious

---

[21] As Seow and Spiekermann have stressed, *yôtēr* "advantage, benefit" (Eccles. 6:8, 11 and 7:11), and *yitrôn* "profit" (Eccles. 1:3; 2:11, 13; 3:9; 5:8, 15; 7:12 and 10:10f.) are neologisms in Ecclesiastes.

[22] H. Spiekermann, "Gott und der Mensch am Markt: Krise des Glaubens und Sprache der Ökonomie in der Bibel," in *Evangelium und Effizienz: Zur Geldförmigkeit des Denkens in Religion und Gesellschaft* (BThZ 21; 2004 Supplement), 32–49.

[23] See T. Hölscher's contribution to this volume, Chapter 6 below.

communication, and the religiously charged representation of the formative potential of money, could almost be seen as a counter-strategy against Kohelet's resigned attitude. Public buildings and public rituals establish new models of orientation and a security of expectation which are compatible with the experienced, regular, public appropriation of personal and familial means of subsistence as well as the experienced, short-lived, personal and familial models of success and a religiosity bound to them. Whether it is fruitful to relate these models to each other (since in many respects they stem from very differing contexts), and whether we will truly uncover insightful connections which might help us toward careful, general considerations about the co-evolution of economics, religion, law, politics, and morality remains to be seen from further discussion. The following chapters will give substantial impulses to this discourse.

Monetary exchange: historical and social roots

6 | Money and image: the presence of the state on the routes of economy

TONIO HÖLSCHER

Introduction

Coined money was invented and introduced in the seventh century BC by the Lydians, a small people at the edge of Greek culture. They first created a currency of so-called *electron*, an alloy of gold and silver, mainly for local circulation within Western Asia Minor. From the sixth century BC, however, coinage as a means of economic exchange, mostly in silver, rarely in gold, was increasingly introduced by various Greek city-states in Asia Minor as well as in Central Greece, and soon afterwards also among the daughter cities of Western Greece, in Sicily and Southern Italy. After its preliminary stage in Lydia, it was in the Greek world that coined money became the basis of economy in its most important aspects: payment and exchange, storing wealth, and measuring value. Late archaic Greece was the first society with a considerably monetized economy.[1]

The surprising fact about the origins of coined money is that they occurred not in one of the great empires of Mesopotamia or Egypt, with their monarchical structures and their unparalleled political and economic dominance, but in relatively small city-states without any firmly centralized political power. As is well known, in these so-called *poleis* there were neither firmly established rulers nor powerful priests who might have organized centralized economic structures, but a changing number of competing aristocratic families and an increasingly self-confident middle class, the members of which seem to have been concerned mainly with the micro-economic issues of their

---

[1] General introduction to Greek and Roman coinage: C. Howgego, *Ancient History from Coins*, London: Routledge 1995; S. von Reden, *Money in Classical Antiquity*, Cambridge University Press 2010. For a general theory of money, see the monumental work of K.-H. Brodbeck, *Die Herrschaft des Geldes*, Darmstadt: Wissenschaftliche Buchgesellschaft 2009. I owe this reference to Ulrich Duchrow.

individual households. This leads to the general question of the historical conditions in which a money economy first originated and developed. Ancient thinkers and authors were particularly impressed by the experience of how much money stamped the social world. As historians, however, we have first to ask the reverse question, which is rarely reflected in ancient sources, about the social world that created money.

Methodologically, this means to clearly distinguish three levels of investigation: first, the general historical conditions and exigencies that favored the introduction of coined money; second, the immediate purposes, concrete devices, and general cultural concepts of this first phase of coinage; third, the general consequences of monetization in the realms of economy, lifestyle, ethics, religion, politics, and society.[2] It is the aim of this chapter to demonstrate that it was precisely the political weakness and decentralization of early Greek city-states which was at the origins of coined money in ancient Greece: a view in accordance with the general theoretical framework developed in the contribution of Jürgen von Hagen.[3]

The historical context of the origins of coined money

The historical background of monetization in ancient Greece was the emergence, from the ninth to the seventh centuries B C, of a specific kind of city-state, the so-called *polis* (plur. *poleis*). The earlier great Bronze

---

[2] Most important recent work on this issue: R. M. Cook, "Speculations on the Origins of Coinage," *Historia* 7 (1958) 257–62. C. M. Kraay, "Hoards, Small Change and the Origin of Coinage," *Journal of Hellenic Studies* 84 (1964) 76–91; M. J. Price, "Thoughts on the Beginnings of Coinage," in: C. N. L. Brooke, B. H. I. H. Stewart, J. G. Pollard, and T. R. Volk (eds.), *Studies in Numismatic Method Presented to Philip Grierson*, Cambridge University Press 1983, 1–10; J. H. Kroll and N. M. Waggoner, "Dating the Earliest Coins of Athens, Corinth and Aegina," *American Journal of Archaeology* 88 (1984) 325–40; S. von Reden, *Exchange in Ancient Greece*, London: Duckworth Publishers 1995, 171–94; T. R. Martin, "Why did the Greek *Polis* originally Need Coins?" *Historia* 45 (1996) 257–83; L. Kurke, *Coins, Bodies, Games, and Gold*, Princeton University Press 1999, esp. 3–37; J. K. Papadopoulos, "Minting Identity: Coinage, Ideology and the Economics of Colonization in Akhaian Magna Graecia," *Cambridge Archaeological Journal* 12 (2002) 21–55; R. Seaford, *Money and the Early Greek Mind*, Cambridge University Press 2004, esp. 88–95, 125–46. Most important is D. M. Shaps, *The Invention of Coinage and the Monetization of Ancient Greece*, Ann Arbor: University of Michigan Press 2004.

[3] See above. In numismatic research on ancient Greece, see Martin, "Why did the Greek *Polis* originally Need Coins?"

Age cultures of the second millennium in Minoan Crete and Mycenaean Greece had developed around strong ruler palaces, seats of a centralized economy, and towering over tightly dependent "cities". This structure can be termed a *pyramidal* system of society and its living spaces. The palaces were centers of economy, engaged in far-reaching trade with partners in the eastern and western Mediterranean. The ruler assumed the function of collecting and redistributing all commodities in the frame of a centralized economic organization.

After the collapse and disintegration of these Bronze Age civilizations, around 1200 BC, the following so-called "Dark Ages" were characterized by small scattered settlements where the chiefs of leading families must have held a position of more-or-less independent power over the local village population; the structure of this period is a *disconnected* system of hierarchically conceived societal and dwelling units.

At the end of this period, through the ninth to the seventh centuries, the Greek world recovered economically, not least through a new growth of "international" trade, leading to increasing wealth, labor division, social stratification, and concentration in larger settlements, as centers of autonomous territorial city-states. The emerging structure of the *polis* was characterized by a connective organizational concept of a citizens' community which was more than the sum of its parts. The decisive phenomenon in this process was the transition from a single-level society, dominated by mighty families and their chieftains (*basileus*, plur. *basileis*) with their clans and their followers, to a double-level society where families and their chiefs were – more or less – integrated into a conceptually egalitarian body of citizens. This fundamental change found its clearest expression in the development of settlements during this crucial period of the genesis of Greek society and culture.

Most clearly, the idea of a second-level community is documented in the planning of newly founded "colony" cities in Sicily and South Italy, with a grid of orthogonal streets, defining blocks of equal estates, given to the basic units of the community, to families in a restricted sense; the same principles of orthogonal division, with larger units, were adopted in assigning the arable land of the territory for cultivation. Such communities disposed of two sorts of communal spaces where civic life developed: on the one hand the *agora*, serving for all public matters, i.e. of a communitarian character, the people's assemblies, jurisdiction,

market, common festivals, etc., and on the other hand the *polis* sanctuaries, serving communitarian religious rituals. In the old cities of the
Greek mother-country the urban layout was determined by long periods
of irregular growth, but the structural development, with an *agora* and
one or more city sanctuaries, corresponded precisely with the "colonies". This structure can be defined as an *egalitarian and reciprocally
communicative* system.[4]

The typical form of economy in the first phase of *polis* culture,
through the ninth to seventh centuries BC, was exchange trade and
gift.[5] There existed some general value units, like cattle or bronze
tripods, and some pre-monetary means of pay, like iron spits (*obeloi*)
or silver bullion,[6] but their adoption must have been difficult in differentiated mercantile activities: they cannot have helped much more than
to supplement and rationalize the prevailing practice of exchange.
A crucial precondition in economic exchange was the basic incompatibility of commodities and services: a fisherman who needs a boat
acquires at one moment a precious object for which he can pay only
later, and only in small quantities, with his daily yield of fish. In this
sense, exchange trade is fundamentally asymmetrical, with short-term
services on the one side and long-term obligations on the other. As a
consequence, it is based strongly on personal reliability and mutual
trust.

A specific form of economic exchange, typical of this phase, was gift
and counter-gift. Gifts were given, and answered by counter-gifts,
among the dominant chiefs as the basic symbols of long-term relations.
This practice, too, was not based on one-to-one equivalence, but was

---

[4] For the urban structure of early *poleis*, see R. Martin, *L'urbanisme dans la Grèce
   antique*, Paris: Oicard 1956, 75–96; E. Greco and M. Torelli, *Storia
   dell'urbanistica: Il mondo Greco*, Roma-Bari: Laterza 1983, 65–148; T. Hölscher,
   Öffentliche Räume in frühen griechischen Städte, 2nd edn., Heidelberg: Winter
   1998; D. Mertens, *Städte und Bauten der Westgriechen*, Munich: Hirmer 2006.

[5] See recently von Reden, *Exchange in Ancient Greece*; B. Wagner-Hasel, *Der Stoff
   der Gaben: Kultur und Politik des Schenkens und Tauschens im archaischen
   Griechenland*, Frankfurt: Campus 2000, esp. 27–76 with a critical assessment of
   theories of gift.

[6] Pre-monetary "media": I. Strøm, "Obeloi of Pre- or Proto-monetary Value in
   Greek Sanctuaries," in: T. Linders and B. Alroth, *Economics of Cult in the Ancient
   Greek World*, Proceedings of the Uppsala Symposium 1990, Uppsala:
   Gustavianum 1992, 41–50; Seaford, *Money and the Early Greek Mind*, 102–24;
   Thesaurus Cultus et Rituum Antiquorum V, 2.b (2005) 329–33 (S. Th.
   Schipporeit).

embedded in a comprehensive social system of dominance and dependence, in which the folks provided their lord with supplies and commodities, while the lord offered protection and justice to his followers. Exchange, therefore, was not immediate and piece-for-piece, but was a long-term interaction belonging to a *système de prestations totales.*[7]

National economists like Karl Bücher, social historians like Marcel Mauss and Louis Gernet, classical historians like Moses I. Finley, recently followed by Sitta von Reden and Beate Wagner-Hasel, have insisted on this "embedded" social character of gift culture and exchange trade and the deeply rooted fiduciary and moral aspects of this system.[8]

On principle, the relationship of long-term exchange and mutual support was also the basis of the interrelation between gods and mortal men. Here, too, the gifts of men, veneration through rituals and sacrifices, and those of the gods, such as welfare, richness, and success, did not result from one-to-one negotiations; the traditional principle of "*do ut des*" was no trade transaction of goods, but was a reciprocal establishment of long-term confidence and support.

A second phase of the archaic Greek *polis*, beginning in the decades around 600 BC, was marked by an increasing consolidation of the entire body of citizens, in which the prosperous middle classes played an essential role. The main concern was to integrate the mighty aristocratic leaders politically and mentally into the citizens' community, through efficient legislation based on reflection on the ethical and religious foundations of the *polis*. The effect was a considerable increase in civic coherence. It was in this period that the exigencies of economy within the community as well as the collective tasks of the citizen-body became more and more complex. However, there was no "state" institution, whether an individual monarch or a collective steering group, that had the power of organizing the community's economy. In the Bronze Age palace systems the ruler had assumed the function of organizing the economic preconditions of great collective activities.

---

[7] M. Mauss, *The Gift: The Form and Reason for Exchange in Archaic Societies,* trans. W. D. Halls, New York: W. W. Norton 1990 (orig. pub. 1925).

[8] K. Bücher, *Die Entstehung der Volkswirtschaft* I, Tübingen: Laupp 1893; M. Mauss, "Essay sur le don: Forme et raison de l'échange dans les sociétés archaiques," in: *L'année sociologique* n.s. 1 (1923/24) 30–196; M. I. Finley, *The Ancient Economy,* London: Chatto & Windus 1973; Wagner-Hasel, *Der Stoff der Gaben,* esp. 27–76.

Now, in the developed *polis* of the late seventh and early sixth centuries, there emerged again great challenging exigencies and tasks – for which, however, the structures of the *polis* state were insufficient. In this situation, new forms of economy were required.

The gradual development of "money" in seventh- and sixth-century Greece corresponds precisely to this new stage of social and economic life. The pre-monetary means of paying that hitherto were in use had a practical function as well as a symbolic significance which determined their value: cattle were the primary riches of agrarian societies; bronze tripods and iron spits might be adopted as cooking vessels and roasting instruments for meat at religious festivals; bullion of precious metal could be melted down and used for various purposes. There was not yet a difference between exchange of goods and payment of value.

The first issues of stamped coinage, the Lydian *electron* coins of the seventh and early sixth centuries BC, still seem to have been used in a sort of gift system, in "an intermediate stage between 'pure' exchange of goods and the development of all-purpose money".[9] Monetization of the market in its proper sense was only – partly – achieved in sixth-century Greece. Even then, money economy did not replace the practice of exchange trade, but complemented the traditional system. Nevertheless, the new currency implied a historical change of great impact.

The immediate aims in the introduction of coined money

The decisive new step of coined money was that *the state* created an artificial system of economic exchange. Recent approaches to this phenomenon see the principal goal of this initiative in the aim of "the *polis*" to promote commerce and to control the economy:[10] the community of the middle classes, as the core of the citizen-body, is conceived of as the initiator of an egalitarian system of short-term exchange by which the traditional elite system of long-term gift exchange was efficiently fought

[9] Price, "Thoughts on the Beginnings of Coinage," 5–8; Kurke, *Coins, Bodies, Games, and Gold*, 10 (quotation); Papadopoulos, "Minting Identity: Coinage, Ideology and the Economics of Colonization in Akhaian Magna Graecia," 41–2.
[10] See (critically) Cook, "Speculations on the Origins of Coinage," 259: "Most Classical students assume that coinage was invented to assist commerce". Contra, e.g. Kraay, "Hoards, Small Change and the Origin of Coinage."

against and ultimately superseded.[11] In this sense, "coinage as a recompense" is thought to have become a symbol of "the *polis* as an institution that controlled justice and prosperity". And the traditional system of gift exchange, based on agrarian wealth and ancestral treasure, is seen as a concept referring to "a divine order of justice", favoring the mighty clan leaders in their privileged positions, while "the introduction of coinage indicates a shift of authority over social justice from the gods to the *polis*".[12]

All this may in a higher sense be true. But it is difficult to imagine that such theoretical considerations corresponded to the explicit discourses and intentions of archaic Greek statesmen and citizens. Probably the introduction of coined money is one of the most striking cases of discrepancy between the concrete intentions of historical actors and the implicit consequences of their action. Both of these phenomena are highly relevant, but they should be kept and considered apart.

The state's "promotion of economy" seems to be a rather abstract and anachronistic concept of economic theory: who, in this period, is the "state" that exerts control? What is "the economy" that is to be promoted? In which way is this "control" conceived? And for what immediate purpose? It seems rather improbable that general concepts of "trade" and "market" were already in existence, and that specific structural measures were taken, aiming at steering "the economy".[13] As soon as one tries to substantiate such explanations, difficulties arise. On the one hand, trade with external partners does not seem to have been of primary importance for the introduction of a money economy.[14] Far-distance trade had already been effectuated in similar dimensions in the Bronze Age and again increasingly since the early Iron Age – without coined money. Carthage, with its powerful trade activities, did not coin money until the late classical period. In Greece, after the introduction of coinage, circulation was more-or-less confined to the issuing *polis* territory. Only in a few mighty *poleis*, like

[11] Kurke, *Coins, Bodies, Games, and Gold*, 19–22; Papadopoulos, "Minting Identity: Coinage, Ideology and the Economics of Colonization in Akhaian Magna Graecia," 42–3.

[12] von Reden, *Exchange in Ancient Greece*, 175.

[13] On the absence of an abstract concept of "market" see Finley, *The Ancient Economy*, esp. 17–34.

[14] Kraay, "Hoards, Small Change and the Origin of Coinage," 76–85; Papadopoulos, "Minting Identity: Coinage, Ideology and the Economics of Colonization in Akhaian Magna Graecia," 40–1.

Athens, and to some degree Aigina and Corinth, did far-distance trade develop more and more, and the distribution of their coins testifies impressively how much this was facilitated by the new currency. But this was not the normal case. Therefore, the first motivation for the introduction of a money economy must be sought in new internal developments and exigencies of the *polis*. Promotion of "trade" in general can hardly have been a major concern of those who introduced coined money.

Regarding the practical use of coinage, it has often been assumed that the denominations of early Greek coinage were too high for retail trade in local markets. Recent research, however, seems to suggest the existence of rather substantial quantities of fractional coinage. Thus, the use of coins in individual economic practice cannot be excluded.[15]

Further questions arise regarding social and political explanations of coinage as an economic tool in favor of justice regarding the middle classes: did anybody intend or realize a direct connection between coinage and justice? Moreover, could anybody think of the possibility of shifting the authority of social justice away from the gods? Why, then, the overwhelming presence of divine images on Greek coins? Thus, if the aforementioned interpretations imply some higher truth, they probably do not correspond to the explicit intentions and aims but, rather, mark the inherent consequences and theoretical implications of early Greek money economy. Equally problematic are explanations of the introduction of money as expressions of a city-state's sovereignty, autonomy, and identity.[16] Apart from the question why so many city-states for a long time did without this means of self-assertion, it is difficult to imagine that a *polis* changed its entire economic behaviour out of a purely symbolic motivation. Thus, before reflecting on such abstract second-level issues, some simple considerations seem to be appropriate.

The basic goal of the introduction of coined money was probably much more concrete and circumscribed; for the "state" had not only a monopoly in issuing money and in controlling and granting its value, but must above all have been the first distributor and "user" of the new currency. Thus, obviously, the introduction of coined money must have served the exigencies of a new kind of public enterprise and expenses

---

[15] Howgego, *Ancient History from Coins*, 6–8.

[16] Thus Finley, *The Ancient Economy*, 166. Contra: Martin, "Why did the Greek *Polis* originally Need Coins?" 259–64.

which could no longer easily be fulfilled by the pre-monetary means of exchange. Since the first currencies, even in their smallest units, consist of relatively high values, coins must have served to recompense some precious commodity or long-term service. Because of their occasional application, coins seem not to have been issued with continuous regularity, but in response to specific needs.[17]

Early Greek city-states fulfilled only few tasks for which public recompense of major volume had to be paid.[18] Political and sacred administration was accomplished by members of the wealthy classes, equipment for the citizen's army had to be provided by the citizens themselves, while the employment of mercenaries was a restricted practice in a restricted number of city-states.[19] Higher state expenses regarding warfare were probably needed for warships, the costs of which must have exceeded the possibility of private financing. Doubtless, however, the most expensive field of state projects was public building. Indeed, it was in the period of the late seventh and the sixth centuries BC that Greek cities were transformed through new devices of urban monumentalization: the civic centres (*agorai*) were enlarged and equipped with public buildings, the main streets were paved, abundant water supply with pipelines was provided and water-houses were built, drainage systems were constructed, the urban settlements were encircled with mighty city walls. And above all, the great *polis* sanctuaries were provided with monumental and richly adorned temples, altars, porticoes, banquet halls, entrance buildings, some of them also with installations for athletic training and competition.[20] Such constructions were

[17] Kraay, "Hoards, Small Change and the Origin of Coinage," 320–8.

[18] On financial practice and purposes of coinage in archaic Greek city-states, see C. Starr, *The Economic and Social Growth of Early Greece 800–500 B.C.*, New York: Oxford University Press 1977, esp. 97–117; Martin, "Why did the Greek *Polis* originally Need Coins?"

[19] Hiring mercenaries as the purpose of early Lydian electron coinage: Cook, "Speculations on the Origins of Coinage," 259–61. The examples of state financing of warfare cited by C. M. Kraay, "Greek Coinage and War," in: W. Heckel and R. Sullivan (eds.), *Ancient Coins of the Graeco-Roman World: The Nickle Numismatic Papers*, Ontario: Wilfried Laurier University Press 1984, 3–18, are all post-archaic.

[20] In this sense, see Starr, *The Economic and Social Growth of Early Greece 800–500 B.C.*, 113; Martin, "Why did the Greek *Polis* originally Need Coins?" 267–72. See also Seaford, *Money and the Early Greek Mind*, 75–87. In general on money in religious contexts, see von Reden, "Monetary Economy in the Greek World," in: *Thesaurus Cultus et Rituum Antiquorum* vol. VIII (2012), 11–127.

designed for the consolidated civic communities of this period, and they served public purposes which afforded additional financing by the *polis*: in particular, the great religious festivals with athletic and musical competitions, sacrifices, public meals and banquets which, besides the irregular efforts of building projects, constituted a high regular burden.

For all such projects, storage of financial resources and continuous payment to large numbers of workmen was necessary. In this regard, the traditional exchange economy did not constitute a sufficient basis; minted coinage was much better suited to fulfill these needs.

Precise chronological correspondence between the origins of coinage and urban monumentalization in stone is difficult to prove. Firstly, the emergence of monumental architecture occurred gradually, not in a definite step towards a higher level of monumentality; in addition, there are few cities where investigations give a comprehensive insight into this development. Within this change of urban centres there is no moment when the introduction of coined money became "necessary": we can only determine periods when coining money became a plausible solution to increasing problems. On the other hand, dates of the origins of coining within the various Greek cities are still, within certain limits, controversial among numismatists.

With these precautions, some figures may be given as a framework for substantiating the interrelation between sacred architecture and coinage:

	Coinage	Temples
Ephesos	600 BC (*electron*), 540 BC	560 BC
Samos	7th century (*electron*), 530 BC	570–560 BC
Miletos	600–575 BC (*electron*)	550 BC (Didyma)
Athens	570–550 BC	580–560 BC
Aigina	580–560 BC	570 BC
Corinth	570–550 BC	540 BC
Taras/Tarentum	500 BC	560 BC
Metapontion	550 BC	570–560 BC
Poseidonia	530 BC	540 BC
Syracuse	530 BC	580 BC
Akragas	520–510 BC	530 (?) BC
Selinunt	520 BC	560–540 BC

Obviously, in some places like Aigina, Corinth, or Athens, the origins of coinage occurred roughly at the same time or slightly earlier than monumental temple building; in Eastern Greek places like Ephesos, Samos, and Miletos, the monetary conditions had already existed for some decades, while in Western Greece cities like Taras, Syracuse, or Selinus started monumental temple building without coined money, and only later seem to have felt the need for supporting their great building programs with coinage of their own. All this, however, does not contradict the general interrelation between coinage and monumental urbanization, of which temple building was only one of several factors.

Generally speaking, not only was the society of the *polis* state a higher, second-level community, but also the common exigencies and tasks changed from the production for individual persons and families to the enterprises of and for the whole community.

Contrary to the great centralizing monarchies of ancient Mesopotamia and Egypt, with their powerful system of collecting and redistributing material goods, early Greek cities did not have a sufficient economic infrastructure in order to accomplish public enterprises of such dimensions. While formerly, individual craftsmen or workshops, busy with short-term production, were remunerated by individual customers, now the community had to pay great numbers of workmen for more-or-less long-term work. Remuneration in commodities would by far have exceeded the capacities of early Greek *poleis* with their yearly changing non-professional magistrates. To cope with such problems, a means was created by which the property of the community could be accumulated, stored and paid out in small units to individual persons according to their individual quantity of labour. Thus, it was the specific lack of political power and the infrastructural weakness of Greek *poleis* that was the basis of the introduction of a money economy. Instead of the powerful organization of redistribution, a slim system of "abstract" payment was installed. On the other hand, this makes it clear why a money economy did not spread out through the Near East and Egypt: there, under the conditions of hierarchical monarchic power, public labor and exchange were differently organized; there was no market in which free convertibility of coined money was needed.

For the recipients, payment by money must soon have become attractive. Whereas in the traditional exchange and gift culture the recompense depended on the specific goods that one's partner could offer, money was a completely abstract potential, allowing conversion of labor or commodities into all kinds of goods, in any place and at any time. Thereby, the bonds and dependencies between patron and employee, buyer and seller, became looser. Money was – for those who disposed of it – a vehicle of social autonomy.

It may be doubted, however, whether coined money was conceived of as a weapon in the struggle of the middle classes against the traditional elite. For it seems to be a rather modern and theoretical idea that this struggle was consciously and intentionally fought as a battle of economic systems. In fact, if one of the basic functions of coined money is its capacity for storing wealth, then this new economic instrument served the purposes of the prosperous elite very well. On the whole, the leading classes were always successful in adapting themselves to new social and economic situations, exploiting new means of cultural practice, putting themselves at the head of new developments, and thereby maintaining, defending and even strengthening their social position. They will have played a leading role in the introduction of coined money.

Compared with pre-monetary objects of value, like tripods or spits, not to speak of cattle, coined money had several advantages. It consisted of precious metal, rarely gold, mostly silver, both of which had hitherto been an exclusive exchange property of the elite: this must have granted a certain confidence in the new currency. But unlike pieces of metal, which were necessarily of uncertain weight and purity and had to be controlled in every transaction, coins were given a standardized form and a conventional value. This change from intrinsic to socially conferred values was the decisive phenomenon in the genesis of money.

The value of coins lay somewhat above bullion value, which means that it was fixed by convention.[21] This was on the one hand an advantage, since it prevented coins from being converted into bullion. On the other hand, however, this must have created problems, since for their reduced metal value their recognition was at risk: therefore, the convention of coins' value had to be guaranteed by some "public" authority. If certain goods or labors were to be paid with coins, this

---

[21] See J. H. Kroll, "Silver in Solon's Law," in: R. Ashton and S. Hurter (eds.), *Studies in Greek Numismatics in Memory of Martin Jessop Price*, London: SPINK 1998, 231.

presupposes a market, accessible to everybody, where the acceptance of coins was granted and where coined money could be converted into commodities for everyday life. How was collective confidence to be achieved in a value which so evidently was based on pure convention? The crucial point in this cannot have been the purity and the weight of the metal, since this was difficult to control (and moreover would have made the grant useless), but the certainty that the coin would be taken back by the issuing authority. Here again, the institutional weakness of Greek city-states turned out to be a strength. In the absence of strong central powers like monarchies or mighty priesthoods, there was no independent authority which could grant the value of coinage to the community of its users – except the community itself. It is the community of citizens that assures itself and others of the validity of its coins, by images and inscription, typically in the genitive plural: e.g. (coin) "of the Syracusians". Paradoxically, this is precisely where the force of the whole concept seems to lie: since it was the same community that on the one hand fixed and on the other hand acknowledged and accepted the coinages' value, this was a highly stable system.

In this sense, the introduction of coinage, first of all, served civic communities to accomplish their communitarian enterprises and to facilitate their economic communication, in particular within their own realm, but also beyond in economically dynamic city-states. It was the result of a far-reaching process of depersonalization and decentralization, by which all participants of economic transactions were freed from hierarchically imposed authorities and long-term dependencies, through which they became equal partners, acting in immediate independent exchange. The trustworthiness of this system was based on a high degree of social coherence and reciprocity, insofar as coined money was an important step towards and a firm element of an egalitarian civic society.

Roots of this kind of community sense have been convincingly seen in sacrificial rituals.[22] Sacrificial meals at the great *polis* festivals were occasions of egalitarian division of meat among all citizens, who constituted the *polis*' central sacrificial community. Such sacrifices had to be paid for by the community, with equal contributions, which then were converted into equal distributions. For that purpose, too, a currency of equal units was very useful. That the origins of money are indeed

[22] Seaford, *Money and the Early Greek Mind*, 48–67.

connected with the sphere of sacrifice becomes clear from the name of the most common coin, *obolos*, originally meaning the spit used for sacrificial meat consumption. Indeed, the great political reformer and poet Solon, who fixed the sacrificial calendar of his mother-city Athens, also determined prices of victims for public sacrifices. Thus, sacrifice seems to have been "an early agent of monetization".[23] From these origins, temples became the main places for storage of a city's treasures. An impressive inscription from the temple of Artemis at Ephesos records silver and gold coming from various sources: "from the *polis*", "from the wood", "from here", "from the naval", "from the salt", etc.[24] Thus, temples became places of egalitarian, communal distribution for religious, political and other communitarian purposes.

Even more, and to an amazing degree, the fully developed democracy of classical Athens was based on money: law courts in which thousands of members were involved every day, citizens' assemblies which gathered on average every ninth day, and many other institutions were paid in order to make participation possible for all citizens.

In this sense, Plato and Aristotle consider trade and money fundaments of communitarian life. Money makes things commensurable and thus promotes exchange and community, *koinonia*.[25]

This community, at least in its first phases, above all was the community of the individual *polis* citizens. As we saw, coins were first primarily designed and used for payment and exchange within the issuing state's territory. This was enhanced by the fact that many cities used their own weight standards, which must have considerably impeded conversion. On the other hand, this fact must have led to the result that the citizens considered "their" coinage as their own property. It was *their* collective good, and it was *their own* responsibility that granted this good's reliability and stability. In fact – if we don't ask for specific intentions but for general implications – coinage could become a sign of the city's self-assertion and a symbol of its identity. Not as a political propaganda message, but as a sign of the community's richness, distributed and floating among individual owners.

---

[23] Seaford, *Money and the Early Greek Mind*, 75–87; R. Parker, *Athenian Religion*, Oxford: Clarendon Press 1996, 43–55; Kroll, "Silver in Solon's Law," 225–32.
[24] *Inschriften von Ephesos* I (1979), Nr. 1.
[25] Plato, *Republic* 371b; Aristotle, *Nicomachean Ethics* 1133b.

Structural implications

Beyond the immediate intentions and purposes of the introduction of coined money there occurred some basic structural changes inherent in the process of monetization in early Greece which cannot, from the beginning and in every respect, have been obvious to its participants, but became implicitly efficient in the course of time. In the form of coinage, the accumulation of wealth tended to become an end in itself, independent of former social interrelations. Certainly, this is not a substantialistic quality of coinage as such, implying necessary conse-quences in social behavior.[26] Like all cultural goods, coined money attained its significance via changing cultural practice: on the one hand money could be used to create and ensure social connections, and on the other hand the accumulation of wealth could also become an autonomous practice without, and before the introduction of, coin-age. Nevertheless, coined money had some qualities and aspects that might at least have served such tendencies.[27]

Whereas the traditional exchange of goods and gifts had been a specific act, confined to specific occasions, effectuated through specific objects with specific symbolic meanings for specific purposes, particu-larly for creating personal bonds and relations between the donor and the receiver of the object, money more-or-less excluded such symbolic values. Exchange on the basis of money was universal: money had no special purpose, it could be applied to all things, to all subjects, in all contexts. Consciously or unconsciously, this was in various respects a far-reaching process of abstraction.

First: Transactions on a monetary basis tended to be basically non-personal: whereas gifts are personal acts directed to personal addressees, commodities may be bought from and sold to anyone. Gifts, being not immediately compensated by counter-gifts, create long-term obligations; goods, being exchanged on the basis of trust-worthiness, presuppose long-term relations; while acquisition by and sale for money do not create any specific relationship between the

---

[26] This is particularly stressed by von Reden, *Exchange in Ancient Greece*, 171–216. See also Papadopoulos, "Minting Identify: Coinage, Ideology and the Economics of Colonization in Akhaian Magna Graecia," 39.

[27] With what follows, compare Seaford, *Money and the Early Greek Mind*, 147–72, with substantialistic tendencies.

respective actors – on the contrary, payment by money, as an immediate compensation of a debt, terminates any such interrelation.

Second: Whereas the exchange of gifts is effectuated with things and activities of specific cultural or psychological valor, money does not allow for measuring the price of things that are at one's heart or have a personal significance – on the contrary, money constitutes a measure that applies to all objects and actions of human life alike. The most varied of things are deprived of their specific emotional or symbolic qualities and character by measuring and evaluating them according to their monetary value.

Third: This reduction and neutralization of individual persons to subjects and of things to objects is made possible by a general and neutral measure of value. Representing conventionally fixed values, and therefore being of no concrete use, money is the clearest expression, and at the same time the most effective promoter, of a specific kind of abstract thinking – which concerns not only the economy, but the whole society with its specific concepts of man, social values, and social interaction.

Fourth: A decisive new step consisted in extrapolating this value from the objects into a medium of its own. Whereas formerly value was inherent in valuable objects, now it became an autonomous system. This does not mean to deny preliminary stages of this development, e.g. silver bullion or spits used as currency; but it was only in the form of coined money that "value" became a system with its own, self-regulating rules. In principle, this has not changed even in the present development towards a moneyless credit economy where mere numbers like the Dax or the Dow Jones have taken over the function of an autonomous value system. Anyway, this is the precondition under which money could be valued as an autonomous factor of social development and social crisis.

Without any doubt, the introduction of coinage was a great intellectual and cultural achievement. As we have seen, a similar kind of rational thinking underlies the design of newly founded cities and their territories. Moreover, as has been acutely observed, pre-Socratic philosophy, with its reduction of the multiplicity of existing things to a unique principle, like water, corresponds closely with the abstract concept underlying the monetization of early Greek economy.[28]

---

[28] Seaford, *Money and the Early Greek Mind*, 175–291, with stimulating exaggerations.

Homogenization of persons and objects, universality and pervasiveness of coins and money: these were achievements that could be conceived, and were in fact evaluated, as progress towards social equality, justice, and free communication. However, as we shall see, the same phenomena also became the goals of sharp criticism.

An unconscious consequence of this development was the fact that the exchange of goods among men became fundamentally different from the exchange of reciprocal support between men and gods. Whereas the religious relationship of mortal men to their gods remained a long-term connection based on the principle of gift exchange, veneration and benevolence, the market of money-based trade and short-term exchange obeyed totally different rules which essentially belonged to the human world. It is true that some Greek sanctuaries, with their accumulating wealth, adopted functions of banking on a monetary basis; but these economic activities were a game with different rules than the religious interactions between men and gods through traditional votive-offerings.

Images

A specific quality of coins, which in antiquity was exploited even more than today, resulted from the combination of two of its features.

First: Coins were authorized by political units, states or rulers; they embodied their authorities, in a sense. This becomes particularly obvious in the marks of authentication they are distinguished by. The authority that issued money as today, made itself "present" on its coins, by inscriptions and images. Such images are highly interesting testimonies of how ancient cities and states aimed to present themselves within their own realms as well as towards the external world. These are images of political identity.

Second: Coins were an official medium with the widest diffusion conceivable. The routes of internal exchange and external trade became routes of coins, and by implication, routes of presence of those states by which these coins had been issued. In a world without mass media, coins were a uniquely ubiquitous means of official self-presentation through images.

The choice of a motif of "identity" implied two perspectives: towards the interior and towards the exterior. Regarding the home city, a motif had to be found that was acknowledged by the whole community;

regarding the surrounding world, this motif had to define the home city in relation to other cities, either by distinction or by assimilation.

Archaic and classical Greek city-states

The first phase of Greek coin issuing was shaped by the competitive situation within and among the countless larger and smaller city-states. Images, being the most conspicuous features of coins, were used on the one hand in order to visualize an individual *polis* identity, and on the other to signal distinction as well as interconnections among various city-states.

Most cities relied on gods to whom they reserved the obverse side of their coins, while the reverse side was often decorated by some other characteristic motif, symbol, or other. On principle, this must have been intended to put the city's money under divine protection. How these decisions were taken can only be guessed at. In Athens the choice of the city's name-goddess Athena on the obverse and of the goddess's owl on the reverse was probably uncontroversial. Normally, however, Greek cities had not one major "city-god(dess)" but many gods and goddesses of public importance; therefore they had to decide to which god they were to entrust their money. In Syracuse, for example, Apollo and Athena had old temples in the city centre; for what reason the local nymph-goddess Arethusa was chosen to adorn the city's lavish coins – perhaps as a compromise between different groups – is a matter of pure speculation.[29]

Other cities had symbols of their wealth on their coins: thus, Sybaris issued with a bull and Metapontion with a corn-ear, documenting agricultural richness, while Kroton had a tripod, perhaps indicating access to mineral resources and metal industry.[30] But again, we will never know how much these motifs were contested by groups other than the rich landowners or metal merchants.

Besides the city's internal identity, there were the relations to the surrounding world.[31] A city might choose a deity who was present on an allied city's coins, thus expressing positive political relations; or a

[29] See the complicated explanation given by E. Boehringer, *Die Münzen von Syrakus*, Berlin: Walter de Gruyter 1929, 95–102.

[30] Papadopoulos, *Money and the Early Greek Mind*, 28–39, with whom, however, I do not agree regarding possible references to Bronze Age traditions.

[31] S. Ritter, *Bildkontakte: Götter und Heroen in der Bildsprache griechischer Münzen des 4. Jahrhunderts v. Chr.*, Berlin: Reimer 2002.

deity of an adversary city, indicating political opposition. Accordingly, the choice of the same deity could demonstrate alliance as well as opposition. Athens created for her coins a new type of Athena with an open, so-called "attic" helmet, while soon afterwards her great economic rival Corinth also chose Athena, but with a closed, so-called "Corinthian" helmet, pushed backwards over her forehead. That this is not a negligible detail is shown by the fact that later the Athenian daughter-city Thurioi and the Athenian ally Neapolis took over the Athenian version of Athena, while the Corinthian daughter-cities Leukas and Ambrakia followed the Corinthian version. Political affiliations were expressed through the assimilation of coin images. On the other hand, a blatant example of *polemic* reception is given by Syracuse, after the glorious defeat of the Athenian fleet (413 BC), through a new series of splendid silver coins where the traditional version of Arethusa is changed into a spectacular representation of Athena – with an Athenian-type helmet! Thus, the images of a city's gods or goddesses were received and imitated by political allies and friends, opposed by political rivals, and "occupied" by political enemies.

Hellenistic monarchies

The rulers of the great Hellenistic monarchies made extensive use of coins in order to make themselves "present" through their vast empires. Alexander the Great in many places of his realm, from Greece and Macedonia to Alexandria, Beirut and Babylon, installed highly efficient mints producing a unified currency, authorized in the king's name: silver coins with his alleged father, Zeus, on the obverse and his ancestor, Herakles, on the reverse, and gold coins with his tutelary goddess, Athena, and the victory goddess, Nike. This was probably Alexander's most far-reaching measure in order to unify his immense empire with its extremely heterogeneous political and cultural traditions: coined money allowed and encouraged boundless economic communication, and the coins' images testified to the ubiquitous "presence" of the ruler who granted the trustworthiness of material value. This communicative force of circulating coinage must have been particularly efficient in the newly conquered lands of the former Persian Empire, east from Asia Minor and Phoenicia, where coined money was hitherto practically unknown. Thus, the gods of the new ruler circulated on the coins in the contexts of new forms of trade.

Alexander's successors, the rulers over the great empires of the Hellenistic age, even put their own images on the coins: these became the most obvious demonstration that the king, in the form of "his" money, was efficiently present in all parts of his realm and permeated the life of all his subjects.

Roman Republic

These possibilities of coins were exploited to an extreme degree in ancient Rome.[32] During the Roman Republic, images of gods and goddesses testify to the various goals images could serve. As a norm, coin values were distinguished by different gods: the *denarius*, the main coin, was marked by the goddess Roma, the *quinarius* by Hercules, the *as* by Ianus, and so forth. Thus, the system of coinage was visualized with a stable constellation of gods and goddesses. On principle, this multifaceted stability corresponded to the "system" of coin images of Hellenistic monarchies.

Nevertheless, when Roman armies conquered Greece and installed Roman rule from the second century BC, this was not followed by an expansion of Roman money:[33] finds of Roman coins from the period of the republic are rare in Greece. This does not imply that Rome did not interfere in the economic system of the conquered East. The first victorious general, T. Quinctius Flamininus, probably stopped the circulation of coins of Macedonia, Rome's immediate enemy, but a little later Rome accepted and promoted a powerful local coinage, the Athenian "new style silver coins". A similar situation is to be observed in other parts of the Eastern Mediterranean that had come under Roman rule. And even in Spain where the use of coinage had formerly been very restricted, the Roman conquest of the second century BC did not entail a wide diffusion of Roman money; towards the middle of the century, Rome even initiated a local coinage, based on the Roman weight system, but with local images. Obviously, the truly Roman *denarius* and *as* system, with its characteristic imagery, was mainly destined for circulation and comprehension within the realm of the capital and Italy.

[32] The whole repertoire is readily accessible, with commentaries, in
M. H. Crawford, *Roman Republican Coinage*, Cambridge University Press 1974.
[33] M. H. Crawford, *Coinage and Money under the Roman Republic*, London: Methuen 1985, 116–32.

During the last century of the Roman Republic, this relatively stable system of coin images was rapidly changed into an extremely flexible instrument for political messages.[34] The struggle of mighty army commanders for political power and the ensuing competition for social prestige within the upper classes resulted in an increasing public demonstration of personal claims and achievements in all realms of life. For this purpose, coins were a particularly efficient medium. Although the office of the three magistrates responsible for coin issuing was a rather low rung at the beginning of a political career, moneyers used coins for highly specific political messages: either promoting their own interests and careers, by depictions of their political activities, legislation, organization of public games, erecting public buildings, and so forth; or by glorifying and supporting one of the great protagonists of political life, the triumph of Marius, or the symbols of charismatic world-rule of Julius Caesar. To this end, a most complex imagery of political themes, allegories, and symbols was created, through which coins became a medium of a widely dispersed political discourse. Finally, Julius Caesar was given the right to put his own portrait on his coins, as Hellenistic kings used to do.

Scholars like to speak of this practice as "propaganda" – which, however, implies some misleading connotations. The images as such are in part not very clear, difficult to understand, and therefore lacking the self-explaining evidence and convincing power that is to be expected from "propaganda". And regarding the users of money, one may doubt whether they normally studied coin images with such intensity that they might be influenced by them in their political positions. More adequate are the notions of "self-assertion" and "claim". Impressing one's own figurative motif and script on the public medium of coinage means to occupy this medium for a symbol of one's own person and thus imposing one's own claims by forcing the community to acknowledge this

---

[34] A. Alföldi, "The Main Aspects of Political Propaganda on the Coinage of the Roman Republic," in: R. A. G. Carson and C. H. V. Sutherland (eds.), *Essays in Roman Coinage presented to Harold Mattingly*, Oxford University Press 1956, 63–95; Crawford, *Coinage and Money under the Roman Republic*, 712–44; T. Hölscher, "Die Bedeutung der Münzen für das Verständnis der politischen Repräsentationskunst der späten römischen Republik," in: T. Hackens and R. Weiller (eds.), *Actes du 9ème congrès international de numismatique, Bern 1979*, Louvain-la-Neuve: Association Internationale des Numismates Professionels 1982, 269–82.

self-assertion. In this sense, the distribution of coinage within the political community makes these images and their implied claims universally present.

Roman Empire

The Roman emperors monopolized this unique medium of political publicity. With great iconographic skill whole programs were displayed, changing according to the vicissitudes of historical events and the ideological and mental moves of the time: the emperor's heroic feats, in particular military campaigns and triumphs; his significant political acts, like public sacrifices, distribution of money, speeches to the army; personifications of his ideological issues, like *Virtus, Pietas, Concordia, Fides, Felicitas*, and so forth. By this example, coins became a most manifold panel of imperial policy.[35]

Even here the term of "political propaganda" is misleading. Certainly, there was no central institution for steering public opinions; nor was there any aim of ideological infiltration in the sense of Christian mission (from where the term "propaganda" is derived: *propaganda fide*) or even of modern dictatorial regimes, addressing potential opponents. More appropriately, we might speak of panegyric exaltation aiming at creating an atmosphere of general consent. Much more interesting, however, and highly debated, is the problem of the efficiency of this medium. Were coins intensely observed? Were their messages eagerly received, enthusiastically or critically interpreted and commented on? By whom? With what results? Leading to what kind of reactions? All this would be a matter of high-level theory about low-level political communication, which is an important task for future interdisciplinary research between art history, political science, and semiotics: a theory which would have to consider on the one hand the extraordinarily complex imagery of the emperor's and the state's political presence in this medium, and on the other hand the normal situations of low attention in this medium's use – but always keeping in mind that it must have been an efficient medium, as is testified by its endurance through the centuries.

---

[35] *Coins of the Roman Empire in the British Museum* I (1923)–VI (1962); C. H. V. Sutherland, *Coinage in Roman Imperial Policy 31 B.C.–68 A.D.*, London: Methuen 1951.

The consequences of coined money in ancient judgments

Ancient authors, critical authorities, as well as low-level observers and participants in economic life, were well aware of the great changes, in part revolutionary in part structural and processual, that were implied by the introduction of money: with consequences that not only concerned the economy, but in many respects deeply affected social, cultural, and even religious life, attitudes, and mentality.

Homer, the great representative poet of "heroic" values in a world of the emerging *polis*, marginalized the world of trade although this was one of the seminal factors of his time. Nevertheless, his hero, Achilleus, defends, in a symptomatic way, the values of his "self", his *"psyche"*, against the tempting offers of wealth: when Agamemnon takes away his maiden who had been given to him as a reward for his bravery in battle and who thus was the sign of his *time*, his social excellence, he resisted all compensation, saying that no wealth could ever have so much value as his *psyche*, his personal "self".[36]

From that time, there emerges a broad tradition of far-reaching criticism of wealth in Greek literature, particularly of its universal and pervasive character, which undoubtedly implies coined money.[37] This criticism is to be seen in the horizon of a society in which property was in fact the undisputed basis of social rank, even in the periods of the most radical form of Athenian democracy. Against this background, such criticism may seem at first sight somewhat hypocritical, but on the other hand it is this horizon which gives criticism of wealth its sharpness.

Money acquires everything. For money one can have beauty, health, noble birth (by paying the dowry for a noble bride), the favor of gods (by acquiring an expensive sacrifice victim), even human beings: prostitutes. Ares, the god of war, is a trader, exchanging even corpses for wealth.[38] Thukydides is particularly bitter: "No currency ever grew up among humankind as evil as money: This lays waste even cities, this expels men from their homes, this thoroughly teaches and transforms good minds of mortals to set themselves to disgraceful acts; it showed men how to practice villainies and to know every act of impiety".[39] And Sophocles concludes: money creates friends, honor, political power

---

[36] Homer, *Iliad* 9, 401 ff.
[37] Seaford, *Money and the Early Greek Mind*, 147–72.   [38] Ibid., 157–65.
[39] Aischylos, *Agamemnon* 438.

near to tyranny, physical beauty, wise speech, and pleasure even in disease.[40]

As a consequence, money becomes a goal in itself. The acquisition of tripods has a natural limit set by their use (to boil meat, as gifts, etc.) and by the problem of storing them. Equally, according to Aristophanes, the purchase of all other goods – sex, bread, music, glory, warfare, and so forth – has an end in satiety. But money is accumulated without limits.[41] While commodities are normally sold for money in order to acquire other commodities (C – M – C), now money is invested in commodities in order to make more money (M – C – M – C – M). And whereas the first of these sequences finds a natural end in the acquisition of the desired commodity, the second sequence is fundamentally unlimited.

Alkaios, the early archaic poet, already assured: "Man is wealth".[42] Not much later, the poet Pythermos says: "All other things than gold were nothing".[43] Still more radically, Aristophanes concludes: Wealth "is the unique source of all things, good as well as bad".[44]

However, the position of Achilleus in Homer was not forgotten. Solon, who had already created a new class-system on the basis of property, insists that there are limits to the desirability of wealth.[45] The myth of Midas who miraculously transformed everything he touched into gold, but almost starved to death because his food was transformed too, was a popular warning. The same Solon, when he was asked by Kroisos, the richest king of his age, about the happiest of men, is reported to have surprised his partner by not naming Kroisos because of his immense riches, but a certain Tellos of Athens who had lived in a prosperous city, was the father of noble sons, saw children born to all of them, and having had as much wealth as a man may "among us", crowned his life with glorious death in war for his fatherland, for which he was given the great honour of a public burial.[46] This text is particularly interesting because it does not create a fundamental

---

[40] Sophocles, frg. 88.   [41] Aristophanes, *Ploutos* 189–97.

[42] Alkaios, frg. 360.

[43] Pythermos: D. L. Page, *Poetae Melici Graeci*, Oxford: Clarendon Press 1962, nr. 910.

[44] Aristophanes, *Ploutos* 182.   [45] Solon, frg. 24.

[46] Herodotus 1, 30. On Tellos see also the interesting interpretation by L. Kurke, "The Economy of *Kudos*," in: C. Dougherty and L. Kurke (eds.), *Cultural Poetics in Archaic Greece: Cult, Performance, Politics*, New York: Oxford University Press 1998, 153f.

antithesis between material riches and ethical values, but acknowledges moderate wealth, together with a thriving family, as a prerequisite of happiness; indeed, Tellos was a member of the Athenian upper class which defined its rank through its material property and its ensuing freedom from physical labor. But this wealth is neither excessive nor competitive, it keeps within the norms that prevail "among us". And, above all, as a measure of happiness it is superseded by merits for the fatherland, in opposition to the false self-evidence of material riches.

Later, in tragedy, it is frequently asserted which goods and values are never and under no condition to be submitted to the power of wealth and money: a trouble-free life, a good wife, a genuine friend, the fatherland, wisdom; on the other hand, essential goods cannot be acquired by money: youth, peace, virtue.[47]

Conclusion

From what we have seen, it becomes evident that Michael Welker's distinction between such commodities that may and should be submitted to the mechanisms of money and market, and such values that should be excluded from the dynamics economy,[48] has explicit precedents in ancient Greece. There is no question that a certain measure of prosperity and property is a desirable fundamental of human happiness. But there are two basic limitations to accumulating riches: first, the acquisition of wealth should not become an end in itself, obeying only an autonomous market's rules; and second, wealth should not be acquired at the costs of essential goods and values of human societies and individuals.

From this, one might deduce a proposal for the problems of the present: a project of anthropological research on how much wealth an individual person can – anthropologically – use and exploit for his own and his relatives' physical subsistence and moreover for their physical,

---

[47] Aischylos, *Hiketidai* 935; *Persai* 842; Euripides, *Alkestis* 56–9; *Elektra* 941; *Herakles* 643–8; *Ion* 629–31; *Medeia* 598–9; *Phoinissai* 552–4. Seaford, *Money and the Early Greek Mind*, 162, with further testimonies.

[48] M. Welker, "Ab heute regiert Geld die Welt: Die Einführung der Geldwirtschaft und ihre Auswirkungen auf religiöses Denken und ethische Orientierung," in: C. Gestrich (ed.), *Gott, Geld und Gabe*, Berlin: Wichern Verlag 2004, 52–66.

intellectual, and ethical pleasure.[49] What should be opposed is the function of wealth as a symbol of social status, since this is the starting point of an abstract valuation of money as an end in itself. By such an investigation, it might be possible to fix a scientifically founded and socially acceptable maximum limit of personal wealth. If a project of this kind were installed by political authorities and realized by independent scholars of international renown, there might be a chance for transferring its results to the realm of public policy. Perhaps the authority of respectable ancient authors helps to make this proposal less naïve than it might appear to modern finance politicians.

---

[49] An attempt in this direction is made in the Report: *Churches Addressing Greed: The Work of the Greed Line Study Group of the World Council of Churches (WCC)*, not yet available (draft made available to me by Ulrich Duchrow).

7 | *The social world of Ecclesiastes*

CHOON-LEONG SEOW

Some forty years ago, Elias Bickerman characterized Kohelet, the author of Ecclesiastes, as "a sage who in an age of investment teaches not dissipation, but the enjoyment of wealth."[1] Dating the book to the Hellenistic period, Bickerman imagined Kohelet addressing a "new business class" ever concerned with the acquisition of more wealth and constantly worried about the possibility of the loss of it. Bickerman's provocative formulation of the issues represents the first-ever attempt to consider the book in the light of its socio-historical context. His cue led Frank Crüsemann in 1979 to further argue that the historical context of Ecclesiastes – to him, Ptolemaic Palestine – was the key to understanding its teachings.[2] This approach received a further boost in a 1991 study by C. Robert Harrison, wherein he endorses the view that Ecclesiastes is thoroughly pessimistic and argues that the affinities between Ecclesiastes and other pessimistic texts from the Mediterranean world indicate that broadly similar socio-historical conditions in various periods and cultures may yield similar literature.[3] Accordingly, Harrison believes, one should not ask if the worldview in Ecclesiastes was primarily a result of Greek, Mesopotamian, or Egyptian literary or philosophical influence. Rather, similar socio-historical conditions generated similar responses in literature. Moreover, against the common assumption that the book was written for an aristocratic audience, Harrison maintains that Kohelet's audience – "the people" of 12:9 – was "a new indigenous middle class," a

---

[1] E. Bickerman, *Four Strange Books of the Bible*, New York: 1967, 165.
[2] F. Crüsemann, *Die unveränderbare Welt: Überlegungen zur "Krisis der Weisheit" beim Prediger (Qohelet)*, in: W. Schottroff and W. Stegemann (eds.), *Der Gott der Kleinen Leute: Sozialgeschichtliche Bibelauslegungen*, vol. 1: *Altes Testament*, Munich/Gelnhausen: 1979, 80–104.
[3] C. R. Harrison, "Qoheleth in Social-Historical Perspective," unpublished Ph.D. dissertation, Duke University: 1991. See also his essay, "Qoheleth Among the Sociologists," *Biblical Interpretation* 5 (1997), 160–80.

group of people that he characterizes, anachronistically, as "petite bourgeoisie."[4]

These scholars made significant contributions to the study of Ecclesiastes insofar as they have brought the issue of the question of socio-historical context to the fore. After all, in some twenty-six instances, Kohelet is the explicit or implicit subject of the verb *r'h*, "to see."[5] More precisely, Kohelet *observes* the happenings in the world (1:14; 7:13; 8:9), human preoccupations and strivings (3:10; 4:4, 7; 5:12–13; 8:16), divine arbitrariness as reflected in the unequal lots of individuals (2:24; 6:1), society turned upside down (3:16; 10:7), the prevalence of injustice and oppression (3:16; 4:1; 8:9), and how the traditional rules are contradicted in reality (7:15; 8:10; 9:11, 13). Admittedly, these are situations that one may find in many periods in history and virtually anywhere in the world. Still, they are what the author tells us that he himself has personally witnessed. Some of these observed situations, moreover, are quite specific. Hence, one notes the case of the parsimonious man who hoarded wealth only to lose it all in a single "bad venture" (5:12–13). Or the example of the single man who was unable to stop striving even though there was no one with whom to share the fruit of his labor (4:7). Or the powerful man who committed an inadvertent error and suffered its consequences (10:5). Or the situation where the poor and the rich seem to have traded places (10:7). All of these are reported as situations that Kohelet has observed; they are situations that he reportedly encountered in his lifetime, his context.

Moreover, Mitchell Dahood has pointed out that there is in the book an impressive list of commercial terms that, to him, reflects a "distinctly commercial environment."[6] Dahood's overall thesis that the mercantile environment suggested by this vocabulary implies a Phoenician provenance in the fourth century BCE cannot be sustained. Still, he is right that the vocabulary of the book indicates a deep concern with economic

---

[4] Indeed, the common assumption that Israel's wisdom literature stems from the social elite cannot be sustained – at least not for Ecclesiastes, which refers to a sage who is a commoner, *miskēn* (9:15–16), and notes that the wise are not assured of wealth (9:11).

[5] 1:14, 16; 2:1, 3, 12, 13, 24; 3:10, 16, 22; 4:1, 4, 7, 15; 5:12, 17; 6:1; 7:15; 8:9, 10, 16, 17; 9:11, 13; 10:5, 7.

[6] M. J. Dahood, "Canaanite-Phoenician Influence in Qoheleth," *Biblica* 33 (1952), 220–1.

issues. That concern suggests that the author was addressing a particular environment.

That is not to say, however, that Kohelet's epistemology is entirely empirical. He does draw upon traditional and literary sources as well, specifically, wisdom teachings, materials found in the Torah, and, of course, traditions about Solomon. There are suggestive parallels, too, with various ancient Near Eastern literary works, most notably, the *Gilgamesh Epic* and the Aramaic *Proverbs of Ahiqar*, the earliest witness to which is found on a papyrus dated to the late fifth century BCE.[7] So there is, indeed, much that one may learn through an understanding of Kohelet's "intellectual background," as it were. Nevertheless, one can hardly ignore his own insistence that his conclusions are derived from what he has observed and experienced: that is, his socio-historical context.[8]

Provenance

I have previously argued on linguistic grounds for a Persian period provenance for the book.[9] While I readily acknowledge that a Hellenistic date cannot be precluded on linguistic grounds alone, I find no reason to follow scholars who privilege such a conclusion. Indeed, the number of terminological and thematic links with Aramaic documents of the Persian period is without parallel. There is, to my knowledge, no similar clustering of idioms in the Hebrew and Aramaic dialects of later periods. Terms like *yitrōn* ("surplus"), *ḥesrôn* ("deficit"), *ḥešbôn* ("account"), *nĕkāsîm* ("assets"), *šlṭ* ("to have right of disposal"), *ḥēleq* ("lot"), *ḥōpen* ("fistful") and *kap* ("handful") used as small measures, *ṭaḥănâ* ("mill"), and *bêt hasûrîm* ("prison") all have cognates in Persian-period Aramaic.[10] To be sure, some of these terms do occur in the Hebrew and Aramaic of other periods, but we do not

---

[7] C.-L. Seow, *Ecclesiastes: A New Translation with Introduction and Commentary*, Anchor Bible 18C, New York: 1995, 60–5.

[8] Contra: M. Sneed, "The Social Location of the Book of Qoheleth," *Hebrew Studies (HS)* 39 (1998), 41–51. Sneed is entirely skeptical about locating Qohelet's work in a socio-historical context, concluding without argumentation that the author was a "filthy rich" intellectual and that "intellectuals are known for becoming cynical dissidents who 'bite the hand that feeds them.'"

[9] C.-L. Seow, "Linguistic Evidence and the Dating of Qohelet," *Journal of Biblical Literature (JBL)* 115 (1996), 643–66.

[10] Ibid., 651–4.

find them together in a single period, other than the fifth and fourth centuries. By the same token, the expression *hašlîtô lašē't mattat* ("to authorize to take up a grant") in 5:18 reflects an equivalent technical expression in Persian-period Aramaic, *šlyṭ lmnś dšn'* ("authorization to take up the grant").[11] The expression *'ăšuqîm 'ăšer na'ăśîm* ("injustices that were done") in 4:1 is paralleled by *'šq 'byd* ("injustice was done"), an expression found repeatedly on a fifth-century Aramaic petition by a farmer for an injustice to be rectified.[12] Interestingly, too, the injustice in this case was perpetrated with the collusion of the *dyny mdynt'* ("judges in the province"). The text echoes Kohelet's reference in 5:7 to the *'šq* ("injustice") that his readers may be *observing* in the *mědînâ*. Again, it is not that oppression is not a common phenomenon in other times and places. Rather, it is the coincidence of terms being used to describe the phenomenon that prompts one to consider the Persian-period setting compelling.[13]

Money and commerce

Historians have long touted the administrative reforms of the Achaemenid government, notably the infrastructural innovations (like its postal system) and renovations (like its elaborate network of roads), reforms intended to unify the empire but that invariably facilitated economic development as well. Under Darius I (522–486 BCE), the Persians instituted a highly efficient system of taxation throughout the empire. Imperial taxes, ordinarily to be paid in precious metal, were determined for each region according to the region's size and productivity. Locally, the taxes were often paid in kind, some of which were retained for the maintenance of local government facilities and garrisons, while the rest were kept in royal storehouses and subsequently converted into cash, either through export or through the sale of the

---

[11] *TAD* I, 6.4.3–4. See H. Z. Szubin and B. Porten, *Royal Grants in Egypt: A New Interpretation of Driver 2 Journal of Near Eastern Studies (JNES)* 46 (1987), 39–48.

[12] *TAD* I, 5.2.5, 8.

[13] I have previously dated Ecclesiastes broadly to between the mid-fifth century to the first half of the fourth (Seow, *Linguistic Evidence*, 666). I now think the upper end of my date too early. A Persian date in the fourth century seems to me now more in conformity with the evidence, particularly the socio-economic picture I paint here.

goods in urban markets.[14] Then, to facilitate trade, especially international trade, as well as the payment of imperial taxes, the government
began minting coins. Thus, under Darius I, a gold coin known as the
"Daric" was struck by the central government some time after 515 BCE,
along with silver *sigloi*, bimetallism being an idea borrowed from the
Lydians.[15]

Darius was not the first Persian ruler to mint coins, for silver *sigloi*
have been discovered antedating his issue by some three or four decades,[16] but his was the first attempt at standardization for the sake of
international trade, especially with the Greeks, and in support of his
reforms of the imperial tax system. The transition from a largely non-
monetary economy to a monetary one is evident in the government
records uncovered at the imperial city of Persepolis. The Persepolis
Fortification Tablets from the late sixth century indicate that payments
then were made entirely in goods, such as grain, flour, sheep, wine, and
beer.[17] Even taxes were paid in kind and account records mention only
goods. The Persepolis Treasury Tablets, however, suggest that by the
first decade of the fifth century, the economy was beginning to become
monetized. The earliest records indicate that payment was still made in
kind but, importantly, the *cash values* of the goods were invariably
stipulated.[18] Clearly, cash had become the principal method of accounting by the government. Indeed, Cameron points to the gradual monete-
rization of the economy at Persepolis, noting that in 479 BCE, payment

[14] M. W. Stolper, *Entrepreneurs and Empire: The Murāšû Archive, the Murāšû
Firm, and Persian Rule in Babylonia*, Uitgaven van het Nederlands Historisch-
Archeologisch Instituut te Istanbul 54, Leiden: 1985, 28, 146.

[15] Herodotus, 1.94; E. Herzfeld, *Notes on the Achaemenid Coinage and Some
Sassanian Mint-Names*, in: J. Allan, H. Mattingly, and E. S. G. Robinson (eds.),
Transactions of the International Numismatic Congress 1936, London: 1938,
413–26; E. S. G. Robinson, "The Beginning of Achaemenid Coinage,"
Numismatic Chronicle (1958), 190; M. C. Root, "Evidence from Persepolis for
Dating of Persian and Archaic Greek Coins," *Numismatic Chronicle* (1988),
8–12.

[16] See S. P. Noe, *Two Hoards of Persian Sigloi, Numismatic Notes and Monographs
1936*, New York: 1956; I. Carradice, "The 'Regal' Coinage of the Persian
Empire," in: I. Carradice (ed.), *Coinage and Administration in the Athenian and
Persian Empires: The Ninth Oxford Symposium on Coinage and Monetary
History*, Oxford: 1987, 73–95.

[17] R. T. Hallock, *Persepolis Fortification Tablets*, University of Chicago, Oriental
Institute Publishers: 1969.

[18] G. Cameron, *The Persepolis Treasury Tablets*, University of Chicago, Oriental
Institute Publishers: 1948, 2–3.

was two-thirds in kind, by 470 BCE, it was half in kind, by 466–467 BCE most records mention only payments in cash, and finally, by 469 BCE, we have the first tablets recording payment made entirely in cash. The economy appears to have become fully "monetized" in that city at least.

The evidence in the material culture of Palestine, too, matches what one finds in the inscriptions. Whereas coins have been found only sporadically in Palestine from the end of the sixth century on, they did not become common until late in the fifth and early in the fourth, from which period archaeologists have uncovered numerous hoards all over Palestine, mostly produced by local mints all along the coast.[19] The fact that the local mints produced coins of the Greek and Persian designs suggests, surely, some standardization of currency. In any case, by the end of the fifth and the beginning of the fourth century, money had become more than a convenient medium of exchange even in agrarian Yehud. To be sure, people still bartered their wares and services throughout the empire, but for the purposes of taxation and business transactions, goods and services were typically assessed monetary values. Money was both a measure of value and the standard medium of exchange. Not surprisingly, therefore, the extra-biblical inscriptions from this period are replete with references to money, most frequently mentioned in connection with taxes, wages, rents, loans, fines, dowries, divorce payments, inheritances, and, of course, the prices of goods and services. Money was used in everyday business transactions both large and small, given as gifts and bribes, and hoarded. Money was no longer just a convenient medium of exchange; it had become a commodity, something desired for what it could bring. The numerous hoards of coins found at various sites in Palestine are, indeed, testimony to the love of money for its own sake.

In light of such a monetized economy, it is perhaps not surprising to find Kohelet saying in 5:9, "one who loves money will not be satisfied

---

[19] E. Stern, *Material Culture of the Land of the Bible in the Persian Period 538–332 B. C.*, Jerusalem: 1982 (Hebrew original, 1973), 217–28; L. Mildenberg, "Über das Münzwesen im Reich der Achämeniden," in: U. Hübner and A. A. Knauf (eds.), *Vestigia Leonis: Studien zur antiken Numismatik Israels, Palästinas und östlichen Mittelmeerwelt*, NTOA, Göttingen: 1998, 3–29; Y. Meshorer and S. Qedar, *The Coinage of Samaria in the Fourth Century BCE*, Beverly Hills: 1991; J. Bentlyon: *The Coinage and Mints of Phoenicia: The Pre-Alexandrian Period*, Harvard Semitic Monographs (HSM) 26, Chicago: 1980.

with money." Elsewhere in the book, too, he alludes to how "money preoccupies everyone" (*hakkesep ya'ăăneh 'et-hakkōl*, 10:19). Such an indictment is all the more poignant when one realizes that the Hebrew words may be taken also to mean "money answers everything," suggesting that Kohelet may have turned a cliché about the efficacy of money ("money answers everything") into a criticism of those who subscribed to such a notion ("money preoccupies everyone"). A similar sort of subversion may be evident in 7:12, where the author seems to equate the security afforded by money with the security of wisdom. Here the term used for the protective power of money and wisdom is *ṣēl*,[20] a term that elsewhere in the book connotes transience (6:12; 8:13). The point is that money, like wisdom, affords neither real protection nor permanent shelter after all, but only the temporary relief like that provided by a shadow. Kohelet suffers no illusions about the reliability of money or wisdom, even though he acknowledges, perhaps tongue-in-cheek, that "wisdom is as good as inheritance and an advantage to those who see the sun" (7:11). Ironically, the saying points to the fact that *both* wisdom and wealth are, in fact, ephemeral, like *ṣēl*. That skepticism is derived not from philosophical antecedents, but from the reality of the author's socio-historical context.

There can be little doubt that Ecclesiastes presumes an audience deeply concerned with economic matters. Besides general terms like *kesep* "money," *'ōšer* "riches," *'āšîr* "rich," *sĕgullâ* "private possession," *śākār* "compensation," *naḥălâ* "inheritance," and *kišrôn* "success, accomplishments," one finds a number of terms in the book that suggest a lively economic environment: *yitrôn* "surplus, advantage," *ḥesrôn* "deficit," *ḥešbôn* "account," *nekāsîm* "assets," *tebû'â* "yield," *hāmôn* "wealth," *'inyān* "venture, business," *'āmāl* "toil, fruit of toil," *'ōbēd* "worker," and *ḥēlæq* "lot, portion." Indeed, Kohelet often sounds like a pragmatic entrepreneur, ever concerned with the "bottom line": *māh-yitrôn* "what is the profit?" (1:3; 3:9; 5:15). The term *yitrôn* has its Aramaic equivalent found in an accounting document from the late fifth century, where it indicates "net gain."[21] Thus, Kohelet is talking about the net gain of labor, as it were. If there is no profit in a particular investment, one should not waste the effort.

---

[20] There is no need to amend the text to read *k^eṣēl*, as some commentators do. The preposition *be-* here is *beth essentiae* (GKC 119.i).

[21] *TAD* III, 3.11.6.

Moreover, when Kohelet speaks of humanity's desperate search for wisdom, he draws on the image of a merchant or an accountant frantically checking a ledger to explain some discrepancy, examining the account item by item, "one by one to find an accounting" (7:27). The term "accounting" (*ḥšbn*) is, again, a commercial term found among the Aramaic documents of the Persian period.[22] Kohelet makes the point that those who seek to clarify the distinction between wisdom and folly will be frustrated. They will not be able to find a clear accounting of it all. There will always be discrepancies in this confusing ledger.

Ecclesiastes reflects an economic environment that is different from the largely subsistence agrarian culture of preexilic Judah. In the first half of the sixth century, commerce was the domain of the royal sector and trade was still largely conducted by barter. International commerce was carried out by the state, primarily from taxes-in-kind paid into the royal storehouses. As Ezekiel has it, various nations exchanged their goods with Tyre, bringing precious metal, horses and mules, ivory and ebony, precious stones, textiles, aromatics, and so forth (Ezek. 27:12–25). As for Israel and Judah, they brought only agrarian products which they exchanged for Phoenician merchandise (Ezek. 27:17). The cities of Judah, including Jerusalem, were essentially agricultural cities, producing for subsistence and for state taxes.[23] In the fifth century, however, commerce was democratized and no longer primarily a royal enterprise. Indeed, the Persian period is distinguished from the preceding epochs by the widespread use of money and the democratization of commerce.

This extensive commercialization of postexilic Palestine is partly documented by archaeological evidence. The coastal areas saw a rise in population, perhaps indicating the increasing importance of mercantilism in this period. For instance, in a survey of the coastal region of Sharon, scholars found numerous Persian period sites, five in 'Atlit and its vicinity alone.[24] Acco, though poorly settled in earlier times, prospered during the Persian period, when it became a thriving commercial center and sea-port. Apollonia-Arsuf was an important trading center specializing in the production of purple dye in that period. At Tell Megadim, archaeologists found evidence of a well-planned, rectangular

---

[22] *TAD* III, 3.28.79.

[23] H. Kreissig, *Die sozialökonomische Situation in Juda zur Achämenidenzeit,* Schriften zur Geschichte und Kultur des Alten Orients 7, Berlin: 1973, 64.

[24] Stern, *Material Culture,* 18.

town dating to the Persian period, with a street 90 meters long and two side streets running to it at right angles.[25] Excavations at Tell Dor suggest that the ancient city was a major trading center in the Persian period, as evidenced by the number of large storage jars found there, as well as the largest assemblage of foreign ceramic wares found anywhere in Israel.[26] In the Persian period stratum, a purple-dye manufacturing installation was discovered in 1986. Recent reinvestigations of Tell Abu Hawam, the original harbor town of Haifa, have led to the conclusion that the site was a thriving regional granary and a center of maritime trade during the Persian period, the settlement having been revived despite the marshes growing to the southwest of the site.[27] A large Persian-period settlement is found at Tell Michal, where there was an industrial quarter.[28] At Tell Shiqmona, where there had been a thriving town with paved streets in the fifth century, a large subterranean storehouse has been uncovered containing scores of storage jars of various types.[29] Among the finds were two Phoenician inscriptions on a jar handle dealing with the delivery of wine from a settlement known as Gat Karmel.[30] Further south, at Ashkelon, a series of warehouses have been uncovered, including a large building "with at least six magazines, each with about 30 sq m of storage space on the ground floor."[31]

In site after site along the coast, then, there are signs of an expanding and vibrant mercantile economy. Yet, there are signs of commerce inland, as well. Foreign coins and imported wares are common among the Persian period artifacts found everywhere in Palestine, notably in the fifth and fourth centuries, indicating that in this period international trade penetrated deep into the hinterland of the ports.[32] Storage jars designed for the transportation of goods, which had hitherto tended to be concentrated along the coast and have been found underwater, have also been uncovered at several inland sites, suggesting that agrarian products from inland were being exported.[33] Evidence of commercial agriculture has been found at Tell el-Hesi in the foothills of Judah,

---

[25] *The New Encyclopedia of Archaeological Excavations in the Holy Land* (NEAHL) III, (eds.) E. Stern et al., Jerusalem: 1993, 1002–3.
[26] Ibid., I, 361. [27] Ibid., I, 9. [28] Ibid., III, 1038–9. [29] Ibid., IV, 1375–6.
[30] F. M. Cross, "*Jar Inscriptions from Shiqmona,*" *Israel Exploration Journal (IEJ)* 18 (1968), 226–33.
[31] NEAHL I, 108. [32] Stern, *Material Culture*, 137–57.
[33] K. Hoglund, "The Achaemenid Context," in: P. R. Davies (ed.), *Second Temple Studies: I, Persian Period*, JSOT.S 117, Sheffield: JSOT Press, 1991, 60–1.

where a series of pits used for storage of grain have been uncovered, in
addition to a significant number of amphorae and jars designed for the
transportation of goods. Here again the large assemblage of imported
pottery bears witness to significant commercial activity in the Persian
period.[34]

The evidence points to an expanding monetary and commercial
economy in Achaemenid Palestine, as also elsewhere in the empire.
While the mainstay of the economy in Yehud was still agrarian, it is
also clear that agriculture was privatized and largely for profit.
Collection and distribution centers were established everywhere. With
the rise of commerce, cities took on new importance. Jerusalem in the
fifth century was a thriving cosmopolitan marketplace where the
Judeans, even on the Sabbath day, worked in the wine-presses, brought
in heaps of grain, loaded the animals with goods, and hawked their
agricultural products and sold food, while Tyrian residents brought fish
and all kinds of merchandise (Neh. 13:15–16). Competition from the
gentiles living in the city probably prompted the Jews to disregard the
Sabbath injunction. Indeed, when Nehemiah ordered the city gates to be
closed for Sabbath, "traders and the sellers of all kinds of merchandise"
camped outside the city to wait for the market to open (Neh. 13:20).
That was the kind of competitive commercial atmosphere that existed in
fifth-century Jerusalem. The world of Ecclesiastes presumes such a lively
and competitive economic environment. For Kohelet, the silencing of
the mill, perhaps meaning the commercial mills, and the closing of the
doors leading to the street-bazaar was an ominous sign of the end of the
world, the human existence (12:4).[35] Certainly, an urban audience is
presumed in the book. For the author and his audience, it was axiomatic
that only the fool would not know the way to the city (10:15).

Opportunities and risks

The Persians instituted an elaborate system of property grants under
which rights over various properties were given to favored individuals,
to military personnel, or to temple communities. Most generous were
the royal grants that were given outright to relatives and friends of the

---

[34] W. J. Bennett and J. A. Blakely, *Tell el-Hesi: The Persian Period* [Stratum V] III,
ASOR Excavation Reports, Winona Lake: 1989, 342–6.
[35] C.-L. Seow, "Qohelet's Eschatological Poem," *JBL* 118 (1999), 216–18.

crown. One gathers from the Persepolis Fortification Texts that recipients of such royal grants had the responsibility for collecting the taxes from their domains, but the grant meant that they were also entitled to retain a sizable portion of the revenues.[36] The grantees sometimes further divided grant portions of their fiefs to those whom they favored, in return for annual taxes and military services as needed. Such grants included movable and/or immovable property, that is, the land and all the assets that go with it.

One recipient of a royal grant was Arsames, the satrap of Egypt, who, according to Greek and cuneiform sources, was a wealthy landlord possessing assets throughout the empire. Certainly he also owned estates in his satrapy of Egypt, some of which he gave to those retainers whom he favored. In a letter dated to the end of the fifth century, one learns that a grant had been given to a certain Egyptian named Aḥḥapi, an administrator of Arsames' estates in Egypt.[37] The grant is said to have been given (*yhb*) by the king and by Arsames, meaning that it was given by Arsames from a part of his own royal grant. When Aḥḥapi died, he was succeeded in his position by his son, Psamshek, who requested that the grant be transferred to him. So Arsames, who was in Babylon at that time, sent this letter to his representative in Egypt, giving Psamshek the legal authority (*šlyṭ*) to assume the grant (*lmnš' dšn'*): "Let Psamshek his son be authorized to take up the grant there in Egypt".[38] From this text it is clear that a grant was not automatically transferable to one's heirs. The heir had to be given the legal right of proprietorship (*šlyṭ*).[39]

The Persian system of royal grants provides a backdrop against which to interpret Ecclesiastes 5:17–18. Kohelet affirms that it is appropriate to enjoy the fruit of one's toil, for God has authorized one to do so:

Here is what I have observed is good: that it is appropriate [for people] to eat, drink, and to enjoy good in all their toil that they toil under the sun, during the few days of their lives, which God has given them, for this is their portion. Indeed to all people God has given wealth and assets, and he has authorized

---

[36] Stolper, *Entrepreneurs and Empire*, 53.   [37] *TAD* I, 6.4.   [38] Ibid., 6.4.4.
[39] For similar issues pertaining to the proprietary rights to a priestly office with rights over the income and assets that came with the office, see Porten, Bezalel et al. (eds.), *The Elephantine Papyri in English: Three Millennia of Cross-Cultural Continuity and Change*, Leiden/New York/Cologne: 1996, 351–5. The text, written in Demotic, dates to the year 460 BCE.

them to partake of them, to take up their portion, and to have pleasure in their toil. This is the grant of God.

Several terms in this passage echo the language of the royal grant: *ntn* "give," *šlṭ* "to have right," *nś'* "to take up," *mattat* "grant."[40] Kohelet presents life's possibilities in terms of such grants. The deity has granted humanity certain gifts, including wealth and various assets, and the recipients of this favor are authorized to exercise proprietorship (*hišlīṭ*) over this divine grant (*mattat hā'ĕlōhîm*).

The divine sovereign may be just as arbitrary as the Persian ruler who issues royal grants, however. Kohelet speaks of the case of someone who somehow is not permitted to enjoy the grant:

There is a person to whom God gives wealth, assets, and plenty, so that there is nothing lacking of all that is desired, yet God does not authorize that one to partake of them, but rather, a stranger consumes it. (Eccles. 6:2)

There was a considerable amount of arbitrariness in the Persian system of royal grants. The Great King gave grants to his relatives, friends, and favorite subordinates, but others were left out. The king's powerful relatives and allies who received the large grants also parceled out their assets to their friends and favorites, apparently with the same arbitrariness. It must have appeared to the "have-nots" that what one receives was entirely dependent on the whim of the giver. There were fortunate people who fared extremely well, and there were the unfortunate ones who received little or nothing. Life is like that to Kohelet: people receive whatever portion the divine sovereign chooses to give. So Kohelet speaks of those who are favored by God and those who are not so fortunate (2:24–26; 7:26). The former are lucky enough to be favored with the good life; the latter are just unlucky people who will miss the mark. The former are given wisdom, knowledge, and joy, but the latter are given the task of collecting and gathering for others to enjoy. God is seen here to be like the human sovereign, the Great King of the empire, or the powerful satrap, who arbitrarily gives grants to favorite friends and courtiers, while others are left out. Divine grants, like royal grants, created a distinction between the "haves" and "have-nots" – those who could enjoy and those who could not.

---

[40] Szubin and Porten, *Royal Grants in Egypt*, 47.

Besides the royal grants given by the king to family, friends, and other favorites, there were also grants given to various people on condition of military service and/or payment of an annual tax. The most important evidence for such grants comes from various collections of neo-Babylonian texts, notably from the archive of the Murashu business house in Nippur.[41] The lands so acquired were initially not alienable, but in time the proprietors were permitted to sublet or pawn their lands. These fiefs were sometimes shared by a number of co-proprietors, with the rights of proprietorship being transferable in each case by inheritance. And through the division of inheritances, the average size of properties available for economic exploitation became smaller and smaller, thus reducing the efficiency of the lots, while encouraging even the lowliest people in society to harbor hopes that they, too, might have a chance to improve their lot. To meet the demand for taxes paid in silver, fiefs were often converted into cash-producing rental properties. In all cases, taxes and services remained obligatory. The tenant farmers and workers paid their dues to the smallholders whose property they rented, and the smallholders in turn paid those above them, and so forth. Through this elaborate system of land grant, then, the Persian rulers were able to control and exploit the provinces.

The multi-level economic exploitation in fifth-century Palestine is partly attested by Nehemiah: "the former governors who were before me laid heavy burdens upon the people, and took from them food and wine, besides forty shekels of silver." Even their retainers "exercised proprietorship [šālĕṭû] over the people" (Neh. 5:15). Taxes were extracted at several levels: local, regional, provincial, satrapial, and imperial. And there were taxes of various kinds, three of which are mentioned in the book of Ezra (4:13, 20; 7:24). This system caused the stratification of society, as a number of dependent classes were created.

There were ample opportunities for people to ascend the financial pyramid. Neo-Babylonian documents from the period show that there were slaves who borrowed substantial sums of money or otherwise accumulated enough wealth to buy their own slaves, trade independently, participate in all kinds of business ventures, hold various assets,

---

[41] Stolper, *Entrepreneurs and Empire*, 24–7.

rent property, and even acquire expensive property.[42] Slaves could borrow money for investment. Some bought or leased property, which could then be rented out or subleased. Others leased storehouses. Still others owned or leased workshops, farms, orchards, and livestock. It was possible, in fact, for slaves to become quite rich. From the Murashu archive, for instance, one learns of a certain Ribat, son of Bel-eriba, a slave of Rimut-Ninurta of the business firm of Murashu and Sons. Ribat paid taxes for an office that he held, loaned large sums of money and amounts of grain and dates to various individuals (including Rimut-Ninurta!), leased out several workers and 416 head of sheep and goats in the space of a single day, rented land to others, leased access to a canal with other assets that went with it, and served as a guarantor for various debtors. Ribat had become a rich entrepreneur. In one text, one learns that Ribat, together with Raḥim, another slave of Rimut-Ninurta, subleased a piece of land for three years, together with live-stock, equipment, and seed. Thus, Rimut-Ninurta, who had the land rented or mortgaged to him, subleased it to his slaves, who later sub-subleased part of that land, together with some livestock, equipment, and seed, to their own slaves.[43]

Certainly the opportunities were there during the Achaemenid period for people to climb the ladder of success, but they were also easily exploited. In a tantalizing but textually problematic passage, Kohelet seems to allude both to the economic exploitation and the opportunities in such a society:

If you see the oppression of the poor and the violation of justice and right in the province, do not be surprised over the matter – for an arrogant one is above an arrogant one, [and] arrogant ones have watched over them all. (Eccles. 5:7–8)

The latter part of the passage has traditionally been interpreted to be a reference to the imperial bureaucracy. For that interpretation to work, however, the word *gābôah* (literally "high one") must be taken to mean "a high official," a meaning it does not have anywhere in Hebrew. Moreover, the text is about economic exploitation and personal ambi-tion. It seems likely, therefore, that it is referring not to government

---

[42] M. A. Dandamaev, *Slavery in Babylonia: From Nabopolassar to Alexander the Great (626–331 B.C.)*, rev. edn. trans. V. A. Powell, DeKalb: 1984 (Russian original, 1974), 320–97.

[43] See Stolper, *Entrepreneurs and Empire*, 148–9.

bureaucrats, but to ambitious people, who are climbing the socio-economic ladder. The arrogant ones keep ascending, but no matter how high they climb, there are always people higher up than they, who look down on them. The text goes on to speak of the insatiability of the greedy: "the one who loves money will not be satisfied with money, and whoever loves abundance will not be satisfied with yield" (5:10). These people keep consuming more and more, but they never seem to have enough. Elsewhere in the book, Kohelet says it is envy that drives people to vain pursuits (4:4). For them, Kohelet counsels that it is better to have the smallest amount of anything with rest than to have twice as much with "toil and pursuit of wind" (4:6). The author addresses those whose "eyes are not satisfied with wealth," who toil and toil even though they have neither descendants nor kinfolks with whom to share their wealth (4:7–8). The fear of poverty and the possibility of wealth prompted people to be excessively driven and to be ever discontented with what they had.[44] So they were unable to enjoy their present lot, because they were trying to move ahead and climb up the socio-economic ladder. Kohelet's repeated exhortation, however, is to enjoy what is before one's eyes and partake of the fruit of one's toil (2:24; 3:12–13, 22; 5:17–18; 6:6; 7:14; 8:15; 11:7–9). For him, the grant that one receives from God is meant to be enjoyed. Indeed, enjoyment itself is a grant from God (3:13; 5:18). It is humanity's portion.

Kohelet's audience does not seem secure with what they have. Rather, they are constantly toiling to acquire more and more, and they are worried about the possibility of losing what they have. They do not appear to be among the wealthiest in their society. They are paranoid about disparaging remarks that their subordinates may be making about them (7:21). At the same time, they themselves are making disparaging remarks about their bosses, the rich and powerful (10:20). They are people who are socially and economically in the middle, having subordinates beneath them but also superiors in wealth and power. Kohelet distinguishes them from the nobles, the princes, and

---

[44] A fifth-century Demotic text from Egypt indicates the same environment: "Wealth was given to you in order that you [might] reveal your character." See Porten et al., *Elephantine Papyri in English*, Text C26, line 9 (S. 341). The same sentiment is echoed in Papyrus Insinger, col. 15, line 19: "money is the snare the god has placed on the earth for the impious man so that he should worry daily," trans. M. Lichtheim, *Ancient Egyptian Literature III: The Late Period*, Berkeley: 1980, 197.

the rich (10:16–20), but he never implies that they are poor. The recipients of Kohelet's instructions are commoners – the small smallholders, homesteaders, and people of the middle classes. They are susceptible to the various occupational hazards that the ordinary workers face: they are perfumers whose precious products could be contaminated by a single dead fly (10:1), hunters who dig pits to trap animals, farmers who remove stones from old fences in order to build new ones, wood-cutters and quarry workers (10:8–10). They are ordinary citizens facing the vagaries of a rapidly changing social world. They are people of the middle classes who are trying to scale the social pyramid without sliding down into poverty. They are people caught between the impulse to protect and conserve whatever they have (5:12–16; 11:1–2) and the desire to get rich (4:4–6). They are a people caught between the opportunities and risks of a volatile economy.

Among the various social classes mentioned in the book are the *šallīṭīm*. Most commentators have assumed that these *šallīṭīm* were political figures of some sort and, hence, the word is usually translated as "rulers," "tyrants," "governors," or the like.[45] But the term *šallīṭh* probably refers to wealthy land barons of the time, people who have been given the right of disposal over movable and immovable property. A *šallīṭ* is a proprietor – someone who has the right over property (7:19; 8:9). This meaning is evident in various texts from the Persian period.[46] The point that Kohelet makes is that proprietors may be rich and powerful, but no one has proprietorship over the *rûaḥ*, "life-breath." No one can detain it.[47] No one owns the day of death. When the time comes for one to fight the battle with Death, no one can hire a substitute. No one can buy life. Thus, this passage is a social commentary. Kohelet refers to the terrible things done in his generation, a time when people "exercise proprietorship" (*šlṭ*) over one another (8:9).

---

[45] The verb *šlṭ* is "to have right (of disposal)," and occurs in Ecclesiastes in reference to the disposal of inheritance and assets (2:19; 5:18; 6:2). See J. Greenfield, "Two Biblical Passages in the Light of Their Near Eastern Background – Ezekiel 16:30 and Malachi 3:17," *Eretz Israel* (*EI*) 16 (1982), 56–61. The fact that there could be a plurality of *šallīṭīm* in a single city (7:19) indicates that the term could not be referring to local rulers.

[46] See *TAD* II, 2.3.9–10; *TAD* II, 2.6.17–22; *UET* 4, 109.

[47] Hebrew *klʾ* corresponds to Akkadian *kalû*, the verb used in the cuneiform documents for the detention of debtors who default on their payments.

The economy provided opportunities for the ambitious. Poorer people could begin by borrowing, or by hiring themselves out to acquire capital, as Tirakam the home-born slave did. They could begin with smaller lots or with rental property. Or they could pool their capital with others in various joint ventures. There are many examples of joint ventures in Akkadian texts from the same period.

Kohelet complains of injustices being done (*hāʿăšūqîm ʿăšer naʿăśîm*) and he observes that those who have been treated unjustly have no one on their side (4:1–3). The problem seems to have been the competitive culture, in which people are driven by envy to strive for success and they do not seem to be satisfied (4:4–8). In that environment the poor could not count on the legal system to protect them (3:16), undoubtedly because of corruption in the courts. Elsewhere, Kohelet speaks of oppression (*ʿšq*) of the poor and the taking away of justice in the province (*mdynh*), while the arrogant protect one another (5:7–8). There, again, the problem is that people are driven by greed and ambition, and the evil of their greed is portrayed in terms reminiscent of the gaping mouth of personified Death, attempting to swallow up the whole cosmos (6:7–9). In 7:7, Kohelet again alludes to injustice (*ʿšq*) and the taking of a bribe (*mtnh*). The impression one gets is that there are people who are willing to do anything in order to get ahead in that competitive economic environment, and the rich are somehow circumventing the law at the expense of others. Moreover, even though it was possible to appeal the decision of a lower court, a drawn-out legal process would certainly have favored the rich. Indeed, according to Kohelet, the slow legal process encouraged people to act wickedly: "Since sentence for evil work is not executed quickly, people dare to do evil; an offender does the evil of hundreds but endures" (8:11–12a).[48] In context, it seems likely that the author has in mind the rich proprietors who seem to think that they can exercise their power at will (8:7–9).

The ordinary citizen was at the mercy of the rich and powerful proprietors, the provincial judges, and other officials. They had also to be wary of the government, with its host of spies. Hence, Kohelet warns his audience to watch what they say: "Even in your intimacy do not disparage a king, nor in the bedroom disparage a rich person, for a bird

---

[48] Reading *rā' me'ōt* in verse 12a, instead of *rā' me'at* in MT.

of the sky may carry the utterance and a winged-creature may report any matter" (10:20).[49]

Kohelet taught at a time when the average citizen felt vulnerable and powerless before the rich and the political elite. So when the author speaks of humanity's helplessness before the whim of the sovereign deity, he draws on the social experiences of his audience: "Whatever happens has already been designated; the course of human beings is known, and they cannot dispute with the one who is stronger than they" (6:10).[50]

The economy in the Persian period was volatile. With the high interest rates, the smallholder became extremely vulnerable. Those who were unable to pay their debts were seized and put in debtors' prison, known in Egyptian Aramaic as *byt 'sryn*. One example of such an imprisonment is found in fragmentary texts from North Saqqara that tell of prisoners being registered and put to work.[51] The Aramaic term for prison here is comparable to Hebrew *bêt 'ăsûrîm* in Ecclesiastes 4:14, a text contrasting a poor but wise individual with an old but stupid king. The former went forth from the *bêt 'ăsûrîm* to become king, while the latter was born a king but became poor. Kohelet does not indicate in this case that the situation is something that he has observed (contrast 10:5), so one cannot be sure if the instruction here is simply a literary *topos* or if it reflects a historical occurrence as well. If it reflects Achaemenid realities, one should think of the deposed king not in terms of the Great King of the Achaemenid line, but of a local "king" who has fallen out of favor. Like other subjects of the "Lord of Kings" in Susa, local rulers may also be recipients of royal grants, as we know Eshmunazor of Sidon was in the fifth century BCE.[52]

It was an unreliable world in which Kohelet and his audience lived, for those who were rich and powerful could suddenly find themselves impoverished, while those who were poor might suddenly come into great wealth and prestige. Elsewhere in the book, Kohelet describes a world turned upside down:

---

[49] The instruction echoes a passage in the Aramaic *Proverbs of Ahiqar*. See *TAD* III, 1.1.80–2.

[50] See Seow, *Ecclesiastes*, 230–3.

[51] J. B. Segal, *Aramaic Texts from North Saqqâra*, London: 1983, 3.1 (S. 15f.); 8.10 (S. 23); 50.9 (S. 69).

[52] *KAI* 14.18–19.

There is an evil that I have observed under the sun, a veritable mistake stemming from the proprietor. The simpleton is set in great heights, but the rich abide in low estate. I have seen slaves on horses, but princes walk on foot like slaves. (Eccles. 10:5–7)

This description of a topsy-turvy world is commonly identified as another wisdom *topos*, and that is, indeed, correct. The presence of a literary *topos* does not mean, however, that it has nothing to do with historical context; sometimes a *topos* is employed precisely because it is poignant and timely. This is, after all, reported as something the author observed. The allusion to the downfall of a certain "proprietor," in fact, has a certain historical ring to it. Perhaps the author has in mind a wealthy individual who has lost everything because of an inadvertent error (see 5:12–14). In any case, he goes beyond the particular case to reflect on an unpredictable world where events seem to spin out of control and social order is completely disrupted. Individuals are vulnerable to all kinds of dangers in the rapidly changing economic world, it seems. At a macro-level, there are social, economic, and political forces at work that are beyond the control of individuals (10:5–7). At a micro-level, professionals face everyday occupational hazards: the hunter who digs a pit to trap animals is liable to fall into one of such pits, the farmer who removes rocks from fences is vulnerable to snakes that lurk in the nooks and crannies, one who quarries stones is susceptible to certain industrial accidents, as is the one who splits wood (10:8–9). There is also the perfumer, whose precious product may be ruined by the presence of a single fly (10:1). There are risks everywhere and at every level in the new economic world.

Kohelet's characterization of this world is not a figment of his imagination. It is drawn from the wisdom tradition, but it is not merely rhetoric. His use of the tradition reflects the volatile economy of his time. Here, again, the Murashu archive is a valuable resource. Stolper points to an oddity in the archive: in the first year of the reign of Darius II Ochus (423–404 BCE), the number of texts dealing with mortgages rose by over 300 percent.[53] The number of lands pawned as well as the number of loans rose dramatically. One may observe, too, that a large number of texts mentioning "prison" are dated to the years 423–422 BCE. It appears that something was happening in that period that

---

[53] Stolper, *Entrepreneurs and Empire*, 104–24.

suddenly caused people to lose their holdings. Those who once possessed property had to give it up and many found themselves imprisoned for debt or enslaved. In Stolper's reconstruction, the phenomenon was a direct result of political realities attendant upon the accession of Darius II Ochus, who had to fend off several contenders to the throne. To Stolper, the increased indebtedness in Babylonia is evidence that the financial resources of the rivals and their clients were exhausted in the political battles that took place as Darius came to power. The Murashu archive may support Stolper's claim in part, but the Murashu business house, specializing in certain types of leases, bears only partial testimony to the socio-economic picture. One wonders if some people were not losing their fiefs and other assets because they happened to be on the wrong side of the struggle. Certainly we expect some of the royal grants to have been revoked for political reasons, with consequences for all the dependants of the former grantees and their tenants. It may be noted that there is no comparable sharp increase in the number of mortgages and debts in the satrapy of Egypt from the same period, as there was in Babylonia. That is perhaps no coincidence, since Arsames, the satrap of Egypt and presumably the recipient of significant royal grants in the satrapy, was an ally of Darius II. By the same token, one may observe that Artarios, the satrap of Babylonia, supported Sekyndianos, a brother and rival of Darius. Whatever the explanation, it seems clear that land tenure and its privileges were somehow susceptible to the unpredictable wind of political change. The already volatile economy was made even more volatile by the fortunes of the various levels of proprietors who issued the grants. Given such uncertainties, it is no wonder that we find in the book a concern with ephemerality. Nothing seems permanent. Nothing seems reliable in such a world. Even those who have their grants given to them could not count on having their assets forever.

Kohelet speaks of the person who was so afraid of losing his wealth that he hoarded it:[54]

There is a sickening tragedy that I have observed under the sun: wealth was hoarded by one who possessed it, to his own hurt. That is, that wealth disappeared in a terrible venture. Then he sired a son, but there was nothing in his possession. Just as he came forth from the womb of his mother, so he

---

[54] Compare the numerous hoards found in Palestine in the late fifth and early fourth centuries BCE.

will return naked, going as he came. And he will carry away nothing for his toil that he may bring in his hand. (Eccles. 5:13–14)

We do not know what that terrible business was that caused the man to lose all his wealth. The point is that the man did not enjoy his wealth while he was able to. Somehow he had made a bad financial decision and, in consequence, lost everything for which he had toiled. Whatever Kohelet's intent in telling this story, it illustrates the volatility of the economy that his audience knew. They were cognizant of the fact that what they had one day might be gone the next.

Elsewhere in the book, Kohelet urges people not to be too tight-fisted with their money. People should take the risk to be generous, even though tragedies – and surely he includes economic tragedies – may happen in the future. They should take a chance and throw away a good deed, as it were:

Release your bread upon the waters,
after many days you will find it.
Give a portion to seven, or even eight
you do not know what misfortune may come about. (Eccles. 11:1–2)

This text goes on to note that people cannot watch for the perfect conditions. The farmer who watches the wind will never sow, those who watch the clouds will not harvest. Kohelet urges spontaneity instead: sow at any time (11:6). Or, as the Aramaic *Proverbs of Ahiqar* has it, "Harvest any harvest and do any work. Then you will eat and be satisfied and give to your children."[55] Both Ecclesiastes and the Aramaic *Proverbs of Ahiqar* must be read in the light of the volatility of the economy in the last one hundred and eighty years of the Achaemenids, a time of great economic opportunities and equally great risks.

In such a world of tremendous opportunities and risks, it is easy to understand how Kohelet's audience could never feel secure with what they had. They strove for success out of envy (4:4), hoarded out of a sense of insecurity (5:12), and toiled out of concern about their own financial well-being and the security of their descendants (2:18–23) or simply out of habit, even when they have no one with whom to share the fruit of their labor (4:7). Slaves were able to borrow substantial sums of money or otherwise accumulated enough wealth to buy their own slaves and

---

[55] *TAD* III, 1.1.11.2.7.

participate in all kinds of business ventures. Some were able not only to break out of poverty, but even to become wealthy, as in the case of Ribat and some of his friends. No doubt such rags-to-riches stories must have spurred people to yearn and strive for success. The new monetary economy created the impression of equal opportunity for wealth for one and all; it fostered a sense that people who were born poor need not always remain so. As the inscriptions amply attest, there were various possibilities of employment, tenant farming, small-capital businesses, joint ventures, silent partnerships, and so forth. It was a world in which there was, it seems, hope of success for any who would strive hard enough.

The free market that Kohelet observes is an unpredictable arena, however. It was a time for heady optimism about hitherto unimaginable opportunities. Yet, that optimism was offset by socio-political and economic realities on the ground, for there were no fail-safe rules that worked every time. It was a perplexing new world of rapid political, social, and economic innovations, many of which were initiated and determined in seats of power that the ordinary citizens of the vast empire could hardly comprehend.

The discoveries at a cave in Wadi Dâliyeh (halfway between Samaria and Jericho) provide us with an unforgettable vignette of the late Persian period. Archaeologists have uncovered in that cave the skeletons of some two hundred men, women and children, along with scores of stamp impressions (the ancient equivalent of credit card imprints!), exquisite gold signet rings (the equivalent of credit cards), personal jewelry, and an assemblage of coins that must have been part of a much larger hoard. There were also found the now famous "Samaria Papyri," all dating to the final decades of the Persian period, all of which are legal and administrative documents recording various economic transactions. These are the remains of a group of Samarian *šallīṭīm* (proprietors) who were fleeing Alexander's army and who were eventually hunted down and massacred. These proprietors brought their families and all their money, jewelry, and title deeds to various assets. They brought all the legal evidence that they were *šallīṭīm* over these assets. And there, in the cave, they perished with all their wealth – a veritable testimony to the truth of what Kohelet taught in their generation or a little before: no one is a proprietor over death and no one can send a substitute to that decisive "battle." Wealth is to be enjoyed in the present and people cannot bring their wealth with them when they die. Indeed, "everything is vanity."

8 The development of monetary systems in Palestine during the Achaemenid and Hellenistic Eras

ULRICH HÜBNER

The oldest coins in Palestine

Coins (Hebr. and Aram. *ṭbʾ*, *ṭbʾʾ*, *ṭbyʾ*; Phon. ṭbʾ, Gr. νόμισμα, Vulg. *moneta, nummus*) are a specific type of money (Hebr. *ksp*; Gr. χρῆμα; Vulg. *pecunia*). They appear mostly as round, standardized pieces of metal, often containing an amount of precious metal guaranteed (nominally or factually) by a ruler, a state, a tribe, or a city. This value is certified by their symbol – an image or an inscription (see Matt. 22:20 et seq.; Mark 12:16; Luke 20:24 ʾεικών and ʾεπιγραφή; Vulg. *imago* and *suprascriptio/inscriptio*). At the beginning of monetary developments in Palestine, as elsewhere, we find the use of pre-monetary forms of payment such as silver fragments, pieces of jewelry, metal bars, and others.[1] The lentil-shaped silver discs bearing the name of the ruler Barrākib found in Sam'al (Zincirli) in northern Syria are an example of pre-monetary objects.[2] They are 8.4–8.7cm in diameter, weighed about 440–497g, and date to the second half of the eighth century BCE. Interestingly, the widely known Semitic word *kkr, kikkār* can refer to a "round loaf of bread," or a "round disc made of lead, silver, or gold."

In the fourth century BCE, Aristotle provided a historical summary of comparable monetary developments: "When trading, it was agreed

---

[1] U. Hübner, "Die Münzprägungen Palästinas in alttestamentlicher Zeit," *Trumah* 4 (1994): 119–45; Hübner, "Münze," *Neues Bibel-Lexicon* 2 (1995): 850–3; Hübner, "Maße, Gewichte und Münzen in der Bibel," *Lexikon für Theologie und Kirche* 6 (1997): 1460–2; Hübner et al., "Numismatik," *Religion in Geschichte und Gegenwart* 6 (2003): 423–34.

[2] F. von Luschan, *Die Kleinfunde von Sendschirli*, ed. W. Andrae, Berlin: de Gruyter, 1943, 119–21, Abb. 170–1, Taf. 58 t-v; cf. the seal Taf. 38b bzw; J. Tropper, *Die Inschriften von Zincirli*, Abhandlungen zur Literatur Alt-Syrien-Palästinas 6, Münster: Ugarit-Verlag, 1993, 151–2. Cf. W. B. Henning, "The 'Coin' with Cuneiform Inscription," *Numismatic Chronicle 6th Series* 16 (1996): 327–8; P. Hulin, "An Inscribed Silver Piece of Darius," *Orientalia Loveniensia Periodica* 3 (1972): 121–4.

upon to receive and to give an object that proved useful in itself as well as manageable in daily affairs, such as iron or silver ... In the end, this object was stamped with a symbol so it would no longer have to be weighed; the stamp was seen as the sign of its value."[3]

In the fifth century BCE, Herodot[4] described the casting of metal bars[5] in clay molds, a practice acquired from Mesopotamia. "This is how the King Darius I, 522–486 BCE governs the contributions to his treasury: the metal is melted down and cast into vessels of clay. Once a vessel is filled, the clay is removed and an appropriate piece is cut from the whole each time money (χρήματα) is needed."[6] According to some literary sources, the first coins (made of electrum) originated primarily in Lydia in the seventh century BCE. This claim was already disputed in antiquity.[7] As the earliest evidence for coins, archaeological sources point to the Artemision in Ephesos; the precise dating and function of the coins found here is a matter of heated discussions.[8] In the sixth century, coins – especially silver coins – became dominant in the most important Greek cities. From there they spread across the ancient Near East. The introduction of coins, however, was not a revolutionary innovation, but rather, the next step in the development and improvement of existing pre-monetary systems. On the whole, the economy moved towards a monetary system based solely on silver coins.

[3] Aristotle, *Politeia* 1,9,1257a–b.   [4] Herodotus, *Hist.* 3,96.

[5] E. Lipiński, "Les temples neo-assyriens et les origins da monnayage," in: *State and Temple Economy in the Ancient Near East II*, Orientalia Lovaniensia Analecta 6, ed. Lipiński, Leuven: Peeters, 1979, 565–88; A. C. V. M. Bongenaar, "Money in the Neo-Babylonian Institutions," in *Trade and Finance in Ancient Mesopotamia*, Uitgaven van het Nederlands Historich-Archaeologisch Instituut te Istanbul 84, ed. J. G. Derksen, Leiden: Netherlands Instituut vor het Nabije Oosten, 1999, 159–204; K. Radner, "Money in the Neo-Assyrian Period," in: *Trade and Finance in Ancient Mesopotamia*, 127–57; E. Haslauer, "Edelmetall als Zahlungsmittel im alten Ägypten: Bemerkungen zu zwei Ringbarren aus Silber und zu Goldringen." *40 Jahre Institut für Numismatik und Geldgeschichte der Universität Wien 1965–2005, Numismatische Zeitschrift 113–114*, Vienna: Osterreichische Numismatische Gesellschaft, 2005, 37–46.

[6] Cut bars, e.g. in the early Achaemenid hoard from Ugarit: R. A. Stucky, *Ras Shamra – Leukos Limen*, Bibliothèque Historique et Archéologique 110, Paris: P. Geuthner, 1983, 28–43.

[7] Alkaios, *frag.* 69; Xenophanes, *frag.* 4; Herodotus, *Hist.* 1,94; cf. Pollux, *Onom.* 9,83; Strabo, *Geogr.* 8,358.376.

[8] N. Cahill and J. H. Kroll, "New Archaic Coin Finds at Sardis," *American Journal of Archaeology* 109 (2005): 589–617; A. Bammer and U. Muss, *Das Artemision von Ephesos*, Mainz: Zabern, 1996, 89–90, Abb. 115.

The earliest coins found in Palestine are of Greek origin: archaic and early classical coinage of the late sixth and early fifth centuries BCE, especially from Athens, Kos, Thasos, Corinth, Stagira, Aigina, Milet, Chios, and Phokaia, including also Lycian coins. The archaic and classical coins found in Palestine (all, without exception, silver coins in a country without any silver mines) were all found in major centers in southern and northern Palestine. It is noteworthy that hardly any hoards of coins from the sixth and fifth centuries BCE were found in ancient Palestinian soil. This might indicate a comparatively low circulation of Greek coinage in Palestine during this time due to the low economic potential of the region; it is hardly a mere coincidence.

The *Dar(e)ikosi*, the Persian gold coin weighing 8.4g. and the state currency of the Achaemenid Empire, was hardly in circulation in Palestine at all.[9] Until now, only one Achaemenid coin (or, rather, an imitation of an Achaemenid coin) has been found in Palestine: a double-Dareikos (16g.) from Samaria that imitates the equivalent coins of Darius III (336–331 BCE) and was minted under the rule of the satrap Mazaios shortly after 331 BCE in Babylon.[10]

Achaemenid σίγλοι/σίκλοι, coinage in silver, were also not found in Palestine in any significant number.[11] The numerous occurrences of σίκλοι in the Septuagint always refer to the weight (or the value) of a *šql*.

---

[9] See the anachronistic passage in Josephus, ant. 3,8.10 §220.

[10] F. Zayadine and Samaria-Sebaste, "Clearance and Excavations," *Annual of the Department of Antiquities of Jordan* 12–13 (1967–1968): 78, Pl. 51b; W. J. Fulco and F. Zayadine, *Annual of the Department of Antiquities of Jordan* 25 (1981): 197–225, esp. 199–202, No. 2, Pl. 50:1; A. S. Arif, *A Treasury of Classical and Islamic Coins: The Collection of Amman Museum*, London: Foster & Jagg, 1986, 22 (J.11235). For finding sites of *dareikoi* see e.g., M. Thomason et al., *An Inventory of Greek Coin Hoards*, New York: Augustin, 1973, Nos. 1278, 1654, 1656, 1822. For the coins of Mazaios, see L. Mildenberg, "Notes on the Coin Issues of Mazday," in: *Vestigia Leonis Studien zur aniken Numismatik Israels: Palästinas und der östlichen Mittelmeerwelt*, Novum Testamentum et Orbis Antiquus 36, eds. U. Hübner and E. A. Knauf, Fribourg; Göttingen: Vandenhoeck and Ruprecht, 1998, 43–53; P. Bordreuil, "Une nouvelle monnaie babylonienne de Mazday," in: *Collecteana Orientalia Historie, arts de l'espace et industries de la terre: Études offertes en homage à A. Spycket*, Civilisations du Proche-Orient I, 3, eds. H. Gasche and B. Hrouda, Neuchâtel; Paris: Recherches et Publications, 1996, 27–30; J. Elayi and A. G. Elayi, "Le monnayage sidonien de Mazday," *Transeuphratène* 27 (2004): 155–62.

[11] F. M. Cross, "Coins," in: *Discoveries in the Wâdī ed-Dâliyeh*, Annual of the American Schools of Oriental Research 41, eds. P. W. Lapp and N. L. Lapp, Cambridge, MA: Furst, 1974, 57–9, No. 2, Pl. 80:2. Coins from the environs of

The mention of '*drknym* or '*ardarkonīm* [< Gr. δαρ(ε)ικοί] in Ezra
8:27 (and, anachronistically, for the time of David in 1 Chr. 29:7) does
not necessarily refer to the coin of the same name (a dareikos), but may
merely signify its weight. The same is true for the Greek gold drachmas
(Gr. δραχμαί > Hebr. *drkm(w)nym* or *darkemōnīm*, sg. **darkmān* or
*darkemāh) mentioned in the list of returnees from Babylonian exile in
Ezra 2:69 and Nehemiah 7:7–20, which were hardly in circulation in
Palestine. In Ezra 2:69 and Nehemiah 7:7–20, these coins are mentioned
alongside high-quality textiles as especially valuable gifts to the temple.

The first coins in Achaemenid Palestine

The Phoenician coins of the fifth and fourth centuries BCE

Around the mid-fifth century BCE, coins were minted in the harbor and
trade centers along the Phoenician coast: in all likelihood, first in Byblos
and soon thereafter in Tyros, Sidon,[12] and Arados. All of this coinage
was markedly different from the coins originating in other cities. The
Sidonian coins preferred the image of a warship on the obverse side, the
Tyrian coin a dolphin or the hippocampus on the obverse side and
the Athenian owl with an Egyptian hooked staff and whip on the
other side. In addition to Greek coinage, the Sidonian, and especially
the Tyrianian, coins became the leading currencies in Palestine[13] and
played an important role far into the Roman era: "Wherever the Torah
talks of money, it refers to Tyrian money" (bBek 50b); in evidence from
the Roman period, such as from the Wādi al-Murabaʿāt and the Naḥal

Palestine, e.g. Thompson et al., *An Inventory of Greek Coin Hoards*, Nos. 1481–
1483. 1644 u.ö.

[12] J. Elayi and A. G. Elayi, *Le monnayage de la cite phénicienne de Sidon à l'époque
perse (V^e-VIe siècles avant J.-C.), I–II*, Suppl. à *Transeuphratène* 11, Paris:
Gabalda, 2004.

[13] For circulation, see J. Elayi and A. G. Elayi, *Trésors de monnaies phéniciennes et
circulation monétaire (V^e-VIe siècles avant J.-C.)*, Paris: Gabalda, 1993; see my
review in *Zeitschrift des Deutschen Palästina-Vereins III* (1995): 193–5; J. Elayi
and A. G. Elayi, "Nouveau trésors de monnaies phéniciennes (CH VIII),"
Transeuphratène II (1996): 95–114; J. Elayi and A. G. Elayi, "Nouveau trésors de
monnaies aradiennes, athéniennes et/ou pseudo-athéniennes," *Transeuphratène*
18 (1999): 75–85. Cf. e.g., R. S. Hanson, *Tyrian Influence in the Upper Galilee*,
Meiron Excavation Project 2, Cambridge, MA: American Schools of Oriental
Research, 1980; Y. Meshorer, "One Hundred Ninety Years of Tyrian Shekels,"
in: *Numismatik, Kunstgeschichte, Archäologie: Festschrift für L. Mildenberg*,
eds. A. Houghton et al., Wettern: Cultura Press, 1984, 171–9.

Ḥever, the currency is referred to as τυριος. In Persian times, the Phoenician mints all produced common silver coins, and not merely small change as was the case in Samaria and Judah. It is also likely that their output was considerably higher. In addition, the minting of bronze coinage started in the middle of the fourth century BCE but apparently only in small amounts.

The (Philisto-Arabian) coins from Gaza, Ashdod, and Ashkelon

The so-called Philisto-Arabian coins are among the oldest in Palestine. The mints were located in Gaza, Ashkelon, and Ashdod.[14] The minting privileges were conferred on these sites by the Achaemenid rulers. These coins were produced between circa 450/420 and 332 BCE. The Philisto-Arabian production took its lead from the Attic coinage standard, without imitating it exactly. The only coins minted were silver coins (putting aside the silver-plated bronze or copper coins), particularly the middle and smaller values; they all bore exclusively Semitic legends. The silver content was about 94 percent.

The images used are horse protomes, falcons, and sphinxes, as well as the heads of Bes, Janus, and Athena. The motive of the camel-rider in a šadād-saddle is reminiscent of later Arabian gods on horseback.

The production of Philisto-Arabian coinage was discontinued by Alexander the Great. Gaza was only re-established as a minting site under Ptolemy II (283–246 BCE) and Ashkelon under Ptolemy IV (221–205/4 BCE). Ashdod never again became a site of coin production.

The coins in the Achaemenid province of Shomron (Samaria)

In the Persian province of Shomron (Sāmerīna), coins were minted between circa 375/360 and 332 BCE.[15] Here, too, Alexander's

---

[14] See H. Gitler and O. Tal, *The Coinage of Philistia of the Fifth and Fourth Centuries BC: A Study of the Earliest Coins of Palestine*, Milan; New York: Edizioni Ennere – Amphora, 2006; L. Mildenberg, "Notes on the Coin Issues of Mazday," 1998, passim. H. Gitler, M. Ponting, and O. Tal, "Metallurgical Analysis of Southern Palestinian Coins of the Persian Period," *Israel Numismatic Research* 3 (2008): 13–27.

[15] Y. Meshorer, *Ancient Jewish Coinage, Vol I*, Dix Hills; New York: Amphora, 1982, 31–2, 98, 160; Y. Meshorer and S. Qedar, *The Coinage of Samaria in the Fourth Century BCE*, Jerusalem: Ben-Zvi, 1991; Y. Meshorer and S. Qedar, *Samarian Coinage*, Numismatic Studies and Research 9, Jerusalem: Graphit

campaign led to the cessation of production. In Samaria, coins were only minted once again during the reign of Herod the Great in 40 BCE.

The Shomron coins existed only in small values. Their silver content was almost 92 percent. The impressions were based on a local Phoenician–Attic coinage standard. Almost all known coins were passed through art dealers; only minute amounts were actually found during controlled excavations (e.g. *Horvat Rāqīt, Gan Sōrēq, "Nāblus"-Hort, Garizim, Rāmat ha-Nādiv*). Their iconography followed Cilician, Phoenician, and Athenian prototypes as well as motives from the ancient Near East, especially Persia. Some of them were imprinted with legends in Aramaic, Greek, or cuneiform[16] symbols; on a few, we find Paleo-Hebrew letters. The imprints display the provincial name Samaria (Hebr. *Šomrōn*; aram. *Šamrayn*) and the geographical or personal name *Mbyg*, as well as the name of various governors and the Satrap *Mazaios* (abbreviated *Mz* for *Mzdy/Mazday*). We also find the names of the gods Zeus and Heracles (?) in Greek. Zeus is the Greek term for Baal or Baalšamem, who was already known before the Persian era and whose image could also be used in connection with Yahweh. Iconographically, we also encounter Athena, Aphrodite (or Hera?), a god on a winged sun, the Persian great king, and a few chimeras. The iconographic repertoire of the Shomron coins was much larger and richer than that of the Yehud coins.

Aside from local coinage, Greek imports could also be counterstamped. A few Athenian tetradrachmas display an Š for Samaria. In addition to his own coinage, one of the provincial governors, Sanballa, also counter-stamped foreign coins such as the Athenian tetradrachma. On the same location in a small rectangle, the counter-stamp shows the two Aramean letters *SN* as an abbreviation of his name.

We find very few silver-plated copper or bronze coins among the Shomron coinage. It is not quite clear whether these coins are forgeries or official coinage. A comparison of various impressions shows that these silver-plated coins were imprinted with official stamps. It is hardly

---

Press, 1999; Y. Ronen, "Twenty Unrecorded Samarian Coins," *Israel Numismatic Research* 2 (2007): 29–33; H. Gitler and O. Tal, "Coinage with the Aramaic Legend Šhrw and other unrecorded Samarian Issues," *Schweizerische Numismatische Rundschau* 85 (2006): 47–60.

[16] W. Horowitz, T. Oshima, and S. Sanders, *Cuneiform and Canaan: Cuneiform Sources from the Land of Israel in Ancient Times*, Jerusalem: Old City Press, 2006, 116–17. Cf. J.-P. Fontantille and C. Lorber, "Silver Yehud Coins with Greek or Pseudo-Greek Inscriptions," *Israel Numismatic Research* 3 (2008): 45–9.

likely that they are private forgeries. We are also probably not dealing with cost-cutting measures by the state itself; rather, these coins may be the result of corrupt mint officials who used the excess silver for their own gain.

The coins in the Achaemenid province of Judah/Yehud

Since the second quarter of the fourth century, coins were also minted in the province of Judah – most of it small change (*minutiae*) in silver (i.e. hardly any drachmas, almost exclusively oboloi and their subdivisions, ø *c.*5–8 mm).[17] The mint was probably located in Jerusalem. Most of these coins are highly provincial. They are badly centered and inaccurately imprinted; the planchets are uneven and chapped. The specific weight of each coin, even those of the same nominal, varies to such an extent that the coins would have had to be weighed during each business transaction. Their silver content lay at about 95–96 percent. As in the case of the Shomron coins, the Yehud coins were hardly circulated outside of the province itself; they were only intended for the domestic market. They follow primarily Greek, Cilician, and (following Achaemenid rule) Ptolemaic prototypes. The iconographic repertoire is comparatively small.

The Yehud coinage is the youngest group of regional coins within Achaemenid Palestine. It is unclear why minting was started at all and at precisely this point in time in Jerusalem. Perhaps this fact was due to inter-regional pressure and reasons of prestige and image that forced Judah to adopt this political and economical innovation. The iconographic program contributed to shaping an ethnic and administrative identity separate from contemporary neighboring cultures. Explanations that have proven helpful for other regions of the eastern Mediterranean do not apply to Judah. Those Achaemenid provinces did not have to pay mercenaries[18] and did not have to finance wars and

---

[17] Mildenberg, "Notes on the Coin Issues of Mazday."

[18] On J. Hyrcan I as the first Jewish ruler who paid for mercenaries see Josephus, *Bell. Iud.* 1,2,5 §61; ibid., Ant., 13,8,4 §249. He certainly had precursors, see for example, Ri. 9,4; (1 Chron. 19:6f.); 2 Chron. 25:6, and the Jews in Elephantine, who were paid by the Achaemenids during their occupation of Egypt. According to the letter of Aristeas §13, Jewish mercenaries already earned their wages in Egypt during the Nubia campaign of the Psammetichs (I and II). The first literary evidence for coins as payment for mercenaries is found in the Babylonian army,

large construction projects. The temple in Jerusalem had been re-dedicated in 515 BCE,[19] and the city walls had been rebuilt under Nehemiah's rule. There is no discernible connection to the Tennes revolt of 351 BCE. As in other regions in earlier times, coins made of precious metal convinced all participants in economic exchanges of their usefulness. They were durable, manageable, and, as such, ideal for measuring value and facilitating trade. In addition, they themselves were merchandise and items for the treasury. At the same time, distrust of coins ran deep, but never deep enough to prevent the introduction of monetary trade in total.

The Paleo-Aramaic and Paleo-Hebrew legends mention the name of the province *Yhd(h)* and the name of the leading provincial officials. The officials responsible for currency export mentioned by name carry the title of *peḥāh* and *kōhen*. The minting in Judah thus operated not only under the auspices of the governor, but also of a priest, most likely the high priest in Jerusalem. In political terms, these coins symbolize the separation of Judean territories from the province of Samaria, to which Judah had belonged up to this point.

Coins from Yehud continued to be produced up to the reign of Ptolemy I (323–283/282 BCE) and his second wife, Berenike I (317–279 BCE). Ptolemy II halted the coin production and substituted Yehud coins with a large quantity of Ptolemaic bronze coins, especially in large nominal. The Yehud coins are thus the only coins where the

---

see Alkaios, *frag. 48, B 16;* cf. Strabo, Geogr. 13,2,3: Antimenidas, the brother of Alkaios, served as a mercenary in the army of Nebukanezzars II during his campaign against Ashkelon in 604 BCE, see J. D. Quinn, "Alcaeus 48 (B16) and the Fall of Ascalon (604 B.C.)," *BASOR* 164 (1961): 19–20. See also W. Helck, "Söldner," *LÄ* 5 (1984): 1051–2; G. F. Seibt, *Griechische Söldner im Achaimenidenreich,* Bonn: R. Habelt, 1977, 23ff.; R. Wenning, "Griechische Söldner in Palästina," in *Naukratis: DieBeziehungen zu Ostgriechenland, Ägypten und Zypern in archaischer Zeit,* eds. U. Höckmann and D. Kreikenbom, Möhnesee-Wamel: Bibliopolis, 2001, 257–68. For Greek mercenaries in Egyptian armies under Psammetich I and II, see *Historische griechische Inschriften in Übersetzung Bd. I: Die archaische und klassische Zeit,* eds. K. Brodersen et al., Texte zur Forschung 59, Darmstadt: Wissenschaftliche Buchgesellschaft, 1992, Nrn. 8–9; Plinius, *Nat. Hist.* 5,14,68.

[19] On the earliest Greek temple in the Levant known to date see E. Stern, "A Gorgon's Head and the Earliest Greek Temples at Dor and on the Coasts of Phoenicia and Palestine," in: *"Up to the Gates of Ekron": Essays on the Archaeology and History of the Eastern Mediterranean in Honor of Seymour Gitin,* eds. Sidnie White Crawford et al., Jerusalem: Old City Press, 2007, 249–57.

provincial stamps of the Achaemenid and the Ptolemaic periods overlap. In this context only, the royal minting monopoly of the Lagids was not enforced from the beginning. Following this time, coins were produced again in Jerusalem under Hasmonean reign from the second half of the second century BCE.

Among the Yehud coins from the Persion period, we also find the famous one-of-a-kind BMC Palestine S. 181, Nr. 29 of unknown origin.[20] The obverse side of the drachma (?) (ø 15mm; 3.29g) displays a bearded face with a Corinthian helmet; in a recessed square on the opposite side, we see a bearded god sitting on a winged wheel with a bird (of prey) on his extended left arm. The lower right shows the head of Bes and above it the letters *yhd* that were incorrectly read earlier as the divine name *yhw*. Nonetheless, we cannot exclude the possibility that the unknown god on the winged wheel is the *interpretation hebraica* of Zeus or another Greek god as YHWH (the Hebrew Bible name for God). In any case, the figure depicted could be seen by Greeks as Zeus, by non-Jewish Semites as Baal, and by "Protohellenistic" Jews as YHWH. Whoever carved the stamp was most likely not a Judean. All of the officials responsible for currency export, including the high priest who had commissioned the subject and accepted it as the official coin image for Judah, belonged to the leading, highly Hellenized social stratum in Judah. There were groups among them who worshiped YHWH exclusively; whether they were willing or able to recognize their God on this coin remains unknown.

The Yehud coins are not "Jewish" coins in a strict sense. They are, rather, provincial examples of Achaemenid coinage, i.e. coins that a respective provincial governor produced with the permission of the satrap of *eber nāri*, or Ptolemaic coins which the Egyptian king commissioned for *Yhd(h)* in Judah. This also explains the anthropomorphic and zoomorphic motives such as Athena and an owl, the Persian great king with a *kidaris*, the god on a winged wheel, the (Egyptian) falcon, the Ptolemaic eagle on lightning bolts, and the portraits of Ptolemaic rulers. The fact that the majority of the governors and most of the coins' end-users were Jews is not a contradiction of their non-Jewish imagery. Beginning with the Hasmonean period, one can speak of "Jewish" coins

---

[20] H. Kienle, *Der Gott auf dem Flügelrad: Zu den ungelösten Fragen der "synkretistischen" Münze*, BMC Palestine S. 181, Nr. 29, Göttinger Orientforschungen VI 7, Wiesbaden: Harrassowitz, 1975.

(to a certain degree) in that, even if the Maccabees started their own production of bronze coins by permission of the Seleucid dynasty, these soon became (at least from a Hasmonean point of view) autonomous coins of the Hasmonean state.

Coins in Hellenistic Palestine

The coinage of Alexander the Great, the Ptolemaic, and the Seleucid Empire

Alexander the Great

The end of Achaemenid rule coincided with the end of coin production in Samaria, Gaza, Ashkelon, Ashdod, and Judah. It was replaced by the currency of the new rulers. From the time of Alexander the Great (356–323 BCE), an international currency was created that soon replaced the gold and silver currency of the Achaemenid rulers, strongly diminished the importance of the Athenian and other Greek currencies, and was circulated throughout the known world.[21] It was issued in large quantities – especially as staters and tetradrachmas – and continued to be minted with the name of Alexander under Philipp III Arridaios (323–317 BCE)[22] and even later, up to the second century BCE. The last known productions from the Syro-Phoenician region are located in Arados and Marathos and date to 166/165 BCE. Even after this time, Alexander coins remained in circulation and were frequently counterstamped, especially by the Seleucid rulers. Following the conquest of Tyros and Gaza in 332 BCE, Alexander coins made of gold, silver, and bronze were minted in Syro-Phoenicia in the *poleis* Sidon (from 333 BCE), Akko-Ptolemy, Tyros, Berytos, and Damascus. In Damascus,

---

[21] See e.g., M. J. Price, "On Attributing Alexanders – Some Cautionary Tales," in: *Greek Numismatics and Archaeology: Essays in Honor of M. Thompson*, eds. O. Mørkholm and N. M. Waggoner, Wettern: Édition NR, 1979, 241–50; M. J. Price, *The Coinage in the Name of Alexander the Great*, Zurich; London: P. Haupt, 1991; O. H. Zervos, "Near Eastern Elements in the Tetradrachms of Alexander the Great: The Eastern Mints," in: *Greek Numismatics and Archaeology: Essays in Honor of M. Thompson*, 1979, 295–305; O. Mørkholm, *Early Hellenistic Coinage from the Accession of Alexander to the Peace of Apamea*, New York: Cambridge University Press, 1991, 41–54.

[22] M. J. Price, *The Coinage in the Name of Alexander the Great*, 1991, 422–4, 433–5, 441: only coins in Sidon, Marathos, and Arados; cf. Mørkholm, *Early Hellenistic Coinage*, 55–62.

Alexander had gained access to a large part of the Persian royal treasure in the local Achaemenid headquarters.[23] On their obverse side, the gold coins tend to show the head of Athena and, on the opposite side, the shape of a double-winged Nike. The silver coins show the head of Heracles on the obverse side and Zeus on his throne on the opposite side. The various Alexander coins are well documented in Palestine in hoards and as single coins.

The Ptolemaic coins in Palestine

The Ptolemaic rulers in Egypt built an economic and administrative system that was largely determined by monopolistic and fiscal concerns. It was controlled by a Dioiketes. From the time of Ptolemy I, gold and silver coins followed the Phoenician coinage standard. The Ptolemaic silver coins (and from the second half of the third century BCE, the Ptolemaic bronze coins as well) became the leading currency in Palestine[24] without completely displacing foreign currencies.[25] The Yehud coins continued to be produced into the early Ptolemaic period. Those Ptolemaic coins that were still in circulation in Palestine were silver and bronze coins, especially from the *poleis* Alexandria, Akko-Ptolemy, Tyros, and Sidon; in addition, coins were also produced in Joppe-Jaffa, Gaza, and Dor.

The Seleucid coins in Palestine

Following the rule of Ptolemy V (205/4–181/0 BCE), Seleucid coins slowly displaced Ptolemaic coins. From the late second century BCE, Seleucid currency was the most widespread, but not the only, currency in Palestine.[26]

---

[23] F. Rebuffat, "Alexandre le Grand et les problèmes financiers au début de son règne," *Revue Numismatique 6ᵉ série* 25 (1983): 43–52.

[24] A. Kromann and O. Mørkholm, *Syllage Nummorum Graecorum Copenhagen: Egypt, the Ptolemies*, Copenhagen: P. Kristensens, 1977.

[25] A. Houghton and C. Lorber, "Antiochus III in Coele-Syria and Phoenicia," *Israel Numismatic Journal* 14 (2000–2002): 44–58; cf. O. Hoover, "Ptolemaic Lead Coinage in Coele Syria (103–101 BCE)," *Israel Numismatic Research* 3 (2008): 81–5.

[26] The most important sources are: A. Houghton, *Coins of the Seleucid Empire from the Collection of A. Houghton*, New York; Wetteren: Cultura, 1983; A. Houghton and C. Lorber, *Seleucid Coins: A Comprehensive Catalogue, Part I: Seleucus I through Antiochus III*, Vols. 1–2, New York; London: Classical Numismatic Group, 2002; A. Houghton, C. Lorber, and O. Hoover, *Seleucid*

Aside from Antiochia, minting sites during Seleucid reign were located in Akko-Ptolemy, Ashkelon, Gaza, Damascus, Tyros, Sidon, and Berytos; Akko-Ptolemy was also the temporary residence of Kleopatra Thea (d. 121 BCE). As early as 169–8 BCE, Antiochus IV Epiphanes had granted several Syro-Mesopotamian and Phoenician cities the right to mint copper coins, among them Byblos, Sidon, and Tyros.

Under the nominal rule of the Seleucid dynasty, the first autonomous city coins appeared in Palestine-Phoenicia during the second half of the second century BCE: in Tyros after 126–5 BCE and in Ashkelon after 103 BCE. From the second half of the second century BCE, coins were also minted once again in Maccabean Judah.

Coin production under Hasmonean rule

Local coin production in Judah started again only with the downfall of the Seleucid Empire.[27] In 139 BCE, Antiochus VII Euergetes (138–129 BCE) wrote a letter promising the Hasmonean Simon (142–135/4 BCE) the right to mint bronze coins if he would provide successful military aid against Tryphon (1 Macc. 15:6). Already around 160 BCE, several rights were granted by letter to Jonathan (161–142 BCE) by Demetrius I Soter (162–150 BCE), without mentioning minting rights specifically (1 Macc. 10:25–45; Josephus, Ant. 13,2,3 §55). In 132/1–131/0 BCE, Antiochus VII probably minted tetradrachmas in Jerusalem with the monogram of John Hyrcan I and, apparently, also bronze coins with a

---

Coins: A Comprehensive Catalogue, Part II: Seleucus IV through Antiochus XIII, Vols. 1–2, New York; London: Classical Numismatic Group, 2008; O. D. Hoover, *Coins of the Selucid Empire in the Collection of Arthur Houghton, Part II*, New York: American Numismatic Society, 2007; A. Spaer et al., eds., *Sylloge Nummorum Graecorum Israel I: The A. Spaer Collection of Seleucid Coins*, London 1998.

[27] See e.g., D. Barag and S. Qedar, "The Beginning of Hasmonean Coinage," *Israel Numismatic Journal* 4 (1980): 8–21; Y. Meshorer, "Again on the Beginning of the Hasmonean Coinage," *Israel Numismatic Journal* 5 (1981): 11–16; Y. Ronen, "The First Hasmonean Coins," *Biblical Archaeologist* 50 (1987): 105–7; Y. Meshorer, *A Treasury of Jewish Coins from the Persian Period to Bar Kokhba*, Jerusalem; Nyack, NY: Amphora, 2001, 23–59; J. C. Kaufman, *Unrecorded Hasmonean Coins from the J. Ch. Kaufman Collection, Parts I–II*, Jerusalem: Graphit, 1995, 2004; S. Ostermann, *Die Münzen der Hasmonäer: Ein kritischer Bericht zur Systematik und Chronologie*, Novum Testamentum et Orbis Antiquus 55, Göttingen; Fribourg: Vandenhoeck & Ruprecht, 2005.

lily, the "crest" of the Hasmonean high priest.[28] The era of Hasmonean coin production began with the end of the Seleucid mint in Jerusalem in 131/130 BCE. From the time of John Hyrcan (135/134–104 BCE) through the time of Antigonos Mattathias (40–37 BCE), coins were issued by the Hasmoneans. Almost all of the Hasmonean coins are bronze coins of small value (lead coins were also produced under Alexander Jannaios (104–76 BCE),[29] with nominals equivalent to the Seleucid lepton and dilepton. These nominal values indicate that Seleucid coinage was used as a reference point. As the Hasmoneans only produced copper (and lead) coins, larger transactions were still done with foreign silver currency or with pre-monetary forms of payment.

The legends printed on Hasmonean coins appear in old Hebrew and/ or Greek script, sometimes bi- or even trilingually with Greek, Hebrew, and Aramaic titles, the name of the respective king, and/or the high priest, or the inscription "counsel of the Jews" [*(w-)ḥbr h-Yhwdym*]. Iconographically, the coins forgo any kind of anthropomorphic imagery and contain next to no allusions to pagan mythology. Instead, they display floral images (flowers, palm branches, wreaths, and cornucopias) as well as other symbols (apex, stars, menorah, or a table for the bread of the Presence). The coins also show a typically Seleucid symbol with the anchor.

Economic documents and hoards from Iron Age, Persian, and Hellenistic Palestine

The following will present a few representative and significant examples. These include various hoards of ostraca and papyri that contain delivery orders, tax lists, lists of rations, bills, receipts, etc., in addition to hoards of coins. In an attempt to show long-term development, we

---

[28] The lily was already a motif on the Yehud coins and also appears on several other Palestinian and non-Palestinian coins, see U. Hübner, "Tradition und Innovation: Die Münzprägungen der Hasmonäer im Alltagsleben des 2. und 1. Jahrhunderts v. Chr. als Massenmedien," in: *Medien im antiken Palästina? Materielle Kommunikation and Medialität als Thema der Palästinaarchäologie*, Forschungen zum Alten Testament 2, 10, ed. C. Frevel, Tübingen: Mohr, 2005, 171–87.

[29] These lead coins may also have been copies, test coins, or tokens. Such items similar to money are also known from other periods in the history of Palestine.

will compare findings from Iron Age II, the Persian, and the Hellenistic periods. These findings grant us some insight into economic factors that are important for understanding the slowly developing monetary systems in Palestine. From the Iron Age, a series of hoards have been found including: Bet-Schean,[30] Dor,[31] as-Samūʿa,[32] Arad,[33] Eqron,[34] Geser,[35] Megiddo,[36] Tell Keisān,[37] En-Gedi,[38] and Sichem;[39] they consist mostly of hack silver and hack jewelry.[40] Even though the

[30] P. Vargyas, "Fakes before Coins?: On the Gold and Silver Hoards from Level V at Beth-Shan," in: *"Up to the Gates of Ekron,"* eds. S. White Crawford et al., 2007, 295–304.
[31] E. Stern, "The Silver Hoard from Tel Dor," in *Hacksilber to Coinage: New Insights into the Monetary History of the Near East and Greece*, American Numismatic Society Numismatic Studies 24, ed. M. Balmuth, New York: American Numismatic Society, 2001, 1–26.
[32] R. Kletter and E. Brand, "A New Look at the Iron Age Silver Hoard from Esthemoa," *Zeitschrift des Deutschen Palästina-Vereins* 114 (1998): 139–54.
[33] M. Aharoni, "A Silver Hoard from Arad," *Qadmoniot* 13 (1980): 39–40 (Hebr.).
[34] A. Golani and B. Sass, "Three Seventh-Century B.C.E. Hoards of Silver Jewelry from Tel Miqne-Ekron," *Bulletin of the American Schools of Oriental Research* 311 (1998): 57–81; S. Gitin, "Tel Miqne-Ekron in the 7th Century B.C.E.: The Impact of Economic Innovation and Foreign Cultural Influence on a Neo-Assyrian Vassal City-State," in: *Recent Excavations in Israel: A View to the West, Reports on Kabri, Nami, Miqne-Ekron, Dor, and Ashkelon*, Archaeological Institute of America, Colloquia and Conference Papers 1, ed. Gitin, Dubuque, IA: Kendall Hunt, 1995, 61–79; S. Gitin and A. Golani, "The Tel Miqne-Ekron Silver Hoards: The Assyrian and Phoenician Connections," in: *Hacksilber to Coinage*, ed. M. Balmuth, 2001, 27–48.
[35] R. A. Stewart Macalister, *The Excavation of Gezer 1902–1905 and 1907–1909*, Vol. II, London: J. Murray, 1912, 262.
[36] G. Loud, *Megiddo II: Seasons of 1935–39*, Oriental Institute Publications 62, University of Chicago Press, 1948, 157, Pl. 229:24.
[37] É. Nodet, "Le trésor du loc. 635 (niv. 9a)," in: *Tell Keisan (1971–1976), une cité phénicienne en Galilée*, Orbis Biblicus et Orientalis, Serie Archeologica 1, eds. J. Briend and J.-B. Humbert, Göttingen; Fribourg; Paris: Vandenhoeck & Ruprecht, 1980, 325–6.
[38] R. Kletter and A. de Groot, "Iron Age Hoard of Hacksilber from En-Gedi," in: *En-Gedi Excavations I: Final Report (1961–1965)*, ed. E. Stein, Jerusalem: Old City Press, 2007, 367–76.
[39] M. Balmuth and C. M. Thompson, "Hacksilber: recent approaches to the study of hoards of uncoined silver: Laboratory analyses and geographical distribution," in: *Akten des XII: Numismatischen Kongresses Berlin 1977, Bd.I*, Berlin: Zabern, 2000, 159–69; the precise dating of the hoard (1200–200 BCE) is not clear.
[40] C. M. Thompson, "Sealed Silver in Iron Age Cisjordan and the 'Invention' of Coinage," *Oxford Journal of Archaeology* 22 (2003): 67–107; O. Bulgarelli,

interpretation of their function is controversial, they can be interpreted as a collection of metal pieces that were broken up and weighed and thus served as a pre-monetary form of payment. The fact that these pieces of metal do not have any standardized weight is not a compelling argument for assuming that they were the metal supplies of a precious metal smith. Apart from the fact that each separate piece could easily be broken to match a certain weight, a precious metal smith would have had to do the same to prepare the metal for further use (such as the sale of jewelry).[41] Hack silver and hack jewelry are not standardized by definition – they only become so by being weighed against standardized weights. Metal bars could be, but did not have to be, standardized. Durability and transportability were their main features. They, too, were standardized by denominational division and the process of weighing.

We also know of similar hoards from the Persian period. Whereas in the beginning we find unmixed and mixed hoards consisting of coins, silver bars, silver pieces, and hack silver, the situation changes in the late Achaemenid period. In Palestine itself, hardly any hoards of archaic coins were found,[42] very few hoards were found in the classical era consisting mostly of unmixed coins, most of which were buried between 350 and 332 BCE.[43] The situation changes again in the Hellenistic period: many more hoards were found and almost all of these consisted exclusively of coins.[44]

"Appunti sul'argento come strumento monetario e finanziario nell'economia del Vicino Oriente Antico," *Rivista degli Studi Orientali* NS 79 (2006): 219–29. Cf. F. von Luschan, *Die Kleinfunde von Sendschirili*, 1943, 119–21; Tropper, *Die Inschriften von Zincirli*, 51–152.

[41] For the discussion, see R. Kletter, "Iron Age Hoards of Precious Metals in Palestine – an 'Underground' Economy?," *Levant* 35 (2003): 139–52; Kletter, "Coinage before Coins? A Response," *Levant* 36 (2004): 207–10; S. Gitin and A. Golani, "A Silver-Based Monetary Economy in the 7th Century BCE: A Response to R. Kletter," *Levant* 36 (2004): 207–10; M. Silver, "'Coinage before Coins?' A Further Response to Raz Kletter," *Levant* 38 (2006): 187–9.

[42] Thompson et al., *An Inventory of Greek Coin Hoards*, 200–2. Due to restrictions of space, I will not discuss hoards found after this point in time, see Stucky, *Ras Shamra – Leukos Limen*, 28–43.

[43] Thompson et al., *An Inventory of Greek Coin Hoards*, 202–6; see e.g., P. Visona, "A Hoard of 4th-Century Athenian Tetradrachms from Nablus," *Quaderni Ticinesi: Numismatica e Antichità Classiche* 27 (1998): 141–9; H. Nicolet-Pierre, "Tétradrachmes athéniens en Transeuphratène," *Transeuphratène* 20 (2000): 107–19; H. Gitler, "A Hacksilber and Cut Athenian Tetradrachm Hoard from the Environs of Samaria: Late Fourth Century BCE," *Israel Numismatic Research* 1 (2006): 5–14.

[44] Thompson et al., *An Inventory of Greek Coin Hoards*, 206–24.

In the beginning, contributions to the temple in Jerusalem were payable in natural produce. According to Deuteronomy 14:22–29, produce could later be substituted by *ksp*, "silver"; this passage does not necessarily refer to coins. The payment of temple taxes with silver coins was the obvious course of action only in later times. The melting site at the Jerusalem temple mentioned in 2 Kings 12:5–17 (see 2 Kings 22:3–6),[45] allegedly dating to the reign of Joash, b. Ahaziah of Judah (*c.*840–773 BCE), served the purpose of producing bars from the silver contributed to the temple (see Zech. 11:13).[46] These bars could then be broken up in order to pay the craftsmen at the temple. The passage in Zechariah 11:12 may describe just this practice. The wage (*śkr*) is weighed (*šql*) in silver (*ksp*). The financial function of the temple as a bank did not change substantially once coins were introduced.[47] Tributes owed by various local Palestinian monarchs to the Assyrians, Babylonians, or Persians were paid in metal bars of gold, silver (see 2 Kings 15:19f.), tin, or iron, but also in ivory, wood, textiles, animals, or other types of natural produce, i.e. in pre-monetary form.[48]

Ancient Hebrew ostraca from Iron Age II seldom mention *ksp* and *š(qlym)* alongside the usual goods, wages, or taxes.[49] If it is mentioned at all, then it is in reference to silver of a particular weight, never in reference to minted coins as such.

---

[45] E. Würthwein, *Die Bücher der Könige: 1 Kön. 17–2 Kön. 25,* Das Alte Testament Deutsch 11, 2, Göttingen: Vandenhoeck & Ruprecht, 1984, 352–8; M. Cogan and H. Tadmor, *II Kings,* The Anchor Bible 11, New York: Doubleday, 1988, 135–41.

[46] For Zech. 11:4–17; 13:7–9; Exod. 32:4 (and Matt. 27:3–10), see O. Eissfeldt, "Eine Einschmelzstelle am Tempel zu Jerusalem," (1937) in: *Kleine Schriften II,* Tübingen: Mohr, 1963, 107–9.

[47] R. Bogaert, "Ursprung und Entwicklung der Depositenbank im Altertum und Mittelalter," in: *Essays zur historischen Entwicklung des Bankensystems,* Gesellschaft, Recht, Wirtschaft 3, Bogaert and P. C. Hartmann, Mannheim; Vienna; Zurich: Bibliographisches Institut, 1980, 9–26; N. Lohfink, "Qohelet und die Banken: zur Übersetzung von Qohelet V 12–16," *Vetus Testamentum* 39 (1989): 488–95.

[48] See e.g., J. Bär, *Der assyrische Tribut und seine Darstellung: Eine Untersuchung zur imperialen Ideologie im neuassyrischen Reich,* Alter Orient und Altes Testament 243, Kevelaer; Neukirchen; Vluyn: Butzon & Bercker, 1996; J. S. Holladay, "How much is that in . . .? Monetisation, Money, Royal States, and Empires," in: *Exploring the Longue Durée: Essays in Honor of L. E. Stager,* ed. J. D. Schloen, Winona Lake, Ind: Eisenbrauns, 2009, 207–22.

[49] Y. Aharoni et al., *Arad Inscriptions,* Jerusalem: Ben Zvi, 1981, Nos. 16, 24, 29, 48, 65.

Several ostraca from the late seventh or early sixth centuries BCE were found in Stratum VI in the archives of the Jewish fortress at Arad. These ostraca mention "Kittim."[50] This term refers to Cypriote or other (eastern) Greek mercenaries who were also common in Egyptian, Babylonian, and Persian armies in the seventh to fourth centuries BCE. In Arad, these mercenaries were paid with bread, flour, wine, and oil, i.e. in natural produce.

An ostracon found in *Mesad Hašavyāhū*[51] tells of a legal dispute initiated by a Judean agricultural worker around 600 BCE. The worker attempted to regain his garment that had been used as collateral by his creditor (see Exod. 22:25; Deut. 14:12). The debtor's land, cattle, or manpower could be impounded as security and compensation, despite protective regulations that were not always heeded.

An Aramaic customs tariff from lower Egypt (475 BCE) lists items that were transported to and from Egypt by Ionian (*ywny*) and Phoenician (*sydnyn*) ships; among them natron, cedars, wine, copper, tin, iron, wool, and others, items that also originated in Palestine. The taxes were payable in silver and gold (*krš*, *šql*, *hlwr*). We can no longer determine whether this referred to money, value units, or coins.[52]

Aramaic ostraca of the Persian period from Arad *Tell as-Sebaʿ, Tel ʿĪrā (Khirbet Ġarra)* as well as other locations, mention grain and trade goods as well as mules, horses, and goats; *ksp* ("silver-money") of a precise weight is only mentioned on rare occasions. The same is true for

---

[50] Ibid., Nos. 1–2, 4–5, 7–8, 10–11, 14, 17. Cf. U. Hübner, "Südjordanien in der Eisenzeit als Kontaktzone zwischen Mittelmeer, Arabien und Mesopotamien," in: *Austausch von Gütern, Ideen und Technologien in der Ägäis und im östlichen Mittelmeerraum von der prähistorischen bis zur archaischen Zeit*, ed. Verein zur Förderung der Hellenischen Geschichte, Weilheim; Oberbayern: DZA Druckerei 2008, 205–20.

[51] J. Renz, *Die althebräischen Inschriften I*, Darmstadt: Wissenschaftliche Buchgesellschaft, 1995, 35–329; Ulrich Hübner und Bemerkungen zum Pfandrecht, "Das judäische Ostrakon von Mᶜṣad Ḥašavyāhū alttestamentliches und griechisches Pfandrecht sowie ein Graffito aus Marissa," *Ugarit-Forschungen* 29 (1997): 215–25.

[52] A. Yardeni, "Maritime Trade and Royal Accountancy in an Erased Customs Account from 475 BCE on the Aḥiqar Scroll from Elephantine," *Bulletin of the American School of Oriental Research* 293 (1994): 67–78; B. Porten and A. Yardeni, eds., *Textbook of Aramaic Documents from Ancient Egypt III: Literature, Accounts, Lists*, Jerusalem: Eisenbrauns, 1993, 82–193, XVII–XXI.

š(ql)(ym) (Aram. Arad-Ostracon Nr. 41; Aram. *Tell as-Sebaʿ*-Ostraca Nrs 16–17; *T.ʿĪrā* Inscription Nr. 8).[53]

The ostracon Number 2069 from *Tell Kulēfi* is an Aramaic receipt or the administrative note of a tax collector from the fifth or early fourth century BCE. In Aramaic, the term for his profession mimics a Greek loan word (*qrplgs* < *καρπολόγος*). The taxes were paid in shipments of wine.[54] Another ostracon from the fourth century (Nr. 10.007), which is exceptionally hard to read, may be interpreted as *zzn ksp'*, or as *ttn ksp'*. In the first case, *zzn* could not be a nominal construction, since it is not a term for a particular value.[55]

The copy of a Persian deed of purchase in Babylonian cuneiform and language deals with the purchase of two rams for "money" (KÙ. BABBAR – *kaspu*), which is not specified further.[56] It was drawn up in Harrān between a local native and a man by the name of Qūsu-šāma, son of Qūsu-yadāʿ; it was found, however, in Edomite *Tawīlān*. Many Idumean ostraca of the fourth century written in Aramaic and found in Marissa (and surroundings) were published over the last few years. They hardly ever mention *ksp/ksp'* or use the terms *šql*, *rbʿ*, or *m(ʿh)*, which probably corresponded to the division 1:4:24, i.e. the increments of tetradrachma, drachma, and obol, without referring to specific coin values.

In contrast, natural goods such as wine, grains, flour, oil, straw, and others are mentioned frequently with precise designation of weight (especially *kr/kōr*, *qb/qab*, and *s'h/se'āh*),[57] It is uncertain whether we

---

[53] J. Naveh, "The Aramaic Ostraca from Tel Arad," in *Arad Inscriptions 168*, No. 41; Naveh, "The Aramaic Inscriptions," in *Beer-Sheba I: Excavations at Tel Beer-Sheba 1969–1971 Seasons*, ed. Y. Aharoni, Tel Aviv: Peli Printing, 1973, 81, Nos. 16–17; Naveh, "Aramaic Ostraca," in: *Tel ʿĪrā: A Stronghold in the Biblical Negev*, Tel Aviv Monograph Series 15, ed. I. Beit-Arieh, Tel Aviv: Graphit Press, 1999, 412–13, No. 8.

[54] R. A. DiVito, "The Tell el-Kheleifeh Inscriptions," in: *Nelso Glueck's 1938–1940 Excavations at Tell el-Kheleifeh: A Reappraisal*, ed. G. D. Pradico, Atlanta, GA: Scholars Press, 1993, 58–9, Pl. 81:A.

[55] Ibid., 60, Pl. 83:C.

[56] S. Dalley, "The Cuneiform Tablet," in: *Excavations at Tawilan in Southern Jordan*, British Academy Monographs in Archaeology 8, eds. C.-M. Bennett and P. Bienkowski, Oxford University Press, 1995, 67–8.

[57] See I. Ephʿal and J. Nevah, *Aramaic Ostraca of the Fourth Century BC from Idumaea*, Jerusalem: Magnes Press, 1996; A. Lemaire, *Nouvelles inscriptions araméenes d'Idhumée au Musée d'Israel*, Paris: Gabalda, 1996; S. Ahituv and A. Yardeni, "Seventy Aramaic Texts on Ostraca from Idumea: The Late Persian to the Early Hellenistic Periods," *Maarav* 11 (2004): 7–23.

should read *zuzn* on ostracon 61.2.[58] One of the editors, André Lemaire, summarizes the situation as follows: "Au total et jusqu'à maintenant, ces ostraca ne semblement pas attester explicitement l'usage de la monnaie. L'existence probable d'une capitation de deux quarts de shéqel (= didrachme) et la mention d'oboles et de quarts d'oboles peuvent se comprendre aussie bien d'un metal monnayé."[59] We are faced with a similar situation on other documents. An Aramaic papyrus from the vicinity of the monastery of St. George, west of Jericho/*Tell as-Sulāān* from the second half of the fourth century BCE, contains the three abbreviations: *š(qlyn)*, *r(b'yn)*, and *m('ā)*. They might refer to coin values equivalent to tetradrachma, drachma, and obol,[60] but also to other values or weight measurements.

Among the Aramaic papyri of *Wādī d-Dāliye* are documents describing the lending or sale of slaves between the years 354 and 335 BCE. These documents contain the specifications *ksp(')*, *šql bzw*, *šql ksp(')*, and *mnh/mnm*. The two latter terms were never made into coin values. Whether the sheqels refer to coin values or are an indication of price is not clear. In part, they describe the value of a slave in the sense of a pledge.[61]

Three examples, representative of many others, should be mentioned from the Hellenistic period.

[58] Lemaire, *Nouvelles inscriptions araméenes d'Idumée*, 58–9.

[59] A. Lemaire, *Nouvelles inscriptions araméenes d'Idumée, Tome II*, Paris: Gabalda, 2002, 229.

[60] H. Eshel and H. Misgar, "A Fourth Century B.C.E. Document from Ketef Yeriho," *Israel Exploration Journal* 38 (1998): 158–76. The Roman documents from the *Wādi al-Murabba 'āt* and *Naḥal Ḥever* mention several value terms (in Aramaic, Nabatean, Hebrew, and Greek) such as *'αργύριον*, *'αργύρους*, *δενάριον*, *δραχμᾱ*, *λεπτον*, *mélas*, *στατῆρ*, *τύριος*, *dnr/dnyr*, *zwz*, and *sl'*. The term *ksp* could either refer to "silver," "money," or "sum," and the verb *šql/tql* to the activity of weighing or counting (?) *ksp* or another value; see Pierre Benoit et al., eds., *Les Grottes de Murabba 'at*, Discoveries in the Judaean Desert 2, Oxford: Clarendon Press, 1961; Y. Yadin et al., eds., *The Documents from the Bar Kokhba Period in the Cave of Letters: Hebrew, Aramaic, and Nabatean-Aramaic Papyri*, Judean Desert Studies 3, Jerusalem: Old City Press, 2002; N. Lewis, Y. Yadin, and J. C. Greenfield, eds., *The Documents from the Bar Kokhba Period in the Cave of Letters: Greek Papyri, Aramaic, and Nabatean Signatures and Subscriptions*, Judean Desert Studies 2, Jerusalem: Ben-Zvi Printing, 1989; cf. E. Eshel, "A Late Iron Age Ostracon featuring the Term *l'rrk*," *IEJ* 53 (2003): 151–63.

[61] D. M. Gropp et al., eds., *Wadi Daliyeh II: The Samaria Papyri from Wadi Daliyeh and Qumran Cave 4 – XXVII, Miscellanea, Part 2*, Discoveries in the Judean Desert 28, Oxford: Clarendon Press, 2001.

- An Aramaic–Greek bilingue from *Khirbet al-Kōm* (Ostracon Nr. 3) from the third century BCE is a receipt issued by a money lender. His job title *qpyls* is based on the Greek loan word καπῆλος. The Aramean value term *zwzn* is translated on the Greek side with the known abbreviation for drachmas.[62]
- The famous Zenon papyri, named afer the Carian Zenon, who dwelled in Ptolemaic Syria and Palestine between January 259 and February 258 as Oikonomos in the service of the Alexandrian Dioiketes Apollonios, were written during the reign of Ptolemaios II (284–246 BCE). They witness to the fact that bills could be paid in drachmas, obols, and chalkoi.[63]
- An Aramaic wedding contract from the year 176 BCE found in Marissa mentions the bridal price and specifies its value with the term *zwzyn*.[64]

Especially with these last two examples, one can assume that the value terms do not merely refer to abstract values, but to their concrete form as minted money.

Summary

The development of a monetary system in Palestine finds its precursors in the Bronze[65] and Iron Ages and its beginnings during the Persian period. It began along the Mediterranean coast of Phoenicia and northern Palestine and continued into the interior, first in northern Palestine, including Samaria, and lastly in the remote hill country of Judah with Jerusalem. In other words, the development of a monetary system in pre-Hellenistic Palestine took different directions in various stages in different regions. A few Palestinian regions, especially east of

---

[62] L. T. Geraty, "The Khirbet el-Kōm Bilingual Ostracon," *Bulletin of the American School of Oriental Research* 220 (1973): 55–61.

[63] X. Durand, *Des Grecs en Palestine au IIIe siècle avant Jesus-Christ: Le dossier syrien des archives de Zéon de Caunos (261–252)*, Cahiers de la Revue Biblique 38, Paris: Gabalda, 1997, 297.

[64] E. Eshel and A. Kloner, "An Aramaic Ostracon of an Edomite Marriage Contract from Maresha, dated 176 B.C.E.," *Israel Exploration Journal* 46 (1996): 1–22.

[65] Ü. Yalçin, C. Pulak, and R. Slotta, eds., *Das Schiff von Uluburun: Welthandel vor 3000 Jahren*, Veröffentlichung aus dem Deutschen Bergbau-Museum Bochum 138, Bochum: Cuno, 2005; H. Katz, "The Ship of Uluburun and the Ship from Tyre: An International Trade Network in the Ancient Near East," *Zeitschrift des Deutschen Palästina-Vereins* 124 (2008): 128–42.

the Jordan, did not mint their own coins during the Achaemenid and Hellenistic periods; the circulation in these areas was also much lower than west of the Jordan.[66] Early coin production in Palestine was a relatively late import and thus a secondary cultural phenomenon that was highly dependent on external influence. The Achaemenid rulers granted minting rights implicitly or explicitly to several provinces. Administratively, the coins were an Achaemenid provincial production.

The introduction of coins did not constitute a major innovation, but rather, the continuation and improvement of pre-monetary systems, in which weighed silver was replaced by an exclusively monetary system based on silver coins.

Traditional trade, i.e. non-monetary payment, remained the primary form of transaction. The price and the value of various goods could be recorded in silver, just as it was during the previous Iron Age. During the Persian period, the economy remained focused on agriculture and live-stock farming, and the monetary system was primarily based on silver, not on coins.

The development of a monetary system specific to each region and time remained a partial undertaking.

The various currencies that were simultaneously in circulation served various different purposes. Alongside currencies that were important for international trade (such as Athenian, Sidonian, and Tyrian money), regional currencies were used for economic transactions limited to Palestine (such as the Philisto-Arabian, the Samarian, and the Judean currencies).

The development of a monetary system was primarily an urban phenomenon, especially in the provincial capitals and harbor cities, narrowing the social focus to the urban upper classes that were instituted by the hegemonic powers, recognized provincial governors, or urban administrations. The population of the rural areas was hardly involved in the circulation of coins.

The circulation included silver coins of varied value. They were based on different coinage standards.

The following consequences resulted from this monetary "anarchy," the co-existence of different currencies, standards, and economic systems.

---

[66] C. Augé, "La circulation des monnaies à l'est du Jourdain à l'époque perse," *Transeuphratène* 20 (2000): 167–8.

First, it was necessary to test each coin for its genuineness and its degree of precious metal. A whole host of control stamps, counter-stamps, hallmarkings, and graffiti[67] on the coins bears witness to this fact. The distrust of coins was high and the fear of private and official forgeries, i.e. of silver-plated copper or bronze coins, was widespread.[68] This fear also explains the legal proscriptions that punished coin forgery with the death penalty.[69] The earliest known forgeries in the history of money were located in the Egyptian temple of the eleventh century (?) in Bet-Shean: the hoard found here contained gold-plated silver bars.[70] A modern Palestinian proverb states, "Better to turn a coin over 100 times than to accept a fake coin once."[71] As an example from Haifa in the year 1914 shows, it was not unusual until far into the British Mandate to weigh precious metal coins, "After I brought my Napoleondors to the Bank, where they were not counted due to their large number, but rather weighed, I proceeded to the hospice with heavy money sacks."[72]

---

[67] J. Elayi and A. Lemaire, *Graffiti et contremarques ouest-sémitiques sur les monnaies grecques et proche-orientales*, Glaux 13, Milan: Edizioni Ennere, 1998; A. Lemaire, "Graffito Hébreu sur Tétradrachme Pseudo-Athénien," *Israel Numismatic Journal* 15 (2003–2006): 24–7; J. Elayi, "The Tyrian Monetary Inscriptions of the Persian Period," *Transeuphratène* 34 (2007): 65–101.

[68] See the agreement on coins between Mytilene/Lesbos and Phokaia (early 4th century BCE) or the death sentence from Dyme/Achaia (3rd century BCE); K. Brodersen et al., eds., *Historische griechische Inschriften in Übersetzung, Bd. II*, Texte zur Forschung 68, Darmstadt: Wissenschaftliche Buchgesellschaft, 1996, 4, Nr. 203; K. Brodersen et al., eds., *Historische griechische Inschriften in Übersetzung, Bd. III*, Texte zur Forschung 71, Darmstadt: Wissenschaftliche Buchgesellschaft, 1999, 53, Nr. 446. In an Attic law on coin circulation and control from the year 375/4 BCE, the hallmarking and thus the voiding of silver-plated bronze or copper coins became the legal obligation of coin officials: Brodersen et al., eds., *Historische griechische Inschriften in Übersetzung, Bd. II*, 18f., Nr. 221. See also Dio Cassius, *Hist.* 78,15,3–4; Aristophanes, *Ranae* 718–737; Petronius, *Sat.* 56,1 ("Was aber scheint uns nach der Bücherwissenschaft das schwierigste Handwerk zu sein: Mir scheint, Arzt und Wechsler. ... Der Wechsler, weil er unter der Silberschicht das Kupfer sieht").

[69] In addition to the previously mentioned sources see *Codex Iustinani* 9,24,2 (de falsa moneta); *Digest.* 48,10,8 (Ulpian).

[70] P. Vargyas, "Fakes before Coins?" in: *"Up to the Gates of Ekron,"* eds. White Crawford et al., 295–304.

[71] See L. Haefeli, *Spruchweisheit und Volksleben in Palaestina*, Lucerne: Räber, 1939, 119.

[72] S. Kirchberger and J. Schmitzberger, "Die dritte bayerische Volkswallfahrt ins Heilige Land im Jahre 1914," in: *Bayerischer Pilgerverein vom Heiligen Lande*, 77; cf. König, *Die Deutschen Palästinas in englischer Gefangenschaft*, 25–6.

Second, because of the variety in currencies, it became necessary to weigh the coins. All currencies could be exchanged by means of weighing. Thus, the fear of fake weights became a major concern. It is interesting that the Old Testament does not contain any prohibitions against coin forgery; instead it contains prohibition against the use of fake weights or scales (Lev. 19:35f.; Deut. 25:13–15; Hosea 12:7f.; Amos 8:5; Micah 6:10f.; Ezek. 45:10; Job 31:6; Prov. 11:11; 16:11; 20:23).[73] In addition, the Old Testament does not mention officials to supervise weighing (*šql*; see perhaps Isa. 33:18 *šōqel*)[74] and coin control [*mḥšb(m)*][75] as are known, for example, from Punic inscriptions in Carthage. All of this clearly shows that the new form of payment had a hard time establishing itself in Judah.

For a long time, coins were seen as a kind of silver bar. They did not bear any indication of value or a number. The value of a coin was defined according to the real value of its metal. Thus, coins not only continued to be weighed, they were also divided as needed into thirds, halves, quarters, etc. Breaking up coins was as widespread a practice[76] as it had been previously with silver bars and jewelry. As archaeological and literary sources clearly show (e.g. *'štwt* Kupferrolle 3Q15 I,5; II,4; see *lšwn* Josh. 7:21 and *qšyāh* Josh. 24:32; Job 2:11),[77] metal bars were not merely a pre-monetary form of payment, they continued to be used once coins dominated trade.

The famous inscription on the wall described in Daniel 5:25 (completed during the Seleucid-Hasmonean reign) appeared in the

---

[73] For the coming of standardized weights in the eighth century in Judah, see R. Kletter, *Economic Keystones: The Weight System of the Kingdom of Judah*, Journal for the Study of the Old Testament. Supplement Series 276, Sheffield Academic Press, 1998.

[74] M. Heltzer, *Die Organisation des Handwerks im "Dunklen Zeitalter" und im I. Jahrtausend v.u.Z. im östlichen Mittelmeergebiet*, Padua: Sargen, 1992, 101.

[75] Heltzer, *Die Organisation des Handwerks*, 81, 108–12.

[76] See e.g., J. Elayi and A. G. Elayi, "Trésor d'époque perse et de la region d'Arwad," *RNum 6e série* 32 (1990): 7–16; C. M. Kraay and P. R. S. Moorey, "Two Fifth Century Hoards from the Near East," *RNum 6e série* 10 (1968): 181–235; J. Reade, "A Hoard of Silver Currency from Achaemenid Babylon," *Iran* 24 (1986): 79–89; Stucky, *Ras Shamra – Leukos Limen*, 39–40.

[77] J. Briend, "Le trésor de YHWH en Jos. 6,19–24b," *Transeuphratène* 20 (2000): 101–6. Cf. e.g., E. S. G. Robinson, "Two Greek Coin Hoards," *Numismatic Chronicle* 20 (1960): 31–6; G. Stumpf, "Der Kreuzzug Kaiser Barbarossas: Münzschätze seiner Zeit," Munich: Staatliche Münzsammlung, 1991, 47–8.

residence of the Babylonian King Belshazzar with only three initial letters: *m, t, p*. These letters are interpreted by the narrator as *m^{e}ne' m^{e}ne' t^{e}ql û-parsín>m^{e}nah, tql>t^{e}qîlitā*'; *p^{e}res>p^{e}rîsat* [actually, Mine, Šeqel (aram. *t^{e}qel*) and Halb-Šeqel (*p^{e}res sic!*)]. Daniel unravels the abbreviation and reads the nouns as passive participles, "counted, weighed, and divided," and thus presupposes a well-known pre-monetary procedure.

How many coins were in circulation in early Palestine is not known. The variety of coin images and thus the number of different coin stamps is quite high. It stands to reason that quite a few coins were in circulation. The coins from verified archaeological sites – Gaza is an exception – were all found within the area of their minting press, suggesting that they were only used in the local market. In Samaria and Judah, almost exclusively small coins have been found. The largest, but not most frequent, value was the drachma. Larger transactions were conducted with foreign currencies or pre-monetary payment. Mass-produced bronze or copper coins spread throughout Palestine only from the Ptolemaic period. All this points to the conclusion that economic concerns were not the sole reason that led to the earliest coin production in Samaria and Judah.

The monetary system expanded only with the introduction of coins made of non-precious metals such as bronze, copper, or lead. Even if these token coins were initially based on metal, their real value soon departed from their nominal value. The disadvantage of these face-value coins lay in the fact that their value fluctuated to a much higher degree than that of silver coins during the course of history. It became dependent on the amount of money currently in circulation, the type of product and its availability, and the basic price of metal. Token coins were only a mass phenomenon in the Hellenistic period. Under Hasmonean rule, millions of small coins made of non-precious metals were brought into circulation.

The transition from barter economy to money and coins was a gradual process spanning a long period of time. The various forms of payment were not mutually exclusive, but rather existed side by side. Barter economy was complemented, not supplanted, by money and coins. The payment with coins appeared alongside the traditional pre- and para-monetary economic systems that continued to exist.

Except for the indications of weight and value, a general term for coin (*āaeba'lāib'ā'* (*āb'*, *āb'*, *tby'*); phon. *āb'*) appears in both Hebrew and

Aramaic only in the *Wādi al-Murabbaʿāt* Papyri,[78] the Targumim, the Talmud (e.g. bBM 25a, 44b, 46a; bŠebu 38b; yŠeq 2, 46) and in other rabbinic writings.

A monetary system developed only partially and gradually in Achaemenid and Hellenistic Palestine. From the Hellenistic period, it became a phenomenon encompassing the whole region without supplanting other traditional forms of economy. Coin economy was never exclusive, but rather, a part of the whole. Already in the ancient economic history of Palestine and other regions, we know of periods of demonetization and the return to barter economy.[79]

---

[78] Phon. *ṭbʿ ṣr* in RÉS No. 1204:2. P. Benoit et al., eds., *Les Grottes de Murabbaʿāt, Discoveries in the Judaean Desert 2*, Oxford: Clarendon Press, 1961, No. 20:5.

[79] e.g. in the late Roman Empire after the mid-third century or in the Byzantine Empire in the time after *c.*580 CE, see C. Morrisson, V. Popovic, V. Ivaniševic et al., *Les trésors monétaires byzantines des Balkans et d'Asie Mineure (491–713)*, Réalités Byzantines 13, Paris: Lethielleux, 2006, 59f.; R. Wolters, *Nummi Signati: Untersuchungen zur römischen Münzprägung und Geldwirtschaft*, Vestigia 49, Munich: Beck, 1999, 410.

9 | Fate's gift economy: the Chinese case of coping with the asymmetry between man and fate

RUDOLF G. WAGNER

The problem

A parallelism has been observed by many scholars between the perception of the interaction of the individual in China with the state and that with forces in the Beyond such as gods, spirits, ancestors, and ghouls. This parallelism pertains to the power, the hierarchical organization, and the impact of the respective realms on the individual, but also to the forms of interaction in a legalized and monetized bureaucratic form replete with contracts and money. Since Arthur Wolf's pioneering article in 1974,[1] it has become a generally accepted notion among China scholars that the practices dealing with the Beyond are extrapolated and derived from the experiences with the "real world." The primacy of the real-world experience is treated as self-evident and in no further need of proof beyond showing the parallelism mentioned.[2]

The relevance of this parallelism is heightened by a very peculiar feature in Chinese religious practices. In many Eurasian cultures it has been a practice since early times to give some money and provisions to

---

[1] A. P. Wolf, "Gods, Ghosts, and Ancestors," in A. P. Wolf, ed., *Religion and Ritual in Chinese Society*, Stanford University Press, 1974, 131–82. On money, for example, Wolf writes: "The offerings made to the various forms of supernatural usually include several types of "spirit money" [gun-cua], as well as food and incense. The different categories of spirit money reflect the division of the supernatural world into spirits modelled on senior kinsmen, on strangers, and on the imperial bureaucracy" (179).

[2] Examples for the way in which this assumption has become a commonplace figure of thought might be V. Hansen, *Negotiating Daily Life in Traditional China. How Ordinary People Used Contracts 600–1400*, New Haven, CT: Yale University Press, 1995, 3, referring to tomb contracts as replicas of contracts between people; R. von Glahn, *The Sinister Way: The Divine and the Demonic in Chinese Religious Culture*, Berkeley: University of California Press, 2004, ch. 7, links the emergence of the cult of the God(s) of Wealth to the commercialization of Song and Ming society.

the deceased for their trip into the nether world. In the Chinese realm, this practice has also been documented since the Shang dynasty. In Shang tombs we find gifts of kauri shell "money" as well as grains and beverages in bronze vessels. They imply the assumption of a certain continuity of needs, material values, and social structures between this world and the other. There is, however, nothing in the early Chinese written record to flesh-out these assumptions in words.

Accordingly, while there seems to be little difference between China and the other early Eurasian cultures with regard to gifts accompanying the dead, any visit to a Chinese temple today will also show a very distinctive Chinese feature: the pervasive presence of paper money that is being burnt there. At sometimes spectacular funerals this money is supplemented with specific valuables such as Mercedes cars, television sets, fancy interior decoration, and credit cards. These are made of coloured paper and are burnt together with the paper money. Looking back, there is a rich record of monetary and contractual dealings with the Beyond since very early times that is qualitatively different from the practices elsewhere. As Anna Seidel has observed, this is a unique Chinese feature in world religion that will be found neither in the central Asian and north Indian homelands of Buddhism nor in societies adjacent to China such as Japan, Vietnam or Korea, which in other aspects have incorporated many ideas, institutions and practices from China into their own environment.[3]

A second feature particular to the Chinese world is the ubiquitous presence of supernatural forces in written contractual relations as guarantors of covenants and as counterparts of contracts, often in association with money.

There are various problems with the common-sense assumption of the primacy of the "real" against the "supernatural." First, no convincing and hopefully falsifiable scholarly process has been developed to show how the transfer from the natural to the supernatural might have operated. Second, the explanation presupposes an all-pervasive, powerful, highly invasive, and utterly incalculable presence of state bureaucracies in individual lives that would prompt a psychological need to hypostasize the agents into supernatural beings. While this might be true for the modern and highly invasive nation-state, nothing

---

[3] A. Seidel, review of Hou Ching-lang, *Monnaies d'Offrande*, "Buying One's Way to Heaven: The Celestial Treasury in Chinese Religions," *History of Religions*, 17 (1978) 3(4): 428.

in the Chinese historical record indicates such a penetration of the state into individual lives. The image of society and individual lives in pre-modern history on which this common-sense assumption rests is that of the highly ideological modern inventions of the Chinese past by revolutionaries who used it to mobilize for their cause of radical change, and to highlight their achievements after the success of the revolution by enhancing the contrast with the dark past. This invented history-with-a-purpose has seeped into the common-sense picture of the Chinese past for long enough to become a shared notion that has the additional charm of largely agreeing with "Chinese" pronouncements shared by officials and intellectuals alike instead of landing in the political incorrectness of imperialist or orientalist impositions. As far as I can see, in the area under consideration here, only Hou Ching-lang has refrained from imposing this story on his sources in his pivotal 1975 study, *Monnaies d'Offrande et la Notion de Trésorerie dans la Religion Chinoise (Sacrificial Money and the Notion of the Treasury in Chinese Religion).*[4]

Instead of following the reductionist path of prejudging the primacy of the "real" over the "supernatural," I suggest testing the viability of the inverse hypothesis. The plausibility of such a hypothesis as being not just random, but worth the test, rests on simple observations. Areas of maximum concern for average Chinese that can be documented both from practices and, to a smaller degree, from the written record, would be wealth, social status, health, longevity, and (male) offspring. None of these can be achieved by human effort alone. They show a daily and pressing dependence of the individual on incalculable factors of fate. In all of these realms the state only plays the role of a pale second cousin. If we maintain the bifurcation between the natural and the supernatural for a moment, and use as a yardstick the amount of time, energy and resources put into reducing the unpredictability of the "supernatural" forces compared to that of the "natural" forces, we see a practice that signals higher urgency for dealing with the Beyond. Maspéro has calculated that in pre-modern times (his sources were Ming and Qing), apart from the daily religious ceremonies in home and temple, nearly half of the days of the year were tagged as being under one or the other

---

[4] H. Ching-lang, *Monnaies d'Offrande et la Notion de Trésorerie dans la Religion Chinoise*, Paris: Collège de France, Institut des Hautes Études Chinoises, 1975.

"religious" restriction or mandate.[5] On the birthdays of the kings of hell, sacrifices had to be made for them and the rules against killing living beings were to be more strictly kept, quite apart from refraining from sexual intercourse. On the days when the hungry ghosts roam, good deeds would have to be done and rituals organized in temples to transfer merits to these hungry ghosts, quite apart from sacrifices to feed them. If we compare this to the energy and time spent by little folk on reducing the unpredictability of the pre-modern Chinese state machinery, with which in fact they had minimal contact, the result seems evident. We thus hypothesize that the "real" world is but a small and relatively minor part of the factors determining fate, and that many of the secular practices of reducing randomness in fate are adapted to worldly uses from the interaction with the supernatural rather than the other way around.

To move from plausible hypothesis to convincing and falsifiable analysis, detailed evidence would have to be offered showing the primacy of fate over the state, and documenting how specific processes of the interaction with the supernatural are translated into features of interacting with the "real."

The second problem is one of evidence. Anthropologists, who tend to emphasize the particularity of locality against the elite-dominated unifying features of the state in institutions and ideology, have observed an unusually high homogeneity in religious ritual practices across the Chinese realm.[6] This does not come with an equally homogeneous set of canonical explanations and interpretations. Field research has shown a wide array of different interpretations of the meaning of the same practice in different localities or social groups, and even by different individuals. In addition to this synchronous difference, we have a diachronous continuity of practices that is going far back in time without, especially for the earlier phases, any sort of (surviving) interpretation, but for which certainly a wide range of different interpretations may be assumed.

An argument has been made that Chinese religion is identified by such practices rather than by any interpretation of them. Once such interpretations show up in the historical record they must be read against the

---

[5] H. Maspéro, "Mythologie de la Chine Moderne," in: L. Conchaud, ed., *Mythologie Asiatique Illustrée*, Paris: Librairie de France, 1928.

[6] A good summary of this discussion that involves scholars such as Steven Sangren, Maurice Freedman, C. K. Yang, James Watson, Arthur Wolf, and Robert Weller will be found in: von Glahn, *The Sinister Way*, Introduction.

background of this continuity of practice as an attempt at interpretation with all the particularities of historical circumstance and intellectual orientation this involves. While the practices might be impacted by the interpretation, the two remain essentially independent of each other, and other interpretations of the same practice remain possible. This again is a hypothesis to be tested. It presupposes a willingness to accept as part of the historical religious record not just articulated interpretations, but also practices reconstructed from the archaeological record or fictional narratives.

The third problem is that of the nature of the economic relations with the supernatural in China. Gernet's approach in his seminal *Aspects économiques du bouddhisme dans la société chinoise du Ve au Xe siècle* (1956) is informed by a basic estrangement from and hostility to religious pursuits. While the English translation by Franciscus Verellen has straightened out some of the documentary weaknesses of Gernet's work, this aspect has remained untouched.[7] The Buddhists, in Gernet's opinion, were a "parasitic" body feasting on Chinese society. Hou Ching-lang, by contrast, gives a detailed description of the economic relations with the supernatural, but he does not address the question of the nature of these economic relations. Valerie Hansen in her rich chapter on "Contracting with the Gods," focuses on the parallelism of contracts with the supernatural with contracts among people, but does not deal with the particular kind of contractual relations with the gods as non-signatories of these pacts that fundamentally differentiates them from the regular contracts.[8] A short note in Macdonald's 1956 review of Gernet's work, however, suggests an approach that focuses exactly on the particularity of these monetary and contractual relations. Macdonald wrote: "One might emphasize one aspect of this work that is so full of new information: It provides a set of additional historical information of greatest importance for the "Essai sur le don."[9] The suggestion to treat

---

[7] J. Gernet, *Buddhism in Chinese Society. An Economic History from the Fifth to the Tenth Centuries*, New York: Columbia University Press, 1995. For a critical review of this translation, see J. Silk, "Marginal Notes on a Study of Buddhism, Economy and Society in China," *Journal of the International Association of Buddhist Studies*, 22 (1999) 2: 360–98.

[8] Hansen, *Negotiating Daily Life*, pt. II.

[9] A. W. Macdonald in a review of, among others, J. Gernet's *Aspects économiques du bouddhisme en Chine*: A. W. Macdonald, "Bouddhisme et Sociologie," *Archives de Sciences Sociales des Religions*, 2 (1956) 1: 97. The reference is to M. Mauss, "Essai sur le don," *L'année sociologique*, nouvelle série, 1923/4.

the contractual and monetary relationships with the Beyond in terms of a gift economy is a valid one, and I intend to follow this trail.

The gift economy of Fate: an exercise in coping with asymmetry

From burial practices since at least Shang times, there is evidence that the realm of the living and the realm entered into by the dead were seen as mirror images. The transition from one realm into the other involved communication about the status of the dead in the hierarchy of the living. This was signaled through status emblems accompanying the dead in the tomb. Early Chinese mantic practices such as scapulomancy operate on the assumption that the dead – at least the dead kings – become immortal ancestors endowed with a knowledge that is superior to that of the living by including the future. This practice can be documented only for the Shang kings and their mantic specialists, but it is possible and even plausible that lower nobility and common folk had their own forms of reducing uncertainty through communication with the Beyond.

Part of the communication with the Beyond was monetary. "Money" became an important – and to a degree standardized – medium for commercial exchange only much later. As far as available records show, it was first precious and valuable for its material content and was used alternatively with bronze, silk and perhaps by fiefs as part of a gift economy through which the king reciprocated for services provided to him, such as war deeds. In the early tombs we find kauri shells, which were such "gift" money during the Shang period; later during the Zhou period we find precious metals, sometimes in the standardized form for which the term "money" is often used in scholarly literature, although it definitely was not used as part of regular business transactions. The kauri shells and later precious metals accompanying the (high-ranking) dead into their tombs were part of a gift for which some sort of reciprocity in the form of the treatment of the deceased was expected, but they were not part of a money economy with a fixed commodity or service to be paid for at a price both sides had agreed upon. These "money" gifts where thus part of a gift rather than part of a money economy.

As a rule, the dividing line between the two is described as that between a gift and a money economy. In the Chinese case, however, money remains – as we shall see to this day – a key part of the gift economy. The "money" gifts were never the only precious goods accompanying the tomb lord. Apart from goods such as wine and grain to bridge over some sort of "transition" to a new existence, precious objects might include bronze vessels, jade discs and the like, which were equally important pieces in a gift economy and would enable the tomb lord to make appropriate presents as part of his settling in new circumstances. The valuables were not stones gathered without great effort from the field. They represented the condensation of effort, and could ideally be exchanged into similar efforts by others to provide goods and services. The perceived risk of missing the preferences of the recipient was accordingly low. While the moral qualities of the ways in which these valuables had originally been acquired leaves no trace in the end product, the transfer of the results of these efforts to the recipient is an act that calls for reciprocity from the recipient as well as from those powers to whom he transfers them as gifts.

The insertion of these gifts into the tomb is a service provided by the living to their dead relations. They are to be used by the deceased in the new environment. This means that instead of direct one-to-one gift relations, we have a – silent and unarticulated but very consistent – transfer of the claim to reciprocity coming with a gift from the living to the dead.

While the relative homogeneity of some of the Chinese practices of dealing with the Beyond reflects a social consensus, this consensus itself contains the silent assumption that all the asymmetries notwithstanding, the "other side" was not acting randomly, even if the particulars of this non-randomness eluded the understanding of the living. This assumed non-randomness eventually shows up in the interpretations and in the later narratives about human interaction with the supernatural, which detail the reasons prompting a particular intervention from the supernatural. It is this assumed non-randomness which allowed for the development of repeatable practices in dealing with the supernatural.

From early on the practice in quite a few – but not in all – tombs of using bone imitations instead of the real kauri shells, or coloured clay pieces instead of gold ingots, signals an understanding that in the realm of the supernatural into which, for example, the dead entered, a different valuation might prevail. Not all tombs had such imitation goods. This signals that there was no canonized knowledge about the proper way, but rather, a diversity of specific practices within a common framework. These practices are to be seen as tests of effectiveness. Their falsification came not with a "correct" reading of the canon, but

with the occurrence of the desired effect such as freedom from moles-
tation from the spirit of the deceased. As the efforts going into making
these replicas are definitely lower than those going into the real thing, a
cynical reading might infer that we see here a fading of the belief that
some real efforts were needed to accommodate the supernatural. I see
no other evidence for such a process. There are finds with up to 20,000
such kauri shell imitations and later, since the third century BCE, we
have finds with gold ingot imitations in tombs the lords of which clearly
belonged to the most prestigious and wealthiest men of their time. Given
the public and social nature of such prestigious burials and the fact that
in the same tombs precious bronze vessels might be found, the notion
that this is cheating is not convincing. The practice presupposes an
understanding of a valuation with a mirror inversion much like the
existence after death was imagined as a mirror or shadow of life.

As real kauri shells and real gold pieces were also found, there was no
consent as to the radicalism with which this principle was to be pursued,
but the notion of the mirror inversion must have been accepted enough
not to cause embarrassment at a burial. The silent practice of putting a
definite amount of foodstuffs and valuables into a tomb also signals a
two-stage process after death, the first being a transition, a period for
which food, drink, transport vehicles, horses, servants, and gifts will be
needed; the second being something like a permanent state with much
lower needs that can be satisfied with food sacrifices at greater intervals,
such as once a year.

Written records from the Chunqiu period show that there is substantial risk if the dead are not treated in an appropriate way with gifts. They
might reciprocate for the failure to provide gifts (in the form of burial
goods and sacrifices) through interventions into the world of the living
such as causing disease. Their operation will not be controlled even by
the living with the highest powers. A practice therefore was current
from early on for a new dynasty to continue the sacrifices for the
ancestors of a toppled dynasty.

This observation shows that treatment of these exchanges purely in
terms of a gift economy shortchanges the record. One is not free to give
a gift or withhold it. There is a routinized expectation that a gift will be
given to atone for interfering in the sphere of the counterpart, be it by
dispatching a dead body into the Beyond, or by asking for information,
protection, or support. Withholding a gift is not just the absence of the
positive gesture, but a slight that will call forth a reaction as much as

giving the gift will. It is therefore appropriate to talk of a gift-and-slight economy rather than simply of a gift economy.

Covenants or contracts are an integral part of the practices of inter-action with supernatural forces. Covenants between states in the Chunqiu period and covenants in which loyalty to a lord was sworn, such as the Houma covenants, were concluded with a sacrifice, and a copy of the covenant would be buried together with the victim.[10] For this early period we have no evidence of contracts between private persons. For a later date, ample archaeological evidence is forthcoming, and in the Turfan and Dunhuang troves we have large numbers of such contracts for loans and the like from the seventh to the tenth centuries CE.[11] Interestingly enough, they shared an important feature with the cove-nants mentioned above, namely, there is no worldly authority to enforce adhesion. As opposed to pawn shops where the security is deposited with the creditor, these loan contracts operated with a provision that in case of default the creditor had a claim on such and such a part of the property of the credit-holder, but this provision was not one that could be reliably enforced by recourse to state authorities. The Qin and Han law codes contain no civil law provisions for state-sanctioned enforcement of con-tracts, and in the Tang code their role is only marginally alluded to. The covenants thus did not contain worldly sanctions, but explicitly con-tained the threat brought with a sacrifice that the spirits would punish the transgressor. Susan Weld writes on the Houma covenants: "The burial of the victim together with the inscribed tablets suggests instead a form of communication across the boundary between the human and the spirit worlds: an attempt to elicit the spirits' attention and draw on their power, if necessary, to activate the covenantor's self-curse."[12] While in these covenants "the spirits" in a rather diffuse and collective way were called upon as an authority securing the fulfillment of the covenant, since the first century CE, contracts were found in tombs in which, together with the identification of the name and status of the tomb lord, the subsoil into which the coffin was laid was bought from the particular earth deity

[10] S. R. Weld, "Covenant in Jin's Walled Cities: the Discoveries at Houma and Wenxian," unpub. Ph.D. dissertation, Harvard University 1990.

[11] Y. Tatsuro and I. On, *Tun-huang and Turfan Documents Concerning Social and Economic History*, Tokyo: Toyo Bunko, 1986, 1987, vol. III, Contracts: B, *Plates* and Vol. III, Contracts: A, *Introduction and Texts*. These documents have been studied by Gernet and Hansen.

[12] Weld, "Covenant in Jin's Walled Cities," 63.

to whom it belonged. The contract named a sum for which the land was bought. This sum, always made up of very high lucky numbers such as 99.999 or 99,000 strings of cash independent of the varying local surface land prices over time and widely outside the range of the surface or subface soil prices has, however, never been found in the tombs.[13]

The 9 is a "lucky" number because the pronunciation of its Chinese character, 九 *jiu*, is homophonous with that of the character 久, namely *jiu*, meaning "eternal, long-lasting." The sum thus translates into "forever-ever, ever-ever-ever," which for a contract is a good duration. It is to be assumed that the contract money consisted of some form of burnable imitation (paper was just being invented) that was transferred to the earth god by burning. While technically this looks like a regular commercial transaction, it is not. The practice clearly assumes a different value structure in the Beyond, with land values about a hundred times higher than land prices for the surface soil, and calculated with lucky numbers, as well as an appreciation of forms of payment that are an inverted mirror image of cash in this world. As there was no way to have a negotiated settlement on the price with the counterpart, this huge sum with its symbolic lucky number accoutrements must be seen as a safe gift that is definitely above any value that might be put on this piece of subsoil. In the huge disproportion between the price of the surface land and the subsoil we can find a quantitative assessment of the perceived asymmetry between the contracting partners.

The purpose of this contract and money gift is twofold: to secure a peaceful transition of the tomb lord, and to forestall an angry reaction by the earth god that in turn would transform the tomb lord into a threat to the health and well-being of his living descendants. The gift offered for the subsoil is proportional to the perceived threat to the living in case the gift is considered insufficient.

Such contracts of buying and selling are read by scholars – very much like the use of money – as indicating that they are part of a monetized economy that operates on the assumption of equality between buyer and seller, creditor and credit-taker within a legally secured contractual relationship. As opposed to, for example, the explicit contract between Jahweh and the children of Israel, which defined the duties of both sides

---

[13] A. Seidel, "Traces of Han Religion in Funeral Texts Found in Tombs," in: A. Kan'ei 秋月觀暎, ed., *Dōkyō to shūkyō bunka* 道教と宗教文化, Tokyo: Hirakawa shuppansha, 1987, 21–57.

and the penalty (for the children of Israel alone) for defaulting, none of the contracts with the supernatural realm from China has the other side agreeing. The contracts rest on one-sided gifts together with a description of the hoped-for reciprocal reaction.

A key difference between gift and conventional credit is that the currency of the credit disbursement and that of the return payment tends to be the same, while in a gift economy the goods and services given do not have to be replicated in the reciprocal gift.

There is no assumed equality between the contracting parties, but an assumed total asymmetry that makes these contracts into a form of formalized prayer for a specific favor. Still, as contracts they mark an effort from humans to enhance the agency of their subaltern station, formalize the behavior of supernatural powers into a predictable pattern and in this manner cope with this asymmetry.

This asymmetry has different aspects.

- It is an asymmetry of power, with the authority in the Beyond being able to impact the health and life of human beings while human beings have little power over their counterparts, especially if they are not local goblins, but higher up in an assumed hierarchy.
- It is an asymmetry of knowledge, as the authority in the Beyond is assumed to have knowledge not just of the present and the past, but also of the future, about which human beings are utterly ignorant.
- And finally, it is an asymmetry of information, because it is assumed that the authority in the Beyond has full information about human beings in their past, present, and future in all aspects down to innermost secret thoughts, while human beings have no hard information whatever about their counterpart.

This consistent asymmetry does not deprive human beings of agency. To the contrary, the need to cope with this asymmetry generates a large but highly targeted set of diverse practices that try to reduce the vicariousness of human life. In short, far from reducing human beings to passive victims of unpredictable and unfathomable interventions, this asymmetry prompts and prods human agency, without, however, the prospect of inverting the asymmetry.

This agency is not reduced to various practices designed to preempt damaging interventions; to undo them after they have occurred; to secure beneficial interventions; or to flout all these steps and withhold the expected gift. As there is no clear and falsifiable path to assess the counterpart, practices that have shown to be effective gain wide traction without being dependent on further causal explanation, and are abandoned once the deity concerned did not deliver or the practice used had become ineffective. While this pragmatic approach generally dominates, the extremely high degree of perceived dependency creates a need, a market, and an audience for explanations and interpretations that promise to increase the reliability and effectiveness of practices to influence the counterparts in the Beyond. A very large volume of religious writing consists of efforts to concretize and specify the actors, the dynamics of their interaction, and the most effective practices of this purpose as well as those most damaging.

In the pre-Buddhist practices of the contractual relations with the supernatural, no moral value judgments either about the deceased or the supernatural forces are implied. There is no retribution for good or bad deeds of the deceased person, and the sacrifices to the ancestors of the previous dynasty have to be maintained even though it lost the mandate to rule. In the interpretation of these practices, however, such evaluative elements turn up from early on. A contract partner should abide by the contract with a "virtue" located in his "heart."[14] Knowing about the weakness of human beings, both sides agree to call on the spirits to descend on them if they fail to honor the contract. The content of the contract is not judged in these interpretations in moral terms, but abiding by the contract or not is. The spirits are not to judge the righteousness of the contract content, but that of the partners in abiding by it or reneging on it. In this manner they are contracted not to ease the transition of a deceased into the nether world and prevent him from visiting his descendants with disaster, they are contracted with the gift of a present (the victim) to intervene with exactly such disasters in the world of the living to enforce obedience by a covenant. In a related manner, Heaven, as the ultimate Zhou authority in the Beyond, is interpreted as intervening in the human world by withdrawing the right to rule from a dynasty and giving it to another in a complex interaction with the standing of the respective candidates among the people. According to the earliest documents in the *Book of Odes* as well as the earliest archaeological finds such as the Bin Gong Xu bronze

---

[14] Weld, "Covenant in Jin's Walled Cities," 64.

vessel inscription from the middle of the ninth century BCE,[15] Heaven decides on the basis of a quality in the candidates called *de* 德 (often translated as "virtue" or "charisma"), which is also appreciated by the "people." The total lack of this quality ends with the dynastic house being justly toppled by the new aspirant, as happened when the Shang dynasty was replaced by the Zhou.

While we do have, for example in the *Ritual of Zhou, Zhouli*, descriptions of required burial practices, on the level of explicit interpretations of post-mortem life or the structures of the supernatural, practically nothing for the early pre-Han period is extant.[16] The same is true for the covenants for which descriptions of the practice as well as silent archaeological monuments (such as the Houma covenants) survive, but no interpretations of their implications.

Early Chinese interaction practices with the powers of fate in the forms of material exchanges (sacrifices, money) and of their fixation in contractual terms operate in the mode of a gift economy. This presupposes in the most radical sense actors operating independently of each other in providing services and goods without negotiation but with the implied – and in the shape of a contract, explicit – expectation of reciprocity. The asymmetry in the material structure between the human world and the Beyond translates into a practice of "translation" of worldly services and goods to make them valid in the other realm through burning or other procedures. The asymmetry in the power relations between the authorities of the Beyond and mortal humans translates into the need for the humans to develop proactive agency in forestalling negative and even achieving positive interventions from the Beyond. This human agency is largely defensive and implies an assumption of more-or-less constant threats to wealth, status, health, longevity, and offspring. A wide array of supplementary practices has been developed to undo the worst if one such proactive intervention does not suffice. An example is demonic medicine. Operating on the assumption

---

[15] E. L. Shaughnessy, "The *Bin Gong Xu* Inscription and the Origins of the Chinese Literary Tradition," in: W. Idema, ed., *Books in Numbers*, Cambridge, MA: Harvard Yenching Library, 2008, 3–23.

[16] This is in marked difference to other early cultures in the Near and Middle East. This difference has sometimes been explained by an aversion of "Confucian" men of letters to transmit matters of "superstition." This explanation stipulates a parallel development, which, however, has not found support in the recent excavations of pre-Han texts written on bamboo.

that a disease is caused by demonic impact (later interpreted as hungry spirits), curative practices involved sacrifices to the demon, but also rituals with the power to evict the demon as well as more strictly medical interventions.[17] Risk reduction in such asymmetrical relations is done by hedging the bets by simultaneously or consecutively engaging in a variety of practices of possible effectiveness but without any necessary consistency of meaning.

Life as credit

We have to go one step further back. The entire set of practices hitherto sketched presupposes a more fundamental relationship between humans and the supernatural. While there is an unquestioned assumption that humans are constantly exposed to the random exercise of power from forces beyond their control and while there are efforts visible to manipulate the way in which these interfere in human life, all this operates on the basis of the assumption of an even more fundamental asymmetry. Humans are not just at the receiving end of fate; they are at the receiving end of life itself. They receive it, or it is given, without them asking for it, and it is again taken without them being consulted. The assumption implied in the practices we described is that life and death are just the most radical forms of the gift economy of fate.

The huge original gift of life creates from the outset a debt in the receiver that calls for substantial reciprocity and entitles the giver to some permanent role in the life of the receiver. As the recipient of these gifts lives through the specificity of his body and mind in space and time, fate materializes not in one essentialized moment and place, but in a string of occurrences that are usually inconsistent and full of contradictions. The practices developed to deal with the occurrences of fate react to the inconsistency by assuming a variety of supernatural agents with different powers and agendas as well as different preferences and aversions in terms of the gift-and-slight economy. A hierarchy among the supernatural actors linked to status and territorial sway seems to be implied in practices from early on. Personal idiosyncrasies, conflicts and alliances, however, which in some other environments – such as early Greek mythology – are ubiquitous, are not assumed in either the

---

[17] P. Unschuld, *Medicine in China: A History of Ideas*, Berkeley: University of California Press, 1985.

pre-Buddhist Chinese or the Buddhist Chinese Beyond. Altogether, the Chinese practices deal with a Beyond that impacts the human world according to an exceedingly complex but non-random mechanism. The individualized powers in the Beyond are understood as administering this mechanism, but as being neither able nor interested to change its set-up. This mechanism is operative in a dimension not bound by human time with its precipitous decline in reliable information between the past and the present on the one hand and the future on the other. Its complexity as well as impersonal rationality is mirrored on the elite level in one of the early Chinese key classics, the *Book of Changes*. In principle it follows that the fate of human beings is inserted into a mechanism that leaves little leeway for proactive change. The implied non-randomness of the complex workings of this mechanism on the other hand prompts the search for interventions that will not fundamentally change the mechanism but might be effective in achieving moderate – and reproducible – effects that are due to the inherent instabilities of such extremely complex mechanisms. This instability is articulated through explanations, which see spiritual bureaucratic agents as manning the system. While relatively bland and faceless, they are individualized enough to inadvertently make the generic bureaucratic mistake – such as misfiling a name – on occasion, and might have a weak moment during their birthday, or might be irritated at a lack of veneration.

It is easy to see that specialists will make their appearance, who, on the basis of successfully hitting the taste and preference of the supernatural counterpart who is administering a particular fate event, will claim higher knowledge, and will market themselves in the human world as skilled in this gift economy.

Interpretations and their impact

It is the hypothesis to be tested that the practices described above contain in an open and silent form the potential for the manifold interpretations given in different sectors of society over time. While different interpretations are by definition simultaneously possible and do not have to lead to disagreements as long as the practice stays the same, these interpretations may have an impact on the specific shape these practices assume. At the same time, we have seen variations within a common framework of practice. These must be seen as implicit interpretations the truth of which shows not through an agreement with elite canons, but through the achievement of the desired effect, which often is the non-occurrence of damage.

The notion of life as a powerful and defining gift that comes with a package of fate including at least wealth, status, capabilities, and lifespan is among the earliest to find explicit interpretation in China. The key term to identify this gift is *ming* 命 with the meaning of life mandate, but also a narrower meaning of an order from above. First used in the early Zhou to describe the "mandate" received by a dynasty from the highest celestial authority, Heaven, it had by the Han dynasty moved to describe the endowment received by a human being at birth from the supernatural ("Heaven"), an endowment that included a fixed (if unknown) lifespan.

There is a rich discussion about the impact which elements such as eager study or efforts at moral improvement might have on the particular shape and length of a life, but the basic constellation seems to rest on the shared assumption that life and fate are something that is "received." In terms of the gift economy, this can be read as a huge initial stock invested into an individual or even credit given to that individual that will secure the giver a say in the handling of this gift, but also impose a huge burden on this individual to reciprocate. As the gift economy operates in the mode G-G (gift-gift) and not M-C-M-C (money-commodity-money-commodity), it exchanges goods and services for goods and services mostly of a totally different kind without money as the valuation. Rather, it operates on the basis of a complex implied valuation system in which the assumed subjective appreciation of the recipient becomes a key feature in the gift's assumed value. In the highly personalized and utterly asymmetrical relationships between a human being and the unseen powers that are seen as controlling his or her fate, this value system is more accurate than collective ("market") valuation. Even with the interpretation provided by the concept of *ming*, the practice of handling fate does not gain a secure handle to enhance its effectiveness. Effectiveness in dealing with fate-impacting powers continues to hinge on trial and error. As practices that proved effective for a while might stop doing so, the primacy of practice shows up in the quick willingness to move to other now more successful practices, as evidenced by the shifting fortunes of the worship of supernatural powers credited with a willingness to intervene to improve the fate of a worshiper.

During the later Han (first and second centuries CE), we see a variety of moral interpretations of fate events surface that foster a kind of moral economy. The explicit introduction of a moral economy governing the relationship between fate and the moral quality of one's actions comes with state legislation. It operates on a moral scale of good and bad actions, and links them to promotion or punishment in a basically scaled and quantitative manner. This is clearly present in the newly discovered Han code of 182 BCE with its many laws dealing with actions such as lack of filial piety that other legal systems, which operate on a principle of discouraging and punishing damage to the community, might not consider punishable.[18] For higher officials, the legal option was offered to pay a fine adjusted to the gravity of the offense instead of suffering physical punishment. Here again we find a quantitative relation between money and the moral quality of an action. At the other end, exemplary behavior could be honored by the ruler with a gift. In the emerging Daoist "church" of the Later Han (second century CE) disease and other fate afflictions were interpreted as being caused not by "demonic" intervention, but by morally reprehensible acts. Curing disease was achieved through remedial practices consisting of confessions and morally "good" forms of community service. In terms of a gift economy, restoration of health thus worked through balancing a negative moral account with an appropriate amount of morally positive acts. The pragmatic test for the balance being achieved was the return of health, otherwise more would have to be done to get out of the deficit. The implication was that fate authorities remembered/had records of individual earlier acts and their moral valuation, and would react mechanically by translating the moral deficit into disease. The moral quality of one's actions became a moral currency that had a clearly quantitative aspect. It operated according to an A-Q-E sequence with A being the action, Q being its value translated into moral currency, and E being the translation of this value in the form of returning fate effects.

The tomb contracts for buying the subsoil from the earth spirit on the other hand came with a proactive gift to prevent revenge for an equally proactive human interference in the powerful domain of the supernatural.

---

[18] U. Lau and M. Lüdke, *Exemplarische Rechtsfälle vom Beginn der Han-Dynastie: Eine kommentierte Übersetzung des Zouyanshu aus Zhangjiashan/Provinz Hubei*, Tokyo: Research Institute for Languages and Cultures in Asia and Africa, 2012.

The earliest exemplars we have were written as orders from the highest supernatural authorities to these earth spirits. It is to be assumed that this was not simply an arrogation by their author, but that a procedure had preceded the burial to secure the agreement of Heaven or the highest god, most probably through a sacrifice or other gift. The contract assumes a hierarchy in the powers of fate that made it possible to appeal to the highest levels to help solving problems with local spiritual powers.[19] The contract in this context has the purpose of fixing the otherwise diffuse recipient of the gift, and of identifying the very specific purpose addressed with this gift together with the value of the gift. But while these contracts operate within the general framework identifiable from earlier practices, they do not yet engage in a moral gift economy, but assume the form of a monetary transaction with lucky money that tries to cut down the leeway of the counterpart by inserting the gift into the language of a legally "binding" contract guaranteed by a superior.

Buddhism filtered into the Han territory along merchant routes mostly linked to Central Asia with a small inflow also coming via Canton. With the overpowering package deal of the karma doctrine, it brought a highly systematized interpretation of the interaction of humans with fate that had not been new for India when Buddhism came, but was new for China. It verbally fleshed out, theorized, and systematized elements silently implied in existing practices: the basic asymmetry between human beings and the factors influencing their lives; the impersonal and non-random mechanism controlling fate; the use of the powerful currency of moral action as not just an expected gift to an unpredictable recipient, but as a secure capital input into the economy of fate; and the negative consequences incurred for not starting to pay back one's huge initial debt. It provided, with the monasteries, an institutional environment for the maximization of karmic capital. And it offered with its purgatory and Western Paradise, hungry ghosts and bodhisattvas, magical powers and sangha rituals the wherewithal to make very abstract concepts palpably understandable to the proverbial village granny. In its most abstract form, this doctrine read fate as a blind mechanism, in which the moral qualities of one's actions (in a Buddhist definition) would end up materializing into a next body in the cycle of rebirth. The overall quality of the karmic endowment would

---

[19] Seidel, "Traces of Han Religion."

decide on the type of living being that was to emerge. Such a being would be on a gradient anywhere between a turtle and a male human being. This very abstract and blind mechanism presupposed some sort of record-keeping, in which acts of beings were translated into an abstract karmic currency. As a strictly moral economy, it does not operate on the M-C-M (money-commodity-money) model Marx proposed for the capitalist economy, but in a cycle B-K-B (being-karma-being) based on a mechanical computation of the deeds of sentient beings translated into karmic currency. Karma is the abstract and trans-cultural moral currency that links existences of sentient beings ("being") over time within the cyle of transmigration.

This Buddhist reading of the dynamics of interaction with the Beyond highlights the assumption of non-randomness and rationality already implied in earlier practices, and provides a tight set of rules that binds both sentient and supernatural beings. While this reading creates a slightly claustrophobic and overdetermined environment, it in fact enhances the agency of human beings. They gain the option to directly and reliably impact their long-term existence over several generations through the karmic capital (for good deeds) or debt (for bad) accumu-lated through their personal actions, over which they indeed have control.

The karmic plot machine of transmigration offers an explanation for the particular shape and fate of sentient beings and for their develop-ment over time. All its tight logic notwithstanding, the hard proofs are buried in the dark of the forgotten past and the not-yet-materialized future. The moral currency of karma is funny money of uncertain validity, but comes – in the case of good deeds – with the subjective value of having done all in one's power. The claim of the universal rule of karma notwithstanding, the moral economy with karmic currency operates within a gift-and-slight economy that has no control over the reaction of the counterpart in the Beyond. This sheds some light on the nature of money gifts (and their withholding). They are not payment for services or goods, but defined in their value through the effort that went into their acquisition, and the respect expressed through their being given or withheld as gifts. This use in the gift economy cleans the money from potential pollution occurring during the acquisition. While not originally defined in the tight sense of karmic positive values, the money gifts and their withholding fall into the same category of being abstract values of benevolent deeds and intentions (or their opposite).

The enhanced predictability and agency offered by the explanatory model of the karma doctrine had a huge impact in China. The ease of the transcultural migration of this doctrine signals the energetic pull with which it was absorbed by Chinese agents who directly saw it as a sophisticated explanation for a prevailing and accepted practice. The process highlights the fact that among the push-and-pull factors in transcultural flows, the pull always dominates. The doctrine was integrated into the Daoist understanding of fate, and eventually became a background feature of all currents of Chinese popular religion, providing even the plot engine for most works of fiction.

Early Chinese sources already claim the ubiquity of the underlying thinking across the different schools and currents. Daoist handbooks of moral economy such as the *Taiwei xianjun gongguo ge* 太微仙君功過格 (*Ledger of merits and demerits of the immortal Lord of the Taiwei Constellation*) of 1171 in the Daoist canon would refer to a statement in the *Wenyan* Commentary to the second hexagram of the *Book of Changes* attributed to Confucius: "A family that accumulates goodness will be sure to have an excess of blessings. A family that accumulates non-goodness is sure to have an excess of disasters."[20] They would juxtapose this with a statement in the *Daoke* 道科, a text dated in the middle of the seventh century (Ofuchi Ninji) or around 550 (Yoshioka Yoshitoyo), "Accumulating good will have bliss descend on one; doing evil will burden one with misery."[21] On this basis they claim that there was agreement between the Confucians who count the *Zhouyi* as a book of their tradition, and the Daoists who did the same for the *Daoke*, the main work outlining accepted Taoist practices for the Tang Dynasty.[22] Below the highly documented and verbalized Buddhist and Daoist teachings which dominated Chinese intellectual life between the fourth and ninth centuries, we thus have a continuity of older shared practices that have gradually and slowly evolved in the *longue durée* and that have survived to this day in what is generally referred to as "Chinese popular religion."

In this wider elite and popular context, other levels of reading the law of karma developed in which this was interpreted as working through

---

[20] *Taiwei xianjun gongguo ge* 太微仙君功過格, Daozang TT 186; *Zhouyi yinde*, Harvard-Yenching Institute Sinological Index Series, 4/2/言.
[21] *Dongxuan lingbao sandong fengdao kejie yingshi*, TT 1125.
[22] Beginning of the preface.

the efforts of a large number of individual supernatural agents. These would report on the thoughts and actions of the individual to record-keeping authorities situated either in heaven or in purgatory. These in their turn would translate them into some sort of point system that would lead to a final judgment at the death of the person that would translate into the level in the hierarchy of living beings where the new being would emerge and the circumstances it would confront. In between two existences, ample good karma points would translate into temporary rebirth in the Western Paradise, while karmic debt would translate into a lengthy period in purgatory. A rich array of narratives fleshed out and personalized the anonymous operations of the karmic law and showed the impact of human action. With it came the interpretation that meritorious deeds including money could be enhanced in their karmic value by being presented within the spatial environment of a religious setting with its high load of positive karma, and the time framework of added-value days in the religious calendar such as the birthdays of the kings of purgatory.

These practices would, above all, allow individuals to be proactive in reducing threats to their fate and improving their chances for luck through exchanges that did not exclusively hinge on the heavy burden of moral perfection. There is no need for unification in these interpretations, and the Buddhist doctrine of *upāya* (teaching adjusted to the level of understanding of the audience) quite explicitly links the different levels of religious sophistication into a cohesive "Buddhist" framework. A monk might go to extremes in keeping to the Vinaya rules of discipline for monks, but he might also be officiating at a religious ritual where paper money was burnt. A householder who works as a butcher killing living beings might go on a pilgrimage crawling up a mountain on his knees to reach a Buddhist temple at the top where he would donate money for a ritual, but would return after this merit-accumulating exercise in Buddhist morality to being a butcher professionally killing living beings, the worst of karmic infractions. In this context, the question of the economic equivalences between moral currency and money gifts is broached.

The seventh-century collection, *Records of Karmic Retribution, Mingbao ji*冥報記, offers the first known explicit interpretation of the transfer of money and other valuables to the supernatural known to us. Most importantly, the source of this interpretation is a supernatural agent. This is insider information coming directly from the fate-deciding powers. We have records of works described as being authenticated directly by gods or spirits since the second century (Later Han). An important text of the period, the *Classic of Great Peace, Taiping jing* 太平經, was submitted to the court with the claim that it originated in writing directly inspired and dictated by supernatural beings.[23] Zhang Daoling, the first-century CE founder of the Daoist "church," wrote a commentary to the Laozi that claimed direct inspiration from the Laozi – by then the highest god in the emerging Daoist pantheon – who appeared to him. The large fourth-century *True Announcement, Zhengao* 真誥, records a number of descents of gods into human mediums who then would write down the gods' communication about the structure and hierarchy of the Beyond.[24] The practice of mediums going into trance and writing down whatever was fed to them by the being possessing them is familiar from China and Taiwan to this day and is well documented.[25] I have not seen pre-Han records mentioning it.

The credibility of these testimonies as coming from the spiritual authorities themselves hinges on the credibility of the medium's being transformed and blindly writing down whatever the god makes him write. As this spirit writing, at least nowadays, is a very public activity with many bystanders as witnesses, the credibility of the trance has to be authenticated with proofs enough to convince a public that might be willing to be credulous but is unwilling to be duped in matters of the greatest gravity. What is important for the present context is the fact that these records were believed, and that they confirmed as true what the practice of dealing with the fate authorities had always assumed to be the fact.

In the *Mingbao ji*, Cheng Jing, the chief scribe of the netherworld in the state of Hu, instructs a man who is in the world of the living and always doubted whether there are spirits at all, in the proper manner of making sacrifices. This man then advises a patron: "The things used by

---

[23] B. Kandel, *Taiping jing: the Origin and Transmission of the "Scripture on General Welfare": the History of an Unofficial Text*, Hamburg: Gesellschaft für Natur- und Völkerkunde Ostasiens, 1979.

[24] Tao Hongjing 陶弘景, ed., *Zhengao*. I use the edition *Shinkō kenkyū (yakuchū hen)* 眞誥研究 (譯注篇), Tadao Yoshikawa 吉川忠夫 and Kunio Mugitani 麥谷邦夫, eds., Kyoto: Kyōto Daigaku Jinbun Kagaku Kenkyūjo, 2000.

[25] D. K. Jordan and D. Overmyer, *The Flying Phoenix: Aspects of Sectarianism in Taiwan*, Princeton University Press, 1986.

the spirits and by humans differ. Only gold and silk may circulate in both realms; but it is better if these were imitations. Imitated gold produced by spreading yellow color on a piece of tin, and papers offered instead of silk and other cloth are considered worth more [in the netherworld than the real thing]."[26] Another man learns when he has landed in purgatory that he can buy his freedom for money, and that the netherworld economy essentially operates with paper money: "We are not using the copper money that you employ. What we like better is money made with white paper."[27]

One should not assume that the taboos relating to cash in European contexts, which are most visible in the exclusion of cash from the gift economy, are shared by mankind at large. In the Chinese gift economy, cash in gaudily visible red envelopes is all-present to this very day on occasions as varied as marriage ceremonies, seasonal festivities, and on the occasion of graduations, burials, or births. Cash gifts are given to reciprocate for the efforts and expenses of organizing the respective ceremonies.

To be rich in cash, *fu* 富, is homophonous with living in blissful happiness, *fu* 福. There is no shyness in talking about money, and striking it rich at a casino or at the stock market is a daydream of many Chinese, who will prepare this with offerings to especially potent supernatural beings, and thank them in case of success with a substantial gift both in real cash for example, to gild the temple roof, and in paper money. In Taiwan today, the government is printing special money bills – fully legal tender – to be used for New Year gifts.[28] The seemingly deep abyss separating money from morality and the intrinsic moral suspiciousness of cash is absent in Chinese tradition to this very day.[29] The lucky red envelopes serve the purpose of inserting the "real" paper money into the gift economy.

Money in the Buddhist doctrine was not a privileged place of evil. It was just one of the common elements trapping people in this world.

---

[26] Tang Lin唐臨, *Mingbao ji*, Beijing: Zhonghua shuju, 1992, 27. The story is also given in the *Fayuan zhulin*, T53n2122.p0315c09(01)f.

[27] D. E. Gjertson, *Miraculous Retribution: A study and translation of T'ang Lin's Ming-pao chi*, Berkeley: University of California Press, 1989, 100.

[28] H. Gates, "Money for the Gods," *Modern China*, 13 (Jul., 1987) 3: 259–77.

[29] For discussions of this issue in the Hebrew and Protestant traditions, see the studies by M. Welker and C.-L. Seow, Chapters 5 and 7, respectively, in this volume.

Sexual attraction easily tops money in this respect, and slaughtering sentient beings incurs far greater karmic debt than plundering the poor or cheating at business. Intrinsically Buddhism is not anti-commercial or anti-merchant. The positive elements of wealth, namely, the option to become a donor to the Buddhist community, were very much appreciated. Many of the most prominent early laymen supporting the Buddha and the Sangha were merchants. The new area to which Buddhism came, China, was different in many respects, but not in this one. While the lure of money is acknowledged in China and sometimes satirized, and while a substantial part of the elite for many centuries kept at a distance from commercial activities, there is a quite unabashed glorification of wealth in popular culture. But this is wealth described as the result of luck granted by higher powers, and of hard work, not as the result of reckless exploitation. This attitude marks a big difference to the Christian dispensation.

The practice of using "spirit-money" in the gift-and-slight economy with the supernatural is not only one in "folk religion," but has been officially sanctioned by the Tang court since at least 739.[30] It was criticized by many scholars at the time for being a vulgar custom, but was also being used in state rituals for high officials of the Song dynasty.[31]

Managing life credit

Enhanced by the Buddhist *karma* doctrine, which was widely accepted as a credible interpretation of the life-endowment, *ming*, an interpretation spread that life altogether was something like a credit. It operated in a gift economy in the sense that the creditor and the recipient were not negotiating the terms, but at the same time established an asymmetrical contractual relationship by saddling the recipient with a huge burden to pay back or to make worse. The authority giving this credit was the very same authority that tracked and recorded the karmic performance of sentient beings, helped by a vast array of spies within the body, in the house and in the locality.

In Buddhist textual environments, the fate administration was situated in purgatory under the management not of a devil, but of the bodhisattva Ksitigharbha; in more Daoist contexts, the records were

---

[30] Hou, *Monnaies d'Offrande*, 127.   [31] Hansen, *Negotiating*, 164.

kept in heaven with the Jade Emperor presiding. In this latter reading, which is documented since the twelfth century and has been studied in detail by Hou Ching-lang, the life-fate-credit emanates from a central bank, the Treasury of Celestial Jurisdiction, *tiancao ku* 天曹庫, that also is referred to by some other terms using *ku*, treasury. The particular features of the credit (such as life duration, or wealth) derive not from the random pleasure of the creditor – which would make rebellion an option – but result from the recipient's own previous record.

The fate accounts are managed not by an abstract law, but by individualized actors on the basis of the universal law of karmic retribution. This verbalized the tradition contained in archaic practices of dealing with an assumed variety of supernatural counterparts with different powers and qualities, and inserted them into a new explanatory context. The ambivalence about the time-frame of the reactions of the supernatural counterpart that is visible from early records, which mention immediate interventions but also interventions for earlier hurts even several generations later, is maintained and rationalized into two types of retribution, in this life, and in the endowment for the next.

The endowment itself is therefore not a fixed credit given to any new sentient being, but rather, a credit line with a steep hierarchy that furthermore might shrink and expand with the debtor's performance. A disastrously poor karmic record will lead to a shortening of the credit line and with it of the lifespan. In terms of the gift economy, this initial endowment thus imposes from the outset the burden of reciprocity on the recipient to select from different offerings on the market those that might be the most effective set of practices for balancing the fate account. The critical and very practical importance this had for one's life militated against considerations of canonic orthodoxy and in favor of a pragmatic and ideologically wholly opportunistic search for effectiveness.

This pragmatic urgency and the basic incalculability of the supernatural counterpart favored, and does so to this day, a risk-hedging strategy, by combining elements from all recipes on the market to make sure that at least one of them would work. As far as the individual was concerned, these strategies involved gifts in the form of spirit money and/or foodstuffs to be burnt and/or deposited before the image of the supernatural authority, and/or good deeds. To maximize impact and effectiveness, these would preferably be offered or done on days of high attention such as the birthdays of the different kings of purgatory, days of high risk such as the year end, when annual karmic records were presented for entry into the central ledgers, or during the days when hungry spirits where known to roam. The good deeds might involve abstention from sex, not killing living beings, or even buying living beings such as fish that had been caught for consumption and releasing them, but it also often involved giving "real" money to temples for buildings or printing of morality books, or to religious specialists to perform rituals with impact on the treasury. As all these gifts enter into a mode of reciprocity, G-G, the diversity of G and the necessity of humans to make a choice prompt a translation into a quantitative system. A Catholic priest calculating the gravity of an offense in the number of Ave Marias that are needed to atone for it follows a similar track, and he would insist that the prayers be spoken with fervor and concentration.

This quantification is again a matter of intense and diverse interpretive activity. For human actions, since the Song dynasty we have a quickly growing number of handbooks of the *Gongguo ge* 功過格-type (ledgers of merit and demerit) quantifying – each different from the other, but within a basic framework of values – the karmic load of actions through a point system and offering the user some inkling of the state of his fate account. In these handbooks, burning paper money does not figure, and the authors might have discounted this as a crass and helpless effort to outwit an iron law, but the accounting system they use is clearly introducing the point as a gradable moral currency allowing for the exchange into fate-benefits of an utterly different kind than the action (or non-offense) prompting it, very much in the manner in which money mediates the transition between different commodities.

If we look at the particulars of the spirit money in the context of the management of the fate account, its relative status will become clearer.[32] Spirit money comes in huge denominations and is burned in thick packs. This shows a sober assessment of its point value which is totally out of proportion to its nominal value. It is burnt not somewhere at random, but in a special vessel in temples. Temples are seen as natural abodes of the supernatural, often present through statues or descending into the premises through mediums. The money is burnt in a ritualized action with the worshiper praying while the money burns and it is transformed through

---

[32] For the discussion during the Song dynasty about the use of paper money for conventional economic purposes, see Chapter 10 by H.-U. Vogel in this volume.

the fire into supernatural currency. The combination of critical space (temple), critical time (such as a birthday of a king of purgatory), and critical (that is, momentary) devotional mindset, are all there to enhance what is the pretty miserable effective earthly value of the spirit money itself. The simultaneous application of these very diverse procedures, which all had their particular interpretative framework, shows a primacy of practice in this gift economy, a primacy which reacts to the asymmetry in power and in verifiable predictability.

The assumption of the non-randomness of supernatural interventions which we have extracted from the early practices found a variety of interpretations. These range from the link between the moral qualities of individual actions and the fate of the person to the descriptions of the iron law of karma. The blandness and absence of strong individual traits in Chinese deities and saintly figures compared to the very idio-syncratic character of, for example, Near and Middle Eastern and Greek gods has often been observed. On the level of high interpretation, this is read from early on as a sub-segment of the non-randomness (and unfathomable complexity) of the universe altogether.

Obviously, the term non-randomness used here is purely descriptive and calls for more analysis, especially insofar as it pertains to the behavior of the fate administrators in the gift economy studied here. Non-randomness in the behavior of a participant in a gift economy means that this participant will not let petty and personal whims and fancies cloud the judgment of the fair value of the gift presented. A story such as the one about the bet between Jahweh and the devil concerning Job's behavior by contrast signals idiosyncratic randomness of fate-managing authorities and with it an immeasurably enlarged asymmetry of powers.

With the insertion of these Chinese fate-administrators into the karmic law, they were endowed with a kind of Weberian bureaucratic rationality that involved a highly professional disregard for petty personal interests in the management of human fates. Given the huge asymmetry in which these authorities were dispensing and controlling life credits for unending numbers of humans, who in their turn were only free to work on the repayment of the credit extended to them, this assumption of bureau-cratic rationality in behavior imputed an attitude of responsibility that kept the bank with its huge capital clean and free from abuse.

The efforts to reach these authorities with gifts during short moments of personal weakness (their birthdays) reflect on their otherwise impla-cable correctness in applying the law of karma, and the hope that on such moments they might be willing to be a bit more lenient. A reading of these practices as transposing an earthly practice of corruption to the super-natural realm misreads the evidence on both ends. The earthly officials are only minor players in fate-management and both their attitudes and those of their subjects are better read as subsets of the larger story.

In the interpretations, the non-randomness returns in the figures identified as chief administrators of fate. The Buddhist purgatory is not administered by a vicious and flippant devil, but by bodhisattva Ksitigharbha, who stays in this world of red dust to fulfill his vow not to enter Nirvana before all sentient beings have shed the iron chains of karma. The purgatory with its terrible punishments is his benevolent effort to teach humans not to commit transgressions again after they have left purgatory and enter the next stage in the chain of rebirth. As a bodhisattva above the seventh stage in the bodhisattva ladder, he has long left behind all idiosyncratic and personal concerns. The Daoist interpretation is less clear. While also positing a didactic purgatory, the karmic records in this reading are kept in heaven and are administered by the Jade Emperor as the central banker.

Credit transfer

We have seen that many of the early practices for the dead had the living endowing the dead with the wherewithal to make gifts. This transfer has surfaced in many interpretations. In the Buddhist context it has led to the rich Chinese development of a marginal earlier doctrine that allowed for the transfer of karmic merit to relatives. This option puts a huge burden on the living, namely, to accumulate merits with which to endow their deceased relatives with the wherewithal to be spared some of the tortures of purgatory. In terms of the gift economy, this merit transfer extends the parent–child gift-and-slight economy with its shift of dependency of the parents to their children's services beyond their death. A very large part of Chinese religious activities goes into this type of collective fate-credit servicing by the family members. The Buddhist communities have offered an effective and extremely popular enhance-ment of this merit transfer since the Tang dynasty in the Ullambana festival.[33] It builds on the assumption that the merit valuation of the acts

[33] S. F. Teiser, *The Ghost Festival in Medieval China*, Princeton University Press, 1988.

of Buddhist monks is particularly high because of their following monastic rules that mandate abstention from sex and meat. The story of Mulian on which the Ullambana festival is based has Mulian try to get his mother, who during her life has been a butcher, out of purgatory, but his strength was not enough to open the doors. He then went to ask the Buddha for help, and with the collective merit power of the Buddhist sangha, the doors opened and the mother got out. During the Ullambana festival, the faithful make substantial "real" gifts to the sangha to get help in facilitating the passage of their relatives through purgatory with an elaborate collective ritual. Here we have real money translating into real merit, multiplied through the moral purity of the sangha into a huge karmic gift that rebalances the fate account of the dead enough to end the torture in purgatory.

Laundered money

As we have seen, the gift economy, whether read as a moral economy or not, operated, all asymmetry notwithstanding, with hard basic structures that were even apt to be formalized in contracts. The personal disinterest of the administrators of fate was as much a key factor in the successful operation of this economy as the in-life or post-mortem sanctions imposed for the failure to fully repay the life credit.

For the much smaller and less critical economy of the human world, this prefigured a pattern to follow. The Buddhist doctrine developed in an environment in northern India where much of the support for the monks' community, *sangha*, came from wealthy merchants. In a famous case, one of these merchants, Vimalakīrti, was even depicted as a bodhisattva in disguise whose religious insights were of such a high level that none of the Buddha's disciples was his match.[34]

Buddhism spread into Central and East Asia not only along the trade routes, and merchants had monks in their retinue as much as they had the preciousnesses of the Western paradise for religious purposes in their trade bags.[35] While the accompanying monks were reputed to have magical powers to ward off robbers and monsters, they also

---

[34] E. Lamotte, *L'enseignement de Vimalakirti (Vimalakirtinirdesa)*, Louvain: Publications universitaires, 1962.

[35] For the religious valuation of the goods transported on the Silk Road, see Liu Xinru, *Ancient India and Ancient China: Trade and Religious Exchanges AD 1–600*, Delhi: Oxford University Press, 1988.

gave an air of respectability to traveling caravans in areas where even the robbers most likely were Buddhist enough to rather not wreck their karma accounts by killing monks. The monasteries acted as important *entrepôt* stations and guest houses for these caravans in Central Asia. It is in this context – if not already in India – that the big Central Asian monasteries started to lend money from their treasury. While in some cases this money was lent to monks or to serfs of the monastery without interest, in most cases the records from Khotan and Dunhuang show that these treasuries acted as regular banks with interest fixed, security given, and contract made.

The institution of the bank is thus a religious institution that owes its capital stock to meritorious donations, is managed by managers who are not the owners and who draw no personal profit from this managing activity, and lend money for the purposes of increasing the capital that is allowing monks to leave the world, and is useful to other sentient beings within the world through rituals and the like. The documentation on these monastery banks was made available by Chavannes many years ago in the appendix to Stein's volume, *Ancient Khotan*.[36] The Buddhist monasteries in China brought this Central Asian institution with them. For the Buddhist communities this was no easy matter. The early communities had very minimalist accommodations with little need of cash for building and repair. Only when fully developed monastic communities were established did the question of a capital stock come up on which to draw for buildings and repairs. The key type of text to broach the subject are the monastic rules, Vinaya. There are different sets of such rules, and by the early fifth century some of them had been translated into Chinese. The most important of them is the Vinaya of the Mūlasarvāstivāda. After many trips by different Chinese monks to India in search of a manuscript copy of this Vinaya, which was considered the most authoritative, the monk Yijing 義淨 (635–713) finally produced a Chinese translation early in the eighth century.[37] It only survives in the

---

[36] E. Chavannes, in Mark Aurel Stein, *Ancient Khotan: Detailed Report of the Archaeological Explorations in Chinese Turkestan*, Oxford: Clarendon Press, 1907, Appendix vol. 1.

[37] From the side of Buddhologists with a focus on India, Gregory Schopen and Jonathan Silk have dealt with the sections about economic activities of monasteries in this vinaya text, see G. Schopen, "Doing Business for the Lord: Lending on Interest and Written Loan Contracts in the Mūlasarvāstivāda-vinaya,"

Chinese and Tibetan translations.[38] The key passage that has been crucial for Buddhist commercial enterprise and philosophy runs as follows:

The Buddha, the Blessed One, was staying in *Vaiśālī*, in the hall of the lofty pavilion on the bank of the monkey's pool. At that time the Licchavis [wealthy members of the ruling elite] of *Vaiśālī* lived in grand houses with six or seven upper chambers (pura). When they saw the lowly buildings the monks lived in, they proceeded to also build for them beautiful buildings with six or seven upper chambers. As these buildings were aging and many of them started to crumble, the donors saw this and thought: "Now as we are still alive already these monasteries are all crumbling, what will happen once we have passed away? We should make a gift of a perpetuity 無盡物 ["an inexhaustible thing," aksaya] to allow [the monastic communities] to do construction work." Whereupon they brought this "gift-thing" [施物] to the monks' place and addressed them thus: "Noble Ones, this is a gift in perpetuity, please accept it for repair purposes!" The monks responded: "The Blessed One has promulgated a rule of discipline that it is inappropriate for us to accept this." When the monks reported the matter to the Buddha, he said: "If it is for purposes of buildings for the Sangha a perpetuity is to be accepted. However, [155a] a vihara for a community of monks should be made with only three upper chambers and for nuns with two." Thereupon the monks accepted the perpetuity and placed it into the depository (*kosthika*). Thereupon the donors came and asked: "Noble Ones, why is it that there are still no repairs being done on the vihara?" The monks answered: "Gentlemen, because there is no money [*kdrsdpana*]." "But have we not given you perpetuities?" The monks answered: "Gentlemen, how could the perpetuities possibly be spent? Placed into the community's depository, they are to this day untouched." The donors said: "Such perpetuities should not be handled like this. They would have been as safely kept in our houses! Why do you not lend them out to get profit [=interest] on them [*prayojayati*]?" The monks said: "The Buddha has enjoined us not to strive for profit." The monks for this reason reported the matter in detail to the Blessed One. The Blessed One said: "As long as it is for the benefit of the Sangha, you might strive for profit. Once devout brahmins and householders hear of these words of the Buddha, they will make donations of perpetuities to the Buddha, the Dharma and the Sangha.

These three jewels [Buddha, Dharma and Sangha] also may lend out [money] to make profit. The profits generated return to the Buddha, the

Journal of the American Oriental Society, 114 (Oct.–Dec., 1994) 4: 527–54, and Silk, "Marginal Notes on a Study of Buddhism, Economy and Society in China."
[38] The Chinese version is *Genben shuo yiqie youbu pinaiye* 根本說－切有部毘奈耶, T.1442.

Dharma and the Sangha to take care of things needed for worship [such as incense, candles etc.]." Thereupon the monks returned the perpetuities among those same donors [as credit]. But when the interest was due to be collected it caused disputes with them. "Noble Ones," they said, "How is it that disputes have arisen from our own wealth?" The monks reported the matter in detail to the Blessed One. The Blessed One said: "Perpetuities should not be placed among these people for interest." The monks thereupon placed them for interest among wealthy persons. But when they came due, relying on those possessed of power, those wealthy persons did not repay them. The Buddha said: "They should not be placed among such people as credit." The monks in their turn placed them among poor people for interest. But when they came due, they had nothing. The Buddha said: "When giving the money things should be clearly spelled out. A pledge [*ddhi/bandhaka*] should be made with twice the value [*dviguna*], this should be written up in a contract [*likhita*], a guarantor should be installed, the year and month should be recorded, with the name of the institution as well as the debtor written on it. That pledge of twice the value is also to be placed with a devout lay-brother who has under-taken the five rules of training [if he gets such a credit].[39]

The passage maps the transition from a gift economy to an economy that looks like a "real" economy but retains all the markers of its origin. Lending money for personal profit is something a monk should not do. The money generated by the merchants, however, has been accumulated in this way. It is purified through its being made into a donation to the monastery. In terms of the gift economy of fate, this gift produced substantial karmic merit, and once this option was opened, many laymen made use of it. The money that is purified by being given to the Sangha, the Buddhist community, is not allowed to become the private possession of the monks, but the interest generated from it may be used for the purposes of the Sangha. In this manner, the management of this money, although seemingly no different from money managed by bankers, is cleaned of any personal interest. The text does not include threats of karmic retribution for failure to repay the loans, but in a very businesslike manner secures collateral in the form of a land deed as well as the services of a guarantor.

---

[39] *Genben shuo yiqie youbu pinaiye* 根本說一切有部毘奈耶, Taishō Daizōkyō, T.1442.0743b11. The relevant excerpt from the Tibetan version is translated in Schopen, "Doing business for the Lord," 529–30. The differences between the Tibetan and the Chinese versions are insignificant. The Sanskrit equivalents follow Schopen's identification.

Such karmic threats, however, will be found in many Chinese texts about visitors to purgatory who were sent back to report what they had seen. And in many cases they reported having seen the sufferings of those who failed to repay their loans to the monasteries. They endow the proper behavior towards a creditor with a moral flavor. We thus see the gift economy, in this case the Buddhist monasteries, as the testing ground for banking institutions. Many years ago, Yang Lien-sheng already pointed to the fact that all major Chinese financial institutions have their origin in Buddhist monasteries.[40]

The operations of these Buddhist banks with their laundered money made full use of the particular religious value attached to the treasury of the monasteries. As this was purified money, a borrower's failure to repay a loan would not only land him before the magistrate for infringement of a contract, but would also incur a hefty karmic penalty. Buddhist narrative literature is full of stories of borrowers who came to a dreadful death as a consequence. In one such case a monk had borrowed a fagot of firewood from the monastery's treasury. Such loans to monks would not carry interest. However, he failed to return his loan. A monk who was visiting purgatory on one of the regular organized tours designed to make known in the world what horrors awaited the sinners, ran into this fellow, who in earlier time had been his cell companion, and was now being tortured in purgatory. This companion implored him to pay back his debt so as to relieve him from his suffering.

To do so, this monk in his turn took out a loan of a hundred fagots to atone for the infraction of his colleague. In quantitative terms, the failure to repay the one fagot borrowed from the treasury came with a karmic debt worth one hundred times the amount.[41] The theme of an unpaid debt to the monastic treasury leading to rebirth as an animal, slave, or infernal being is common in Chinese Buddhist folklore. The karmic law thus operated to enhance compliance with the terms of the commercial loan.

The functioning of this karmic system of enforcing credit discipline hinged on the purity of the money, and many efforts were made to

[40] Yang Lien-sheng, "Buddhist Monasteries and Four Money-raising Institutions in Chinese History," *Harvard Journal of Asiatic Studies*, 13 (Jun., 1950) 1(2): 174–91.

[41] Quoted in Gernet, *Buddhism in Chinese Society*, 178.

secure it. There was a constant danger that the monks administering the treasury would become corrupted and would work for their own accounts. The potential pollution from unclean money was such that some communities entrusted the management of these loans to closely supervised laymen. But the monasteries made great efforts to keep the credit business clean. Interest rates were in effect around 20 percent per annum, well below the regular 50 percent for loans to peasants in the form of grain. The system was effective enough in an economy that was permanently cash-strapped to be officially sanctioned during the Tang dynasty. The dynasty not only capped interest rates at 20 percent, it also set up its own treasuries, which emulated the system of the monasteries. The regional governments received a basic capital. They were entitled to lend this against interest, with the interest then serving to prop up the very low official salaries in a manner that was neither corruption nor extortion.

The particular monastic background of the institution of the bank and the magic transformation of money with all the grime of real-life business transactions attached to it into clean money managed by managers who themselves do not personally benefit from the business transactions has established a system of a relatively high stability and credibility that has greatly helped the banks to assume the functions and public role they enjoy to this very day.

Yang Lien-sheng refers to Max Weber when he states: "Together with paper notes, Chinese banking practices became known in the West. Max Weber states that the accounting system (*Verrechnungswesen*) of the old Hamburg bank was set up on a Chinese model. Robert Eisler suggests that the Swedish system of banking and money deposit vouchers may have been influenced by Chinese examples, transmitted by medieval merchant-travelers and, possibly, by Jewish silk merchants."[42]

---

[42] Yang Lien-sheng, *Money and Credit in China*, Cambridge, MA: Harvard University Press, 1952, 65, referring to M. Weber, *Gesammelte Aufsätze zur Religionssoziologie*, Tübingen: Mohr, 1920, 2.2767. R. Eisler, *Das Geld: seine geschichtliche Entstehung und gesellschaftliche Bedeutung; Ein wirtschaftswissenschaftlicher Lichtbild-Lehrgang*, Munich: Verlag der Diatypie, 1924 (Lichtbildlehrbücher. Abteilung Wirtschaftslehre und Staatswissenschaft, 1), 217.

Conclusion

It would be an interesting question whether the money laundering functions of the bank, together with the religious honesty and disinterestedness of the banker in administering other people's money, is part of the religious package coming with this Buddhist heritage. As far as China is concerned, it has often been observed, and Yu Yingshi has offered a detailed study of to what lengths the later Shanxi banks went to secure a public image of rigorously controlled honesty as the very basis of their business.[43] Could this be read as a secular continuation of the Buddhist antecedents, reinforced by ample religious activities of these bankers themselves and adumbrated by giving a Confucian education to their descendants and heirs?

The Song dynasty was the first state institution worldwide experimenting with paper money. Altogether the experiment was not too successful, as the state could not resist the temptation to print ever-larger amounts to pay its debts and as at the time there was no international economy to buy up Chinese treasury notes. However, it seems plausible that the key features of this enterprise have been developed and tested in the gift economy of fate. This is true for the basic trust in the validity of the credits and repayments in all their multifarious forms including paper money. It is true for the presumption of a personal disinterestedness of the state administrators of the paper money in this business, which owes much to the management style of the monastery banks. Finally, the institutions set up to administer the paper money took their names directly from the Buddhist treasuries and the fate bank.

---

[43] Yu Yingshi, *Rujia lunli yu shangren jingshen (Confucian ethics and the spirit of merchants)*, in: *Yu Yingshi wenji* 3, Guilin: Guangxi shifandaxue chubanshe 2004.

10 | *"Mothers and children": discourses on paper money during the Song period*

HANS-ULRICH VOGEL

Paper money originated in China during the Northern Song period (960–1127) and was then used for about five hundred years during the Jin (1115–1234), Yuan (1271–1368), and Ming (1368–1644) empires. The experiences with paper money created a rich and lively discourse by which the contemporaries voiced their concerns about the adoption of this type of money. During the Song dynasty, when paper money was still new, a wide spectrum of diverse opinions was voiced by different protagonists, ranging from scholars and officials who declined paper money and urged its abolition, to those who favoured its adoption and an expansion in its use. In this chapter, I will present a first insight into these discussions. The main aim is to introduce the most important arguments and theoretical concepts that were developed during that period, often in response to practical problems arising from the use of paper money.

In the following, it will first be made clear that paper money was a private invention which emerged in Sichuan and which was then taken over by the state. Secondly, I will point out that while paper money was accepted for Sichuan province, the introduction of paper money in other regions proceeded not without difficulties. Thirdly, military needs and the abuse of paper money as a means to produce more fiscal income will be investigated as a further topic through which both benefits and harms of the paper money regime become obvious. A fourth item considered in this chapter and closely related to the aforementioned is the problem of the excessive issue of paper money or, in other words, the lack of a sufficient reserve in bronze coins to back these issues. What, after all, was considered to be a reasonable stock of real cash to keep up public trust in the system? A fifth theme to be addressed is the contents and structures of the arguments proffered by the various thinkers in their attacks or defences of the paper money regime. This includes a first analysis of the metaphors used in the context of discussions about paper

219

money, such as the benefit–harm dichotomy and binominal metaphors like "mother and child" and "real and empty."

The various discussions held by Song scholars and officials illustrate that the issue of paper money, affecting the lives of the masses and the conjuncture of public finances, prompted lively and sometimes even heated debates. They also show that in the course of time multifaceted and more or less solid discourses emerged which adequately reflected the importance of paper money in the innumerable transactions taking place on markets and in public finance.

Understanding the discourses of the Song period, when real paper money was invented in China, is certainly a justified aim in itself. At the same time, analyzing the Song period will also help us to better understand the developments in the Yuan period, which was the time when paper money was most intensively used in Chinese history.

Sichuan in 1023: a private innovation taken over by the state

It is well known that paper money had its origin in the private realm, but was soon taken over, in 1023, by state institutions. This all took place in Western China, in Sichuan, where "exchange notes" (*jiaozi* 交子) had already been current before being appropriated by the state. The use of paper notes in Sichuan was quite probably favoured by the currency system of this province, in which iron coins were legal tender. The weight of these heavy coins and the costs involved in their transportation were one reason for the spread of paper money in this province. Xue Tian 薛田,[1] the promoter of the takeover of the exchange notes by the state, argued in the following way:

Within the confines of Sichuan iron cash is used. Ten strings of small cash (*xiaoqian* 小錢) weigh 65 *jin* ["pounds"], which are exchanged for a string of large cash (*daqian* 大錢) weighing 12 *jin*. When on streets and markets transactions of 3 to 5 strings are carried out, it is difficult to carry them along. Thus, the exchange notes, having come along by themselves, have been of convenience for the people for a long time. . . .

Since the exchange notes have been stopped, those undertaking sales and purchases at the stalls and markets have become very rare. If now private

---

[1] Xue Tian, style (zi 字) Xiji 希稷, was from Hedong.

exchange notes are abolished and made by officials instead, this will provide great stability and convenience.[2]

Apart from the legitimating argument of bringing stability and convenience to the people, the state administration of the paper money was, no doubt, also considered a means of generating benefit for the public finance system.

Shaanxi in 1071 and 1074: futile attempts at expanding paper money

In the 1070s, during the reform period of Wang Anshi 王安石 (1021–86), two attempts were undertaken to expand the use of paper money to the northern province of Shaanxi. During the first attempt, in the beginning of 1071 (Xining 4/1), the government planned to allot the exchange notes to the population and to collect all the bronze and iron coins. This aroused great unrest among the people so that after only four months this attempt was aborted. A statement of Emperor Shenzong reveals the fiscal intentions behind the whole operation: "To have exchange notes circulate [there] just does not work. If the usual legal restrictions are adopted so that there is enough for public expenditures, then naturally these [notes] are not needed."[3]

In 1074, a second attempt was undertaken in connection with the need to procure ready cash for the garrisons at the northern frontier. Thus, in order to save transportation costs,[4] for a beneficial price the government issued exchange notes to merchants who had transported cash to the garrisons. These exchange notes were then carried back by the merchants who cashed them in Xi'an or had them circulated in other places in Shaanxi province. In this way the government not only saved transportation costs, but also promoted the circulation of the exchange notes.[5]

The implementation of this system proceeded, however, not without difficulties. The salt ticket system, i.e. another logistic and fiscal system

[2] Li You 李攸, *Songchao shishi* 宋朝事實, ch. 15; Xiao Qing 蕭清, *Zhongguo gudai huobi sixiang shi* 中国古代货币思想史, Beijing: Renmin chubanshe, 1987, 174.

[3] *Xu zizhi tongjian changbian* 續資治通鑑長編, ch. 221 (Xining 4/3/*xuzi*); Xiao Qing 蕭清, 175.

[4] Xiao Qing 蕭清, 176, speaks of transportation costs of 2,600 to 2,700 strings for transporting 1 million strings from Xi'an to Qinzhou 秦州, which does not seem to be an excessively high amount.

[5] Xiao Qing 蕭清, 176.

of the government, was negatively influenced by the issue of exchange notes – at least in the eyes of Wang Anshi. From a discussion led at the court of the Shenzong emperor we learn some interesting details about how the working and function of paper money were perceived by the people ruling the empire:

The emperor said: "The exchange notes (*jiaozi*) naturally are exchanged (*dui* 對) with cash, while the salt tickets (*yanchao* 鹽鈔) are exchanged with salt, hence both obviously will not obstruct each other."

[Wang An]shi said: "But where can one get so much reserve (*ben* 本) [to back them]?"

The emperor said: "Just by issuing and taking them in, one will cause the people to have trust (*xin* 信) in them, and one thus naturally does not waste reserve [funds]."

Qian 僉 said: "In the beginning, however, one needs a reserve, but as soon as trust is there, they can be circulated permanently."

I [i.e. Lü Huiqing 呂惠卿][6] said: "We should do it in the way as it was done in Western Sichuan. When now the people bring cash, they can ask for exchange notes (*jiaozi*) or payment notes (*huizi* 會子). If the people have cash, they will just get their payment notes. If they have no cash, who then would come forward to bring cash for getting payment notes?"

[Wang An]shi said: "But eventually the salt ticket system will be obstructed. The reason for this is that in the salt ticket system [the salt harvest] is uneven each and every year. Moreover, searching out and arresting salt smugglers is also of utmost importance, which means that salt is not a fixed amount. If too much [salt] is produced, then cash is obtained, but if too little, then unfortunately, the proceeds and profits from the salt sales are lost in the dark. Hence it should be permitted to issue somewhat more [salt] tickets to be sold at a moderate price on an official auction."

I said: "This is not so. Even if [salt] harvests are uneven year by year, this is not the case in the consumption of salt. This is not comparable with liquor, because [salt] is a good used by the people in a constant way. Even if it is abundant, some mean value can be established as a standard. Even in good years increases are thus not much. And if one has [really] the impression that people suffer from a lack of salt and that tickets are too few, then issuing more is not difficult. [Thus salt] tickets possess a permanently high value and because this is so, their price cannot be artificially raised when selling them officially. Hence it is better to issue fewer tickets and to adopt exchange notes."[7]

---

[6] Lü Huiqing (1032–1111) was one of the reformers during the New Laws period and thus an adherent of Wang Anshi.

[7] *Xu zizhi tongjian changbian*, ch. 255 (Xining 9/1/*jiashen*); Xiao Qing 蕭清, 175.

The discussion, as Lü Huiqing recorded it, makes clear that some scholar-officials were aware that the issue of paper money had to be backed by "reserve cash" (*benqian* 本錢). Only after trust had been established could relatively more paper money be issued in proportion to the "reserve cash." The crucial importance of "reserve cash" was also stressed by Pi Gongbi 皮公弼, an official responsible for the financial affairs of Shaanxi: "The method of the *jiaozi*, a piece of paper of a square *cun* [inch], consists of making cash flying to far-away places. However, if no reserve cash were accumulated, one would not be able to have such an empty document circulated."[8] The emperor, however, seems to have been convinced that by the state's issuing and taking in paper money alone could trust be established in the population, and that it was not necessary to build up a reserve.

With regard to the debate about the relationship between the salt tickets and the exchange notes, the emperor was certainly right in stating that these two items are backed by two different things: salt on the one hand and cash on the other. Nonetheless, both functioned as "convenient cash" (*bianqian* 便錢) and were used as such. The merchants who brought cash from Yongxingjun 永興軍 (Xi'an) to Qinzhou 秦州 preferred to buy the reasonably prized exchange notes to the salt tickets, resulting in the latter's accumulation and fall in value. This was the reason why Wang Anshi wanted to dispose of the exchange notes and admit only the salt tickets. As a matter of fact, this attempt to use the exchange notes in Shaanxi failed, and it was finally by way of the consolidation of the salt ticket system by which the situation in Shaanxi province was attempted to be resolved.[9]

Military needs and their consequences in 1136: "Where there is profit, there is also harm"

Compared with the Northern Song period (960–1127), discussions and evaluations of paper money during the Southern Song period (1127–1279) became much more intense and elaborate. In the Southern Song period, when the Jurchens had conquered the north of China and the dynasty had to retreat to central and southern China, the use of paper money was expanded. The reason for this expansion was clearly rooted

[8] *Xu zizhi tongjian changbian*, ch. 259 (Xining 8/1/*dingsi*); Xiao Qing 萧清, 176.
[9] See ibid., 178.

in the increase of military expenditure. As a consequence, in Hangzhou, where the provisional court of the Song had been set up, a special office was established in the second month of the sixth year of the Shaoxing reign-period (1136). The task of this office was to print official paper money according to the model provided by private payment notes (*huizi*). However, because the government issued exchange notes without sufficient backing by reserve money, this plan had to be given up after only three months.

This attempt to issue paper money also in the southeast of China was met with resistance by many scholars and officials. An unknown scholar-official, by listing two advantages and four disadvantages related to paper money, proffered a relatively systematic and thorough critique of the paper money regime during the beginning of the Southern Song:

I have heard that when matters in this world produce profits, they necessarily also have harms. … Those who today are discussing the exchange notes mention two benefits and four harms. One benefit is that grain in the frontier regions is plentiful and transportation costs are reduced. The other benefit is that [paper money is constantly] circulating by being issued and taken in, and [though reserve] cash is few, the usefulness [and benefits] are many. These are the [the two] benefits of the exchange notes. As to their disadvantages, the first one is that there are two prices and that all things have become more expensive. The second is that people cheating and counterfeiting have become numerous and with them judicial cases and imprisonment. The third harm is that when people get exchange notes, they cannot use them for small transactions. Moreover, if they want to transfer them, they fear that nobody will buy them. The fourth problem is that as cash and things are becoming more and more valuable, people increasingly will hold them back. With all the exchange notes flowing back to the authorities, they too have difficulties in spending them for payments.

While all the harms are presently fully there, it is far from sure that one of the benefits, i.e. that of [constant] circulation is [now really] at hand. How do we know this? We know because exchange notes are issued in large numbers and that people thus know for certain that the authorities have no [adequate] reserves (*ben*). Even if merchants and traders buy such [paper notes], how could they be willing to keep them in their own homes? By all means they have to try to exchange them for real cash (xianqian 現錢). But even if they have piles of these [paper notes], they are not able to exchange them. As a consequence of this, the system of exchange notes suffers heavy damage.

Since antiquity it has always been like this that in times of war one had to be extremely meticulous in matters of finance and spending. Let us assume that with a piece of paper of only a few inches one could really cover the needs of a whole period, why then did the ancients refrain from issuing several millions [of them] in order to fill all the gaps, instead of discussing to such detail the art of how to regulate finances?[10]

In the view of this unknown scholar, paper money could have had some benefit, not only for the exchange and transaction business related to the logistics of the frontier garrison armies, but also by providing a convenient and easily circulating means of payment, even in the case of a limited amount of reserve cash backing it. But this would only be the case with a sufficient cash reserve, because otherwise paper money would not be accepted at its original value, but would depreciate and thus accumulate in huge piles difficult to dispose of in exchange for real cash. In such a situation of ever-more depreciating paper money, people necessarily tended to hold back and treasure the valuable money, namely, cash coins, which became rare in circulation, especially in the areas of small transactions. Hu Jiaoxiu 胡交修[11] described the results of this development in the following way:

For today's exchange notes no expenses are incurred for copper and charcoal and no costs for smelting and casting like in the case of the large cash [of the Chongning reign period]. In one day one man can make several 100,000 notes, and none of the gods and ghosts is able to inspect this. Nobody can distinguish between real and counterfeit notes, and it easily happens that when the notes are transferred from one hand to the next, punishment is meted out to the innocent, because he happened to be implicated with the crime of having falsified notes in his hands. After some time real cash will all have been treasured in the houses of those with stores of cash strings, and because merchants and traders do not release them into circulation, the ordinary people have to live in strained circumstances.[12]

"Mother and child," "real and empty": positive and negative metaphors

In traditional Chinese monetary theory the metaphor of the mother and the child was often used to describe relationships between differently

---

[10] *Jianyan yilai xinian yaolu* 建炎以來系年要錄, ch. 101, Shaoxing 6/5/*yiyou*; Xiao Qing 蕭清, 179–80.

[11] Hu Jiaoxiu (style: Jimao 己楙) was a man from Jinling 晉陵. He was then a scholar of the Hanlin Academy (Hanlin xueshi 翰林學士).

[12] *Jianyan yilai xinian yaolu*, ch. 101, Shaoxing 6/5/*yiyou*; Xiao Qing 蕭清, 180.

valued kinds of currencies. The first to have used this metaphor in the field of paper money was Yang Wanli 楊萬里 in the late twelfth century.[13] When serving as an official for the supply of horses and grain in Huaixi 淮西 and Jiangdong 江西, he submitted a memorial in 1192 in which he compared the relationship between real cash and payment notes (*huizi*) with the time-venerated concept of the mutual balancing between mother and child. However, during his time, there were two mothers, namely, the copper coin of Jiangnan 江南 and the iron coin of Huaishang 淮上; and, Yang Wanli said, these two mothers had two different children: The payment note of Hangzhou was the child of the bronze coin, while the new payment note was the child of the iron coin. If mother and child, so Yang Wanli said, are not distant from each other, then cash and payment are not of mutual use for each other.[14]

Yang Wanli's idea was that both the mother and the child should circulate and be exchangeable for each other, less by exchange operations carried out by the state, but exchangeable for each other on the market.[15] The reason for bringing this concept of mothers and children to the fore was because Yang opposed the plan of reintroducing *huizi* backed by iron currency in eight departments and military departments in the Jiangnan region, i.e. in an area where iron money was forbidden to circulate. This meant that iron-coin-backed paper notes, the child, could not be balanced with their mother, as this mother, the iron coins, were not allowed to circulate in this region. Hence, this would have been a child without a mother.[16] It is perhaps not too far-fetched to state that what Yang Wanli supported was the idea of convertible paper money and that he stood in strict opposition to inconvertible paper notes.[17]

A rather negative metaphor was the equation of coin with "real" and that of paper money with "empty." This characterization was first adopted for paper money by Yang Guanqing 楊冠卿 (1139–?) before the reforms of the years 1166–67, a time when paper money had lost over ten percent of its value. This depreciation of paper money prompted the people to decline paper money in payment and to treasure bronze coins which were driven out of the markets. Moreover, counterfeiting of paper money appears to have been widespread. Yang

---

[13] Yang Wanli 楊萬里 (1124–1206) was from Jishui 吉水 in Jizhou 吉州. Apart from being an official he was also a famous poet.

[14] See *Chengzhaiji* 誠齋集, ch. 30; Xiao Qing 蕭清, 183.   [15] See ibid.

[16] See *Chengzhaiji* 誠齋集, ch. 30; Xiao Qing 蕭清, 184.   [17] See ibid., 184–5.

Guanqing saw the reason for this development in the different nature of cash coins and paper money:

The people all say that the iron [coins] of Sichuan are the same as the bronze [coins], not knowing that these are two different things. I heard an old man of Sichuan saying that iron is easily worn and thus cannot be stored for such a long time like bronze. This is the reason why men appreciate bronze and despise iron. And this is also why in Sichuan bronze [coins] and paper [notes] circulate side by side without abuse. Bronze [coins] are daily more lacking because rich families and big merchants profit by treasuring them and by being reluctant in easily spending them. This can be said in this way: Paper [notes] are empty, and thus all the abuses related to them are beyond description. Cash coins, however, are real and are thus stored and not related to any abuse. Moreover, while the authorities issue daily more and more paper [notes] without restraint, they only appreciate bronze currency when the people pay [their dues]. But what is it like if we have to take something real to exchange it against their empty [things]! This is the reason why cash becomes increasingly rare and paper money becomes lighter every day. Departments and prefectures all hold these empty notes and transfer them to each other without even seeing one hundred cash coins per day. Why then should one wonder about all these abuses?[18]

Sichuan excepted: specific regional conditions and the question of adequate cash reserves

It was a common argument during the Northern and Southern Song period that Sichuan was some sort of special case that made the adoption of paper money in that province acceptable, while at the same time it was stressed that such conditions did not prevail in other places, which, as a consequence, were thus not suitable for the circulation of paper money. Already in 1071 Zhang Jingxian 張竟憲 (1004–80) stated that exchange notes should be circulated in Sichuan, but not in Shanxi.[19] Li Gang 李綱 (1083–1140) used a similar argument during the Southern Song dynasty when he opposed the introduction of paper money in the southeastern regions. In addition, however, he provided a

---

[18] Keting leigao 客亭類稿, ch. 9, "zhong chubi gao" 重楮幣說; Xiao Qing 蕭清, 186.

[19] *Xu zizhi tongjian changbian*, ch. 222, Xining 4/4/*guihai*; Xiao Qing 蕭清, 181. Zhang Jingxian's style was Zhengguo 正國. He came from Henan.

clear idea in which proportion the amount of paper money should stand
to the amount of reserve cash backing the paper notes:

In my opinion, having the method of exchange notes operated in Sichuan is of
benefit, while it is a catastrophe for other administrative routes. The mountain
roads in Sichuan are very steep and dangerous. Because iron cash is heavy and
difficult to be taken along and transported [to other places], the use of exchange
notes is convenient. Those who once had set up the system did this in an
appropriate way, because they permanently provided and retained a stock of
reserve cash to the amount of one million strings which they used to balance
three million strings of exchange notes. As both public and private were of one
[mind], the notes circulated without obstruction and for the convenience of the
people of Sichuan. ... In Jiangnan, however, the roads are safe and convenient
and the weight of bronze cash is light. If one wishes to make it convenient for
the people, then one should not have the exchange notes circulated there by
themselves. [Moreover,] presently the financial resources of the Ministry of
Revenue are in a desperate state, but it would [nonetheless] have to provide a
cash reserve of several million [strings for backing the notes]. If the circulation
of the exchange notes would be only based on a piece of paper ... the harm for
the population would be beyond description.

Thus, in the eyes of Li Gang the issue of paper money had to be backed by
real cash in the order of 33.33 percent. When the system of governmental
exchange notes was established in Sichuan for the issue of one cycle (*jie*
界) of paper money amounting to a value of 1.256 million strings, a cash
reserve of 360,000 strings, or 28 percent, was earmarked. Li Gang had
probably aligned his conception with this policy as it had been carried out
in Sichuan. At any rate, he proposed a lower, and probably more realistic,
cash reserve than Zhou Xingji 周行己 (1067–?), who had earlier opted
for a percentage of two-thirds, or 66.66 percent.[20]

Li Gang also described that when he served as a military official in
Zhenzhou (Zhenzhou sifa canjun 真州司法參軍) and at the same time
as administrator for the ordinary granaries during the Daguan period
(1107–11), the court had also introduced exchange notes there. The
result of this was that powerful households vied with each other for
getting them for a cheap price, then using them instead of ready cash
(*xianqian* 現錢) for the payment of taxes. As paper notes were considered state money, they had to be accepted by the authorities, with the
result that the granaries were depleted of any real cash. This shows, says

---

[20] See Xiao Qing 蕭清, 182.

Li Gang, that the introduction of paper money was not only of no convenience to the people, but also detrimental to the authorities.[21]

Ma Duanlin (1254–1323): a balanced account of Song paper money

Ma Duanlin 馬端臨, the author of the famous historiographical encyclopaedia *Wenxian tongkao* 文獻通考 (*Thorough Investigation of [Historical] Documents*) commented on the paper money experience of the Song period in a clear-cut manner. Different from other writers, his evaluation appears to be rather balanced, pointing out both negative and positive aspects of the Song paper money regime. As we will see, he did not bluntly oppose the adoption of paper money, although he made clear why the Song experience ended in inflation and failure. Moreover, he made a refreshing attempt to define the characteristics of paper money, for instance, in contrast with tea or salt certificates.

Living as a retired scholar under the Mongol Yuan dynasty, Ma Duanlin described the monetary inflation towards the end of the Song period and its negative impact on the lives of commoners, soldiers, and officials in the following terms:

State purchase of rice was based on paper money (chu 楮); salt was based on paper money; rations paid to soldiers were granted in paper money; there was not any single item purchased from us by departments and districts which was not paid in paper money. Bronze cash became a treasure as it was rarely seen any more, while the accumulation and storage of a reserve [for paper money], as had been done in earlier times, disappeared in statements and were not mentioned any more. Under these conditions prices obviously soared and the paper money suffered depreciation. The people lived in desperate conditions, soldiers were often worried because they had not enough food, and the petty officials of the departments and districts complained because of a lack of means that would have nourished their incorruptibility. This all was due to the abuses of paper money. And from the abuses of paper money also the abuse of cash coins arose. In former times, because cash was heavy [i.e. valued], paper money was restrained and was thus really convenient. Now, however, because cash is lacking, paper money is restrained and hence really constitutes an illness.[22]

---

[21] *Liangxi xiansheng wenji* 梁溪先生文集, ch. 104, "Yu you xiang qi baxing jiaozi zhazi" 與右相乞罷行 交子札子; Xiao Qing 蕭清, 181.

[22] *Wenxian tongkao*, ch. 9, "Qianbi er" 錢幣二; Xiao Qing 蕭清, 215.

In spite of his negative account of the monetary conditions and policies of the late Song period, Ma Duanlin nonetheless highlighted the advantages of a paper money currency when compared with bronze coins:

The things by which the life of the people is supported are clothes and food. Things, which are not related to clothes and food, but are really appropriate for use are pearl, jade and gold. The former kings, being aware that clothes and food were not yet sufficient for providing everything for the overall use of the people, took the things that were of appropriate use and made them to currencies in order to balance them [i.e. clothes and food] ... However, pearl, jade and gold are items difficult to obtain. Thus, when the heavy and the light were balanced and when wealth and poverty were equalized, this could only be done in a thorough manner with copper. Hence, since the Zhou dynasty no change took place with regard to the issue of coins by the Nine Storehouses ...

... It was only when payment notes and exchange notes were put in circulation that one started to make paper (chu 楮) to cash (qian 錢). Now while pearl, jade and gold are items that are treasured, copper is an item that is appropriate for use in spite of not being sufficient to be treasured [like pearl, jade, and gold]. To take the items that are treasured and are of appropriate use and make them into currency (bi 幣) for wide circulation was the intention of the ancients. Making paper into currency marks the beginning of putting the useless to use. Taking now a [paper] note of one chi square which can easily break and have it circulated everywhere during a whole age is comparable to taking cold for clothes, hunger for food and poverty for wealth, i.e. something that never had happened before. However, copper is heavy and paper light, and casting coins is troublesome and difficult, while printing [notes] is easy. To choose the light and easy and to get rid of the heavy and difficult, to avoid that people infringe upon the law because of copper prohibitions and to see to it that the authorities are spared the troubles of copper requisitions is indeed a convenience.[23]

In this passage, by assigning "appropriate use" to pearl, jade, gold, and copper, Ma Duanlin not only broke with the traditional concept in which all items besides clothes and food were considered "useless things," but also singled out copper as an adequate material for making money because it was much less rare than the precious goods mentioned. At the same time he went a step further and extended the idea of making something useful out of a useless item to the realm of paper money, acknowledging its advantages over bronze coins, i.e. being light

---

[23] *Wenxian tongkao*, "zixu" 自序; Xiao Qing 蕭清, 216.

and easy to make. Thus, in Ma Duanlin's view, under the precondition that enough reserve cash was allotted, paper money no doubt could function as currency.

Ma Duanlin argued for a unified control in the production of paper money. Moreover, he was of the opinion that paper money should circulate everywhere, making use of its advantages:

These paper notes measure one chi only, but represent several jin of copper. Thus they are light for transport, but heavy [valuable] in their use. With the force of one man a value of several ten thousand strings can be transported over a way of one thousand li within a few days only. Therefore, what need is there for that Sichuan [notes] are limited to Sichuan, those of Huai to Huai, and the ones of Hu 湖 to Hu, and why sometimes abolish them and then reintroduce them again, rescinding orders time and again, and thus arousing the people's doubt when they hear about it?[24]

For Ma Duanlin paper notes were not real cash, but only representative of it. He was of the opinion that when paper notes were established, this was not done in order to make them cash. Rather, they resembled the certificates or tickets for salt and tea, inasmuch as they served to balance (i.e. represent) cash. But, on the other hand, salt and tea certificates clearly differed from paper notes in several respects. First, the value of certificates was very high, sometimes representing a value of 200 *jin* of salt, while paper notes only had a value of 200 coins to one string. Second, certificates were held only by the merchants who were permitted to sell salt in well-defined regions only. Paper notes could be sold and purchased privately and publicly, and they could be used everywhere. "Thus, with them clearly ready cash (*xianqian*) was represented."[25]

Conclusions

Although in this chapter only a part of the debates and arguments proffered by Song scholars on the characteristics of the paper money regime could be introduced, it has become evident that the adoption of paper money had a deep influence on the daily life of all the people of all social groups as well as on public finances, which were so crucial for raising enough revenue for the pressing military needs. The examples

---

[24] *Wenxian tongkao*, ch. 9; Xiao Qing 蕭清, 217.
[25] *Wenxian tongkao*, ch. 9; Xiao Qing 蕭清, 217.

that I have chosen for a more intense analysis show that a wide range of arguments was presented, some of them in support of paper money, others much more critical and dismissive. Very often, judgements by scholars and officials were directly influenced by recent events in monetary conditions, especially with regard to inflationary developments in the paper money sector and the concomitant phenomenon of the growing scarcity of bronze coins. While not all of the arguments brought forward by different scholars and officials – even if measured according to their contemporary standards – can be considered solid, reasonable or objective, from time to time scholars, such as Ma Duanlin, succeeded in offering a more balanced and analytical view of the characteristics of paper money.

The growing intensity of the debates is also reflected in the elaboration of language and metaphors. To be sure, none of the expressions and concepts on which I have concentrated here, i.e. the dichotomy of "benefit and harm" as well as the metaphors of "mother and child" and of "real and empty," were new *per se*. What was new, however, was their creative adaptation to a new monetary situation that many considered as radically new. How could it be that something as "useless" as paper could act as a representation of money? This was something which not only had to be explained, but for which some empirical understanding also became necessary, like, for instance, regarding the question of how much of a paper money issue had to be covered by a reserve fund. Yet, even if most of the Song scholars and officials adhered to the idea that paper money should be convertible, this eventually did not prevent the excessive issue from playing havoc with the Song paper money regime.

Finally, we should not forget that the Song period is considered a period of veritable revolutions. Apart from the revolutions in agriculture, science and technology, and in society at large, the dramatic changes in the degree of commercialization and monetization have to be highlighted. No doubt, the adoption of paper money, as well as the practical policies and theoretical debates, form an indispensable part of this development.

11 | "Buying Heaven": the prospects of commercialized salvation in the fourteenth to sixteenth centuries*

BERNDT HAMM

It is striking how uninhibitedly religious sources in the late medieval period – even those written by theologians – describe the relationship of humanity to divine grace and the heavenly Hereafter in terms of commercial exchange and financial transactions. Statements from the pen of theologians about the advantageous trade with the other world are by no means uncommon towards the end of the Middle Ages. In devotional literature, too, there is regularly talk of a profitable, meritorious acquisition, collection and accumulation of pious works which can be related as commendable wares to imperishable heavenly treasures. A typical example is how the much-read *Imitatio Christi* gives instructions for a well-prepared death. It is a product of the Dutch "Devotio Moderna" of the early fifteenth century and consequently grew out of the milieu of a flowering commercial culture. One can hear in the commercial maxim "time is money" – every period of time must be used profitably with clever, planned foresight – when the author warns his readers: "The present is the most valuable time [...]. But unfortunately you are not using it profitably enough: you could be acquiring merits to enable you to live forever."[1] "Work, be industrious now, my dearest, achieve whatever you can; for you do not know when you will die! [...] While you have time gather everlasting treasures!"[2]

---

* This text was first published in German in 2006. See B. Hamm, "Den Himmel kaufen: Heilskommerzielle Perspektiven des 14. bis 16. Jahrhunderts," in: *Jahrbuch für Biblische Theologie 21*, Neukirchen-Vluyn: Neukirchener Verlag 2006, S. 239–75.

[1] "Nunc tempus est valde pretiosum, nunc sunt dies salutis, nunc tempus acceptabile. Sed pro dolor quod hoc utilius non expendis, in quo promereri vales, unde aeternaliter vivas." *Imitatio Christi*, Book I c. 23, nr. 29f.; bilingual edition by F. Eichler, *De Imitatione Christi/Nachfolge Christi*, Munich: 1966, 106f.

[2] "Age, Age nunc, carissime, quidquid agere potes, quia nescis, quando morieris; nescis etiam, quid tibi post mortem sequetur. Dum tempus habes, congrega divitias immortales," ibid. nr. 41f. (108f.).

The shaping of theology and piety by the commercial logic of a profitable transaction

One could play down the significance of such statements to the level of a metaphorical, figurative manner of expression, e.g. by stressing: of course every medieval theologian is aware that the infinite divine sovereignty, righteousness, compassion and mercy is so exalted over every creature any commercial logic of trade is totally inappropriate for describing the relationship between God and humanity. If, in spite of this, theologians make use of a commercial terminology in relation to salvation, then it is only because – following Jesus' parables about money, traders, and stewards and his talk of heavenly treasures and reward hereafter – they desire to express allegorically that, with regard to a man's position before God, it is a matter of the responsibility and aim of the Christian life and the steadfast reliability of the God who rewards richly. Such an interpretation could justifiably be supported by several medieval theological voices which stress precisely this figurative use of concepts such as reward and merit;[3] on the whole, however, this would lead to a kind of minimizing of the commercial terminology which would not do justice to the actual close connection of theology, piety, ecclesiastical practice and the socio-economic facts of the Late Middle Ages. Consequently my alternative thesis is that a particular conception is insolubly connected to the semantics and imagery described, and this moves, with regard to its content, within the coordinates of commercial thinking and calculation. From the twelfth century, ecclesiastical theology and piety were more and more characterized by a mercantile logic. This means the logic of the traffic in goods and money oriented on trade took over humanity's relationship to God both in the form of theological thinking and in the way in which the faithful actually developed this relationship – whereby they were taught by theologians.

A particular part of "mercantile logic" is that God takes on characteristics of a calculating, counting and weighing merchant, bookkeeper or bank director, and that man's relationship to this God is regulated by

---

[3] See e.g., the extremely remarkable reflections of Cardinal Laborans in his tract "De iustitia et iusto" (between 1154 and 1160), ed. A. M. Landgraf, *Laborantis Cardinalis Opuscula*, Florilegium Patristicum 32, Bonn: 1932, 6–42; also B. Hamm, *Promissio, Pactum, Ordinatio: Freiheit und Selbstbindung Gottes in der scholastischen Gnadenlehre*, Tübingen: 1977, 53–6 and 465f.

principles of *"Do ut des"*, of barter or exchange, i.e. like a transfer of goods or money from this world to the next. The special distinguishing mark of this exchange-logic in the sense of commercial calculation is that it is not a question of the exchange of goods of like value, but of a business to a high degree oriented on profit which makes as much as possible from as little as possible – whereby in relationship to God all earthly proportions are transcended. A truly fortunate deal is possible because in this transaction one exchanges the earthly, which is transitory and consequently worthless, for the infinite value of heavenly glory. The proportions of earthly profit are broken asunder, but the mercantile logic of the profitable exchange with the aim of maximization of profit is preserved.

The economic change in the eleventh to thirteenth centuries and the new business mentality

This far-reaching change in ecclesiastical thought and attitude can be understood only against the background of those economic changes which have been called a "commercial revolution" between the eleventh and thirteenth centuries.[4] Characteristic of this period in European history above all is a remarkable demographic upswing, the flowering of the cities and therewith the transition from the natural economy of the feudal life to an increasingly organized economic form of trade. The cities were, as we know, the centres of craft and trade, the seat of merchants, bankers, moneylenders, moneychangers, and other rich burghers. Now they become sites of money and banking, accounting, bills of exchange and the giro system, of amassed capital and dealing in credit.[5] But this means the cities are sites of an intensified literarization and intellectualization of life, but at the same time also of a new kind of

---

[4] J. le Goff, *Kaufleute und Bankiers im Mittelalter*, Frankfurt am Main: 1989 (French edn., Paris 1956), 12.

[5] See P. Spufford, *Handel, Macht und Reichtum: Kaufleute im Mittelalter*, Darmstadt: 2004; H. Kellenbenz, "Geldwirtschaft," *Lexikon des Mittelalters* (München: reprint 2002), Vol. IV, cols. 1201–1204; Kellenbenz, "Giroverkehr," in ibid., col. 1463f.; E. Pitz "Frühkapitalismus," in ibid., cols. 998–1001; G. P. Massetto, "Bankwesen," in ibid., Vol. I, cols. 1410–1414. On money and the use of coinage, see also K. Grubmüller and M. Stock (eds.), *Geld im Mittelalter: Wahrnehmung – Bewertung – Symbolik*, Darmstadt: 2005; on further more recent literature on the same topic, see the review by H. Mäkeler in: sehepunkte 6 (2006), Nr. 3, available at www.sehepunkte.historicum.net/2006/03/9358.html.

objectification and reification of culture. For with the intensified turn to the market, trade and money two different things are connected: on the one hand a spiritualization and internalization to the extent that dealing with goods and money demands enormous intellectual abilities of fore-thought in planning, calculation, evaluation and assessment, and in all this the ability to think abstractly; but on the other, this economic change means an increased magnetism of the material, the constant preoccupation with ever-new, improved goods, luxury articles and precious objects, and the increase of money and wealth as a purpose in life. In this way there develops a kind of early capitalist mentality.

Ecclesiastical criticism and support of the new money economy

When one considers how intensely the religiousness of the bourgeoisie was interwoven with their economic livelihood, it is not surprising that the basic features of the commercial professions and the mercantile industry outlined above can also be found in the area of the Church – in the new Scholastic and Canonist theory, in the financial policy of the clerics, in preaching and pastoral care and in the pious attitude of the faithful. The encounter of the Church and the new money economy, however, was by no means without complication. Because of its biblical and patristic tradition, the medieval Church appeared initially to be a spanner in the works of the expanding money economy. In particular, money-lending and the charging of interest proved to be a troubled area.

Because of the canonical ban on interest and the ecclesiastical verdict on any kind of increased pursuit of profit, the merchants were denounced as profiteers who were up to their necks in the deadly sin of *avaritia*, greed. Consequently trade and wealth were in principle considered as morally disreputable and were at least socially controversial.[6] Since the "dirty" business of money-lending

---

[6] See H. Fuhrmann, *Überall ist Mittelalter: Von der Gegenwart einer vergangenen Zeit*, Munich: 1996, 123–36, particularly 130: "A high point of the exclusion of the usurer from the human ecclesial community is the Council of Vienna (1311) – the 15th Ecumenical Council: The statutes of those cities which allow an interest on a loan are invalid, and any judge who awards interest to a creditor should be excommunicated; anyone who dares to act against the ban on interest or who raises doubt about its legitimacy should be regarded as a heretic and treated as such. But the convicted heretic – so runs the order from the time of the 13th

and interest-charging was quite readily left to Jewish merchants, these became the preferred target of the disapproval of the money economy.[7] It is known that there were fervent forces of reform which countered the maelstrom of monetarism with new ideals of evangelical and apostolic poverty. Waldensians, Franciscans and other Church reformers opposed a monetization of the Church conditioned by wealth with the poverty called for by the emulation of Christ.

In the thirteenth and particularly in the fourteenth and fifteenth centuries, however – in spite of continuing resistance – those powers in the Church which developed a positive attitude to the acquisition of capital gained the upper hand, among them the influential municipal Mendicant Orders and, of all people, even the Franciscans. They opened for the rich merchants the possibility of liberating themselves from their notoriously bad consciences and their fears of Hell and Purgatory, of feeling at home in the Church and reaching Heaven without difficulty through trade. The attitude to begging and the alms (endowments) of the wealthy created a plausible cycle of piety so that a kind of symbiosis, interaction and reciprocal reinforcement of the wealth won by trade and the piety demanded by the Church came into being. The new municipal economy combined with the dominance of the Mendicant Orders brought it about that the exchange-system of earthly gifts and heavenly gifts in return also changed: this took place less in the traditional form of donations of land but now, above all, in capital-oriented forms of endowment. To this extent one can say that in central areas the Church turned from a pact with the feudal social order to an alliance with the early capitalist economic way of the merchants and bankers.[8]

---

century – was to be handed over to the secular power which committed him to the stake."

[7] See ibid., 137–46 (with literature 288f.); M. Toch, *Die Juden im mittelalterlichen Reich*, Munich: 1998, 7–9 and 96–100.

[8] Thus Le Goff, *Kaufleute und Bankiers im Mittelalter*, 93. On the phenomenon of the amalgamation of piety and financial capital, see also M. Clévenot, *"Lieber Jesus, mach mich reich!" Geschichte des Christentums im XIV. und XV. Jahrhundert*, Lucerne: 1993 (French edn., Paris 1987), esp. 11–17; A. Angenendt, *Geschichte der Religiosität im Mittelalter*, Darmstadt: 1997, esp. 496–9 (on the financing of the Mass in the Mendicant Orders); Angenendt, "Stiftung und Fürbitte," in: G. Litz, H. Munzert, and R. Liebenberg (eds.), *Frömmigkeit – Theologie – Frömmigkeitstheologie: Contributions to European Church History, Festschrift for Berndt Hamm*, Leiden/Boston: 2005, 3–15; B. Pohl-Resl, *Rechnen mit der Ewigkeit: Das Wiener Bürgerspital im Mittelalter*, Munich: 1996;

Religious factors which furthered a reception of mercantile logic

On the part of the Church the following four factors furthered a convergence of piety, wealth, and mercantile ideas.

A Religion of Preciousness: In the Church there was a general conception that the Holy has a particular affinity to what is exquisite, precious and richly embellished. Consequently, in the imagination of the faithful Heaven was a place of boundless treasures and radiant splendour, and as a result, relics were covered with the most expensive materials,[9] priests wore costly vestments during the liturgy and church buildings were furnished like great treasure chambers, just as the aura of the Holy on religious paintings was symbolized by the most exquisite robes and brilliantly furnished rooms, through velvet, silk, brocade,

---

Martial Staub, "Stifter als 'Unternehmer': Frömmigkeit und Innovation im späteren Mittelalter am Beispiel Nürnbergs," in: K. Schreiner and M. Müntz (eds.), *Frömmigkeit im Mittelalter: Politisch-soziale Kontexte, visuelle Praxis, körperliche Ausdrucksformen*, Munich: 2002, 155–76; B. Hamm, *Theologie und Frömmigkeit, Religiösität im späten Mittelalter: Spannungspole, Neuaufbrüche, Normierungen*, Tübingen: 2010, 293–6.

[9] See the impressive, richly illustrated accompanying volume for the exhibition "De Weg naar de Hemel. Reliekverering in de Middeleeuwen," Amsterdam/Utrecht: 2000/2001, German edn., H. van Os (ed.), *Der Weg zum Himmel: Reliquienverehrung im Mittelalter*, Regensburg: 2001, with the striking intermediate title (113): "The most precious receptacle was not yet good enough"; cf. 159: "The art historian Johan Huizinga talking of the painter, Vermeer, spoke of 'the holiness of everyday things'. In the Middle Ages, on the other hand, we see the holiness of things which are not everyday." On the symbolism of the holiness of precious materials, see Bruno Reudenbach, "Heil durch Sehen: Mittelalterliche Reliquiare und die visuelle Konstruktion von Heiligkeit," in: M. Mayr (ed.), *Von Goldenen Gebeinen: Wirtschaft und Reliquie im Mittelalter*, Innsbruck, etc.: 2001, 135–47; C. Meier, *Gemma Spiritalis: Methode und Gebrauch der Edelsteinallegorese vom frühen Christentum bis ins 18. Jahrhundert*, Munich: 1977. On the contemporary criticism of the religion of preciousness from a Cistercian perspective, see B. of Clairvaux, "Apologia ad Guillelmum abbatem" (*c.*1125), ch. XII, 28, in: B. von Clairvaux, *Sämtliche Werke lateinisch-deutsch*, ed. G. B. Winkler, Vol. II, Innsbruck: 1992, 192–7, particularly the sentences (195): "Thus is wealth creamed off from wealth, thus money attracts money because – I do not know why it happens – more generous donations are given where greater wealth is observed. The eyes feast on relics covered with gold and the purse opens of its own accord. One points out the beautiful picture of a male or female saint and its sanctity seems even greater the more lustrous the colours are. The people come in their crowds to kiss it, and they feel required to offer their own contribution. [. . .] O vanity on vanity, but it is no less crazy than vain! On her walls the Church shows her splendour, on her poor her meanness. She clothes her stones with gold, her children she leaves naked."

gold and precious stones. In so doing, the Church conveyed the message: there is not only a proximity of God's grace to poverty, but also a proximity of the holiness of grace to wealth and the proximity of wealth to grace. One only needs to cast a glance at the many late medieval representations of the Three Kings: they approach the Child in the manger in fairytale splendour and present to him their precious gifts – a symbol of the donor religiousness of the high-ranking and wealthy.[10] In manifold ways Christianity thus presents itself as a religion of luxuriousness in which the wealth of Heaven combines with the riches of the earth.

Wealth as a Gift of God: Closely connected to this was the conception – strongly supported by the Church – that economic prosperity, increasing of capital and wealth, should be understood as an effect of divine blessing – a blessing which, however, only remains beneficial if a part of the profit is used to provide for the Hereafter by means of gifts and endowments, i.e. serves in the form of good works for the placatory cancellation of punishment and the meritorious augmentation of the capital laid up in Heaven. Hence money leads to Hell or to Heaven, depending upon whether it is greedily misused or used to win salvation.

New Teaching about the Hereafter: From the early thirteenth century the teaching about the judgement of every individual, Purgatory, indulgence, and the treasure of the Church made up the theological framework for the logic of securing the Hereafter: God decides the fate of the person in the Hereafter, not only in the universal Last Judgement of Doomsday, but already in the moment of death, when each person will be weighed in an individual *"iudicium particulare"* according to his spiritual quality and morality[11] – a conception which complied with the commercial mentality of weighing and measuring. The outcome of this judgement determines not only the decision for Heaven or Hell, but also the exact calculation of the duration of the stay in Purgatory. The indulgence offers the possibility of shortening this period of time by a particular quantum of days, weeks and years, or of setting it aside

---

[10] See e.g., the predilection of the Medici family in Florence for the cult of the Three Kings; also, in particular, C. A. Luchinat (ed.), *Benozzo Gozzoli: La Capella dei Magi*, Milan: 1993; H. R. Bleattler, "Adoration of the Medici: fifteenth century construction of a princely identity through the expropriation of Magian iconography," Dissertation, Florida State University: 2001.

[11] See P. Dinzelbacher, *Die letzten Dinge: Himmel, Hölle, Fegefeuer im Mittelalter*, Freiburg, etc.: 1999, 47–57: Personal Judgement.

completely. Because the Church grants indulgence, she draws from her treasure, i.e. from the enormous capital of vicarious satisfaction provided by Christ and the saints. It is quite understandable that this construction of the Hereafter was an invitation to mercantile speculation, counting, and calculation. The Church's treasure in the Hereafter functions like a colossal bank-account from which particular sums can be debited in the form of the amount of the indulgence. So Letters of Indulgence can be compared to those letters of exchange which came into use from the thirteenth century on as instruments of national and international payment by cashless transactions.[12]

The Doctrine of Merit and the Idea of Contract: During the thirteenth century, Scholastic theology also constructed its Doctrine of Merit which, like the teaching about satisfaction and indulgence, consolidated in the minds of both clerics and laymen the idea that the relationship of a person to the rewarding God should be structured as a kind of binding business and commercial relationship. If one talks of the heavenly reward as one reads in the Bible, one must, according to the Scholastic theologians, also speak of merits. The possibility of gaining merit, however, always presupposes a kind of relationship of obligation, i.e. that the one awarding is indebted to the one earning merit.[13] But how should God become a debtor for the reward over meritorious human beings? The theologians' answers were varied and ingenious. One influential pattern, which was supported above all by representatives of the Franciscan order and which towards the end of the Middle Ages was in general circulation up to and including in the theology which was preached, operated along the lines of a legal mercantile contract – with reference to the agreement between the householder and the labourers in the vineyard in Matthew 20: 2–13: In his free, sovereign grace, God has made himself a partner of humanity in the Covenant and business. In a kind of Bill of Sale (*pactum, conventio*) he has promised heavenly reward for a person's good works – in themselves by no means meriting reward – which have taken place out of love for God and neighbour. By virtue of this voluntary commitment of God, good works now count as merit, now have a "purchasing power" for the

---

[12] See M. A. Denzel, "Wechsel, -brief, Wechsler," *Lexikon des Mittelalters* (reprint 2002), Vol. VIII, cols. 2086–2089.

[13] See Hamm, *Promissio, Pactum, Ordinatio*, 437–62 on elements and changes in the concept of merit in the Middle Ages.

Hereafter.[14] In fact, some theologians from the end of the twelfth century compare commendable works with low-value coins which have a high purchasing power because of the conditions of the contract, while conversely, the heavenly reward should be likened to valuable currency which is earned with minimum exertion. The point of the comparison with money lies in the discrepancy in value between deed and reward and a relationship of obligation, justice, and reward which nevertheless exists.[15] All this corresponds to the commercial profit principle, which aims for the maximum profit with the greatest possible safety guaranteed by a contract. Jesus' parable of the labourers in the vineyard is made in this way to serve an argument which runs contrary to its original intention. Hence Scholastic theology in its own way supported the need of contemporary commercial piety to interpret its striving after profit on earth and in Heaven, linked to God's blessing and grace, in a regular trade-agreement with the heavenly business partner.

The interconnection of Church and early capitalist money economy

It should now be clear to what extent particular ecclesial-theological developments furthered the complex coalescing of late medieval religion and economy. The decisive point lies not only in the fact that in its internal structure theology itself was open to a mercantile logic and developed into a kind of capitalistic format with its conceptions of the relationship between God and humanity; it was also significant that, because of this, it established, legitimated and drove early real capitalist practice forward in a sanctifying way and thereby allowed it to settle in the Church. The Scholastic theologians in the thirteenth century formulated the principle that works produced by the traditional justifying grace bring the person closer to heavenly salvation than simple grace itself.[16] In the commercial environment of the towns, these good works

---

[14] See ibid., and the register of biblical texts 520 on Matt. 20. See also B. Hamm, *Frömmigkeitstheologie am Anfang des 16. Jahrhunderts: Studien zu Johannes von Paltz und seinem Umkreis*, Tübingen: 1982, subject index 378 on the concept of *Vertrag Gottes*.

[15] See W. J. Courtenay, "The King and the Leaden Coin: The Economic Background of 'Sine qua non' Causality," *Traditio* 28 (1972), 185–209.

[16] Thus, e.g. Odo Rigaldi, one of the most important masters of the older Franciscan School, who, as occupant of the Franciscan chair in Paris, formulated in his *"Quaestiones de gratia"* written around 1245–7 the sentences: "Immediate

were increasingly equated with expenditure for alms, indulgences, gifts to the Church, social and memorial endowments, i.e. with financial investments in the Hereafter. The endowment of the Heilig-Geist-Spital in Nuremberg is a good example of this connection between earthly and heavenly capital. The Church shows the founder how the exchange functions. Indeed, it becomes a speciality of church authorities, to place a "calculated piety",[17] i.e. a particular quantity of money payments, prayers, liturgical contributions or other pious deeds, in a calculated value-relationship to gain church treasure in the Hereafter and to shorten the period of punishment in Purgatory. Here we can see that the Church's talk of heavenly treasures and riches means something not simply symbolic or metaphorical, but something very real, because the capital in the Hereafter will be divided into portions just like the economic capital of the merchants. In the Hereafter, too, things will be quantified, weighed, counted, and measured. To this extent the heavenly treasure is connected to the earthly by a continuum of reality. This holds true not only for the quantities of Purgatory and the treasure of the Church, but also for the graded hierarchy of eternal bliss, and even on the negative scale for the degrees of infernal damnation. The real connection between the earthly and the heavenly capital is particularly clear in the fact that the capitalization of the Hereafter impacts upon the kind of religious financial investments, i.e. controls the stake of the expenditure and regulates its amounts. The present and the Hereafter form one world of economic calculation.

The extent reached by the amalgamation of the Church with the new money economy of the big merchants and bankers can be seen at all levels of the hierarchy and in the whole breadth and variety of Church religiosity. In particular, it is known with what perfection and consistency the financial administration of the Avignon papacy during the first half of the fourteenth century adopted the early capitalist methods of maximization of profit and siphoning off of money.[18] The financial

tamen opus informatum praemii causa est et magis assimilativum est gloriae opus tale quam gratia in se." *Quaestio* 26, ad 5, Cod. Toulouse Ville 737, fol. 218d–219a; for the longer context, see Hamm, *Promissio, Pactum, Ordinatio*, 207–10.

[17] See A. Angenendt, T. Braucks, R. Busch, T. Lentes, and H. Lutterbach, "Gezählte Frömmigkeit," *Frühmittelalterliche Studien*, Vol. 29, Berlin/New York: 1995, 1–71.

[18] See G.-R. Tewes, *Die römische Kurie und die europäischen Länder am Vorabend der Reformation*, Tübingen: 2001; Tewes, "Deutsches Geld und römische Kurie: Zur Problematik eines gefühlten Leides," in: Brigitte Pflug, Michael Matheus, and

politics of the Church were pushed through right down to the level of the parishes and their financial income. More significant perhaps, however, is the progress of new, money-oriented processes of sacralization which need to be examined more closely. I would only mention that now merchants and bankers were also canonized, increasingly, members of the rich commercial bourgeoisie become priests or monks,[19] and that above all, money itself gains a new kind of quality of holiness: not only as the offering which is brought to the altar during the Mass – i.e. not only as secular money which is sanctified by a spiritual use[20] – but also as coinage which is hallowed by its appearance and its special quality. Particular coins are now worshipped as protective relics[21] and currency with inscriptions relating to Christ appears upon the market. The French King, Louis IX (*Saint Louis*), in the thirteenth century had gold coins minted with the circumscription "Christus vincit, Christus regnat, Christus imperat". Throughout the century these remain the ideal of every royal coinage.[22]

Thereby it was impressed upon the subjects: anyone who defiles this money by counterfeiting it, scraping off the precious metal or making excessive interest with it, does injury not only to His Majesty the King, but is unfaithful as Judas was to Christ. Such a crime against the sacrosanct royal coinage would be punished with the heaviest penalty.[23] From this standpoint, late medieval anti-Semitism moves into a new light: in one breath the Jews were branded as counterfeiters and

Andreas Rehberg (eds.), *Kurie und Region: Festschrift für Brigide Schwarz*, Stuttgart: 2005, 209–39; see also Part II: *Geldgeschäfte und Kurie* in that volume.

[19] Cf. le Goff, *Kaufleute und Bankiers im Mittelalter*, 87 and 92.

[20] See T. Rainer, "Judas, der König und die Münze: Zur Wunderkraft des Geldes im Spätmittelalter," in: M. Mayr (ed.), *Von Goldenen Gebeinen: Wirtschaft und Reliquie im Mittelalter*, Innsbruck, etc.: 2001, 28–65, here 33f. and 39.

[21] Cf. ibid., 29–32 and 39.

[22] Ibid., 35. On the origin of the wording "Christus vincit, Christus regnat, Christus imperat" and its re-minting in parody, provable already in the twelfth century: "Nummus vincit, nummus regnat, nummus cunctis imperat" (in Walter von Châtillon), see Dieter Katschoke, "Regina pecunia, dominus nummus, her phenninc: Geld und Satire oder die Macht der Tradition," in: K. Grubmüller and M. Stock (eds.), *Geld im Mittelalter: Wahrnehmung – Bewertung – Symbolik*, Darmstadt: 2005, 182–203. Here it may be recalled that the medieval coin most widespread from the thirteenth century, the Florenus, bore the portrait of John the Baptist, the patron saint of Florence. From this phenomenon combining money with the sacred, we can trace a tradition right up to the US dollar notes with their inscription "In God we trust".

[23] Rainer, "Judas, der König und die Münze," 35.

violators of the consecrated host, wanton defilers both of the Body of
Christ and the sacred coins, dragging what is sacrosanct through the
dirt of their betrayal.[24]

Commercialization of religion and religious domestication of the capital economy

The amalgamation of Church and money economy has two complementary consequences which one can describe as the commercialization
or monetization of religion, and conversely as a religious penetration of
the capital economy. There appears a double declivity of influence or a
twofold dynamic: the secularizing dynamic of the mercantile in the area
of what is sacred, and the sanctifying dynamic of ecclesial-religious
standards in the secular business of the merchants and wealthy skilled
tradesmen.

On the one hand the Church is imbued with the calculating rationality of the financier; she becomes a great economic business oriented
on capital and profit. Greed and usury have the Church under their
control. On the other hand the Church succeeds in domesticating
wealth to some degree in the direction of religion. An army of preachers,
father confessors, and spiritual authors attempt to put the reins of
moderation, ecclesial awareness and ethical responsibility on the new
economy, to use the exorbitant profits of the rich for pious purposes,
and to turn their attention particularly to those in need, i.e. the poor,
sick and old – according to the principle: "Who gives to the poor, gives
to God." Indeed, many rich merchants in this way involved God in
their business (as a heavenly partner in the contract), of course,
above all because they could in this way make provision for their own
spiritual salvation and secure the divine blessing on further successful
transactions, as well as increase their measure of social recognition. The
extremely expensive foundation of the Heilig-Geist-Spital in
Nuremberg clearly shows in exemplary fashion how the Church
managed to unite the thirst for acquisition and desire for honour on
the part of the merchants with her spiritual ideas of the adoration of
God, orientation to the Hereafter and social awareness.

[24] Rainer, "Judas, der König und die Münze," 36–8.

A redemptive commercial orientation as a religiosity of achievement and compassion

The symbiosis of Church and mercantile striving for profit reveals bilateralism in yet another respect. The redemptive commercial orientation of theology and piety to the acquisition of heavenly treasure is on the one hand the driving force of a propagated religiosity of achievement, but on the other hand it can be connected with an extremely trenchant religiosity of mercy and compassion. As far as the achievement side is concerned, it is clear that the religious logic of the Church invites this and strives to change earthly, sinful, conscience-burdening property into investments in the Hereafter – as many and as effective as possible – and thus, by the accumulation of expensive good works, to lessen the fears of the Hereafter and increase the expectations of reward. The person then really seems like a merchant who arrives in the Hereafter with a store full of valuable goods.

But the connection of religious and mercantile logic can also, for some theologians interested in pastoral care, tend conversely towards an intensified logic of God's mercy, if they put the main emphasis on the complete discrepancy between the divine gift and the human contribution towards salvation. This consequence of commercial redemptive thinking, which should not surprise us after what has been said, is almost always overlooked in research on the Late Middle Ages. The argumentation of such theologians of mercy then reads basically as follows: because God in his infinite mercy desires to shower gifts beyond measure on humanity, the person can trade like a clever, successful merchant and with very little expenditure can gain immense wealth in the Hereafter, i.e. liberation from all temporal punishments for sin and immediate entry into eternal bliss.

The metaphor of the divine treasury of grace

We already encounter the metaphor of treasure in the Scholastic canonical doctrine of the Church's treasury (*thesaurus ecclesiae*), which was the foundation of Indulgences. But the metaphor of the immeasurable treasure is also used diversely beyond this doctrinal connection. In an age of growing accumulation of money and a corresponding religious ideal of poverty, it is not surprising that the message of God's liberal mercy is also visualized theologically as an encounter of an enormously

rich treasure with the most extreme poverty, particularly by the municipal theologians of the mendicant orders. Those who are poor in goods,
and particularly those who are poor in spirit who find themselves in a
state of insufficient piety and lacking a credit of good works and who
crave grace without any special prior effort, are told that their loving
desire and ardent longing are sufficient; for the great riches and treasure
of divine mercy, particularly the Passion of Christ, which compensates
for all human inadequacy and opens the way to Heaven, are within their
reach.[25]

The paradox between the logic of gift and the logic of exchange in the Reformation

The motif of joyful exchange or barter takes us right into the middle of
the Reformation, to that oft-quoted passage from Luther's 1520 tract,
"On the Freedom of a Christian", in which he described the relationship
between the believing soul and the divine man, Christ, as a "joyful
exchange and strife" and a "happy economy".[26] He speaks of an
exchange or transfer of property between the sins of the poor bride
and the goods of her noble bridegroom, Christ, who endows her with
his own "wealth of righteousness". Several traditions build the historical background to this text: the Early Church Christology with its
conception of the exchange of the divine and the human nature, the

---

[25] Very characteristic in this respect is the metaphor of treasure and gold in a
Dominican sermon in 1324: see C. Burger, "Gottes Gnadenangebot und der
Erziehungsauftrag der christlichen Kirche im Konflikt: Die Predigt über den
goldenen Berg des Nikolaus von Straßburg," in: Litz, Munzert, and Liebenberg
(eds.), *Frömmigkeit – Theologie – Frömmigkeitstheologie*, 65–79. The
overwhelming abundance of grace which is available for all wretched, contrite
sinners thanks to Christ is compared by the preacher with a mountain of gold as
big as the city of Cologne which a king puts at the disposal of everyone so that
they can "take as much of it as they need to pay off their debts and henceforth live
from it" (72).

[26] M. Luther, *Von der Freiheit eines Christenmenschen*, German version, §12:
"Here arises the joyful exchange and dispute." "Is this not a happy economy that
the rich, noble, pious bridegroom Christ weds the poor, despised, wicked little
whore and frees her from all ill, adorns her with all kindness. Thus it is impossible
for sins to condemn her because now they belong to Christ and swallow up in him
(cf. 1 Cor. 15, 54). Consequently she has such rich righteousness in her
bridegroom that in future she will be able to resist all sin though it already lies
upon her." WA 7, 25, 34 and 26, 4–10; *Martin Luther Studienausgabe*, ed. H.-U.
Delius, Vol. II, Berlin (East): 1982, 277, 1 and 9–15.

"admirabile commercium" of the Latin liturgy, the medieval mysticism of the bride, and the legal marital understanding of community of property – but clearly also the economic imagery of barter, joyous trade, and lucky exchange. This can be found in the theology of the Augustinian Order before Luther, but above all in the writings of Augustine himself, which were read with great enthusiasm.

Elsewhere, too, Luther had a special liking for the graphicness of the riches of treasure and poverty in Christological and soteriological contexts. A good example of this is the sixth verse of the Christmas hymn of 1523–24, "Gelobet seist du, Jesus Christ":

> Er ist auff erden kommen arm,
> das er unser sich erbarm
> und in dem hymel machet reich
> und seynen lieben engeln gleych.
> Kyrieleys.[27]

("He came in poverty to earth in order to have mercy upon us, and makes us rich in heaven and like his beloved angels. Lord have mercy!")

But a comparison of such texts – and above all that central passage in the tract on freedom – with the medieval tradition of the salvatory commercial market relationship between humanity and God, reveals very quickly that Luther's motif of the exchange or barter now has a considerably altered significance. Here Luther is very close to his Superior in the Order, Johannes von Staupitz, and their common authority, Augustine.[28] Augustine had already introduced the metaphors of Christ the heavenly merchant, of the wondrous relationship of exchange and of the commodity of eternal life, but only in order to be able to show, as preacher and biblical interpreter, that the relationship between God and sinful humanity is quite a different matter from earthly commercial dealings. In a similar manner, in Luther the

---

[27] Quoted from: *Archiv zur WA*, Vol. IV (1985), 166 (cf. 60); see also WA 35, 435, 6–10 (cf. 147f.). On this verse, see particularly 2 Cor. 8, 9.

[28] One must see Luther and Staupitz as being very close in this regard. Even before Luther, Staupitz depicted the blessed exchange or barter between Christ and the soul, without any trace of a salvatory commercial metaphor or logic, as a deed of unadulterated grace accomplished by the merciful God on the wretched person, and in so doing – as later Luther did – took as his starting-point the theology of the Incarnation and the Two Natures of Christ and the metaphor of the spiritual marriage (based on Eph. 5: 30–32). In this way, Staupitz and Luther carry on the tradition of the father of their order, Augustine.

economic language of wealth, treasure and exchange excludes any kind of mercantile logic of exchange, every human acquisition, every earning, buying and profiting. It becomes a language solely of receiving gifts without any preliminary effort whatever. Like the stars raining gold in the fairytale, Luther would put it, so the divine riches of salvation are poured out through Christ upon the poor so that "we receive such grace free of cost and without merit, yes, with great lack of merit and even though we are unworthy" ("wir solch gnade umbsonst und on vordienst, ia mit grossem unvordienst und unwirdickeit empfahen").[29]

The only preparation for grace lies with God himself: in his election of predestination. On the part of the human being only a total indisposition precedes grace, i.e. not only his poverty, in which he stands before God with empty hands and has not the least quality and morality which could open for him the heavenly riches; but also his *"rebellio gratiae"*: that he defiantly rebels against the pure mercifulness of Salvation.[30] The gospel gives the believer knowledge: the one who pays and acquires in this whole event of grace and salvation is not the human person – not even in the smallest sign of a free stirring of volition – but Jesus Christ alone: the sinner will be "ransomed" through Christ's laying down of his life. With his death the price of redemption is paid once and for all.[31]

In Luther, and in the Reformation as a whole, other than was generally the case in the Middle Ages, the religious logic of the gift came into radical competition with the mercantile logic of the exchange of goods. A tradition more than a thousand years old of meriting, atonement and satisfaction which wiped out sin, the acquisition and collection of heavenly treasure, came to an end. But at the same time, the Reformation also continued a tendency which already existed: it continued and promoted the strong dynamic of mercy running counter to all earthly calculation which was contained in certain strains of both Mystic and Scholastic theology in the Middle Ages in such a way that

---

[29] M. Luther, *Kirchenpostille* (1522), on Tit. 3: 6; WA 10/I/1, 123, 16–19.

[30] Cf. M. Luther, *Disputatio contra scholasticam theologiam* (4 September 1517), theses 29 and 30: "Optima et infallibilis ad gratiam praeparatio et unica dispositio est aeterna dei electio et praedestinatio. Ex parte autem hominis nihil nisi indispositio, immo rebellio gratiae gratiam precedit." WA 1, 225, 27–30.

[31] Augustine, particularly e.g. in *Sermo* 130, 2 took this thought – following 1 Cor. 6: 20 and 7: 23 – and passed it on to Luther through the medieval tradition. See C. Gestrich (ed.), *Gott, Geld und Gabe: Zur Geldförmigkeit des Denkens in Religion und Gesellschaft* – 2004 Supplement to the *Berliner Theologische Zeitschrift*: Gestrich's introduction to the theme 9–15, here 14.

the idea of a divine gift connected to a human acquisition became impossible. Consequently, the idea that money and alms could buy Salvation was excluded, and the total rejection of the previous symbiosis of a religion of grace and a logic of earning could be compressed, as by Zwingli in 1522, into the polemical formula: for the followers of the Pope there is no grace without money. "One must have money, because without money, they say, God can not be appeased."[32] And the furrier from Memmingen, Sebastian Lotzer, added in a pamphlet in 1524: "If one must buy heaven with money, where do the poor go? They must all go to hell."[33]

The Reformers' criticism of the symbiosis of the Roman Catholic Church and money economy: the dimension of the break in the ecclesiastical system

We know that such polemical tones in the Reformers' tracts were grievously unjust to the previous ecclesiastical constitution. No medieval cleric whom one can take seriously thought that the poor are in a worse position than the rich in God's eyes. On the contrary: while a pious prayer was sufficient for a poor man, rich merchants and entrepreneurs had to invest huge sums in order to achieve satisfaction before God for their sinfully acquired wealth. And yet the Reformers' polemic in regard to money hits the centre of the image of medieval Christianity. As we have seen, it presented itself by and large as a religion of wealth and sumptuousness, as the earthly reflection of heavenly splendour, and in this respect as the combination of divine holiness and material wealth. This desire for luxurious representation of the holy was integrated in the cycle of expensive provision for the Hereafter, for particularly characteristic of the Late Middle Ages was how strongly the role of the hierarchy as a mediator of Salvation and the need of the faithful to acquire Salvation mediated by the Church were connected to the new burgeoning economy and to the enormous need for money on the part of the ecclesial institutions. Though she claimed that she remained a Church of the materially

---

[32] "Pecuniam omnino habere oportet, qua sine deum negant propiciari posse." Huldrych Zwingli, *Apologeticus Archeteles*; Zwingli, *Sämtliche Werke*, Vol. I (= Corpus Reformatorum 88), Berlin: 1905, reprint Zurich 1982, 302, 20f.

[33] "Dann solt man das himelreych umb gelt erkauffen, wa kamen die armen hin? Mießten all gen hell." S. Lotzer, "Beschirmbüchlein," in: *Sebastian Lotzers Schriften*, ed. Alfred Goetze, Leipzig: 1902, 47–75, here 56, 30–2.

and spiritually poor, in fact she became through the combination of fear of the Hereafter, securing of Salvation and financial investments, an enormous mercantile apparatus and a Church of wealth in which the prosperous with their pious disbursements and their religiously heightened family honour could feel more at home than others. Consequently, the picture of the Church immediately prior to the Reformation in the eyes of many critical contemporaries was characterized by the features of consistent skimming-off of money, enormous expenditure of money and money-devouring transactions in grace and Salvation. The sale of Indulgences to finance the new building of St. Peter's in Rome from 1515 was a phenomenon in which the connection of these three aspects of the Church's relation to money was particularly evident.

The Reformation was able to take up the critical, frequently anti-clerical attitude to the Roman Catholic financial practices and the mastery of money in the Church. But its criticism did not stop at the outrages of the creaming-off and waste of money – that everything was for sale in the Church and no saint was so adored as St. Quaestus – but was concerned above all about the salvatory-commercial core of the Church's financial transactions: the combination of the question of grace and Salvation with the mercantile logic of buying, acquiring, and earning; and with an ecclesial authority which, by virtue of its jurisdiction, stimulated and served precisely these needs for afterlife security on the part of the faithful. Only when the Reformation totally rejected this exchange-logic of "*Do ut des*" with regard to the relationship of human beings to God came the break with the earlier Church system.[34] To this extent a new classification of money was central to the Reformation: it cannot serve to buy Salvation, but solely for a way of life in the service of God and one's neighbour.

Eberlin of Günzburg, a one-time Franciscan who wrote tracts, summed up theologically the extent of this radical change when he differentiated between two Gods in the tract which appeared in 1524: "I am surprised that there is no money in the country."[35] There was the God

---

[34] See B. Hamm, "Die Stellung der Reformation im zweiten christlichen Jahrtausend: Ein Beitrag zum Verständnis von Unwürdigkeit und Würde des Menschen," in: *JBTh 15* (2000): Menschenwürde: Neukirchen-Vluyn 2001, 181–220, here 194–8 with the title: Die Reformation als Unterbrechung der religionsgeschichtlichen Logik von Gabe und Gegengabe.

[35] Edition: J. E. von Günzburg, *Sämtliche Schriften*, Vol. III, ed. L. Enders, Halle a. d. Saale: 1902, 147–81; repr. in: A. Laube et al. (eds.), *Flugschriften der frühen Reformationsbewegung (1518–1524)*, Vol. II, Vaduz: 1983, 1123–55. See also

previously worshipped and the true God.[36] The God worshipped up to this point, behind whom the Devil is concealed, has dragged the Church's endeavours into the *"pracht dißer werlt"* (splendour of this world) which devours money[37] and taken all the money of the faithful "nit allein auß dem land, sonder auch auß dißer werlt" (not only out of the country but also out of this world),[38] i.e. misused it for purposes of the Hereafter.[39] The author has no desire to be in such a Heaven.[40] The God whom he wants to accept is the true God of whom one reads in the Bible:[41] "Der

C. Peters, *Johann Eberlin von Günzburg, ca. 1465–1533: Franziskanischer Reformer, Humanist und konservativer Reformator*, Gütersloh: 1994, 222–36.

[36] On the differentiation between two Gods, the true, biblical God, and the God erroneously worshipped, see the Reformation tract first published pseudonymously in 1521 (under the name Judas Nazarei) and then reprinted several times: "Vom alten und neuen Gott, Glauben und Lehre"; also H.-J. Köhler, *Bibliographie der Flugschriften des 16. Jahrhunderts* I/3, Tübingen: 1996, nr. 3433–3442. See also a sermon by Johannes Brenz, "Von zweierlei Gott, dem irdischen und dem himmlischen" (*c.*1522), in: Brenz, *Frühschriften*, Part 1, ed. M. Brecht et al., Tübingen: 1970, 1–3.

[37] Enders, 173, 37f.; Laube, 1142, 28f.

[38] Enders, 170, 21–3; Laube, 1140, 5–7.

[39] Cf. Enders, 178, 1–8; Laube, 1145, 36–1146, 2: "Durch solche mittel kommen wir dahin, das wir gottis, der heilgen und yhrer prokuratorn gantz eigen werden; und so Got und seine heilgen in einer andern werlt wonend, so fehrt all unser gut auß dißer werlt dahin in ihene werlt, und bleibt zu letzt kein pfennig mehr ym lannde, dan allein, was gottis procuratores haben, pfaffen, munch und nunnen. Und das ist die ursach, warumb ietzt alles der pfaffen ist." (By such means it comes about that we become completely the property of God, the Saints and their procurators; and because God and his Saints live in another world, all our property goes out of this world to their world, and in the end there is not a penny left in the land except that which God's procurators have, priests, monks and nuns. And that is why everything now belongs to the priests.)

[40] Cf. Enders, 179, 17–23; Laube, 1146, 42–1147, 3: "Auch wollt ich mir nicht wunschen, in einem solchen himelreich zu sein, als seine heilgen haben, das man mir erst mueste ewigen bettel anrichten auff erden und ich muste den bettel durch mancherley plagen von den leuten schrecken; ich wolt lieber unsers bruders Clausen zu Reinfelden odder schwester Walburgen leben furen, wie ubel tage sie haben." (I, too, would not wish to be in such a heaven as his saints have, for which I must first eternally beg on earth and I must scare up the beggary by many a torment of the people; I would rather live the life of our brother Clausen of Reinfelden or sister Walburgen, whatever bad days they may also have.)

[41] Cf. Enders, 180, 22–5; Laube, 1147, 34–7: ". . . so befind ich, das der biblisch got der recht got ist, thut yederman guts und liebt das gut und die gerechtikeit; darum sag ich unserm [bisher verehrten] got ab und ergibe mich an den biblischen got im namen Jesu Christi." (And thus I deem that the God of the Bible is the true God who does good to everyone, loves what is good and justice; consequently I decline the God [whom we have previously worshipped] and devote myself to the biblical God in the name of Jesus Christ.)

thut seinen leuten vil guts umbsonst und will nichts darfur nehmen; er vorgibt yhn yhre sund; sein son ist fur sie gestorben; er erlaubt yhnen zu essen alles, das sie haben mogen, zu der noth und zu nutz." (He bestows many gifts upon his people for free and does not want anything in return; he forgives them their sins; his son died for them; he allows them to eat all they want for their need and use.)[42]

The Protestant alliance with the money economy: the dimension of continuity

The radical change from the Church system which commercialized Salvation is admittedly only one side of the Reformation relationship to money and the economy. The other side, to which I can only briefly draw attention, lies in the remarkable continuity which characterized its dealings with the world of the rich merchants, the pre-industrial or early industrial entrepreneurs and bankers. Clearly the intertwining of money economy and Church continued to exist in the new Protestantism, too, but also the reciprocity of the vectors of influence: the religious manners determined by the Church continued to influence how money was dealt with, and a money economy oriented on profit continued to characterize the structure of the churches and the behaviour of their followers.

Luther's fierce polemic against commercial companies and monopolies, the taking of interest and usury, is certainly very close to his theological anthropology and is to this extent not a minor theme for him,[43] but was not generally characteristic of the course of the Reformation and the development of Protestant confessionalization. In Lutheranism and even more clearly in Calvin's sphere of influence, there grew up a great deal of understanding for the requirements of the modern money economy.[44] A glance at Reformation Nuremberg shows that the rich tradesmen and master-craftsmen could feel themselves just as much at home in the frame of evangelical preaching in a Lutheran Church as under the Papacy – or perhaps even more so. Consequently, in 1524 Hans Sachs already feels

---

[42] Enders, 179, 4–7; Laube, 1146, 30–3.

[43] See R. Rieth, "*Habsucht*" *bei Martin-Luther: Ökonomisches und theologisches Denken, Tradition und soziale Wirklichkeit in der Reformation*, Weimar: 1996; R. Mau, *Evangelische Bewegung und frühe Reformation 1521 bis 1532*, Leipzig: 2000 (= Kirchengeschichte in Einzeldarstellungen II/5), 126–9.

[44] Thus C. Strohm, "Götze oder Gabe Gottes? Bemerkungen zum Thema 'Geld' in der Kirchengeschichte," *Glaube und Lernen* 14 (1999), 129–40, here 139.

himself led to denounce the exploitive financial and management practices of his wealthy co-religionists who call themselves "evangelical" but offend against Christ's commandments with shameless greed.[45]

Such a call for a curbing of sinful greed and for the use of wealth for the good of the community and support of those in need of help remains fervent in all denominational forms on the Protestant side. But there was such a socio-ethical sensibility in the medieval church as also found support in the new Roman Catholic denomination; and it made no difference that the Protestants, too, made their peace with the early capitalist economy. In the Protestant sphere, too, wealth was understood as a blessing, and impoverishment as God's punishment;[46] and here, too, endowments and gifts continued to be made – a kind of religious patronage – which, it is true, was no longer intended to make provision for the Hereafter of the soul, but was a sign of an intensive interconnection of Church and wealth and the manifold channels for religious elevation of worldly honour.[47] Consequently, Jacques le Goff is quite correct when he observes on the success of the Reformation, "sometimes we meet a strange alliance between earth and heaven, religion and business, God and a merchant"[48] – but there was nothing strange at all here, for this alliance, like the alliance of the Reformation with the political

---

[45] See the reforming tract by Hans Sachs, *Ein Dialogus ... den Geiz ... betreffend* (preface dated 29 September 1524), the best edition in: Sachs, *Die Wittenbergisch Nachtigall: Spruchgedicht, vier Reformationsdialoge und das Meisterlied, Das walt Got'*, Stuttgart: 1974 (Reclam Universal-Bibliothek Nr. 9737 [3]), 93–117, and B. Hamm, *Bürgertum und Glaube: Konturen der städtischen Reformation*, Göttingen: 1996, 202–11.

[46] On the relevant idea of the benevolent God who bestows earthly prosperity and the avenging God who punishes the sins of humanity by poverty, failed harvests, plagues and the misery of war in the Reformed as well as in the Lutheran church, see B. Hamm, *Die Stellung der Reformation im zweiten christlichen Jahrtausend*, 181–220, here 196f. (with literature).

[47] Monographic researches on the Protestant nature of endowment and gift are few and far between. On the Swabian area, see M. Scharfe, *Evangelische Andachtsbilder: Studien zur Intention und Funktion des Bildes in der Frömmigkeitsgeschichte vornehmlich des schwäbischen Raumes*, Stuttgart: 1968; F. Strecker, "Bilderstreit, Konfessionalisierung und Repräsentation: Zur Ausstattung protestantischer Kirchen in Augsburg zwischen Reformation und Restitutionsedikt," in: R. Dellsperger et al. (eds.), *Wolfgang Musculus (1497–1563) und die oberdeutsche Reformation*, Berlin: 1997, 246–78.

[48] Le Goff, *Kaufleute und Bankiers im Mittelalter*, 96.

powers and cultural forces of the time, was the normal case which safeguarded their worldly survival.[49]

On the other hand, to continue the debate on the theory proposed by Max Weber and Ernst Troeltsch, one must also say that no denomination, in particular not even the reformed, became the driving-force of modern capitalism.[50] Certainly, there were particular religious factors which could have strengthened the striving for profit which accumulated capital and a calculating mentality of gain; but such impulses existed at least as strongly in the medieval alliance between economic success and the forces which could bring blessing mediated by the Church, between entrepreneurial capital and the commercial logic of acquisition of Salvation.[51] Modern Roman Catholicism, too, proved in many ways to be an understanding and helpful partner of the activity and mentality of capital economy. Two prominent voices from the anti-Reformation camp, Johann Eck's plea for the taking of interest[52] and Konrad Peutinger's defence of the large commercial companies,[53] pointed to the future. It is typical that the Augsburg

---

[49] See on this problem area as a whole in the age of the Reformation (with particular consideration of Strasbourg and its leading politician, Jakob Sturm): T. A. Brady Jr., *Zwischen God und Mammon: Protestantische Politik und deutsche Reformation*, Berlin: 1996.

[50] Cf. F. W. Graf and T. Rendtorff (eds.), *Ernst Troeltschs Soziallehren: Studien zu ihrer Interpretation*, Gütersloh: 1993; F. W. Graf, "Weber, Max," in: *Religion in Geschichte und Gegenwart*, 4th edn., Vol. VIII (2005), cols. 1317–1320 (with literature).

[51] Gerhard Besier stresses this: "Zur kirchlichen Wertschätzung von Erwerbsmentalität. Die 'Weber-Troeltsch-Theorie' auf dem Hintergrund eines akzeptierten Kapitalismus im Spätmittelalter," *Glaube und Lernen* 2 (1987), 136–46, with the striking conclusion (143) that the so-called "soul" of Capitalism has no specific affinity to Calvinism, as Weber and Troeltsch assumed, but is good late-medieval, and therefore is "older than ascetic Protestantism".

[52] Eck had good contact with the merchants in Augsburg, at their head, Jacob Fugger. From the end of 1513 – particularly in a great disputation in the University of Bologna in 1515 – he supported the idea of freeing interest from the stigma of sinful usury. A moderate interest rate of 5% is ethically legitimate if it is connected with a good intention on the part of the merchant and does not serve usurious purposes. This position was pioneering for a capital-friendly Roman Catholic social ethics in the age of the Reformation. See E. Iserloh, *Johannes Eck (1486–1543): Scholastiker, Humanist, Kontroverstheologe*, Münster: 1981, 20–2; J. P. Wurm, *Johannes Eck und der oberdeutsche Zinsstreit 1513–1515*, Münster: 1997; H. A. Oberman, *Werden und Wertung der Reformation: Vom Wegestreit zum Glaubenskampf*, Tübingen: 1977, 161–200: Oeconomia moderna.

[53] See Fuhrmann, *Überall ist Mittelalter*, 146; H. Lutz, *Conrad Peutinger: Beiträge zu einer politischen Biographie*, Augsburg: 1958, 73–7, 106–9, 136–41, 214–22, 300–7.

town clerk, Peutinger, jotted down the conclusion that nothing makes people less tired than profit. In 1530 he could praise the legitimation of the commercial striving for profit in a report with the words: "Clerics and laymen of all ranks and professions are not prohibited by any legal clause from making a lot of money and becoming rich or being intent on making a profit with what they have. And it is honourable to serve one's own profit because this is beneficial to all realms, provinces and domains for the general and particular advantage, and the state, too, has an interest in wealthy subjects."[54] Even if Peutinger occasionally mentions the name of God – may he bestow blessing for good business and preserve from bankruptcy – his economic outlook is not characterized by religious principles, but by the calculations of worldly rationality.

On the whole, when considering the Middle Ages and Early Modern Age, one can well say that religion was never the decisive power behind a capital-oriented way of thinking and acting, but again and again and in different ways it became the desired ally. The medieval Church and the denominations of the Modern Age received, internalized, promoted, moulded and domesticated the spirit and practice of capitalism; only rarely – and then for the most part from the position of outsiders and fringe groups – did they combat it. Theologically judged, the minority voices – Peter Waldes, Francis of Assisi, John Wyclif, or Thomas Müntzer, and their followers – have weight as evidence of a powerful biblical radicalism; yet in the history of Christianity, the symbiosis of capital and Church won through.

A capital-oriented money economy was and is no unknown force for convinced Christians. In the past and present they belong to its supporters and maintain a thrifty, speculating, investing, and consuming contact with it. In this process the churches as institutions of middle-class cultural and economic enterprises developed into a kind of capital conformity,[55] just as, conversely, the capitalist economy certainly to an ever-greater extent withdrew from the influence of the churches, but at the same time took on religious characteristics: characteristics of an all-powerful, globally omnipresent, invisibly active, security-promising, sacrifice-demanding, heart- and trust-claiming authority behind all

---

[54] Sources for Peutinger ibid., 140.
[55] See F. Wagner, *Geld oder Gott? Zur Geldbestimmtheit der kulturellen und religiösen Lebenswelt*, Stuttgart: 1985; see also the contributions in Gestrich (ed.), *Gott, Geld und Gabe*.

realities in this world.[56] The alliance of religion and money established in the Middle Ages thus led long-term to the imbalance of the present: while the position of the churches was weakened by their increasing capital conformity, the religious contours of capitalism appear to demonstrate its immensely heightened power. But it can be that in future its weakness lies precisely here. It appears contradictory that capitalism is not aware of any divine transcendence, yet has appropriated for itself functions of a transcendent nature.[57] But this religiously analogous character makes the financial world susceptible to collapse of trust, the withdrawal of credibility, and a critical destruction analogous to modern criticism of religion. It could suffer the same fate as the flourishing trade in Indulgences, which collapsed from one day to the next when it lost its goodwill.[58]

---

[56] On Capitalism as a cult religion, see W. Benjamin, "Kapitalismus als Religion," Fragment 74, in: Benjamin, *Gesammelte Schriften VI*, eds. R. Tiedemann and H. Schweppenhäuser, Frankfurt am Main: 1991, 100–3. On the combination of Capitalism and Religion, see also N. Bolz, *Das konsumistische Manifest*, Munich: 2002; D. Baecker (ed.), *Kapitalismus als Religion*, Berlin: 2003; T. Ruster, *Der verwechselbare Gott: Theologie nach der Entflechtung von Christentum und Religion*, 7th edn., Freiburg; Basle; Vienna: 2004.

[57] See J. Hörisch, *Kopf oder Zahl: Die Poesie des Geldes*, Frankfurt am Main: 1996.

[58] I wrote these sentences in 2006 in the German edition of *Jahrbuch für Biblische Theologie* 21 (2006), 239–75. The English text was shortened at many points compared to the German version.

Monetary exchange: ethical limits and challenges

12 The monetization and demonetization of the human body: the case of compensatory payments for bodily injuries and homicide in ancient Near Eastern and ancient Israelite law books

KONRAD SCHMID

I

The legal requirement to pay compensation for injuries and homicide has a long tradition, even longer than the *ius talionis*, which is generally understood as more archaic. Until the middle of the twentieth century, an almost canonical perspective reigned about the development of "primitive law" regarding injuries and homicide. According to this line of thinking, the development started with the concept of unlimited revenge (see Gen. 4:23f.), proceeded then to the *lex talionis*, which limited the extent of the revenge to the extent of the crime ("an eye for an eye"), and concluded with the system of compensatory payments.[1] While a number of law historians in the first half of the twentieth century were uncomfortable with this linear development,[2] the 1948 publication of various cuneiform law books, especially the Code of Ešnunna and the Code of Ur-Nammu[3] provided the means to empirically falsify this theory.[4]

---

[1] See the examles provided by R. Yaron, *The Laws of Eshnunna*, Jerusalem: Magness, and Leiden: E. J. Brill, 1988, 263 n. 20; E. Otto, "Zur Geschichte des Talions im Alten Orient und Israel," in: *Ernten, was man sät: Festschrift Klaus Koch*, ed. D. Roger Daniels et al., Neukirchen-Vluyn: Neukirchener, 1991, 109.

[2] A. S. Diamond, "An Eye for an Eye," *Iraq* 19 (1957); see also idem, *Primitive Law: Past and Present*, London: Methuen, 1971, pp. 97–102, 142f., 398–9.

[3] A. Goetze, "The Laws of Eshnunna Discovered at Tell Harmal," *Sumer* 4 (1948); F. Rue Steele, "The Lipit-Ishtar Law Code," *AJA* 52 (1948); S. N. Kramer, "Ur-Nammu Law Code," *Or.* 23 (1954); Yaron, *Laws*; M. T. Roth, *Law Collections from Mesopotamia and Asia Minor*, Atlanta: SBL, 1997.

[4] Otto, "Geschichte des Talions," 108f. Remarkably, the speech of Diodotus formulated by Thucydides (3.45.3) regarding the execution of the Mytilenaeans because of their revolt against Athens already exhibits an early detractor from this common misunderstanding: "All men are by nature prone to err, both in private

The Code of Ešnunna (CE)[5] and the Code of Ur-Nammu (CU)[6] are both older than the Code of Hammurabi (CH)[7] and these older codices provide many more regulations regarding compensatory payments than the later CH, which is famous for its extensive use of the *lex talionis*. Of course, the consequence of these discoveries cannot be just to turn the old linear development scheme of the early history of law upside down. Rather, they show the need to be cautious about simplistic interpretations.

At any rate, it is safe to assume that these law books were not written in complete and splendid isolation from one another, despite different historical and geographical origins. They participate in a shared scribal law culture, and their changes and accentuations can therefore be compared.

Some comments on the legal status of these codices may prove helpful at this point. Although there has been an extended discussion on the function of ancient Near Eastern law collections,[8] there is a growing consensus that these collections had primarily a *descriptive* rather than a *normative* status. They do not contain rules for every life situation. Instead, they seem to be products of learned scribal traditions that dealt primarily with complicated and extraordinary cases. Everyday conflicts were usually solved according to the customary legal traditions, which did not need to be fixed in writing, but were part of a legal "common sense."

---

and in public life, and there is no law which will prevent them; in fact, mankind has run the whole gamut of penalties, making them more and more severe in the hope that the transgression of the evil-doers might be abated. It is probable that in ancient times the penalties prescribed for the greatest offences were relatively mild, but as transgressions still occurred, in course of time the penalty was seldom less than death. But even so there is still transgression."

[5] CE, ca. 1770 BCE; Roth, *Law Collections*, 57; Yaron, *Laws*, 19–20.

[6] CU, written in Sumerian, ca. 2100 BCE; Roth, *Law Collections*, 13.

[7] CH, ca. 1750 BCE; Roth, *Law Collections*, 71; M. E. J. Richardson, *Hammurabi's Law: Text, Translation and Glossary*. BiSe 73, Sheffield: Sheffield Academic Press, 2000; copies of the CH have been known since the discovery of Ashurbanipal's library in Nineveh in the mid-19th century; the well-known stela was excavated in Susa in 1901; for variant readings see Richardson, *Hammurabi's Law*, 15–19.

[8] See e.g. Roth, *Law Collections*, 4–7; E. Otto, "Recht/Rechtstheologie/ Rechtsphilosophie I," TRE 28, Berlin and New York: de Gruyter, 1997; idem, "Recht und Ethos in der ost- und westmediterranen Antike: Entwurf eines Gesamtbildes," in *Gott und Mensch im Dialog: Festschrift Otto Kaiser*. BZAW 345/I, ed. M. Witte, Berlin/New York: Walter de Gruyter 2004.

Therefore, the common designation of ancient Near Eastern law collections as "code" (e.g. "Code of Ur-Nammu," "Code of Lipit-Ishtar," etc.) is rather misleading.[9] The notion of a "code" implies normativity and completeness, but these texts are collections of exemplary cases rather than "normative law." It is more suitable to call them "law books."[10] They provide "help, but not rules in the finding of justice."[11] Their language is *informative* rather than *performative*. If these codices were authoritative, their authority was not rooted in their character as codified texts. Rather, it was dependent on the authority of the king, who repeatedly re-enacted these laws. The case of pre-Demotic ancient Egypt, where no written laws at all are extant,[12] is therefore not an exception in the history of ancient Near Eastern law, but only a very poignant example: the legislative authority was the king and not a text.[13]

The CH usually differentiates between three classes of persons: the free person (*awilum*), including men, women, and minors; the "commoner" (*muškenu*), who is hard to define in a specific way, but is certainly inferior to the *awilum*;[14] and finally, the slaves, both male

[9] K.-J. Hölkeskamp, *Schiedsrichter, Gesetzgeber und Gesetzgebung im archaischen Griechenland*. Historia Einzelschriften 13, Stuttgart: Franz Steiner, 1999, 16; S. Greengus, "Law. Biblical and ANE Law," AncBD 4, New York: Doubleday, 1992, 243; S. Greengus, "Legal and Social Institutions of Ancient Mesopotamia," in *Civilizations of the Ancient Near East II*, ed. J. M. Sasson, Peabody, MA: Hendrickson, 2000, 471–2.

[10] Cf. C. Houtman, *Das Bundesbuch: Ein Kommentar*. DMOA 24, Leiden: E. J. Brill, 1997, 18; J. Assmann, *Herrschaft und Heil: Politische Theologie in Ägypten, Israel und Europa*, Munich: Beck, 2000, 178–89; R. Rothenbusch, *Die kasuistische Rechtssammlung im "Bundesbuch" (Ex 21, 2–22.18–22, 16) und ihr literarischer Kontext im Licht altorientalischer Parallelen*. AOAT 259, Münster: Ugarit, 2000, 408–73.

[11] Assmann, *Herrschaft*, 179 (translation mine); for the "Code of Hammurabi" as "memorial"/"commemorative inscription" see H.-J. Gehrke, ed., *Rechtskodifizierung und soziale Normen im interkulturellen Vergleich*. ScriptOralia 66, Tübingen: Narr, 1994, 27–59; Assmann, *Herrschaft*, 179–80.

[12] With the one exception of a decree of 18th dynasty King Haremhab; see Otto, "Recht und Ethos," 105.

[13] Greengus, "Law," 244; as the Greeks and Romans later put it: the king as *nomos empsychos* or *lex animata*, see J. Assmann, "Gottesbilder – Menschenbilder: anthropologische Konsequenzen des Monotheismus," in: *Gottesbilder – Götterbilder – Weltbilder: Polytheismus und Monotheismus in der Welt der Antike, Band II: Griechenland und Rom, Judentum, Christentum und Islam*. FAT II/18, ed. R. G. Kratz and H. Spieckermann, Tübingen: Mohr Siebeck, 2006, 321.

[14] See the discussion in Yaron, *Laws*, 132–46, especially 139; in German often rendered as "Palasthöriger."

(*wardu*) and female.[15] It is noteworthy that legal regulations concerning bodily injuries to slaves are not treated among the laws concerning damage of objects or injuries of animals, but among injuries to persons. Furthermore, injuries caused by slaves are separated from injuries caused by animals.[16]

When looking at the CH alone, it already suggests that the *lex talionis* is only extant within the *awilum* class:

§ 196:   If a man (*awilum*) puts out the eye of another man, his eye shall be put out.

§ 197:   If he breaks another man's (*awilum*) bone, his bone shall be broken.

§ 200:   If a man (*awilum*) knocks out the teeth of his equal, his teeth shall be knocked out.

Furthermore, CH § 200 shows that there are also social differentiations within the *awilum* class, in that the talion as for knocking out teeth is only applicable for peers (*awilim meḫrišu*).[17]

The application of the talion further seems to be dependent on the amount of intent. CH §§ 206 and 207 regulate the case where injuries or homicide occur "during a brawl" (*ina riṣbatim*), which is the common wording for acts without intention:

§ 206:   If during a brawl one man (*awilum*) strikes another man (*awilum*) and wounds him, then that man (*awilum*) shall swear, "I did not strike intentionally," and pay the physician.

§ 207:   If he dies of his wound, he shall swear similarly, and if he (the deceased) was an *awilum*, he shall pay 30 shekels of silver.

The redactional juxtaposition of these regulations in §§ 206–7 in the literary vicinity of those in §§ 196, 197, and 200 implies that the extremely severe punishments in §§ 196, 197, and 200 are limited to actions committed intentionally as well (which in these cases seems to be rather self-evident, anyway).

In dealing with criminal actions committed by an *awilum* ("free man") which harm a member of the lower *muškenu* class ("commoner") or a slave, the CH provides regulations for compensatory payments:

---

[15] *amtu*; see Yaron, *Laws*, 161–5.

[16] G. Ries, "Körperverletzung," RLA 6, Berlin and New York: de Gruyter, 1980–1983, 174.

[17] Ries, "Körperverletzung," 174.

§ 198: If he puts out the eye of a commoner (*muškenum*), or breaks the bone of a commoner (*muškenum*), he shall pay 60 shekels of silver.

§ 199: If he puts out the eye of a man's (*awilum*) slave, or breaks the bone of a man's slave, he shall pay one-half of its value.

§ 200: If a man (*awilum*) knocks out the teeth of his equal, his teeth shall be knocked out.

§ 201: If he knocks out the teeth of a commoner (*muškenum*), he shall pay 20 shekels of silver.

Several problems arise when trying to determine the economic status of such a fine.

Firstly, it is difficult to determine the monetary value of a shekel of silver[18] because there are regional and temporal differences in the exact weight of a shekel (usually 8.3 grams = 0.28 oz in Old Babylonian times, but e.g. 11.3 grams = 0.38 oz in monarchic Israel according to weight stones).[19] Furthermore, for comprehensible reasons the shekel of the dealer when selling was often a little heavier than the shekel used when buying. Finally, the prices could vary significantly in different time periods.[20] For example, Sin-Gashid from Uruk (*c.*2200 BCE) stated that during his reign, 3 Kur of grain, 12 minas of wool, 10 minas of copper, or 30 sila of oil could be bought for 1 shekel of silver (1 Kur = 180–300 sila (72–120 liters = 19–31 gallons); 1 mina = 60 shekels). Meanwhile, under Shamshi-Adad I (*c.*1800 BCE), 1 shekel of silver bought 2 Kur of grain, 12 minas of wool, or 20 sila of oil.[21] However, these prices are probably propagandistically low. In Old Babylonian times, the usual price for grain was 1 Kur of grain for 1 shekel (362), and a day laborer could earn 6 shekels in one year (163). An idea of the value of silver can also be deduced from exchange rates with bronze, tin or gold:[22]

---

[18] See M. A. Powell, "Weights and Measures," AncBD 6, New York et al.: Doubleday, 1992, 904–8; CAD 17, 96–9 s.v. *šiqlu*.

[19] See R. Kletter, *Economic Keystones: The Weight System of the Kingdom of Judah*. JSOT.S 276, Sheffield: Sheffield Academic Press, 1998; for changes during the history of Judah, see Y. Ronen, "The Enigma of the Shekel Weights of the Judean Kingdom," *BA* 59 (1996).

[20] F. Joannès, "Metalle und Metallurgie. A. I.," RLA 8, Berlin and New York: de Gruyter, 1993–1997.

[21] B. Meissner, *Babylonien und Assyrien*. Kulturgeschichtliche Bibliothek 3, Heidelberg: Carl Winter, 1920, 361.

[22] Joannès, "Metalle und Metallurgie," 99–100.

Table 12.1 *Exchange rates between 1 shekel of silver and corresponding quantities of bronze, copper, tin, and gold (in shekels)*

	Bronze	Copper	Tin	Gold
Mari (*c.*1800 BCE)	120	150	8–15	1/4, 1/6
Old Babylonian (18th–12th century BCE)	360	180	8–16	1/3, 1/6
Neo-Babylonian (7th–5th century BCE)	?	180–200	20–100	1/5

Secondly, it is not completely clear whether these fines were really applied or rather, whether they were conceived as *maximum amounts*. There is only one document concerning bodily injuries extant from Old Babylonian times.[23] In this document, the offender, who slapped the cheek of another man, is sentenced to pay a sum of 3⅓ shekels of silver, which is significantly less than CE § 42 (10 shekels) or CH § 203 (60 shekels among members of the *awilum* class, 10 shekels among the *muškenum* class) allot for this case.

It is striking that there are hardly any regulations affecting commoners (*muškenum*) or slaves who commit crimes causing injury or homicide. The only instances are related to offending a person's honor, which is a bagatelle physically, but socially a very severe crime:[24]

CH § 202:   If a man (*awilum*) strikes the cheek of a man (*let awilim imtaḥaṣ*) higher in rank than he, he shall receive sixty blows with an ox-whip in public.

CH § 203:   If a man (*awilum*) strikes the cheek of another man (*let awilim imtaḥaṣ*) of equal rank, he shall pay 60 shekels of silver.

CH § 204:   If a commoner (*muškenum*) strikes the cheek of another commoner (*let muškenim imtaḥaṣ*), he shall pay 10 shekels of silver.

CH § 205:   If the slave of a man strikes the cheek of a man (*let awilim imtaḥaṣ*), his ear shall be cut off.

---

[23] UCBC 756, see Ries, "Körperverletzung," 177.

[24] E. Otto, *Körperverletzungen in den Keilschriftrechten und im Alten Testament: Studien zum Rechtstransfer im Alten Orient*. AOAT 226, Kevelaer: Butzon & Bercker and Neukirchen-Vluyn: Neukirchener, 1991, 67.

The non-specific formulation of § 195, which also concerns a specific instance of offending a person's honor – namely, one's father's – can be added here:

CH § 195: If a son strikes his father, his hand shall be cut off.
The punishment of "cutting off a hand" seems to be applied especially when a specific action is not to be repeated, as becomes clear from the following examples:

CH § 218: If a physician performs major surgery with a bronze lancet upon an *awilum* and thus causes the *awilum*'s death, or opens an *awilum*'s temple with a bronze lancet and thus blinds the *awilum*'s eye, *they shall cut off his hand* (emphasis added).

CH § 226: If a barber shaves off the slave-hairlock of a slave not belonging to him without the consent of the slave's owner, *they shall cut off that barber's hand* (emphasis added).

CH § 253: If a man hires another man to care for his field ... if that man steals the seed or fodder and it is then discovered in his possession, *they shall cut off his hand* (emphasis added).

To sum up this first glance at the CH, the *lex talionis* is specifically and exclusively valid among the *awilum* class. Assaults perpetrated by members of the *awilum* class on lower classes are always punished by payments, while assaults by lower classes (like slaves) on members of the *awilum* class are penalized by punishments above the equality ratio of the *lex talionis*, illustrated by looking again at CH § 205: if the slave of a man strikes the cheek of a man, his ear shall be cut off.

In the older law books like the CE and CU, the *lex talionis* plays nothing more than a marginal role. If the case of the death penalty for murder is excluded from the definition of talion, then it is completely absent.[25] Be this as it may, only CU § 1 provides a tit-for-tat punishment, i.e. the death penalty, for homicide.[26]

---

[25] See B. S. Jackson, "The Problem of Exod. XXI 22–25," *VT* 23 (1973): 281 n. 1: "(T)he term talion is rightly applied only when non-fatal bodily injuries are involved, and where the offender is punished by suffering the same injury as he inflicted. Thus the death penalty for murder is not an example of talion," followed by Yaron, *Laws*, 263.

[26] On CU § 1 see Yaron, *Laws*, 263 n. 22; as for R. Westbrook, *Studies in Biblical and Cuneiform Law*. CRB 26, Paris: Gabalda, 1988, 39–83, see the objections of Otto, *Körperverletzungen*, 66 n. 1.

Table 12.2 *Fines and punishments for injuries and homicide in the CH*

	Free man (*awilum*)	Commoner (*muškenu*)	Slave (*wardu*)
eye	eye	60 shekels	50% of slave's value
bone	bone	60 shekels	
teeth	teeth	20 shekels	
slap on cheek	60 shekels		
homicide without intent	30 shekels	20 shekels	

If a man commits a homicide, they shall kill that man.

These law books exclusively treat the bodily injuries of the *awilum* [in the Sumerian CU: *lú*] class[27] and always provide for compensatory payments. These payments are measured primarily in accordance with the extent of the damage, while the question of guilt plays hardly any role:[28]

CU § 18:   If [a man] cuts off the foot of [another man with ...], he shall weigh and deliver 10 shekels of silver.

CU § 19:   If a man (*lú*) shatters the ... bone of another man (*lú*) with a club, he shall weigh and deliver 60 shekels of silver.

CU § 20:   If a man (*lú*) cuts of the nose of another man (*lú*) with [...], he shall weigh and deliver 40 shekels of silver.

CU § 22:   If [a man knocks out another man's] tooth with [...], he shall weigh and deliver 2 shekels of silver.

The CE does not treat homicide in general, mentioning only unintentional homicide (CE § 47, see below). It does, however, provide a broad passage on injuries:

§ 42:   If a man (*awilum*) bites the nose of another man (*awilum*) and thus cuts it off, he shall weigh and deliver 60 shekels of silver; an eye – 60 shekels; a tooth – 30 shekels; an ear – 30 shekels; a slap to the cheek – he shall weigh and deliver 10 shekels of silver.

§ 43:   If a man (*awilum*) should cut off the finger of another man (*awilum*), he shall weigh and deliver 20 shekels of silver.

---

[27] Yaron, *Laws*, 286, thinks that the CE makes no legal distinction between *awilum* and *muškenum* for these cases, but this does not seem completely convincing.

[28] Ries, "Körperverletzung," 176.

Table 12.3 *Fines and punishments*
for injuries and homicide in the CU

Homicide	Death penalty
Foot	10 shekels
Bone	60 shekels
Nose	40 shekels
Tooth	2 shekels

§ 44: If a man (*awilum*) knocks down another man (*awilum*) in the street (?) and thereby breaks his hand, he shall weigh and deliver 30 shekels of silver.

§ 45: If he should break his foot, he shall weigh and deliver 30 shekels of silver.

§ 46: If a man (*awilum*) strikes another man (*awilum*) and thus breaks his collarbone, he shall weigh and deliver 20 shekels of silver.

These regulations do not differentiate explicitly between intentional and unintentional actions. It is unclear what role premeditation plays in these cases, although it is very hard to imagine some of the referred injuries happening unintentionally.[29] At any rate, these regulations are conceived according to *Erfolgshaftung* rather than guilt, although it is very difficult to determine the rationale of the specific amounts of payments allotted to the different injuries. Is it the loss of working power that is compensated? Or is the loss of a body part, as such, compensated? The fines for knocking out a tooth or biting the nose which, at least for most professions, do not constitute a diminution of working power, suggest that, at least in part, the second option is more probable.

The presence or lack of intention seems to be fully relevant for the case of homicide:

CE § 47: If a man (*awilum*), in the course of a brawl (*ina riṣbatim*), should cause the death of another man (*awilum*), he shall weigh and deliver 40 shekels of silver.

CE § 48: And for a case involving a penalty in silver in amounts ranging from 20 shekels to 60 shekels, the judges shall decide his case; however, a capital case is only for the king.

---

[29] E.g. "biting the nose," see the discussion in Yaron, *Laws*, 264–7.

Table 12.4 *Fines for injuries and unintentional homicide in the CE*

Nose	60 shekels
Eye	60 shekels
Tooth	30 shekels
Ear	30 shekels
Slap to cheek	10 shekels
Finger	20 shekels
Hand	30 shekels
Foot	30 shekels
Collarbone	20 shekels
Homicide without intent	40 shekels

By means of an *argumentum e silentio*, it is possible to conclude from CE § 47 that the crime of *intentional* homicide was expected to be punished by the death penalty. As a self-evident case, this might not have needed to be mentioned explicitly in the CE. However, there was obviously a need to state that capital punishment can only be proclaimed by the king, which seems to be an innovation over CU § 1.

So far one can say that the stress on the *lex talionis* for injuries among members of the *awilum* class in the CH is more of an innovation than a traditional element, at least as far as the written sources are concerned. Especially the CU, but also the CE witness an earlier legal order that punishes deliberate injuries with compensatory payments rather than in a tit-for-tat mode.

The introduction of the talion for the *awilum* class in the CH is therefore not the result of the domestication of unlimited revenge, but instead develops out of regulations providing compensatory payments. The talion seems especially designed to protect the members of the *awilum* class from injuries,[30] and therefore may be interpreted as a legal element privileging a certain social class, since assaults by these members on other classes were regulated by payments.

When comparing the fines for bodily injuries in the CU, CE, and CH, it becomes evident that the fines are generally *higher* in the *later* law books. This may be partly explained by the inflation of silver due to the

---

[30] Otto, *Körperverletzungen*, 74.

increase in silver circulation in the Mesopotamian economies between 2100 and 1750 BCE. However, three observations problematize any explanation based on economic history alone.

Firstly, the increases of the fines is not linear: a broken nose costs 40 shekels according to the CU, 60 shekels according to the CE (60 shekels (= 1 mina, *c.* 0.5kg) according to § 48 is probably the maximum fine in the CE), which is an increase of 50 percent. A knocked-out tooth is 2 shekels according to the CU, 30 shekels according to the CE, which means an increase of 1,500 percent. A broken foot is compensated by 10 shekels according to the CU and by 30 shekels according to the CE, which is an increase of 300 percent. Therefore, the higher fines cannot be explained by referring to economic changes alone. Apparently, the rise of the fines is due to other, conceptual reasons as well.

This might also be corroborated by the introduction of the talion in the CH, which can be interpreted as a drastic intensification of the fine compared with the payments provided in the CU and the CE. Apparently the fines take on additional functions beyond merely covering the damage in terms of *Erfolgshaftung*.

Thirdly and finally, it can be seen that the *higher* fines in the CE for injuries remain within a significantly *smaller range* than in the CU. In the CE the range of fines for injuries is 20 to 60 shekels (a factor of

Tabel 12.5 *Comparative Listing of fines and punishments for injuries and unintentional homicide in the CU, in the CE, and in the CH*

	CU 2100 BCE	CE 1770 BCE	CH 1750 BCE *awilum* (*muškenum*)
Nose	40 shekels	60 shekels	
Eye		60 shekels	(60 shekels)
Tooth	2 shekels	30 shekels	(20 shekels)
Ear		30 shekels	
Slap on cheek		10 shekels	60 shekels
Finger		20 shekels	
Hand		30 shekels	
Foot	10 shekels	30 shekels	
(Collar)bone	60 shekels	20 shekels	(60 shekels)
Homicide without intention		40 shekels	30 (20) shekels

3) – if we put the 10 shekel fine for the slap on the cheek aside for a moment, since it is not an injury but an offense against a person's honour. In the CU the range is much broader, reaching from 2 to 60 shekels (a factor of 30). This also may suggest that the fines are not just determined by the value of the loss.

How are these developments to be interpreted? As already mentioned, the fines in the CE, and especially in the CH, are apparently not only based on considerations regarding compensation, but also seem to fulfill the function of prohibition and deterrence. The fines are so high that crime is not only punished when having occurred, but virtually prohibited from being committed at all. In this respect, it is interesting to compare the fines for offending a man's honor ("slap to the cheek") in the CE ("10 shekels") and the CH ("60 shekels"): 60 shekels is not an adequate, but rather, a draconian fine for a bagatelle like a slap to the cheek. This is intended to make it an efficient medium to prevent such assaults. In the CE and especially the CH, it is therefore possible to observe a development from a compensatory law towards a criminal law, at least on the *awilum* level. As for the *muškenu* level, the law continues to be driven mainly by the principle of compensation.[31]

The preceding discussion suggests that despite the remarkable economic development between the time of the CU, the CE, and the CH – a bit less than four centuries – the perception of the value of the human body (at least, of the human body of an *awilum*) seems to have been de-economized, even de-monetized. This is supported by the prohibitively high fines for injuries in the CE, which are all within a relatively small range, and especially the abandonment of the compensatory payments in favor of the talion (among members of the *awilum* class) in the CH.

One might ask whether the execution of the talion in the CH or the high fines in the CE are the more severe punishment, as the raising of the compensatory payments must have equaled a life sentence, whereas the execution of the talion ended the case immediately. However, as in other cultures, the mutilation of a body is a very hard punishment that hardly overrides the economic "advantages" entailed in the execution of the talion.

---

[31] Otto, *Körperverletzungen*, 74.

II

How do the biblical legal regulations, especially in the so-called Covenant Code (CC, Exod. 20–23) relate to these findings?

When looking at the CC in the Hebrew Bible, a law book originating from the eighth to the sixth century BCE,[32] a more complicated picture emerges with regard to fines and punishments for bodily injuries and homicides. Nevertheless, as has often been noted, the CC shares many variously explained commonalities with ancient Near Eastern law books.[33] The ancient Near Eastern legal tradition was most likely handed down to and in ancient Israel within the framework of scribal education.[34] Therefore, it is only to be expected that the legislation of the CC shows similarities to its ancient Near Eastern predecessors, while providing its own interpretations and accentuations. Turning to the punishments for homicide and injuries, there is a strict regulation in the CC providing the death penalty for homicide.

Exod. 21:12 Whoever strikes (*mkh*) a person mortally shall be put to death.

Whether this homicide had been committed intentionally is not stated explicitly, although the action of "striking" in most cases is not really conceivable as an accident.[35] However, the following verses specify:

Exod. 21:13f: If it was not premeditated, but came about by an act of God (*wh'lhym 'nh lydw*), then I will appoint for you a place to which the killer may flee. But if someone willfully attacks and kills another by treachery, you shall take the killer from my altar for execution.

---

[32] Y. Osumi, *Die Kompositionsgeschichte des Bundesbuches Exodus 20, 22b-23, 33*. OBO 105, Fribourg: Universitätsverlag and Göttingen: Vandenhoeck & Ruprecht, 1991; F. Crüsemann, *Die Tora: Theologie und Sozialgeschichte des alttestamentlichen Gesetzes*, Munich: Kaiser, 1992, 132–8; Houtman, *Bundesbuch*; Rothenbusch, *Rechtssammlung*.

[33] Crüsemann, *Tora*, 170.

[34] L. Schwienhorst-Schönberger, *Das Bundesbuch (Ex 20, 22–23, 33): Studien zu seiner Entstehung und Theologie*. BZAW 188, Berlin and New York: de Gruyter, 1990, 260–8; K. van der Toorn, *Scribal Culture and the Making of the Bible*, Cambridge, MA and London: Harvard University Press, 2007.

[35] C. Houtman, *Exodus. Volume 3: Chapters 20–40*. HCOT, Leuven: Peeters, 2000, 135f.

According to this statement, offenders guilty of manslaughter do not have a legal guarantee to be spared the death penalty; however, they do have the chance to flee to a certain cultic place.[36] Exodus 21:12 therefore seems to be a general rule that may be applied to any homicide, be it committed on purpose or not. Yet for homicides resulting from an "act of God," there is the possibility legally to avoid the death penalty.

Furthermore, the CC extends the death penalty to other offenses:

Exod. 21:15:   Whoever strikes (*mkḥ*) father or mother shall be put to death.
Exod. 21:16:   Whoever kidnaps a person, whether that person has been sold or is still held in possession, shall be put to death.
Exod. 21:17:   Whoever curses father or mother shall be put to death.

Like the older Mesopotamian law books, the CC also differentiates between different classes of humanity. In ancient Israel, however, there are only two classes – free and slave. Homicide of slaves is treated in Exodus 21:20, but the wording of this verse does not make immediately clear how the offender should be punished:

Exod. 21:20:   When a slaveowner strikes a male or female slave with a rod and the slave dies immediately, the owner shall be punished (*nqm ynqm*).

The formulation rendered "he shall be punished" has led some scholars to conclude that a fine is in view, but this is not clearly stated. Moreover, to whom should such a compensatory payment be made? The slave was the owner's property and so, probably – at least in most cases – is his family.

It is also possible to interpret the regulation in Exodus 21:20 as a specification of the overall rule in Exodus 21:12: "Whoever strikes a person mortally, shall be put to death." Already the Samaritan Pentateuch reads "shall be put to death" instead of "shall be punished"[37] and thus clarifies the meaning.[38] Understood in this way, the intention of Exodus 21:20 seems to be the following: the death penalty applies even to cases *where the victim is a slave.*

However, this interpretation is contested. Houtman,[39] for example, thinks otherwise. He notices that Exodus 21:20 lacks the specific formulation *mot yumat* "shall be put to death." Nevertheless, the

---

[36] Houtman, *Exodus*, 140–1.   [37] Houtman, *Exodus*, 157.
[38] B. Jacob, *The Second Book of the Bible. Exodus*, Hoboken: Ktav Publications, 1992, 648.
[39] Houtman, *Exodus*, 158–9.

semantics of *nqm* still point to the death penalty. Leviticus 26:25 interprets *nqm* with the expression "to bring the sword upon you," i.e. killing. Schwienhorst-Schönberger[40] and Westbrook[41] think of "vicarious punishment": "the appropriate member of the creditor's family is liable to be killed by way of revenge: if the victim were a son – his son; if a daughter – his daughter" (ibid.).

In sum, it seems more plausible to assume that Exodus 21:20 has the death penalty in mind, although this is not explicitly stated. When read in this way, the continuation in Exodus 21:21 also makes good sense:

Exod. 21:21:   But if the slave survives a day or two, there is no punishment (*l'yqm*); for the slave is the owner's property.

A slaveowner is to be executed when intentionally and brutally he beats his slave so that he or she dies immediately. If the blow does not cause immediate death, then the owner goes free. Exodus 21:20f therefore seems to be a regulation protecting slaves – it is striking that there is no difference between male and female slaves – from excessive physical violence on the part of their owners. Furthermore, the specification "the slave is the owner's property" again suggests that the interpretation of Exodus 21:20 as a monetary payment is hardly possible.

Compensatory payments are only provided in the CC for cases involving injuries, but not intention (*yrybn* "quarrel") or homicide:

Exod. 21:18f: When individuals quarrel and one strikes the other with a stone or fist so that the injured party, though not dead, is confined to bed, but recovers and walks around outside with the help of a staff, then the assailant shall be free of liability, except to pay for the loss of time, and to arrange for full recovery.

The payment in this case covers only what has been lost; there is no additional fee. The payment has a purely compensatory function. Apparently this is sufficient because there are no lasting damages (*rp' yrph'* "full recovery").

For more complicated cases (where no "full recovery" is possible), the following regulation seems to provide a model for decisions:

---

[40] Schwienhorst-Schönberger, *Bundesbuch*, 70–4.   [41] Westbrook, *Studies*, 91.

Exod. 21:22–25:   When people who are fighting injure a pregnant woman so
                   that there is a miscarriage, and yet no further harm (*'swn*)
                   follows, the one responsible shall be fined what the wom-
                   an's husband demands, paying as much as the judges
                   determine. If any harm (*'swn*) follows, then you shall
                   give life for life, eye for eye, tooth for tooth, hand for
                   hand, foot for foot, burn for burn, wound for wound,
                   stripe for stripe.

This of course is rather a specific case, and it is unlikely that it happened
very often. However, it may have served as a sample case that helped to
decide similar matters.

The regulation includes the following premise: if a third party is
injured in a fight (which again means unintentionally), then a judge
may set a specific sum *which may be more* than merely the amount for
covering the damage. The legitimation for this seems to lie in the fact
that the pregnant woman is not involved in the fight and therefore
carries no responsibility.

This is followed in Exodus 21:23–25 by the most prominent mention
of the *lex talionis* in the Old Testament:[42] if there are further damages,
"then you shall give life for life, eye for eye, tooth for tooth" and so
forth. What does that mean?

First, one must ask about the meaning of the term *'swn*, often
rendered as "harm." Is it only a harm if death results, or also a harm
in a wider sense?[43] The term *'swn* is used in the Hebrew Bible on only
three other occasions, all within the Joseph story – in Genesis 42:4 ("But
Jacob did not send Joseph's brother Benjamin with his brothers, for he
feared that *harm* might come to him"), 42:38 ("But he said, 'My son
shall not go down with you, for his brother is dead, and he alone is left.
If *harm* should come to him on the journey that you are to make, you
would bring down my gray hairs with sorrow to Sheol'"), and 44:29
("If you take this one also from me, and *harm* comes to him, you will
bring down my gray hairs in sorrow to Sheol"). These instances seem to

---

[42] See Otto, "Geschichte des Talions;" A. Graupner, "Vergeltung oder
      Schadensersatz? Erwägungen zur regulativen Idee alttestamentlichen Rechts am
      Beispiel des ius talionis und der mehrfachen Ersatzleistung im Bundesbuch,"
      EvTh 65 (2005), 459–77.

[43] See Schwienhorst-Schönberger, *Bundesbuch*, 89–94; Otto, *Körperverletzungen*,
      119–20; Crüsemann, *Tora*, 190 n. 266; Houtman, *Exodus*, 163–4; Graupner,
      "Vergeltung," 467.

reckon with the fact that *'swn* implies death. But *'swn* is also found in parts of the deuterocanonical book of Sirach (written around 180 BCE) preserved in Hebrew – in Sirach 38:18 ("Out of grief results harm [*'swn*]"); 41:9 ("if you increase, then for harm [*'swn*]") which witness to a broader understanding. However, these findings do not help much further, because the possibility cannot be excluded that the term *'swn* underwent some changes in meaning between the CC and the book of Sirach. It is not possible to decide about the meaning of the term *'swn* with certainty. Reading Exodus 21:22–25 in context, *'swn* seems to have a lasting, incurable injury to the mother or the future child in view, perhaps even death. It treats a counter-case to Exodus 21:18f, where "full recovery" is possible.

Far more important is a second observation: it is crucial to see that *ntn*, "to give" (Exod. 21:23: "then you shall give life for life, eye for eye"), in the CC always refers to *paying* a specific sum (Exod. 21:19, 22, 30; in all these instances, the New Revised Standard Version renders *ntn* "to give" correctly with "to pay"), like the Akkadian equivalent *nadanu* in the corresponding contexts.[44] Where the CC envisions a refund, it uses *šlm* "to refund" (see Exod. 21:36, 37; 22:4). But lost "health" cannot be "refunded" as such; therefore, there is a payment for the lost value.

The specific formulation in Exodus 21:23 therefore seems to point quite clearly to a metaphorical interpretation of the *lex talionis* as an accordingly assigned fine. Who should, otherwise, be the addressee of "then you shall give life for life" if this regulation should imply the death penalty? Is it the executor? But how should he "give" a life? The process of execution is, as Exodus 21:14 shows, formulated differently. Is it the offender? How shall he "give" his life? Shall he sacrifice himself?[45] The verbatim understanding of Exodus 21:23 does not make much sense. These observations suggest that the *lex talionis* here is conceived in a monetized way: you *shall pay* as much as a life is worth, you *shall pay* as much as an eye is worth, etc. But, of course, this interpretation of the *talio* as a *payment* shall still be recognizable *as an interpretation* to

---

[44] See D. Daube, *Studies in Biblical Law*, Cambridge: Cambridge University Press, 1947, repr. 1963, 137–8; H.-W. Jüngling, "'Auge für Auge, Zahn für Zahn': Bemerkungen zum Sinn und Geltung der alttestamentlichen Talionsformeln," *ThPh* 59 (1984), 19–20; Schwienhorst-Schönberger, *Bundesbuch*, 101–2; Graupner, "Vergeltung," 469–70.

[45] Schwienhorst-Schönberger, *Bundesbuch*, 99.

the reader, as the concrete formulation shows. Exodus 21:21–25 is both tradition and innovation; it relies on the old tradition of the talion, but interprets it in terms of monetary payments.

Interestingly, the Babylonian Talmud in its exegesis of this passage strongly insists on the interpretation of the talion as payment and provides several arguments for the conclusion that only payments are a just application of the talion. For example, if the offender has a small eye and the victim has a big eye, how can the small eye compensate for the big one? Or, what if the offender was already blind? Therefore, according to the Babylonian Talmud, the talion needs to be understood as referring to payments.

On the other hand, the Greek legislation of Zaleukos, according to Demosthenes, feels the need to exclude explicitly the possibility of a payment of the talion in replacement: "If someone puts out an eye, his own eye shall be put out, and there shall be no possibility of a material substitute."[46]

Moreover, such an interpretation of Exodus 21:23–25 in the sense of a payment would be in accordance with the preceding regulations. Especially the "life for life" sentence as understood literally contradicts Exodus 21:13 and 21:21. This collision can be avoided if "life for life" is conceived as a regulation including a compensatory payment.

Finally, this interpretation clarifies why the statements in Exodus 21:26f. follow these regulations:

Exod. 21:26f: When a slaveowner strikes the eye of a male or female slave,
                destroying it, the owner shall let the slave go, a free person, to
                compensate for the eye. If the owner knocks out a tooth of a
                male or female slave, the slave shall be let go, a free person, to
                compensate for the tooth.

Because slaves are not entitled to their own money, they cannot be compensated by payments. Instead they should be released if their owner destroys their eye or knocks out one of their teeth. Apparently Exodus 21:26f follows Exodus 21:22–25 in order to provide a sub-case.

Finally, the famous regulation about the "goring ox"[47] provides guidance on how to deal with unintentional homicide due to

---

[46] Crüsemann, *Tora*, 175 n. 203.
[47] Exod 21:28–32, see the corresponding paragraphs in CE §§ 53–5 and CH §§ 250–2; Schwienhorst-Schönberger, *Bundesbuch*, 129–62.

carelessness or negligence. Again, this case seems to be very specific, but it owes its explicit regulation in the CC to the fact that it provides guidelines for similar cases.

Exod. 21:28–32: When an ox gores a man or a woman to death, the ox shall be stoned, and its flesh shall not be eaten; but the owner of the ox shall not be liable. If the ox has been accustomed to gore in the past, and its owner has been warned but has not restrained it, and it kills a man or a woman, the ox shall be stoned, and its owner also shall be put to death. If a ransom (*kwpr*) is imposed on the owner, then the owner shall pay whatever is imposed for the redemption of the victim's life. If it gores a boy or a girl, the owner shall be dealt with according to this same rule. If the ox gores a male or female slave, the owner shall pay to the slave-owner thirty shekels of silver, and the ox shall be stoned.

Accidents resulting from a goring ox do not in and of themselves produce any liability for the owner. But if the owner knows that his ox gores, and proceeds to act carelessly, he is liable to the extent of the death penalty. In this case, the accident is not treated as a lethal accident, but as homicide. There is the possibility of a payment ("ransom"), but there is no guarantee of this. The more specific regulation, "If it gores a boy or a girl, the owner shall be dealt with according to this same rule," clarifies that a ransom shall *always* be imposed in the case of the death of a child (rather than a vicarious punishment). In contrast to the case of intentional homicide of a slave which is also punished by the death penalty (Exod. 21:20), the accidental killing of a slave due to carelessness and negligence does not result in the death penalty for the responsible person, but rather, in a payment of 30 shekels.

The "stoning of the ox" may sound atavistic,[48] but the practical sense of this measure is apparently to render impossible another such incident caused by this ox. Other instances of "stoning" in the Hebrew Bible (Exod. 8:22; 17:4; 19:12f; Josh. 7:24f; 1 Sam. 30:6) suggest that the meaning of "stoning" is not a punishment subsequent to a trial, but an immediate action designed to protect the community from a deadly danger. Nevertheless, there may be some religious overtones in Exodus 21:28–32, since the ban on eating the flesh of

---

[48] See the scholarly discussion in Schwienhorst-Schönberger, *Bundesbuch*, 132–6.

the ox is present as well. But this may also be understood as a fine – the owner is not allowed to take advantage of any benefits the dead ox might provide.

III

What are the profile and the inner logic of these regulations in the CC, especially in light of the legal tradition witnessed by CU, CE, and CH?

Firstly, homicide is generally punishable by the death penalty even if the victim is a slave. The loss of a human life – be it of a free man or a slave – cannot be "compensated." In the legislation of the CC, the idea might have played a role that every slave – due to the law of the manumission of the slaves – is potentially a "free man." Even the lack of intention does not guarantee protection from prosecution and punishment. As mere exceptions, compensatory payments for homicide are only possible where a third party is affected and where no intention is given ("pregnant woman"). If the case involves carelessness or negligence ("goring ox"), then the death penalty applies, but the possibility of a ransom remains. It is interesting that the Hebrew Bible is reluctant to *guarantee* exceptions from the death penalty, even one providing the possibility of such exemptions.

Secondly, it is noteworthy that the CC rarely sets any fixed amounts for payments even when fines are allotted. The fine must be fixed by a judge, apparently taking into account the circumstances of the case (amount of intention and/or carelessness), the economic situation of the offender, and the needs of the victim. The only fixed price is the value of a slave (30 shekels). The mention of the talion in Exodus 21:23–25 (bodily injury or homicide of a third party without intention) should be understood as a monetized transformation, and therefore might be interpreted as a guideline for the amount of the compensatory payments in the following manner: to put out an eye entails a fine corresponding to the value of that eye, but this value cannot be fixed in an absolute, monetized way. The process of a systemic de-monetarizing of the human body conceived in the ancient Near Eastern law tradition continues into the Hebrew Bible, but the Hebrew Bible seeks solutions other than a verbatim executed talion in the case of bodily injuries. There are payments, but their amount is not fixed. (So, in another respect, one could also speak of a re-monetization.)

Thirdly, there are hardly any regulations extant for cases of bodily injuries among free persons. The CC is especially concerned with cases of injuries to slaves, which are also fined "draconically" in order to prevent mistreatment of slaves (Exod. 21:26f). An injured slave is rewarded by freedom, which at the same time means a loss of his or her value (30 shekels) to the owner.

When looking back over these findings in ancient Near Eastern and ancient Israelite law books, it is noteworthy that the developing economization of a society does not necessarily entail a thorough and consequent monetization of all of its parts. There are also counter-examples of processes of de-monetization, especially in the regulations on homicide and bodily injuries in these various law books.[49] Apparently monetization is not only a development to measure everything in terms of money, but seems to be capable of sharpening the perception of non-monetary values as well.

IV

When speaking of "monetization," "demonetization," etc., in the realm of ancient Israel and Judah, it needs to be kept in mind that the CC probably developed before "coined" money found its way to Palestine in the fifth century BCE.[50] Nevertheless, one has to acknowledge that the existence of a "monetized" economy *in a broader sense* in ancient Israel and Judah is older. The beginnings of an economy that exceeds the possibilities of a system based primarily on the non-pecuniary exchange of goods and services seems to have co-emerged with the formation of the "nation state" in ancient Israel.[51] It is, more or less, a shared assumption in recent Hebrew Bible scholarship that Israel became a "state" in the ninth century BCE. In Judah – which was politically and economically less significant than Israel – this

---

[49] These findings from the ancient world shed some new light on current discussions on comparable problems, see the contribution by Günter Thomas in this volume. On the stunningly high amount of sophistication in biblical discussions on "money," see M. Welker's article on Kohelet in this volume.

[50] U. Rappaport, "Numismatics," in: *The Cambridge History of Judaism 1*, ed. W. D. Davies and L. Finkelstein, Cambridge: Cambridge University Press, 1984, 25. See especially the article by U. Hübner in this volume.

[51] H. Weippert, "Geld," BRL, Tübingen: Mohr, 1977, 88.

happened about a century later.[52] Domestic (buildings: 2 Kings 12:5–
15; 22:3–7; horses and chariots: 1 Kings 10:28) as well as foreign affairs
(toll payments: 2 Kings 12:19; 14:14; 15:20; 16:8; 18:14) required the
king to have certain amounts of "money" at his disposition; and this
certainly contributed to the rise of a monetized economy.[53]

However, it is clear that "money," *in a narrower sense* of coins,
does not appear in Judah before the Persian Period,[54] which is, of
course, also true for the Mesopotamian cultures. Nevertheless, in
earlier times there were already certain kinds of materials that could
be used as "money" – rings, disks, bars, wedges (*tongues*, Josh. 7:21,
24), etc., as a number of biblical texts suggest. Since there were no
standardized weights and measures for metals, one had to use scales to
determine the value of merchandise in relation to the precious material
that was used for payment. This preliminary form of "money" seems
to be of Egyptian origin, whereas hacked precious metals (bullion)
were used in Mesopotamia, but were also well known in Syria and
Palestine: hack-silver has often been found in excavations[55] and is also
attested in biblical texts (e.g. Isa. 46:6; Jer. 32:9–10). Moreover, one
should keep in mind that there is no clear terminological distinction
between "money" and "silver" in biblical Hebrew.[56]

This corresponds with the fact that coins in ancient Israel were never
fully taken for their par value. Their value was also, or even mainly,
dependent on their concrete weight and material, as traces of hacking
on several coins and mixed finds of coins and bullions indicate.[57]

---

[52] D. W. Jamieson-Drake, *Scribes and Schools in Monarchic Judah: A Socio-
Archaeological Approach.* JSOT.S 109 and SWBA 9, Sheffield: Sheffield
Academic Press, 1991.

[53] For the pre-history of money before the state formations of Israel and Judah see
K. Jaroš, "Geld," NBL 5, Zurich: Benziger, 1991, 773.

[54] Y. Meshorer, *Jewish Coins of the Second Temple Period*, Tel Aviv: Am Hassefer,
1967; G. Mayer, "*ksp*," ThWAT IV, Stuttgart et al.: Kohlhammer, 1984;
L. Mildenberg, "Yehud-Münzen," in: *Palästina in vorhellenistischer Zeit.*
Handbuch der Archäologie Vorderasien II/1H, ed. H. Weippert, Munich: C.H.
Beck, 1988; U. Hübner, "Münze," NBL 5, Zurich: Benziger, 1995, 850–53, and
especially idem, "The development of monetary systems in Palestine during the
Achaemenid and Hellenistic Eras" in this volume.

[55] Beth-Shean, Megiddo, Ein-Gedi (Weippert, "Geld," 89).

[56] *ksp*, see Mayer, "*ksp*"; J. W. Betlyon, "Coinage," AncBD 1, New York:
Doubleday, 1992, 1076; Ezr. 2:69 and Neh. 7:70–71 mention *darkmomim*, i.e.
Drachmai.

[57] W. Schwabacher, "Geldumlauf und Münzprägung in Syrien im 6. und 5.
Jahrhundert," *Opuscula Archaeologica* 6 (1950), 139–49.

Zech. 11:13, a late third-century BCE text, points to the existence of an official melting down of coins in the Jerusalem temple,[58] a process which only makes sense if the material that was melted down retained its value. Similarly, Herodotus reports on the tribute received by Darius I from the 20 satrapies (*Hist.* III 96): "This tribute the king stores up in his treasure house in the following manner: He melts it down and pours it into jars of earthenware, and when he has filled the jars he takes off the earthenware jar from the metal; and *when he wants money he cuts off so much as he needs on each occasion.*" This process of "cutting off money" shows that Darius I himself relied on hacked silver as opposed to coined "money."

Moreover, the appearance of coined money under the rule of Darius I seems to be an innovation that was foremost due to *political* rather than to *economic* circumstances.[59] Already Herodotus notes: "Darius wished to perpetuate his memory by something no other king had previously done." The coining of money seems not only to have been a revolutionary act in the economic realm; it also serves as a political demonstration of the power and sovereignty of the Persian king. It is, therefore, not altogether surprising that the first coining of *high* values in Judah – as late as the Jewish War (66–70 CE) (shekels and half-shekels) – served the same purpose: it demonstrated the power of the Jewish revolutionaries. The coins of that time show inscriptions like "Jerusalem the holy one," "Shekel of Israel," "Liberty of Zion," "For the liberation of Zion."[60]

Therefore, one should keep in mind that *coined* "money," even in Persian times, was not yet an indispensable economic instrument. Coins from the Persian period in ancient Judah are almost exclusively of local origin – coined by the local governor – and represent only small values. Hardly any Persian imperial coin or coins from Egypt, Cyprus, or Asia Minor (only a few from Greece) have been found in Judah.[61]

---

[58] O. Eissfeldt, "Eine Einschmelzstelle am Tempel zu Jerusalem" (1937/1939), in *Kleine Schriften II*, ed. idem, Tübingen: Mohr Siebeck, 1963, 107–9.

[59] L. Mildenberg, "Über das Münzwesen im Reich der Achämeniden," in *Vestigia Leonis: Studien zur antiken Numismatik Israels, Palästinas und der östlichen Mittelmeerwelt*. NTOA 36, ed. U. Hübner and E. A. Knauf (Fribourg: Universitätsverlag and Göttingen: Vandenhoeck & Ruprecht, 1998), 3–29; P. Briant, *From Cyrus to Alexander: A History of the Persian Empire*, trans. by P. T. Daniels (Winona Lake: Eisenbrauns, 2002), 409.

[60] Betlyon, "Coinage."   [61] Rappaport, "Numismatics," 29.

13 | *What price do we place on life? Ethical observations on the limits of law and money in a case of transitional justice*

GÜNTER THOMAS

I. Introduction: money in transitional justice and reparatory justice

What happens when money is used for non-marketable goods, such as a lifetime? How can an awarded amount of money "compensate" for lost time, such as, for example, for a false conviction resulting in months or years of hard labor in prison? Money can never carry the same value as a real, lived life, so what is life's monetary value, and how can it be measured in a standardized way?

Such questions become prominent in situations of transitional justice and at the intersection of politics, law, moral communication, and financial transactions. Whenever societies come to the end of a period of injustice and "illegal rule," they face problems of transitional justice. In these times of transition, one crucial question recurs: how should societies deal with evil actions in their recent history, especially when there can be no rerun of that history? Furthermore, how can these deeds be redressed in a manner which reflects not the injustices of the past, but manifests the values and principles of the new rule?

In this chapter I would like to analyze one specific process within the larger issue of transitional justice: the use of money in the specific search for reparatory justice. This process of monetization operates at a very peculiar cultural point, namely, at the dynamic and indeterminable intersections of the law with other social institutions such as politics, art, history, and religion. This investigation will highlight the theologically relevant ethical problems which occur at the limits of jurisprudence occasioned by its search for reparatory justice. It will then systematize these problems, and make them accessible both to cultural analysis and to genuine theological reflection.

Methodologically, I will combine an inductive approach to these far-reaching theoretical problems, and will do so by use of a very limited historical case study: the program of compensation offered by the Federal Republic of Germany to those who were politically persecuted and were forced to work in prisons by the ruling SED party in the former Eastern German Democratic Republic.

In terms of the widely criticized "economization of social spheres," this approach starts with a rather "indirect," even inverse, view of the problem.[1] The matrix of problems surrounding the issue of economic compensation locates the "economization of life" in a dynamic interaction between politics, law, economics, religion, and individual concern. In addition, the issue arises within a framework of compensation in which people have high expectations concerning the socio-cultural power of money. Although all parties affirm this process of "economization" as an appropriate means to deal with past injustices, and although it is instituted by political representatives and regulated by law, it is not without severe shortcomings. One finds in the discussion of legal regulations regarding compensation the primary entry point to this dynamic interaction. My own conviction is that the theological debate regarding the "monetization" of life must appropriately perceive the complexity of that life, and that a satisfactory solution can only be found in the creative tension between these complexities and an adequately complex theoretical endeavor.[2]

I will proceed in four steps: in section II I lay out the issue of transitional justice in the twentieth century. I then turn to a very specific example: the way in which the German government dealt with political

---

[1] For sharply critical perspectives, see the contributions in J. Ebach, ed., *"Leget Anmut in das Geben": Zum Verhältnis von Ökonomie und Theologie.* Jabboq, Gütersloh: Kaiser, 2001. For an attempt to offer a more nuanced and diversified view, see M. Welker, "'Ab Heute regiert Geld die Welt . . .' Die Einführung der Geldwirtschaft und ihre Auswirkungen auf religiöses Denken und ethische Orientierung," in: *Gott, Geld und Gabe: Zur Geldförmigkeit des Denkens in Religion und Gesellschaft,* ed. C. Gestrich. Berlin: Wichern Verlag, 2004, 52–66.

[2] On the limits of monetary rationality in the field of non-economic goods, see M. J. Sandel, *What Money Can't Buy: The Moral Limits of Markets.* New York: Farrar, Straus and Giroux, 2012; with a feminist perspective, see D. Satz, ed., *Why Some Things Should Not Be for Sale: The Moral Limits of Markets,* Oxford Political Philosophy. New York: Oxford University Press, 2010; against the background of the green movement, see J. Mulberg, *Social Limits to Economic Theory.* London; New York: Routledge, 1995; and in the context of arguing for a democratic "politics of the common goods," see R. Keat, *Cultural Goods and the Limits of the Market.* New York: St. Martin's Press, 2000, 167ff.

prisoners in the former East Germany (German Democratic Republic). In this section I also analyze the specific types of monetization and standardization employed in this empirical case.[3] Based on this, I assess possible media for compensation and reconciliation. In the final section, I discuss possible intersections between the political process of reconciliation, law, and religion.

The approach favored in this chapter is necessarily multi-systemic, since the particular strengths and weaknesses of a standardized monetary system become visible in situations (a) where several forms of standardization intersect, and (b) where, sociologically speaking, a conversion of systemic "currencies" occurs.

II. Transitional justice in the twentieth and twenty-first centuries

1. Historical changes and the need for transitional justice

"Over the past two decades, all over the world, newly emergent liberal democracies with long, dolorous pasts of injustice – under communism, under military dictatorship, under apartheid – have sought to confront and to overcome these persistent legacies. From these episodes has emerged a concept relatively new to the vocabulary of liberal democracies, but now the subject of a global conversation: reconciliation."[4] With these remarks Daniel Philpott points to a debate about reconciliation which, in fact, has not quite made it into the ethical conversation within academic Protestant theology in Germany.[5] In the second part of

---

[3] For the issue of standardization in law and economy, see Chapter 4 in this volume by B. Hess.

[4] D. Philpott, "Introduction," in: *The Politics of Past Evil: Religion, Reconciliation, and the Dilemmas of Transitional Justice*, ed. D. Philpott. University of Notre Dame Press, 2006, 1.

[5] The only notable exception is the broad historical and descriptive study by R. K. Wüstenberg, *Die Politische Dimension Der Versöhnung: Eine theologische Studie zum Umgang mit Schuld nach den Systemumbrüchen in Südafrika und Deutschland*, Öffentliche Theologie. Gütersloh: Kaiser, 2004. More recent treatments of German unification are offered by A. J. McAdams, *Judging the Past in Unified Germany*. Cambridge; New York: Cambridge University Press, 2001. A summary can be found in A. J. McAdams, "The Double Demands of Reconciliation: The Case of Unified Germany," in *The Politics of Past Evil*, 127–49. Interesting observations can be found in G. Sauter, "What Does Common Identity Cost? Some German Experiences and Provocative Questions," in: *Peace*

the twentieth century, a considerable number of nations were forced to face issues of what has become known as transitional justice; for example, South Africa, Northern Ireland, Argentina, Guatemala, Spain, Poland, El Salvador, Brazil, and finally, Germany.[6] It is a striking fact that the second part of the twentieth century saw a historically unusual concentration of societies that passed from authoritarianism to democracy, from war (even civil war) to peace. Nations in Eastern Europe, Latin America, East Asia, and South Africa have sought to move away from various forms of non-democratic regime that persistently denied human rights to their citizens: military dictatorships, apartheid or communism. In some cases, such as North Korea and Cuba, significant transformations may yet take place. These historical transitions opened up a large range of conversations between religion, law, and the political sciences.[7]

These states needed to respond to their pasts and did so in a variety of ways, combining an array of approaches which we could place on a broad spectrum.[8] At one end of the spectrum we find highly pragmatic

---

and Reconciliation: In Search of Shared Identity, eds. S. C. H. Kim, P. Kollontai, and G. Hoyland. Aldershot, England; Burlington, VT: Ashgate, 2008, 21–33.

[6] For a broad overview of cases with an analysis of the structure of transitional justice, see J. Elster, *Closing the Books: Transitional Justice in Historical Perspective*. Cambridge University Press, 2004, and the collection of cases in Elster, *Retribution and Reparation in the Transition to Democracy*. Cambridge; New York: Cambridge University Press, 2006. The concept of transitional justice is clarified by Elster, *Closing the Books*, 79–135; R. G. Teitel, *Transitional Justice*. Oxford University Press, 2000, chs. 1 and 7; M. R. Amstutz, *The Healing of Nations: The Promise and Limits of Political Forgiveness*. Lanham, MD: Rowman & Littlefield Publishers, 2005, 17–40. For case studies related to identity processes, see P. Arthur, *Identities in Transition: Challenges for Transitional Justice in Divided Societies*. Cambridge; New York: Cambridge University Press, 2011.

[7] The enormous body of literature cannot be listed here. See e.g., the conceptual studies and historical analyses in N. Biggar, *Burying the Past: Making Peace and Doing Justice after Civil Conflict*, expanded and updated edn., Washington DC: Georgetown University Press, 2003. The role of religion in violence and peace-building is lucidly reflected in R. Scott Appleby and Carnegie Commission on Preventing Deadly Conflict, *The Ambivalence of the Sacred: Religion, Violence, and Reconciliation*, Carnegie Commission on Preventing Deadly Conflict Series. Lanham, MD: Rowman & Littlefield Publishers, 2000. As an example of the many publications on the transition in South Africa, see R. G. Helmick and R. L. Petersen, *Forgiveness and Reconciliation: Religion, Public Policy & Conflict Transformation*. Philadelphia: Templeton Foundation Press, 2001.

[8] The strength of the study by Elster, *Closing the Books*, is that it offers a systematic comparison of the highly varied ways of dealing with the past. For a general

compromises which come close to a continuation of the old regime. In such cases there are no trials, no "truth commissions," no punishment, and finally, no procedures or rituals for reconciliation with, and recognition of, the victims. No public authority addresses the problems of past injustices in a meaningful way. A concern for peace and social stability, fear both of the old powers and certainly of long conflicts, might be the reason for this seemingly pragmatic approach. The old regime and its representatives are still too powerful to allow for an official examination of the past and of those crimes committed by past powers. In many cases, it takes a significant amount of time to search for the perpetrators of the most egregious human rights violations.

At the other end of the spectrum, we find more "idealistic" attempts which display their own problems, such as addressing the crimes of the past by disclosing procedures, either through the use of punitive justice and/or non-legal forms such as truth commissions, or by attempting to move society toward peaceful futures without reversing the original mechanisms of exclusion.[9]

2. Shadows of the past in shaping the future

Situations of transitional justice exemplify two interconnected yet simple facts with far-reaching implications. First, deep systemic political changes aim at altering the possible and likely futures of a nation and its social institutions. In shaping the future, transitional justice must address the problems of the past. Second, the past, or the history of a social entity, is not just a blessing, but in many cases also a burden. The "hot memory" of a culture preserves and regenerates not only that culture's identity, but also its divisions and supporting bitterness, and this quite often fuels violent conflict.[10] Given that the experience of a

---

systematization, see A. M. Khazanov and S. G. Payne, "How to Deal with the Past?" *Totalitarian Movements & Political Religions* 9, no. 2/3 (2008), 411–31.

[9] For this differentiation, see Teitel, *Transitional Justice*, 3. Teitel unfolds this double dimension on the basis of an analysis of "biblical reparations" mentioned in Genesis 15:13–14 (120ff.).

[10] For the distinction between a (at least potentially dangerous) *hot memory*, which forms current identity, and *cold memory*, which serves a more archival purpose, see J. Assmann, *Das Kulturelle Gedächtnis: Schrift, Erinnerung und politische Identität in frühen Hochkulturen*, C.H. Beck Kulturwissenschaft. Munich: C.H. Beck, 1992, 66–86. He bases this differentiation on Claude Lévi-Strauss's concept of hot and cold societies.

history of severe injustice is a seedbed for future conflict, dealing with the past is an essential requirement for a peaceful future. In the face of the thoroughly ambivalent nature of "having a history and remembering it," it seems quite understandable that Niklas Luhmann would recommend the absolute disappearance of the individual histories of nation states as a requirement for an emerging "world society."[11] It is this "hot memory" in a given culture that helps to perpetuate conflicts and violence – even if these conflicts take many years to erupt.[12]

Without forms of transformative remembrance, the past can become a haunting and destructive shadow. Conversely, situations of transitional justice are a litmus test of society's temporal structures and a revelation of a culture's understanding of history. In addition, claims of transformation lose their credibility if the new government fails to seek justice for those who suffered from past injustices. Dealing with the victims of the past becomes a litmus test for a new government's moral credibility and an indicator of its long-term political capital.

3. Many agents of multiple types, and the search for moral agency: challenging complexities and a systematic prospect

3.1 Multiple agents

In all cases of such major political and cultural transitions, the *various agents* involved form a dynamic constellation:

(i) the *present power* in charge of shaping the future (the general culture, as well as the institutional and administrative powers of the new government);

(ii) the *living or dead perpetrators* of past crimes (and their institutions); and

(iii) the *living or dead victims* (individual as well as institutional) who suffered under the past regime.

---

[11] N. Luhmann, "Die Weltgesellschaft," in: *Soziologische Aufklärung: 2 Aufsätze zur Theorie der Gesellschaft*, ed. N. Luhmann. Opladen: Westdt. Verl., 1975, 51–71.

[12] This issue is a constant theme in Y. Gutman, A. D. Brown, and A. Sodaro, eds., *Memory and the Future: Transnational Politics, Ethics and Society*, Palgrave Macmillan Memory Studies. Houndmills, Basingstoke, UK; New York: Palgrave Macmillan, 2010.

However, this triadic constellation becomes more complex in the following cases:

(iv) when *past perpetrators* had themselves been victims in another, former past or "prehistory" (as with some communists in the GDR, who were themselves persecuted by the Nazi regime);

(v) when transitional justice is directed toward *new states or institutions* created in that transition;[13]

(vi) when (as became the case after the dissolution of the GDR) the *current regime holds multiple roles simultaneously*. For example, the Federal Republic of Germany (FRG) is the legal successor and therefore the compensating institution, while also being the long-time observer of the GDR and its historical transition. By being involved in the transition, the FRG embodies aspects of both continuity and discontinuity. Put more bluntly: why should the FRG take responsibility for the past GDR?

3.2 Different agent types

These short remarks reveal what is a serious theoretical challenge for many approaches taken by moral philosophy and theological ethics (though less problematic for political and social philosophy): in situations of transitional justice, not only individual people and individual victims (so-called natural persons) are affected, but also states, institutions, companies and their legal successors as acting entities (all non-natural persons).[14] Hence, situations of transitional justice cannot be conceptualized exclusively within the framework of person-to-person relationships, frameworks often basic for moral philosophy and theological ethics. The issue here is whether non-natural persons can be moral agents. Who can speak on their behalf? Can non-natural

---

[13] This was the case when the German government paid compensation to the Israeli State, which itself emerged out of the conflict: Teitel, *Transitional Justice*, 122f.

[14] On the issues of non-natural persons as moral agents, see R. Stoecker, "Können Institutionen Handeln?" in: *Institutionen und ihre Ontologie*, ed. G. Schönrich. Frankfurt: Ontos Verl., 2005, and in the same volume, N. Strobach, "Juristische Personen." Contrast this with E. Hankins Wolgast, *Ethics of an Artificial Person: Lost Responsibility in Professions and Organizations*, Stanford Series in Philosophy. Stanford University Press, 1992, 81–95, who is rather critical about the blurring of responsibilities.

persons forgive, repent or be sinners?[15] If one denies that non-natural, legal persons are morally responsible actors, then the issue of transitional justice almost disappears.

If one agrees that non-natural persons are moral agents, what, then, are the systemic or institutional equivalents of guilt, shame, contrition, repentance, forgiveness, and responsibility? What are the requirements for adequate forms of representation? Can non-natural persons die, or do they live on forever?[16] In some cases, non-natural persons have died and the acting legal person has disappeared. In those cases, to what extent can a legal successor be held responsible? Is public opinion and its media-managed attention a responsible moral agent?

Even if these questions cannot be answered easily in terms of social philosophy, three phenomena are noticeable in times of transitional justice: (i) individual victims expect distinct reactions *from public and social institutions*: Parliament, the courts, foundations, the state, or churches; (ii) individual perpetrators fear the reactions of these public and social institutions; (iii) individual victims organize themselves along the lines of certain markers of victimization for reasons of representation, group identity, and solidarity. In many cases, they already have a collective identity, since the political oppression targeted them as a specific group; and (iv) in many cases unjust regimes with many supporting institutions (parliaments, courts, administrative regional bodies such as city councils, etc.) act as non-natural persons – even though they are, in specific ways, not only legal and political agents, but also moral agents.

[15] For a fascinating example of an attempt to avoid critical reflection on the difference between these two types of persons, see the conversation in A. Köpcke-Duttler, *Schuld, Strafe, Versöhnung: Ein Interdiziplinäres Gespräch*. Mainz: Matthias-Grünewald Verlag, 1990. However, the problem was seen quite clearly by Dietrich Bonhoeffer in his *Ethics*, where he even distinguishes the non-natural persons of the Church and the Nation: "For the nations there is only a healing of the wound, a cicatrization of guilt, in the return to order, to justice, to peace. . . . Thus the nations bear the inheritance of their guilt." See D. Bonhoeffer, *Ethics*, eds. E. Bethge and N. Horton Smith, Macmillan Paperback. New York: Macmillan, 1965, 117. The issue of the various types of agencies is only touched on in passing by both M. Beintker, "Remembering Guilt as a Social Project: Some Reflections on the Challenge of Working through the Past," *Studies in Christian Ethics* 24, no. 2 (2011), 210–31; and G. Scarre, "Political Reconciliation, Forgiveness and Grace," ibid., 171–82.

[16] This is a pressing issue in claims put forth by Native and African-Americans against the United States of America. These issues also arise in debates about colonialism. If non-natural moral agents "live forever," moral claims against them might span hundreds of years.

These four observations demonstrate how the two levels of individual life and institutional action are intimately intertwined. The shift from systemic political injustice to a constitutional democracy points to the problem of individual "repercussions" from unjust non-natural persons and systemic formations, and the responsibility of individual natural persons in emergent structures of injustice and oppression. Most dehumanizing regimes emerge out of numerous elements and from minor decisions – their properties are only loosely related to the individual intentions of individual people. Thus it becomes difficult to locate responsibility for certain actions of the state. And yet, non-democratic as well as democratic states depend on mechanisms of substitution and representation that operate as structural forms for the coupling of individual and structural responsibility.

In sum, it is this complex nexus of problems into which the following, specific problem will be located and in which the problems of standardization and monetization occur.

III. United Germany's treatment of political prisoners of the GDR regime

1. The political and legal frameworks

"Coming to terms" with the history of the GDR is one of the greatest tasks facing German federal politics, after the post-World War II attempts to cope with the history of National Socialism.[17] People had been imprisoned for minor reasons and without adequate trials. The numbers vary, but between 1945 and 1989 about 200,000 people had been political prisoners.[18] Given a population of approximately 17

---

[17] For a general view of the transition, see A. J. McAdams, *Judging the Past in Unified Germany*. Cambridge; New York: Cambridge University Press, 2001; "The Double Demands of Reconciliation. The Case of Unified Germany," in: *The Politics of Past Evil*, 127–49; J.-W. Müller, "East Germany: Incorporation, Tainted Truth, and the Double Division," in: *The Politics of Memory: Transitional Justice in Democratizing Societies*, eds. A. B. de Brito, C. Gonzalez Enriquez, and P. Aguilar Fernandez. Oxford; New York: Oxford University Press, 2001, 248–74.

[18] Official source of the number: http://www.bpb.de/themen/6X7JLZ,4,0,Glossar. html (last accessed August 20, 2009). See also J. Raschka, *Justizpolitik im SED-Staat: Anpassung und Wandel des Strafrechts während der Amtszeit Honeckers*, Schriften des Hannah-Arendt-Instituts für Totalitarismusforschung, vol. XIII. Cologne: Böhlau, 2000.

million people, more than one percent of the GDR's population had been imprisoned for political reasons. In the period before 1989, approximately 30,000 political prisoners had been ransomed by the West German government and transferred to the West. An unknown number of political prisoners were assigned to forced labor.

The political actors involved in the national agreement on economic, currency, and social unification (from May 15, 1990) found themselves confronted with the task of establishing legal regulations for the entire public sector – and were immensely pressed for time in doing so.[19] After reunification, dealing with the past of the GDR was recognized as an urgent task for both federal politics and German law. An important step lay in the decision that the FRG would assume the costs of the now dismantled or "defunct" state of the GDR. Thus the FRG – as the legal successor of the GDR – took upon itself not only the minor assets of the GDR, but primarily its "bad legal debts." Article 17 of the German Unification Treaty lists the duty of the FRG to provide for the rehabilitation of, and appropriate compensation for, the politically persecuted:

The parties to the agreement affirm their intention, that a legal foundation shall be created immediately so that all persons who became the victims of politically motivated persecution or any other legal decision contrary to the state under the rule of law or contrary to the constitution shall be rehabilitated. The rehabilitation of these victims of the SED regime of injustice shall be connected to an appropriate compensatory regulation.[20]

---

[19] With regard to the rehabilitation law issued by the Parliament of the GDR shortly before unification (September 6, 1990), see J. Goydke, "Rehabilitierung als Justizaufgabe," in: *Vertrauen in den Rechtsstaat. Beiträge zur deutschen Einheit im Recht; Festschrift für Walter Remmers*, eds. J. Goydke et al., Cologne; Berlin; Bonn; Munich: Heymann, 1995, 369–81. In the period leading up to September 1991, 10,800 applications for rehabilitation had already been submitted to the courts, up to 1995 in the state of Saxony-Anhalt alone; approximately 25,000 rehabilitation proceedings had to be dealt with by the courts.

[20] "Art 17 Rehabilitierung: Die Vertragsparteien bekräftigen ihre Absicht, daß unverzüglich eine gesetzliche Grundlage dafür geschaffen wird, daß alle Personen rehabilitiert werden können, die Opfer einer politisch motivierten Strafverfolgungsmaßnahme oder sonst einer rechtsstaats- und verfassungswidrigen gerichtlichen Entscheidung geworden sind. Die Rehabilitierung dieser Opfer des SED-Unrechts-Regimes ist mit einer angemessenen Entschädigungsregelung zu verbinden" (http://bundesrecht.juris. de/einigvtr/art_17.html, last accessed 20 November, 2011).

Here, in a very specific sense, the FRG officially assumed the heritage of the GDR. In the following months and years, this led to a first (1992) and then a second (1999) "Redress of Socialist Unity Party Injustice Act."[21] The Criminal Law Rehabilitation Statute created by Article 1 of the first version of the Redress of Socialist Unity Party Injustice Act provided compensation at the level of 600 Deutschmarks (DM) for each calendar month of imprisonment in the GDR contrary to the state under the rule of law. It is interesting to note that the victims saw this regulation as unsatisfactory for various reasons. When we look more closely, the reasons seem obvious.

(a) The first issue regards the way in which this amount of financial compensation was calculated. The amount corresponds exactly to compensation set out in § 7 of the Statute for the Compensation of Criminal Prosecution in West Germany (FRG). However, this law (from the West) relates to unjust imprisonment under the conditions of a modern and fairly humane penal system in Western Europe. The accusation leveled against lawmakers was that the penal system in the GDR was never equivalent to that in the FRD. In addition, most political prisoners in the GDR were subjected to forced labor. Thus both before and after the statutory process, victims of illegal persecution (i.e. those who were imprisoned and subjected to forced labor) demanded financial compensation in the amount of 1,000 DM (510 euros) for each month of imprisonment, plus a so-called honorary pension of 1,000 DM. However, the second Redress of Socialist Unity Party Injustice Act set the payment at 600 DM, 400 DM less than was being claimed. The legislative body of the unified Germany did not accept the argument that the payment of 600 DM rendered comparable events that could not be compared.

(b) The second point of critique also arose from a problematic comparison: the FRG repeatedly (and most recently in the year 2000) declared its interest in moral, political, and legal responsibility for the victims of National Socialism in a statute for the establishment of a fund, entitled "Remembrance, Responsibility and the Future." Forced laborers during the Nazi period could receive a payment of up to 15,000 DM. The victims of the GDR dictatorship now claimed that

---

[21] For detailed commentaries, see J. Herzler, ed., *Rehabilitierung* (StrRehaG/ VwRehaG/BerRehaG). *Potsdamer Kommentar*, 2nd edn., Stuttgart; Berlin; Cologne: Kohlhammer, 1997.

they had been deprived of compensation for forced labor in GDR prisons – because the position of victims in totalitarian systems is always comparable. For this reason, prisoners subject to forced labor claimed – and continue to claim – an additional amount of compensation between 1,000 and 15,000 DM, depending upon the length of forced labor. Aggravating this problem is the manner in which the revenues of forced labor were credited to the penitentiaries, and then found their way into the state coffers of the GDR.[22] As a consequence, former prisoners demand that this money be returned by the legal successor of the GDR: West Germany, that is, the FRG.

The plans for a third version of the Redress of Socialist Unity Party Injustice Act sought to recognize and address these concerns. It aimed to provide a so-called honorary pension of 1,000 DM and an additional increase in financial compensation from 600 to 1,000 DM per month. The corresponding bill was voted on in the Bundestag on May 18, 2001 and rejected by the then ruling coalition (Social Democratic Party and Green Party) – even though all parties appeared to agree (with an almost cynical tone) "that the suffered fate, the injustices added to those involved cannot be offset and made good again with any amount of money."[23]

The deep jurisprudential issues beneath these debates come down to the so-called Sacrificial Entitlement Doctrine (*Aufopferungsanspruch*) which will now underlie any future attempts to develop a compensatory regulation for forced labor. The Sacrificial Entitlement Doctrine is a compensatory claim with a legal foundation in common law.[24] In cases of sacrificial loss, compensation is awarded when – and this is crucial – it involves sovereign intrusions into a citizen's legally protected yet non-capital assets or non-tangible goods (such as life, health, physical inviolability, personal freedom or honor). The underlying idea is that a particular sacrifice was inflicted upon the affected person for the benefit of the general public (!). In particular, the Sacrificial Entitlement

[22] See U. Bastian, *Schamlos Ausgebeutet: Das System Der Haftzwangsarbeit Politischer Gefangener Des SED-Staates*. Berlin: Bürgerbüro, 2003.

[23] W. Mäder, "Die Entschädigung der Opfer politischer Verfolgung in der DDR im Spannungsfeld von moralischer Verpflichtung und Anforderung des Rechts (1)," *ZFSH/SGB* 42 (2003), 152.

[24] See ibid., 153f., and Mäder, "Entschädigung von Opfern politischer Verfolgung in der DDR für Freiheitsentzug und Haftzwangsarbeit (4)," *ZFSH/SGB* 42 (2003), 653, for the legal discussion and further references.

Doctrine operates by providing financial, asset-based compensation for "legally protected yet non-capital assets." This leads then, consequently, to financial transactions in which non-monetary entities are somehow transformed into monetary ones. But what amounts correspond to or even outweigh such non-monetary loss?

To do justice to the political process, part of the political agenda was to uncover historical truth about acts and structures of serious injustice. In 1992, the German Bundestag established a so-called "Study Commission for the Assessment of History and Consequences of the SED Dictatorship in Germany" (Enquete-Kommission, "Aufarbeitung von Geschichte und Folgen der SED-Diktatur in Deutschland"), specifically tasked with shedding light on mechanisms of injustice, investigating and providing an accurate record of the events and practices that took place in East Germany under communist rule, and opening up a moral discourse about the past. In the end, the commission proposed (successfully) the establishment of a foundation dedicated to ongoing work on the past GDR regime.[25] And yet, this Enquete-Kommission was no "Truth Commission": historical elucidation, not the encounter between victims and perpetrators, constituted the central task of its many hearings.

2. Socio-philosophical and ethical problems and perspectives

(a) Prima facie evidence

As is clear from the many studies on transitional justice and the process described above for the rehabilitation, and compensation of the GDR

---

[25] Members of the commission included 14 representatives of Parliament and 9 experts – chaired by the human rights activist, Rainer Eppelmann. At the end, 32 volumes with 30,000 pages documented 300 expert opinions, 68 public hearings, and approximately 600 hearings by eyewitnesses and politicians. But again, the dimension of a public life, of interaction and encounter so crucial for truth commissions, was deliberately avoided in favor of "objectivity." For a view on the striking differences, see e.g., Priscilla B. Hayner, *Unspeakable Truths: Confronting State Terror and Atrocity*. New York; London: Routledge, 2001. It is telling that in the 2011 second edition of the book, Hayner departed from her earlier opinion that regarded the Enquete-Kommission as a truth commission. See Priscilla B. Hayner, "Fifteen Truth Commissions – 1974 to 1994: A Comparative Study," *Human Rights Quarterly* 16 (1994), 626f., and Priscilla B. Hayner, *Unspeakable Truths: Transitional Justice and the Challenge of Truth Commissions*, 2nd edn., New York: Routledge, 2011, 52f.

victims, injustice can be observed from different points of view. What ethical and socio-philosophical problems arise at the limits of legal regulation – particularly in view of monetary compensation via quantified monthly payments? I believe that the case of compensation for victims of injustice is particularly instructive because it works with the self-evident moral and political conviction that some financial compensation is indeed appropriate, even while the consensus exists that the theft and destruction of life as a non-tangible good through unjust imprisonment and forced labor "cannot be offset" by money.

(b) Justice for victims: but only for victims?

In seems noteworthy that, in the present case, the search for justice is directed toward victims rather than perpetrators. Neither punitive justice with respect to the perpetrators, nor reconciliation between the oppressor and the victim (or even a meeting of both) is sufficient. The willingness for compensation transcends any notion of punitive justice and brings into attention the still-living victims of the past. These persons continually make the past present in the present attempt to shape the future. However, is it possible to achieve justice for the victims by ignoring the actions of perpetrators; that is, simply by reducing rehabilitation and compensation to an "administrative act"?[26]

(c) Non-monetary damages to living victims

Furthermore, of crucial importance is the turn to living rather than dead victims. At stake here is their future life in the light of their past in prison. They must live with the burden, the limitations and the suffering stemming from their time in prison. The damages they suffered are partially pecuniary and partially non-monetary. Pecuniary damages include lost income, property seized by the state, the forced payment of penalties and the loss of revenue from forced labor. However, attention focused on non-monetary damages: the loss of freedom and the loss of real lifetime. It is the specific case of living victims which

---

[26] Punitive justice was only directed toward politicians responsible for the order to shoot citizens attempting to flee to the West. The law of the GDR was basically respected, except in cases of gross violations of human rights – which was the basis for the so-called "*Mauerschützenprozesse.*" This interpretation of the GDR law was confirmed by the Constitutional Court of the FRG (BVerfG, 24.10.1996, Az. 2BvR 1851/94; 1853/94; 1875/94; and 1852/94).

confronts situations of transitional justice with the danger of a double or "renewed" stigmatization and victimization. Furthermore, it remains unclear whether the money primarily compensates for the victim's past life or helps them live a future life.

(d) Standardized solutions for large numbers of individual cases

Compensation in the context of transitory justice must face the problem of large numbers and individual lives. In situations of state-wide transitions, it is literally impossible to evaluate and judge every individual case. As Burkhard Hess points out in Chapter 4 above, it is the enormous power of the law to standardize the complexity of real life into cases. Confronted with a large number of individual cases of injustice, standardized legal procedures working with standardized cases have the ability to operate at very high "speed." The standardization procedures of legal systems are intensified in the specific case under investigation here: the laws regulating compensation cover all relevant cases without asking people to state their claim in court. Without giving the thousands of victims the chance to present their story and without taking into account their individual story and history, the normally public transformation of an individual case into a legal (standardized) case in the courtroom becomes "invisible."

(e) De-individualization in legal cases and standardized compensation

However, based on "intensified standardization" legal procedures face a very specific dilemma which clearly appeared in the public debate surrounding the issue of unjust imprisonment. The very application of formal procedures within this framework of standardized cases makes each case comparable and strips it of its uniqueness: *individuum est ineffabile*. This de-individualization is the price which must be paid in situations under the pressure of limited time and in dealing with large numbers. This paradox reappears if the rehabilitation is accompanied by compensation mechanisms. When compensation is assigned, legal standardizations encounter monetary standardizations. Even if the calculus for translation is highly culturally dependent, compensation works on the basis or on the assumption of a convertibility of aspects of the legal problem into a monetary solution.[27] The combination of legal

---

[27] That this issue reaches back to ancient legal traditions can be seen in Chapter 12 by Konrad Schmid in this volume.

entitlements and monetary payments creates a double bind: the victim of past injustices is denigrated either by the public neglect of the loss of life or by stripping away the uniqueness of his or her own fate and destiny by transforming it into "a case."

(f) Comparability of compensation on a moral market

Comparability is an essential feature of the nature of money. As soon as a monetary price is fixed, products and their prices can be compared with other similar products. This comparison of compensation is in addition to comparisons of the different punishments for different crimes (calculated using the unit of years or months in prison). Hence, the introduction of a specific amount for each month of forced labor in prison immediately intensified comparisons and opened up a parallel "moral market of victimhood." In particular, comparisons with victims of the National Socialist regime were immediately raised.

(g) Disjunction of rehabilitation and compensation without the performance of recognition

The public reaction of former prisoners points to a systemic vagueness in the whole political process after the fall of the GDR. It remained unclear how rehabilitation and reparation or monetary compensation relate to each other. Without doubt, obviously there is and was a clear moral belief that legal rehabilitation alone does not sufficiently account for past injustices.[28] We observe here a specific intrinsic limit of the law: the disastrous consequences of past "legally based injustice" cannot be addressed simply through the building up of "legal justice" in the present alone. However, at this point it is worth noting that in working out and executing the program of compensation, the legal system was lacking any performative dimension as condensed in the formal acts in the courtroom. As a consequence, the compensation of 300 euros for

---

[28] One might question whether rehabilitation is the adequate term for this situation of transitional justice. The term comes from the legal system of the GDR and extends back to Soviet laws concerning the "rehabilitation" of victims of the Stalin era after 1953, and rehabilitation processes after 1989 in the context of perestroika. Resulting from this context, rehabilitation has a strong moral undertone – something recognized very early by legal scholars. Built into the idea of "rehabilitation" is a hidden implication: an acknowledgment of the very same state power which first caused the loss of legal security and that initial public degrading.

each month spent in prison had to carry the burden of being both real practical reimbursement and at the same time an act of public – thus symbolic – honoring and recognition. Against that reduction, Martha Minow states: "Spreading knowledge of the violations and their meaning in people's lives may be more valuable, ultimately, than any specific victory or offer of a remedy."[29]

(h) Moral, legal, and economic reparation

At the time of the unification of both German states, the public discussion was marked by repeated calls for "moral, legal, and economic reparation." This frequently used triad forces to ask us what moral reparation consists of. Does moral reparation occur (i) through the legislative process, (ii) through legal reparation, i.e. a formal act of rehabilitation, or (iii) through, or in the medium of, economic reparation? How are these processes related?[30] The underlying assumption of the whole process seemed to be that the legal rehabilitation through the Bundestag simultaneously communicates a moral acknowledgment – even though the non-human person or political agent "GDR" had already "disappeared." Seen in this way, the protest of former prisoners is misplaced. And yet, the protest of the former prisoners clearly pointed to another dimension of the conflict, such as a violation of their human dignity – something which cannot be dealt with by means of financial transactions and administrative acts without any performative dimension or encounter between victim and perpetrator. The protests signalled that moral reparation had no specific place.

(i) Monetary compensation: gift or quantifiable claim?

At this point, we touch again upon the issue of standardization: is the reparation payment or financial compensation a symbolic "gift of acknowledgment" and thereby an act of honoring performed by a political agent not responsible for atrocities and false imprisonment – such as the FRG? Or does it stand in a strictly quantitative relation of exchange correlating with the number of months of experienced injustice and the possibilities destroyed by that time in prison? The former

---

[29] M. Minow, *Between Vengeance and Forgiveness: Facing History after Genocide and Mass Violence*. Boston: Beacon Press, 1998, 93.

[30] Even the process of legal rehabilitation points to paradoxes, since the recognition of the GDR as a "regime of injustice" declares the convictions "en bloc" unjust and that specific rehabilitation does not appear necessary.

prisoners seemed to operate with the second interpretation, yet in the public debate "in the West" as well in Parliament, the first interpretation seemed to dominate. And yet, the problem for the former prisoners was that quantitative changes can trigger qualitative steps. When victims receive financial compensation reflecting a manifest disregard for the loss of earnings during periods of false imprisonment, and perceive the situation as "degrading" and "lacking in respect," then it may in fact stem from the insufficient quantitative amount, which is then perceived not as an honoring gift, but as a degrading action.[31] At least below and above certain thresholds, economic communication itself happens to be the medium for communicating respect or disrespect. Due to the subtle subject of critical thresholds, which combine quantity and dignity or disrespect, economic compensation can literally backfire if it becomes (quite accidentally) the medium for providing moral and political honor. But in light of the dictum "compensation can never compensate," one might ask: why should the financial transaction carry all the weight of communicating respect, honor, and appreciation?

(j) Moral obligation versus legal right
A subtext of the debate about proper compensation was a conflicting interpretation of the conclusions drawn from the underlying moral right and the corresponding moral obligation: does the moral right and the moral obligation for compensation result in a legal right on the victims' side or just in some form of gift from the legal (not moral) successor of the GDR: the FRG?

(k) Competitive self-victimization
Though one can never gain back a lost period of life, how might unrealized possibilities be calculated into a model that would do justice to the individual?[32] The strict focus on money, and then on

---

[31] Hayner, *Unspeakable Truths*, 2nd edn., 178ff., under the heading "Reparations without Truth-Telling: Possible but Precarious," critically reconstructs several similarly failed attempts of isolating and thereby overburdening monetary compensation.

[32] Daniel Philpott argues that religion can bring something to the table on the issue of reconciliation. See D. Philpott, "What Religion Offers for the Politics of Transitional Justice," in: *Rethinking Religion and World Affairs*, eds. T. S. Shah, A. C. Stepan, and M. Duffy Toft. New York: Oxford University Press, 2012, 149–61.

monetary quantification, opens up multiple possibilities for comparison: between individual victims, between types and groups of victims of the GDR (religious, non-religious, conscientious objectors, prison with or without forced labor, etc.), between victims of the GDR regime and victims of the National Socialist dictatorship, between victims of the GDR regime and victims of Stalinism, etc. How much have others in these differing groups received? In this case, economic quantification, rather than legal standardization, opens the door to a competitive self-victimization by the victims. Who can stake a claim to being the most victimized victim, and thus the victim most deserving of honor?

IV. At the limits of monetization and law: art, narrative, and religion

The sad and unfortunate story of political prisoners in the former GDR raises a number of questions: what are the possible alternatives to standardized and quantified economic compensation? How can a lost lifetime be valued? What strategies could accompany and supplement monetary means when addressing past evils, and what would be their strengths and weaknesses? How might they deal with the paradox of the simultaneous scarcity and overabundance of trust (i.e. distrust versus overly expectant hopes), which characterize those brief historical moments marking a powerful cultural transition? What media might best communicate dignity and moral estimation?

In short, where did the focus on monetary compensation go wrong? Put simply, the process of addressing past evils when dealing with political prisoners who experienced forced labor: (i) did not make use of all resources, specifically the *multiple social media in differentiated societies*, and (ii) failed to take into account the *complexity of Christian anthropology*.

1. *Neglect of collective and individual symbolism*

In light of the problems sketched above, it is clear that monetary compensation was forced to carry a weight it could not bear and to fulfill multiple functions it could not fulfill. Broadly stated, it missed a distinct yet multi-layered communal and individual *symbolic dimension* vis-à-vis the *material dimension of monetary compensation.*[33] When dealing with lost periods of life due to injustice, the communication of honor, appreciation, and the affirmation of human dignity required a medium other than money alone. Furthermore, this communication process needed both a distinct collective and distinct individual dimension. In hindsight, we see that there was no orchestrated response using the various communication media available to modern societies.

First and foremost, the indirect, yet powerful, symbolic dimension of the legal system itself was not put to work. Politicians and the courts in the West sent out a double message: while the GDR was an unjust and totalitarian regime, punitive justice will be directed only very selectively against persons responsible for *gross* violations of human rights. As a result, those responsible for political imprisonments and forced labor acted, so to speak, below the radar of later punitive justice – they were not even awarded amnesty. Furthermore, since the application and approval process for reparation payments was an administrative act (processed solely through paperwork, without physical interaction), no use was made of the legal system's ability to provide a semi-public and highly ritualized space for the telling of individual stories, or for encounters between victims and perpetrators. Thus, even the legal means for symbolically restoring "justice" were ignored.

From the outside, unjust regimes give the impression of being built on many seemingly minor contributions by individual agents – agents who appeared to bear no responsibility for the overall effect. Consequently, one major problem faced by transitional justice is the moral and legal accountability of these "minor players."[34] In our case, the identification of the perpetrators was not part of the rehabilitation and compensation

---

[33] In a similar vein, the political scientist Ernesto Verdeja suggests a very simple matrix of four dimensions when addressing past evil: E. Verdeja, "A Normative Theory of Reparations in Transitional Democracies," *Metaphilosophy* 37, no. 3/4 (2006). Reparation or compensation must take into account *symbolic* as well as *material* acknowledgment. These represent two quite different "ideal types" for addressing past victims. At the same time, there is always the second typology of victims (or the recipient of acknowledgment): the *individual* victim as well as the *collective* entity. When combined, these two axes create four spaces, which call for different responses.

[34] This problem of individual agents encountering systemic injustice by non-natural agents is not sufficiently taken into account when person–person encounters are compared with relations between nations. For such an approach, see Bonhoeffer, *Ethics*, 116f.

process.[35] Intense forms of public, symbolic recognition and honoring of victims could have counterbalanced the widespread "dropout" of victimizers. However, without the clear separation of this dimension, the process of monetary reparation became semiotically "overloaded" – and remained within the limits of monetization.

2. *The symbolism of public art*

Recognizing that lost periods of life cannot be regained through retributive or punitive justice should have stimulated the search for more adequate symbols acknowledging this humiliating and depressing fact. The intentional theft of life, along with acts that disable the flourishing of life, needed a specific medium for its public and symbolic recognition. This need, however, transcended the abilities of the political and legal systems.

Art is a very powerful medium for communicating the collective attribution of honor and dignity. Through monuments, songs, literature, and performative media, artistic communication can help construct a culture of remembrance which simultaneously honors the victims. The symbolic and lasting recognition of groups subject to targeted victimization can take many forms, for example the creation of monuments, parks or more elaborate historical memorial sites. Naming buildings, streets or institutions after individual victims can lead to individual symbolic recognition. These measures nourish cultural memory, and preserve and maintain a culture of remembrance.

With regard to the remembrance of victims, the twentieth century has seen a significant shift: attempts to deal with the bloodshed and atrocities of the twentieth century dealt with so-called negative memory.[36]

---

[35] The public debate regarding the ongoing openness of the secret service archives and files (the so-called *Gauck-Behörde*) centered on the ongoing *possibility* of identifying the victimizers. Interestingly, this debate was personified in the struggle between two Lutheran pastors: Friedrich Schorlemmer and Joachim Gauck. For the arguments in this debate, see McAdams, "The Double Demands of Reconciliation: The Case of Unified Germany," 127–49.

[36] See R. Koselleck, "Formen und Traditionen des negativen Gedächtnisses," in: *Verbrechen Erinnern: Die Auseinandersetzung mit Holocaust und Völkermord*, eds. V. Knigge, N. Frei, and A. Schweitzer. Munich: Beck, 2002, 21–32. In the past, artistic *public* remembrance was geared toward (a) the "winner," and (b) his or her heroic deeds. It contributed (at least inside the social entity) only to the affirmation of identities.

One challenge facing contemporary public art in all nations that have experienced such dramatic transitions is the cultivation of a negative memory as well as a means of public mourning.[37]

However, even public artistic communication cannot replace the dimension of individual recognition. Art must work with typifications, with abstractions and standardizations. Individual symbolic recognition tends to privilege "heroes" among the victims – a practice which can reinforce or continue victimization. In addition, artistic communication is always based on scarcity and, as such, is vulnerable to inflation.[38]

3. Communication of dignity in narratives: between psychology and religion

During past decades, the so-called truth commissions have opened a particular space of narration and of the symbolic communication of personal dignity. While such commissions played no role in the transition from the rule of the GDR, they did take center stage in the South African process of transitional justice. Their strength came from their ability to communicate individual recognition by offering to those who had been silenced a public voice for their individual narrative. Without doubt, the strength of this form lies in its focus on the details of history. In doing so, it works on restoring the human dignity of *individuals.* They effectively work against any form of standardization.[39] And yet, truth commissions have another side. Dealing with past evils can include a highly moral discourse of public shame: major perpetrators can be invited by an institution to confess their wrongdoings and to show signs of shame and repentance in public. Yet these confessions can be highly ritualized and routinized, thus oscillating between an encouraging social form and an invitation to personal insincerity.[40]

---

[37] See the contributions in B. Liebsch and J. Rüsen, eds., *Trauer und Geschichte*, Beiträge Zur Geschichtskultur. Cologne; Weimar; Vienna: Böhlau, 2001.

[38] See e.g., the inflation of "monumental remembrance" in non-democratic states as an attempt to manipulate cultural memory.

[39] We might, however, assume that the narratives of victimhood and victimization themselves become highly standardized.

[40] For a very critical view on the encounters and the often false hopes attached to them, see A. E. Acorn, *Compulsory Compassion: A Critique of Restorative Justice.* Vancouver: UBC Press, 2004, chs. 1 and 3.

In that amnesty from legal prosecution only applied when the perpetrator confessed, the South African Truth Commissions inherited at
least some aspects of "public confession." In this respect, truth commissions combine religious and psychological forms. They use the
religious and therapeutic idea that truth and transparency, repentance
and contrition are necessary preconditions for any serious transformation.[41] In addition, they draw on the religious insight that reconciliation
and forgiveness require at least some form of encounter between the
perpetrator and the victim. At the same time, and in contrast to the very
intimate public sphere found in the therapeutic process or in religious
confession before a priest or a minister, they locate that confession
before a much larger public. However, this helpful instrument was not
utilized in the case of the GDR.

4. The role of religion and churches in situations
of transitional justice

Over the past decades, Christian churches have facilitated and productively accompanied a variety of political transitions. Historically speaking, Protestant churches played a crucial role in the peaceful transition
in the GDR, not only during the weeks before the fall of the Berlin Wall,
but also in the preceding decade.[42] However, collectively they were
a major voice neither in the restoration of justice nor in the process of
coming to terms with the past, even though individual pastors made
significant contributions. Thus, a degree of self-criticism accompanies

---

[41] R. Daye, *Political Forgiveness: Lessons from South Africa*. Maryknoll, NY: Orbis
   Books, 2004; D. Tutu, *No Future without Forgiveness*. New York: Doubleday,
   1999.

[42] Among the vast body of literature, see G. Hofmann, *Mutig gegen Marx & Mielke:
   Die Christen und das Ende der DDR*. Leipzig: Evangelische Verlagsanstalt, 2009;
   T. Mayer, *Helden der Friedlichen Revolution: 18 Porträts von Wegbereitern aus
   Leipzig*, 2nd edn., Leipzig: Evangelische Verlagsanstalt, 2009; W. J. Everett,
   *Religion, Federalism, and the Struggle for Public Life: Cases from Germany,
   India, and America*. New York: Oxford University Press, 1997, 28–62, on "The
   Churches and Germany's 'Peaceful Revolution' 1989–90"; G. Sauter, "What
   Does Common Identity Cost? Some German Experiences and Provocative
   Questions," in: *Peace and Reconciliation: In Search of Shared Identity*, eds.
   S. C. H. Kim, P. Kollontai, and G. Hoyland. Aldershot, England; Burlington, VT:
   Ashgate, 2008, 21–33; McAdams, *Judging the Past in Unified Germany*; "The
   Double Demands of Reconciliation: The Case of Unified Germany," in: *The
   Politics of Past Evil Justice*, 127–49.

the following remarks on the contribution made by the churches. In addition, the role of religion in general and of the Christian churches in particular, when considering transitional justice, depends heavily on the given society: its type and degree of secularization, its religious heritage and theological tradition, the role the churches played at the time of systemic oppression and injustice, as well as the cultural and legal aspects of the Church's place in the new society. In the words of the Barmen Declaration (1934): what does it mean for the Christian Church to remind the state of "the Kingdom of God, God's commandment and righteousness"?[43] There seem to be at least three key issues that provide some profile for the role of the Church.[44]

(a) Churches as instruments in the socio-cultural "orchestra"

The Christian churches do not primarily serve themselves, but rather, the people in their society – hence, they do not advertise themselves as institutions. Instead, the churches are a reminder of the multidimensionality of life, and they help us to see the richness of social symbolism. They support the development of a working, reliable and just legal system and the flourishing of civil society. With regard to processes of monetization in material compensation and reparation, the churches reveal both their necessity and their intrinsic limitations. In pointing out the dangers inherent in these processes, the churches must combine their vision of justice with a self-critical patience. At the same time, this view of the complexity and multidimensionality of life also reminds the churches of the limits of religion.[45] The churches find themselves in an "orchestra" of social institutions – without being the conductor. Not as

---

[43] R. Ahlers, *The Barmen Theological Declaration of 1934: The Archaeology of a Confessional Text*, Toronto Studies in Theology. Lewiston, NY: Edwin Mellen Press, 1986.

[44] The following remarks represent a normative and constructive description of the Church, that is to say, a theological proposal.

[45] This "orchestrated" coordination was clearly seen by Dietrich Bonhoeffer. Within the model of divine mandates he affirms what could be said today about social subsystems and their respective media of communication: "It is only in conjunction, in combination and in opposition with one another that the divine mandates ... declare the commandment of God as revealed in Jesus Christ. No single one of these mandates is sufficient in itself or can claim to replace all the others. ... Moreover, within this relation of conjunction and mutual support, each one is limited by the other ..." Bonhoeffer, *Ethics*, 286.

conductor, but as a faithful, critical and listening player, the churches build up what is missing most: trust.[46]

(b) Searching for metaphors of the kingdom by searching for helpful analogies

Truth commissions emerged as semi-religious or quasi-religious forms of communication. The churches should critically analyze and reflect upon such religious forms and processes in order to stimulate analogous forms and processes in the wider culture and society. To use again the language of the Barmen Declaration: what could act as metaphors of the kingdom of God, identified by a Church which is a reminder of this kingdom? What are (or what could become) suitable, comparable forms for public, individual as well as social, manifestations of forgiveness or repentance that could supplement political processes? What can be "learned" from the study of divine remembrance, which is always transformative and future oriented?[47] Interestingly enough, the theological or semi-theological categories of repentance, guilt, and forgiveness which played a part in the struggles of other countries were, quite literally, absent from the attempts to deal with forced labor imprisonment in the GDR. Here, the churches lagged far behind the complexity of their own symbolic material and traditions of reflection. This is not to say that the churches knew the answers and simply needed to teach the public, but rather that, informed by the rich texture of religious tradition, the churches needed to raise questions and enable the open search for adequate answers. For instance, in the process of healing the wounds of the past, does forgiveness require at least the public legal *identification of guilt* (and the identification of perpetrators) and at least the *possibility of punitive justice* (eventually rejected by means of an amnesty)? Without a publicly identifiable "other," the dynamic but highly vulnerable process of reconciliation seems to lack a substantive element – something that cannot possibly be substituted for with any amount of money. Reconciliation and forgiveness both need an

---

[46] For illuminative and insightful observations on the non-instrumental role of trust, see C. Murphy, *A Moral Theory of Political Reconciliation*. Cambridge; New York: Cambridge University Press, 2010, 71–93.

[47] B. Janowski, "Schöpferische Erinnerung. Zum 'Gedenken Gottes' in der biblischen Fluterzählung," in: *Die Macht der Erinnerung*, ed. M. Ebner. Neukirchen-Vluyn: Neukirchener Verlag, 2008.

"other" – be it natural persons or symbolic representatives of non-natural legal persons and institutions. It seems that this systemic disregard concerning the perpetrator violates and breaks much more than state forgiveness in amnesties – it impinges on the trust of its citizens.[48] However, it remains a substantial challenge to use these theological concepts in dealing with non-natural persons such as states and institutions – even though these entities are considered moral agents.

(c) Rejecting false reconciliation and opening spaces for analogies of lament and hope

At the end of the twentieth century, the Christian churches dealt with a double challenge: the course of political history made it painfully clear that there can be no redemption *of* history *in* history. At the same time, this course of history calls into question classical notions of divine providence. Again, the churches share key questions regarding the redemption of past injustices and, yet, are called to keep alive the search for an answer. In this situation, the task of the churches could well consist of keeping the search for meaning in individual as well as

---

[48] The crucial issue of "identifying" the perpetrator is mostly overseen in the large body of literature which positions "forgiveness" and a "theology of embrace" over "punitive justice." See M. Volf, *Exclusion and Embrace: A Theological Exploration of Identity, Otherness, and Reconciliation.* Nashville: Abingdon Press, 1996, 125ff., and "Forgiveness, Reconciliation, and Justice: A Christian Contribution to a More Peaceful Social Environment," in: *Forgiveness and Reconciliation: Religion, Public Policy & Conflict Transformation*, eds. R. G. Helmick and R. Lawrence Petersen. Philadelphia: Templeton Foundation Press, 2001, 27–49; but also A. J. Torrance, "Theological Grounds for Advocating Forgiveness and Reconciliation in the Sociopolitical Realm," in: *The Politics of Past Evil*, 45–85. The very metaphor of "embrace" presupposes an identifiable other, as Volf indeed implies with his frequent use of the phrase "the other." Even the idea that repentance is secondary to forgiveness and the result of it requires the clear identification of "the doer" (Volf, "Forgiveness, Reconciliation, and Justice," 45). The problem is clearly seen by Daye, *Political Forgiveness: Lessons from South Africa*, 60–78, who includes this "identifying" action in the process of truth telling. Illuminative in this regard is N. Wolterstorff, "The Place of Forgiveness in the Actions of the State," in: *The Politics of Past Evil*, 87–111. If models based on forgiveness as an I–Thou encounter are clearly insufficient, another even wider question remains on the table: can individual victims forgive non-natural persons or only their (former, or current) representatives? This problem arises not only in cases of "institutional actions," but also in cases where the individual perpetrator has already died and the institution is the only "survivor."

collective history open and unanswered. The meaning provided by the Christian churches could restrain us from giving quick answers, barring us from glossing over pain and loss, and holding us back from accepting false reconciliation.[49] Religious communities could help to open an experiential and conceptual space which corresponds to negative memory, thereby helping to break the spell, not only of secondary victimization through repressive silence, but also of continuous and strategic self-victimization. In keeping the question of historical justice open, the churches encourage analogies of lament. The churches then act as a reminder both of the importance for the search for justice through monetary and non-monetary means, and of the finite and incomplete character of all justice achieved by human beings.

At the same time, the churches are challenged to search for secular analogies of divine honoring and ennobling. The dignity of human persons, which was called into question through the violation of their "intangible goods," calls for vital forms of communication that remind the victims of its indestructible nature. Analogous to the public work of the Holy Spirit, the churches might work toward a public climate in which future-oriented forms of remembrance can be found. To rephrase, and at the same time expand upon, the Barmen Declaration, we could say that: the churches not only remind the state, but also art, law, economy, civil society, and finally the Church itself of the kingdom of God. And yet the churches remind us of the present and the coming kingdom of God, and they productively make use of the difference between both dimensions of God's work and presence. In doing so, they witness to their hope in God's faithfulness to this world and eventually are reminiscent of what money can do and cannot do.[50] They can be living reminders for God's own future action in situations where the processes of restorative justice and the search for reconciliation fail.

---

[49] Such a posture would take up many concerns rightly put forth by Acorn, *Compulsory Compassion: A Critique of Restorative Justice.*

[50] In doing that, the churches also remind us of the wide horizon of forgiveness. See S. N. Williams, "What Christians Believe About Forgiveness," *Studies in Christian Ethics* 24, no. 2 (2011), 147–56, and T. Brudholm and A. Grøn, "Picturing Forgiveness after Atrocity," ibid., 159–70.

14 Standardized monetization of the market and the argument for preferential justice

PIET NAUDÉ

The series of discussions on standardized monetization (SM) that led to the publication of this book have focused on historical and conceptual analyses of how systems of monetization came into being; the nature of the cultural-intellectual achievement implicit in setting up systems of monetization, and the implications for law, politics, and particularly religion. This chapter is an attempt to bring the "ethics" of the theme of our book into the discussion, and has a threefold purpose.

First, to interpret standardized monetization in modern and contemporary terms for the period between 1878 (introduction of the Gold Standard) and 1971 (free-floating monetary exchange).[1]

Second, to advance three related arguments from theology, philosophy, and economics, respectively, of why preferential or prioritarian distributive justice is required by these forms of standardized monetization.[2]

Third, to draw a few brief conclusions from the foregoing arguments for our understanding of ethics and policy.

Standardized monetization and the evolution of the global financial system

The expansion of global trade and the migration of people, goods, and technology across international borders have increased dramatically

---

[1] See the historical perspectives on monetization in the contributions by Peter Bernholz, Tonio Hölscher, Ulrich Hübner and Hans-Ulrich Vogel, Chapters 2, 6, 8, and 10, respectively, in this volume. An abbreviated version of the evolution of the modern financial system appeared in Piet Naudé, "Fair global trade: A perspective from Africa," in: G. Moore (ed.), *Fairness in International Trade*, London: Springer 2010, 106–9.

[2] See the link between monetization and questions of legal justice in the contributions by Burkhard Hess and Günter Thomas, Chapters 4 and 13, respectively, in this volume.

since significant advances in transportation and communication were made. One can refer to the development of shipping since the seventeenth century, the laying of transatlantic and transpacific telephone cables in the 1950s; fiber-optic communications in the 1970s, and the revolution caused by personal computers, electronic mail and the launch of the Internet in the 1980s. Communication technology has brought people progressively closer together and has led to a situation of increasing economic interconnectedness.[3]

This growing economic integration implies that the decisions taken by one actor in the economic sphere affect other actors much more directly and intensely than ever before. It has necessitated certain forms of cooperation to ensure orderly trade, generally accepted trade rules, and regulations regarding the stabilization of various monetary systems through the "standardization" of exchange rates.

Economic historians[4] generally agree that three such attempts at SM developed between 1870 and the present time: the first was the Gold Standard (GS), formalized in 1878, after the Paris Monetary Conference of 1867, which remained in force until the advent of the First World War, although fractional support continued up until 1933.[5] In simple terms, the standardization at work here linked the value of major currencies to a fixed price of gold, setting up a system of regulated exchange rates. Initially, the USA, Australia and leading European countries participated. They were joined early on in the twentieth century by Latin America and other colonial territories. The initial key currency areas committed themselves to a free flow of gold, and to convert national currencies at a fixed rate into gold when requested to do so.[6] This created a system of standardized monetization, facilitating international transactions and protecting participants against currency volatility.

---

[3] A. Madison, *The World Economy: A Millennium Perspective*, Paris: OECD, 2001 shows how this integration has grown by indicating that for the world as a whole the ratio of merchandise exports to GDP rose from 5.5% in 1950 to 17.2% in 1995.

[4] For this section I rely strongly on the exposition by P. Isard, for many years a senior adviser at the IMF, and writer of *Exchange Rate Economics*, Cambridge University Press, 1995, in his *Globalization and the International Financial System*, Cambridge University Press, 2005.

[5] Ibid., 15 (footnote 5).

[6] For a simple explanation of the orthodox account of the Gold Standard, see D. Held, A. McGrew, D. Goldblatt, and J. Perraton, *Global Transformations: Politics, economics and culture*, Stanford University Press, 1999, 196.

In theory at least, the GS was the first example of a system embodying globally integrated financial markets, where domestic or national economies were subject to international financial discipline, to which they were required to conform. The maintenance of currency convertibility and macro-economic stability took precedence over other possible goals of national economic policy.[7] One might refer to the GS as the origin of what has become known as economic globalization, i.e. "the increasing flow of goods and services, financial resources, workers, and technologies across national borders".[8]

Both Isard and the more critical account of Held, McGrew, Goldblatt, and Perraton[9] point out that the GS was only possible under the specific economic and political conditions of late nineteenth-century Europe. There was not yet a clear insight in the link between a tightened monetary policy and unemployment. Workers were not yet empowered to protest effectively against a system that left them vulnerable; and in the context of limited government and limited social programs, there was not yet pressure for increased public spending. In such a situation it was generally accepted that national priorities were subject to international control.[10,11]

Standardized monetization based on the GS was slowly eroded, and eventually disintegrated due to a combination of factors. These included the financial crises arising during and after the World Wars, the impact of the 1929 stock market crash in the USA, and the effects of the Great Depression. This led to a restriction in international capital flows, national priorities gained ascendancy, and members of the GS began resorting to protectionism. Countries started to unpeg their currencies from gold, and when the USA, under Roosevelt, abandoned the GS in April 1933, it spelt the end of the system.[12,13]

However, the collapse of the GS did not remove the need for international monetary cooperation. During the Second World War, negotiations had already commenced that eventually led to a monetary agreement amongst 44 nations at a conference in Bretton Woods,

---

[7] Isard, *Exchange Rate Economics*, 17.   [8] Ibid., 4.
[9] See Held et al., *Global Transformations*.
[10] Isard, *Exchange Rate Economics*, 17–18.
[11] Held et al., *Global Transformations*, 195.
[12] L. B. Yeager, *International Monetary Relations: Theory, history and policy*, 2nd edn., New York: Harper & Row, 1976, 299.
[13] Isard, *Globalization and the International Financial System*, 25.

New Hampshire, in July 1944. This became known as the Bretton Woods System (BWS) and entailed the declaration of fixed exchange rate parities by a substantial group of countries.[14]

In contrast to the GS, the BWS is a managed multilateral system that leaves individual countries with considerable autonomy to pursue national economic goals, whilst they subject their exchange rate and international trade practices to international agreements. Two important institutions embodied the BWS: The International Monetary Fund (IMF) focused on monetary cooperation and an orderly exchange rate system, whereas the World Bank financed economic reconstruction and development.[15]

Gold still played a role, although a somewhat different international gold standard was established in this exchange rate system. The USA was the only country that actually pegged its currency to gold (at a par value of \$35 per ounce), and other countries in turn pegged their currencies to the dollar. The BWS was thus a system of SM based on the dollar. In this system, private financial flows were restricted, and to diminish market volatility, the USA undertook only to sell gold to foreign central banks and governments, and to licensed private users.[16]

According to Held et al.,[17] the BWS broke down under exactly the same three forces that shaped the current situation of financial globalization.

First, the dramatic increase in highly mobile private capital put the control systems of the BWS under severe stress. Second, the emerging euro currency markets (dollar deposits in European banks from multinational companies and the Soviet Union) were also not easily subjected to national capital controls. The dollar itself became the object of speculative market activity, and in 1971 President Nixon announced that the dollar would no longer be freely convertible to gold. This destroyed the very basis of the fixed exchange rate system envisaged by the BWS. Third, the Organization of Petroleum Exporting Countries (OPEC) crisis of 1973 resulted in a huge flow of funds from oil-exporting to oil-importing countries. This increased the liquidity of international banks with an even greater flow of capital across national boundaries, and higher speculative trading. In short,

---

[14] Held et al., *Global Transformations*, 199–201.
[15] Isard, *Exchange Rate Economics*, 27–9; 69–118.   [16] Ibid., 29.
[17] Held et al., *Global Transformations*, 201–2.

the intensity and increasing diversity of global financial flows broke the back of the BWS and its intended stable system of SM that operated formally from 1946 to 1971.

However, the same question remained: how can an increasingly integrated global financial and economic system be managed so as to ensure relative stability, orderly exchange rates, rules of trade, and economic growth?

In the place of a fixed system, where the value of gold or the dollar acted as the "standardization measure", emerged a floating exchange rate system where the only remaining "standard" was the value assigned to a particular currency by the day-to-day trading on foreign exchange markets.[18] Needless to say, in such a system, volatility is higher, and the power to determine market perceptions is a crucial factor in who will gain or lose. The "hot money" of private speculators moves with great velocity around the world. This has been shown to have a significant impact on financial markets, in some cases leading to currency crises that threatened national and regional economies, due to the contagion effect of emerging market economies.[19,20]

This third, and still emerging, evolution of the international monetary system, retained the major institutions of the BWS (the IMF and World Bank), although their roles were redefined as lessons were learnt about currency instability and development economics. To ensure some coherence in the increasing volume and extent of trade, the World Trade Organization (WTO) replaced the failed General Agreement on Tariffs and Trade (GATT), and has become the only global international organization dealing with the rules of trade between nations, acting as a tribunal in the case of disputes. General trade agreements reached at the WTO are ratified in the parliaments of participating nations, of which there were 146 in 2003.[21]

In the first era, the GS was fairly tightly controlled with restricted national autonomy. In the BWS, there was more freedom to pursue national economic goals, but the stability was provided by the gold – dollar price and restrictions on private capital flow. In the current era, there is such a high degree of interconnectedness, and such a rapid flow

---

[18] Ibid., 209.   [19] Ibid., 209, 213.

[20] For a discussion of the different currency crises between 1994 and 1999 in Mexico, the Asian countries, and Russia, see Isard, *Globalization and the International Financial System*, 119–51.

[21] J. Bhagwati, *In Defense of Globalization*, Oxford University Press, 2004, 270.

of (speculative) capital, that national autonomies are severely restricted – especially for weaker nations.

Consequently, there has been a structural shift in the balance of power between public and private authority in the global financial system. This shift is a matter of fierce debate, but without being "hyper-globalist", one must admit that: "there is much compelling evidence to suggest that contemporary financial globalization is a market-driven rather than a state-driven phenomenon".[22] The nation-state, according to Stiglitz, is squeezed between political demands at local level and the economic demands of a global system. The problem is that economic globalization has outpaced political globalization, resulting in uncoordinated systems of global governance, which are particularly evident in issues of global health and the environment,[23] and as is evident from the current Eurozone crisis where political union is too weak to ensure concerted action on the economic front. This power vacuum has been filled by powerful proponents of unlimited trade liberalization, such as the USA, which is a staunch believer in the unfounded "trickle-down" economic paradigm.[24]

It is perhaps too early to fully interpret most recent events since the financial crisis of 2008 and the shift in economic power from West to East and South.[25] Questions about the role of the state in the economy have been deepened by banking bail-outs with public money as well as the bail-out of whole nations like Ireland and Greece. There are new signs of "currency wars" between China and the USA, and serious questions are asked of trade liberalization policies in post-socialist economies of former East European states[26] and of "market society" as such.[27]

---

[22] Held et al., *Global Transformations*, 234.
[23] J. E. Stiglitz, *Making Globalization Work*, New York: W.W. Norton, 2006, 21.
[24] Ibid., 23.
[25] See D. Moyo, *How the West was Lost*, London: Penguin, 2011, 3–130 for an economic analysis of why the West is fast losing its dominant power.
[26] See the incisive analysis by Polish economist, Kolodko, of the failures in post-socialist economies due to trade liberalization: G. W. Kolodko, *Truth, Errors and Lies: Politics and economics in a volatile world*, New York: Columbia University Press, 2011.
[27] R. Patel, *The Value of Nothing: How to reshape market society and redefine democracy*, London: Portobello Books, 2011.

For the purposes of this chapter, I wish to point out a common element in all three systems of standardized monetization as they developed up to the late twentieth century: *From the beginning they created a fundamental differentiation between "central" and "periphery".*

The GS was managed by the Bank of England in London; the BWS was dependent on dollar policies in Washington; the emerging financial system is determined by the triad of New York, London, and Tokyo. The poorer countries of today were for the most part still colonized when these monetary systems took shape and played only a marginal role in their origin and current direction. This differentiation between countries is expressed in terms such as: core-currency countries and marginal currencies, industrial nations and non-industrial nations, developed economies and underdeveloped or poor nations. This language has become part and parcel of the way we think and speak, assuming the nature of "fact" – and for many this "fact" is devoid of ethical content. This is not to say that developing countries are less integrated in the global economy than developed nations, or that foreign direct investment and other forms of capital do not flow in and out of developing nations. The point is that a hierarchical, uneven and asymmetrical system has emerged[28] with clear democratic deficits in decision-making power, and trade agreements that make the poorest countries worse off.[29]

These historical examples, and especially the current system of monetization, challenge our traditional notions of justice. It introduces new kinds of justice that were previously absent or under-represented. One thinks, for example, of emerging debates about ecological justice, intergenerational justice, cultural justice,[30] and participative justice.[31] For

---

[28] Held et al., *Global Transformations*, 213, 224.

[29] Stiglitz, *Making Globalization Work*, 58.

[30] This is a form of justice that is not as widely discussed in literature yet. I have found the essay by C. V. Kwenda, "Cultural justice: the pathway to reconciliation and social cohesion," in: *What Holds Us Together: Social cohesion in South Africa*, eds. D. Chidester, P. Dexter, and J. Wilmot, Cape Town: HSRC Press, 2003, 67–80, very helpful in this regard. He argues that cultural justice is established when people are allowed unselfconscious living, i.e. live in acceptance and appreciation of their own identity. For an analysis of the link between cultural justice, identity, and globalization, see P. J. Naudé, "The ethical challenge of identity formation and cultural justice in a globalizing world," *Scriptura* 89 (2005): 536–49.

[31] H. Bedford-Strohm makes the astute observation that both material and socio-cultural poverty find their origin in "fehlende Teilhabe"; see *Vorrang für die Armen: Auf dem Weg zu einer theologischen Theorie der Gerechtigkeit*,

the sake of this chapter, I will not focus on these complex new dimensions of justice, but will point to a redefinition of distributive justice in the context of an integrated global monetary system.

Distributive justice[32] is a form of socio-economic justice that regulates the distribution of goods and services amongst the people of a specific society or amongst societies in a regional or global context. The result of such a distribution will obviously depend on the notion of justice and the specific theory of justice adopted. Egalitarian understandings of justice will, for example, seek to spread benefits more equally than entitlement notions of justice.[33]

Arguments for preferential justice: theology, philosophy, economics

There is a growing consensus that in order to make the emerging global monetary system moral and sustainable, special focus on disadvantaged nations is needed. In historical order, this notion of "preferential"[34] treatment has been expressed in different ways by theologians, philosophers, and economists over the last few decades. In the second section of this chapter each of these three viewpoints is briefly expanded.

Latin American liberation theologians developed "the preferential option for the poor" as a prophetic critique against failed development and structural adjustment policies in Latin America in the 1960s and early 1970s. John Rawls developed his ideas about "justice as fairness" and the priority of the least-advantaged persons in the early 1970s. He based this on his judgment that a utilitarian ethic that simply maximizes

---

Gütersloh: Chr. Kaiser Verlag, 1993, 169. People are poor because of a lack of participation in the (in)formal economy and lack of power to influence decisions. This is one of the most urgent issues in discussions of global economic justice today.

[32] For a definition and wide-ranging discussion of different theories of distributive justice, see J. E. Roemer, *Theories of Distributive Justice*, Cambridge, MA: Harvard University Press, 1998.

[33] This difference is, for example, illustrated in the debate between John Rawls (egalitarian view) and Robert Nozick (entitlement view).

[34] For an earlier discussion of this theme, see Piet Naudé, "In defense of partisan justice – an ethical reflection on 'the preferential option for the poor'," *Verbum et Ecclesia* 28(1): 166–90.

happiness will not create just societies, and later stated that burdened societies need special assistance in a new global order.[35] Joseph Stiglitz recently made a strong economic argument to replace "reciprocity for all" with the dictum of "special and differential treatment" for the poor nations of the world.[36]

Latin American liberation theologians: the preferential option for the poor

Reading the works of these theologians, one could construe at least four theological arguments that cumulatively provide a rationale and simultaneously express a preferential option for the poor:[37] methodological, hermeneutical, theological, and ecclesiological.

The methodological argument

The advent of a cluster of liberation theologies – Latin American, black, African, feminist/womanist, gay/lesbian, and ecological – was accompanied by a specific self-understanding that what is at stake is not just new theological themes on liberation, but the very way of constructing theology. Despite the inner complexities of and differences amongst this pluralistic array of liberation theologies, there is a specific methodological convergence: liberation theologies generally take as a methodological point of departure the oppressive experience of those who fall within the focus of that particular theology. These focal points explain in each case who should be regarded as "poor, marginalized and oppressed". The poor, marginalized and oppressed include economically or materially poor people, racially oppressed black people, culturally marginalized or colonized people, middle-class women and poor black women, gay and lesbian people, people suffering from HIV/AIDS, as well as the

---

[35] J. Rawls, *The Law of Peoples*, Cambridge, MA: Harvard University Press, 1999. For a recent discussion of fairness in trade from different global perspectives, see Moore (ed.), *Fairness in International Trade*.

[36] Stiglitz, *Making Globalization Work*.

[37] There is a certain circularity involved here: the option for the poor historically predates the development of Latin American liberation theologies (see below). Therefore, these theologies are expressions of different ways of the underlying option; but in turn, these "expressions" become arguments for a reinforcement of the option.

oppression of animals and the non-human world via a narrow anthro-
pocentric construction of reality.[38]

For the purposes of this chapter, a very general description of Latin
American liberation theology is undertaken.[39] There is a twofold motivation of this particular choice: first, the historical origin of the specific
terminology, "the preferential option for the poor", lies in Latin
American Catholicism. What later became Latin American liberation
theology stands the closest to these historical roots. The first indications
of the term are already present in *Gaudium et Spes*, emanating from
Vaticanum II (1965). It found its way in more explicit forms into the
second general conference of Latin American bishops at Medellin
(1968), and was taken up explicitly as a chapter entitled "the preferential option for the poor" in the final document of the third bishops'
conference in Puebla, Mexico (1979).[40]

Second, although "the option for the poor" has been adopted by
other liberation theologies, and later by the ecumenical movement,[41]
Latin American liberation theology is, in my view, the best example of a
theology constructed specifically around this option as a prism through
which all theological loci are viewed.

---

[38] Literature in each case is too vast to cite here. For a very useful overview of some
of these theologies from a South African perspective, see the first part of
S. Maimela and A. König, *Initiation into Theology*, Pretoria: Van Schaik, 2001.

[39] It must be made clear: one cannot write a few paragraphs on such a vast theology
(or theologies) without fairly sweeping generalizations and loss of specifics. It is
also impossible to refer to all relevant literature at each point. The value of the
"generalist" approach here, though, is that it serves a heuristic function in the
elucidation of a specific focal point. It is for the reader to judge whether the
exposition below contradicts the general thrust of liberation theologies from
Latin America.

[40] See a discussion of the original documents by G. Gutierrez, "Option for the
poor," in: *Mysterium Liberationis: Fundamental concepts of liberation theology*,
eds. I. Ellacuria and J. Sobrino, New York: Orbis, 1993, 239–40, and the more
detailed overview and analysis by Bedford-Strohm, *Vorrang für die Armen*,
151–66.

[41] This theological view is, for example, echoed by the Ecumenical Church in an
exposition of the Nicene Creed: "In the particular case of human oppression, the
victim is assured that God is never on the side of the oppressor, the bringer of
death, but will, in justice, protect the rights and lives of the victims." See World
Council of Churches, *Confessing the One Faith: An ecumenical explication of the
Apostolic faith as it is confessed in the Nicene-Constantinopolitan Creed (381)*,
Geneva: WCC, 1991, 63.

In a short, illuminating passage, Gutierrez explains the preferential option for the poor: "The very term *preference* obviously precludes any exclusivity; it simply points to who ought to be first – not the only – objects of our solidarity". He points out that liberation theology "has insisted on the importance of maintaining both the universality of God's love and the divine predilection for 'history's last'".[42] What the word *option* seeks to emphasize is "the free commitment of a decision. The option for the poor is not optional in the sense that a Christian need not necessarily make it, any more than the love we owe every human being, without exception, is not optional. It is a matter of a deep, ongoing solidarity, a voluntary daily involvement with the world of the poor."[43] The reference to *the poor* denotes at least three forms of poverty: material poverty (physically poor), social poverty (being marginalized due to racial, cultural or gender oppression), and spiritual poverty (openness to God's will and solidarity with the poor).[44,45]

The methodological renewal, brought about by liberation theology, was formulated by Gustavo Gutierrez in a classical exposition in 1971. According to him, liberation theology "offers us not so much a new theme for reflection as a *new way* to do theology".[46] He thus formulates: "Theology is a critical reflection on Christian praxis in the light of the Word."[47] The starting point of theological reflection is not revelation or tradition, but "purely and simply, the daily experience of the unjust poverty in which millions of our fellow Latin Americans are obliged to live".[48] What informs this theological reflection at the beginning are the facts and questions derived from the world. And this world is the world of the poor and the marginalized, a reality of social misery. It is the experience of these poor and marginalized people from "the underside of history" that informs theology as a liberating process.

There are actually three forms of theologies inherent in "liberation theology". Clodovis Boff[49] names them metaphorically as the roots, the

---

[42] Gutierrez, "Option for the poor," 239.   [43] Ibid., 240.   [44] Ibid., 235–7.

[45] See the discussion below where the first two forms of poverty are linked to two different forms of justice: distributive and cultural.

[46] G. Gutierrez, *A Theology of Liberation*, London: SCM, 1973, 15 (emphasis in original).

[47] Ibid., 13.

[48] Oliveros, "History of the Theology of Liberation," in: *Mysterium Liberationis*, 4.

[49] C. Boff, *Theology and Praxis: epistemological foundations*, New York: Orbis, 1987.

trunk, and the branches in the tree of liberation theology. The "roots" are popular liberation theology undertaken by ordinary Christians in base communities in a diffuse and less organized manner, with the basic method of confronting life conditions with the message of the gospel. The "trunk" refers to pastoral liberation theology by church assemblies, (lay) pastors and religious orders with a basic three-step method of seeing, judging, and acting. The branches – best known outside Latin America – are professional theologians who follow developed and rigorous academic arguments in a threefold mediation of theology, namely, socio-analytical, hermeneutical, and practical.

The socio-analytical mediation constitutes the material object of theology in its relation to the social sciences ("see"). The hermeneutical mediation constitutes the formal object of theology in its relation to Scripture and tradition ("judge"). The practical mediation constitutes the concrete object of theology in its relation to pastoral and historical action ("act").[50]

The metaphor of the tree already points out that the very methodological structure of liberation theology reflects and supports the preferential option for the poor. It is their experiences that inform liberation theology and provide pastoral and academic theologians with the core material for reflection in the light of Scripture and tradition. Liberation theology is therefore much more dialectical[51] than analogical, and more historical–practical than merely analytical. This in turn implies both an epistemological and a methodological break with mainline, traditional (Western) theology.[52]

---

[50] See L. Boff and C. Boff, *Salvation and Liberation*, New York: Orbis, 1984, 5–11, 49–55, and L. Boff and C. Boff, *Introducing Liberation Theology*, New York: Orbis, 1987, 24, as well as the very structure of C. Boff's *Theology and Praxis*. This latter book is for me the most illuminating and penetrating discussion of the concept of a praxis-oriented theology. Perceptive liberation theologians are obviously aware of the fact that the very "starting point" in socio-political realities or "experience" presupposes some *interpretation* of those realities. "Hermeneutics" in the sense of "reflective interpretation" indeed underlies the whole liberation theological enterprise. See the discussion that follows below.

[51] This term should not be interpreted in the Barthian sense of the word. Its origin lies in left-Hegelian and Marxist thought and refers to the development of history via dialectical movements of thesis, antithesis, and synthesis.

[52] See how Gutierrez in *A Theology of Liberation*, 3–15 attempts to link classical theologies to a liberation theology. For more detail, see J. Sobrino, *The True Church and the Poor*, New York: Orbis, 1984, 7–38, for an interesting and illuminating juxtapositioning of liberation and Western theologies.

We can thus attempt a first reply to the question: why this preferential option for the poor? The methodological answer is: because the lived realities of the poor impose themselves as the starting point of reflection on faith, and constitute the "hinge" of the praxis[53] process toward the liberation of the oppressed.[54]

The hermeneutic-exegetical argument

If the methodological starting point is the experiences of the poor, a hermeneutical discussion of liberation theology must commence with the poor, ordinary people as primary readers of the Bible. The methodological option for the poor here turns into an epistemological and hermeneutical privilege: we learn the truth of the Bible through the eyes and life histories of the poor. "No theoretical reading or quest for ideas is involved. The reading of the Bible as done by the poor is a matter of life and death, freedom and domination."[55] The primary context is the base communities and not the seminary or the university; and the "source" of biblical and exegetical reflection should be the readings as read through the eyes of the poor.

The implications are that the Bible is not read as history, but as a mirror of the present. The chief aim is not an isolated interpretation of the Bible for the purpose of erudition, but an interpretation of life with the aid of the Bible which itself becomes a source of life. There is no search here for a "neutral" reading – the poor engage in a committed reading as they search their way out of oppression toward liberation.[56]

One of the most significant shifts in twentieth-century hermeneutical studies occurred with the locus of meaning shifting from the text to the reader.[57] Meaning, it is argued, does not reside somewhere "in the autotelic text" where it is merely "retrieved" through historical,

---

[53] The word "praxis" refers to the continuous movement from practice ("experience") to theory ("reflection") and back ("action"). For a detailed philosophical discussion, see ch. 1 of the unpublished thesis by P. J. Naudé, "Ortopraksie as metodologiese prinsipe in die sistematiese teologie." D.Th. thesis, University of Stellenbosch, 1987.

[54] Sobrino, *The True Church and the Poor*, 27.

[55] G. da Silva Gorgulho, "Biblical hermeneutics," in: *Mysterium Liberationis*, 124.

[56] Ibid., 124–5.

[57] B. C. Lategan and W. S. Vorster, *Text and Reality: Aspects of reference in biblical texts*, Atlanta: Scholars Press, 1985.

grammatical and structural analysis. Meaning is constructed by an interaction between text and reader. Without the reader the text is voiceless. In some extreme reader-oriented views, the text is in fact constructed by the reader.[58] Thus, the important question is no longer: "What is read?", but rather, "Who reads?" And the answer from liberation theology is straightforward: the poor and the marginalized are the preferred readers.

Where a reader-oriented approach is coupled with a hermeneutics of suspicion[59] – specifically those from a Marxist or neo-Marxist origin – two crucial insights come to the fore: first, in what has become known as materialist readings, the production of the biblical text is itself viewed with "suspicion" based on who owns the means of production in the text-producing communities. Where a text originates or is edited over time by people in positions of political and economic power, they tend to show features of "status quo" texts. The opposite is naturally also true, so that the reader should rather seek out and follow the guidance of texts reflecting the views "from the underside" of society. Second, in what has become known as social constructivist readings, the socio-economic position of the reader is itself of crucial importance. If the reader is the primary locus of meaning, such meaning will tend to reflect her/his social position. In short, rich and powerful people construct different meanings than the poor and the marginalized.[60] And as many texts seem to address the needs of the latter, the epistemological privileged position now becomes one of hermeneutical privilege.

Based on these hermeneutical arguments, the exegetical key consequently shifts from notions such as "justification by faith alone" (dominant in Reformed exegesis), including the two kingdoms, or the creative tension between law and gospel (arising from Lutheran work), to "liberation of the poor and the marginalized".

---

[58] For a concise discussion of hermeneutical approaches that emphasize the role of the reader, see L. Jonker and D. Lawrie, *Fishing for Jonah (anew): Various approaches to biblical interpretations*, Stellenbosch: Sun Press, 2005, 112–28.

[59] See ibid., 167–228, for a general overview of "suspicion-hermeneutics" with a specific discussion by Lawrie of Marxist approaches on 189–99.

[60] See the many fruitful analyses of the insight by "ordinary readers" as set out by South African Old Testament scholar, Gerald West. See, for example, G. West, *Biblical Hermeneutics of Liberation: Modes of reading the Bible in the South African context*, New York: Orbis, 1995, and G. West, *Academy of the Poor: towards a dialogical reading of the Bible*, Sheffield Academic Press, 1999.

Boff and Boff state that: "From its point of departure in the anguish of the poor of this world, the whole biblical message emerges as a proclamation of liberation".[61] Themes from the Old Testament are liberation from Egypt, the special care for foreigners, widows, and orphans in the law, social criticism against oppressing the poor in the prophets, and the admonitions against riches and care for the poor in the wisdom literature. In the New Testament, much is made of Jesus' relation and ministry to sinners and marginalized people. In Luke – Acts, the emphasis is on the physically poor, the sharing of goods, and care for the widows in the earliest Christian communities. There is emphasis on the egalitarian elements in the Pauline corpus (like Galatians 3 and Ephesians 2), and the obvious option for the poor in the book of James.[62]

Why this preferential option for the poor? A second answer, highly simplified, is: "Because the Bible tells us so."

The Trinitarian argument

The interpretation of the Trinity is in many ways an extension of the hermeneutical views discussed above, though they represent the "doctrinal" dimension of the option for the poor.

God

If you live under wretched socio-economic, or marginalized, or oppressive conditions, and if you then read the Bible from the perspective of the poor, the very image of God that appears, is "the God of the oppressed". Gustavo Gutierrez calls this the theocentric basis of the option for the poor.[63] And Jon Sobrino writes: "In my opinion, God's manifestation, at least in Latin-America, is his scandalous and partisan love for the poor and his intention that the poor should receive life ... The mediation of the absolutely Other takes the form of those who are really 'other': the oppressed."[64]

---

[61] Boff and Boff, *Salvation and Liberation*, 26.

[62] As indicated above, the primary literature here is once again overwhelming. For an excellent summary and overview, see G. V. Pixley and C. Boff, *The Bible, the Church and the Poor*, New York: Orbis, 1989, esp. 17–52 ("The option for the poor in the Old Testament"), and 53–67 ("The option for the poor in the New Testament").

[63] Gutierrez, "Option for the poor," 239.

[64] Sobrino, *The True Church and the Poor*, 2, 33.

Here hermeneutics becomes theology. In situations of entrenched economic injustice, God is on the side of the poor and is a different God from the God of those who proclaim a prosperity gospel, perceiving God as guarantor for privileges and power. A theology that defends oppressive conditions is a false theology. "God" turns into idolatry; religion turns – as Marx rightly observed – into the opium of the people.

Jesus Christ

Liberation theologians have made rich contributions to our understanding of Christ.[65] One could point to a number of common emphases[66] that reinforce the option for the poor.

There is a definite return to the historical Jesus, although not in the "archaeological" or "historicist" sense of the word. Jesus is primarily seen as being materially poor. His seeking out and healing of marginalized people demonstrates his own commitment to the poor. He is as "Word made flesh" the incarnation and revelation of God, as the God of the poor. His ministry and preaching points to the coming kingdom of God with its radically inverted value system, where the first will be last, and the last first.

Latin American liberation theology moves away from explaining the cross in terms of expiatory theories of reconciliation, to an historical recovery of the cross, as the world's condemnation of the poor and at the same time judgment against the sin of marginalization. There is an intrinsic link between cross and resurrection. The latter stands as the triumph of justice over injustice, and as a sign of hope for those crucified in history. Christology is not merely constructed by theories about Jesus or the post-Easter Lord, but by following Jesus in his solidarity with the poor. The only way to Christology, i.e. knowledge about Christ, is via discipleship, the following of Christ.

Holy Spirit

The Holy Spirit is the One who fills the prophets who speak against oppression; who prompts the songs of liberation sung by Miriam,

---

[65] One immediately thinks of the seminal works by J. Sobrino as published in English: *Christology at the Crossroads* (1978), *Jesus the Liberator* (1993), and *Christ the Liberator* (2001), all published by Orbis Books in New York.

[66] I roughly follow the exposition by J. Lois, "Christology in the Theology of Liberation," in: *Mysterium Liberationis*, 168–93, but add interpretations based on my reading of primary literature.

Simeon, and Mary; who creates the church as an egalitarian prophetic community (Acts 2); who groans with the whole of creation, crying for justice and truth (Rom. 8). Based on these biblical insights, the Spirit is the divine force that works in history toward the radical transformation of society. The poor experience this Spirit as the Spirit that spurs them on to action; that delivers them from slavery and lets them experience freedom; that leads them from oppressed silence to the freedom of the word, crying out "Abba Father"; that makes possible the experience of a new community; that brings – amidst death – living waters of life.

Trinity

Not only as separate Persons, but also in community, the Trinity[67] serves as an example of self-donating love, non-hierarchical communion, and as a basis for our critique of society. To create social embodiments of the Trinitarian communion would require a new society that avoids the aberrations of both excessive individualism underlying capitalism and the collectivism of socialism: "The sort of society that would emerge from inspiration by the Trinitarian model would be one of fellowship, equality of opportunity, generosity in the space available for personal and group expression."[68]

Why this preferential option for the poor? A third reply provided by liberation theology is: because this is how God, as Trinitarian God, has revealed God-self. As Boff puts it: "Oppressed Christians find an incomparable inspiration for the liberation struggle in the God of their faith."[69]

The ecclesiological argument

The church is not so much a church for the poor as a poor church.[70,71] This argument is strengthened by Moltmann, who states that: "Poverty

---

[67] Perhaps one could say that Leonardo Boff has done the most interesting work on Trinitarian theology from amongst the liberation theologians. See his *Trinity and Society*, New York: Orbis, 1988, and his *Holy Trinity, Perfect Community*, New York: Orbis, 2000, as examples of what has become known as "social trinitarianism".

[68] Boff, *Trinity and Society*, 151.   [69] Ibid., 152.

[70] Sobrino, *The True Church and the Poor*, 84–124.

[71] Sobrino develops his ecclesiological views in this regard with strong reliance on Western theologians like Moltmann (see next quotation) and Hans Küng, but obviously adds his own perspectives from the Latin American situation.

is not a virtue unless it leads to the fellowship of the really poor. The poor church will therefore have to be understood as the church of the poor ..."[72,73]

Sobrino attempts to overcome three obstacles in understanding the church as a church of the poor: an idealist universalism, an ethical approach to the poor, and a segment approach to view the poor in the church as part of a wider sociological group.

First, the Second Vatican Council reintroduced the metaphor "people of God" for the church, and although this is clearly a move away from the strict hierarchical and mystical understandings of the church to a more democratic or participative notion, Sobrino maintains that a universalistic understanding of the people of God is still too vague. He argues that – as in the times of Isaiah and Jesus – the good news is for the poor a locus where God is found (Matt. 25). Therefore, the poor have the sacramental value of being "a structural channel for the coming into being of the true Church".[74] The church was historically born of the poor and they remain the theological locus of the church.

Second, a "church of the poor" is not an expression of the idea that the church has an ethical obligation to assist the poor whilst ignoring poverty. Yes, one can build a church for the poor, but that is not synonymous with a church *of* the poor, because the first assumes that "the Church is constituted in logical independence of the poor, and then goes on to ask what this Church must do for the poor. However, a Church *of* the poor poses a strictly ecclesiological problem; it concerns the very being of the Church."[75]

Third, "Church of the poor" does not simply imply that the poor are part of the church alongside others who are non-poor and who remain unaffected by the plight of the poor segment of the church. The Spirit of Jesus who is in the poor recreates the entire church to become a church of the poor. The poor are the theological source of the entire church and

---

[72] J. Moltmann, *The Church in the Power of the Spirit: A contribution to messianic ecclesiology*, London: SCM, 1981, 336.

[73] This is a quotation from Moltmann's exposition of the marks of the church that, according to him, is holy in poverty. He argues that because Christ has been made poor "so that you might become rich" (2 Cor. 8:9), the church is sanctified "wherever it participates in the lowliness, helplessness, poverty and suffering of Christ": see Moltmann, *The Church in the Power of the Spirit*, 355.

[74] Sobrino, *The True Church and the Poor*, 93.   [75] Ibid., 92.

being a church of the poor is the only way to seek and find God. Solidarity with the poor by being poor is an expression of the church's own kenosis.[76]

A fourth reply to the question, "Why is there a preferential option for the poor?" would be: the poor church expresses the essence of being church in the world today. The implications of this theological construct for our understanding of justice are profound. For the sake of focus, let us look at the views expressed by Jon Sobrino in his discussion of the integral relationship between faith and justice.

He takes the kingdom of God as a point of departure: because God's reign embraces the totality of human relations and includes all of history, justice – as the concrete embodiment of love – must be understood in equally holistic terms. Therefore, justice concerns itself not merely with interpersonal relations, but with structural relations as well. As humans are divided into "oppressor and oppressed", justice must concretely address the sin of structural economic disparity.

The partisan nature of this justice is expressed unreservedly: "Love in the form of justice has meant historically doing justice to the vast majority of the human race, namely, the poor.... Historically, therefore, the concretization of love as justice is a necessary and effective way of giving flesh to the great Christian truth that God is partial to the poor majority."[77]

Let us now attempt to establish whether and in what manner the same kind of preference emanates on different grounds, from the philosophical theory of justice, as presented by eminent political philosopher, John Rawls. In other words, what are the philosophical grounds – if any – for preferential justice?

John Rawls: the priority of "the least advantaged representative man" and "burdened societies"

In his well-known *A Theory of Justice*, Rawls develops a difference principle,[78] in which redistributive policies allow for social and economic inequalities, but only if they result in compensating benefits for everyone, "and in particular for the least advantaged members of society".[79] The protection or improvement of the circumstances of the

---

[76] Ibid., 95.   [77] Ibid., 77.
[78] J. Rawls, *A Theory of Justice*, Oxford University Press, 1971, 60–90.
[79] Ibid., 14–15.

least advantaged therefore receives absolute priority in determining justice.

Rawls' defense of this priority is philosophically based on his choice against sum-utilitarianism and his preference for the contract tradition stemming from Hobbes, Locke, Rousseau, and Kant. His methodological defense is based on his strategy to show that the difference principle (or maximum criterion) would be the rational choice for members of a future society who find themselves behind a veil of ignorance[80] in an original contract position.[81] The (re)distribution of primary goods, identified by Rawls as "rights and liberties, opportunities and powers, income and wealth",[82] must always satisfy the criterion of improving the circumstances of the person who is the worst off in society.

The identification of this "worst off" person, or what Rawls calls "the least advantaged representative man",[83] may be determined by economists in terms of the Gini-index, coupled to social welfare functions, or by the Lorenz curve, which depicts the percentage of the total amount of income possessed by any given percentage of the poorest amongst the population (e.g. the poorest 20% of people share in 4% of total income).[84]

In his later book, *The Law of Peoples*,[85] Rawls extends his notion of "justice as fairness" to an international society composed of different peoples who have "distinctive institutions and languages, religions and cultures, as well as different histories".[86] In an initial compact (the second original position) where representatives of the peoples meet behind a thick veil of ignorance,[87] eight principles of the "Law of Peoples" would hypothetically be agreed upon.[88] This is not an agreement between free and equal individuals as in Rawls' "domestic version", but an agreement reached by distinct peoples via their rationally inclined representatives.

In what way could Rawls' "international" version of justice as fairness be interpreted as prioritarian, as described above? Let us look at the

---

[80] Rawls, *A Theory of Justice*, 136–42.   [81] Ibid., 17–22.   [82] Ibid., 62, 92.
[83] Ibid., 91.
[84] Frankfurt argues that this "priority" of those "worst off" should be given only to those below a certain threshold: see H. G. Frankfurt, "Equality as a moral ideal," *Ethics* 98 (1987): 21–43. One could apply his view to the current distinction between people living in poverty and those living in absolute poverty.
[85] J. Rawls, *The Law of Peoples*, Cambridge, MA: Harvard University Press, 1999.
[86] Ibid., 54–5.   [87] Ibid., 32–3.   [88] Ibid., 37.

principles of justice among free and democratic peoples as formulated by Rawls:

(1) Peoples are free and independent, and their freedom and independence are to be respected by other peoples.
(2) Peoples are to observe treaties and undertakings.
(3) Peoples are equal and are party to the agreements that bind them.
(4) Peoples are to observe a duty of non-intervention.
(5) Peoples have the right of self-defense but no right to instigate war for reasons other than self-defense.
(6) Peoples are to honor human rights.
(7) Peoples are to observe certain specified restrictions in the conduct of war.

Whereas the first seven principles all presume equality and non-partisanship, the addition of the last principle[89] is significant:

(8) Peoples have a duty to assist other peoples living under unfavorable conditions that prevent their having a just or decent political and social regime.[90]

According to my interpretation, this is the only law that moves Rawls' egalitarianism toward its special version of prioritarianism, namely, "a duty" toward those "living under unfavorable conditions". Rawls refers to these as "burdened societies",[91] because they "lack the political and cultural traditions, the human capital and know-how, and often, the material and technological resources needed to be well-ordered".[92]

Buchanan argues that Rawls does not adequately address the inequities built into the "global basic structure". The latter is seen as "a set of economic and political institutions that has profound and enduring effects on the distribution of burdens and benefits among peoples and individuals around the world".[93] Therefore, Rawls' laws do not

---

[89] Rawls himself remarks: "This principle is especially controversial" (see ibid., 37, note 43).

[90] Ibid., 37.

[91] A well-ordered and even rich society may become a burdened society through a natural disaster. Irrespective of the cause, Rawls argues that a rational view of reciprocity would agree to the principle that peoples have a duty to assist burdened societies.

[92] Rawls, *The Law of Peoples*, 106.

[93] A. Buchanan, "Rawls's *Law of Peoples*: Rules for a vanished Westphalian world," *Ethics* 110 (2000): 705.

adequately address issues of distributive justice in the current global order. Buchanan subsequently adds three further laws pertaining to: (1) global equality of opportunity, (2) democratic participation in global institutions, and (3) a principle designed to limit inequalities of wealth among nations.

However, it may be argued that a strong interpretation of the eighth principle does, indeed, imply redistributive action. The "duty to assist" can hardly be practically conceived without some "transfer" or "sacrifice" from decent peoples living under more favorable conditions than those in the opposite situation.[94] Anton van Niekerk argues convincingly that this duty is not merely a duty of charity, but indeed, of justice. And that this law – even if construed as a duty of charity – has no diminished moral force.[95]

The difference principle returns with a special and exclusive focus on "peoples living under unfavorable conditions". In this "universal" version of Rawls' theory, the individuals who are worst off in a specific society are replaced by peoples who are comparably worst off in the global system.

However, some qualification is required: Rawls does not accept a blanket global difference principle.[96] "Well-ordered peoples have a duty to assist burdened societies. It does not follow, however, that the only way, or the best way to carry out this duty of assistance is by following a principle of distributive justice to regulate economic and social inequalities among societies."[97]

The three guidelines[98] for the duty to assist[99] clarify this: the aim of assistance is not primarily to reach greater equality in, for example, economic wealth, but to ensure that burdened societies are able

---

[94] The G-8 debt relief program, or South Africa's contributions to the South Africa Development Community Countries are cases in point.

[95] A. A. van Niekerk, "Principles of global distributive justice: moving beyond Rawls and Buchanan," *South African Journal of Philosophy* 23(2) (2004): 183.

[96] Here Rawls differs from Charles Beitz, whom he discusses in *The Law of Peoples*, 115–19.

[97] Ibid., 106.

[98] Simply put, these guidelines are as follows: assistance is not aimed at reduction in wealth inequalities per se, but in establishing just institutions; the establishment of a political culture and political virtues are crucial, and, despite being relatively poor, the inclusion of the burdened society in the Society of Peoples is the ultimate aim.

[99] Rawls, *The Law of Peoples*, 106–13.

"to establish reasonably just basic institutions for a free constitutional democratic society and to secure a social world that makes possible a worthwhile life for all its citizens".[100] Therefore, the duty to assist is a transitional duty linked to a specific target after which the duty is no longer in force, as the former burdened society is now able, or has become a member of the Society of Well-ordered Peoples.[101]

This does not imply that redistributive justice or the reducing of inequalities is at stake. It also does not exclude direct financial assistance, although Rawls is at pains to focus on political culture rather than economic aid.[102] The Society of Peoples may and will probably have members that are rich and poor in relative terms, but the latter will not be so poor (burdened) as to make the establishment and maintenance of a well-ordered society impossible.

Rawls explains that one of the preconditions for establishing basic institutions is by meeting peoples' basic needs. "By basic needs I mean roughly those that must be met if citizens are to be in a position to take advantage of the rights, liberties, and opportunities of their society. These needs include economic means as well as institutional rights and freedoms",[103] and may (in my interpretation) be linked to the presence of adequate "primary goods" to secure a social world in which just political institutions can be built.

Therefore, the duty to assist in the context of relations amongst peoples – despite qualifications and restrictions – carries the same egalitarian consequences as the difference principle in domestic societies.[104] The principle, if applied to asymmetrical power relations, implies the following.

---

[100] Ibid., 107 (see also 5).   [101] Ibid., 117–19.

[102] "What must be realized is that merely dispensing funds will not rectify basic political and social injustices (though money is often essential)." A focus on human rights and the establishment of a democratic political culture is more important (Rawls, *The Law of Peoples*, 108–9). Rawls takes his cue, inter alia, from Amartya Sen's case studies of famine that show that political and economic factors are often more important than "natural" factors such as droughts; see Amartya Sen, *On Ethics and Economics*, Oxford: Blackwell, 1988. This reinforces Rawls' view that assistance amongst peoples must carry political consequences, i.e. the creation of just institutions.

[103] Rawls, *The Law of Peoples*, 38, note 47.

[104] Rawls remarks that among various interpretations of liberalism, "justice as fairness is the most egalitarian" (ibid., 14, note 5).

In situations where, for example, indigenous people share member-
ship of a domestic society with better-off persons, and they happen to be
in the worst-off position (which is mostly the case), the difference
principle would require that such people receive absolute priority in
any redistributive policy decision. And in situations of global distributive decision-making, Rawls' principle of assistance requires that,
whatever the outcome of such a decision, it should not diminish the
fulfillment of the basic needs of the poorest people to the point where
citizens are unable to build just institutions, or take advantage of
available rights and opportunities. The rational and just thing to do in
the (second) original position is to maximize the minimum, where the
latter has the potential to build a well-ordered Society of Peoples,
because the people you represent in the second original position might
find themselves, in reality, to be a burdened society.

We now look at the work of well-known economist, Joseph Stiglitz,
to discern whether and in what way he expresses the idea of prioritarian
justice.

Joseph Stiglitz: the differential treatment of the poor

It has to be said clearly that Joseph Stiglitz, winner of the Nobel Prize for
Economics and chief economist of the World Bank until January 2001,
does not assume an ideological anti-globalization position. He would,
I assume, not be comfortable with some of the Christian prophetic
critiques against globalization that are strong in rhetoric, but in some
cases weak in discernment and policy.[105] He is committed to a market
position and understands that economic globalization is a complex
phenomenon with both positive and negative consequences.[106] His
critique of economic globalization, eloquently detailed in his bestseller,
Globalization and its Discontents,[107] is fierce, but his ultimate aim is
"to make it work".

Stiglitz commences his book *Making Globalization Work* with his
interpretation of "Another world is possible", the motto of the World

---

[105] On the strengths and weaknesses of prophetic critique, read P. Naudé, "Is
    prophetic discourse adequate to address global economic justice?" in:
    H. Bedford-Strohm and E. de Villiers (eds.), *Prophetic Witness: An appropriate
    contemporary mode of public discourse?*, Muenster: Lit. Verlag, 91–108.
[106] Stiglitz, *Making Globalization Work*, 22–3.
[107] J. E. Stiglitz, *Globalization and its Discontents*, New York: W.W. Norton, 2002.

Social Forum, a gathering of 100,000 people in Mumbai, in January 2004. One could isolate a number of important convictions that underpin his argument for a differential economic treatment of poorer nations. In arguing for such a differential trade system, he challenges a number of traditional, conservative economic views on market fundamentalism.

He rejects the separation of efficiency and equity considerations in a market economy. He states that the belief that markets and the pursuit of self-interest would – via an invisible hand – lead to economic efficiency is only partially true. Furthermore, he states that if markets by themselves lead to socially unacceptable income distributions, questions around equity arise. And to address equity, economic policy has to include appropriate government interventions and regulations (see the reference to Keynes on page xvii!). Stiglitz argues that economic efficiency should not be isolated as the sole criterion of economic performance, but that so-called non-economic values like "social justice, the environment, cultural diversity, universal access to health care, and consumer protection" should be co-determinants of economic success.[108]

Stiglitz further rejects two long-standing premises of trade liberalization: first, that liberalization of trade automatically leads to more trade and higher economic growth. Second, that such growth inevitably leads to a "trickle-down" benefit for all.[109] Apart from his own research in information economics, he argues that neither economic history nor current economic theory supports these two premises. There are consequently no grounds to believe that the best way to help the poor is simply to strive for more liberalization of trade and higher growth. Opening up the markets *alone* will not solve the problem of poverty, but may even make it worse.[110]

In his only reference to Rawls,[111] Stiglitz does intimate that a fairer and more equitable trade system would "entail putting ourselves in others' shoes: what would we think is fair or right if we were in their position?"[112] What type of international trade regime would we, in Rawlsian terms, choose behind the veil of ignorance? It is in this context that Stiglitz argues for his differential option for the poor

---

[108] Stiglitz, *Making Globalization Work*, xvii; see also xiv, 17, 22.
[109] Ibid., 23, 99.   [110] Ibid., 14.
[111] Ibid., 22 (referring to Rawls, *A Theory of Justice*, 296, note 15).   [112] Ibid., 58.

and – reminiscent of Rawls – suggests that we judge trade regimes by the criterion of whether they do not make the poorest countries actually worse off.[113]

When trade agreements were established between advanced industrial nations, under GATT, the principles of nondiscrimination, equality, and reciprocity were upheld. Such countries would not discriminate against other members of GATT and each country treated all others the same – all were considered to be "the most favored". This system of multinational trade was founded on strict reciprocity. Each country agreed to lower tariffs and to open up markets if the others reciprocated.[114] Coupled to these arrangements was the principle of national treatment: foreign producers were subject to the same regulations as domestic ones.

When GATT was replaced by the WTO in 1995, these principles were carried over into the new, much more expanded trade regime. There is much hard, empirical evidence listed by Stiglitz[115] to show that an asymmetric system, with grossly uneven playing fields and uneven implementation, evolved and that it actually made developing countries worse off.[116] What is needed is a global trade regime "that promotes the well-being of the poorest countries and that is, at the same time, good for advanced industrial countries as a whole", although current special corporate interest groups might suffer and lose some of their unfair advantages.[117]

In what he calls "fair trade for the poor", Stiglitz suggests a reform of international trade. This reform entails that the principle of "reciprocity for and among all countries – regardless of circumstances" be replaced by the principle of "reciprocity among equals, but differentiation between those in markedly different circumstances".[118]

In practice, Stiglitz (and Charlton)[119] proposes a three-tier system of rich, middle-income and poor countries – a classification based on agreed empirical norms. The rich countries open up their markets to others in their own group, but also to the middle-income and poor countries, but without reciprocity, or political conditionality expected

[113] Stiglitz, *Making Globalization Work*, 75.   [114] Ibid., 77–8, 85–97.
[115] Ibid., 58.   [116] Ibid., 82; on special interests see also 13, 24.
[117] Ibid., 83 (emphasis added).
[118] J. E. Stiglitz and A. Charlton, *Fair Trade for All: How trade can promote development*, Oxford University Press, 2005.
[119] Stiglitz, *Making Globalization Work*, 83.

from the latter two groups. The middle-income group opens trade to all in its own group and to the poor countries without conditionality, but is not required to extend such preferences to the rich countries. In such a system, developing nations will receive "special and differential treatment", as has already happened in some bilateral trade agreements (see the European Union (EU) in 2001).[120] However, such preferential treatment should not be voluntary, but should become part and parcel of WTO negotiations and be enforced in fields such as agriculture, tariffs, and non-tariff barriers.

On what grounds would this proposal be accepted? Stiglitz consistently argues for two grounds: conscience/morality and self-interest. Concerning self-interest, he notes that greater stability and security in the poor and developing nations will contribute to stability and security in the developed world.[121] The flood of immigrants from poor to rich countries might be slowed down if the circumstances compelling people to leave are improved. Obviously there are also responsibilities on poor countries with regard to governance.[122] A fairer trade regime would, in the long run, diminish the need for development aid and debt write-offs – mainly sponsored by developed countries. In fact, rich countries have cost poor countries three times more in trade restrictions than they give in total development aid.[123] The growth attained under a differential system has a far greater chance of actually benefiting everyone (excluding special interest groups).

The emphasis on morality must be seen in the context of Stiglitz's introduction of non-economical values as well as the retention of equity with efficiency. He does not argue his case at length, but simply states that to create a trade regime with differential and special treatment is a moral issue and a matter of conscience.[124] The empirical and social realities of poverty amongst and inside countries are socially unacceptable and constitute moral appeals in themselves. "It appears that it is better to be a cow in Europe than a poor person in a developing country", he writes,[125] referring to agricultural subsidies for cows in the EU that are equivalent to the poverty line of $2 a day per person in poor countries. One might (with some hesitation) conclude that Stiglitz adds economic flesh to the theological and philosophical bones of the

---

[120] Ibid., 59.   [121] Ibid., 58.   [122] Ibid., 78.   [123] Ibid., 100–1, 59.
[124] Ibid., 85.   [125] Bedford-Strohm, *Vorrang für die Armen*, 306–13.

preferential option for the poor and the priority of the least advantaged representative man, or special assistance to burdened societies.

This concludes the trilogy of views that contends that under a system of standardized monetization (as has emerged over the last century) a particular form of prioritarian distributive justice is morally defensible.

Implications of preferential justice for local and global policies

What are the policy implications of the theological, philosophical, and economic arguments for this specific form of partisan justice? Following some of Bedford-Strohm's points,[126] the following are listed as a conclusion to this chapter.

First, there are obviously differences of content, interpretation, and motivation amongst the three positions outlined above. Some might even suggest that my exposition suffers from a strong antecedent bias! Whatever these differences are, it is possible to see a synergy between a global ecumenical consensus, one of the most plausible political philosophies of the twentieth century, and a leading economist. This gives social and political credence to the notion of a preferential option for the poor. This synergy is no small achievement, as it witnesses the influence of theological ethics (broadly speaking) on political theory; but in turn it provides evidence of secular arguments for and confirmation of a primary theological notion. The option for the poor is obviously open for different interpretations, and some may even speak up against it; but the fact of the matter is that this option can no longer be ignored. Partisan justice is firmly on the international political and economic agenda – and it has legitimacy.

Second, one of the strongest criticisms against the option for the poor, by theologians, has been that it may be tough prophetic talk, but unless given more precise content regarding principles and procedures of (re-)distribution, it would only serve as a narrow rhetorical function. Poverty is obviously a relative concept: the poor in one society (Belgium) may be rich when compared with another (Somalia). Liberation theologians particularly attempted to define "the poor" in material, socio-cultural and spiritual terms. It is possible today to extend definitions of the poor to our global society and work with adjusted empirical data of the baseline (expressed in, for example,

---

[126] Stiglitz, *Making Globalization Work*, 99.

dollar terms) under which people will be considered poor. The value that Rawls adds to this is to develop a universal criterion, which formally addresses any situation, no matter how and where this baseline is set. Inequalities are allowed only insofar as they benefit the least advantaged representative person in a particular society, or the least advantaged peoples in a global setting. And the value that Stiglitz adds is that he is able to integrate differential treatment of poorer nations into the very procedures and agendas of current trade negotiations.

Third, all three proponents of the option for the poor emphasize that – contrary to popular perception – this option is not exclusive, but exactly inclusive. Liberation theologians argue that God's solidarity with the poor – so clear in the biblical trajectories – is a pastoral and not a salvation-historical notion. It needs to be made a priority and not excluded. That Jesus sides with the poor and was himself poor in no way detracts from the universal significance of his cross and resurrection. Showing no preferential treatment for the rich serves the whole faith community, and is the mark of a sincere religion before God, teaches James. Rawls has similar intentions: the choices made in the original position, according to the maximin principle, are designed precisely to contribute to a stable, well-ordered society, locally as well as globally. This links up with the interplay between conscience and self-interest that Stiglitz puts forward. A differential treatment of poor countries includes and, in the long run, actually benefits the rich. It is aimed at a global system in which trade is not a zero-sum, but a positive-sum, game.[127] Whether you argue from a theological, deontological or instrumental ethical perspective, the option for the poor is an inclusive strategy worthy of universal support.

Fourth, it must be evident that the option for the poor is a critical policy concept. It is not just another interesting theory amongst others. It has the ability to judge current socio-economic policies and outcomes. In terms of Gustafson's[128] stratification of moral language, the option for the poor can make the transition from prophetic to policy statements. There are certain interpretations of Rawls that turn his ideas into policy (for example, see Hayden[129]), and the core of international trade

---

[127] J. M. Gustafson, *Varieties of Moral Discourse: Prophetic, narrative, ethical and policy*, Grand Rapids: Calvin College, 1988.
[128] P. Hayden, *John Rawls: Towards a just world order*, Cardiff: University of Wales Press, 2002.
[129] See Bedford-Strohm, *Vorrang für die Armen*, 317.

negotiations centers on exactly how agreements should be shaped to eliminate uneven playing fields. It has been suggested[130] that the core indicator of public policy should not be economic GDP growth, but whether (for example) the past financial year has led to an improvement in the position of the least advantaged persons/groups in society, locally or globally. An annual "poverty report" should be the primary driving factor behind public and global policy, as well as the basis for a policy scorecard – for example, the Millennium Goals (2000) that set specific targets over a certain timeframe.

It does not take a lot of imagination to see the radical impact on global policies of the preferential option for the poor, as expressed in the notion of preferential justice. It is hoped that an important ethical dimension of "standardized monetization" has been firmly established herewith.

15 | Religious faith and the market economy: a survey on faith and trust of Catholic entrepreneurs in China

GAO SHINING AND YANG FENGGANG

It is nearly thirty years since China adopted the policy of reform and opening-up in the 1980s. This new policy has clearly brought about favorable changes in various aspects of society, though there have also emerged some negative effects. For example, social ethics and morals have been rapidly declining, and for certain areas, it would not be an exaggeration to use the word "crisis".

This decline became evident in the 1990s: the whole society became so "money-oriented" that all social classes and groups would take advantage of, or even abuse, their power to obtain wealth. As a result, injustice quickly found its way into society, and immoral or even malign conduct became prevalent. In fact, society has already witnessed the crossing of bottom-line ethics in some areas: the person who breaks the law does not have the least sympathy or shame about what he does, while onlookers, and even the general public, feel apathetic or indifferent. This phenomenon is characterized by a weakening, or even disappearance, of the sense of shame and guilt, and, in some cases, human nature.[1]

Consequences of moral decline can also be found in the market economy: society has been experiencing a trust crisis – a widespread social distrust, from goods and services, to administration, law-enforcement, laws and regulations, even basic values. This may be best represented by a joking remark of the public, "now nothing is real except for a cheater". This may sound sad, but it shows vividly how much most Chinese have suffered from this crisis. Trust, which is unfortunately absent in the country's market economy, has become a rare resource in today's China.

Many economists have commented on the relationship between trust and market economy: trust is an effective lubricant in economic

---

[1] The earthquake in Wenchuan brought new hope to people.

transactions;[2] trust is a public good necessary for economic transactions;[3] and the trust between social members is culture's way of influence on and representation of economy, which has a direct effect on, or even determines, economic efficiency.[4] The trust held by a society is not only a factor for economic development, but may also have a direct impact on the operation of the economy. In fact, it has been proved that absence of trust will not only bring a drastic increase in transaction cost and impede social division of labor, but also pose a fundamental threat to the market and transactions. Thus, market economy and morality are related to each other. In other words, that a smooth market operation and good order should be supported by morals and trust is the foundation for morals.[5]

Many religious believers have taken advantage of the policy of reform and opening-up and have been very active in China's market economy. After years of hard work, they have now become entrepreneurs (or "bosses", as the Chinese like to say) who represent well an emerging class in the transition of China's economic system and society. But how do they deal with a market economy that is not equipped with a sound legal system? Do their faiths help them re-establish the widely missing trust, especially social trust? Can religious faith play its own role in China's market economy? These are questions this survey and research has been asking, and the questions it intends to answer.

Situations of the subjects

Basic situations

This survey was carried out by interviewing some Catholic entrepreneurs in China: all of the subjects here were baptized and became Catholic; at the same time, all of them are entrepreneurs or senior managers in enterprises with at least ten employees. Semi-structured

---

[2] K. Arrow, *The Limits of Organisation*, New York: Norton, 1974.

[3] F. Hirsch, *Social Limits to Growth*, Cambridge, MA: Harvard University Press, 1978.

[4] F. Fukuyama, *Trust: The Social Virtues and Creation of Prosperity*, Yun Fang Press, 1998.

[5] See Zhang Weiying et al., "Trust and Its Interpretation: A Survey and Analysis in Several Provinces in China," *Economic Research Journal*, issue 10 (2002).

interviews were held for the survey, each of which lasted over seventy minutes.

This project started in September 2006 and was completed at the end of July 2007. The subjects are from Shijiazhuang and Hejian in Hebei province, Xi'an, Xingping, Zhouzhi, Wugong, and Fufeng in Shanxxi province, as well as other Chinese cities like Guiyang and Beijing.[6] Of all the forty-four Catholic subjects interviewed, forty-three are bosses or entrepreneurs, and the other is a senior manager; thirty-eight are male and six female. They have an average age of around forty, with the oldest being seventy-five and the youngest twenty-four. As for education, one is illiterate, seven have primary school degrees, nine are junior high school graduates, six senior high school graduates, two are graduates from technical secondary school, four from junior college, six are college graduates, and one postgraduate (the educational background of the other eight is not available). In terms of wealth, most of those interviewed have assets of several million RMB, ranging from more than 100,000 RMB to more than 10 million RMB; and they employ from fourteen to more than 300 people in their enterprises. Interviews, with the consent of the subjects, were recorded, and all of them are good and sound.

Common characteristics

All of the subjects here are from private businesses, most of whom did not start their initiatives until the mid and late 1990s. The following common characteristics are common to them: (1) they became Catholic under family influence: with the exception of two, all forty-six interviewed became Catholic under family influence and were baptized when they were very young; their core family members are Catholic, as well as their relatives; (2) during business activities they never hide their faith from people; (3) all represent themselves as conforming with laws and requirements of administrative organs and doing their best to support administrative work; (4) all put the Ten Commandments as a standard and caution of their behavior, claiming that they are "honest" to people and never cheat; (5) each one agrees that after attending religious

[6] Traditionally, Catholics don't like to engage in business, and the number of Catholic businessmen who would not say no to interviews, because of various reasons, is small. Therefore, though the researcher is based in Beijing, this survey failed to concentrate there as a result of many restrictions.

activities, he/she feels freed from trouble and gains peace of mind, ready for future hard work; (6) nearly all of the entrepreneurs interviewed, after their businesses prospered, are paying back to society, though to different degrees and in different ways; and (7) all of them agree that faith is the fundamental basis on which their enterprises develop.

The scope of human relations of the subjects in market economic activities

Research on "trust" has become more and more popular: it has been conducted from various perspectives, including psychology, sociology, culturology, and economics. Though they may define trust differently, these perspectives or disciplines share the consensus that trust is the result of human relations. As we all know, Robinson Crusoe on the desert island did not have a trust issue until he met "Friday". Thus, this chapter agrees with the following definition of trust: trust is an interpersonal attitude determined by rational calculation and emotional connection in interpersonal relations.[7]

Starting from this perspective, by looking at their economic activities, we can easily summarize the subjects' scope of human relations into the following: employer–employee, entrepreneur–administrative organs, and entrepreneur–clients and suppliers.

Employer–employee
The employees here can roughly be divided into three groups: managing staff in key departments, technical staff, and ordinary workers. The nature of an enterprise's main structure is decided by what kind of managing staff is employed for key departments. As one of the subjects put it, "there are three core departments for an enterprise: finance, purchase and sales". From the 44 entrepreneurs interviewed, four types of business structure can be identified in their management of these three departments.

When employing technical staff, all interviewed shared the consensus that a person's integrity comes before technique, because technical staff are key to an enterprise. As for ordinary workers, most of those interviewed would follow an order of fellow believers (including also

[7] J. D. Lewis and A. Weigert, "Trust as a Social Reality," *Social Forces* 63(4) (1985): 967–85.

Table 15.1 *Business structure of enterprises*

Type	Definition	Number of interviewees	Proportion
A. Family members	All three departments are managed by family members	15	34%
B. Relatives or friends	All three departments are managed by relatives or friends	13	29.6%
C. Competent employees	All three departments are managed by competent employees	10	22.7%
D. Mixed	The three departments are managed by a mixture of A, B, and/or C	6	13.7%

Table 15.2 *Relations with administrative organs*

Forms	Number	Proportion
A. Nothing except normal contact	11	25%
B. Besides A, extra gifts and treats	27	61.4%
C. Granted privileges	3	6.8%
D. Did not answer this question	3	6.8%

relatives, friends and those coming from his/her hometown), poor men, people with religious faith and non-religious people.

Entrepreneur–administrative organs

The entrepreneurs interviewed have a diversified business scope; none does the same as the others. As private enterprises, they are under the authority of the administration of industry and commerce. In addition, they have to deal with a wide range of government organs, including tax, health, quarantine, quality control, public security, and others. During the interview, all of the entrepreneurs said that they paid tax on time and actively supported administrative work. However, different forms of contacts can be found in the entrepreneur–administrative organs relations.

The survey shows that of those who answered the question, type B accounts for the majority. During the interview, entrepreneurs who ticked this type had some complaints to make about enterprise–administrative organs relations: these government organs "don't miss any opportunity to squeeze money from us ... I spend more time on them than on my business. With 1,000 RMB of tax, I also have to give away 1,000 to relevant officials. Honesty and trustworthiness is not only a personal problem, it is also a social problem, an institutional problem"; "if you don't know anyone in an administrative department, it will be very difficult even for normal contacts"; "relations are very important: the health and quarantine bureaus, television stations, all areas. Relations with television stations must also be good because we have to put on advertisements"; "to do business, you have to deal with relations, relations in all areas. If you fail in one area, it will instantly bring you trouble. Doing business is indeed difficult"; "for example, when festivals come, we would have to give them something as a token of appreciation, the administration of industry and commerce, public security, tax, etc. If you don't do it, sooner or later they will find a way to give you a ticket or other penalty. We have had a lot of things like this, the administration of industry and commerce, tax bureau ... and no one can do anything about them. It is like gift or penalty."

Of course, contacts between enterprises and administrative organs are supposed to be normal and restricted to business. However, only 25 percent of those interviewed are enjoying this situation, some of whom also used to adopt the gift-and-treat approach to "forging good relations" with government organs and only rejected it after administrative reform in some of them.

Only three enterprises chose type C, two of which are worth further discussion. The first interviewee is the president and engineer of a provincial food company: she has received many honors and awards, including the State Woman Pace-Setter ("March 8" Red Flag Bearer), National Outstanding Female Entrepreneur, as well as other honors and titles in her province, such as one of the "Ten" Provincial Female Model Workers, member of the Executive Committee of her province's Federation of Industry and Commerce, member of the Standing Committee of her province's International and National Public Relations Association, and Chairman of the Provincial Association of Industry and Knowledge Economy. The other has been awarded Advanced Individual Worker in both his city and province. His enterprise has received honors from the city's administration of industry and commerce for the past eight years and his products have also been praised in various media, including the Hong Kong press and *South*

China Post. From the two examples above, we can see that the titles and social status earned by an entrepreneur become extra intangible assets for his/her enterprises, so in terms of relations with administrative organs the entrepreneur gains not only respect but also monetary support from the state.

Entrepreneur–clients and suppliers

Compared with the first two kinds of relations, the relations between the entrepreneur and his clients and suppliers are less complicated, and can be summarized in three types: (A) friends or acquaintances; (B) temporary partners; and (C) long-time partners. These relations are never static: entrepreneurs always start with friends, acquaintances or people introduced by them for goods supply and sales, and sometimes they themselves may have to look among strangers for possible suppliers and buyers; but once the enterprise is on track, clients and suppliers will gradually become his long-time partners who share with him both benefits and risks. Every entrepreneur understands that clients and suppliers are vital to the enterprise and "the people on whom his livelihood depends", so they are very careful in dealing with these kinds of relations.

Religious faith and enterprises

The boss's religious faith is supposed to be something very personal, but we have found in our survey that such "personal matters" have more or less become the enterprise's concepts and values in economic activities.

Incorporating the entrepreneur's faith into corporate management

For example, entrepreneur D said "I take my Catholic faith as my theory, management ideas and standard of behavior and at the same time, I try to influence my employees and always ask them to conform to it". Entrepreneur G's "way of management is to teach his employees to read the Bible ... we read the Bible and say prayers together and our business has been very good". According to entrepreneur ZH1, "meetings are held at most every two weeks; managers meet every morning before work starts to discuss company matters but we say prayers every evening".

Taking religious festivals as company holidays

For example, in entrepreneur GO's company, "besides national holidays, our employees enjoy one more holiday: Christmas. It has become a company tradition that a company dinner is held several days before Christmas every year: we have a big dinner, report what we have done during the past year and most importantly, give honors and awards to hardworking employees. We would also invite priests and government officials. On Christmas Eve, all the employees must go to church . . . Christmas carols will be sung by a choir of employees who receive training in their free time. And as another example, entrepreneur W said "in our company, employees don't have to work on a Sunday or Great Feast Days".

"Faith" weighing in employment[8]

Entrepreneur S said: "I choose these brothers and sisters as employees because we are family and we can have better communication between us. Besides, they don't speak rudely, as some non-believers do . . . and they would be honest and work very hard. Another reason is, they would bring me less trouble. So when choosing employees, I would first go to fellow believers." Entrepreneur Y explained: "why do I choose someone with religious faith? Because I do hold better opinions of and attitudes towards believers, for example, I would give them more respect because they are honest and sincere citizens. Why do I think so? From my experience, believers always remember there is God: God comes before laws in governing people. However, non-believers don't have the idea of God and only know laws. Take me as an example, even if there is no law enforcement, I can feel that God is before me, so whatever I do I first have to obey God and then laws. So sometimes I say to my employees that a believer will always make a good employee." Entrepreneur M "also prefers those with the same faith because a lot of trouble can be avoided when people with the same faith are working together". Entrepreneur W also remarked that "generally speaking, I would feel a kind of affection if an applicant is a fellow believer. I would ask him to stay and try for some time. But if he does a bad job, I would not keep him either, even if a fellow believer."

"Faith" also weighing in choosing managers and staff

Entrepreneur W said: "I would try to use believers for my purchase department: they follow public morals and at the same time are bound by church commandments and other requirements, so they would not cheat." Entrepreneur ZH1 also remarked that "there are fellow believers, acquaintances and friends working in my company, but of

---

[8] It's a pity that I have no statistics.

them all, fellow believers are the most reliable: they are trustworthy because they have ethical bottom-lines and know what is right and what is wrong". According to entrepreneur D, "of course, believers are more trustworthy. Take Mr. Jing as an example; he is also Catholic, my father knows him very well, and I regard him as my elder brother. In fact, he has been an important friend for two generations in my family, so after he retired I invited him to run my company. I would discuss the top secret technology only with him."

The weight of "faith" in relations with clients
Entrepreneur W, for example, would say to his clients: "I am Catholic and you may believe in me on account of this alone. If I fail you, you can stop coming to me, but if I keep my word, you are welcome to keep doing business with us." And it is like this that his company has prospered. Entrepreneur C explained that "after establishing relations with clients, we would give 'love for love': we would provide the best service and when there is a quality problem, we would immediately offer to deal with it ourselves so as to win trust from the market. Once, a client came to my office and saw an icon hanging on the wall. He immediately recognized it and said 'Catholic!' Yes I am Catholic! People have a very good impression of Catholics: they think Catholics, unlike ordinary people, are more trustworthy. With this trust, we have successfully kept our clients and don't have to travel and discuss face-to-face whenever something comes up. Instead, a telephone call will do." Entrepreneur ZH3 also said that "if my client is a fellow believer, I would immediately give him more trust. For example, I would not press him to sign a formal contract, while for others I would not show the same degree of trust. Once a fellow believer asked me to design his house, but it turned out that he gave up the construction. He still paid me: just a few phone calls and he was here with money. But other people are different: I did design for all kinds of companies and government organs and whenever a contract was absent they would not pay me. It is because they have no faith."

Participation in religious activities

Although entrepreneurs are generally very busy, over half of those interviewed said that they would not miss the weekly activity on Sunday, which has already become a part of their life or custom. For example, entrepreneur X said that he would go to the six o'clock

Table 15.3 *Participation in religious activities*

Regularity	Number	Proportion
A. Every religious activity	24	54.5%
B. Whenever there is time	14	32%
C. Great Feast Days only	4	9%
D. Rarely	2	4.5%

(morning) Mass if he had an appointment at eight o'clock, and the evening Mass if he was fully occupied during the day; "whenever I travel to a new place, one of the first things would be to find a church". According to entrepreneur D, "unless I am away on business, I would attend Mass every week ... If I ever fail to attend it, then it would be a rough week". Moreover, those who chose B, "whenever there is time", or C, "Great Feast Days only", feel a sense of guilt about their failing to "keep the Sabbath" and "breaking commandments".

Analysis of the survey

All enterprises share the same goal, that, by providing products and services society needs, they would gain profits and establish themselves in the market. Of course, it takes a lot of factors to realize this goal, an important one of which is that an entrepreneur is able to mobilize all relevant forces. In this sense, his trust of people – people of all relevant areas – in market economic activities is very important, as it is relevant to the survival of his enterprise. This trust is established with the help of the entrepreneurs' religious faith, which in turn is supported by their participation in religious activities.

Trust established in various relations

Analysis of trust of employees

Weber proposes two kinds of trust in his book, *The Religion of China: Confucianism and Taoism*: particularistic trust and universalistic trust. The first kind of trust is rooted in blood, resting upon personal, familial and semi-familial relationships, while the latter is based upon the community of faith. Weber concludes that what is in Chinese society is particularistic trust: trusting no one but people with whom one has personal relations.[9] The same view is expressed in the book, *The Spirit of Chinese Capitalism*, in which Redding points out that one of the characteristics of Chinese family businesses is that people outside the family are extremely distrusted.[10]

This view seems to have been proved in our survey: in entrepreneur–employee relations, over 63 percent of the enterprises interviewed put family members, relatives or friends in key departments, while only 22.7 percent "appoint people according to their ability". This seems to suggest that Catholic entrepreneurs trust their family and relatives more, but in our survey there is also something that may supplement the above-mentioned views of Weber and Redding.

Nearly all the family members of these Catholic entrepreneurs share their faith, as do the majority of their relatives and friends. In this way, the core structure of the enterprise, which is based on employment of family members, relatives, and friends, is overlapped with a structure based on common faith in Catholicism. As believers are bound by Catholic doctrines and the Ten Commandments in their marriage, family, and conduct, this structure is always very stable and well established: the entrepreneurs don't have to worry about the trust issue. In other words, a trust based on blood or affection becomes even more reliable after it gains the second foundation of faith. For example, none of the forty-four entrepreneurs interviewed has ever been betrayed by family members, relatives, or close friends; in fact, all of them think that with this common ground in faith, their family life is smooth and happy, and they have had very good partnerships with relatives and close friends.

Furthermore, there is an interesting phenomenon: in today's rural areas, many kinds of traditional values, such as filial piety, have declined with the development of urbanization and the move of the younger generation to the cities. And it is Catholics and Christians who are practicing these traditional values of Confucianism.

However, for other enterprises where such common religious faith is absent, it is not unusual that an entrepreneur's spouse, relative, or good friend, after having been put in charge of the company's finance or other

---

[9] *The Religion of China: Confucianism and Taoism*, New York: The Free Press, 1915/1951.
[10] G. Redding, *The Spirit of Chinese Capitalism*, Berlin: Walter de Gruyter, 1990.

key departments, secretly transfers money to his/her own account or establishes his/her own relations with clients, which leaves the entrepreneur with a bitter break-up and no money. For them, there is no trust, but only benefits between people.

Thus, for Catholic entrepreneurs, the trust shown in the core structure of an enterprise, which is based on employment of family members, relatives, and friends, is built upon two pillars: particularistic trust (which is built on personal relations such as blood or affection) and universalistic trust (which is based on common faith). This trust, which combines the two, is even stronger than either of them alone; it is based on the faith of the entrepreneur.

One of the entrepreneurs interviewed explained how he looked at and treated his employees: "man is created by God and everyone is equal. Though I am the boss, I have no privilege as a man; every one of my employees has to be respected. My men are on an equal footing with me: When times were hard I myself was ill-paid too but in them I have very deep trust ... private enterprises in China often face a lot of difficulties and conflicts ... without a firm faith, it is very hard to overcome one's human nature of selfishness and vanity. That is why I spend more time on my faith and I would never have achieved what I have today without the kind words from my fellow believers and support from everyone." This remark shows that Catholic entrepreneurs give more trust to their employees, which is based on a sense of equality learned in their faith, while in general cases a boss has more power and higher status than his employees in the company and does not show his trust until the latter exhibit their "loyalty and competence". In other words, for Catholic entrepreneurs, blood or personal relations, through common faith, can be generalized or extended to strangers.

Analysis of trust of administrative organs

The trust established during contacts with administrative organs is one for relations with social roles, i.e. this trust is based upon the social role played by the trustee. Administrative organs are "authorities" and, generally speaking, are supposed to have normal contacts with enterprises. In China, however, administrative organs play the role of a "leader", which results in some tension between them and enterprises. For example, our survey shows that over 61 percent of the enterprises interviewed are trying to relieve this tension with gifts and treats or, as the entrepreneurs complained, "every relevant organ has to be attended". This not only proves ethical decay and moral decline in today's China, but also shows the enterprises' distrust of administration. As entrepreneur H put it, "there is no trust; just half-hearted must-dos".

However, as previously mentioned, three enterprises interviewed manage to receive favorable treatment from administrative organs. Two of them share the same characteristics: (1) the entrepreneur has been hailed as a model and enjoys high social status; and (2) the entrepreneur's personal faith has already become a kind of social capital, which in turn earns him support from the administration. Of course, there is no easy or quick way for faith to change into social capital.

As entrepreneur G explained, "you must start from relations with the local community: every year when Spring Festival comes, we would send some necessities, like rice, flour and oil, to sub-district offices and those poorly off in the local community. Last year, we gave relief of 10,000 RMB to support ten middle school and university students in Weiyang district. And on the 20th Anniversary of Teacher's Day, we donated 500 eye-protection desk lamps to outstanding teachers in the city (including four districts and six counties) and a visual acuity chart light-box to every one of the 100 primary schools in Weiyang, as well as 100 eye-protection desk lamps to doctors in these primary schools. Besides, we have also offered our hands to the society. For example, the year before last when Weinan was stricken by a huge flood, the biggest for the past fifty years, I went there four times for flood relief: the first time, on September 8, we brought with us 10,000 steamed bread leaves and 580 packets of instant noodles; the second time, when a new school was being built, I donated 5,000 RMB; the third time I went there it was around the Mid-Autumn Festival and National Day, so, in addition to the 500 pieces of clothing donated by our employees, we invited a heart-to-heart art troupe to put on a performance for local villagers; and this Spring Festival, I myself gave 15,000 RMB to support 50 poverty-stricken families in Weiyang district (with financial aid of 300 RMB for each family). There are a lot of things like this, and enterprises should be active in contacts and communication with the local government . . ."

Moreover, entrepreneurs interviewed never overlook publicity: they announce their faith, or even give thanks to God in public occasions, particularly those when authorities and officials from administrative organs are present. Entrepreneur D said "once our company held a celebration and there were a lot of guests, including many officials. I said in my speech that I am Catholic and I am thankful to God for what he had done for us. In fact, I never hide the fact that I am Catholic. My whole family has been Catholic for generations." Such open expression of one's personal faith, when it is an entrepreneur with some social status, will inevitably push it to change into social capital. As it turned out, administrative organs have given great support and honor to these two enterprises, which in turn results in their extreme confidence in the administration.

Analysis of trust of clients and suppliers

Most of the entrepreneurs interviewed have long-term partners as clients and suppliers, who can be defined as total "strangers" (people who are not the entrepreneurs' family, relatives or friends). In interpersonal relations with the clients, these entrepreneurs win trust not only with their quality products and services, but also their religious faith. The role it plays may be illustrated by the clients' comments: "people with religious faith are trustworthy because they will not cheat or misbehave ..." After the first deal, these entrepreneurs will do their best to "keep" the clients; sometimes they even offer such concessions as delivery-before-payment. On the other side, these entrepreneurs also distinguish their clients in terms of trustworthiness: state-owned enterprises or units are the most reliable, followed by big companies, small companies and self-employed people. This order shows that "state-owned" remains the equivalent of trustworthy in China and, in line with the mentality of an individual's trust of objects, larger-scale companies are more trusted because it is generally thought that big companies rarely cheat, and even if someone from the big companies cheats, "there will always be a big entity who can shoulder the responsibilities". In the same sense, it is easy to understand why self-employed people are least trusted: this is a new kind of business which did not exist until the reform and open-up, and individuals, compared with entities employing several people, are more prone to a "one-shot deal".

In sum, entrepreneurs interviewed, with their own honesty, have earned loyal clients as their enterprises get on track. As for suppliers, they also share the view that Catholic entrepreneurs "never delay payment; if they are in trouble they will carefully explain the situation and pay us once they have money in hand ..." The Catholic entrepreneurs, on the other hand, take several factors into account for purchase: besides cost, their number one consideration is quality. If the quality of the products provided is satisfactory and will not fail the entrepreneurs, they will always show trust to the suppliers.

Religious faith and public value

Uniqueness in the faith-holding of Catholic entrepreneurs

Unlike other religious believers like Protestants, Catholic entrepreneurs have their faith handed down from previous generations of the family; some of them have had this tradition for several generations.[11] They got to know Catholicism when they were young and have seen, heard and practiced it for years, so, instead of "choosing" a faith to support themselves[12] or "finding themselves an ultimate support" to "deal with various crises",[13] they have, unconsciously, had their faith deep-rooted in their life. This has gone beyond a practical effort to pray to God for good luck, blessing, and safety. In fact, none of the entrepreneurs interviewed (except for one whose business is named "Gao Manna's Shop of Baked Wheaten Cake with Donkey Meat")" gives a religious name to their companies:[14] it seems to suggest that they no longer need to announce their religious faith with a company name, as their faith has already been closely related to, or is even a part of, their life and enterprise. That is why among the entrepreneurs interviewed, "coming to God only at the last moment" is rare; for the majority of

[11] G. Shining, "Christianity and Christians in Today's Beijing," in: *External Factors for Establishing Belief*, the Institute of Sino-Christian Studies in Hong Kong, Hong Kong: Institute for Sino-Christian Studies 2005; Li Xiangping, "Belief and Practice of Entrepreneurs in Today's China," *China Ethnic News*, March 4, 2008.

[12] In Li Xiangping's article, Christian entrepreneurs are quoted as saying that they "chose Christianity because they, based on their small capital, ventured into a highly competitive and risky world and had to find a belief to support themselves".

[13] Niu Song, "Religion and Belief of Entrepreneurs," *China Ethnic News*, March 4, 2008.

[14] This is also a difference between Catholic and other Christian entrepreneurs. See Li Xiangping, "Belief and Practice of Entrepreneurs in Today's China."

them, saying prayers, reading the Bible and participating in religious activities has already become a part of their life and the enterprise. For example, many entrepreneurs said in the interview that if they were too busy "to go to church, they would go the next day to make up for it. Sometimes they were even too busy for that, then they would feel regret and uneasy about it."

The social expression of personal faith

Religion has two dimensions: personal and social. Deep down in people's hearts, religion is something very personal: it is a direct communication between man and God, which can be done by individuals in many ways. On the other hand, religion, which cannot stay in the realm of private life forever, can be expressed to society. Generally speaking, an individual's faith is expressed to society through groups, the best representation of which is religious groups. Religious groups, through various activities related to their faith, exhibit this private thing directly and together to society. Through this, individual faith is strengthened within a group and further extended to more people.

Of course, enterprises are not religious groups, but we have found in our survey that most entrepreneurs interviewed purposely announce their personal faith in economic activities and have made their companies more or less religious. Among our subjects, the external expression of this religiousness, besides announcement of their faith in the enterprise, is Madonna, scrolls with quotes from the Bible, and other things related to Catholicism which are found in their office, meeting room and restaurants. Internal expressions are various, from company rules and regulations, unwritten rules for employment, and holidays, to contacts with people from outside the company, some of which have already been discussed in our summary of the survey.

By being involved in the enterprise's economic activities, the entrepreneurs' personal faith is expressed to society. What makes such social expression possible is (1) it is hardly detrimental to anyone (nonbelievers don't feel any pressure); (2) the behavior of the entrepreneur is consistent with his open expression of personal faith, which makes people realize that religious believers are "truly different" from non-believers, "believers are reliable", and "see what Catholics are like and in turn see what God is like"; (3) such expression strengthens the entrepreneurs' sense of social responsibility: "[we] have the responsibility to influence and teach people around us to stay away from evil" and with profits made, "we should do our best to support charity and help the needy". That is why this open expression of faith is always appreciated and admired by people; and (4) this social expression of faith has in fact worked as a restriction on these entrepreneurs in business activities: "to live up to our name as a model, we may not do anything bad or associate with evil persons". This power of restraint has been very inspiring in today's world where moral decline and corruption rage.

There is no denying the fact that such open expression may put the entrepreneurs in an embarrassing or awkward situation: for example, they may take a long time to force themselves, or find a proper excuse when they find that they have to offer gifts or treats, or when they have to treat clients or officials to a sauna or nightclub, they have to wait outside. What we have found in our survey is that once personal faith is announced and works in the survival and management of the enterprise, it gains public value.

The public value of personal faith

The entrepreneurs' combination of their faith and business activities can be summarized as "first learn how to behave, then how to do business". For example, entrepreneur D said "my enterprise has a history of more than 20 years. If a company can last that long, it must have something deeply rooted in it and that is all about the entrepreneur, which, in my case, is my faith." We have found in our survey that once faith becomes the fundamental principle for an entrepreneur's conduct and business, many values highlighted in that faith, for example "gratitude", "love", "honesty and trustworthiness", and "confidence", are accepted by the entire company. The fact that these values play a role in the enterprise's development gives them a public nature.

Nearly all of the entrepreneurs interviewed feel deep and sincere "gratitude" about what they have achieved today. Many of them always give grateful remarks, for example "I have always thought about what I have gone through during the years. Now when I look back, I see clearly, in the series of events, that every single step is governed by God." Sometimes, when they get a bit carried away by their success, "God" will immediately "remind us to stay modest, just like a parent will do to a child".

"Love" is important for the enterprise's development. As one of the entrepreneurs interviewed said, "our church talks about love: we should love everyone; and love is what our company's development relies on". These entrepreneurs not only care about the employees, but also their families, which makes the staff feel "at home". Love also extends to partners, for example entrepreneur ZH1 said that his enterprise has a goal of four kinds of profits: profits in transparency – money is earned in a transparent way; profits in morality – the other side (the clients) feels happy about the transaction; profits in conscience – we ourselves are happy and contented about the business; and monetary profits. This placement of monetary benefits last is without doubt due to the influence of his faith.

Every entrepreneur interviewed talked about the value of "honesty and trustworthiness": "if you want others to trust you, you must first win trust from them". To employees, they try to win trust by "never delaying salary payment, keeping their word, enjoying the same standard of food and accommodation with staff, and working and relaxing with them". To administrative organs, they would pay tax on time and do their best to support the administrative work. And to partners, they try to convince them, with quality products and service, that "we are the most trustworthy as partners". All these efforts are based on an enterprise that has "honesty" running through everyone and everything. As the entrepreneurs interviewed said, "Honesty is from your faith; without faith, it is really difficult to maintain honesty". An entrepreneur interviewed whose company produces fertilizers, summarized the relationship between "honesty" and faith like this: "if I wanted to get very high profits, I could have cheated in my products. But as a man of religious faith, I would not do such a thing; on the contrary, I would work to improve the quality, though sometimes that means I will earn less."

"Confidence" has also been hailed by the entrepreneurs as key to the development and success of an enterprise: "sometimes when you keep pouring money in and don't see anything coming out, you are definitely basing your confidence and persistence on your faith"; "I have seen many enterprises that are not guided by faith, whose behavior or ways of doing things I don't quite agree with. I don't know what I would be like if I hadn't believed in God. But one thing is clear, whenever I falter or am about to be overcome by my greed, there is only one thing that can save me – my faith. This is fundamental."

As these principles, which are born of religious faith, become key public values for an enterprise, its entrepreneur would have a very different attitude toward money and see his sense of social responsibility heightened. For example, one of the entrepreneurs interviewed said that "business has been good for the past few years and I have earned quite some money, so now I start to think of doing something for society, building a Catholic church, natural disaster relief, or supporting a few poor students. I would like to help those in need and don't care what it would cost me. Now, for me a great sum of money is not helpful at all; it will only lead to crimes." Another example is the "Association of Catholic Businessmen" in Hejian, Hebei province. They meet on the first Sunday of every month and "do charity work to pay back society".

The importance of religious activities not to be underestimated

As is often remarked in China, "business is like war". Businessmen in today's world are always exposed to the cruel side of life: cheating, risks, and crisis. That is why it is easy to understand that they are constantly under great pressure. For Catholic entrepreneurs, however, there is a second source of stress: in addition to that of trying to lead their enterprise to survive fierce competition and to prosper, they also have to avoid "being forced to do something bad because most people do". Such efforts are voluntary and purposeful, because they know those things would be against their religious faith. It would amount to great tension when these entrepreneurs are under the double pressure of making money and maintaining their integrity, particularly in the business world where "every man is wicked". To relieve such pressure and tension, these Catholic entrepreneurs go to church to attend religious activities, which for them are even more important than reading the Bible and saying prayers. As entrepreneur ZH said, "I go to church for several reasons: first to revitalize myself and second to confess. We spend nearly all the time on worldly affairs and stay with God only once every week ... this is for my soul (we believe in the soul) and I should definitely spare one day to go to church. When you think like this, you will manage to spare some time for that."

Although not every one of the entrepreneurs interviewed can do that, the majority of them manage to go to church every week. Therefore, in these enterprises, Sundays and Big Feast Days are holidays; even their clients and suppliers know about and follow such practice. Many interviewees express such feelings when they come out of the church: "when I go to church, I would reflect on what I have done during the past week and after that I would feel revitalized and renewed, ready for another week's work"; "when I walk into the church, it is like a lamp is lighted in darkness – I am no longer afraid or bewildered and I would know where I would go and which road I should take"; "in the church, I feel my soul has been purified and it is detached, though temporarily, from the outside world; besides, when I say prayers with my fellow believers, I feel greatly inspired and encouraged"; "you will know what interpersonal harmony is when you are in a church".

This function of religious activities has been summarized by Durkheim like this:

no matter how complicated religious life appears to be, it is in essence unitary and united. No matter where or when it is, it corresponds to one need and comes from one state of mind. Whatever form it takes, the goal of religious life is to elevate man above himself to live a life which is more than personal opinion and drifting: faith, in its expression, demonstrates such life, which is organized by ceremony and goes in strict accordance with it.[15]

The Catholic entrepreneurs interviewed all hope to go beyond themselves and the reality of society. Though not everyone names religious activity as the number one issue in their Catholic life, they all feel the same when they walk out of the church. In other words, when the Catholic life is conducted in accordance with rules and practice, it makes integration and stability of society possible.

Conclusion

Trust under the restriction of relations and the expansion of trust

The Catholic entrepreneurs interviewed see their trust restricted by "relations" – under the restriction and influence of first-blood relations and then pseudo-kin ties that are results of the expansion of the blood relations. The "trust" research has often failed to note the importance of the factor "faith", and during our survey, we have found that faith

---

[15] E. Durkheim, *The Elementary Forms of the Religious Life*, Shanghai People Press, 1999, 541.

also has an extremely important influence on trust. It is faith that safeguards and at the same time leads to changes in trust which is restricted by these relations: on one hand, trust is cohesive and closely glues trust to these relations, and on the other hand, it is a tester, with which the entrepreneurs differentiate between people from "inside or outside their religious faith". As analyzed above, people from "inside their faith" may well include those with no personal relations with them. In this sense, then, trust becomes a regulator: entrepreneurs expand their trust from blood relations to strangers who don't have any personal relations with them, but who share with them the same religious faith; some of them, based on the fact that they are "honest" because of their religious faith, even assume that "people who are neither blood relations nor fellow believers" may also be honest and trustworthy. Therefore, though Weber and other researchers comment that the essence of trust of Chinese people (entrepreneurs) is based on the "standard of blood relations", trusting only those who have personal relations with them, what we have found in our survey can supplement or even modify this view.

A clear interaction between trust and the transformation of social structure and the social system

In a time when a person's social role is relatively fixed, people are more certain about and willing to trust others. It was so in the early days of reform and opening-up. Entrepreneurs who started their business then all mentioned that, as business was mainly done among a few local residents, "everyone knew everyone else", so oral promises were made and there was no need for a written contract because there was hardly any cheating. With the development of the market economy, however, people constantly change their jobs and a person's social roles become far more complicated. Moreover, the market expands to new areas which businessmen may not be so familiar with, and as competition intensifies, companies have to fight hard to survive. All of these social changes result in a new attitude of trust: nearly all entrepreneurs feel that they are "uncertain" about people. Catholic entrepreneurs are no exception: they remember the good old days "when everything was much easier"; and now they all have to spend time on things not directly related to business, and always to be "on guard" against others.

A life attitude based and centered on religious faith

Though the Catholic entrepreneurs interviewed also share uncertainty about people and would "put everything in a written contract once agreement is made", most of them "still believe in people even after being cheated" and claimed to remain "kind" or "tender-hearted".

Among theories about trust,[16] that of "moralistic trust" seems to explain the Catholic entrepreneurs' view of it: "moralistic trust shows a person's life attitude, which is not built upon his experience in dealing with people, but his optimistic view of the world".[17] The trust held by these Catholic entrepreneurs shows a life attitude, but more specifically, it is based and centered on their religious faith, which asks them first to be "honest" themselves and then believe that others will be the same. This is from the belief that God knows about anyone's dishonesty and that everyone will face the Last Judgment – "those who do evil things will definitely be punished by God". It is with this faith that, although most of the entrepreneurs interviewed have been cheated in business (twenty-seven have been cheated, three have never been cheated, and fourteen did not answer this question), the majority of them did not go after the cheaters for revenge: they either try to explain and understand the cheaters' behavior from experience – "he would not have cheated if he had not been in real trouble" – or assure themselves with the idea of the "Last Judgment" – "God will punish him".

Personal faith changing into social capital

When Catholicism, the personal faith of an entrepreneur, becomes the public value of his enterprise, the company will be endowed with a soul, a goal which goes beyond economic benefits. In addition, this faith, which becomes the company's public value, brings considerable social capital to it: a fairly permanent staff – employees "trust their boss 100%" and "rarely leave for other companies"; "assured

---

[16] These theories include "altruistic trust", "trust culture", "trust based on cognition", "rational choice", "institutionalism", "moralistic trust", and a new rational explanation. Wang Shaoguang and Liu Xin, "The Basis of Trust: A Rational Explanation," in: Zheng Yefu, Peng Siqing et al., *Trust in the Chinese Society*, Beijing: China City Publishing House, 2003, 220–34.

[17] Ibid., 227.

and confident"[18] during contacts with the administrative organs – they pay their tax on time and try their best to support the administrative work; recognition which helps them in competition – clients and suppliers trust "Catholicism" and in turn, Catholics; reflection and peace of mind in both good and bad times – they draw calmness, confidence and alertness from religious activities; a force to resist bad social practices – the entrepreneurs will not do anything that is against their faith; a good reputation in society – which is the reward for their constant and long-term charity efforts. Such social capital has helped with the development of the enterpreneur interviewed and with the accumulation of such capital, and it will play a positive role in changing China's religious environment. Maybe in the future what is now the personal faith of these entrepreneurs will become a "citizen faith" based on the community of work.

In short, we have found in our survey that religious faith helps the entrepreneurs establish their view of "trust", and to some extent promotes the standardization of activities in the market economy.

---

[18] Though over 60% of the entrepreneurs interviewed said that they would "offer gifts and treats to establish good relations" with the administrative organs, they all claimed to be "assured and confident" in front of them.

Money, wealth, and desire

16 | *"Do not sell your soul for money"*: economy and eschatology in biblical and intertestamental traditions

ANDREAS SCHÜLE

Introduction

In his famous essay, "The Protestant Ethic and the Spirit of Capitalism," Max Weber claims that Protestants of Western Christianity – especially in the Calvinist tradition – introduced the idea that a person's economic welfare was, to some degree, indicative of his or her state of election. The implicit assumption of Weber's (today, certainly contested) theory is that the Reformed doctrine of double predestination created an existential anxiety in the individual Christian that led to a desire to come to some assurance about his or her status regarding the "divine decree." Obviously, there was no way in which a human being could influence God's choice, since God's decrees about the world and about every individual soul were eternal and unchangeable. Nonetheless, the desire to "read" God's mind was a matter of gaining clarity about one's place in the eternal scheme of things.

John Calvin made it precisely the point of his doctrine of election that lingering over the divine decrees was a devilish snare. In fact, he compares any attempt to "break into" the divine wisdom to falling into a bottomless abyss.[1] According to Calvin, the only assurance of God's love and mercy that faith can gain is through beholding Christ as the "mirror of election." Yet, according to Weber, the doctrine of double predestination had fallout in the praxis of Christian life that ran counter to its original purpose. If one was among the few elect, it was hardly conceivable that this would not have at least *some* effect on one's present life.[2] Weber then moves on to his claim that it was faith seeking

---

[1] J. Calvin, *Inst.* III 24.4.
[2] Perhaps the most influential attestation of the so-called "syllogismus practicus" is found in the Westminster Confession of Faith (1647), ch. 18/3: "And therefore it is the duty of everyone to give all diligence to make his calling and election sure; that thereby his heart may be enlarged in peace and joy in the Holy Ghost, in love and

certainty in economic productivity that supported and even caused the rise of modern capitalism.[3] This claim has frequently, and probably also rightly, been criticized for its monocausal account of a complex phenomenon such as early modern capitalism. Nonetheless, Weber's theory is instructive, because it focuses on specific *points of contact* between religious and economic systems. In his view, the influence of the economy and of money on religion is not simply the result of hidden or overt forms of cultural hegemony. Weber considers the possibility that economic and monetary thinking is not only what challenges religion, but what can be employed by the religious system for its own specific purposes.

It is the task of this volume to identify such points of contact between religion, and specifically the monetary aspects of the economy, and one might start such an endeavor with the assumption that these points of contact between the two systems allow for traffic in both directions. Turning to my own subject, the texts and worlds of the Old Testament/ the Hebrew Bible, one notes that there was economy and religion long before there was money. As a matter of fact, money, as we understand the term, occurs only relatively late on the horizon of the Hebrew Bible.[4] Professor Seow's chapter above addresses this in greater detail with regard to the Book of Kohelet/Ecclesiastes. While the dating of this particular book (late Persian or early Hellenistic) remains under debate, it is clear that here, probably for the first time in the Bible, we find money as an integral part of the author's reasoning about the purpose

thankfulness to God, and in strength and cheerfulness in the duties of obedience, the proper fruits of this assurance: so far is it from inclining men to looseness."

[3] Here, I am not referring to Weber's theory of "inner-worldly asceticism" but, rather, its underlying assumption that in the Reformed faith the question of election was closely tied to economic success. An interesting passage in this regard is Weber's explanation of why the Puritans had high regard for the Book of Job, especially its epilogue, where Job is rewarded beyond what he originally possessed: "The Puritans repudiated the Apocrypha as not inspired, consistently with their sharp distinction between things divine and things of the flesh. But among the canonical books, that of Job had all the more influence. On the one hand it contained a grand conception of the absolute sovereign majesty of God, beyond all human comprehension, which was closely related to that of Calvinism. With that, on the other hand, it combined the certainty which, though incidental for Calvin, came to be of great importance for Puritanism, that God would bless His own in this life – in the Book of Job only – and also in the material sense": M. Weber, *The Protestant Ethic and the Spirit of Capitalism*, New York: Macmillan, 1976, 164.

[4] See S. Schwartz, *Were the Jews a Mediterranean Society? Reciprocity and Solidarity in Ancient Judaism*, Princeton University Press, 2010; G. G. Aperghis, *The Seleucid Royal Economy: The Finances and Financial Administration of the Seleucid Empire*, Cambridge University Press, 2004.

of life.[5] As such, money also becomes the subject of Kohelet's reflections on the possibility (or impossibility) of human happiness (Eccl. 5:9; 7:12; 10:19).

Kohelet and the Wisdom of Solomon

In the following, I want to focus on a development in the religion of ancient Judaism that occurred in the time of Kohelet, but that seems to have become even more dominant in the so-called intertestamental period, especially the second and first centuries BCE. One of the major religious innovations of this period is an emerging belief in the afterlife and in the immortality of the soul, both of which are practically entirely absent from the Semitic religions of the area of the Fertile Crescent. In these religions, death was essentially understood as the point when the *nefesh*, the "life force" of a person (in Bible translations, mostly rendered "soul"), departed the dead body and drifted away to an area that the Hebrew Bible calls "Sheol," the underworld. There it continued to "exist," although in a shadowy, lifeless form. In some periods of ancient Israelite religion, one also finds the idea that the "souls" of the deceased temporarily returned from the netherworld to haunt the living.

Although the belief in an afterlife and immortality is not characteristic of all of second and first century Judaism, it seems to have been widespread among rather different groups of that period. It plays a significant role in what one might call "upper-class" educational literature, such as Ben Sira and the Wisdom of Solomon, but also in sectarian communities like Qumran.

One gets a sense of what seems to have been a rather heated debate about the emerging belief in an afterlife, if one compares Kohelet – certainly a traditionalist in matters of eschatology – with the Wisdom of Solomon. In a passage following Kohelet's famous poem on the time and season that are allotted to all things under the sun, Kohelet meditates on the fate that all living beings share, namely, that eventually, they all go to the same place.

For the fate of humans and the fate of animals is the same; as one dies, so dies the other. They all have the same breath, and humans have no advantage over

---

[5] C.-L. Seow, *Ecclesiastes*, The Anchor Bible 18C, New York: Doubleday, 1997, 21–36.

the animals; for all is vanity. All go to one place; all are from the dust, and all turn to dust again. (Eccl. 3:19–20)

Ecclesiastes highlights what was held as common belief in most of pre-Hellenistic antiquity (with Egypt as an exception). However, in the sentence that follows the above quotation, Kohelet raises a question that goes beyond this frame of reference:

Who knows whether the spirit of man goes upward and the spirit of the beast goes down to the earth? (Eccl. 3:21)

There is reason to assume that this is a rhetorical question to which the implied answer is that no one knows whether the human spirit goes up, i.e. returns to God, whereas the spirit of animals goes "down."[6] Kohelet's interest in this question seems to suggest that there were people in his time who believed that human beings, after their bodily life, would continue to exist in a spiritual or angelic form. Within the Hebrew Bible, such a belief is attested in the book of Daniel (Dan. 12:3),[7] but it is even more prominent in the apocryphal Wisdom of Solomon (Wisd. Sol.), which reads almost as a direct refutation of Kohelet's position:[8]

For they reasoned unsoundly, saying to themselves, "Short and sorrowful is our life, and there is no remedy when a life comes to its end, and no one has been known to return from Hades. For we were born by mere chance, and hereafter we shall be as though we had never been, for the breath in our nostrils is smoke, and reason is a spark kindled by the beating of our hearts; when it is extinguished, the body will turn to ashes, and the spirit will dissolve like empty air. Our name will be forgotten in time, and no one will remember our works; our life will pass away like the traces of a cloud, and be scattered like mist that is chased by the rays of the sun and overcome by its heat. For our allotted time is the passing of a shadow, and there is no return from our death, because it is sealed up and no one turns back . . .

---

[6] Seow, *Ecclesiastes*, 176.

[7] J. J. Collins, *Daniel*, Hermeneia, Minneapolis: Augsburg Fortress, 1993, 393–8.

[8] See M. Kepper, "Hellenistische Bildung im Buch der Weisheit: Studien zur Sprachgestalt und Theologie der Sapientia Salomonis," *BZAW* 280, Berlin/New York: De Gruyter, 1999, 98–146; V. D'Alario, "La réflection sur le sens de la vie en Sg 1–5: Une réponse aux questions de Job et de Qohélet," in N. Calduch-Benages and J. Vermeylen (eds.), "Treasures of Wisdom: Studies in Ben Sira and the Book of Wisdom," *BETL* 143, Leuven University Press/Peeters, 1999, 33–329.

Thus they reasoned, but they were led astray, for their wickedness blinded them, and they did not know the secret purposes of God, nor hoped for the wages of holiness, nor discerned the prize for blameless souls; for God created us for immortality, and made us in the image of his own eternity, but through the devil's envy death entered the world, and those who belong to his company experience it. ... But the souls of the righteous are in the hand of God, and no torment will ever touch them. (Wisd. Sol. 2:1–5; 2:21–24; 3:1 NRSV)

Building on the idea of human beings as images of God (see Gen. 1:26–28), the author of this text seeks to establish the notion that human beings have immortal souls and are thus made for more than their earthly, bodily existence.[9] The soul is that aspect of a human being that shares God's eternity; and a "blameless soul" that did not corrupt itself during the person's lifetime will never lose this connection with its creator – not even in death.[10]

Beyond the reference to the *Imago Dei*, Wisd. Sol. does not provide any metaphysical argument why humans should be regarded as equipped with immortal souls. Rather, the focus here is on the ethical implications of such a notion: if Kohelet and, with him, most of the Hebrew Bible traditions, were right that "all creatures go to the same place," then social fatalism would be the consequence. In the passage I have left out in the above quotation, the author of Wisd. Sol. pictures how, in his view, most people would lead their lives, if the ethical presupposition were true that everything was going to end badly anyway:

Come, therefore, let us enjoy the good things that exist, and make use of the creation to the full as in youth. Let us take our fill of costly wine and perfumes, and let no flower of spring pass us by. Let us crown ourselves with rosebuds before they wither. Let none of us fail to share in our revelry; everywhere let us leave signs of enjoyment, because this is our portion, and this is our lot. Let

---

[9] See M. V. Blishcke, "Die Eschatologie in der Sapientia Salomonis," *FAT* 26, Tübingen: Mohr Siebeck, 2007; L. Ruppert, "Gerechte und Frevier (Gottlose) in Sap 1,1–6,21: Zum Neuverständis und zur Aktualisierung alttestamentlicher Traditionen in der Sapientia Salomonis," in: H. Hübner (ed.), *Die Weisheit Salomos im Horizont Biblisher Theologie*, Neukirchen-Vluyn: Neukirchener Verlag, 1993, 20.

[10] There is little doubt, however, that the authors of Wisd. Sol. were not aiming at changing their inherited belief system, but saw themselves as faithful interpreters of the "canonical" scriptures; see Kepper, "Hellenistische Bildung," 204, who suggests that the Jewish authors of Wisd. Sol. understood their attempt at appropriating and reworking ideas from Hellenistic philosophies as an educational exercise on the basis of their inherited traditions.

us oppress the righteous poor man; let us not spare the widow or regard the grey hairs of the aged. But let our might be our law of right, for what is weak proves itself to be useless. (Wisd. Sol. 2:6–11)

It seems that Wisd. Sol. employs the idea of the afterlife as a pedagogical tool or moral corrective.[11] It seeks to challenge a worldview that one could characterize as a combination of hedonism and social Darwinism. It addresses those who have the means to enjoy their lives and, in turn, hold the power to make other people's lives miserable.

Wisd. Sol. says little to nothing about the afterlife itself;[12] there is no depiction of the "world to come" as one finds in parts of the apoc-alyptic intertestamental literature. Wisd. Sol.'s approach to what comes after or, more adequately, what *lies beyond*, our physical existence, focuses on the *unscathedness* of the immortal soul. The place of a person's soul is "in the hands of God"[13] – this is a theological, anthropological, and also eschatological statement. Consequently, the principal objective of one's life should be to avoid anything that could damage the soul and estrange it from its creator. This is also the point where "money" comes into focus. Wisd. Sol. offers a nuanced account of the dangers that wealth in general, and the possession of money in particular, hold for one's immortal soul. The bottom line of this argument is the following: money gives the one who has it the power to recreate the social world according to his or her own preferences, desires, and values, which even includes fashioning God according to one's own image. Wisd. Sol. draws an interesting parallel between the gold and silver that are used to manufacture idols and the money that is used to take advantage of the poor:

But the workers are not concerned that mortals are destined to die or that their life is brief, but they compete with workers in gold and silver, and imitate workers in copper; and they count it a glorious thing to mold counterfeit gods.

---

[11] On the connection between the just and immortality in Wisd. Sol., see F. Raurell, "From ΔΙΚΑΙΟΣΥΝΗ to ΑΘΑΝΑΣΙΑ," in Calduch-Benages and Vermeylen (eds.), *Treasures of Wisdom*, 331–49.

[12] For obvious reasons, much of the secondary literature clusters around this particular aspect; particularly helpful in this regard are Blischke, *Eschatologie*, 50–88; L. L. Grabbe, *Wisdom of Solomon*, Sheffield Academic Press, 1997, 53–7; J. J. Collins, "Apocalyptic Eschatology as the Transcendence of Death," *CBQ* 36 (1974): 21–43.

[13] On this and related phrases, see D. Winston. *The Wisdom of Solomon*, Anchor Bible 43, New York: Doubleday, 1979, 125–6.

Their heart is ashes, their hope is cheaper than dirt, and their lives are of less worth than clay, because they failed to know the one who formed them and inspired them with active souls and breathed a living spirit into them. But they considered our existence an idle game, and life a festival held for profit, for they say one must get money however one can, even by base means. (Wisd. Sol. 15:9–12)

Reading between the lines, one gets the impression that the author of Wisd. Sol. regards money as something that does not really belong in God's creation. It potentially subverts or undercuts the relationships among humans and also their relationships with God. One certainly also finds a critical approach to money in Kohelet. Kohelet holds that money can ease some of life's burdens and should, therefore, not be dismissed altogether, but it becomes a deceitful friend when one expects it to make one happy or to add even an inch to one's lifespan. However, Kohelet is not nearly as suspicious of the potentially demonic power of money over people's lives as is Wisd. Sol. According to the latter, money is not only deceitful, but has the power to damage and eventually even destroy what is infinitely more precious than money and all temporary possessions, namely, the immortal soul.

It seems clear that both Kohelet's and Wisd. Sol.'s reasoning about wealth and poverty have the economically wealthy in mind, those who not only possessed more land, material goods, etc. than others, but who were also in a position to use money as a means to increase their profits beyond what was possible in a traditional, exchange-based economy. In Wisd. Sol.'s view, money was a powerful tool that was not bound by any moral principles and controls and could, thus, lead to reckless exploitation and oppression, especially if combined with Kohelet's seemingly fatalistic doctrine that, in the end, "all go down to the same place." It is against this backdrop that Wisd. Sol.'s teaching of an immortal soul and of judgment after death has to be understood. The idea of retribution in the afterlife introduces balance to a world that was otherwise perceived as unbalanced and unjust.[14]

---

[14] On the "act-consequence" involving the notion of an afterlife in ancient Egypt, see J. Assmann, *Maat: Gerechtigkeit und Unsterblichkeit im Alten Ägypten*, Munich: Beck, 1995; for the late-biblical and intertestamental traditions, see S. L. Adams, *Wisdom in Transition: Act and Consequence in Second Temple Instruction*, Leiden/Boston: E. J. Brill, 2008.

The discourse between Kohelet and Wisd. Sol. might suggest that the belief in the immortal soul and an afterlife had a specific social location, namely, the education of future economic and intellectual leaders – in other words, people who would be the likely candidates to have money and to use it in ways that, especially Wisd. Sol. sees as a perversion of the social and cultural order. In this view, the controversy about money and eschatology would have played itself out among the elites. However, as we shall explore below, looking at the lower end of the social spectrum, one finds that the nexus between the use of money and the welfare of the soul also played a significant role in the life of those who identified themselves as "the poor" – namely, the community of Qumran and the groups with which they interacted. The fact that Wisd. Sol. and the texts from Qumran are associated with groups at opposite ends of the social spectrum suggests that religious reflection on money was framed, to a major extent, by the new eschatology that emerged in the Hellenistic period and that focused on the non-negotiable value of the human soul.

Money and the ethos of poverty in 4QInstruction

Returning to our initial discussion of Weber, one can see how a partic-ular idea such as the "immortal soul" affects the perspective that a religious community has of the role of money in their lives and how, in turn, the increasing significance of money during the Persian and Hellenistic periods challenged the religious system. Another invaluable resource in this respect is some of the texts from the caves of Khirbet Qumran. Among them is the recently edited text 4QInstruction, the main purpose of which is to instruct the "poor" to accept their lot and resist the temptation of chasing after material goods in general and money in particular. It has been debated whether the addressees of 4QInstruction were economically poor, or if the Hebrew term *dallim* is used here in a more spiritual sense, not unlike the beatitude given to the poor in the Sermon on the Mount (Matt. 5:3).[15] Looking at the

---

[15] See B. G. Wold, "Metaphorical Poverty in 'Musar le Mevin'," *Journal of Jewish Studies* 58 (2007): 140–53. For a critique of Wold's position, see S. L. Adams, "Poverty and 'Otherness' in Second Temple Instructions," in D. C. Harlow et al., (eds.), *The "Other" in Second Temple Judaism: Essays in Honor of John J. Collins*, Grand Rapids: Eerdmans, 2011, 189–203. Adams characterizes the situation of the addressees of 4QInstruction as follows: "References in the extant

social milieu around the Qumran community, it seems that poverty, understood as people living at or below the existential minimum, was not a pressing issue of the time. However, it is also clear that the Qumran people and their associates stuck to traditional forms of economic production and trade that were not aimed at accumulating wealth.[16] In that respect, they might have considered themselves as "poor" as against the "rich," whose economic aspirations they did not share. Archaeological evidence has provided a fairly consistent picture of the Qumranites' deliberately modest lifestyle:[17] the pottery found at Qumran is of good quality, but of a very simple and "sleek" style;[18] burial sites do not show any ornaments or decorations, although they are not the mass graves of poor people either. With regard to money, the coinages found at Qumran were those of the outside economy,[19] suggesting that money was used for tax purposes (especially the half-shekel and the Roman *denarius*), rather than for economic transactions.[20] In other words, it seems that the Qumran people themselves used money only when they had to in order to avoid conflicts with Jewish or Roman authorities; as such, money was a means to interact with the outside world, but it was not supposed to play a role in the inner circle of the community.

Due to its largely fragmentary state, 4QInstruction poses several challenges to its interpreters. However, the overall literary character and content seem to be basically clear. 4QInstruction presents its teachings as "mysteries"; here, one encounters the much-debated term *raz*

---

fragments depict the specific situations of farmers, low-wage artisans, and poor families, facing the risk of debt-slavery."

[16] See C. Murphy, *Wealth in the Dead Sea Scrolls and in the Qumran Community*, Studies on the Texts of the Desert of Judah 40, Leiden/Boston/Cologne: E.J. Brill, 2002, 451: "The archeological evidence from Qumran compound and vicinity displays features consistent with the thesis that a community lived here, that they were religious in nature, and that their economy, though engaged with other sites, was not characterized by commerce traditionally defined."

[17] Ibid., 452–3.   [18] See Magness, *The Archaeology of Qumran*, 73–9.

[19] Murphy, *Wealth in the Dead Sea Scrolls*, 305–17, 451.

[20] Much debated in this respect is a hoard of silver coins, contained in three pots, that was found in room L120. While it has been argued that this could have been a "treasure," indicating that accumulating money was not so alien to the Qumranites after all, most scholars prefer a different view: "I believe that the character and composition of the hoard are best understood in connection with the sect's interpretation of the temple tax as a one-time payment made when a man reached adulthood and his name was recorded for the first time in the census registers" (Magness, *The Archaeology of Qumran*, 193).

nihyah, "the mystery that is to be."[21] A detailed account of this phrase cannot be provided here. Most likely, the authors seek to present their Sapiential instruction as *addenda* to the Mosaic Torah, which had not been revealed at Mount Sinai, but were meant for later revelation to the Israelites.[22] As part of this, 4QInstruction seeks to provide a deeper level of understanding than one finds in "traditional" wisdom. As Goff points out, "Acquiring wisdom entails learning the divine plan that orchestrates reality. By combining teachings on various topics with the mystery that is to be, 4QInstruction urges the addressee to comprehend the deterministic framework of creation in a way that shapes his conduct. Unlike traditional wisdom, in 4QInstruction, the divine plan is a hidden truth."[23]

What necessitates a new understanding of reality is that Sapiential instruction is not only limited to the here and now, but extends to an eschatological future. In other words, the wisdom that 4QInstruction provides is intended to ensure that a person will persevere in the face of God's eschatological judgment, which will bring death to some, but immortality to those who live their lives in accordance with the particular instructions that documents such as 4QInstruction provide. The main concern that echoes throughout 4QInstruction is to become a "spiritual people,"[24] as opposed to a merely fleshly existence that will not continue beyond the death of the physical body. Every ethical, cultural, and religious activity had to be oriented towards that goal, whereas deviating from it was to give in to a type of existence that was inevitably doomed. It is in this context that 4QInstruction entertains the idea that human beings have immortal souls that extend their existence beyond their physical lifetime. Thus a person's primary

---

[21] F. G. Martínez and E. J. C. Tigchelaar, *The Dead Sea Scrolls*, vol. II, Leiden: E.J. Brill and Grand Rapids: Eerdmans, 1998, 851, 855, translate "the mystery of existence."

[22] As B. M. Levinson has pointed out, later scribes did not feel at liberty to change, add to, or alter the Sinaitic Torah as God's word to Moses (Levinson, *Deuteronomy and the Hermeneutics of Legal Innovation*, Oxford University Press, 1997, 24–50). However, one of the "strategies to avoid a potential conflict" in that regard was to consider the revelatory process that started at Sinai as yet incomplete. God himself would reveal more of the "full" Torah as Israel was in need of it in any given historical situation.

[23] 4Q418 10, 13; see M. Goff, *The Worldly and the Heavenly Wisdom of 4QInstruction*, Leiden/Boston: E.J. Brill, 2003, 79.

[24] Ibid., 214.

concern in life should be the *unscathedness* of the soul. There are several key phrases that underline this concern and, strikingly, they all indicate that the striving for "money" is a way of damaging one's soul and, as such, of missing eternal life: "Do not sell your soul for money!"[25] and "Do not exchange for any money your holy spirit, for no price is adequate!"[26]

4QInstruction does not seem to draw a clear distinction between "soul" (*nefesh*) and "spirit" (*ruach*), which is consistent with many of the wisdom texts from the late- and post-biblical periods.[27] However, what one finds in only very few texts is the idea that humans not only possess a spirit that God sends to enliven physical bodies, but that they have His own "holy" spirit in them.[28] It seems that 4QInstruction understands the immortal soul as a manifestation of God's holy spirit in a human being. This seems significant, because the idea of an individual soul as the manifestation of God's spirit implies the notion that one can lose this spirit, that it can be withdrawn if one acts counter to its presence in one's own life. All these dangers echo in 4QInstruction. There is a very real sense that one's deeds in life, even seemingly trivial ones, can tarnish, damage, or even destroy one's spirit/soul. For example, 4QInstruction provides instruction about the safekeeping of a stranger's money:

Also, do not receive money from any man unknown to you, lest he add to your poverty. But if he places it at your disposal until death, deposit it, and do not corrupt your soul with it. Then you may lie down with the truth, and when you die your memory will blossom forever, and your succession will inherit joy.[29]

One can assume that instructions like these respond to real-life scenarios, in this case, of someone who agreed to safeguard somebody

---

[25] 4Q417 1/II, 21 (translations are taken from Martínez and Tigchelaar, *The Dead Sea Scrolls*).

[26] 4Q416 2/II, 6.

[27] For the increasing significance of "spirit" as an anthropological notion, see A. Schüle, "The Divine-Human Marriages (Genesis 6:1–4) and the Greek Framing of the Primeval History," *THZ* 65 (2009): 120–1; Schüle, "Der Prolog der Hebräischen Bibel: Der literar- und theologiegeschichtliche Diskurs der Urgeschichte," *Arbeiten zur Theologie des alten und Neuen Testaments*, Zurich: TVZ, 2006, 295–8.

[28] The only two texts in the Hebrew Bible that mention that humans are endowed with God's "holy spirit" are Ps. 51:1 and Isa. 63:11.

[29] 4Q416 2/II, 5–8.

else's money, which he then lost through bad investments or due to some other reason. Although the text does not go into any details, it is conceivable that some of the "poor" in 4QInstruction succumbed to the temptation of speculating with other people's money, which pushed them into even deeper poverty than before. Reading through 4QInstruction, one cannot avoid the impression that the addressees of the text had some bad experience with money, perhaps because some of them sought to work their way up the social hierarchy in their own lifetime – one of the promises of a monetized society in contrast to economic systems in which change of social status was practically impossible to accomplish.

It is important to understand that 4QInstruction does not limit its eschatological vision to an *apocalyptic* scenario in which the faithful will be rewarded and sinners punished.[30] What makes this text theologically intriguing is the fact that it develops an eschatology that is based on *sapiential* reflection, which is quite unusual, given the almost complete absence of eschatological motifs from the Sapiential literature of the Hebrew Bible. Wisdom, in 4QInstruction's view, is not limited to empirical knowledge, commonsensical savvyness, etc.[31] but includes an awareness that, through the divine spirit that resides in them, human beings already – in the here and now – participate in the reality of the eschaton. If one wants to use theological jargon, 4QInstruction has a "realized eschatology," complementing the "future eschatology" that it shares with apocalyptic traditions, making the divine spirit/the immortal soul the crucial link between this life and the one to come. As a consequence, seeking to accumulate wealth and improve one's social status appears as a way of missing the mark, and it is in this context that 4QInstruction exhorts its audience not to succumb to the temptation of what money can offer:

Do not in your affairs demean your spirit; do not for any money exchange your holy spirit, for no price is adequate. . . . Do not reach for what is beyond

---

[30] One needs to say, however, that the idea of a Last Judgment at the end of history is very much alive in 4QInstruction and other literature associated with the Qumran community (especially in the "War Scroll" 1QM); cf. 4Q418 1,4–6; 4Q418 19,2–15.

[31] See J. E. Burns, "Practical Wisdom in 4QInstruction," in *DSD* 11 (2004): 12–42; D. J. Harrington, "Wisdom at Qumran," in E. Ulrich and J. VanderKam (eds.), *The Community of the Renewed Covenant: The Notre Dame Symposium on the Dead Sea Scrolls*, University of Notre Dame Press, 1994, 137–52.

the range of your power, lest you stumble, and your disgrace becomes exceedingly great. Do not sell your soul for money. It is better that you are a servant in the spirit, and that you serve your overseers for nothing. And for money, do not sell your glory, and do not mortgage your inheritance, lest you bequeath your body.[32]

The language here clearly suggests that the addressees of the text were engaged in financial activities, involving loans, mortgages, etc., which the authors of the text view as risking one's true inheritance in heaven. The appeal of money to their audience also explains why the authors employ economic language to depict the promise of a God-fearing life:

If you are poor, do not long for anything but your inheritance, and do not get consumed by it, lest you displace your boundary. And if he [God] restores you in glory, walk in it, and investigate its origins through the mystery of existence. Then you will know his inheritance, and walk in justice, for God will lighten his ... on all your paths. Give honor to those who glorify you, and praise his name continuously. For from poverty he lifted your head, and seated you among nobles. And over an inheritance of glory he has given you dominion.[33]

The key phrase in this passage is the "inheritance of glory" as that which will outshine the deceitful allure of money. It needs to be added that 4QInstruction does not at all glorify poverty; in this respect it is very much in line with the older wisdom of Proverbs, where it is made clear that there is nothing desirable about poverty.[34] But if "poverty," to whatever extent and in whatever form, happens to be one's lot in life, then it is crucial to remain within one's "boundaries," because someone poor is no less entitled to the "inheritance of glory" than someone rich.

If one were to look at 4QInstruction now from the perspective of the history of early Judaism, a few conclusions can be drawn. Whereas the idea of the spirit of God as the life force in human beings or even in all living creatures (see Ps. 104:29) occurs in several late-biblical texts, this spirit never assumes an eschatological role. There is no expectation that God's spirit provides life beyond physical death. This, however, is the case in 4QInstruction. Living in this spirit as a "spiritual people," even possessing it as one's individual soul, characterizes the purpose and meaning of human existence in this life and the next. As in other texts

---

[32] 4Q417 2/I, 8–23.   [33] 4Q416 2/III, 8–12.
[34] Cf. Adams, *Poverty and "Otherness."*

from the Dead Sea, "spirit" is a dynamic principle that shapes human lives according to the sovereign will of the creator. It is instructive to place this dynamic view of human existence in the context of an equally dynamic, monetized economy. Money accelerated the pace of the economy in Syria-Palestine and, therefore, had a tremendous impact on the social systems of that area. The boundaries between societal classes had become more permeable than ever before. The new, money-based economy even challenged the family systems, since property was no longer solely defined in terms of commodities that were handed down from one generation to the next.[35] Put more pointedly, for better or worse, money had the power to shape and change the lives and fortunes of individuals, and it seems to have been this potency that the Qumran authors viewed with great suspicion. Thus it seems reasonable to assume that these authors modeled their understanding of the spirit and the individual soul as a counter-proposal to the economic reality of their time. This does not mean that the eschatology that one finds in these texts could or should be reduced to being merely a reaction to an outside world that the Qumranites experienced as threatening. However, it is safe to say that money was a determining factor in a world in which the idea of an immortal soul as something infinitely precious took shape.

---

[35] Thus it is not surprising that 4QInstruction emphasizes the importance of the family hierarchy between parents and children (4Q418 9,17–10,8), which might have been an issue in situations when children had become economically independent of the family "inheritance" (נתלה).

17 | "Businessmen and merchants will not enter the places of my Father":[1] early Christianity and market mentality

EDMONDO F. LUPIERI

Premise

At the time of the redaction of the New Testament (NT), the relatively newly constituted Roman Empire seems to have brought some sort of political uniformity to the whole Mediterranean world. This phenomenon must have had some kind of financial repercussions due to a more centralized administration and a relatively larger diffusion of a standardized monetary system. Can we understand if this had any impact on the preaching of (the historical) Jesus? Did his early followers have the memory of any teaching of his regarding money, its possession or its use? And, in the times and areas they were living in, did they develop any reflection on these subjects, which can testify to the new economic situation?

Introduction

The first century CE was a period of consolidation of the Roman Empire in the East. After the collapse of the two kingdoms of Syria and Egypt, the shift in the political panorama was dramatic. While the Empire of Persia still extended its influence up to the borders of India, all the rest of the "inheritance" of Alexander the Great had been swallowed by Rome.

In the Middle East the political and administrative situation was very diversified. We find the descendants of Herod the Great, a plethora of other kinglets (who were more or less willingly vassals to the Romans), and/or Roman functionaries who were all in charge of the administration of the territory. They were often involved in complicated relationships with extraneous political bodies, such as neighboring principalities and kingdoms that were always ready to change

---

[1] Gos. Thom. 64 (NHC II, 2; 44:34f.).

allegiance, or semi-independent cities that were usually under the governance of a political and economic oligarchy.

Each political entity was able to mint its own coins according to local traditions. Overarching the whole system, however, was the Roman coinage:[2] through sets of exchange rates based on the intrinsic value (weight and alloy) of each coin, all the local coinages were connected to this system.[3] It was the furthest the Romans could go to impose a standardized monetization system in the first century.[4]

We may suppose that the very existence and relative abundance of Roman coins,[5] the value of which was universally recognized, facilitated commercial and financial transactions in all regions of the empire and beyond its official borders. This must have had a stabilizing effect on the markets, even if it did not impede fluctuations of prices, especially on the occasions of extraordinary events such as droughts, wars,

[2] Inside the Roman Empire there were 500–600 mints. Only the most important centers were allowed to mint silver coins (in the first century, golden ones were usually minted in Rome or in the West, particularly at Lyon; in the East this happened only exceptionally at Pergamum or in other centers), while coins of bronze and other copper alloys could be struck in many cities in every province.

[3] After Augustus and through the first century (with some small changes in the weight of the silver coins, beginning with Nero), the main Roman coins were as follows: the golden *aureus*, corresponding to 25 silver *denarii*; the *denarius* (also called *argýrion* in Greek texts), corresponding to four brass *sestertia*; the *sestertium*, corresponding to four copper *asses* or *assarii* (the old *pondus* or *pound*); and the *as*, corresponding to four copper *quadrantes*. To these were to be added the brass *dipondium* ("two pounds"), corresponding to two *assarii*, and the bronze *semis*, half an *assarius*.

[4] Even after Augustus and his reform, in the Eastern part of the empire two systems basically coexisted: the Greek and the Roman. The Greek system was centered on the silver *drachma*, roughly corresponding to the *denarius*, with its silver multiples (the *didrachma* and the *tetradrachma*, corresponding to 2 and 4 *drachmas*), the golden *stater* (20 silver *drachmas*) and smaller coins: the silver *obolós* (one-sixth of a *drachma*), corresponding to eight bronze *chalkoí* (one *chalkós* corresponding to seven copper *leptá*). According to Mk. 12:42, two *leptá* make one *quadrans*. Local coinages usually corresponded to the Greek system.

[5] It is very difficult to know what level of liquidity there was at any given time. It seems that under Nero a great number of new coins were struck, but, generally speaking, "In currency terms, the Roman world was above all things undermonetised" (R. Duncan-Jones, *Money and Government in the Roman Empire*, Cambridge: 1999, 21; see also esp. 3 and 32; for Nero, see 31, Fig 2.2). "Surface, excavation, and hoard finds in Jerusalem" and in Jewish Palestine have brought out a surprisingly low number of Roman coins minted before the war of 66–70: F. E. Udoh, *To Caesar What Is Caesar's: Tribute, Taxes, and Imperial Administration in Early Roman Palestine (63 B.C.E.–70 C.E.)*, Brown Judaic Studies, 343, Providence: 2005, 233f.

earthquakes, etc. Further, it was in the interest of the Roman administration to have an equally distributed and possibly florid market economy in all the provinces.[6]

Besides the availability of money, a flourishing market economy in the first century was also favored by the Roman road system and, after the war against the so-called "pirates," by the security of the sea: the Mediterranean had become the *mare nostrum*.[7] All this allowed quick fortunes to be built and destroyed, especially those based on shipments of durable goods.[8] The scenario for such sudden wealth was no longer that of the traditional agricultural society, with wealth slowly growing in the hands of the landowners, but that of the cities, some of which had been newly founded or rebuilt, often planned to serve as harbors or commercial centers.

This was the environment in which Paul and his fellow missionaries went on to preach in the squares and in the markets, both in Jewish and Greek areas.[9] The world of the cities soon became the world of the followers of Jesus, but it had not been the world of Jesus. As far as we can see from our sources, Jesus avoided the cities; and, in the NT as a whole, not a single scene depicts him in a market.[10]

---

[6] The increasing importance of the equestrian class in the public administration since the end of the Republic should be noted. The knights were more likely to support mercantile activity – to make money and attain power, directly or through their friends – than the senatorial class, traditionally tied to landed property (notoriously, Roman senators were not even allowed to own ships).

[7] We should not imagine, though, a homogeneous monetized market economy. Barter, and in general, pre- or non-monetary ways of exchange and lending were diffused, as noticed by Strabo (see R. Duncan-Jones, *Structure and Scale in the Roman Economy*, Cambridge: 1990, esp. Ch. 2 ("Trade, Taxes and Money"), 30–47.

[8] As an example of first-century cargo, see the impressive list of (imported) goods enjoyed by "the city" in Rev. 18:12f. Notoriously, the figure of Trimalchio, in Petronius' novel, *Satyricon*, is a literary example of the sudden changes in one man's destiny, due to a change of fortune in maritime commerce.

[9] Not by chance was it in Antioch that for the first time some followers of Jesus, probably converted from paganism, were called "Christians": Acts 11:26.

[10] This attitude may be connected with a traditionally Jewish conservative worldview, similar to the one voiced by Josephus in a famous passage of *Contra Apionem* I, 60: "Well, ours is not a maritime country; neither commerce nor the intercourse which it promotes with the outside world has any attraction for us. Our cities are built inland, remote from the sea; and we devote ourselves to the cultivation of the productive country with which we are blessed. Above all we pride ourselves on the education of our children, and regard as the most essential task in life the observance of our laws and of the pious practices, based thereupon,

Therefore we must suppose a socio-cultural shift from the years and
the world of Jesus to those of the authors of the NT and of the earliest
Christian "apocryphal" works. This renders a comprehensive picture of
the sociological dimension of early Christian groups extremely complex
and multifaceted,[11] even if we get the general impression that there was
some sort of critical reaction to a widespread "market mentality," some
kind of mistrust towards "businessmen and merchants," or even traces
of some possible discomfort with the very use of "money." The various
assertions on these subjects that we find in the NT and in other
"Christian" texts of that period, though, if framed in their contexts,
show their true nature as religious and theological reflections. They aim
more at explaining the history of salvation than at voicing socio-
economic criticism.

Criticism of wealth

Criticism of wealth is largely attested in religious and philosophical
literature of the time and is by no means exclusively Jewish or
"Christian." To remain in our cultural framework, though, we can
easily find passages in the Book of the Similitudes (1 En. 37–71)
which parallels the Infancy Gospel of Luke in its perspective on the
eschatological destiny of the rich and powerful.[12] Also at Qumran,

which we have inherited" (trans. H. St. John Thackeray). See B.-Z. Rosenfeld
and J. Menirav, *Markets and Marketing in Roman Palestine* (Supplements to *JSJ*,
99), Leiden-Boston: 2005. The times Jesus is reported to have mentioned a
"market house" (John 2:16) or a private "business" (Matt. 22:5; a shop?), the
context is very critical (see the discussion below on the "Cleansing of the
Temple"). For Jesus' avoidance of cities, see A. Destro and M. Pesce, *Encounters
with Jesus: The Man in his Place and Time*, Minneapolis: 2011 (orig. pub. as:
L'uomo Gesù: Giorni, luoghi, incontri di una vita, Milan: 2008).

[11] See E. and W. Stegemann, *The Jesus Movement: A Social History of Its First
Century*, Minneapolis: 1999 (orig. pub. as: *Urchristliche Sozialgeschichte: Die
Anfänge im Judentum und die Christengemeinden in der mediterranen Welt*,
Stuttgart: 1995).

[12] As an example, cf. 1 En. 38:4f. and Luke 1:51ff. The presence of such criticism in
the Apocalyptic literature (the Book of the Similitudes was part of the Enochic
"Pentateuch," but was not found in Qumran and is dated to the first century CE)
should not be surprising, since, maybe for the first time in Jewish literature,
Apocalyptic texts do not seem to proceed from politically and/or economically
leading sectors of the Jewish population. It is very possible that the earliest among
those texts are also the cultural result of impoverishment and deprivation
experienced in post-exilic times by part of the (former) Jewish intelligentsia. The
exclusion of some of the acculturated people from power and wealth continued

"wealth" is one of the "three nets" used by Belial (the Devil) to catch Israel and cause its ruin (CD IV:15–19). Similarly, the "risk" caused by wealth is present in almost every level of the NT. The "lure of riches" (Mark 4:19; Matt. 13:22) or simply the "riches" (Luke 8:14) are able to "choke" the word of God or those who have accepted it. That the problem is felt inside the communities of believers is clear from many passages of James (1:9–11; 2:2–7). The epistle strongly criticizes the iniquity which is supposed to be the basis for the acquisition of wealth, and at a certain point seems to criticize some mercantile activity in some "city" far away.[13] We can also read in a similar way a quite famous passage of Revelation, rebuffing the believers in Laodicea (3:17).

In the Jewish pre- or non-Christian world, there were also more-or-less realistic descriptions of ideal communities, like that of the Essenes, which fascinated both pagan and Jewish writers with their absence of money,[14] community of goods,[15] and total abstention from any form of commercial trade, including navigation.[16] In the NT literature, the most striking similarities can be found in Acts' idealized description of the community in Jerusalem.[17]

We must notice, however, a basic ambiguity in the judgment of wealth and in the use of terminology related to it. Even if there seems to be an incompatibility between the dimension of God and that of wealth (Luke 16:13 and Matt. 6:24) and if rich people face difficulties in entering the kingdom announced by Jesus (Luke 6:24; 16:19; 18:23; Matt. 19:23f.), nevertheless some of them can convert (Zacchaeus in Luke 19:2) and also become some sort of disciple (Joseph of Arimathea in Matt. 27:57). Furthermore, in the language of the parables, God can be not only a king, landlord, and slave-owner, but even a "rich man" (see esp. Luke 16:1–13, with the almost positive evaluation of "mammon" at v. 9, and 19:11–27). And, curiously enough, in Paul

---

under the Hasmoneans and under the Romans, while the divisions in the priestly class culminated in a self-centered and extortive policy of tithing by the high priests that damaged the other priests and was bitterly criticized by Josephus (*Ant. Jud.* XX, 180–207).

[13] See esp. 5:1–6 and 4:13f. (The rich have killed the just and stolen "the hire of the laborers," and are blind in programming their future, without taking into consideration their finitude.) At the same time we already find in these passages (and others, such as 1 Tim. 6:9, 17–19) a nucleus of catechesis for the rich, which will be developed in the following centuries.

[14] Pliny the Elder, *Nat. Hist.* V, 15,73.   [15] Josephus, *Bell.* II, 127.

[16] Philo, *Quod omnis probus* 78.   [17] Acts 2:44f.; 4:32–34f., 37.

the words connected with "wealth" (πλοῦτος and its homoradicals) are always and only used by him to describe the positive values of faith, virtue, religion, etc. In other words, the only "rich" people are the faithful.

Luke, though, in a couple of scenes which he uses to reconstruct the life of the early Church, takes his meditation a step further. In the episode involving Ananias and his wife Sapphira (Acts 5:1–11), and especially in that dedicated to Simon, the sorcerer of Samaria (Acts 8:9–24), the point is not simply or only a negative judgment on the use of money and wealth, but involves a reflection on their wrong use in things related to God. This is an aspect characteristically present in much of Luke/Acts, but may also introduce us to a more general "Christian" idea of the incompatibility between a human commercial attitude – what I would call a "market mentality" – and salvation brought by God. Not the use of money *per se* seems to be criticized, but a series of activities (especially spiritual or religious) in which money is involved.

Market mentality

The negative appreciation of such "market mentality" appears in some cases as an appreciation of non- or pre-monetary situations. Luke 6:30 seems to exclude the use of money in the lending that is praised by Jesus,[18] while the lending activity by the others is actually practiced by "sinners," even when they charge no interest (and therefore it seems to be fully monetized: Luke 6:34f.).[19] Explicit avoidance of money is recommended in the Synoptics, as a teaching of Jesus for his disciples involved in missionary activity. Interestingly, Mark 6:8 prohibits the taking of any *chalkón* ("bronze"; probably any coin in copper alloy) in the "belt" (which is where one kept one's money), while Luke 9:3

---

[18] The parallel passage in Matt. 5:42 may involve the use of money.

[19] The lending without interest suggests that those "sinners" are Jews lending to other Jews and avoiding the risk of usury. Nevertheless, we must remember that the big "credit crunch" of the year 33 CE was finally solved when Tiberius lent 100 million sesterces for three years at zero interest, allowing the recovery of the credit market in Rome. I doubt, however (and apart from the time difficulty), that any echo of the financial crisis in Rome could have reached the agricultural and pastoral world of the historical Jesus in the kingdom of Antipas or in the province of Judaea.

prohibits any *argýrion* (properly any silver coin, be it a *denarius* or not). Matthew 10:9 goes on to specify: no gold, no silver, no bronze are allowed. Matthew seems willing to clarify that no money whatsoever should be in the possession of the missionary, who should abandon himself[20] completely to the providence of God and be like the "lilies of the field" (6:28; no parallel in the other gospels).[21]

Selling and buying, though, and some uses of money are not only allowed, but suggested in some cases. Unique among the gospels, it is Matthew again that shows in a relatively clear way a double level of positive meaning of selling and buying. The "selling" is that which involves the selling of all personal belongings. The first meaning is a spiritual/parabolic one: when one identifies the "kingdom," in the form of a "treasure buried in a field" or of a "pearl of great price," one is expected to sell everything and buy that field or that pearl (Matt. 13:44–46: a passage with no parallel in the other gospels). Here we find the idea and the wording of a financial transaction (selling and buying) applied to a spiritual reality.[22] More concretely, there is another set of passages where Jesus is presented as inviting his followers in general, or some person in particular, to "go, sell all [their] belongings" (Matt. 19:21; Mark 10:21; Luke 18:22[23] and Luke 12:33) and give everything to the poor, in order to obtain treasure in heaven. This is probably the ownership of the kingdom or the "inheritance" (Mark 10:17; Luke 18:18).[24] In these cases, property is sold and *money* (though not explicitly mentioned) is distributed to the

---

[20] I say "himself," since Matthew doesn't seem to envision a strong presence of women with such functions in his communities.

[21] In the final part of this chapter, I will come back to the peculiar attitude towards money, as shown in some passages by Matthew.

[22] In Matthew, both "treasure" and "pearls" (see 7:6; only Matt.) can and should signify a spiritual reality. See esp. 12:35 (Luke 6:44f. specifies "treasure of the heart") or 13:52 (a treasure with "new and old things"; only Matt.) or 6:19–21 (the two treasures, "on earth" and "in heaven"; Luke 12:33f. mentions only a treasure in heaven). See also further, n. 95 below.

[23] Luke is the one who stresses the necessity to sell "all" one's belongings.

[24] There are indications that there were discussions in the communities of the early followers of Jesus about exactly the point of selling everything for the poor or for the communities: 1 Cor. 13:3 considers it an extreme case, but stresses that the gesture is not sufficient; on the other side, the story of Zacchaeus, as told by Luke 19:2–10, shows that a donation in good faith of half of one's belongings (together with the restitution of the illegally owned) is sufficient for the owner to be considered again a "son of Abraham" (therefore, to enter into the inheritance). In Acts, the case of Barnabas who sold "a field he owned" (Acts

poor. Possibly because of practical reasons,[25] then, the property should not be donated directly to the poor, but the money obtained by selling it should be distributed.

In order to donate, you should always be allowed to sell what you have, especially if it is precious. Nevertheless, the scene of the anointing in Bethany seems to go further. While it is true that the vase of alabaster could have been "sold" for a good price[26] and the money could have been distributed to the poor, the need to anoint the body of Jesus before his burial creates an exception.

If this is the case for "selling," "buying" also has some apparently contrasting functions. It is certainly and always was permissible to "buy" spiritual treasures, but, generally speaking, what can we do with the money we (already) own? Immediately before the so-called "Feeding of the Five Thousand," in all four gospels there is a rhetorical opposition between going to "buy" enough food and simply distributing what there is to everybody. Apart from the Eucharistic symbology involved in the scene, it is quite clear that only through the sharing (*condivisio*) of what is already owned by the followers of Jesus (and obviously thanks also to the presence of Jesus), can the mercy of God feed the thousands and allow commensality.[27]

The underlying teaching seems to be that you can either sell your worldly property to buy spiritual treasures for yourself, by donating the

4:37: was it the only field he owned?) is contrasted with that of Ananias and Sapphira, who sell some "property" (Acts 5:1–11). And it is still Luke (8:1–3) who stresses that the women who followed Jesus from Galilee helped him and his disciples "out of their belongings."

[25] *A house or a piece of land cannot be divided to help all people in need.*

[26] Matt. 26:9, Mark 14:5, and John 12:5 offer the indicative figure of 300 *denarii*.

[27] In the Synoptics, the disciples think that "the crowds" should "buy" food for themselves (Matt. 14:15; Mark 6:36. Luke 9:12 does not use the verb "to buy," but "to find [food]"); in John 6:5f. from the beginning the responsibility to "buy" food for the masses falls on the disciples (who probably represent the community and possibly its leaders), who need – but don't have – at least 200 *denarii* (thus Mark 6:37 and John 6:7). The scene is also very similar in the "Second Multiplication of Loaves and Fishes," even if the verb "to buy" does not appear in that context (see Matt. 15:33 and Mark 8:4). From a practical point of view, 5 loaves and 2 fish, or 7 loaves and some fish, can be directly divided and distributed: there is no need for "selling" an indivisible property. For the connection between commensality and kingdom, see Destro and Pesce, *Encounters with Jesus*, and, for the possible specific meaning of meals in Johannine communities, E. Kobel, *Dining with John: Communal Meals and Identity Formation in the Gospel of John and its Historical and Cultural Context*, Leiden: 2011.

money you get from the sale, or, more usually, you need to be able to share (with the poor, with the community, with everyone) whatever you already own: if you (con)divide what you have, independently from its amount, you will multiply it.

Real purchase and true possession

At this point in our reasoning, two further steps are expected. The first is to understand how we enter into the possession of something. How do we own what is ours? The answer seems to be that one only really owns what one receives from God. God, however, donates everything, including salvation. He does not "sell" anything.

The second step, therefore, is to understand that we are supposed to do the same since, ultimately, we do not give away what is our inherent possession, but what was donated to us by God. This is explained in many different contexts in early "Christian" literature, from Paul to John to Revelation,[28] or in passages like Matthew 10:8: "Freely you have received, freely you give."

The model is Jesus Christ. According to Paul, Jesus is the one who was able to "buy." His buying "at a great price" was the buying of the faithful, at the price of his own blood (see esp. 1 Cor. 6:20 and 7:23). Therefore, the transaction accomplished by Jesus was his free gift (Gal. 2:21) of himself on the cross. Through such acquisition, a faithful person now "belongs" to him, he or she is his "slave," but this makes him or her a "free person." Not only this, but whatever their ethnic/religious origin, thanks to the sacrifice of Jesus, the believers are now part of "the seed of Abraham" and therefore are entitled to the inheritance and can be saved (see esp. Gal. 3:29 and also 3:8 and 13f.). The other Jews do not believe that the non-Jews can be saved immediately, but think that the Gentiles must undergo proselytism and its rites and the acceptance of circumcision and the Torah. They ignore or don't understand the novelty brought by Jesus, the Anointed of God: therefore, they try to administer the salvation, which God had put in their hands, in the old, traditional, wrong way, based on ethnicity (see esp. Rom. 2:17–24 and 11:13–24). The

---

[28] See e.g., 1 Cor. 4:7; 2 Cor. 11:7; John 4:13f. or 7:47f.; Rev. 21:6 or 22:17. Please note in many of the passages quoted in our discussion the theological use of the adverb "freely" (δωρεάν).

key question for Paul seems to be that of who is the instrument of salvation for the non-Jews. This appears quite clearly also in the canonical gospels and elsewhere:[29] the other Jews sell salvation in the wrong way. Particularly, there are numerous passages in Revelation that, though apparently oriented towards the criticism of the surrounding social world, refer to a religious polemic against the other Jews. I will analyze two contexts: the dirge of the merchants over the fall of the "great city,"[30] and the reflection on the relationship between the markets and the Beast.

The dirge of the merchants is pronounced by "the kings of the earth," the "merchants of the earth," the helmsmen, the seamen and all those who "practice trade by sea" (Rev. 18:9–17), therefore involving "earth" and "sea," while "heaven" is invited to "rejoice."[31] The "kings" who lament the fall of the city-woman are among those with whom she used to prostitute herself (17:2; 18:3) and are afraid "of her torment."[32]

---

[29] See Gos. Thom. 102 and cf. 39, where the Pharisees are depicted like dogs "sleeping in the manger of oxen." They don't eat and do not allow others to eat. Under the cover of the Pharisees, the text as it is now refers to the authorities of the "Great Church." It is not impossible, however, that the probably proverbial expression derives from some ancient tradition, rooted in the first generations of followers of Jesus, who struggled with pharisaic proselytism (notice also the possibly ironic choice of potentially impure animals, like dogs, about which see Matt. 7:6; Mark 7:27/Matt. 15:26; 2 Pt. 2:22, and Rev. 22:15 with Phil. 3:2).

[30] I belong to a minority of scholars who believe that "the city, the great one, which spiritually is called Sodom and Egypt, where also their Lord was crucified" (Rev. 11:8) remains the same throughout the whole book and can only be Jerusalem (or, in any case, a Jewish reality, and not Rome). See E. Corsini, *The Apocalypse: The Perennial Revelation of Jesus Christ*, Wilmington: 1983; A. J. Beagley, *The "Sitz im Leben" of the Apocalypse: With Particular Reference to the Role of the Church's Enemies* (BZNW, 50), Berlin, New York: 1987; E. Corsini, *Apocalisse di Gesù Cristo secondo Giovanni*, Turin: 2002; E. Lupieri, *A Commentary on the Apocalypse of John*, Grand Rapids: 2006.

[31] There, opposed to kings, merchants and sailors, we find "the holy ones (saints and/or angels) and the apostles and the prophets" (18:20). This corresponds to the usual cosmological view of Revelation, at least since 12:12, where, thanks to the fall of Satan, the "heavens" can rejoice, while "woe" reaches "the earth and the sea."

[32] Rev. 18:10; therefore they cannot be the same "kings," who are the "ten horns" of the Beast, in charge of the destruction of the city/prostitute (17:12) and who were also expected to do battle against the Lamb and be defeated (17:14). There the kingdom of Evil appears to be divided, with some of its components destroying others. This is typical of apocalyptic context, where often the felons

John's explanation of the deeper meaning of the scene is probably offered at 18:14: "And your seasonal fruit, your soul's desire, has departed from you, and all the sumptuous things and the splendid things are lost for you, and they will never find them again."[33] What is the "fruit" which was supposed to be the "seasonal produce of the desire" of the city? If the city is Jerusalem, my hypothesis is that this is the whole of the Jewish religion, the cultic dimensions of which are "all the sumptuous things and the splendid things," which are going to be lost. The loss has two levels: the historical one, with the destruction of Jerusalem in the year 70 CE, and the spiritual one. The "seasonal fruit" was the only produce the city had to give in exchange for the goods of the cargo.

I am inclined to interpret the passage as an allegory in the following way: the city in her prostitution gave away her seasonal produce, that religion of salvation she had received as a present from God and which was actually the only real instrument of cosmic salvation. But she did not give it away freely. Instead, she did it to receive all the goods of the earth, including "souls of men" (this should again be a violent criticism of Jewish proselytism). Instead of donating her seasonal fruit, like the tree in the eschatological Jerusalem (22:2), she exchanged it as at a market, and therefore she is now doomed, like the fig tree of Mark 11:13 (and Matt. 21:18), unable to bring fruit (in season or out of season).[34] And there is no possibility for the historical, earthly city to return to her former status.

destroy each other: e.g. 1 En. 100:2. It can also be considered a sign of the near end: Mark 3:24ff. (cf. Matt. 12:25f. and Luke 11:17f.).

[33] In the form of an apostrophe to the city (the speaking subject of which should be the same Voice from heaven of 18:4 and possibly 18:20), this is inserted between the long list of the cargo, remembered by the "merchants of the earth" (18:12f.), and the shorter one, spoken by the same merchants (18:16). Both lists are very carefully crafted by John, and are full of biblical echoes to the garments of the high priests, to the decorations of the tent/temple and to the materials brought by Hiram, King of Tyre, to the Jerusalem of Solomon. I find particularly striking the double presence of "fine linen" (βύσσινος), at vv. 12 and 16, which is always used by John to define the whiteness and positivity of the saints (19:8, 14). Similarly, "silk" in the OT appears only once, in Ez. 16:8–14, together with "fine linen," in a list of presents Jerusalem receives from God, but then uses for her prostitution; all this makes good sense if the city/prostitute is the degeneration of Jerusalem, and scarcely if she is Rome. See my discussion while commenting on these passages in Lupieri, *Commentary*.

[34] If the woman-city is said to have produced in the past some sort of "*seasonal fruit*," this may signify that she is compared, at least in the mind of the author, to a

These ideas are repeated several times in the book, but possibly the strongest passage is that depicting the activity of "the beast coming up out of the land" (13:11), the one who organizes the cult in favor of "the beast coming up from the sea." In the interpretation I accept, the beast coming from the sea is the pagan power[35] and the one "coming from the land" is the corrupted religious power of Israel. This second beast "was granted [ἐδόθη; the usual *passivum divinum*] to provide Spirit to the image of the [first] beast . . .[36] and it causes all, the small and the great . . . that they should give them a brand on their right hand or on their forehead, and that no one can buy or sell except he who has the brand, the name of the beast or the number of its name" (13:15ff.).

In sectarian apocalyptic imagery, what we see depicted here should be the situation of the temple. John's irony transforms the tephillim, supposed to keep the name of God close to the forehead and the hand (Deut. 6:8; Isa. 44:5), into the "brand/mark" of subjugation to the beast.[37] This "mark," then, is the satanic counterpart of the "seal" the "servants" of God bear on their "forehead."[38]

The seal is explained at 14:1, where we see the 144,000, "who had his name and the name of his father written on their foreheads." The presence of "the name" may be a sign of possession, since the army of the Lamb, we learn from the context, was "purchased and taken away from among men, a first offering for God and for the Lamb" (14:4).

---

fruit tree. This is usual for Israel (the vine, the fig tree . . .) and the possible connection with Mark 11:13 is quite striking. We could be dealing here with the traces of an early Christian speculation on the incapability of Israel to bring fruits out of season (see further discussion on the Withered Fig Tree) and on its rapacity in appropriating them when "in season" (Mark 12:2 et seq.; see further n. 53 below).

[35] At the time of John, it is basically the Roman Empire, but John's beast represents all satanic earthly power, since it is the fusion of all the constitutive elements of the four beasts, corresponding to the four empires in human history, as seen by Daniel in Dan. 7:3–7.

[36] This is the sin of idolatry, repetition of the sin of Aaron in the desert. Corrupted Judaism uses the Spirit of God for the religious cause of the heathen and therefore it is identified as the "Pseudo Prophet" (16:13; 19:20; 20:10).

[37] Although the Bible does not explicitly say which should be the hand with the tephillim, the traditional Jewish usage involves the left hand and not the right. I suppose that in Revelation there is a conscious passage from the hand of the side of the hearth to the hand of economical transactions.

[38] 7:2ff.; 9:4. No hand is ever mentioned for them: perhaps, given the fact that they do not access the markets, they don't need hands to be shaken (to make a valid contract).

The human activity of "purchasing," then, and the related one of "selling," do not concern the saints as subjects. Only evil people seem to be interested in buying or selling (13:17) and only imperfect, "lukewarm" believers are invited by John to purchase from him the real "gold, fired by fire," the one capable of making them "rich" (3:16ff.). The faithful, like the "angel of the church in Smyrna," are already "rich," in spite of their (worldly) "poverty" (2:8f.), and there are some ready to "walk . . . in white garments, since they are worthy" (3:4). Therefore, they don't need anything, but are expected to join the Resurrected Lord in his universal power (2:26ff.).

The saints are rich, not because they have purchased anything, but because they have been purchased: "You [the Lamb] were slaughtered and you purchased for God, by your blood, men of every tribe and language and people and nation . . ." (5:9). As we see in the description of the 144,000, the blood of the Lamb is the "money" used for their purchase "away from the earth" and "away from among [the other] men" (14:3f.).

The only righteous purchase, then, is that completed by Jesus Christ the Lamb, who offers salvation to all (including the nations of 5:9), through his blood. In John's perception, the real followers of Jesus do not care for the square of the market, but for the mountain of Golgotha.

The death of Jesus as gratuitous act of ransom

Although the term "ransom" (λύτρον) appears only twice in the NT,[39] and the term "redemption" (ἀπολύτρωσις) only in texts of Pauline tradition,[40] the idea is widely present in all NT "streams."[41] With or without terms related to buying/selling/redeeming, the main Christian interpretation of Jesus' execution by the Romans is that of a freely accepted sacrifice, therefore having a central function in the cosmic salvific history.[42] According to

---

[39] Mark 10:45 = Matt. 20:28, in both passages supporting the idea of "substitution" (Jesus died "instead of").

[40] Rom. 3:24; 8:23; 1 Cor. 1:30; Eph. 1:7, 14; 4:30; Col. 1:14; Heb. 9:15; 11:35 and Luke 21:28 in an apocalyptical context.

[41] See e.g., John 1:29.

[42] It appears to be *the* explanation of Jesus' death offered by Paul, possibly already "received" by him (1 Cor. 11:25), and accepted by Peter, by the surviving apostles and, at a certain early point, by at least one of the brothers, James (possibly after his experience of the Resurrected Lord: 1 Cor. 15:7). It will be absent, though, in many Gnostic Christianities, where the historical death of Jesus

Revelation, the sacrifice of the Lamb, as well as the constitution of the lists with the names of the saved human beings, has taken place "from the establishment of the world" (13:8; 17:8; see Matt. 25:34). God has planned, decided and already accomplished human salvation through his Son in a meta-historical dimension, even "before" that event (the sin of Satan in Rev. 12), the reparation for which, as an extraordinary program of salvation, had to be planned.

Both the intervention of God and the sacrifice of Jesus are gratuitous. Consequently, the extension to all mankind of the salvation offered by God through Christ must also be a gratuitous act of donation and self-donation. This complex of thoughts seems to be a very old *theologoumenon* in the Christian tradition, the scriptural foundations for which are easily identifiable.[43] In NT contexts, though, it appears to be constantly connected to the bias against "the (other) Jews" and their presumed intention to "sell" salvation. Therefore we should probably conclude that the whole reflection was originated among the early groups of followers of Jesus who could explain in such a way both the death of their master and the incredulity of the other Jews.

Having said this, we should attempt to reach some glimpses of the possible preaching of the historical Jesus regarding money, as well as its reflections upon the early life of his followers. Towards this goal, I would like to concentrate our attention on the well-known scene of the so-called "Cleansing of the Temple" and to other gospel passages involving Jesus and the use of money.[44]

Indeed, the "Cleansing of the Temple" was considered such a meaningful incident in the public life of Jesus that all four evangelists decided to reproduce it in their works. On the one hand, this may signify that the historical tradition or memory of the event was so strong that it could

has little or no salvific dimension, as salvation comes through the illumination and knowledge brought by the Celestial Savior (in some Gnostic contexts, the "cross" may still have a salvific function, but only as the necessary moment of the separation of Christ from Jesus; see e.g., Gos. Phil. 72).

[43] Plenty of passages in the canonical Bible and in the Pseudepigrapha present various forms of God's gratuitous intervention to "redeem" individuals and/or his own people. For the Exodus ideology, see Ps. 74 [73]:2 and Exod. 15:13. Accordingly, it is also acceptable to think of a first-century Jewish preacher announcing a new redemption, even without the superimposition of ideas developed by the church of his followers.

[44] It is worth noticing that, with the exclusion of the parables, the gospel passages which put the figure of Jesus in more-or-less direct contact with money also involve the temple of Jerusalem.

not be obliterated, but on the other it proves that the scene, duly adapted, was useful to the narrative of each evangelist. Over the centuries, then, the episode continued to be read and interpreted, receiving different, and even opposing, explanations. Today, some contemporary readers would incline towards a socio-religious understanding of it: Jesus offered religious motivation for Jewish social uneasiness, and this led to his capture and execution. Others believe that the action of Jesus was a prophetic one, a prefiguration of the destruction of the temple (and possibly of the near end of the world), but that unfortunately, it was interpreted as an obviously menacing action (and perhaps it really was such); therefore, it was the wrong thing to do at the wrong time. And others, finally, would completely deny its historicity.[45]

We should first of all, though, try to understand what each evangelist wants to say with his version of the scene and then see what we can still *suppose* Jesus did and/or wanted to communicate with his action. Therefore I will analyze the content of the four versions of the "Cleansing of the Temple," see whether we can still understand something of Jesus' behaviour, and then follow Matthew in his meditation on the spiritual meaning of the use of money, since his reflections on one hand help to contextualize his version of the "Cleansing of the Temple" and, on the other, are most central to our analysis.

The "Cleansing of the Temple" in Mark

Mark[46] places the "Cleansing of the Temple" in the first part of Jesus' last week in Jerusalem.[47] The section of the story which interests us the

---

[45] See discussion in P. Fredricksen, *From Jesus To Christ: The Origins of the New Testament Images of Jesus*, Introduction to the Second Edition, New Haven: 2000, xx–xxiv.

[46] It is usually accepted that the gospel went through a complex redactional history, with a series of editions or re-writing of the text. For the complexity of the problem, see the recent book by Josep Rius-Camps, *El Evangelio de Marcos: etapas de su redactión*, Estella (Navarre): 2008.

[47] The redactional aspects of this fraction of Mark (11:1–[26]) have been widely studied, and there is a consensus on its structure, crafted by the author. According to Mark, this is the first time Jesus enters Jerusalem and the temple. If we should try to reconstruct the chronology of the presence of Jesus in the Temple of Jerusalem basing our reconstruction on the canonical gospels, our task would be practically impossible. Even if both accept the idea of the "Passion Week," for the presence in the temple, Mark uses a "3-day scheme" and Matthew a "2-day

most takes place on the second and third days of that week.[48] Here the evangelist combines three narrative elements: (a) the Cleansing of the Temple, which is sandwiched[49] between (b) the Cursing and the Withering of the Fig Tree, which is then followed by (c) some Teaching of Jesus to his disciples on faith and prayer. Each of these three elements has its own theological and/or ecclesiological meaning, which explains its narrative function.[50]

The Cursing and Withering of the Fig Tree, given the symbolic value of the tree,[51] appears to be a prophecy of the punishment of the unbelieving Israel.[52] The phrase that is very difficult to understand

---

scheme." Luke not only prolongs the presence of Jesus for an unspecified number of days during his last permanence in Jerusalem, but also considers the presence of Jesus in the temple theologically meaningful when he was a newborn and when he was a child (at least once every year, until he was 12). Both Luke and Matthew also testify to an apparently short presence of Jesus during the temptation narrative and John, finally, describes multiple, prolonged periods of Jesus' presence in different times and years. We can only say that Jesus very probably *was* in the temple.

[48] On the first day we find Jesus' "Triumphal Entry" on a colt (it is not clear where Jesus made his entry; apparently not in Jerusalem, nor in the temple, but on the outskirts of the city); then he reaches the temple, "looks around" and, quite awkwardly, goes away, to spend the night in Bethany, "since it was already late" (Mark 11:1–11).

[49] This kind of "sandwiching" is frequent in Mark, and has been studied by scholars. See e.g., G. Theissen, *The Miracle Stories of the Early Christian Tradition*, Edinburgh: 1983 (1st pub. 1972), 180ff.

[50] Each of these three elements also contains different layers of materials and may have had separate origins before the present literary construction. For this section of my work, see E. Lupieri, "Fragments of the Historical Jesus? A Reading of *Mark* 11,11-[26]," *ASE* 28(1) (2011): 289–311. The Markan text we have, at least in its last part (c), went through a "growth process" of accretion of elements, probably deriving from its interaction with Matthew. The manuscript tradition of Mark 11:26 is not very strong, and the verse is usually considered spurious and derived from reworking Matthew, but vv. 24 and 25 are also full of Matthean expressions, often *hapax* here in Mark.

[51] In the OT, the fig tree is often paralleled with the vine (1 Kings 5:5; 1 Macc. 14:12; Mic. 4:4; Zech. 3:10), so that the fig tree can also represent Israel. This is particularly true when destruction (of the tree-Israel-Jerusalem) is involved: Jer. 5:17; cf. Joel 1:12. For the importance of the fig tree in apocalyptical contexts, see Mark 13:28.

[52] Also the uncomfortable idea that Jesus was hungry for figs finds its explanation in Mic. 7:1f., where the prophet complains against Judah that he can find "no early fig that I crave. The faithful are gone from the earth" (or, maybe better, "from the land [of Judah]").

with a different interpretation is verse 13: "It was not the time for figs."[53] If the fig tree is Israel, then Israel should be ready to offer its fruit whenever the visitation of God comes,[54] especially when it is not the right season for fruits.[55] Since Israel was not able to offer its fruits, its function in the history of salvation will be abolished. No one will eat any fruit from it, until the eon.

Since Mark was very probably written after the fall of Jerusalem, this passage should reflect a typically Christian explanation of the event. In this way the whole context is strongly connected with the final part of Mark 12 and the beginning of Mark 13[56] and, through the end of Jerusalem and the temple, to the end of the world in Mark 13. The end of Israel, though, as frightful as it was, was not to be feared by the followers of Jesus. They had to realize that God was simply maintaining his promises and being faithful to his own

---

[53] This sentence has always created problems for Christian exegetes (and not by chance is avoided by Matthew), while on the other hand, has helped anti-Christian critics. Famously, Bertrand Russell considered this passage, together with that on the drowning of the pigs in the Lake of Gennesaret, as examples of irrational behavior and useless cruelty (in *Why I am not a Christian*, originally a lecture held on March 6, 1927, then published in *Why I am not a Christian and Other Essays on Religion and Related Subjects*. Edited with an Appendix on the "Bertrand Russell Case," by P. Edwards, New York: 1957).

[54] In the Christian interpretation, it is Jesus, impersonating Yahweh, or being his emissary, who brings the time of the visitation.

[55] We must note that Jesus does not curse the tree directly, but says that "no one ever will eat" its fruits "until the eon." This creates a strong connection with one of the final scenes in Revelation (22:2), where in the New Jerusalem (in the new eon) the Tree of Life offers its fruits (and leaves) for the salvation of everyone, Jews and non-Jews. In the closer Markan context, the complementary explanation can be found in the parable of the vineyard, where the tenants keep the fruits for themselves, when it is the right season of the year (Mark 12:2).

[56] In the present subdivision in chapters, Mark 12 opens with the parable of the vineyard and the reflection on the "stone rejected by the builders" (12:10), while Mark 13 opens with the prophecy according to which "there will not be one stone left upon another [stone]" (13:2). This means that the whole of the teaching of Jesus during his third day in the temple is framed by strong supersessionist phrases that criticize non-Christian Judaism. This attitude is particularly strong at the end of Mark 12, where Jesus first attacks the scribes, saying that they "devour the houses of the widows" and therefore "will receive a harsher punishment" (12:40), then shows his disciples the case of the "poor widow" who throws "her whole life" in the treasure of the temple (13:44). But the temple is going to be destroyed, and this is probably the punishment (for this reading of the widow's mite, see S. Häkkinen, "Two Coins Too Many: Reflections on the Widow's Offering," *The Fourth R* 20/4 (2007): 9–12), heralding the end of the world as prophesied in Mark 13.

word.[57] As a result, the fall of Jerusalem, understood as the just punishment for the unbelieving Israel, is something the followers of Christ can only pray for.[58] Therefore, the final teaching of Jesus to his disciples (narrative element c) seems to be the most recent redactional layer of the whole passage and it is there to explain the meaning of the Cursing and Withering of the Fig Tree. The end of Jerusalem is no more immediately connected to the end of the world, but becomes a sign of the power of prayer.[59]

If this is true, then the most recent element (teaching of Jesus, (c) above) is added to offer the correct interpretation of the older one (Cursing and Withering of the Fig Tree, (b) above). I suppose that the Cursing and Withering of the Fig Tree in its turn plays the same role as the Cleansing of the Temple ((a) above). In other words, the narrative of Mark guides us to read the Cleansing of the Temple as a menace or, at least, as a prophetic act focusing on the end of the temple and of Jerusalem.

The hypothesis appears further convincing if we analyze the internal structure of the pericope of the Cleansing of the Temple (Mark 11:15–19). This also seems to reflect at least three levels of composition. Verses 15a and 19, which are the beginning and the end of the scene, connect it with the narrative context and say that Jesus went in and out of the temple and the city, undisturbed. This should be the most recent redactional level of the pericope. What lies in between can be divided into two subsections: verses 15b and 16, which describe the activity of Jesus in the temple (the "Cleansing" proper), and verses 17 and 18, which add some teaching (this time public) by Jesus and record the reaction of the authorities.

Verse 17 puts a modified Old Testament (OT) quotation on Jesus' lips. According to the text (cf. Isa. 56:7 and Jer. 7:11) the temple was

---

[57] The phrase "ἔχετε πίστιν θεοῦ" (11:22b) should not mean "Have faith *in* God," but "You have [here an example of the] trustfulness of God": if God withered the tree, it means that he is ready to allow any miracle, if requested.

[58] This should be the meaning of the passage regarding the destiny of *that* "mountain," that Jesus was able to show his disciples. The Zion (or possibly the Mount of Olives?), which used to be holy, like the other fallen angels had been transformed into one of the devilish mountains well known in Enochic traditions (1 En. 21:3), so that it could be "eradicated" by God and "thrown into the abyss/ sea" (Mark 11:23; cf. Rev. 20:3 and esp. 19:21, where "a millstone, a great one," is "thrown into the sea"). OT texts like Ezek. 6 should have been the scriptural basis for such speculations. For the correspondence between angels and mountains, see Lupieri, *A Commentary on the Apocalypse of John*, 270f.

[59] This appears to be a useful idea in a growing church, more and more aware of its independence from the rest of Judaism, but also from its apocalyptical groups.

destined, in the plan of God, to be "called a house of prayer by/for all the Gentiles," but had instead been transformed by the Jewish authorities into a "den of bandits." This explains why the historical function of the temple is over. Judaism was expected to become the instrument of salvation for "all the Gentiles," offering them the way to worship the only true God. But Jewish authorities considered salvation their own property, so that they acted like robbers or bandits (or the wicked tenants of the vineyard), appropriating what was not theirs.

This brings us back to the discussions on the gratuitousness of salvation and on who is able to save the non-Jews. At this point we can also affirm that the "fruit" Judaism was expected to produce was the salvation freely offered to the Gentiles. The impediment brought by the Jewish authorities to the salvation of the Gentiles is the reason for their punishment by God.[60] In this context, then, the OT quotation of verse 17 is there to connect the Cleansing of the Temple to the Cursing and Withering of the Fig Tree. Accordingly, verse 18 increases the criticism: the religious authorities perfectly understand what Jesus is talking about, but, instead of accepting his words and converting, they immediately plan to kill him. If they had a chance, they burned it. The Fig Tree is fruitless and is going to be withered.[61]

Verses 17 and 18 possibly belong to the same redactional activity that was responsible for inserting the Cleansing of the Temple inside the Cursing and Withering of the Fig Tree. This seems to be the case even more for the end of verse 18, which tries to explain why the Jewish authorities (and the temple police) did not immediately arrest Jesus: "They feared him because the whole crowd was *astonished* at his teaching." Can simple *astonishment* explain the fear of even the high priests?[62]

---

[60] The most explicit text on this subject is 1 Thess. 2:15–16: "The Jews ... who have killed the Lord Jesus and the prophets ... prevent us from speaking to the Gentiles that they may be saved, thus constantly filling up the measure of their sins. But the wrath of God has finally begun to come upon them." Independently of the fact that the last words came from Paul or not, this is also the idea Mark has.

[61] At the time of the redaction of the gospels, the destruction of Jerusalem would have been seen by the followers of Jesus as *the* proof that all Jesus had prophesied was on the way to realization, and particularly that the Gentiles were going to be saved by another providential instrument of God, the new religious reality that we now call "Christianity."

[62] Both the other Synoptics, indeed, do keep the decision to kill Jesus immediately after his teaching, but in Matthew this teaching is notoriously virulent (see Matt. 21:45), and in Luke it stretches over a long period of time (Luke 19:47f.).

The other point is that we should ask ourselves if, in the narration, Jesus had done or said anything to deserve to be executed according to Jewish law. The answer comes from verses 15b–16: all Jesus did or said was *prohibiting*. Three categories of activities are prohibited by him: (a) buying and selling (whatever) in the temple; (b) changing money and selling doves in the temple; and (c) carrying vessels through the temple. The third prohibition[63] is the key to understanding the whole scene.

This prohibition is a "prohibition of carrying" and it is not generic (as it were, had Mark said "burdens"), but precise: Jesus does not prohibit carrying money, foods, offerings ... but "vessels."[64] Further, he does not prohibit "carry out" or "carry in," but "carry through." The space is also clear: "through the temple."[65] Finally, the beginning of the verse ("He did not allow any person to carry ...") reproduces exactly the formulaic structure of sentences in those days used in lively

---

[63] Apparently the most difficult to explain, to the point that no other evangelist saved any mention of it.

[64] The word is technical and can be extended to refer to any container. If strictly observed, the prohibition could have created some restriction in the practical execution of some liturgical activities in the temple, but I want to stress that this is only a consequence. Jesus is not prohibiting the cult and its sacrifices, which can continue, but he seems worried about the level of purity of the "vessels." If applied, his rules would have caused some liturgical changes or return to lost habits (as an example, not to have to transport their blood in vessels through the temple, animals should have been slaughtered by the altar and not in the slaughterhouse built by the high priest John (Hyrcanus)). Since it appears in Strack–Billerbeck (H. L. Strack and P. Billerbeck, *Kommentar zum Neuen Testament aus Talmud und Midrasch*, vol. II, *Evangelium nach Markus, Lukas und Johannes und die Apostelgeschichte*, Munich: 1956), M. Ber. 9:5 is often quoted. The *Mishnah* prohibits one to "make of [the Temple Mount] a short by-path" (H. Danby, *The Mishnah*, Oxford: 1964, 10). This doesn't seem to be the case for Jesus, since the prohibition of carrying "vases" has very little to do with a "short by-path." The *Mishnah* prohibits the transit, with or without carrying anything, according to the intention of the passing person; if Jesus had wanted to prohibit it in the case of anyone who wanted to transport objects through the Temple Mount, why should he have prohibited only "vessels" and implicitly allowed all "burdens"?

[65] With most commentators, I suppose that here "temple" means the whole "Temple Mount," for the extension of which, see J. Schwartz and Y. Peleg, "Are the 'Halakhic Temple Mount' and the 'Outer Court' of Josephus One and the Same?" in S. J. D. Cohen and J. J. Schwartz (eds.), *Studies in Josephus and the Varieties of Ancient Judaism: Louis H. Feldman Jubilee Volume* (AGAJU, 67), Leiden: 2007, 207–22.

halakhic discussions on the exact nature and extension of the "sabbatical prohibition of carrying."[66] We find similar or parallel texts in
Nehemiah,[67] at Qumran,[68] in Jubilees,[69] and in the Mishnah.[70]
The objects, the carrying of which is forbidden, and the location of
the prohibition are different,[71] but the halakhic structure of the sentence is the same ("Allow no person to carry . . ."). Mark 11:16 could
be explained as an example of teaching on "sabbatical prohibition of
carrying," based on a quite common halakhic exegesis which interprets the prohibitions of Jeremiah 17 using the wording of Exodus
16.[72] The divergence from the other examples of this halakhic exegesis
is that Jesus' prohibition does not mention Sabbath. This means that
Jesus is "expanding the Law," by applying his interpretation of the

[66] A. P. Jassen, "Tracing the Threads of Jewish Law: The Sabbath Carrying
Prohibition from *Jeremiah* to the Rabbis," *ASE* 28/1 (2011): 253–78. I want to
thank Dr. Jassen for his kindness in supplying unpublished works of his and for
his personal communications on this subject.

[67] See further discussion below (n. 71).

[68] Most important passages: *CD* XI:7–9 (4Q270 frg. 6, col. V:13f. and 4Q271 frg.
5, vol. I:3f.); *4QHalakhah A* (4Q251) frg. 1–2:4f.; *4QMiscellan. Rules* (4Q265)
frg. 6:4f. (subdivision of the text as quoted in Jassen, "Tracing the Threads of
Jewish Law," according to J. Baumgarten et al. (eds.), *Qumran Cave 4, XXV:
Halakhic Texts* (DJD 35), Oxford: 1999).

[69] Jub. 2:29f. (on carrying burdens) and 50:8 (on buying and selling and carrying
burdens). The latter passage specifies that the punishment for any infraction is
death.

[70] M. Shab. 1:1. The Mishnic text is much more developed and the halakhah
detailed, so that the result appears to be far from the earlier texts, although the
basic question is still that of how to interpret the prohibition of bringing
something into and outside a house on the day of Sabbath.

[71] The strictest parallel is to be found in *4QMiscellan. Rules* (4Q265) frg. 6:4f.: "Let
no on[e] ca[rry out] from his tent any vessel or foo[d] on the day of the Sabbath"
(trans. Baumgarten, "Tracing the Threads of Jewish Law," modified). In the same
fragment (7, col. I:8f. according to F. García Martínez and E. Tigchelaar, *The
Dead Sea Scrolls* (Study edn.), Grand Rapids: 1997, I, 548) there is another
prohibition regarding vessels: "And a vessel no one [. . . on the day] of the
Sabbath" (translation modified), although this may refer to the quite common
prohibition of opening a sealed vessel on a Sabbath.

[72] Jer. 17:19–27 (esp. 21–22) is possibly the most detailed classical biblical text on
sabbatical prohibitions, but has the big disadvantage of not being "Mosaic."
Exod. 16:28f. (esp. 29) is the only "Mosaic" passage on sabbatical prohibitions,
but it is short and generic. Further, it doesn't refer to "carrying," but to "going
out." However, it contains the clear sentence "allow no person to . . ." Therefore,
the Jewish reflection on the "sabbatical prohibition of carrying" usually takes the
"Mosaic" phrasing of Exod. 16 to adapt and apply Jer. 17 to the sabbatical life of
the community. See Jassen, "Tracing the Threads of Jewish Law."

"sabbatical prohibitions of carrying" to the life of the temple on *every day of the week*.

This allows us to immediately and better understand the first prohibition of verse 15: Jesus is the new Nehemiah. The Jewish reformer of old threw (foreign) merchants out of Jerusalem on the Sabbath, to impede any mercantile activity (buying and selling) of the "children of Judah" on that day (Neh. 13:15–22).[73] Jesus throws (Jewish) buyers and sellers out of the temple, and his halakhah should be valid in the temple every day of the week.

The final part of verse 15 explains to what extent the prohibition of mercantile activity was supported by Jesus. He "overturned the tables of the money changers and the seats of those who were selling the doves."[74] For foreign pilgrims, the exchange of currency was the

---

[73] This model is usually little taken into consideration by contemporary scholarship, but Nehemiah notoriously introduced draconian measures in fifth-century BCE Jerusalem to purify the priesthood, the temple, and the city. As it is narrated, he not only obliged the Jews to observe a stricter observance of the Sabbath, but threw out of the city "those who resided in her [Jerusalem] and were carrying fish and were selling any kind of merchandise on the Sabbath to the sons of Judah and in Jerusalem" (v. 16). The LXX does not specify who "they" are, but the MT explains that those merchants are "men from Tyre" (thus further proving the historical mercantile connection between Tyre and Jerusalem). Nehemiah then shuts the doors of the city and puts guards on them (v. 19), to avoid any risk, but "the merchants and the sellers of any merchandise spent the night immediately outside Jerusalem, once and twice" (v. 20), and, according to the Greek: "They all spent the night and made their selling outside Jerusalem once and twice." At that point, Nehemiah menaces them and obliges them to go away from the walls of the city and to come back only after the end of the Sabbath (v. 21). Jassen ("Tracing the Threads of Jewish Law") stresses the fact that Nehemiah criticizes not only the selling and buying, but the *carrying into* the city of all kinds of food and merchandise (esp. in vv. 15f.).

[74] The text does not say that Jesus touched the money that was on the tables, nor the people who sat on the chairs. In this same context, John 2:15 relates that Jesus "made a whip out of cords" to "throw out" of the temple people and animals. John uses the word φραγέλλιον (curiously enough, for the flagellation of Christ, John 19:1 does not use the verb φραγελλόω, like Mark 15:15 and Matt. 27:26, but the verb μαστιγόω). Usually a *flagellum*, technically speaking, is not made of cords, but of leather strings. I wonder if this anomalous detail, instead of being a sign of Jesus' wrath, could strengthen the hypothesis that he was avoiding direct contact, and therefore contamination with people and objects who/which might have been considered impure *in the context of the temple*. Outside of the temple, the Jesus we find in the gospels is not usually worried about being contaminated by even highly polluting people or objects, like lepers or blood, or even

necessary prerequisite for any buying or selling of offering for the temple and could in itself be considered an act of buying and selling Tyrian *tetradrachmae.*[75] The selling (and buying) of doves, even if they were not particularly expensive, exemplify the kind of mercantile transaction that was taking place in the temple. Again, Jesus is not criticizing these activities *per se*, since they were both useful, or even essential to the Jewish cultic life, but because they take place inside an area he considered sacred.[76] Even if in Matthew 5:35 Jerusalem is still "the city of the Great King," Jesus is not presented as particularly concerned about its purity.[77] He does not seem to be interested in expanding the purity of the temple to the whole city. What worries him is the risk brought against the temple and its parts (altar, offering, treasure) even by some otherwise licit activity.[78]

human cadavers (see T. Kazen, *Jesus and Purity* Halakhah: *Was Jesus Indifferent to Impurity?* (Coniectanea Biblica, NT Series, 38), Stockholm: 2002). While outside the temple polluting agents are purified by the power of Jesus, in the temple these are "thrown out" by him.

[75] It was the right of any adult male circumcised Jew in a state of purity to bring into the temple his own offerings (living animals and food or money and gold, or even the wood to burn his offerings, if that be the case), as long as they were all in the prescribed state of purity and perfection. Nevertheless, especially for pilgrims coming from a distance, it was easier to buy whatever was needed on the spot. There was therefore the possibility to buy everything needed, the purity and perfection of which was checked and guaranteed by the Levites (the animals, which had to be physically "blameless," usually came from the rearing farms owned by the priestly families – and so did the wood, only twelve kinds of which were allowed to be burned in the temple). To stabilize the prices, the use of money in the temple had been standardized: for the various transactions the silver *stater*, or shekel, from Tyre should have been used. In Greek terms it was a *tetradrachma*, and had probably been chosen because of its good and constant alloy and because of the traditional importance of Tyre as a mercantile and commercial center, the ties of which with Jerusalem were old and solid (actually from the times of King Hiram, who helped Solomon build the temple). It is worth noting that no purity or religious rule was involved in the choice, since the coin bore the image of the god Melkart. According to some scholars, this last detail may have caused the reaction of Jesus. In any case, if the faithful man did not already own Tyrian coins, he could exchange his currency (whatever this was) on the tables of the money changers, who rented some allotted space from the administration of the temple for their activity.

[76] And this is why he throws the people "outside," where we can suppose they could continue with their activities, if not forbidden for different reasons.

[77] Possibly because its end is near, at least according to the gospels: Luke 13:34f.; 19:41–44; Matt. 23:37ff.

[78] Other traces of this can be spotted in other NT passages, notably Matt. 5:23f.; 23:16f. and 18–22. Regarding Jerusalem, there were ample discussions about

The historical Jesus and the Cleansing of the Temple

The earliest redactional layer of the Markan version of the Cleansing of the Temple allows us slowly to unearth the figure of a Jewish teacher of halakhah, very concerned with the purity of the temple. The way Jesus acts and talks in this context is not at all "revolutionary," but could be considered ultra-conservative. He is stricter than the Sadducees and the Pharisees[79] and presents himself as a defender of the temple, not as an attacker. The mercantile attitude which characterizes the religious life of his time could bring impurity inside the temple, and stricter sabbatical rules had to be applied. But why *sabbatical* rules?

I see two possible explanations, which do not exclude each other. The basis is a reflection on the presence of God in the temple.[80] If the presence is in the temple, its space belongs to God, and the time of the temple becomes the time of God. But what is the time of God? The time of God is His day, and His day can only be the Sabbath. Wherever God is, there it is the Sabbath. Therefore, in the space of God the sabbatical rules must be implemented every day.

The second explanation is a further step in a similar way of thinking, just more connected to apocalyptic-eschatological reflections. The presence of God on earth is the beginning of the cosmic Sabbath. The temple, on its sacred mountain, is the point of contact between the two eons. On that sacred spot the space/time of God touches the earth. It is always Sabbath there, and this is or should be the beginning of the eternal Sabbath on earth.

If we can accept that these or similar ideas determined the action of Jesus, then, besides the model offered by Nehemiah, the apocalyptic ending of Zechariah could have offered further scriptural support for his behavior: "On that day... the *vases* in the house of the LORD ... and every vase in Jerusalem and in Judah shall be holy to the LORD of

which rules of purity should apply to the city, which objects could or could not be brought inside the city, and which levels of purity should be kept by people entering it. On the "geography of purity" in Jerusalem and in the temple, see M. Kel. 1:8f. Cf. E. Schürer, *The History of the Jewish People in the Age of Jesus Christ (175 B.C.–A.D. 135)*, eds. G. Vermes et al., vol. II, Edinburgh: 1979, 285, n. 58.

[79] Pharisees' halakhot had not been fully implemented in the temple yet, but they where criticizing the Sadducees on similar subjects.

[80] The Presence of God in the temple, before and after the destruction by the Babylonians, was a very important subject of texts of visions like those of Isa. 6:1–7 and Ezek. 8:1–11:25 MT.

hosts ... on that day there shall no longer be any *merchant* in the house of the LORD of hosts" (Zech. 14:20f.).

Jesus presents himself as a new Nehemiah who realizes the prophecy of Zechariah and openly protects and expands the sanctity of the temple. His behavior is coherent with that of a concerned and observant Jewish teacher of halakhah not deprived of prophetic-apocalyptic ideas.[81] The "crowds" understand it, and the temple police do not intervene. Finally, if this is true, the behavior of Jesus does not reflect any concern regarding the use of money or commercial transactions in everyday life. His concern is the purity of the temple.

The Cleansing of the Temple in Luke

The atmosphere in Luke is different. When Jesus arrives near Jerusalem and gets the "colt," he does not seem to enter the city, and especially not the temple, but to climb the Mount of Olives instead (Luke 19:28–40). Possibly from there he already has the chance to utter a lament over the fall of Jerusalem, which includes the statement about the enemies not leaving "one stone upon another stone" (vv. 41–44). The withering of the fig tree disappears, substituted in a different context[82] by the beautiful parable of the barren fig tree, which the owner (God) would like to eradicate, but is, however, saved by the servant of the landlord.[83]

The scene of the "Cleansing of the Temple" is also reduced to a minimum (Luke 19:45–48). When Jesus enters the temple for the first

---

[81] After his death, his followers may very well have obliterated the purely halakhic explanation and stressed the apocalyptic potentiality of the scene, by connecting it to the fall of Jerusalem and to the expectation of the eon.

[82] Luke 13:6–9.

[83] Jesus himself? The new leaders of the "Christian church"? The Greek says: "the [man] in charge of the vineyard" (the vineyard is traditionally Israel, but here the meaning could encompass anyone, from the whole of humankind to the community of the believers, including Israel in an ethnic sense). This figure obtains a delay so that conversion is still possible. It seems that in Luke the teaching on the destiny of the fig tree switches from the polemical attitude towards Israel to a more general reflection on human sinfulness and repentance. Different from the other gospels, and possibly developing Pauline teaching, Lukan supersessionism is based more on continuity with Israel than on antagonism. Besides that of the fig tree, the disappearing of the "doves" is another example. How could Jesus throw the sellers of the doves out of the temple, since according to Luke 2:24 his own observant parents, when he was born, probably bought a pair of them from those sellers to be sacrificed for him?

time[84] on the first day, he immediately begins to "throw out those who were selling." According to Luke, therefore, only "sellers" are involved in Jesus' action. The possible buyers (the Jewish people?) are exempted from his wrath and no other human category is mentioned (nor are we told what the sellers were selling). Apparently to those sellers Jesus proclaims a contracted form of Isaiah 56:3 and Jeremiah 7:11: "It is written: And my house will be a house of prayer, but you made it into a den of robbers." The allusion to the Gentiles has disappeared; the polemical discussion is now an intra-Jewish one and Jesus' criticism is directed only against the "sellers." His action does not seem to cause any reaction. Luke goes on, saying that Jesus "was teaching during the day in the temple"[85] and that only after such teaching the Jewish authorities, obviously hurt by Jesus' criticism, "were trying to kill him," but were not able to find the way, since "the whole people" were listening to his words.

The Cleansing of the Temple in Matthew

Also according to Matthew 21:12-14, Jesus acts immediately after having entered the temple,[86] but the people who sell and buy seem to be only one category and certainly face the same criticism, since Matthew stresses that Jesus threw out "all" of them together. Tables and chairs suffer the same destiny as in Mark, but there are no "vases" carried through the temple. The OT quotation, as in Luke, does not mention any Gentile, but stresses that the adversaries of Jesus are

---

[84] Just in this context; see above, n. 47.

[85] The length of Jesus' teaching in the temple remains undetermined; cf. 20:1 and 21:37 (here we learn that Jesus did not spend the nights in Bethany, but on the Mount of Olives).

[86] Matthew first has Jesus enter Jerusalem on a female ass and a colt together, so to fulfill a prophecy constructed from Isa. 62:11 and Zech. 9:9 (Matt. 21:1-9). Then, after noticing two opposite feelings, the negative one of "the whole city" (which is "shaken" as it was at the announcement of his birth: 21:10 and 2:3) and the positive one of "the crowds" (who salute him as a "prophet": 21:11), Matthew depicts Jesus entering "the temple." There he "threw out all those who were selling and buying in the temple and overturned the tables of the money-changers and the chairs of those who were selling the doves and told them: 'It is written: "My house will be called a house of prayer, but you are making it into a den of robbers"', and blind and lame people came to him in the temple and he cured them."

transforming the house into a den at that moment, in the present tense of the narration.

Unique to Matthew is the coming to Jesus of the blind and the lame, who are cured by him right "in the temple."[87] The following confrontation with "high priests and scribes" is also described in a way that is peculiar to Matthew. It takes place when they see all "the wondrous things" that Jesus had just done and when they hear "the children scream in the temple and say: 'Hosanna to the son of David'" (v. 15). When the authorities protest to Jesus, his answer, a quotation from Psalm 8:3 according to the LXX, offers the interpretive key to the whole scene: "Out of the mouths of infants and nurslings you have brought forth praise" (v. 16). Then Jesus can leave the temple and spend the night in Bethany (v. 17).

Matthew accepts the Markan point of departure: the temple has become a place for selling and buying, and it is not presently a house of prayer. The Gentiles are not yet in the picture, though,[88] but we are in the eschatological times, at least for Israel. Jesus is the Son of David,[89] and the blind and the lame are healed in the temple, where, finally, the children praise the Lord by recognizing the Davidic descendance of Jesus. In this way, the temple (mentioned in almost every sentence) is offered the possibility of going back to its original function of being the true house of prayer.

Unfortunately, this will not happen, as the withering of the fig tree shows.[90] The following explanation by Jesus doesn't mention the "faithfulness" of God, but the necessity of "faith" in the prayers of

---

[87] They must, therefore, have entered it, although this seems quite improbable for purity reasons (the crippled beggar of Acts 3 does not seem to enter the temple until he is healed, and the same seems to happen with the blind man of John 9).

[88] This is in agreement with Matthew's idea that the person we would call the historical Jesus came basically to save "the lost sheep of the house of Israel" (10:6), while the mission to the Gentiles will be commissioned by the Resurrected Lord to the Eleven in Galilee (28:19).

[89] Matthew shows this from the opening of his narration: 1:1 plus the genealogy of 1:2–17 and the angelic recognition of the legal paternity of Joseph, "Son of David" (1:20).

[90] The morning after, when Jesus and his disciples come back to the temple, he sees a fruitless fig tree. Matthew does not mention that it was not the season for fruits, and therefore, the tree had no possible excuse not to bear fruits. That was *the* moment to show the fruits. The cursing of Jesus is directly against the tree: "May no fruit come from you any more until the eon." And the fig tree dries up on the spot (Matt. 21:18).

the disciples. The withering of the tree, analogous to the throwing of the "mountain" into the "sea," keeps its strong apocalyptic dimension.[91] It must not be feared by the faithful, though. On the contrary, it can be the object of the prayer of any believer who has a true "faith."[92]

To sum up, Jesus is the eschatological figure who offers Israel a last chance to abandon its sinful way, represented by sellers and buyers inside the temple, and to choose the right path of free donation of grace, represented, among other passages, by the healing of the blind and the lame in the temple. This also allows the full and legal reconstitution of the cultic life (in the form of "praise" by children) and the reintroduction of the categories of the excluded Jews, including the children, in the economy of salvation.[93] But the refusal by the Jewish authorities to recognize Jesus will impede Israel from taking advantage of God's offer and will ultimately bring to an end the temple and its function in salvation history. Its destruction will become one of the eschatological signs of the beginning of the end (Matt. 24:2).

The Cleansing of the Temple in John

In John the "Cleansing of the Temple" takes place not at the end of the public activity of Jesus, but at the beginning, when he goes to Jerusalem around "the Passover of the Jews."[94] Jesus finds "in the temple [men] who were selling oxen and sheep and doves and the money-changers who were sitting [there] and he made a whip out of cords and threw them all out of the temple, and the sheep and the oxen and spilled the

---

[91] See Rev. 19:21, mentioned above. It must also be noted that the verbs involved in the descriptions are all passive and may very well be *passiva divina*.

[92] This should be read in parallel with Matt. 24:15–22, where the Matthean Jesus, reinterpreting Mark 13:14–20, says that the prayer of the faithful can "shorten . . . those days" so that the "flight not be on winter or on the Sabbath." I explain this sentence as meaning that the faithful should pray to hasten the coming of the end, so that the great tribulation does not arrive at the scheduled end of time, the "winter" of the eon, which is the last day, "Sabbath," of the last "week" of salvation history; see E. Lupieri, "La fuga di sabato: Il mondo giudaico di Matteo, seguace di Gesù," *ASE* 20(1) (2003): 57–73.

[93] This was both a messianic sign and the subject of extended meditation in the early literary production of the followers of Jesus, especially Luke (see Luke 7:21–22/ Matt. 11:4–5; Acts 3:1–10; 8:26–39; and John 9), also because it was one among the theological and scriptural models for the introduction of Gentiles into the pact of Israel. For the exclusion of "under-age boys" see CD XV:16 or 1QM VII:3.

[94] John 2:13, apparently "many days" after the wedding of Cana (2:12).

money of the money-changers and overturned their tables and to those who sold the doves he said: 'Take them out of here and do not make [= stop making] my Father's house a market house [οἶκος ἐμπορίου]'" (John 2:14–16).

Immediately afterward, quoting Psalm 69:9, John introduces the memory of the disciples and focuses on the "zeal" Jesus shows "for his house" (v. 17). This allows him to continue with a confrontation between Jesus and "the Jews" asking for a "sign," with Jesus uttering the famous sentence: "Destroy this temple and in three days I will raise it up" (vv. 18–20). The concluding reflection again shifts the attention and the level of the theological discussion from the earthly temple of Jerusalem, the destiny of which appears to be relatively unimportant, to the "body" of Christ (vv. 21–22).

In spite of all the diversities, though, we can consider the passage as an additional proof of an ongoing discussion, at least among the believers, about the physical temple of Jerusalem. It had been transformed into a "market house," and this fact was in some way connected to its destruction.

Money and the temple

Jesus' criticism of the use of money in the temple was part of his criticism against a mercantile ideology in religious matters that was putting the purity of the temple at risk. The early groups of Jesus' followers knew that he had spoken against "the merchants."[95] Once the temple was gone and its purity rules became obsolete, the criticism of the mercantile dimension of main-stream Judaism remained the basis for even more elaborate reflections on the proper way for attaining salvation, not only for the Jews, but also for the Gentiles.

---

[95] This should be clear not only from the canonical texts we discussed, but also from passages like the one I chose as a title and which, in spite of the verbal analogy with the canonical passages, comes from a different context in the Gospel of Thomas. It is at the end of the parable of the man inviting people to dinner (64; NHC 2, 44:11–33). The sentence has a strong Gnostic flavor: the "places" of the Father should denote the pleromatic level of spiritual perfection that cannot be reached by the psychical or ecclesiastical Christians excluded from the dinner. The ecclesiastical Christians are the new Jews, "businessmen and merchants." Still, it shows that even among Christian Gnostics there was a lively tradition about some sort of incompatibility between market mentality and salvation. An exception is the merchant of "beautiful pearls" in Matt. 13:45 (see above, n. 22).

In Matthew, these reflections apparently assume the aspect of a direct criticism of the use of money.[96] Indeed, while the Matthean Jesus is able to throw all the people selling and buying out of the temple, the only thing high priests and scribes or Pharisees or elders seem to be able to do effectively to try to combat Jesus is to use money, an act that appears related to deception. This is quite clear already at the end of Chapter 17 when, after the second prediction of the Passion, Matthew describes the discussion of Jesus and Peter about the temple tax. This passage has no parallel elsewhere in the NT and is written in a fantastical style that probably reflects Matthew's own intervention.[97] Matthew 17:24–27 has two main goals. One is to stress the special relationship existing between Jesus and Peter (one single coin suffices for both); the other is what interests us here. The money for the temple, in the concrete form of one *didrachma* per adult male (v. 24), was collected by envoys of the high priest during the month of Adar, the last before Nisan, the month of Passover. This must have been well known and therefore, apart from our uncertainty about the historical basis of the scene, the authority that is criticized by Matthew is the temple authority. Matthew says that "the kings of the earth" do not

---

[96] The use of money is implicit in the parable of the ten virgins (Matt. 25:1–13), which is only Matthean and strongly connected with our discussion. The foolish virgins, not having enough oil, can still go to the "sellers" and "buy" some (even if it is after "midnight"), but their buying is useless. This should mean that the non-believing Israel keeps its habit of buying/selling salvation, even in the dark of the night or when the bridegroom is already there, but it is useless. The text as it is seems to be constructed by Matthew using literary material similar to Mark 13:33–37; Luke 12:35–38, 40 and 13:25–28. The cultural context is strangely polygamous: there is no bride for the groom, but the ten virgins. The five wise ones "entered with him into the wedding and the door was closed," the "remaining" five stayed outside and were not "known" by the groom.

[97] It may very well be a diptych of the Synoptic discussion on the "coin for the [Roman] poll-tax" of Matt. 22:15–22 (see Mark 12:13–17 and Luke 20:20–26). There the discussion involves a Roman *denarius* bearing the picture and the name of "Caesar." Here we have a coin for the temple (see below, n. 100). Recent studies add the extreme scarcity of *denarii* in Jerusalem before the war of 70 CE to the fact that there is no other evidence of the existence in Palestine of a Roman poll-tax (*census*, to be paid with a Roman coin, as Matthew says?) in the years of Jesus, and draw the conclusion that the discussion about Caesar's *denarius* is also historically improbable: Udoh, *To Caesar What is Caesar's*, esp. 207–43. This may very well be the case, but it is a good rule to think that the absence of evidence is not necessarily evidence of absence.

take taxes[98] from "their own sons/children." This means that (a) Jesus and Peter are "sons/children" of the taxing authorities, and that (b) the behavior of temple authorities is wrong, being worse than that of "the kings of the earth." The "sonship" may refer to the real (spiritual?) descent from Abraham (see Matt. 3:9), while the earthly kings are under the power of Satan, as proved by Matthew 4:8.[99] This means that the high priests, asking for money from the sons/children of Israel, are worse than the representatives of Satan on earth. Why? The basic idea is again that salvation cannot be sold, but only donated freely. In particular, the religious duty of the Jewish authorities is to offer salvation to the people, and the Jewish people, in general, are expected to bring salvation to the whole world, for free.[100]

Matthew's version of Judas' story is paradigmatic of the habit of Jewish religious authorities of selling and acquiring everything with money. While Mark 14:11 says that the high priests with "joy" promise Judas they will give him "some money" (ἀργύριον; same as Luke 22:5), Matthew develops the well-known story of the "thirty pieces of silver"

---

[98] Matthew uses two different words for "taxes": τέλη, which are the taxes collected by the tax-collectors (τελῶναι), and κῆνσος, although what it could mean at the beginning of the first century CE in Palestine is not clear (Udoh, *To Caesar What is Caesar's*, 225f.). In any case, Matthew's words are very generic, refer to foreign kings and kingdoms (not only or necessarily the Romans), aim at comparing the temple tax to a foreign poll tax, and seem to describe the time of Matthew more than that of Jesus.

[99] Even more, "kings" usually presented themselves as the human dimension of a god, but for a believing Jew this was nothing else than a fallen angel, which is Satan.

[100] And not with money, the purity of which, after all, could be the object of discussions. It should be noticed that, in our context, Jesus not only does not have the coin, but does not even touch it (acting in the same way he was going to act with the Roman *denarius*; see above, n. 97) after Peter finds it in the mouth of the fish. That coin, since it pays for two, is explicitly called a *stater* (v. 27), which is a *tetradrachma* or, again in this case, the silver Tyrian coin officially used in the temple! Further, Matthew doesn't have any parallel to Mark 12:41–44/Luke 21:1–4, the scene of "the widow's mite," where the collection of money as offering to the treasury of the temple (γαζοφυλάκιον) could have been interpreted by him as having a positive religious value (but see above, n. 56). Matthew's only explicit mention of the temple treasure, for which he uses the Semitic word *korbanàs*, is very critical: Matt. 27:6 (Mark 7:11 uses *korbàn*, but Matt. 15:5 has only δῶρον, which, in the other contexts, means "religious offering, sacrifice": Matt. 5:23f.; 8:4; 23:18f. and cf. 2:11).

(26:15; 27:3–9).[101] According to the narrative, Judas asks the high priests for money and they assign him the sum; he accepts (Matt. 25:14ff.), but, after the betrayal, he "repents" and brings the money back to the high priests (and elders); they refuse to accept the money; Judas throws it "in the temple"; they "take" the money, which they handle as a freewill offering,[102] but cannot put it in the treasury (*korbanàs*; see above), because of its sanctity. At the end, all the authorities apparently gather together again and decide to use the money for a merciful act.[103]

Matthew's irony is merciless. Independently from historical plausibility and biblical foundation in the story, here the Jewish authority is a typically Matthean example of hypocrisy, even as they do their best to protect the temple from contamination and to use that money in a correct way.[104]

---

[101] Matthew never says whether those silver coins were Roman *denarii* or Tyrian *stateres*. If the latter be the case, independently from any historical plausibility that high priests used temple money for such transactions, the Matthean criticism would be simply ferocious.

[102] In the case of animals to be sacrificed, the norms for free-will offerings were slightly less rigid than those for other kinds of sacrifices. According to Lev. 22:18–23 even animals with something "superfluous or lacking" in their limbs could be offered (which was otherwise forbidden). 2 Kings 12:4f. states that King Joash allowed the priests to use the "money" received as a free-will offering for the repairs of the temple (in the age of Joash there probably was no coined money; the text possibly refers to offerings in silver or gold).

[103] They establish a cemetery for the foreigners: Matt. 27:3–10.

[104] There must have been an ongoing halakhic discussion on free-will offerings. The Essenes were stricter than others: "Concerning the regulation for freewill-offerings. No-one should dedicate anything, obtained by unjust means, to the altar. Neither should the [pr]iests take from Israel [anything obtained by unjust means]" (CD XVI:13f. (García Martínez and Tigchelaar, *The Dead Sea Scrolls*, I, 565)). This position is coherent with the Essenic idea that even what we would call "ethical sin" causes some sort of contamination. The ideas reflected in Matt. 27 are more specifically connected with the possibility that money can be contaminated and become contaminating, especially for the sanctity of the temple (which had the highest standard of purity). Deut. 23:19 ("Thou shall not bring the hire of a whore or the price of a dog into the house of the Lord thy God for any vow") proves that the gain from any illegal sexual activity (dogs are probably male prostitutes, and in any case "dogs" were deemed incompatible with the sanctity of the temple and priestly purity: see above, n. 29) could not be brought into the treasury of the temple. On this subject we have an interesting and famous tradition, attributed to R. Eliezer, according to which, he had a discussion with a disciple of Jesus in Sepphoris, a certain "James." The disciple reports the idea of Jesus that it is possible to use money offered by a prostitute to

The question, therefore, is again the same: who really protects the temple from contamination and who contaminates it?

This whole scene with Judas constitutes a kind of preparation for the last appearance of the high priests, together with the elders, in this gospel. After the resurrection of Jesus, some of the guards "announce to the high priests all that had happened" (Matt. 28:11). The fact is quite exceptional: pagan soldiers of the Roman army "announce"[105] "all" that happened to the highest Jewish authorities. They gather together again and decide to give "sufficient money" (ἀργύρια ἱκανά: again pieces of silver) to the soldiers to convince them to tell the famous lie about the disciples stealing the body of Jesus. This originates a false *logos* which still circulates "among the Jews" at the time of Matthew (28:12–15). In this way the Jewish authorities not only do not accept the good news brought by the pagan soldiers and believe, but, thanks to their use of money, they impede the possible salvation of the pagans

build a latrine for the high priest (impure money for an impure goal: see the discussions in the *Baraita* and *Tosefta* to AZ 16b–19b; see also D. Boyarin, "The Talmud Meets Church History," *Diacritics* 28(2) (1998): 59f. According to Matt. 27:6 the reason that the high priests cannot bring Judas' money into the treasury is that it is the "price of blood" (τιμή ααματος). This is possibly an expansion (to blood-related impurity) of the Deuteronomic rule originally conceived for a sex-related impurity (the hire/price of a harlot/"dog"). In both cases, the decision to keep the money out of the treasury reflects a halakhic thinking according to which an impure/sinful activity somehow contaminates the money acquired through that activity. I don't have precise rabbinic parallels, but I think this interpretation of "Judas' money" most probably originated among early followers of Jesus, since it is true that "blood ... of a dead man" contaminates (e.g. Rev. 16:3). Note, however, that (a) at the precise moment of the scene, Jesus is still alive, and (b) we can presume that any high priest would have considered the execution of Jesus perfectly justifiable, which would at least have excluded any idea of "sinful" behavior connected with the acquisition of that money. Curiously enough, in the years Matthew was composing his gospel, a complementary legend originated in Rome, according to which *pecunia non olet*, "money doesn't stink." The Emperor Vespasian, as a matter of fact, reintroduced the (originally Neronian) *vectigal urinae*, a tax on collection of urine from public urinals (still called today *vepasiani* in Italian, and *vespasiennes* in French), when carried out for commercial purposes (such as professional tanning, or whitening of wool). When Titus protested, Vespasian invited him to smell a gold coin obtained thanks to that tax and pronounced the sentence, which immediately became proverbial, as related both by Suetonius (*Vesp*. XXIII) and Dio Cassius (LXVI, 14). In this way the famously greedy emperor refuses any connection, ethical or purity-related, between money and the way it is obtained.

[105] It is the same verb, ἀπαγγέλλω, used for announcing the resurrection on two other occasions in the immediate context: Matt. 28:8 and 10.

(who already knew "all that had happened" and had begun to "announce" it) and also that of their own people.

The whole scene, then, is another example of "blind guides of blind men" (Matt. 15:14), who do not save themselves and impede the salvation of others, in this case, both Jews and pagans.[106]

Conclusion

Monetary standardization, as variously attempted by the Roman Empire, doesn't seem to have had a deep impact on Jewish Palestine before 70 CE. In the texts we have analyzed, all discussions and any criticism of market mentality, as well as use of money, are based on theological or ecclesiological motivations. This seems to apply to traditions that may bear the memory of the actual preaching of Jesus as well as to the reflections developed in the groups of his early followers. We do find traces, though, of discomfort with wealth and with rich people, who are actual or possible members of the community. The mercantile society, with its mobility, especially by boat, is notably depicted as external to early Christianity by the author of Revelation. Various aspects of that society are chosen to describe a godless world, where people can get rich, but are allied to the satanic forces that oppose the true faith.[107] Among the gospels, Matthew is the one who appears to be in many respects close to Revelation, but, like John of Patmos, he does not directly criticize the actual, everyday activity of merchants. His point is directed towards the market mentality applied (by the other Jews) to the religious reality and to salvation, which had been donated by God in the past to Israel and now, through the free and gratuitous self-donation of Jesus on the cross, to everybody.

Possibly in Jesus' preaching, and probably in the early Christian mission, the stress on donation and self-donation may have been

---

[106] See esp. Matt. 23:13 and 14 and the passages already quoted above. In the final part of his gospel, Matthew is claiming the right to the mission among both Jews and Gentiles for his own church, the one which recognizes the authority of Peter and of the Eleven, not for Paul (who is not in the picture) or his church. Therefore the whole scene may also have a polemical value against other groups inside early Christianity.

[107] The use of metaphorical language of wealth/poverty, buying/selling, acceptance/refusal of money shows that the NT authors have absorbed the language of the mercantile society they live in, even when they use it to depict internal religious polemics.

presented or understood as an alternative to an economy based on a selling/buying mentality.[108] Certainly, if practiced by everyone in everyday life, the substitution of any market mentality with a "gift ideology" would have brought the existing social system to its "implosion."[109]

In order to realize the ideal, though, it might have been necessary to attend the *parousia*. 2 Thess. seems to handle groups of believers who were worried about its so-called delay.[110] On the other hand, Revelation 3:17f. shows that most "Christians" at Laodicea, like the other Jews, were on their way towards integration, and maybe assimilation, into their social and religiously tolerant surrounding world.[111] Their "wealth" was still, for John, the sign of the temporary victory of Satan, but by the end of the first century, radical positions appear to be in the minority, at least among the believers in Asia Minor. Later the Great Church, turning into a worldwide institution, was able to marginalize any existing apocalyptic trends and/or organize the most radical Christian positions into special ecclesiastical structures (monasticism, missionary activity, etc.). The potentially revolutionary dimension of Christian utopia remained embedded in the Scriptures, ready to feed, through the centuries, periodic social Christian upheavals. But that is another story.

---

[108] In a slave society, though, self-donation presupposes the acceptance of slavery for oneself (see e.g., Phil. 2:6–11) and therefore not even the concept of slavery was contested on a social basis, as proved by Philemon.

[109] From what I understand, this may not have been the main subject of Jesus' preaching, but a very logical consequence. This would have marked the beginning of the "millennium" and/or of the "end of the world/eon." But since it did not come to pass in those years, the social dimension of the idea may have become more and more secondary in the course of NT redaction.

[110] I would like to stress that the expectation of a *parousia* already shows that most followers of Jesus believed that it was not possible to realize the worldly dimension of his message without his second coming.

[111] "Because you say: I am rich, and I have become rich, and I have need of nothing. And you do not know that you are the wretched one and the pitiable and beggarly and blind and naked; I advise you to buy from me gold fired in fire, so that you may become rich ..."

18 | Desire in consumer culture: theological perspectives from Gregory of Nyssa and Augustine of Hippo

JOHN F. HOFFMEYER

I. Introduction

Let me begin with a caveat. My chapter is not about monetization of markets, whether ancient or modern. My project is a theological reflection upon desire in a consumer society and culture. A consumer society and a consumer culture are neither direct nor necessary consequences of the use of money for market transactions. Societies can develop and use money without becoming consumer societies. Many of the consumer transactions in contemporary consumer societies involve no exchange of money in the sense of cash. Instead consumers hand over plastic credit cards or push buttons to instigate electronic transfers of funds. One can still call these processes monetary transactions, in the sense that monetary units serve as the means of accounting: e.g., a credit card purchase is calculated in euros or rand or yen.

Consumer society and consumer culture are not the direct results of either markets or money. Consumer society and consumer culture arise as markets of a particular kind, commodity markets, become pervasive. Because of the pervasiveness of commodity markets in consumer society, some commentators describe consumer society as a society in which "the market" has become pervasive. This can be misleading. Markets need not be commodity markets. For instance, the "marketplace of ideas" can refer to a public space in which ideas are not bought and sold, but argued. Concretely, those arguments may occur in the same physical space in which other items are indeed bought and sold. You go to the market down the street here in Heidelberg to buy some asparagus, and you may end up arguing with someone – it being Heidelberg – about the adequacy of Gadamer's concept of *Horizontverschmelzung*.

The distinction between commodity markets and other types of markets is especially important for an analysis of consumer society and culture. Consumer society tends toward the reduction of all markets to commodity markets. In order to analyze this process, one must retain a broader analytical vocabulary that recognizes the other forms of markets threatened by consumer commodification.

For the sake of clarity I should point out that I am not using the term "commodity markets" in the narrow sense of markets for, say, wheat and corn. Nor am I restricting the sense of "commodity" to "goods" as opposed to "services." I am using "commodity" in the broad sense of anything that is bought and sold, anything that has a price.

Along with describing consumer society as a society that tends to reduce markets to commodity markets, one could also say that consumer society is a society that tends to reduce consumption to the consumption of commodities. It is not the prevalence of consumption in itself that gives rise to consumer society. There is no human life without consumption. All human beings consume oxygen, water, and food as conditions of our very survival. A distinctive feature of consumer society, in contrast to other society forms, is its dominant casting of objects of consumption as commodities.[1]

I suspect that monetization is a precondition of consumer society. Without money, it is hard to imagine that commodity transactions would have become easy enough to achieve the dominance that they hold in consumer society. However, the focus of my chapter lies elsewhere. I assume that consumer society is a dominant social form operating in and through contemporary monetized markets and expanding the scope of these markets toward increasing commodification of social and cultural forms. Within this general framework, my interest is in a theological exploration of desire in consumer society and culture.

Although there is much talk about consumer society, consumer culture, and consumerism, specifying the reference of these related terms is anything but simple. Don Slater says that there cannot be any single definition of consumer culture, since the latter "is bound up with 'the whole of modernity.'"[2] Frank Trentman develops a more sophisticated analysis in which he argues that the "consumer, like 'class,' 'citizen,' or

---

[1] "Consumer culture marks out a system in which consumption is dominated by the consumption of commodities" (D. Slater, *Consumer Culture and Modernity*, Cambridge: Polity Press, 1997, 8).
[2] Ibid., 24.

'nation,' is no natural or universal category, but rather, the product of historical identity formations in which actors through available traditions make sense of the relationship between material culture and collective identity."[3] In contrast to the strong linkage between "the consumer, individualism, and liberal economics" that stands at the forefront of many contemporary discussions of consumer society, Trentman looks back to a time when the word "consumer" was particularly connected with citizen activism. He recalls "the consumer leagues that sprang up in America and continental Europe in the 1890s, with their emphasis on the social responsibility of consumers to shop wisely. These leagues strove to improve the welfare of workers and small traders by refraining from shopping after 8 p.m., by paying in cash, by planning ahead, and by taming the impulse to buy shoddy, fashionable goods made by exploited labor."[4] In 1940, an anxious article dedicated to the "consumer movement" in the trade journal *Advertising Age* warned that this movement had gone from being a "very tiny blot on the horizon" to becoming "THE major problem facing business – and particularly advertising – as they enter the fifth decade of the twentieth century."[5]

The term "consumer" can suggest a frugal person shopping with care and knowledge in order not to waste resources, be they monetary or ecological. It can suggest an engaged citizen working with others to promote policies that would curb exploitative labor practices or restrict unsafe products. Both of these senses of "consumer" are grounded in real movements of earlier periods and point to parts of consumer practice today. But neither of these senses is what usually comes to mind in association with the phrase "consumerism" in most parts of the world today.

In trying to define consumerism as a contemporary phenomenon of global reach, the sociologist Zygmunt Bauman acknowledges that he can offer no more than an "ideal type." He describes contemporary consumerism as "a type of social arrangement that results from recycling mundane, permanent and so to speak 'regime-neutral' human wants, desires and longings into the *principal propelling and operating*

---

[3] F. Trentman, "The Evolution of the Consumer: Meanings, Identities, and Political Synapses Before the Age of Affluence," in: *The Ambivalent Consumer: Questioning Consumption in East Asia and the West*, eds. S. Garon and P. L. Maclachlan, Ithaca, NY: Cornell University Press, 2006, 42.

[4] Ibid., 36–7.

[5] Cited in L. Cohen, *A Consumers' Republic: The Politics of Mass Consumption in Postwar America*, New York: Alfred A. Knopf, 2003, 57.

force of society, a force that coordinates systemic reproduction, social integration, social stratification and the formation of human individuals, as well as playing a major role in the processes of individual and group self-identification and in the selection and pursuit of individual life policies."[6]

For the purposes of this chapter I will not be evaluating Bauman's overall definition, but only taking from it the necessity of an analysis of desire for any serious engagement with contemporary consumer culture. This may seem to be a trivial point. Of course consumer culture runs on desire. People buy things because they want them. But what exactly do people want when they shop for and buy "stuff"? Several years ago ads for high-end Lexus automobiles explained: "We don't sell cars. We merely facilitate love connections." Do people buy a car because they like "stuff" or because they are longing for love? Playing the role of the realistic social critic, Toyota announced, "Let's face it, there are a lot of similarities when it comes to choosing a car and a mate. While this may seem surprising to some, even more surprising is that in today's society the chances for a lasting relationship just may be greater with a car ... Drive the new Paseo. Fall in love." Chrysler summed up the basic argument as succinctly as possible: "Drive=Love." If you can buy the car to drive, can you also buy love?

Advertisers have long recognized that blurring the distinction between what can be bought and what cannot be bought is a powerful tool. The desire for love is a powerful desire. If an advertisement can suggest that the purchase of a product might be, if not the purchase of love itself, at least the purchase of something to bring love within the buyer's reach, that will be an incentive to buy the product. Helen Landon Cass urged the attendees at a sales convention in Philadelphia in 1923 to look beyond the particular products that they were selling and to focus on the hopes and dreams of consumers.

Sell them their dreams. Sell them what they longed for and hoped for and almost despaired of having. Sell them hats by splashing sunlight across them. Sell them dreams – dreams of country clubs and proms and visions of what might happen if only. After all, people don't buy things to have things. They buy things to work for them. They buy hope – hope of what your merchandise

---

[6] Z. Bauman, *Consuming Life*, Malden, MA: Polity, 2007, 28 (emphasis in original).

will do for them. Sell them this hope and you won't have to worry about selling them goods.[7]

This blurring of the lines between what can be bought and what cannot be bought is essential to contemporary consumer culture. The more the lines are blurred, the more pervasive the market becomes. It is this blurring, this increasing "marketization," that Don Slater has in mind when he writes that "consumer culture denotes a social arrangement in which the relation between lived culture and social resources, between meaningful ways of life and the symbolic and material resources on which they depend, is mediated through markets."[8]

It is important to note that the blurring of the lines between that which can be bought and that which cannot be bought is not identical with the assumption that everything has a price. An important part of the seductive appeal of consumerism depends upon the sense that, by buying, we can somehow attain precisely that which cannot be bought. The lines are blurred, but not erased. An entire series of advertisements for MasterCard plays upon this blurring. The ads list particular items and their prices, as well as one or more experiences that are "priceless." The ad concludes with the statement, "There are some things money can't buy; for everything else there's MasterCard." But the point of the ad is to raise the value of MasterCard's brand by associating it with things that are widely valued as priceless. Moreover, in the ad's story line, making the various purchases that have definite prices are the stepping stones by which the characters in the ad – and by extension, we the viewers – get to that which is priceless. For example, one ad takes place at a professional baseball game. The father has bought his young son a baseball glove, he has bought them both tickets to the game, and he has bought them a hot dog and something to drink. Then a fly ball sails foul and the boy catches it. The father beams at his son's excitement and pride. The priceless moment of "his first fly ball," played out in the mythic scenario of American father–son bonding through baseball, only takes place because of the prior expenditures.

It is the theme of desire in consumer society that draws my attention in this chapter: not just desire for this or that material object to satisfy this or that material desire, but desire in a sense that encompasses the

---

[7] Cited in J. B. Twitchell, *Lead Us Into Temptation: The Triumph of American Materialism*, New York: Columbia University Press, 1999, 271.
[8] Slater, *Consumer Culture*, 8.

rich range of human emotional, psychological, and spiritual longings. In Section II I will examine several features of desire in consumer cultures. Section III will compare some theological perspectives on desire from two early Christian theologians – Augustine of Hippo and Gregory of Nyssa. Section IV will seek general theological orientation for engagement with consumer culture by connecting insights developed in section III with issues raised in section II.

II. Desire in a consumer culture

Consumer advertising is in the desire business. A century ago, *The Thompson Red Book on Advertising*, a leading advertising manual of the day in the United States, said it this way: "Advertising aims to teach people that they have wants, which they did not recognize before, and where such wants can be best supplied."[9] The *Thompson Red Book* sees advertising as an educational force, helping people come to greater consciousness of their desires, and then helping them find the means to satisfy those desires. For example, the product Listerine was once a disinfectant, used to clean the surfaces of hospital operating rooms. In the 1920s, Gerard Lambert took an obscure medical term, "halitosis," and spread it throughout magazines and newspapers in a massive advertising campaign. The ads often depicted unfortunate men and women who, despite an engaging personality and attractive physical appearance, were doomed to failure in realizing their dream of finding a marriage partner because of the affliction of halitosis. Other ads portrayed men who could not find a job because potential employers would rather choose someone not beset with halitosis. Lambert appealed to desires connected with marriage and employment to teach people that they had a desire of which they had previously been unaware: the desire not to suffer from halitosis. In the case of the Listerine ad campaigns, the educational value took a special twist. The disease of halitosis placed a limit on the educational scope of the ads. The ads could not teach you whether you suffered from halitosis, nor could they instruct you how to procure this information. The underlying reason was the nature of the

---

[9] Cited in R. Clapp, "The Theology of Consumption and the Consumption of Theology: Toward a Christian Response to Consumerism," in: *The Consuming Passion: Christianity and the Consumer Culture*, ed. R. Clapp, Downers Grove, IL: InterVarsity Press, 1998, 185.

affliction itself. Halitosis was obvious only to others, not to the person actually suffering from the disease. As one Listerine ad put it, "Since halitosis never announces itself to the victim, you simply cannot know when you have it."[10] Given the embarrassment connected with halitosis, most people would not take up the educational task of telling you, even if they noticed that you suffered from the problem. The reader of the advertisement is now faced with a twofold quandary: what can he do about halitosis, and how can he discover if he needs to do anything about it? The ads informatively answer the first question in the obvious way, by presenting the product – Listerine – as the solution to the problem. Since there is no dependable way to answer the second question, the final educational function of the ads is to advise readers to be on the safe side and use Listerine.

One could interpret those early Listerine ads as doing more than educating consumers about previously unknown desires. Rather than just bringing previously unknown desires to consciousness, the ads might be aiming at creating desires. In 1926 Calvin Coolidge, then President of the United States, told a convention of advertising professionals that advertising, if properly applied, is "the method by which desire is created for better things."[11] Fifteen years earlier, Walter Dill Scott in his book *Influencing Men in Business* had also taken up the theme of creating desire for commodities: "The man with the proper imagination is able to conceive of any commodity in such a way that it becomes an object of emotion to him and to those to whom he imparts his picture, and hence creates desire rather than a mere feeling of ought."[12] Immanuel Kant may have thought that the "ought" of duty had the power to serve as the sole authentic motivation of moral action, but Scott was dubious about its ability to sell products. For that the recipe was desire. To sell more products, bring more desires into play, whether they be desires that were previously unrecognized or desires newly minted in the process of marketing.

One way or another, advertising seeks both to proliferate desires and to present products that promise satisfaction of those desires. Not only do the advertisements promise satisfaction, they promise it quickly. The

---

[10] J. B. Twitchell, *Adcult USA: The Triumph of Advertising in American Culture*, New York: Columbia University Press, 1996, 144–5.

[11] S. Ewen, *Captains of Consciousness: Advertising and the Social Roots of the Consumer Culture*, New York: Basic Books, 2001, 37.

[12] Ibid., 31.

typical figure of consumer society is not the innerworldly ascetic of Max Weber's *The Protestant Ethic and the Spirit of Capitalism,* willing to defer gratification until the distant, heavenly future. It is not the case, though, that consumer society is marked by urgent striving to achieve satisfaction, followed by restful enjoyment of that satisfaction. In consumer society's version of the dialectic of satisfaction and dissatisfaction, it is the latter that sets the tone. An article published in 1930 in the trade journal *Printers' Ink* counseled advertisers to remember that "advertising helps to keep the masses dissatisfied with their mode of life, discontented with *ugly things* around them. Satisfied customers are not as profitable as discontented ones."[13] If advertising educates about previously unknown desires, in so doing it brings to consciousness previously unfelt dissatisfaction. If advertising creates new desires, it does so by making life without the desired goods seem shabby. In a television advertisement that crosses the line into cruelty, the setting is a school classroom where children are doing reports on "What I did on my summer vacation." A boy waits expectantly in the front row, holding the small figurine of an athlete in action that he received for his good showing in a tournament at a summer camp. The presenter before him is a girl who begins with the story of how her family went on a cruise. Instead of simply telling the story, though, she is going to show a video of her vacation. She wheels a cart with a video monitor in front of the class and clicks on a highly sophisticated video of a cruise for a particular cruise line, showing the girl enjoying various amenities of the cruise, such as a jet ski romp. Within the classroom, the camera returns to the boy, who is slinking down in his seat and lowering his modest trophy more and more until it is no longer visible above his desktop. In the face of both the girl's prestigious vacation and the high production values of her technologically complex presentation, the boy's athletic success and his summer camp lose their luster. The ad, sad to say, is for the cruise line depicted in the girl's video.

This advertisement is particularly objectionable because it so callously plays with a child's vulnerability to shame and insecurity. In its fundamental structure, though, the ad is not an anomaly. One of the major dynamics of advertising is the suggestion that the product being promoted is superior to what the viewer/hearer/reader of the ad already has in her possession. The cruise line ad goes beyond suggestion to

---

[13] Ibid., 39.

making an explicit claim. By contrast, many ads operate at the level of subtle suggestion. They do not resort to the cruelty of the cruise line ad. Yet they still contribute to the larger project of advertising, as defined by the article from *Printers' Ink*: "to keep the masses discontented with their mode of life."

Notice that the expression is "to keep the masses discontented," not "to make the masses discontented." Consumer society runs upon an ongoing supply of discontent. On the one hand, products promise satisfaction in order to attract buyers. On the other hand, if they delivered lasting contentment, sales would suffer because it would be too long before the contented buyer felt the need to buy again. As a result, consumers keep making purchases to move from dissatisfaction to satisfaction, only to find themselves again dissatisfied, even with their recently made purchases. This treadmill of chronic discontent is a basic figure of consumer society.

The treadmill keeps going as long as consumers keep desiring more. Although advertisements may promise satisfaction, and although we may buy in the hope of satisfaction, satisfaction always seems to remain just beyond our current possession. Whatever we have is never quite enough. Despite bulging consumer markets, consumer society is characterized by a fundamental lack. It is not a lack of any particular product or material, but the experience that we keep wanting, or feeling that we need, something more. In a felicitous formulation from Lutheran pastor Timothy J. Stein, "The opposite of enough is not too little. The opposite of enough is not too much. The opposite of enough is more."[14]

To the extent that we can never simply say "enough," that we are always wanting more, we cannot be satisfied (*satis* – enough; *factus* – made). The undermining of satisfaction is built into consumer society. Satisfactions of consumer desire can only be fleeting; otherwise, buying would "slump." Consumers need to stay on the treadmill; their desire needs to be insatiable.

One way to assess the phenomenon of insatiable desire in consumer society is to mark desire as a negative, a lack longing to be filled, and to mark the promised fulfillment as a positive, the goal of desire. On this view, the problem lies in the fact that consumer goods do not keep the promise. They do not provide satisfaction – or, more accurately,

---

[14] T. J. Stein, sermon, Faith Lutheran Church, Cambridge, MA, 2006.

consumer society requires that the satisfaction that they do provide be undermined by the creation of new discontent. In an analysis of this rapid cycling from satisfaction to renewed dissatisfaction, the economist Simon Patten wrote: "It is not the increase of goods for consumption that raises the standard of life ... [but] the rapidity with which [the consumer] tires of any one pleasure. To have a high standard of life means to enjoy a pleasure intensely and to tire of it quickly."[15] Patten wrote those words in 1889, but they have lost none of their relevance.

What this line of analysis neglects, though, is the complex structure of desire. The external object of desire is not the only thing that desire can find desirable. Desire itself can become desirable. As Judith Butler observes in her fine book on the twentieth-century French reception of Hegel's philosophy, desire has a two-part structure. In its intentionality, desire aims at an external object. In its reflexivity, desire desires desire.[16] To the extent that desire itself becomes desirable, insatiability is built into desire. To the extent that what I want is more of the experience of desiring, any pretended satisfaction that would quiet desire is undesirable. Using the metaphor of a racecourse rather than a treadmill in his description of consumer society, Zygmunt Bauman writes:

It is the running itself which is exhilarating, and however tiring it may be, the track is a more enjoyable place than the finishing line. ... The arrival, the definite end to all choice, seems much more dull and considerably more frightening than the prospect of tomorrow's choices canceling the choices of today. Solely the desiring is desirable – hardly ever its satisfaction.[17]

Consumer desire can be seductive. The desiring itself can be sweet. This is one reason why shopping is such a popular activity in consumer society. The point is not simply to find the right item, purchase it, and be done with shopping. The process itself is desirable, with its imagination and longing, its thrill of being able to choose, its open-ended dream of something better.[18] Bauman goes too far, though, in placing practically the whole weight of desirability on the desiring itself.

[15] Cited in G. Cross, *An All-Consuming Century: Why Commercialism Won in Modern America*, New York: Columbia University Press, 2000, 51.
[16] J. Butler, *Subjects of Desire: Hegelian Reflections in Twentieth-Century France*, New York: Columbia University Press, 1999, 57.
[17] Z. Bauman, *Liquid Modernity*, Cambridge: Polity Press, 2000, 88.
[18] C. Campbell, "Consuming Goods and the Good of Consuming," in: *Consumer Society in American History: A Reader*, ed. L. B. Glickman, Ithaca, NY: Cornell University Press, 1999, 19–32, argues that the "Romantic ethic" with its

Without an intentional object external to desire, there is no desire to be desirable.

If one backs off from the exaggerated form in which Bauman makes his claim, it is an important one. Coupled with the endless process of desiring is the endless process of making choices, none of which is ever final or irrevocable. Bauman argues that "everything in a consumer society is a matter of choice, except the compulsion to choose."[19] We must choose and keep on choosing in a way that tends toward the perpetual revisability of choice.

Several years ago the slogan for the Pittsburgh Airmall (the shopping center at Pittsburgh airport) trumpeted, "I am what I shop." Identity is not narratively developed in interaction with others. Identity is not fashioned by new appropriation – positive, negative, transformative – of one's past. Instead identity lies in one's own present consumer choices: "I am what I shop." My shopping today – and therefore my identity – may very well be different from my shopping last year or last week. Indeed, without that difference there would be much less shopping going on, since only a portion of shopping is dedicated to replacing items that have worn out or been used up.

This perpetual revisability of choice undermines any lasting commitment. As an ad for Macy's department stores put it, "If it's not new, it's not in fashion." This is why, as Colin Campbell puts it, "consumerism involves a high *turnover* of goods, not merely a high level of acquisition."[20] Yesterday's good is so often no longer good today, because its novelty has worn off. In consumer society, the thrill of novelty trumps commitment and faithfulness.

III. Augustine of Hippo and Gregory of Nyssa on the desire for God

One of the most poignant images for the desire for God in the Bible stands in the opening verse of Psalm 42: "As the deer longs for flowing streams, so my soul longs for you, O God." Perhaps this verse was one of the texts in the back of Augustine's mind when he wrote the famous prayer at the beginning of his *Confessions*: "You have made us for yourself and our hearts are restless until they find

emphasis on imaginative longing and dreaming is essential to modern consumer culture.
[19] Bauman, *Liquid Modernity*, 73.   [20] Campbell, "Consuming Goods," 26.

their rest in you."[21] Augustine's theological point is that because we are created by God, and because of how we are created by God, our fundamental orientation is toward God and our basic desire is for God. To the extent that we veer off from this fundamental orientation and seek to fulfill this basic desire with things other than God, our desire will remain unsatisfied. Other, less fundamental desires are properly fulfilled by other objects. Augustine divides human desires and their proper objects into two categories. Human beings are so constituted that their fundamental desire is for their creator. All other human desires are less fundamental, and correspond to less ultimate objects – objects that, like humans themselves, are created beings.

Problems arise when persons confuse the two categories of objects of desire. Specifically, human beings go astray by seeking to satisfy their fundamental desire, the desire for God, with objects that are created by God. For an Augustinian analysis, this is the root cause of the insatiability of desire in consumer society. People make the mistake of trying to satisfy their desire for God the creator with created objects, which by their very nature can never provide that satisfaction. For the Augustinian, we are, in the words of Waylon Jennings' song, "looking for love in all the wrong places." More to the specific topic of this volume, we have not yet learned the truth sung by the Beatles: "Money can't buy me love." It is because the attempt to satisfy our deepest human desire anywhere other than in God is always a doomed project that Augustine prays: "Our hearts are restless until they find their rest in you."

To the extent that we diverge from our fundamental orientation toward our creator, we are troubled by restlessness or disquieted to the very center of our being (*cor inquietum*). More precisely, we are created in such a way that we come to our own center by being centered in God. In this sense we are ek-centric: we find our center not "inside" ourselves – if "inside" means "on our own" – but "outside" ourselves, in God. When we come to our true center in God, then we are no longer disquieted (*inquietum*), but quieted (*requiescat*).

Augustine's line about the restless heart finding rest in God is one of the most frequently quoted and beloved lines in the Augustinian corpus. The image of quiet resting holds great comfort. The very word that

---

[21] "Fecisti nos ad te et inquietum est cor nostrum, donec requiescat in te" (Aurelius Augustinus, *Confessiones*, Stuttgart: B. G. Teubner, 1981, I,1,12–13).

Augustine uses is the prayer for the deceased in the Latin funeral liturgy: *requiescat in pace*, rest in peace. At the same time, the image of rest is not unequivocally positive. Suspicions about rest emerge when people respond to popular imagery about heaven by saying, "Wouldn't it get boring, just sitting around on a cloud and playing the harp all day?"

It may well be that concentration upon Augustine's famous line about the restless heart finding rest in God leads to an oversimplification of Augustine's concept and enactment of desire for God. Commenting in Book 3 of the *Confessions* on his youthful years of unfulfilled searching in Carthage, Augustine says that he was "in love with love." The philosopher Karmen MacKendrick argues that the mature Augustine who has left the pleasures of Carthage for the delights of God is still "in love with love." More precisely, "he seeks a constant and potent seduction of and by his God."[22] Augustine is in love with God not so much as a final rest for his otherwise restless desires, but as a beloved more seductive than any of the creaturely objects of Augustine's affections. "Augustine's desire is the insatiable demand for desire."[23]

MacKendrick rightly warns against too simplistic a reading of what Augustine means by finding rest in God. At the same time, to characterize Augustinian desire primarily as "the insatiable demand for desire" gives the reflexive component of desire a priority over the intentional component in a way that threatens to reduce "God" in Augustine's writing to a code-word for desire in its desirability. MacKendrick is right that Augustine finds the burning desire for God desirable. But for Augustine the heart of the matter is the God whom he desires and the desirability of God. The desire that Augustine finds desirable is not a desire for his own desire, but a desire for God, a desire for an intentional object that is other than Augustine's desire. One can think that Augustine's "God" is a misnaming of the actual object of his desire, but Augustine certainly does not think so.

Although MacKendrick's privileging of an "insatiable demand for desire" seems to distort the productive tension between the intentional and the reflexive objects of desire in Augustine, her analysis helpfully highlights another tension in Augustine's work that, to my knowledge,

---

[22] K. MacKendrick, "Carthage Didn't Burn Hot Enough: St. Augustine's Divine Seduction," in: *Toward a Theology of Eros: Transfiguring Passion at the Limits of Discipline*, eds. V. Burrus and C. Keller, Transdisciplinary Theological Colloquia, New York: Fordham University Press, 2006, 205.

[23] Ibid., 215–16.

he himself does not explicitly address. On the one hand, Augustine praises rest as the proper condition of the faithful human heart in relation to God. On the other hand, Augustine regards faith's relation to God as an ongoing desiring, an ongoing striving. In the opening section of Book IX of his *De trinitate*, Augustine opposes "seeking" (*quaerere*) and "grasping/laying hold" (*apprehendere*). He cites scripture's injunction to "seek the Lord," then, for those who might have the temerity to think that they have already grasped God, he adds the scriptural admonition to "always" (*sempre*) seek the face of the Lord. Augustine then proceeds to several quotations from Paul, locating the summit of his argument in this passage: "'Brothers,' he says, 'I do not judge myself already to have laid hold (*apprehendisse*); but one thing, oblivious of what is behind, and stretched out (*extentus*) into what is ahead, I follow with the aim (*intentionem*) of the prize of the higher calling of God in Christ Jesus.'" Augustine explicitly holds up this vision from Philippians 3:13 as a description of "perfection in this life," rejecting the alternative that perfection would lie in moving beyond seeking to actually grasping and having hold of what had been sought. Here Augustine commends a life not simply of rest, but of the "tensile" strength of stretching (*extentus*) and aiming (*intentionem*).[24]

This same Pauline quotation from Philippians 3:13 is perhaps the most theologically influential sentence in the Bible for Augustine's older contemporary, Gregory of Nyssa. The Greek participle *epekteinomenos* in that verse has as its root the verb *teinô* – "stretch," "strain." The verb comes into English in Latinate forms like those encountered in the preceding paragraph: "tension," "extend," and "intend." It is no exaggeration to say that the term *epektasis* lies "at the heart of the spiritual vocabulary of Gregory of Nyssa."[25] Gregory returns again and again to forms of *teinô* to commend the ongoing dynamism of the life of faith in relation to God. At the same time, like Augustine, Gregory articulates a tension between rest and dynamism in faith's relation to God. Gregory differs from Augustine in two ways. First, Gregory clearly highlights the element of dynamism, of insatiable desiring. Second, Gregory brings the

---

[24] Augustinus, *De trinitate*, IX,1, http://www.thelatinlibrary.com/augustine/trin9. shtml; last accessed July 22, 2009.

[25] J. Fontaine and C. Kannengiesser, eds., *Epektasis: mélanges patristiques offerts au Cardinal Jean Daniélou*, Paris: Beauchesne, 1972, V.

two positive elements of rest and desire into explicit relation with each other.

Gregory sees ceaseless journeying as a positive mark of a right relation to God. One of his favorite biblical passages is the story of God passing by while Moses was hidden in a rock crevice, covered momentarily by God's hand, so that Moses would only see God's backside (Exod. 33:21–23). In his homilies on the Song of Songs, Gregory comments that this passage shows that "it is in always following God that the one desiring to see God sees the One who is longed for, and that the contemplation of God's face is the unceasing [*apaustos*] journey towards God."[26] If one assumes the trajectory from restlessness to rest – the trajectory of Augustine's famous line from the beginning of *Confessions* – restlessness expresses the frustration of desire. Restless desire is desire that does not yet enjoy. For Gregory, the life of ongoing advance, of movement undertaken ever anew, of freshly engendered desire, of continuously straining forward, is not at all incompatible with the present enjoyment of God. Explaining the phrase "they took away my mantle," spoken by the female protagonist in Song of Songs 5:7, Gregory observes:

> But the mantle of sadness is taken away through learning that the true enjoyment of the One she longs for is always to progress in seeking and never to desist (pauesthai) from the upward path, for desire, always being filled, gives birth to another desire for the One who lies beyond. As the mantle of hopelessness was taken away and she saw the unlimited and uncircumscribable beauty of the Beloved, always being found greater in all eternity of the ages, she is stretched [*teinetai*] with more intense longing.[27]

Gregory describes true enjoyment not as what happens after one finally comes to the end of one's search: true enjoyment is seeking that continually moves forward in its seeking. Enjoyment is not the rest that replaces the search. True enjoyment is never to desist (*pauesthai*). Desire is not frustrated; it is always being fulfilled (*pantote plêroumenês*). But this fulfillment is not the stilling of desire. Precisely in its ceaseless fulfillment, it generates another desire. Seeing the divine Beloved is not the occasion for a quiet beatific vision, but for more intense longing (*en sphodroterô teinetai pothô*). This is not because the seeing is, as it were,

[26] Gregory of Nyssa, *In Canticum Canticorum,* vol. VI of *Opera*, eds.
H. Langerbeck and W. Jaeger, Leiden: E. J. Brill, 1960, 356, 12–15.
[27] Ibid., 369, 22–370, 7.

from a distance, so that the desire connected with seeing could eventually give way to the enjoyment of intimacy. The true reason is that seeing and its desire can never get to the end of divine beauty, because that beauty has no end. It is unlimited (*aoriston*).

Gregory does not use the word "unlimited" in a loose sense to describe God. He is not conjuring up the image of a great panoramic expanse. On the contrary, he means that there can be no panoramic vision of God.[28] However one might define God – whatever *finis*, whatever limit one might attach to God – God is always found to be greater.

For Gregory, not only is ongoing desire not incompatible with present enjoyment of God, the absence of such longing is a sure sign that whatever one is presently enjoying, it is not God, but an impostor that is not genuinely transcendent, not genuinely infinite. Consider Gregory's interpretation of God's words to Moses: "You will not be able to see my face, for no human being who sees my face shall live." In Gregory's view,

The word is not indicating this as a cause of death to those who see (for how would the face of life become a cause of death to those who draw near?). But since the divine is by nature life-giving, and since the distinctive knowable feature of the divine nature is the transcendence of every knowable feature, the person who thinks God to be among the things that are known does not have life, inasmuch as that person has turned away from what truly is toward that which image-based perception thinks has being.[29]

Gregory's insistence that God lies beyond every knowable feature is not a simple theology of negation. God transcends all definition because God has no limit, no *finis*. The unknowability of God is grounded not in the epistemological inadequacy of human beings, but in the infinity that

---

[28] This is one of the important similarities between Gregory and the great twentieth-century philosopher, Emmanuel Lévinas. Lévinas' emphatic privileging of the encounter with the face of the other was a rejection of philosophical views that take a fundamentally third-person position. For Lévinas, the third-person attempt to "see the whole" (panorama) is the perversion of infinity into a closed totality.

[29] Grégoire de Nysse, *La Vie de Moïse, ou Traité de la perfection en matière de vertu*, 3rd edn., intro. and trans. J. Daniélou, Sources Chrétiennes, Paris: Éditions du Cerf, 1968, 404B.

is the most precise statement that Gregory can give of the divine nature.[30]

For the theme of this chapter, the important point is that it is God's infinity that lies at the root of the insatiability of human desire for God. Gregory assumes that what is good or beautiful by nature is desirable in any case. The resulting desire is to participate in that which is good or beautiful. The divine nature is without defining limit. Desire that participates in the divine nature is always stretching with and toward the infinite divine. Therefore such desire is always on the move; it can never stand still.[31]

Because God is infinite, desire for God can never reach a point where it ceases, sated. As one comes closer to God, the intensity of the desire for God increases rather than decreases.[32] Desire does not grow because it is approaching a fulfillment that will bring satiety. Desire grows and will keep on growing because it is longing for the Beloved whose beauty is "ever greater in all eternity of the ages." There is no coming to the end of the beauty and desirability of the infinite God.

The open-endedness of the desire for God does not translate into a restlessness for which God remains unattainable, always receding seductively, inflaming the desire of the creature but always postponing the enjoyment of communion. For Gregory, desire never reaches satiety not because it never comes into communion with God, but because God is infinite, always transcending any *finis*. God is always beyond and going beyond, even as we enjoy communion with the divine. Gregory struggles to find the words to express this complex relation. In his *Life of Moses* he says that God assented to fulfill (*plêrôsai*) Moses' desire to

---

[30] For detailed argumentation of this point, see E. Mühlenberg, *Die Unendlichkeit Gottes bei Gregor von Nyssa: Gregors Kritik am Gottesbegriff der klassischen Metaphysik*, Forschungen zur Kirchen- und Dogmengeschichte, Göttingen: Vandenhoeck & Ruprecht, 1966.

[31] Grégoire de Nysse, *La Vie de Moïse*, 300A–B.

[32] Gregory's theology of infinity and desire bears some similarity with the more recent philosophy of Emmanuel Lévinas. Lévinas contrasts totality and infinity (cf. n. 28 above). Under the rubric of totality, desire is defined by lack. To the extent that one can supply the lack, the desire goes away. Within the system of totality there is no room for transcendence. The desire proper to infinity is a desire beyond satisfaction: "The true Desire is that which the Desired does not fill up, but deepens" ("Le vrai Désir est celui que le Désiré ne comble pas, mais creuse"), Emmanuel Lévinas, "La philosophie et l'idée de l'infini," in: *En découvrant l'existence avec Husserl et Heidegger*, Bibliothèque d'histoire de la philosophie, Paris: J. Vrin, 1982, 175.

see God, but did not promise that Moses' desire would come to a stop (*stasin*) or be satiated (*korov*).[33] A bit later in the same text Gregory turns from subtle terminological distinctions to more paradoxical language when he says that what Moses desires is fulfilled (*plêroutai*), but in such a way that his desire remains unfulfilled (*aplêrôtos*).[34] Because it is impossible to come to the end of the divine infinity, there is no end to the "race" or "course" (*dromos*) of those whose desire, in the image of Gregory's favorite text from Phil. 3:13, stretches forward to what lies ahead. Although Gregory has said that in this ongoing journey into God the desire for God never comes to a stop (*stasis*), in another sense the running itself is also a standing (*stasis*).[35] The running is standing in this second sense, not of standing still, but of sure-footed stability in the very act of running the course.[36]

Yet Gregory wants to convey more than the simultaneity of running and sure-footed stability. His claim is that the never-ending journey of desire toward and into God is not frantic, restless, or exhausting, but provides its own deep rest. He provides an image of the simultaneity of desire and rest when, in his commentary on Song of Songs, he has the bride say: "I am at once shot forth like an arrow and am at rest (*epanapauesthai*) in the hands of the archer."[37] Martin Laird comments: "The bride is at once in movement and at rest. ... Union does not stand at the end-point of a linear ascent but is the context of such ascent. The interior ground of ascent is the union of finite creature and infinite Creator, and the exterior ground of union is continual ascent."[38]

IV. Insatiable desire for God and insatiable consumer desire

What light might these perspectives of Augustine and Gregory, these two early and influential theologians of desire for God, cast upon the

---

[33] Grégoire de Nysse, *La Vie de Moïse*, 404A.   [34] Ibid., 404B.

[35] Gregory is ringing the changes on the word (*stasis*) because he is discussing Exod. 33:21, where God says to Moses (in Gregory's version) "I will set (*stêsô*) you upon the rock."

[36] Grégoire de Nysse, *La Vie de Moïse*, 405B–D.

[37] Cited in M. Laird, *Gregory of Nyssa and the Grasp of Faith: Union, Knowledge, and Divine Presence*, Oxford Early Christian Studies, Oxford University Press, 2004, 94.

[38] Ibid.

workings of insatiable desire in consumer society? For both Augustine and Gregory, the life of faith is a life that combines resting in God with ongoing desire or search for God. Neither of them teaches a fundamental spiritual renunciation of desire. In their estimation of the positive spiritual value of desire, the positions of both Augustine and Gregory are partially compatible with President Calvin Coolidge's statement in the 1920s that "advertising ministers to the spiritual side of trade."[39] Advertising, after all, is in the business of cultivating, inciting, and shaping desire. But the compatibility is only partial. Augustine and Gregory offer resources both for understanding and for finding alternatives to insatiable consumer desires.

Presumably both theologians would discern much misdirection of human desire in consumer society. As noted earlier, the theme of the misdirection of desire is central to Augustine's thought. His classic vocabulary for diagnosing such misdirection is the distinction between enjoyment (*frui*) and use (*uti*). To enjoy something is to love it for its own sake; to use something is to use it, even to love it, for the sake of something else.[40] On this Augustinian view, the problem with the disordered desires of consumerism is that they look for enjoyment in those things that are to be used. We can make the mistake of looking for emotional, psychological, and spiritual fulfillment in, say, an automobile or a particular brand of clothes. In attaching our desire to the wrong things, we are alienated from God: "The more the human soul desires temporal and changeable things, the more it is unlike that One who is incorporeal and eternal and unchangeable."[41] A good deal of Christian critique of consumerism runs along these lines. We love our large flat-screen TVs too much; this crowds out spiritual concerns and keeps us far from God in our hearts.

At the same time, the dichotomizing structure of the Augustinian analysis threatens to undermine its own effectiveness. Have we embraced, or at least tolerated, the wasteful, throw-away culture of consumerism because we love our temporal, changeable earth and its myriad little neighborhoods and ecosystems too much? Perhaps we attach our hearts so much to market commodities because we have

---

[39] Ewen, *Captains of Consciousness*, 32–3.

[40] *De doctrina christiana* I, 4 and 22.

[41] "Incorporali vero illi aeterno et incommutabili tanto est anima hominis dissimilior, quanto rerum temporalium mutabiliumque cupidior" (*De civitate Dei* IX, XVII).

lacked practices and policies that foster gratitude for temporal, mundane realities that cannot be bought, such as topsoil, clean air, and human solidarity. The Augustinian temptation to bifurcate the divine, in its exaltation, eternity, and blessedness, from the human and earthly, in their lowliness, mortality, and misery,[42] results in a lowering of esteem for the earthly, the temporal, the mutable in general, and thus a constricting of gratitude for them.

Augustine's development of the distinction between enjoyment and use reinforces this same problem. For Augustine the only proper object of enjoyment is the divine Trinity.[43] Everything else is to be used. This applies not only to shovels and screwdrivers, but also to mountains, sunrises, other human beings, and oneself. "We have the commandment to love each other, but it is a question whether human beings are to be loved by human beings on their own account or on account of something else. If on their own account, we enjoy them; if on account of something else, we use them. It seems to me that they are to be loved on account of something else."[44] That "something else" is God.

Augustine is not advocating an instrumentalism devoid of love that would treat other creatures, particularly other human beings, simply as tools. He insists at great length on the commandment to love. Yet he establishes a cosmic dichotomy in which there is only One whom we are to enjoy, while everything and everyone else is for use. This dichotomy can easily obstruct the fundamental difference in appropriate gratitude for an iPod and appropriate gratitude for human beings. Consumer culture does not suffer from loving temporal, earthly goods *in general* too much for their own sake. We may be inclined to attach unrealistic hopes and desires to the objects displayed so temptingly in advertisements. We are not as societies inclined to esteem the topsoil or hungry human beings too highly as ends in themselves. Augustine's dichotomy of *uti* and *frui* provides a strong device for orientation in the face of disordered desires. But the orientation comes at the price of a cosmology that is suspicious of love for the earthly, the temporal, and the mutable. The phrase "love for the earthly, the temporal, and the mutable" functions not just as a description of consumerist desires that

---

[42] *De civitate Dei*, IX, 12.   [43] *De doctrina christiana*, I, 5, 22.

[44] "Praeceptum est enim nobis ut diligamus invicem, sed quaeritur utrum propter se homo ab homine diligendus sit an propter aliud. Si enim propter se, fruimur eo; si propter aliud, utimur eo. Videtur autem mihi propter aliud diligendus" (*De doctrina christiana*, I, 22).

idolatrously supplant the proper love for the divine creator. The phrase also names what is lacking in a consumerist way of life that carelessly exploits and destroys "earthly, temporal, and mutable" creatures, both human and non-human, for the sake of the imperatives of the consumer economy.

Gregory shares too much of Augustine's cosmology to provide a solution to this particular deficiency in the face of consumerism. Those who are seeking a whole-hearted embrace of the earthly, the temporal, and the mutable will need to look elsewhere. Where Gregory may offer help to contemporary engagement with consumer society is in his theology of insatiable desire. Gregory shares with consumer society an embrace of insatiable desire. Unlike the earlier theologian Origen, who imagined that creatures enjoying the height of perfection could become satiated with the good and thereby turn away from it,[45] Gregory insists: "This is truly to see God: never to reach satiety [*korov*] of desire."[46] Even if one grants that Augustine is more friendly to a theology of ongoing desire than a focus on the famous quieting of the restless heart might indicate, it is hard to imagine him identifying the vision of God and ongoing insatiable desire as closely and explicitly as Gregory does. In his strong positive valuation of insatiable desire, Gregory agrees with a basic aspect of consumer society, which celebrates insatiable desire because "satisfied customers are not as profitable as discontented ones."

The insatiability of desire is inseparable from consumer society's ethos of restlessness. Whether in the rapid turnover from one intentional object of desire to another, or in the seductive reflexivity of desire, where it is "the running itself which is exhilarating" and "the track is a more enjoyable place than the finish line," consumer society is a restless place. Gregory's theology of desire, by contrast, seeks to combine the ongoing dynamism of insatiable desire with the rest of Augustine's heart that finds its rest in God. The bride in Gregory's commentary on Song of Songs says, "I am at once shot forth like an arrow and am at rest in the hands of the archer." She is "both sent and not distanced from the archer."[47] Rest and the flight of desire are not alternating moments, but

---

[45] Origène, *Traité des principes*, intro. and trans. H. Crouzel and M. Simonetti, Sources Chrétiennes, Paris: Éditions du Cerf, 1978, I,3,8.

[46] Grégoire de Nysse, *La Vie de Moïse*, para. 239.

[47] Gregory of Nyssa, *In Canticum Canticorum*, 129, 14–15.

simultaneous. The desire that Gregory describes is not tantamount to restlessness; the rest that he describes does not clip the wings of desire. Gregory plays with the archery image to bring out the identity in difference of the soul's ongoing trajectory of desire for God and the already existing rest and enjoyment of intimacy with God. Love – which Gregory identifies with God by appealing to scripture, probably thinking especially of 1 John 4:8 and 16 – is the archer who shoots the arrow which, when it strikes and enters the bride/soul, causes her to say, "I am wounded with love" (Song of Songs 2:5). The arrow shot forth by love is "the only-begotten God," while the tip of the arrow's point has been tinged with the spirit of life. This trinitarian archery "brings in the archer together with the arrow, as the Lord says that I and the Father 'will come and will make our dwelling with him.'"[48]

The result is the indwelling of the divine in our humanity. "The fullness of the One whose palm encloses all creation finds room in you and dwells in you and does not find the room for the journey constricted by your nature."[49] God is infinite, yet human finitude is roomy enough for God's whole (*holos*) presence. Precisely in God's transcendence of all creation, God comes to dwell within the human.

However else we may interpret this difficult language, Gregory is wrestling to preserve a tension that is fundamental to his vision of the desire for God. While insisting that finite human beings can never circumscribe or comprehend the limitless God, Gregory is quick to guard against the suggestion that this makes God frustratingly distant, always receding beyond our horizon. Gregory holds that the desire for God is never satisfied, if by satisfaction we mean the stilling of desire. But if satisfaction means enjoyment here and now of that which is desired, then Gregory proclaims satisfaction in abundance.

Both Augustine and Gregory have something to offer contemporary thinking about consumer society. Augustine encourages us to investigate the extent to which the proliferation of our desires stems from the misdirection of our desires. Do we turn from one consumer experience to another because we are restlessly seeking a peace that can only be found in that which transcends any consumer commodity, because we are "looking for love in all the wrong places"? Do we invest in "love connections" with consumer commodities such as cars (as in the Lexus

---

[48] Ibid., 127, 8–17.   [49] Ibid., 68, 14–16.

ad mentioned earlier) as a substitute for a love connection with other persons?

At the same time, Augustine has his own shortcomings in helping to guide such an investigation, because his tendency to set up a dichotomy between the exalted eternal and the lowly mortal fails to aid, and can even discourage, the important work of making distinctions between different earthly, temporal, mutable objects of desire. To take one schematic example, iPods, water, and human persons are all earthly, temporal, and mutable. They can all be objects of desire. But they differ from each other in ways that are important for their potential function as objects of desire in a consumer society. The classification of an iPod as a consumer commodity is unobjectionable. There can be debates about things such as its quality or cultural and environmental impact, but its simple classification as a consumer commodity seems uncontroversial. The very classification of human beings as consumer commodities is objectionable. Attaching a price tag to a human being and saying that anyone who pays this price can use that human being as the purchaser desires is morally repugnant. Water differs from both iPods and human beings. On the one hand, the sale of water is not automatically and always morally repugnant. On the other hand, the thoroughgoing commodification of water would be profoundly objectionable. Unlike iPods, water is a basic necessity of life. The commodification of water in a form that would exclude some human beings from the market for that commodity would be morally repugnant.

An approach that learns from Augustine's strengths will, on the one hand, cultivate a sensitivity to inappropriate instances of commodification.[50] On the other hand, such an approach will recognize that attachment to such commodities is not so much a demonstration of spiritual shallowness as a misdirection of profound spiritual desire. An approach that also learns from Augustine's shortcomings will insist that "misdirection of spiritual desire" does not necessarily mean "overestimation of the value of mundane things." Rather than a moralizing castigation of consumerism, the modified Augustinian approach that I have in mind would have two critical principles. First, misdirected desires are a set-up

---

[50] See, for instance, the work of the author and filmmaker Jean Kilbourne on the commodification of women's bodies, especially J. Kilbourne, *Can't Buy My Love: How Advertising Changes the Way We Think and Feel*, New York: Touchstone, 1999.

for failure. They cannot satisfy their own ends. In this sense, such an approach would take up the question from Isaiah 55:2, "Why do you spend your money for that which is not bread?" Second, the solution to consumerism's overwrought attachment to mundane commodities is not a denigration of all things earthly.

What might this modified Augustinian approach look like in practice? Here are several indications. A community guided by this approach would teach its members to treat advertisements as spiritual appeals. It would teach its members to ask: "What spiritual longing is this advertisement promising to satisfy if I buy the product in question? Is it realistic to think that this product can indeed provide the promised satisfaction?" Such a community would tell stories and shape institutions that cultivate affection for earthly things while challenging the fascination with commercial commodities. As a young girl in my neighborhood once remarked as she sifted through freshly turned earth looking for worms: "There's nothing at the mall as interesting as dirt."

Gregory in turn provides tools for focusing not just on the question of the object to which desire is directed, but on the question of the character of desire. Gregory offers a way to recognize the positive spiritual significance of the insatiable desire at work in consumer society, while at the same time taking a critical stance toward that desire's inability to rest in present enjoyment. The insatiable desire that characterizes consumer society is restless because it keeps latching onto objects that cannot give the life that we consumers seek in them. Because of the inadequacy of the commodities to which consumer desire attaches, it must keep moving restlessly on from one object to the next, never able to rest and enjoy the present, endlessly looking for some new consumer experience. A "Gregorian" therapy of consumer society would want to cure the restlessness, but not the insatiability. From a Gregorian perspective, the restless flitting from one consumer experience to another can never fulfill our desire, because it is a version of trying to see the face of God. Gregory argues that trying to see the face – the defining boundaries – of God is doomed to failure, because the source of life has no such boundaries, no such face. Only that which has no such defining boundaries, only that which transcends objectification – and, to be sure, commodification – can provide rest while simultaneously rekindling desire.

In a short section in the *Life of Moses*, Gregory presents a second reading of God's word to Moses that the latter shall not see God face to face. This second reading, which Gregory presents as including and building upon the first reading, emphasizes the alternative that God provided: namely, for Moses to see God from the back. Gregory interprets this to mean that we are to follow God, to let God be our guide. The one who follows sees not the face but the back of the guide. This following is the true vision of God. As a Christian theologian, Gregory does not miss the opportunity to point to the prominence of the words "Follow me" in Jesus' mouth as a summons to a life of discipleship. The true vision of God lies not in a static theoretical vision, but in the practice of following, which consists in an ever-renewed journey towards and into God.

By combining his two interpretations of the impossibility of seeing the face of God, Gregory offers a theological perspective from which to combine faithfulness with ever-rekindled desire. This is a promising alternative in engaging consumer society, in which the insatiable desire for novelty so often results in the devaluation of commitment and faithfulness. A perspective informed by Gregory's thought could help resist the tendency of consumer society to assume that the alternative to novelty is boredom. Indeed, from such a perspective it would become easier to identify the search for novelty not only as a flight from boredom, but as a form of boredom, a repeated initiation of the same restless quest. By contrast, commitment and faithfulness would show themselves to be the more effective milieu for the ongoing renewal of desire.

A perspective informed by Gregory would, for instance, take a different tack than the religious and moral critique that decries the oversexualization of much consumer advertising. A Gregorian approach would suggest that much consumer advertising suffers not merely from oversexualization, but from shortchanging the sexiness of sex. If commitment and faithfulness are the best milieu for the ongoing renewal of desire, then marriage or parallel relationships of permanent promise and commitment are the most effective environments for the deepening and renewal of sexual desire. From the Gregorian perspective, commitment and faithfulness make for sexier sex.[51]

---

[51] For a more detailed discussion of this point, see J. F. Hoffmeyer, "The Trinity and Sexuality: Grounding Sex in God's Desire for Us," *The Network Letter*, vol. 17:2 (Summer 2008): 7–11; online at http://www.inclusivenet.com/uploads/newsletters/2008-summer.pdf.

The adoption of both the modified Augustinian perspective and the Gregorian perspective that I have presented would bring with it several defining emphases. (1) Human desiring is constitutively related to the ultimate goal of human desiring, which is God. (2) One of the basic confusions in consumer society is the misplacing of desire. The problem is not too much desire. The problem is the pressure to develop habits of seeking to fulfill profound and important desires with objects that are not up to the task. What we in consumer society need is more cultivation of the appropriate matching of desire and object. (3) From a Christian perspective, the human spiritual goal involves both (a) the ongoing renewal of desire and (b) the capacity to rest, to receive the present with gratitude. The habits encouraged by consumer society see these two elements as incompatible – thus the accelerated restlessness of consumer society. In fact, the two elements work together. Ongoing renewal occurs most effectively not by constant chasing after the latest novelty, but by practicing relations of faithfulness and commitment.

Money as God?: conclusions

MICHAEL WELKER AND JÜRGEN VON HAGEN

This volume is the product of a debate between scholars from a variety of academic disciplines about the impact of the introduction of money on society at large, and religion and ethics in particular. As noted in the Introduction, our project started from a tension between the deification of money and its demonization, both of which have a long history in theology, philosophy, and social sciences. Concluding this project, we state three propositions that formed the point of departure and summarize, in very general terms, the answers obtained in the course of our debate.

Proposition 1: Monetization causes far-reaching changes in a society

Result: The interaction between monetization and social changes is neither unidirectional nor mono-causal, and monetization is both the consequence and the cause of social changes. On the one hand, it is true that the spreading of the use of money triggers changes in societies. But, on the other hand, it is also true that a society must undergo certain developments to create the preconditions for the use of money. In particular, the use of money arises in environments where stable and long-lasting credit relationships do not exist. Thus, the anonymity and instability of interpersonal relationships, which are often seen as an adverse consequence of the use of money, should at least partly be regarded as one of its causes.

Proposition 2: Money, by making everything comparable, contributes to the dissolution of valuable social relationships

Result: In every society, the question of what has a price (in terms of money) and what does not depends on what the members of that society regard as tradable and negotiable. This is a question of basic values, not a property or consequence of the use of money. There are ethical and cultural limits to what is negotiable, but these limits are not fixed over time. Yet, the use of money and the assignment of monetary prices suggest the comparability of things that would not seem easily comparable otherwise and, thus, make exchange relations more malleable than those in barter trade.

Proposition 3: Money is dangerous, because it distracts human trust from God to dead material things

Result: That people put their trust in material wealth rather than a transcendent God is a phenomenon observed and bemoaned in many different cultural and historical contexts. It is not specific to societies using money as a medium of exchange. A demonization of money, therefore, is hardly the proper answer to the problem. This is so especially because the use of money also has many positive aspects for society. Instead, what is required is an ethical, cultural and eschatological (re)orientation leading human beings to trust in the true God instead of the false idols of material wealth.

Index

4QInstruction
  ethos of poverty in 372–8

accounting standards 68
accumulation of wealth 7, 125
achievement *see* religion and money
Acorn, Annelise E. 303, 308
advertising 14, 15, 344, 416, 417–18,
    419–22, 432, 433, 437
  oversexualization of 438
agent types *see* transitional justice
Aigina, coinage 118, 120, 121, 161
Albertus Magnus 64
Alexander the Great *see* Palestinian
    Monetary Systems
Ancient Israel *see* compensation
Ancient Near East *see* compensation
Antipas 384
apostolic poverty 237
Archaemenid Era *see* Palestinian
    Monetary Systems
architecture and buildings 108, 119–20,
    131, 209, 213, 214, 238, 280,
    302
Aristophanes 55–6, 134, 180
Aristotle 60–1, 64, 69, 124,
    159–60
Arrow-Debreu economy 29–31
Arrow, Kenneth 340
Arsames 147, 156
Ashdod 163, 168
Ashkelon 145, 163, 166, 168, 170
Assisi, Francis of 255
Assmann, Jan 105, 261, 286, 371
asymmetry *see* Chinese asymmetry
Athens, coinage 117–18, 121, 128, 129,
    161
Augustine of Hippo *see* desire and
    money: in consumer culture

Augustinian Order 247
Augustus 380

banking 65, 235
  bail-outs 314
  Chinese 8, 217
  functions of 127
  institutions 216
barter system 6, 24, 27, 34, 42, 43, 44,
    45, 56, 73, 81, 86, 103, 107,
    142, 144, 182, 183, 235, 246,
    247, 381, 441
Bastian, Uwe 293
Bauman, Zygmunt 416–17, 423–4
Beatles, The 425
'beyond,' the
  asymmetry of power in man's
    relation with 193, 194, 196,
    197, 210
  burial as interference with 192
  contracts with 188, 194
  gift economy in relations with *see*
    Chinese asymmetry
  inverse validation of goods here and
    in 186–7
  non-randomness of interventions by
    190, 198, 202, 210, 211
  reciprocity in exchanges with 189,
    190, 196, 197, 208
  risk reduction in human relations
    with 197
  risk-hedging strategies in relations
    with 208
biblical tradition *see* religion and money
Biggar, Nigel 285
bimetallism *see* measurement (*Mensura
    et Mensuratum*)
Bonhoeffer, Dietrich 289, 301, 305
Bretton Woods System 49, 311–15

Burke, Kenneth 1, 96
Butler, Judith 423

Caesar, Caius Iulius 131, 408
Calvin, John (Calvinism) 10, 252, 254,
    365, 366
Campbell, Colin 423, 424
capitalism *see* religion and money
Caroline of Monaco 90
cash reserves *see* Chinese Song Period
Cass, Helen Landon 417–18
catholic entrepreneurs in China *see*
    entrepreneurship
Catholicism *see* entrepreneurship
characteristics of money *see*
    decentralized market
    economies
China *see* Chinese asymmetry; Chinese
    Song Period; entrepreneurship
Chinese asymmetry 184–218
  credit transfer 211–12
  evaluation 218
  gift economy of fate 189–97
  interpretations, impact of
      198–207
  laundered money 212–17
  life as credit 197–8
    life credit management 207–11
  problem 184–9
Chinese Song Period
  paper money 219–32
    context 219–20
    evaluation 231–2
    expansion of (Shaanxi, 1071 and
        1074) 221–3
    Ma Duanlin (1254–1323) 229–31
    metaphor of "mother and child"
        225–7
    military consequences (1136) 223–5
    regional conditions and cash
        reserves 227–9
    state take-over (Sichuan, 1023)
        220–1
Christianity *see* religion and money
Church, the *see* religion and money
cleansing of the temple *see* religion and
    money
Code of Ešnunna 22, 259, 260, 265
Code of Hammurabi 23, 260
Code of Ur-Nammu 22, 259, 260, 261

coinage/coined money 111–36 *see also*
    Palestinian Monetary Systems
  coined money 111–12
    ancient judgments, consequences of
        133–5
    evaluation 135–6
    historical context of origins 112–16
    images 127–32
    objectives 116–24
    structural implications 125–7
collectivism *see* transitional justice
commercials *see* advertising
compassion *see* religion and money
compensation *see also* monetization;
    transitional justice
  for injuries and homicide 259–81
    coined money 279–81
    Covenant Code (CC) 271–8
    historical context 259–70
    legal tradition 278–9
competitive self-victimization *see*
    transitional justice
consumer culture *see* desire and money
consumerism *see* desire and money: in
    consumer culture
contract *see also* standard terms
  American-style 84
  Aramaic wedding contract 178
  business contracts 84
    enforcement of 8
  conclusion of 30, 82, 83, 85
  consumer goods 29–30, 31
  contract for purchase 83
  contracting individuals 19
  contracts and money 184
  contracts of sale 62
  contractual obligations 82
  contractual relationships 4, 82
    contractual engagement 93
    do ut des principle 9
    transactions 68, 80–1
    with the Beyond 185, 188–9,
        192–6, 207, 244
  contractual standardization 84–5
    commercial contracts 86
  credit contracts, enforcement of 33
  different types of 82
  formalization of 212, 347
  freedom of contract 94
  idea/concept of 240–1, 328

contract (cont.)
  individual commitments 40
  infringement of 216, 347
  likhita 215
  modern contracts and
    standardization 81
  nullity of contract 82
  standard contracts 81, 84
  terms and conditions of 93–4
  tomb contracts 184, 200–1
  trade contracts 38
  validity of 390
  voluntary contracts 56
  written/non-written 359, 360
convertibility 44, 45, 46, 48, 52, 72, 73,
  121, 296, 311
Coolidge, Calvin 420, 432
coordination problem *see* decentralized
  market economies
Corinth, coinage 118, 120, 121, 129,
  161
Covenant Code (CC) *see* compensation
credit money 3, 49
credit relationships 54, 440
credit transfer *see* Chinese asymmetry
criticisms of wealth *see* religion and
  money
Crüsemann, Frank 137, 271, 274, 276
currency *see also* Alexander the Great;
  bimetallism; coinage/coined
  money; electron (coinage);
  gold standard; Palestinian
  Monetary Systems; single
  currency
  Achaemenid Empire, of the 161
  balanced currencies 81
  bronze 227
  bullion-currency 62, 126
  circulation of 106
  convertibility of 311
  core-currency countries 315
  credit disbursement 194
  currency wars (China/US) 314
  debasement of 28
  Eurocurrency markets 312
  European Currency Union 87–8
  "evils" of 133–4
  exchange of 400–1
  export of 166, 167
  financial crisis and 49–50, 313

GDR unification and 291
gold and silver 45, 171, 310, 312
  minted gold coins 70
heavenly rewards and 241
inflation of 36, 50
  Index-currency 76
institutional management of 78
iron 226
karmic 202
marginal currencies 315
mint production, Hellenistic
  monarchies 129
moral 200, 201, 202, 204, 209
paper money 230–1
psychology of 78
reporting currency 67–8
Roman 71, 380
spiritual money as 8
stable value of 8, 50, 313
standardization of 142
supernatural 210
volatility of 310, 313

Dareikos 161, 162
Darius I 39, 141, 160, 281
Darius II Ochus 155–6
Darius III 161
David 162, 405
death penalty 265–6, 267, 268, 271,
  272, 273, 275, 277, 278
debasement 52, 62
decentralized market economies 42–51,
  82 *see also* market economy
  characteristics and perceptions of
    money:
    social consequences 51
  context 42
  coordination problem 42–5
  paper money, development of
    45–54
  pure credit economy 45–54
de-individualization *see* transitional
  justice
democratization of commerce 37, 144
demonetization *see* compensation
demonization of money 441
denarius 61–2, 66, 67, 130, 373, 380,
  385, 408, 409
desire and money 12–15, 365, 441
  in consumer culture 414–39

Augustine of Hippo (desire for
    God) 424–31
  consumerism, context of 414–19
  desire in a consumer culture
    419–24
  Gregory of Nyssa (desire for God)
    424–31
  insatiable consumer desire 431–9
  insatiable desire for God 431–9
difference principle *see* preferential
    justice
divine arbitrariness 138
divine treasury of grace 245–6
do ut des 9, 115, 234
Drachme 177
Dunhuang 192, 213
Durkheim, Emile 358

Ecclesiastes 106, 366, 368
  neologisms in 107
  social world of 6–7, 137–58
ecclesiastical criticism *see* religion and
    money
ecclesiological argument *see* preferential
    justice
Eck, Johann 254
economic analphabetism 97
economic documents *see* Palestinian
    Monetary Systems
electron (coinage) 44, 111, 119, 120
electronic money 54
Elster, Jon 285
endowment 29, 30, 32, 199,
    201, 207, 208, 237, 239,
    242, 253
enjoyment 14, 101, 102, 107, 137, 151,
    369, 421, 428–9, 430, 432,
    433, 435, 437
entrepreneurship *see also* market
    economy
  life attitudes towards faith 360
  religious (Catholic) faith and 339–61
    context 339–40
  religious faith and public value 353–8
    public value of personal faith
    355–7
    religious activities, importance of
    357–8
    social expression of personal faith
    354–5

social capital and personal faith 360–1
social structure/system,
    transformation of 359
subjects, situations of the 340–8
  basic situations 340–1
  common characteristics 341–2
  corporate management and faith
    345
  employer–employee relations
    342–3
  entrepreneur–administrative
    organs relations 343–5
  entrepreneur–clients and suppliers
    relations 345
  faith weighing in client relations 347
  faith weighing in employment 346
  faith weighing in recruitment
    346–7
  human relations, scope of 342
    religious activities, participation
    in 347–8
  religious faith and enterprises 345
  religious festivals as company
    holidays 345–6
  survey analysis 348
trust, relationships of 348–53
  administrative organs 350–2
  clients and suppliers 352–3
  employees 348–50
trust, restrictions and expansions
    358–9
Ephesos, coinage 120, 121, 124, 160
eschatology *see* religion and money:
    bibical and intertestamental
    tradition
ethical perspectives *see* monetary
    exchange; transitional justice

faith/faith relations *see*
    entrepreneurship
false reconciliation *see* religion and
    money
fate accounts 208, 209, 212
fate administrators 210
fiat money *see* measurement (*Mensura et
    Mensuratum*)
fig tree 389, 390, 394–5, 396, 397, 403,
    405
financial crisis 49, 314, 384
Fisher, Irving 75, 76, 78

free person 261, 276, 279
Fukuyama, Francis 340
futility 5, 37, 98–9, 101, 103

Gaza 163, 168, 169, 170, 182
Gentiles 146, 387, 397, 404, 405, 406,
    407, 412
German Democratic Republic *see*
    transitional justice
German Unification 92, 284, 291–3,
    298
Gernet, Jacques 188, 192, 216
Gernet, Louis 115
Gese, Hartmut 102
gift economy of fate *see* Chinese
    asymmetry
gift-and-slight economy 192, 197, 202,
    207, 211
global financial system 313, 314 *see also*
    standardized monetization
    (SM)
globalization 311, 312–14, 315
    anti-globalization 332–3
God 323–4 *see also* desire and money;
    Kohelet; religion and money
    act of 271, 272
    adoration of 244
    attributes of 104, 234, 354, 383, 429
    authority/grant of 147–8, 151
    backside of 428
    belief in 346, 356
    benevolence of 253
    biblical associations with 105
    blessings of 366
    Church prayers 353–4, 357
    coinage, economy of 105–6
    commandment and righteousness
        of 305
    creation and 14, 350, 371
    desire for 14–15 *see also* desire and
        money
    differentiation between Gods 250–2
    dimension of wealth 383
    enjoyment of 428, 429, 435
    eternity of 102, 369
    everlasting 15
    face of 437, 438
    faith in 396, 427
    faithfulness to this world 308, 395–6,
        405

favor of 148
fear of 102, 377
future action 308
gifts of 245
    enjoyment 102
    human possessions 14, 101–2
    Jerusalem 389
    property 5, 103
    rewarding God 234, 240
    salvation 389
    wealth 239
giving thanks to 351–2
"godless world" 412
god-like features of money 4–5
god-self 325
god-term, money as 1, 96
good works of 107, 240
goodness of 102
governance of 355
grace of 9, 239, 240, 241, 247,
    248, 249
hand(s) of 102, 369, 370, 428
human dimension of 409
human oppression and 318
human relationships with 5, 13,
    106–7, 234–5, 241, 247, 250,
    354, 371
    contractual relationship 9, 188, 244
    man's position before 234
    reliance/dependence on God 13
idolatry and 324
images of 369, 370
immortality and 369
"in God we trust" 243
infinity and 429–30, 435
influencing God's decisions 365
intervention of 392
journey towards 428
judgement of 239, 360, 374
Kingdom of 305, 306, 308, 324, 327
Lamb of 390, 391
life-giving 101, 103
love and 240, 319, 365
as "maker of all things" 102
Mammon and 1, 4, 96–7, 103, 104,
    106, 383
merchants and 253
mercy of 245, 247, 386
modesty and 355
on money as a "snare" 151

Moses, God's word to 374, 429,
431, 437
name of 255, 390
"only-begotten" 435
people of 326
plan of 397
poverty and 244, 249, 253, 324,
327, 337
presence of 14, 308, 402
procurators of 251
property of 251
providence of 385, 397
punishment by 253, 397
revelation in Jesus Christ 105, 324
rule of 103
salvation of 384, 387, 389, 392, 412
search for 14
secret purposes of 369
seeking 327
servants of 390
service of 250
sovereign reign of 6, 104, 148,
327, 366
spirit of 375, 377, 390
spiritual return to 368, 375
thankfulness to 365
theology of glory 104–5
"things" related to 384
time of 402
transcendent 441
as Trinitarian God 325
"true" 251, 397, 441
trustfulness of 396
universal presence of 104, 319
value of 99
visitation of 395
will of 319
word of 383
wrath of 397
goddess(es) 128, 129
Apollo 128
Arethusa 128, 129
Athena 128, 129
coin imagery and 130
Nike 129
Roma 130
gods
Arabian, on horseback 163
Ares, god of war 133
authentication by 205

authority over social justice 117, 118
coinage and 128, 129, 130, 167, 401
control of 205
counterfeit 370
cult of the god(s) and wealth 184
descents of 205
earth 193
favor of 133
Greek 210
Heracles 164
highest 201, 205
Melkart, image of 401
and mortal men, relations between
115
reciprocal support 127
Palestinian, on a winged wheel 167
Plutus, God of riches 55
Zeus 164, 167
gold standard 46, 49, 50, 51, 53, 72,
310, 312, 315
Gospel of Thomas 407
governmental contributions *see* nature
of money
Goydke, Jürgen 291
Greece, ancient culture and currency
5–6, 7, 36, 51, 111–35, 137,
141, 142, 147, 160–1, 162,
164, 165, 166, 167, 168, 171,
175, 176, 177, 178, 197, 210,
261, 276, 281, 380, 381, 400,
401, 403, 427
Homeric 21
Ionian 44
Greece, modern, bail-out of 314
Gregory of Nyssa *see* desire and money:
in consumer culture
Günzburg, Eberlin von 250–2
Gutierrez, Gustavo 318, 319, 320, 323

hack 280
jewelry 172–3
silver 23, 172–3
Halakhah 399, 400, 402–3
Harrison, C. Robert 137–8
Hasmonean Rule *see* Palestinian
Monetary Systems
Hayner, Priscilla B. 294, 299
heaven *see* religion and money
Hellenistic Era *see* Palestinian Monetary
Systems

hermeneutic-exegetical argument *see*
    preferential justice
Herod the Great 164, 379
Hirsch, F. 340
hoards *see* Palestinian Monetary
    Systems
Hölscher, Tonio 1, 5–6, 36, 107, 114, 131
Holy Spirit *see* preferential justice
homicide *see* compensation
Hou Ching-lang 186, 188, 208
Hu Jiaoxiu 225
human bodily injury *see* compensation
hyperinflation 51–2, 53
    historical episodes of 51
    periods of 50
Hyrcanus, John 398

image and money *see* coinage/coined
    money
imaginary money *see* measurement
    (*Mensura et Mensuratum*)
imprisonment *see* transitional justice
index numbers 75–6
individualism *see* transitional justice
infinity 429, 430–1
insatiability *see* desire and money: in
    consumer culture
intertestamental tradition *see* religion
    and money
investments in the Hereafter 242, 245
Iron Age *see* Palestinian Monetary
    Systems
Isard, Peter 310, 311, 312, 313
iudicium particulare 239

Jade Emperor as central banker 208
Janowski, Bernd 105, 306
Javolen 61
Jennings, Waylon 425
Jesus Christ *see* preferential justice;
    religion and money
Jevons, W. St. 31, 46
John of Patmos 412
Josephus 161, 165, 170, 381–2,
    383, 398
Judah coins *see* Palestinian Monetary
    Systems
judgement of every individual 239
Jurchens 223

justice *see* monetization; preferential
    justice; standardization;
    transitional justice

Keynes, John M. 68, 78, 333
Khotan 213
Kohelet
    religion and monetary economy, co-
        evolution of 96–108
    god-term, philosophical tradition
        of 96–8
    religious perspectives 104–8
    theoretical doctrine 98–104
    Wisdom of Solomon and
        367–72
Koselleck, Reinhardt 302
Kroisos 134
Ksitigharbha 207, 211

Lambert, Gerard 419–20
Latin American liberation
    theologians *see* preferential
    justice
laundered money *see* Chinese
    asymmetry
leasehold system 100
ledgers of merit and demerit (*gongguo
    ge*) 209
legal right *see* transitional justice
legal system(s) 4, 33, 80, 82, 84–5, 86,
    93, 100, 153, 200, 296, 297,
    301, 302, 305 *see also*
    compensation; rehabilitation
Lewis, J. D. 342
Li Gang 227–9
libra 66–7
life attitudes *see* entrepreneurship
life credit *see* Chinese asymmetry
logic of gift 246–9
long-distance trade 7
Lotzer, Sebastian 249
love 56, 97, 104, 105, 106, 142, 240,
    319, 323, 325, 327, 347, 355,
    356, 365, 417, 425, 426,
    432–6
    as justice 327
Luhmann, Niklas 1, 82, 96, 287
Luke 1, 22, 96, 97, 159, 323, 384,
    403–4, 406

Luther, Martin/Lutheran ideology 1, 4, 10, 96, 97, 98, 104–5, 246–7, 247–8, 252–3, 302, 322, 422

Ma Duanlin 229–31
MacKendrick, Karmen 426–7
Mäder, Werner 293
market economy 12, 14, 333, 381 *see also* decentralized market economy; entrepreneurship
market mentality *see* religion and money
market transactions 414
markets and money *see* measurement (*Mensura et Mensuratum*); monetization; nature of money; Kohelet; standardization
  philosophical foundations 2–5
material wealth 249, 441
Matthew 14, 22, 102–3, 326, 393, 404–6, 408–12
Mauss, Marcel 115, 188
McAdams, James 284, 290, 302, 304
measurement function (*Mensura et Mensuratum*) 60–79
  bimetallism, problems of 64–6
  context 60–1
  evaluation 78–9
  fiat money, value of 72–4
  imaginary money 66–9
  Middle Ages 61–4
  psychological processes 77–8
  purchasing power of money 74–7
  variable value of coins 69–72
memory 74, 281, 286–7, 302–3, 308, 375, 392, 407, 412
Mendicant Order 237
mercantile ideas *see* religion and money
merchant(s) 9, 65, 85, 86, 128, 144, 201, 207, 212, 215, 217, 218, 221, 223, 224, 225, 227, 231, 234, 235, 236–7, 242, 243, 244, 245, 247, 249, 252, 253, 254 *see also* religion and money: early Christianity and market mentality
merits 135, 187, 211, 233, 240
metaphor *see* Chinese Song Period; religion and money: divine

treasury of grace, metaphor of: metaphors of "Kingdom of God"
methodological argument *see* preferential justice
Middle Ages *see* measurement (*Mensura et Mensuratum*)
military considerations *see* Chinese Song Period
military service 100, 149
Mingbao ji 204, 205–6
Minow, Matha 298
Mises, Ludwig von 73–4, 75
Mommsen, Theodor 71
monarchy, hellenistic 129–30
moneta imaginaria 66–9, 76
moneta usualis 67
monetary compensation *see* compensation
monetary exchange
  ethical limits and challenges 10–12, 259
  historical and social roots 5–10, 111, 256
monetary trade 2, 166
monetization *see also* compensation; nature of money; standardized monetization (SM)
  quest for justice and 93–5
  societal change and 440
  standardization and 80–95
  within legal systems:
    compensation and rehabilitation 86–93
money, nature of *see* nature of money
moral obligation *see* transitional justice
Moses 23, 115, 374, 428, 429, 430–1, 437–8
mother and child metaphor *see* Chinese Song Period
Mulian, story of 212
multiple agents *see* transitional justice
Müntzer, Thomas 255
Murashu Archives 149, 150, 155–6

nature of money 19–41
  evaluation of 40–1
  government, role of 35–6
  monetary confusions 20–5
  monetization, implications of 19–20
  nature and origin of money 25–8

nature of money (cont.)
    money as social institution 25–8
    pure exchange economy 28–31
    Standardized Monetization of
        Markets, implications for 37–40
    trading frictions 32–5
Near East *see* compensation
Nehemiah 146, 149, 166, 399, 400,
    402, 403
Nero 380, 411
New Testament *see* religion and money
non-monetary damages *see*
    compensation
non-natural persons 288–90, 301, 307

obolos 124
Otto, Eckart 259, 260, 261, 264, 265,
    268, 270, 274

pactum 240
pagamentum 67
Palestinian Monetary Systems
    Achaemenid and Hellenistic Era
        159–83
        oldest Palestinian coins 159–62
    Achaemenid Palestine, first coins in
        162–8
        Judah/Yehud coins 165–8
        Philisto-Arabian coins 163
        Phoenician coins (5thC/4thC BCE)
            162–3
        Shomron (Samaria) coins 163–5
    evaluation 178–83
    Hellenistic Palestine, coins in 168–71
        Alexander the Great 168–9
        Hasmonean Rule, coin
            production under 170–1
        hoards 171–8
        Ptolemaic coins 169
        Seleucid coins 169–70
    hoards and economic documents
        171–8
    iron age 171–8
    Persian 171–8
paper money *see* Chinese Song Period;
    decentralized market
    economies
Patten, Simon 423
Paul 381, 383–4, 387, 391, 397,
    412, 427

pecunia numerata 62, 159
perceptions of money *see* decentralized
    market economies
Persepolis 141–2, 147
Persian period *see* Palestinian Monetary
    Systems
personal faith *see* entrepreneurship
Peter (1st disciple) 250, 391, 408–9, 412
Peutinger, Konrad 254–5
Philisto-Arabian coins *see* Palestinian
    Monetary Systems
Philpott, Daniel 284, 299
Phoenician coins *see* Palestinian
    Monetary Systems
picciolo 66 *see also* denarius
piety *see* religion and money
Pirenne, Henri 45–6
Plato 56, 124
Pliny the Elder 383
Plutus 55–6
polis (Greek) 36, 112, 114, 115–18,
    120, 123, 124, 128, 133
political prisoners *see* transitional justice
poverty, ethos of *see* 4QInstruction
predestination 248
    doctrine of double 365
preferential justice 309–38 *see also*
        standardized monetization (SM)
    implications for local and global
        policies 336–8
    John Rawls:
        difference principle 327–32
    Joseph Stiglitz:
        differential treatment of the poor
            332–6
    Latin American liberation theologians
        317–27
        ecclesiological argument 325–7
        God 323–4
        hermeneutic-exegetical argument
            321–3
        Holy Spirit 324–5
        Jesus Christ 324
        methodological argument 317–21
        Trinitarian argument 323
        Trinity 325
    theoretical arguments for
        316–17
preferential option for the poor 316,
    317–27, 335, 338

pre-Socratic philosophy 126
price, monetary
  social relationships, dissolution of
    440–1
prima facie evidence *see* transitional
    justice
privacy (protection of) 33, 83, 88,
    89–91
profitable exchange 235
property as wealth vs. as God's gift 5
property grants 146–7
Protestantism *see* religion and money
proverbs of Ahiqar 139, 154,
    157
Psamshek 147
psychological processes *see*
    measurement (*Mensura et
    Mensuratum*)
Ptolemaic coins *see* Palestinian
    Monetary Systems
public art *see* transitional justice
public value *see* entrepreneurship
purchasing power *see* measurement
    (*Mensura et Mensuratum*)
pure credit economy *see* decentralized
    market economies
pure exchange economy *see* nature of
    money
purgatory 201, 204, 206, 207, 208,
    210, 211, 212, 216, 237,
    239, 242

Qumran 12–13, 367, 372–3, 376,
    378, 382–3, 399

ransom, acts of *see* religion and money
Rawls, John 11, 316–17, 327–32,
    333–4, 337
real purchase *see* religion and money
reconciliation *see* religion and money
Redding, G. 349
Reformation Protestantism *see* religion
    and money
regional conditions *see* Chinese Song
    Period
rehabilitation *see* monetization;
    transitional justice
religion and money *see also* desire for
    money; entrepreneurship:

religious (Catholic) faith and;
    preferential justice: Latin
    American liberation
    theologians; Kohelet;
    transitional justice: law and
    monetization, limits of
  alliance of 256
  biblical and intertestamental tradition
    365–78
    Christian context 365–7
    ethos of poverty in 4QInstruction
      372–8
    Kohelet and the Wisdom of
      Solomon 367–72
  Church and early capitalism:
    interconnection of 241–4
  commercialization of 244
  commercialized salvation
    (14thC–16thC) 233–56
    heavenly Hereafter 233
  divine treasury of grace, metaphor of
    245–6
  early Christianity and market
    mentality 379–413
    cleansing of the temple in John
      406–7
    cleansing of the temple in Luke
      403–4
    cleansing of the temple in Mark
      393–401
    cleansing of the temple in Matthew
      404–6
    criticism of wealth 382–4
    death of Jesus as gratuitous act of
      ransom 391–3
    evaluation 412–13
    historical context 379–82
    historical Jesus and cleansing of the
      temple 402–3
    market mentality 384–7
    money and the temple
      407–12
    real purchase and true possession
      387–91
    Roman Empire, influence of 379
  ecclesiastical criticism 236–7
  economic change (11thC–13thC)
    235–6
  mercantile ideas 238–41

religion and money (cont.)
   new money economy, support of
     236–7
   Protestant alliance with money
     economy 252–6
   Reformation criticism of Catholic
     Church/money economy
     symbiosis 249–52
   Reformation, logic of gift and
     exchange 246–9
   religiosity of achievement and
     compassion 245
   theology and piety, transactional
     logic of 234–5
   transitional justice, role of 304–8
     churches as sociocultural
      instruments 305–6
     false reconciliation 307–8
     metaphors of "Kingdom of God"
      306–7
religion of preciousness 238–9
religiosity of mercy and
   compassion 245
religious activities *see* entrepreneurship
religious domestication of the capital
   economy 244
religious faith *see* entrepreneurship
religious logic 245, 248
reparation *see* transitional justice
reserve cash 223, 225, 228, 231
Ribat, son of Bel-eriba 150, 158
Ricardo, David 72
Roman Empire *see* religion and money
Russell, Bertrand 395

Sabbath 146, 348, 399–400,
   402, 406
Sachs, Hans 252–3
sacrifice(s) 115, 123–4, 187, 191,
   205, 275, 293–4, 387,
   391–2, 398, 403, 409, 410
salt ticket system 221–2, 223
salvation, commercialization of *see*
   religion and money
   Samaria/Shomron 158, 161,
     163–5, 166, 168, 178,
     179, 182, 384
Sandel, Michael 25, 81, 88, 283
Sangha, moral credit of 201, 207, 212,
   214–15

satisfaction 14–15, 240, 248, 249,
   420–1, 422–3, 430, 435, 437
Satz, Debra 283
Schwienhorst-Schönberger 100, 101,
   271, 273, 274, 275, 276
SED Dictatorship 292, 294, 300
Seleucid coins *see* Palestinian Monetary
   Systems
Seow, Choon-Leong 5, 6, 13, 37, 38, 39,
   99–101, 107, 139, 140, 146,
   154, 206, 366
sex
   abstention from 209, 212
   oversexualization of consumer
     advertising 438
   purchase of/prostitution 134,
     410–11
   sex-related impurity 411
     sexual assault 88
     sexual attraction 206–7
     sexual intercourse 187
Shaanxi (Province) *see* Chinese Song
   Period
Shenzong 9, 221, 222
Shomron coins *see* Palestinian
   Monetary Systems
Sichuan (Province) *see* Chinese Song
   Period
Sidon 7, 154, 162, 168, 169, 170, 179
silver *see* hack
Simmel, Georg 1, 56, 58–9, 77, 96
single currency 86
slavery/slaves 100, 149–50, 153, 155,
   156, 157–8, 177, 216, 262–3,
   264, 265, 266, 272, 273, 276–9,
   325, 383, 387, 413
Sobrino, Jon 320, 321, 323, 324, 325–7
social capital *see* entrepreneurship
social commentary 152
social consequences of money *see*
   decentralized market
   economies
social expression of personal faith
   354–5
social institution of money *see* nature of
   money
social mobility 7, 38, 40
social-historical context 137, 143
socio-philosophical perspectives *see*
   transitional justice

solidus 66, 67
Solomon, Wisdom of *see* religion and
    money
Song Period *see* Chinese Song Period
Sophocles 134
spirit money 184, 208, 209–10
standard terms (contracts) 84–5, 93–4
standardization
    legal technique, as a 82–6
    monetization and 80–95
    quest for justice and 93–5
    theoretical context 80–1
standardized monetization (SM) *see also*
    monetization; preferential
    justice
    global financial system, evolution of
        309–16
    of the market 309–38
    perspectives 309
Standardized Monetization of
    Markets *see* nature of money
state intervention *see* Chinese Song
    Period
Staupitz, Johannes von 247
Stein, Timothy J. 213, 422
Stiglitz, Joseph 11, 314, 315, 317,
    332–6, 337 *see also*
    preferential justice
Strabo 160, 166, 381
stratification of society 113, 149, 417
supernatural world 7–8, 184, 185–8,
    190–1, 192, 194, 195–6, 197,
    198, 199, 200–1, 202, 204–5,
    206, 207, 208, 209, 210, 211
symbolism *see* transitional justice
Syracuse, coinage 120, 121, 128, 129

Taiwei xianjun *gongguo ge* 203
Teitel, Ruti G. 285, 286, 288
temple cleansing *see* religion and money
theology *see* religion and money
Thomas Aquinas 3, 63, 64
Thucydides 259–60
Tiberius 384
token money 60, 72 *see also* fiat money
trade
    bags 212
    barter 6, 144, 441
    channels of 103
    commercial logic of 234

concept of 117
decentralized 37
differential system of 333
economic form of 235
equitable system of 333–4
everyday 6
exchange 114, 115, 116
external 127
fair trade for the poor 317,
    334, 335
    trade negotiations 337
far-reaching 113
forms of 129
global 133, 309
    positive-sum game 337
Heaven, trade agreement with 233,
    237–41
in indulgences 256
international 113, 141, 145,
    179, 312
    trade agreements 315, 334,
        337–8
    bilateral 335
    WTO and GATT 313, 334
inter-temporal 52
joyous 247
liberalization of 314, 333
local and regional 7
long-distance/far-distance 7,
    117–18
maritime trade:
    Persian period 145
    sea trade 388
metal bars, exchange of 7
monetary 2, 166, 181
money and 26–7, 124, 127, 236
navigation 383
Palestinian development of 13
Phoenician coastal trade centers 162
promotion of 118
reciprocal 33, 334
retail 118
routes 212
rules and regulations of 310, 313
specialization and 31
spiritual dimension of 432
terms of 40
time and 2, 26
trade credit 28, 37–8
trading frictions 32–5

trade (cont.)
   traditional (non-monetary) 179
   transaction of goods 115, 175
   wealth and 236, 373
trading frictions *see* nature of money;
     trade
transactional logic *see* religion and
     money
transitional justice 282–308 *see also*
     religion and money
   German Democratic Republic,
       political prisoners of 290–300
   comparability of compensation
      297
   competitive self-victimization
      299–300
   de-individualization in legal cases
      296–7
   justice for victims 295
   monetary compensation 298–9
   moral obligation vs. legal right 299
   non-monetary damages to living
      victims 295–6
   political and legal frameworks
      290–4
   prima facie evidence 294–5
   rehabilitation 297–8
   reparation (moral, legal, economic)
      298
   socio-philosophical and ethical
      perspectives 294–300
   standardized solutions 296
  in 20thC and 21stC 284–90
   agent types 288–90
   future implications 286–7
   historical changes 284–6
   multiple agents 287–8
  law and monetization, limits of
     300–8
   psychology and religion 303–4
   religion and churches, role of
      304–8
   symbolism of public art 302–3
   symbolism, neglect of collective and
      individual 300–2
   transitional and reparatory justice
      282–4
treasure of the Church 239, 242
Treasury of Celestial Jurisdiction,
     tiancao ku 208

Trentman, Frank 415–16
Trinitarian argument *see* preferential
     justice
Trinity *see* preferential justice
Troeltsch, Ernst 254
true possession *see* religion and money
trust and lack of trust *see*
     entrepreneurship
Tutu, Desmond 304
Tyros 162, 168, 169, 170

Ullambana festival 211–12
unit of account 3, 20, 21–2, 29, 42, 55,
     57–8, 59, 68, 76, 81

value
   abstract value 178, 202
   Aramean value term *zwzn* 178
   assignment of 67
   cash value 141–2
   of coins/coinage system 69–72,
      118–19, 122–3, 126, 171,
      176, 177, 181, 280, 380
   commodity value 44, 60, 68, 71, 73,
      74
   of compensatory payments 10
   of the dollar 313
   of drachma 182
   dviguna 215
   equal 46
   exchange value 76
   expression of value 74
   felt value of money 77
   of fiat money 72–4
   fluctuation of 46
   in the gift economy 199, 201, 210
   of God 99
   of gold 27, 72, 312, 313
   of good deeds 8
   of goods and services 55, 57
   of Greek money 6
   high-value obligations 62
   of human life 282
     human body 270
     human soul 372
   of income 53
   intrinsic 23, 26, 27, 42, 43, 44, 45, 52,
     58, 72
   loss of 4, 26, 34, 270
   of major currencies 310

market value (price) 25
measure of 3–4
of melted down material 281
of merchandise 280
of metallic coins 36
of money 24, 57, 58, 59, 76, 77–8
of mundane things 436
nominal 42, 44, 45, 66, 76, 78,
    182, 209
pre-monetary 116, 122
of salt 231
of silver 65, 71, 72, 163, 164, 179,
    181, 182, 263
of slaves 266, 278
of spirit money 210
of a *šql* 161
stable currency 8, 9
of stamping 160
standardization and 22
store(s) of 20, 22, 26, 42, 57, 81
symbolic value 125, 159
    of the fig tree 394
terms of value 177
translation of 200
value of exchange 72, 74–5, 76
value structure in the Beyond 193
value theory 30–1
value units 114, 175
variable value *see* measurement
    (*Mensura et Mensuratum*)
Verdeja, Ernesto 301
Vespasian 55, 411
Vinaya of the Mūlasarvāstivāda 204,
    213–15
Volf, Miroslav 306, 307

Wagner, Adolph 46, 49, 77
Wagner, Falk 1, 96, 255
Wagner, Rudolph 7–9, 14
Wagner-Hasel, Beate 114, 115
Waldes, Peter 255
Wang Anshi 221, 222, 223
wealth and money 12–15,
    365, 441
wealth as a gift of God 239
wealth, criticisms of *see* religion and
    money
Weber, Max 210, 217, 254, 348–9,
    359, 365–6, 372, 421
Weigert, A. 342
Welker, Michael 4–5, 13, 37,
    39, 97, 105, 106, 135, 206,
    279, 283
Wicksell, Knut 53, 69
Wisdom of Solomon *see* religion and
    money
Wolterstorff, Nicholas 307
work relations *see* entrepreneurship
Wyclif, John 255

Xenophon 65
Xue Tian 220–1

Yang Wanli 226
Yaron 259, 260, 261, 262, 265,
    266, 267
Yehud/Judah coins *see* Palestinian
    Monetary Systems
Yuan Period 219, 220, 229

Zwingli, Huldrych 249

Lightning Source UK Ltd.
Milton Keynes UK
UKOW06f0758051016

284472UK00011B/346/P